PLA
CRICKET
5
EDITED B
All statistics by the

PREFACE

Playfair goes to press just as Michael Vaughan has launched England's Caribbean mission with an 82-ball hundred before lunch against Jamaica. Hopefully the captain's epic innings will prelude a successful defence of The Wisden Trophy and an outstanding summer's cricket. On the international front New Zealand (three Tests) and West Indies (four) should provide challenging opposition, a tempting menu indeed. Then we have three internationals against India as a curtain-raiser to the ICC Champions Trophy in September. Should England reach that final they will have been continuously engaged for almost seven months.

On the domestic front things are less certain, with the fixture list yet again a prolonged and confused mishmash without any set pattern of days for each competition. Far more worrying is the influx of overseas players. Apart from the permitted two per county (to be halved next year) plus stand-ins, there appears to be a limitless supply of foreign cricketers with passports of convenience. The County Championship is in great danger of becoming the European or Universal Championship. Bombarded with readers' requests to denote those players not qualified to play for England I have tagged each one in the County Register. The exercise produced some alarming facts. Seven of the first nine players on Derbyshire's list are not qualified, while Middlesex boast a similar tally of South African-born cricketers. On rainy days readers can amuse themselves by compiling a variety of county and national tables featuring the foreign legion. Pity the England selectors with an ever dwindling number of players to choose from as we hone the skills of their overseas contemporaries. Incidentally, in response to other readers' requests, the Register now includes dates of each county's inaugural first-class match and the identity of their head groundsman.

Many congratulations to Sussex for winning their first Championship. Mushtaq Ahmed richly rewarded their faith in his wrist-spin with the first 100-wicket haul since Andrew Caddick took 105 in 1998. Last season saw the astonishingly successful launch of Twenty20 Cup cricket. Boosted by exceptional weather it attracted capacity attendances and, most essentially, it quickly won the support of the players. For detractors of the instant game, a 20-overs affair has the great advantage of leaving most of the day free for other activities. Intriguingly batsmen tended to play authentic cricket strokes and bowlers relied on accuracy, variety and swing. Jimmy Ormond's final-winning return of 4 for 11 provided a prime example.

Peter West, founding editor of *Playfair* and conceiver of its title, sadly left us last year. A favourite broadcaster and friend, he was always tremendously supportive and generous. A tribute follows.

After an association lasting 15 editions, Ian Marshall moves to new masters as their Non-Fiction Publishing Director. My best wishes are accompanied by hearty thanks for his vital expertise, quiet humour, friendship and calm control.

A brace of viruses slightly delayed the final stages of this production, one attacked me, the other effectively sealed off all *windows*-based files in my laptop. Fortunately most of my programmes are *dos*-based. The brainchild of my first computer guru, Pete Thirlby, they have served me extraordinarily well for two decades. I am indebted to his locally based successor, David Court, for many hours of methodical repair work.

Juliana Lessa has taken over as Headline's editor. With David Mitchell's assistance she has proof-read every digit and calmly steered the vessel through production. Chris and Caroline Leggett's team at Letterpart has skilfully and enthusiastically coped with my eccentricities for the eleventh time.

As ever we have had invaluable support from the County clubs' administrators, scorers and statisticians, as well as Alan Fordham, Andy Smith and Janet Fisher (ECB), and a faithful coterie of overseas correspondents including Rajesh Kumar, Francis Payne, Andrew Samson, John Ward and Charlie Wat. Many thanks to Philip Bailey, a tower of strength and a fount of data, and to Robin Abrahams (CricInfo), Ric Finlay and David Fitzgerald (Tastats), Ron Nuttall and Debbie Frindall.

BILL FRINDALL
Urchfont
Wiltshire
2 March 2003

PETER WEST (1920-2003)

A chance meeting with C.B.Fry, the legendary England cricketer, all-round athlete, scholar and writer, changed Peter West's life. When Fry's copy telephonist failed to appear in the press box at Taunton one Saturday in 1947, Peter, then an Exchange Telegraph Agency reporter, offered his services. Fry was so taken with the clarity of West's voice and his enthusiastic and courteous manner that he recommended him to the BBC. That single action launched one of televised broadcasting's most varied careers. Enduring 40 summers until his retirement in 1986, it embraced cricket, rugby, tennis and six Olympic Games, in addition to hosting a fleet of panel games and 16 years of 'Come Dancing'.

Peter's publishing company, Playfair Books of Haymarket, published its inaugural cricket annual in 1948. Printed in quarto format, it cost three shillings and sixpence and its 164 pages included a 16-page section of black and white photographs. Many small portrait photos were spread around the pages of articles and statistics.

That first edition was entitled 'Playfair Books Cricket Annual 1948', 'Books' being omitted thereafter. Writing in the 1997 edition to celebrate the Annual's half-century, Peter revealed the title's origins:

"When ideas for a title were being tossed around I recalled the name of Sir Nigel Playfair, actor/manager between the wars. In due course, it received the endorsement of C.B.Fry, who declared in his foreword to the first issue that it was a very proper title for a book about the noble game."

An outstanding games player, Peter had captained Cranbrook School in five sports in spite of being affected by spondylitis, the back condition that compelled Michael Atherton to retire prematurely from cricket. His active experience of these sports was a considerable asset during his long broadcasting career. Another major one was his unflappability. Once, during an interview on the pavilion roof at The Oval, the Surrey secretary's voice boomed from a closely adjacent loudspeaker. The deafening interruption would have panicked or angered many interviewers but Peter just laughed heartily. He always appeared totally at ease behind a microphone and his linking of live action and interview established a format for modern television coverage.

A former Rugby Correspondent of The Times, he wrote on both rugby and cricket for the Daily Telegraph. It was for the latter that he made his final tour. Fittingly it was to Australia to cover England's last successful Ashes expedition.

In partnership with Patrick Nally, Peter set up a sports events agency that helped to organise two football World Cups, a World Athletics Championship and the first rugby union World Cup. It also ran Cornhill's 131-match, 23-year sponsorship of Test cricket.

For many years he was the leading light behind the Cheltenham Cricket Lovers' Society and many members of the Test Match Special team will have fond memories of evenings spent in his company there.

BILL FRINDALL

ENGLAND v NEW ZEALAND

SERIES RECORDS

1929-30 to 2001-02

HIGHEST INNINGS TOTALS

England	in England	567-8d		Nottingham	1994
	in New Zealand	593-6d		Auckland	1974-75
New Zealand	in England	551-9d		Lord's	1973
	in New Zealand	537		Wellington	1983-84

LOWEST INNINGS TOTALS

England	in England	126		Birmingham	1999
	in New Zealand	64		Wellington	1977-78
New Zealand	in England	47		Lord's	1958
	in New Zealand	26		Auckland	1954-55

HIGHEST MATCH AGGREGATE   1294 for 36 wickets   Christchurch   2001-02
LOWEST MATCH AGGREGATE   390 for 30 wickets   Lord's   1958

HIGHEST INDIVIDUAL INNINGS

England	in England	310*	J.H.Edrich	Leeds	1965
	in New Zealand	336*	W.R.Hammond	Auckland	1932-33
New Zealand	in England	206	M.P.Donnelly	Lord's	1949
	in New Zealand	222	N.J.Astle	Christchurch	2001-02

HIGHEST AGGREGATE OF RUNS IN A SERIES

England	in England	469	(av 78.16)	L.Hutton	1949
	in New Zealand	563	(av 563.00)	W.R.Hammond	1932-33
New Zealand	in England	462	(av 77.00)	M.P.Donnelly	1949
	in New Zealand	341	(av 85.25)	C.S.Dempster	1929-30

RECORD WICKET PARTNERSHIPS – ENGLAND

1st	223	G.Fowler (105)/C.J.Tavaré (109)	The Oval	1983
2nd	369	J.H.Edrich (310*)/K.F.Barrington (163)	Leeds	1965
3rd	245	J.Hardstaff jr (114)/W.R.Hammond (140)	Lord's	1937
4th	266	M.H.Denness (181)/K.W.R.Fletcher (216)	Auckland	1974-75
5th	242	W.R.Hammond (227)/L.E.G.Ames (103)	Christchurch	1932-33
6th	281	G.P.Thorpe (200*)/A.Flintoff (137)	Christchurch	2001-02
7th	149	A.P.E.Knott (104)/P.Lever (64)	Auckland	1970-71
8th	246	L.E.G.Ames (137)/G.O.B.Allen (122)	Lord's	1931
9th	163*	M.C.Cowdrey (128*)/A.C.Smith (69*)	Wellington	1962-63
10th	59	A.P.E.Knott (49)/N.Gifford (25*)	Nottingham	1973

RECORD WICKET PARTNERSHIPS – NEW ZEALAND

1st	276	C.S.Dempster (136)/J.E.Mills (117)	Wellington	1929-30
2nd	241	J.G.Wright (116)/A.H.Jones (143)	Wellington	1991-92
3rd	210	B.A.Edgar (83)/M.D.Crowe (106)	Lord's	1986
4th	155	M.D.Crowe (143)/M.J.Greatbatch (68)	Wellington	1987-88
5th	180	M.D.Crowe (142)/S.A.Thomson (69)	Lord's	1994
6th	141	M.D.Crowe (115)/A.C.Parore (71)	Manchester	1994
7th	117	D.N.Patel (99)/C.L.Cairns (61)	Christchurch	1991-92
8th	104	D.A.R.Moloney (64)/A.W.Roberts (66*)	Lord's	1937
9th	118	J.V.Coney (174*)/B.L.Cairns (64)	Wellington	1983-84
10th	118	N.J.Astle (222)/C.L.Cairns (23*)	Christchurch	2001-02

BEST INNINGS BOWLING ANALYSIS

England	in England	7-32	D.L.Underwood	Lord's	1969
	in New Zealand	7-47	P.C.R.Tufnell	Christchurch	1991-92
New Zealand	in England	7-74	B.L.Cairns	Leeds	1983
	in New Zealand	7-143	B.L.Cairns	Wellington	1983-84

BEST MATCH BOWLING ANALYSIS

England	in England	12-101	D.L.Underwood	The Oval	1969
	in New Zealand	12-97	D.L.Underwood	Christchurch	1970-71
New Zealand	in England	11-169	D.J.Nash	Lord's	1994
	in New Zealand	10-100	R.J.Hadlee	Wellington	1977-78

HIGHEST AGGREGATE OF WICKETS IN A SERIES

England	in England	34	(av 7.47)	G.A.R.Lock	1958
	in New Zealand	19	(av 19.00)	D.Gough	1996-97
		19	(av 19.84)	A.R.Caddick	2001-02
New Zealand	in England	21	(av 26.61)	R.J.Hadlee	1983
	in New Zealand	15	(av 19.53)	R.O.Collinge	1977-78
		15	(av 24.73)	R.J.Hadlee	1977-78

RESULTS SUMMARY

ENGLAND v NEW ZEALAND – IN ENGLAND

	Tests	Series			Lord's			The Oval			Manchester			Leeds			Birmingham			Nottingham		
		E	NZ	D	E	NZ	D	E	NZ	D	E	NZ	D	E	NZ	D	E	NZ	D	E	NZ	D
1931	3	1	–	2	–	–	1	1	–	–	–	–	1	–	–	–	–	–	–	–	–	–
1937	3	1	–	2	–	–	1	–	–	1	1	–	–	–	–	–	–	–	–	–	–	–
1949	4	–	–	4	–	–	1	–	–	1	–	–	1	–	–	1	–	–	–	–	–	–
1958	5	4	–	1	1	–	–	–	–	1	1	–	–	1	–	–	1	–	–	–	–	–
1965	3	3	–	–	1	–	–	–	–	–	–	–	–	1	–	–	1	–	–	–	–	–
1969	3	2	–	1	1	–	–	1	–	–	–	–	–	–	–	–	–	–	–	–	–	1
1973	3	2	–	1	–	–	1	–	–	–	–	–	–	1	–	–	–	–	–	1	–	–
1978	3	3	–	–	1	–	–	1	–	–	–	–	–	–	–	–	–	–	–	1	–	–
1983	4	3	1	–	1	–	–	1	–	–	–	–	–	–	1	–	–	–	–	1	–	–
1986	3	–	1	2	–	–	1	–	–	1	–	–	–	–	–	–	–	–	–	–	1	–
1990	3	1	–	2	–	–	1	–	–	–	–	–	–	–	–	–	1	–	–	–	–	1
1994	3	1	–	2	–	–	1	–	–	–	–	–	1	–	–	–	–	–	–	1	–	–
1999	4	1	2	1	–	1	–	–	1	–	–	–	1	–	–	–	1	–	–	–	–	–
	44	22	4	18	5	1	7	4	1	4	2	–	4	3	1	1	4	–	–	4	1	2

ENGLAND v NEW ZEALAND – IN NEW ZEALAND

	Tests	Series			Christchurch			Wellington			Auckland			Dunedin		
		E	NZ	D	E	NZ	D	E	NZ	D	E	NZ	D	E	NZ	D
1929-30	4	1	–	3	1	–	–	–	–	1	–	–	2	–	–	–
1932-33	2	–	–	2	–	–	1	–	–	–	–	–	1	–	–	–
1946-47	1	–	–	1	–	–	1	–	–	–	–	–	–	–	–	–
1950-51	2	1	–	1	–	–	1	1	–	–	–	–	–	–	–	–
1954-55	2	2	–	–	–	–	–	–	–	–	1	–	–	1	–	–
1958-59	2	1	–	1	1	–	–	–	–	–	–	–	1	–	–	–
1962-63	3	3	–	–	1	–	–	1	–	–	1	–	–	–	–	–
1965-66	3	–	–	3	–	–	1	–	–	–	–	–	1	–	–	1
1970-71	2	1	–	1	1	–	–	–	–	–	–	–	1	–	–	–
1974-75	2	1	–	1	–	–	1	–	–	–	1	–	–	–	–	–
1977-78	3	1	1	1	1	–	–	–	1	–	–	–	1	–	–	–
1983-84	3	–	1	2	–	1	–	–	–	1	–	–	1	–	–	–
1987-88	3	–	–	3	–	–	1	–	–	1	–	–	1	–	–	–
1991-92	3	2	–	1	1	–	–	–	–	1	1	–	–	–	–	–
1996-97	3	2	–	1	1	–	–	1	–	–	–	–	1	–	–	–
2001-02	3	1	1	1	1	–	–	–	–	1	–	1	–	–	–	–
	41	16	3	22	8	1	6	3	1	5	4	1	10	1	–	1
Totals	85	38	7	40												

ENGLAND v WEST INDIES

SERIES RECORDS
1929-30 to 2000

HIGHEST INNINGS TOTALS

England	in England	619-6d	Nottingham	1957
	in West Indies	849	Kingston	1929-30
West Indies	in England	692-8d	The Oval	1995
	in West Indies	681-8d	Port-of-Spain	1953-54

LOWEST INNINGS TOTALS

England	in England	71	Manchester	1976
	in West Indies	46	Port-of-Spain	1993-94
West Indies	in England	54	Lord's	2000
	in West Indies	102	Bridgetown	1934-35

HIGHEST MATCH AGGREGATE 1815 for 34 wickets Kingston 1929-30
LOWEST MATCH AGGREGATE 309 for 29 wickets Bridgetown 1934-35

HIGHEST INDIVIDUAL INNINGS

England	in England	285*	P.B.H.May	Birmingham	1957
	in West Indies	325	A.Sandham	Kingston	1929-30
West Indies	in England	291	I.V.A.Richards	The Oval	1976
	in West Indies	375	B.C.Lara	St John's	1993-94

HIGHEST AGGREGATE OF RUNS IN A SERIES

England	in England	506	(av 42.16)	G.P.Thorpe (6 Tests)	1995
	in West Indies	693	(av 115.50)	E.H.Hendren	1929-30
West Indies	in England	829	(av 118.42)	I.V.A.Richards	1976
	in West Indies	798	(av 99.75)	B.C.Lara	1993-94

RECORD WICKET PARTNERSHIPS – ENGLAND

1st	212	C.Washbrook (102)/R.T.Simpson (94)	Nottingham	1950
2nd	266	P.E.Richardson (126)/T.W.Graveney (258)	Nottingham	1957
3rd	303	M.A.Atherton (135)/R.A.Smith (175)	St John's	1993-94
4th	411	P.B.H.May (285*)/M.C.Cowdrey (154)	Birmingham	1957
5th	150	A.J.Stewart (143)/G.P.Thorpe (84)	Bridgetown	1993-94
6th	205	M.R.Ramprakash (154)/G.P.Thorpe (103)	Bridgetown	1997-98
7th	197	M.J.K.Smith (96)/J.M.Parks (101*)	Port-of-Spain	1959-60
8th	217	T.W.Graveney (165)/J.T.Murray (112)	The Oval	1966
9th	109	G.A.R.Lock (89)/P.I.Pocock (13)	Georgetown	1967-68
10th	128	K.Higgs (63)/J.A.Snow (59*)	The Oval	1966

RECORD WICKET PARTNERSHIPS – WEST INDIES

1st	298	C.G.Greenidge (149)/D.L.Haynes (167)	St John's	1989-90
2nd	287*	C.G.Greenidge (214*)/H.A.Gomes (92*)	Lord's	1984
3rd	338	E.de C.Weekes (206)/F.M.M.Worrell (167)	Port-of-Spain	1953-54
4th	399	G.St A.Sobers (226)/F.M.M.Worrell (197*)	Bridgetown	1959-60
5th	265	S.M.Nurse (137)/G.St A.Sobers (174)	Leeds	1966
6th	274*	G.St A.Sobers (163*)/D.A.J.Holford (105*)	Lord's	1966
7th	155*	G.St A.Sobers (150*)/B.D.Julien (121)	Lord's	1973
8th	99	C.A.McWatt (54)/J.K.Holt (48*)	Georgetown	1953-54
9th	150	E.A.E.Baptiste (87*)/M.A.Holding (69)	Birmingham	1984
10th	70	I.R.Bishop (44*)/D.Ramnarine (19)	Georgetown	1997-98

BEST INNINGS BOWLING ANALYSIS

England	in England	8-103	I.T.Botham	Lord's	1984
	in West Indies	8- 53	A.R.C.Fraser	Port-of-Spain	1997-98
West Indies	in England	8- 92	M.A.Holding	The Oval	1976
	in West Indies	8- 45	C.E.L.Ambrose	Bridgetown	1989-90

BEST MATCH BOWLING ANALYSIS

England	in England	12-119	F.S.Trueman	Birmingham	1963
	in West Indies	13-156	A.W.Greig	Port-of-Spain	1973-74
West Indies	in England	14-149	M.A.Holding	The Oval	1976
	in West Indies	11- 84	C.E.L.Ambrose	Port-of-Spain	1993-94

HIGHEST AGGREGATE OF WICKETS IN A SERIES

England	in England	34	(av 17.47)	F.S.Trueman	1963
	in West Indies	27	(av 18.66)	J.A.Snow	1967-68
		27	(av 18.22)	A.R.C.Fraser	1997-98
West Indies	in England	35	(av 12.65)	M.D.Marshall	1988
	in West Indies	30	(av 14.26)	C.E.L.Ambrose	1997-98

RESULTS SUMMARY

ENGLAND v WEST INDIES – IN ENGLAND

	Tests	Series			Lord's			Manchester			The Oval			Nottingham			Birmingham			Leeds		
		E	WI	D	E	WI	D	E	WI	D	E	WI	D	E	WI	D	E	WI	D	E	WI	D
1928	3	3	–	–	1	–	–	1	–	–	1	–	–	–	–	–	–	–	–	–	–	–
1933	3	2	–	1	1	–	–	–	–	1	1	–	–	–	–	–	–	–	–	–	–	–
1939	3	1	–	2	1	–	–	–	–	1	–	–	1	–	–	–	–	–	–	–	–	–
1950	4	1	3	–	–	1	–	1	–	–	–	1	–	–	1	–	–	–	–	–	–	–
1957	5	3	–	2	1	–	–	–	–	–	1	–	–	–	–	1	–	–	1	1	–	–
1963	5	1	3	1	–	–	1	–	1	–	–	1	–	–	–	–	1	–	–	–	1	–
1966	5	1	3	1	–	–	1	–	1	–	1	–	–	–	1	–	–	–	–	–	1	–
1969	3	2	–	1	–	–	1	1	–	–	–	–	–	–	–	–	–	–	–	1	–	–
1973	3	–	2	1	–	1	–	–	–	–	–	1	–	–	–	–	–	–	1	–	–	–
1976	5	–	3	2	–	–	1	–	1	–	–	1	–	–	–	1	–	–	–	–	1	–
1980	5	–	1	4	–	–	1	–	–	1	–	–	1	–	1	–	–	–	–	–	–	1
1984	5	–	5	–	–	1	–	–	1	–	–	1	–	–	–	–	–	1	–	–	1	–
1988	5	–	4	1	–	1	–	–	1	–	–	1	–	–	–	1	–	–	–	–	1	–
1991	5	2	2	1	–	–	1	–	–	–	1	–	–	–	1	–	–	1	–	1	–	–
1995	6	2	2	2	1	–	–	1	–	–	–	–	1	–	–	1	–	1	–	–	1	–
2000	5	3	1	1	1	–	–	–	–	1	1	–	–	–	–	–	–	1	–	1	–	–
	70	21	29	20	6	4	6	4	5	4	6	6	3	–	4	4	1	4	2	4	6	1

ENGLAND v WEST INDIES – IN WEST INDIES

	Tests	Series			Bridgetown			Port-of-Spain			Georgetown			Kingston			St John's		
		E	WI	D	E	WI	D	E	WI	D	E	WI	D	E	WI	D	E	WI	D
1929-30	4	1	1	2	–	–	1	1	–	–	–	1	–	–	–	1	–	–	–
1934-35	4	1	2	1	1	–	–	–	1	–	–	–	1	–	1	–	–	–	–
1947-48	4	–	2	2	–	–	1	–	–	1	–	1	–	–	1	–	–	–	–
1953-54	5	2	2	1	–	1	–	–	–	1	1	–	–	1	1	–	–	–	–
1959-60	5	1	–	4	–	–	1	1	–	1	–	–	1	–	–	1	–	–	–
1967-68	5	1	–	4	–	–	1	1	–	1	–	–	1	–	–	1	–	–	–
1973-74	5	1	1	3	–	–	1	1	1	–	–	–	1	–	–	1	–	–	–
1980-81	4	–	2	2	–	1	–	–	1	–	–	–	–	–	–	1	–	–	1
1985-86	5	–	5	–	–	1	–	–	2	–	–	–	–	–	1	–	–	1	–
1989-90	4	1	2	1	–	1	–	–	–	1	–	–	–	1	–	–	–	1	–
1993-94	5	1	3	1	1	–	–	–	1	–	–	1	–	–	1	–	–	–	1
1997-98	6	1	3	2	–	–	1	1	1	–	–	1	–	–	–	1	–	1	–
	56	10	23	23	2	4	6	5	7	5	1	4	4	2	5	6	–	3	2
Totals	126	31	52	43															

TOURING TEAM REGISTER 2004

Neither New Zealand nor West Indies had selected their 2004 touring teams at the time of going to press. See page 9 for key to abbreviations. The following players are available and have represented these countries in Test Matches since October 2002:

NEW ZEALAND

Full Names	Birthdate	Birthplace	Team	Type	F-C Debut
ASTLE, Nathan John	15.09.71	Christchurch	Canterbury	RHB/RM	1991-92
BOND, Shane Edward	07.06.75	Christchurch	Canterbury	RHB/RF	1996-97
BUTLER, Ian Gareth	24.11.81	Auckland	N Districts	RHB/RFM	2001-02
CAIRNS, Christopher Lance	13.06.70	Picton	Canterbury	RHB/RFM	1988
FLEMING, Stephen Paul	01.04.73	Christchurch	Wellington	LHB/RSM	1991-92
HART, Robert Garry	02.12.74	Hamilton	N Districts	RHB/WK	1992-93
HORNE, Matthew Jeffery	05.12.70	Auckland	Auckland	RHB/RM	1992-93
JONES, Richard Andrew	22.10.73	Auckland	Wellington	RHB	1993-94
McMILLAN, Craig Douglas	13.09.76	Christchurch	Canterbury	RHB/RM	1994-95
ORAM, Jacob David Philip	28.07.78	Palmerston North	C Districts	LHB/RM	1997-98
RICHARDSON, Mark Hunter	11.06.71	Hastings	Auckland	LHB/LM	1989-90
SINCLAIR, Matthew Stuart	09.11.75	Katherine, Australia	C Districts	RHB/RM/WK	1995-96
STYRIS, Scott Bernard	10.07.75	Brisbane, Australia	N Districts	RHB/RMF	1994-95
TUFFEY, Daryl Raymond	11.06.78	Milton	N Districts	RHB/RFM	1996-97
VETTORI, Daniel Luca	27.01.79	Auckland	N Districts	RHB/SLA	1996-97
VINCENT, Lou	11.11.78	Warkworth	Auckland	RHB/OB/WK	1997-98
WISEMAN, Paul John	04.05.70	Auckland	Auckland	RHB/OB	1991-92

WEST INDIES

Full Names	Birthdate	Birthplace	Team	Type	F-C Debut
BANKS, Omari Ahmed Clemente	17.07.82	Anguilla	Leeward Is	RHB/OB	2000-01
BAUGH, Carlton Seymour	23.06.82	Kingston	Jamaica	RHB/LBG/WK	2000-01
BERNARD, David Eddison	19.07.81	Kingston	Jamaica	RHB	2000-01
BEST, Tino la Bertram	26.08.81	St Michael	Barbados	RHB/RFM	2001-02
BREESE, Gareth Rohan	09.01.76	Montego Bay	Jamaica	RHB/OB	1995-96
CHANDERPAUL, Shivnarine	18.08.74	Unity Village	Guyana	LHB/LB	1991-92
COLLINS, Pedro Tyrone	12.08.76	Boscobelle	Barbados	RHB/LFM	1996-97
COLLYMORE, Corey Dalanelo	21.12.77	Boscobelle	Barbados	RHB/RMF	1998-99
CUFFY, Cameron Eustace	08.02.70	S Rivers, St Vincent	Windward Is	RHB/RF	1990-91
DILLON, Mervyn	05.06.74	Mission Village	Trinidad	RHB/RFM	1996-97
DRAKES, Vasbert Conniel	05.08.69	Springhead	Barbados	RHB/RMF	1991-92
EDWARDS, Fidel Henderson	06.02.82	Gays, St Peter	Barbados	RHB/RF	2001-02
GANGA, Daren	14.01.79	Barrackpore	Trinidad	RHB/OB	1996-97
GAYLE, Christopher Henry	21.09.79	Kingston	Jamaica	LHB/OB	1998-99
HINDS, Ryan O'Neal	17.02.81	Holders Hill	Barbados	LHB/SLA	1998-99
HINDS, Wavell Wayne	07.09.76	Kingston	Jamaica	LHB/RM	1995-96
JACOBS, Ridley Detamore	26.11.67	Swetes, Antigua	Leeward Is	LHB/WK	1991-92
LARA, Brian Charles	02.05.69	Cantaro	Trinidad	LHB/LBG	1987-88
LAWSON, Jermaine Jay Charles	13.01.82	Spanish Town	Jamaica	RHB/RF	2000-01
McLEAN, Nixon Alexei McNamara	20.07.73	Stubbs, St Vincent	Windward Is	LHB/LFM	1992-93
MOHAMMED, Dave	08.10.79	Knolly Street	Trinidad	LHB/SLC	2000-01
NAGAMOOTOO, Mahendra Veeren	09.10.75	Whim	Guyana	LHB/LBG	1994-95
POWELL, Darren Brentlyle	15.04.78	Malvern	Jamaica	RHB/RFM	2000-01
SAMUELS, Marlon Nathaniel	05.01.81	Los Angeles, USA	Jamaica	RHB/OB	1996-97
SANFORD, Adam	12.07.76	Dominica	Leeward Is	RHB/RFM	1996-97
SARWAN, Ramnaresh Ronnie	23.06.80	Wakenaam I	Guyana	RHB/LB	1995-96
SMITH, Dwayne Romel	12.01.83	Storey Gap	Barbados	RHB/RM	2001-02
SMITH, Devon Sheldon	21.10.81	Grenada	Windward Is	LHB/OB	1998-99
TAYLOR, Jerome Everton	22.06.84	St Elizabeth	Jamaica	RHB/RF	2002-03

THE FIRST-CLASS COUNTIES REGISTER, RECORDS AND 2003 AVERAGES

Career records are to the end of the 2003 season (first-class), and to 12 February 2004 (Test Match and LOI).

ABBREVIATIONS – General

*	not out/unbroken partnership	l-o	limited-overs
b	born	LOI	Limited-Overs Internationals
BB	Best innings bowling analysis	Tests	Official Test Matches
Cap	Awarded 1st XI County Cap	Tours	Overseas tours involving first-class
f-c	first-class		appearances
HS	Highest Score		

Awards

BHC	Benson and Hedges Cup 'Gold' Award
CGT	Gillette Cup, NatWest/Cheltenham & Gloucester Trophy Match Award
Wisden 2002	One of *Wisden Cricketers' Almanack's* Five Cricketers of 2002
YC 2003	Cricket Writers' Club Young Cricketer of 2003

ECB Competitions

BHC	Benson & Hedges Cup (1972-2002)
CC	Frizzell County Championship
CGT	Cheltenham & Gloucester Trophy
NL	National League
NWT	NatWest Trophy (1981-2000)
SL	Sunday League (1969-98)

Education

BHS	Boys' High School
C	College
CFE	College of Further Education
CHE	College of Higher Education
CS	Comprehensive School
GS	Grammar School
HS	High School
I	Institute
IHE	Institute of Higher Education
RGS	Royal Grammar School
S	School
SFC	Sixth Form College
SM	Secondary Modern School
SS	Secondary School
TC	Technical College
T(H)S	Technical (High) School
U	University
UMIST	University of Manchester Institute of Science and Technology
UWIC	University of Wales Institute, Cardiff

Playing Categories

LBG	Bowls right-arm leg-breaks and googlies
LF	Bowls left-arm fast
LFM	Bowls left-arm fast-medium
LHB	Bats left-handed
LM	Bowls left-arm medium pace
LMF	Bowls left-arm medium-fast

OB	Bowls right-arm off-breaks
RF	Bowls right-arm fast
RFM	Bowls right-arm fast-medium
RHB	Bats right-handed
RM	Bowls right-arm medium pace
RMF	Bowls right-arm medium-fast
RSM	Bowls right-arm slow-medium
SLA	Bowls left-arm leg-breaks
SLC	Bowls left-arm 'Chinamen'
WK	Wicket-keeper

Teams (see also p 123)

ACT	Australian Capital Territory
ADBP	Agricultural Development Bank of P
B	Bangladesh
CD	Central Districts
DHR	D.H.Robins' XI
EP	Eastern Province
GW	Griqualand West
K	Kenya
KRL	Khan Research Laboratories
NSW	New South Wales
NT	Northern Transvaal
(O)FS	(Orange) Free State
PIA	Pakistan International Airlines
PTCL	Pakistan Telecommunications Co. Ltd.
Q	Queensland
REDCO	Really Efficient Development Company
RW	Rest of the World XI
SAB	South African Breweries XI
SAU	South African Universities
V	Victoria
WA	Western Australia
WAPDA	Water & Power Development Auth.
WP	Western Province

9

DERBYSHIRE

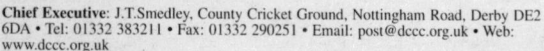

Formation of Present Club: 4 November 1870
Inaugural First-Class Match: 1871
Colours: Chocolate, Amber and Pale Blue
Badge: Rose and Crown
County Champions: (1) 1936
Gillette/NatWest/C & G Trophy Winners: (1) 1981
Benson and Hedges Cup Winners: (1) 1993
National League (Div 1) Winners: (0); best – 4th (Div 2) 2002
Sunday League Winners: (1) 1990
Twenty20 Cup Winners: 3rd in North Group 2003
Match Awards: CGT 49; BHC 71

Chief Executive: J.T.Smedley, County Cricket Ground, Nottingham Road, Derby DE2 6DA • **Tel**: 01332 383211 • **Fax**: 01332 290251 • **Email**: post@dccc.org.uk • **Web**: www.dccc.org.uk

Director of Cricket/1st XI Coach: D.L.Houghton. **Academy Director/2nd XI Coach**: K.M.Krikken. **Captain**: M.J.Di Venuto. **Vice-Captain**: L.D.Sutton. **Overseas Players**: M.J.Di Venuto and *tba*. **2004 Beneficiary**: None. **Head Groundsman**: N.Godrich. **Scorer**: J.M.Brown. ‡ New registration. NQ Not qualified for England.

NQADNAN, Muhammad Hassan Syed (M.A.O. College, Lahore), b Lahore, Pakistan 15 May 1974. 5'10". RHB, OB. Islamabad 1994-95, 2001-02. WAPDA 1997-98 to date (as an overseas player 2002-03 to date). Gujranwala 1997-98 to 1998-99. 49 f-c matches in Pakistan before his Derbyshire debut in 2003. HS 130 WAPDA v Bahawalpur (Bahawalpur) 1999-00. De HS 84 v Hants (Derby) 2003. BB – LO HS 101* WAPDA v Lahore City (Faisalabad) 1999-00.

NQALI, Syed Mohammad Bukhari (Punjab C of Commerce), b Bahawalpur, Pakistan 8 Nov 1973. 6'0". Nephew of Taslim Arif (Pakistan 1979-80 to 1980-81). British passport. RHB, LFM. Lahore 1993-94. Railways 1993-94. Islamabad 1994-95. United Bank 1994-95. Rawalpindi 1995-96 to 1998-99. ADBP 1995-96 to 1998-99. Bahawalpur 1998-99. 55 f-c matches in Pakistan before his Derbyshire debut in 2002. HS 92 Bahawalpur v Lahore (Rahim Yar Khan) 1998-99. De HS 53 v Durham (Derby) 2002 – on debut. 50 wkts (0+1): 56 (1993-94). BB 6-37 Railways v National Bank (Faisalabad) 1993-94. De BB 4-79 v Glam (Derby) 2003. LO HS 19 v Lancs (Manchester) 2002 (CGT). LO BB 4-34 Railways v United Bank (Karachi) 1993-94.

NQBASSANO, Christopher Warwick Godfrey (Grey S, Port Elizabeth; Launceston Church GS; Tasmania U, Hobart), b East London, South Africa 11 Sep 1975. 6'2". British passport (English mother); son of the late B.S.Bassano (cricket writer, historian and broadcaster). RHB, LB. Debut 2001; cap 2002. First to score 100 in each innings on Championship debut – 186* and 106 v Glos (Derby) 2001. Tasmania 2002-03. 1000 (1): 1063 (2002). HS 186* (*see above*). BB – Awards: CGT 2. LO HS 126* v Sussex (Arundel) 2003 (NL).

‡NQBOTHA, Anthony Greyvensteyn (Maritzburg C; Maritzburg Technikon), b Pretoria, South Africa 17 Nov 1976. LHB, SLA. Natal/KwaZulu Natal 1995-96 to 1998-99. EP/Easterns 1999-00 to date. HS 94 Natal B v EP B (Port Elizabeth) 1997-98. BB 8-53 Natal B v Northerns B (Pretoria) 1997-98. LO HS 60* Easterns v EP (Benoni) 2001-02. LO BB 3-16 SA Academy v NZ Academy (Pretoria) 1997.

‡NQBRYANT, James Douglas Campbell (Maritzburg C; Port Elizabeth U), b Durban, South Africa 4 Feb 1976. 6'0". RHB. RM. E Province 1996-97 to date. Somerset 2003. F-c Tour: (SA A): WI 2000-01. HS 234* EP v North West (Potchefstroom) 2002-03. UK HS 109* Sm v LU (Taunton) 2003 – on Sm/UK debut. CC HS 73 Sm v Hants (Taunton) 2003. UK BB – LO HS 105* EP v WP (Cape Town) 2000-01.

DEAN, Kevin James (Leek HS; Leek CFE), b Derby 16 Oct 1975. 6'5". LHB, LMF. Debut 1996. Cap 1998. HS 54* v Worcs (Derby) 2002. 50 wkts (2): most – 83 (2002). BB 8-52 v Kent (Canterbury) 2000. 2 hat tricks (1998, 2000). Award: CGT 1. LO HS 16* v Glam (Cardiff) 1998 (SL) and 16* v Middx (Derby) 2002 (NL). LO BB 5-32 v Glos (Derby) 1996 (SL).

NQDi VENUTO, Michael James (St Virgil's C; Hobart), b Hobart, Australia 12 Dec 1973. 6'0". LHB, RM/LB. Tasmania 1991-92 to date. Sussex 1999; cap 1999. Derbyshire debut/cap 2000; captain 2004. **LOI** (A): 9 (1996-97 to 1997-98); HS 89 v SA (Jo'burg) 1996-97. F-c Tours: Z 1995-96 (Tas); Sc/Ire 1998 (Aus A). 1000 runs (4): most – 1538 (2002). HS 230 v Northants (Derby) 2002. BB (Tas) 1-0. UK BB (Sx) 1-3. De BB 1-16. Awards: CGT 1; BHC 1. LO HS 173* v Derbys CB (Derby) 2000 (NWT). LO BB (Tas) 1-10.

DUMELOW, Nathan Robert Charles (Foremark Hall S; Denstone C), b Derby 30 Apr 1981. 5'9". RHB, OB. Debut 2001. HS 75 v Hants (Southampton) 2003. BB 5-78 (10-160 match) v Northants (Northampton) 2003. LO HS 52 v Surrey (Derby) 2002 (NL). LO BB 3-24 v Sussex (Hove) 2002 (NL).

NQGAIT, Andrew Ian (Kearsney C; UNISA), b Bulawayo, Rhodesia 19 Dec 1978. British passport. 6'1". RHB. Free State 1998-99 to 2000-01. Derbyshire debut 2002. HS 175 v Northants (Northampton) 2002. LO HS 138* FS v GW (Bloemfontein) 2000-01 – Free State l-o record.

GUNTER, Neil Edward Lloyd (The Clere S; Newbury C), Basingstoke, Hants 12 May 1981. 6'0". LHB, RFM. Berkshire 2000-01. Derbyshire debut 2002. MCCYC. HS 20* v Hants (Southampton) 2003. BB 4-14 v WI A (Derby) 2002. CC BB 2-48 v Durham (Derby) 2003. LO HS 5 (Berks CGT) and 5 (NL). LO BB –

HAVELL, Paul Matthew Roger (Mentone GS, Melbourne; Warden Park S; Haywards Heath C), b Melbourne, Australia 4 Jul 1980. 6'3". LHB, RFM. Sussex 2001 (1 non-CC match). Derbyshire debut 2003. HS 7* v Somerset (Taunton) 2003. BB 4-129 v SA (Derby) 2003 – on De debut. CC BB 3-34 v Glos (Bristol) 2003. LO HS – LO BB –

HEWSON, Dominic Robert (Cheltenham C; West of England U), b Cheltenham, Glos 3 Oct 1974. 5'8". RHB, occ RM. Gloucestershire 1996-2001. Derbyshire debut 2002. HS 168 Gs v Derbys (Bristol) 2001. De HS 102* v Glam (Cardiff) 2002 – on debut. BB (Gs) 1-7. LO HS 69 v Kent CB (Canterbury) 2003 (CGT). LO BB 4-25 v Scot (Edinburgh) 2003 (NL).

KHAN, Rawait Mahmood (Moseley S; Solihull SFC), b Birmingham 5 Mar 1982. Elder brother of Z.M.Khan (Derbyshire 2000). 5'10". RHB, OB. Debut 2001. HS 91 v Indians (Derby) 2002. CC HS 76 v Northants (Derby) 2002. BB – LO HS 29 Derbys v Glos CB (Heanor) 2000 (NWT).

LUNGLEY, Tom (St John Houghton SS; SE Derbyshire C), b Derby 25 Jul 1979. 6'1". LHB, RM. Debut 2000. HS 47 v Warwks (Derby) 2001. BB 4-101 v Glam (Swansea) 2003. LO HS 45 v Essex (Chelmsford) 2001 (NL). LO BB 4-28 v Essex (Derby) 2001 (NL).

SELWOOD, Steven Andrew (Mill Hill S; Albany C, Loughborough U), b Barnet, Herts 24 Nov 1979. Son of T.Selwood (Middlesex and C Districts 1966-73). 6'0". LHB, SLA. Debut 2001. HS 99 v Worcs (Derby) 2002. BB 1-8 (CC). LO HS 93 v Glos (Bristol) 2002 (NL). LO BB 1-7 (CGT).

STUBBINGS, Stephen David (Frankston HS, Aus; Swinburne U, Aus), b Huddersfield, Yorks 31 Mar 1978. 6'3". LHB, OB. Debut 1997. Cap 2001. 1000 (1): 1047 (2001). HS 135* v Kent (Canterbury) 2000. BB – LO HS 98* v Lancs (Derby) 2002 (NL).

SUTTON, Luke David (Millfield S; Durham U), b Keynsham, Somerset 4 Oct 1976. 5'11". RHB, WK. Somerset 1997-98. Derbyshire debut 2000. Cap 2002. HS 140* (carried bat) v Sussex (Derby) 2001. LO HS 83 v Lancs (Derby) 2003 (NL).

WELCH, Graeme (Hetton CS), b Durham City 21 Mar 1972. 5'11½". RHB, RM. Warwickshire 1994-2000; cap 1997. Derbyshire debut/cap 2001. F-c Tour: SA 1994-95 (Wa). HS 84* Wa v Notts (Birmingham) 1994. De HS 64 v Warwks (Birmingham) 2001 and 64 v Worcs (Derby) 2002. 50 wkts (3): 65 (1997). BB 6-30 v Durham (Chester-le-St) 2001. Award: BHC 1. LO HS 71 Wa v Kent (Maidstone) 1999 (NL). LO BB 6-31 v Middx (Derby) 2002 (NL).

RELEASED/RETIRED
(Having made a first-class County appearance in 2003)

NQC.Z.Harris and J.I.D.Kerr left the staff having made no f-c appearances in 2003.

CORK, D.G. – *see NORTHAMPTONSHIRE*.

NQ**KAIF, Mohammad**, b Allahabad, India 1 Dec 1980. RHB, OB. Uttar Pradesh 1997-98 to 2001-02. Leicestershire 2002 (one match); cap 2002. Derbyshire 2003. **Tests** (I): 4 (1999-00 to 2001); HS 37 v SL (Galle) 2000. **LOI** (I): 59 (2001-02 to 2003-04); HS 111* v Z (Colombo) 2002-03. F-c Tours (I): E 2002; SA 2001-02 (Ind A); SL 2001. HS 136 India A v SA A (Kimberley) 2001-02. UK HS 77 De v Yorks (Derby) 2003. BB 3-4 Uttar Pradesh v Vidarbha (Kanpur) 2001-02. UK BB 1-21 De v Northants (Northampton) 2003. Award: CGT 1. LO HS 120 Uttar Pradesh v Madhya Pradesh (Udaipur) 2001-02. LO BB 4-23 Uttar Pradesh v Rajasthan (Jaipur) 1998-99.

KRIKKEN, Karl Matthew (Rivington & Blackrod HS & SFC), b Bolton, Lancs 9 Apr 1969. Son of B.E.Krikken (Lancs and Worcs 1966-69). 5'9". RHB, WK. GW 1988-89. Derbyshire 1989-2003; cap 1992; benefit 2002. Academy Director/2nd XI Coach 2003. HS 104 v Lancs (Manchester) 1996. BB 1-54. LO HS 55 v Kent (Derby) 1996 (NWT).

NQ**SHAHID KHAN AFRIDI**, Sahibzaha Mohammad (Ibrahim Alibhai S and Islamia Science C, Karachi), b Kohat, Pakistan 1 Mar 1980. Younger brother of Tariq Afridi (Karachi). 5'11". RHB, LBG. F-c debut (Combined XI v England A) 1995-96. Karachi 1995-96 to 2001-02. Habib Bank 1997-98 to 2001-02. Leicestershire 2001; cap 2001. Derbyshire 2003. **Tests** (P): 14 (1998-99 to 2001-02); HS 141 v I (Madras) 1998-99; BB 5-52 v A (Karachi) 1998-99 – on debut. **LOI** (P): 176 (1997-98 to 2002-03); HS 109 v I (Toronto) 1998-99; BB 5-40 v E (Lahore) 2000-01. Scored a 37-ball hundred (*LOI record*) which included 11 sixes (*equalled record*) v SL (Nairobi) 1996-97 in his first LOI innings. F-c Tours (P): A 1996-97; WI 1999-00; I 1998-99; Z 2002-03; B 1998-99. HS 164 Le v Northants (Northampton) 2001. De HS 67 v Durham (Chester-le-St) 2003. BB 6-101 Habib Bank v KRL (Rawalpindi) 1997-98. CC BB 5-84 Le v Essex (Chelmsford) 2001. De BB 2-29 v Glam (Derby) 2003 – on De debut. Awards: CGT 2. LO HS 112 Pak A v Ind A (Karachi) 1997-98. LO BB 5-36 Habib Bank v Sargodha (Sargodha) 2001-02.

WHARTON, Lian James (Ecclesbourne S; Malkworth C), b Holbrook 21 Feb 1977. 5'9". LHB, SLA. Derbyshire 2000-03. HS 30 v Worcs (Worcester) 2003. BB 6-62 v Middx (Lord's) 2002. LO HS 11* v Essex (Chelmsford) 2002 (NL). LO BB 3-23 v Durham (Chester-le-St) 2001 (NL).

12

DERBYSHIRE 2003

RESULTS SUMMARY

	Place	Won	Lost	Tied	Drew	No Result
County Championship (2nd Division)	**9th**	2	11		3	
All First-Class Matches		2	11		4	
C & G Trophy	Semi-Finalist					
National League (2nd Division)	**6th**	8	8			2
Twenty20 Cup	**3rd in North Group**					

COUNTY CHAMPIONSHIP AVERAGES

BATTING AND FIELDING

Cap		M	I	NO	HS	Runs	Avge	100	50	Ct/St
–	M.H.Adnan	2	4	1	84	189	63.00	–	2	1
2001	S.D.Stubbings	3	6	–	103	306	51.00	1	2	1
2000	M.J.Di Venuto	16	31	–	150	1520	49.03	5	8	25
2002	L.D.Sutton	15	29	4	127	936	37.44	2	2	25/2
–	A.I.Gait	12	24	–	110	662	27.58	1	4	10
–	N.R.C.Dumelow	9	17	3	75	347	24.78	–	3	2
1993	D.G.Cork	16	29	3	92	593	22.80	–	3	11
–	M.Kaif	8	15	–	87	332	22.13	–	1	5
–	R.M.Khan	8	15	–	76	322	21.46	–	2	3
–	S.A.Selwood	9	17	1	88	333	20.81	–	2	3
2001	G.Welch	14	26	5	54	414	19.71	–	2	3
–	Shahid Afridi	3	6	–	67	92	15.33	–	1	–
2002	C.W.G.Bassano	11	21	3	53*	271	15.05	–	2	5
–	D.R.Hewson	8	16	–	57	222	13.87	–	1	4
–	L.J.Wharton	6	9	5	30	46	11.50	–	–	4
–	T.Lungley	5	8	1	29	80	11.42	–	–	2
–	P.M.R.Havell	3	6	5	7*	10	10.00	–	–	2
–	S.M.B.Ali	10	17	3	31	101	7.21	–	–	1
1998	K.J.Dean	15	24	3	30*	148	7.04	–	–	4

Also batted: N.E.L.Gunter (2 matches) 9*, 20*; K.M.Krikken (1 – cap 1992) 14, 1 (1 ct).

BOWLING

	O	M	R	W	Avge	Best	5wI	10wM
G.Welch	455.3	113	1394	53	26.30	6-102	2	–
D.G.Cork	444.1	99	1363	50	27.26	6- 28	3	2
K.J.Dean	421.3	101	1506	41	36.73	4- 39	–	–
P.M.R.Havell	77.4	12	369	10	36.90	3- 54	–	–
S.M.B.Ali	221	36	1060	28	37.85	4- 79	–	–
N.R.C.Dumelow	200.4	39	711	16	44.43	5- 78	2	1

Also bowled:

L.J.Wharton	115	24	364	9	40.44	4- 50	–	–
T.Lungley	66.2	6	350	7	50.00	4-101	–	–

M.J.Di Venuto 6-0-23-0; N.E.L.Gunter 27.1-2-153-3; D.R.Hewson 4-0-14-0; M.Kaif 4-1-21-1; R.M.Khan 3-1-13-0; S.A.Selwood 7-0-28-0; Shahid Afridi 54.4-15-147-4.

The First-Class Averages (pp 123–138) give the records of Derbyshire players in all first-class county matches (Derbyshire's other opponents being the South Africans).

DERBYSHIRE RECORDS

FIRST-CLASS CRICKET

Highest Total	For 645		v	Hampshire	Derby	1898
	V 662		by	Yorkshire	Chesterfield	1898
Lowest Total	For 16		v	Notts	Nottingham	1879
	V 23		by	Hampshire	Burton upon T	1958
Highest Innings	For 274	G.A.Davidson	v	Lancashire	Manchester	1896
	V 343*	P.A.Perrin	for	Essex	Chesterfield	1904

Highest Partnership for each Wicket

1st	322	H.Storer/J.Bowden	v	Essex	Derby	1929
2nd	417	K.J.Barnett/T.A.Tweats	v	Yorkshire	Derby	1997
3rd	316*	A.S.Rollins/K.J.Barnett	v	Leics	Leicester	1997
4th	328	P.Vaulkhard/D.Smith	v	Notts	Nottingham	1946
5th	302*†	J.E.Morris/D.G.Cork	v	Glos	Cheltenham	1993
6th	212	G.M.Lee/T.S.Worthington	v	Essex	Chesterfield	1932
7th	258	M.P.Dowman/D.G.Cork	v	Durham	Derby	2000
8th	198	K.M.Krikken/D.G.Cork	v	Lancashire	Manchester	1996
9th	283	A.Warren/J.Chapman	v	Warwicks	Blackwell	1910
10th	132	A.Hill/M.Jean-Jacques	v	Yorkshire	Sheffield	1986

† 346 runs were added for this wicket in two separate partnerships

Best Bowling	For 10- 40	W.Bestwick	v	Glamorgan	Cardiff	1921
(Innings)	V 10- 45	R.L.Johnson	for	Middlesex	Derby	1994
Best Bowling	For 17-103	W.Mycroft	v	Hampshire	Southampton	1876
(Match)	V 16-101	G.Giffen	for	Australians	Derby	1886

Most Runs – Season	2165	D.B.Carr	(av 48.11)	1959
Most Runs – Career	23854	K.J.Barnett	(av 41.12)	1979-98
Most 100s – Season	8	P.N.Kirsten		1982
Most 100s – Career	53	K.J.Barnett		1979-98
Most Wkts – Season	168	T.B.Mitchell	(av 19.55)	1935
Most Wkts – Career	1670	H.L.Jackson	(av 17.11)	1947-63
Most Career W-K Dismissals	1304	R.W.Taylor	(1157 ct; 147 st)	1961-84
Most Career Catches in the Field	563	D.C.Morgan		1950-69

LIST 'A' LIMITED-OVERS CRICKET

Highest Total	CGT	365-3	v	Cornwall	Derby	1986
	BHC	366-4	v	Combined U	Oxford	1991
	NL	292-9	v	Worcs	Knypersley	1985
Lowest Total	CGT	79	v	Surrey	The Oval	1967
	BHC	98	v	Worcs	Derby	1994
	NL	61	v	Hampshire	Portsmouth	1990
Highest Innings	CGT	173*	M.J.Di Venuto	v	Derbys CB	Derby	2000
	BHC	142	D.M.Jones	v	Minor C	Derby	1996
	NL	141*	C.J.Adams	v	Kent	Chesterfield	1992
Best Bowling	CGT	8-21	M.A.Holding	v	Sussex	Hove	1988
	BHC	6-33	E.J.Barlow	v	Glos	Bristol	1978
	NL	6- 7	M.Hendrick	v	Notts	Nottingham	1972

DURHAM

Formation of Present Club: 23 May 1882
Inaugural First-Class Match: 1992
Colours: Navy Blue, Yellow and Maroon
Badge: Coat of Arms of the County of Durham
County Champions: (0) 8th 1999, 8th (Div 1) 2000
Gillette/NatWest/C & G Trophy Winners: (0); best –
quarter-finalist 1992, 2001
Benson and Hedges Cup Winners: (0); best – quarter-finalist
1998, 2000, 2001
National League (Div 1) Winners: (0); best – 8th (Div 1)
2002
Sunday League Winners: (0); best – 7th 1993
Twenty20 Cup Winners: 5th in North Group 2003
Match Awards: CGT 24; BHC 20

Chief Executive: D.Harker, County Ground, Riverside, Chester-le-Street, Co Durham
DH3 3QR • Tel: 0191 387 1717 • Fax: 0191 387 1616 • Email:
marketing@durham-ccc.org.uk • Web: www.durham-ccc.org.uk
First XI Coach: M.D.Moxon. **Captain**: J.J.B.Lewis. **Vice-Captain**: No appointment.
Overseas Players: H.H.Gibbs and Shoaib Akhtar. **2004 Beneficiary**: J.J.B.Lewis. **Head
Groundsman**: D.Measor. **Scorer**: B.Hunt. ‡ New registration. NQ Not qualified for
England.
*Durham initially awarded caps immediately their players joined the staff but revised this
policy in 1998 and now cap players on merit, past 'awards' having been nullified.*

‡NOBREESE, Gareth Rohan (Kingston U of Technology, Jamaica), b Montego Bay,
Jamaica 9 Jan 1976. 5'7". RHB, OB. Jamaica 1995-96 to date; captain/overseas player
2003-04. British passport. Tests (WI): 1 (2002-03); HS 5 and BB 2-108 v I (Madras)
2002-03. F-c Tours (WI): I 2003-04. HS 124 Jamaica v Lancs (Kingston) 1995-96. BB 7-60
Jamaica v Barbados (Bridgetown) 2000-01. LO HS 44* Jamaica v St Vincent & Grenadines
(Alpart) 2002-03. LO BB 3-24 Jamaica v Leeward Is (Spanish Town) 2001-02.

BRIDGE, Graeme David (Southmoor S, Sunderland), b Sunderland 4 Sep 1980. 5'8".
RHB, SLA. Debut 1999. HS 50 v Yorks (Chester-le-St) 2003. BB 6-84 v Hants (Chester-le-
St) 2001. Awards: CGT 1; BHC 1. LO HS 50* v Leics (Leicester) 2002 (BHC). LO BB 4-20
v Hants (Chester-le-St) 2003 (NL).

COLLINGWOOD, Paul David (Blackfyne CS; Derwentside C), b Shotley Bridge 26 May
1976. 5'11". RHB, RMF. Debut 1996 v Northants (Chester-le-St) taking wicket of D.J.Capel
with his first ball before scoring 91 and 16; cap 1998 ECB contract 2004. Tests: 2
(2003-04); HS 36 v SL (Galle) 2003-04. LOI: 42 (2001 to 2003-04). HS 100 v SL (Perth)
2002-03; BB 4-38 v NZ (Napier) 2001-02. F-c Tour: SL 2003-04. 1000 (1): 1108 (2001).
HS 190 v SL (Chester-le-St) 2002. CC HS 153 v Warwks (Birmingham) 2001. BB 4-31 v
Derbys (Derby) 2002. Awards: BHC 4. LO HS 118* v Notts (Chester-le-St) 2002 (NL). LO
BB 4-31 v Yorks (Chester-le-St) 2000 (BHC).

DAVIES, Anthony Mark (Northfield CS, Billingham), b Stockton-on-Tees 4 Oct 1980. 6'3".
RHB. RM. Durham Academy graduate. Debut 2002. HS 33 v Derbys (Darlington) 2002. BB
5-61 v Glam (Chester-le-St) 2002. LO HS 31* v Warwks (Chester-le-St) 2002 (NL). LO BB
4-13 v Sussex (Chester-le-St) 2001 (NL).

‡^{NO}**GIBBS, Herschelle** Herman (Diocesan C), b Green Point, Cape Town, South Africa 23 Feb 1974. 5'10". RHB, RM. W Province 1990-91 to date. **Tests** (SA): 56 (1996-97 to 2003-04); HS 228 v P (Cape Town) 2002-03. **LOI** (SA): 143 (1996-7 to 2003-04); HS 153 v B (Potchefstroom) 2002-03. F-c Tours (E): E 1996 (SA A), 2003; A 1997-98, 2001-02; WI 2000-01; NZ 1998-99; I 1996-97, 1999-00; P 2003-04; SL 1998-99 (SA A); Z 2001-02; B 2002-03. HS 228 (*see Tests*). BB 2-14 SA A v Somerset (Taunton) 1996. LO HS 153 (*see LOI*). LO BB 1-16 SA A v Essex (Chelmsford) 1996.

‡**HAMILTON, Gavin** Mark (Hurstmere SS, Kent), b Broxburn, Scotland 16 Sep 1974. 6'1". LHB, RFM. Scotland 1993-94. Yorkshire debut 1994; cap 1998. **Tests**: 1 (1999-00); HS 0 v SA (Jo'burg) 1999-00. **LOI** (Scot): 5 (1999); HS 76 and BB 2-36 v P (Chester-le-St) 1999. F-c Tours: SA 1999-00; Z 1995-96 (Y). HS 125 Y v Hants (Leeds) 2000. 50 wkts (1): 59 (1998). BB 7-50 (11-72 match) Y v Surrey (Leeds) 1998. Match double (70, 70; 5-69, 5-43) Y v Glam (Cardiff) 1998 – first instance for Yorks since 1964 (R.Illingworth). Award: BHC 1. LO HS 76 (*see LOI*). LO BB 5-16 Y v Hants (Leeds) 1998 (SL).

HARMISON, Stephen James (Ashington HS), b Ashington, Northumb 23 Oct 1978. 6'4". RHB, RF. Debut 1996; cap 1999. Northumberland 1996. **Tests**: 12 (2002 to 2003-04); HS 20* v A (Sydney) 2002-03; BB 5-35 (9-79 match) v B (Dhaka) 2003-04. **LOI**: 6 (2002-03 to 2003); HS 7; BB 2-39 v SL (Brisbane) 2002-03. F-c Tours: A 2002-03; SA 1998-99 (Eng A); Z 1998-99 (Eng A); B 2003-04. HS 36 v Kent (Canterbury) 1998. 50 wkts (2): most – 64 (1999). BB 6-111 v Sussex (Chester-le-St) 2001. LO HS 11* v Glam (Chester-le-St) 2001 (NL). LO BB 4-43 v Glam (Cardiff) 2001 (NL) and 4-43 v Sussex (Chester-le-St) 2003 (NL).

KILLEEN, Neil (Greencroft CS; Derwentside C; Teesside U), b Shotley Bridge 17 Oct 1975. 6'2". RHB, RFM. Debut 1995; cap 1999. HS 48 v Somerset (Chester-le-St) 1995. 50 wkts (1): 58 (1999). BB 7-70 v Hants (Chester-le-St) 2003. Award: BHC 1. LO HS 32 v Middx (Lord's) 1996 (SL). LO BB 6-31 v Derbys (Derby) 2000 (NL).

LEWIS, Jonathan James Benjamin (King Edward VI S, Chelmsford; Roehampton IHE), b Isleworth, Middx 21 May 1970. 5'9½". RHB, RSM. Essex 1990-96; cap 1994; scored 116* on debut v Surrey (Oval). Durham debut 1997; cap 1998; captain 2000 (*part*) to date; benefit 2004. 1000 runs (4); most – 1252 (1997). HS 210* v OU (Oxford) 1997 – on Du debut. CC HS 160* v Derbys (Chester-le-St) 1997. BB 1-73. Award: BHC 1. LO HS 102 v Glos (Cheltenham) 1997 (NL). LO BB –

LOWE, James Adam (Northallerton C, Yorks), b Bury St Edmunds, Suffolk 4 Nov 1982. 6'2". RHB, WK, occ OB. Debut 2003. Registered but not contracted. HS 80 v Hants (Southampton) 2003 – on debut.

MUCHALL, Gordon James (Durham S), b Newcastle upon Tyne, Northumb 2 Nov 1982. 6'1". RHB, RM. Northumberland 1999-2001. England U-19. Durham Academy graduate. Debut 2002. F-c Tours (ECB Acad): SL 2002-03. HS 127 v Middx (Lord's) 2002. BB 3-26 v Yorks (Leeds) 2003. LO HS 87 v Scot (Edinburgh) 2003 (NL). LO BB 1-15 (NL).

MUSTARD, Philip (Usworth CS), b Sunderland 8 Oct 1982. 5'11". LHB, WK. Durham Academy graduate. Debut 2002. HS 75 v SL (Chester-le-St) 2002 – on debut. CC HS 70* v Derbys (Derby) 2003. LO HS 41 v Somerset (Chester-le-St) 2003 (NL).

‡**ONIONS, Graham** (St Thomas More RCS, Blaydon), b Gateshead 9 Sep 1982. RHB, RMF. Durham Academy graduate. Staff 2004 – awaiting f-c debut. LO HS 5 and BB 2-59 Durham CB v Glam (Darlington) 2003 (CGT).

PATTISON, Ian (Seaham CS), b Ryhope, Sunderland 5 May 1982. 5'10". RHB, RM. Development Player. Debut 2002. HS 62 v Yorks (Leeds) 2003. BB 3-41 v Essex (Chester-le-St) 2002. LO HS 48* and LO BB 1-25 Durham CB v Leics CB (Gateshead) 2000 (NWT).

PENG GILLENDER, Nicky (Newcastle upon Tyne RGS), b Newcastle upon Tyne, Northumb 18 Sep 1982. 6'2". RHB, OB. Durham Academy graduate. Debut 2000. Cap 2001. HS 158 v Durham UCCE (Chester-le-St) 2003. CC HS 133 v Glam (Cardiff) 2003. Scored 98 v Surrey (Chester-le-St) on debut. BB – Award: CGT 1. LO HS 121 v Worcs (Worcester) 2001 (NL).

PLUNKETT, Liam Edward (Nunthorpe SS; Teesside Tertiary C), b Middlesbrough, Yorks 6 Apr 1985. 6'3". RHB, RMF. Durham Academy graduate. Debut 2003. HS 40* v Glos (Bristol) 2003. BB 5-53 v Yorks (Leeds) 2003 – on CC debut. LO HS 3 (Du CB – CGT). LO BB 3-38 v Lancs (Manchester) 2003 (NL).

PRATT, Andrew (Willington Parkside CS; Durham New C), b Helmington Row, Crook 4 Mar 1975. Elder brother of G.J.Pratt. 6'0". LHB, WK. Debut 1997. Cap 2001. MCC YC. HS 93 v Glos (Chester-le-St) 2002. LO HS 86 v Derbys (Chester-le-St) 2001 (NL).

PRATT, Gary Joseph (Willington Parkside CS), b Bishop Auckland 22 Dec 1981. Younger brother of A.Pratt. 6'0". LHB, OB. Durham Academy graduate. Debut 2000. 1000 (1): 1055 (2003). HS 150 v Northants (Chester-le-St) 2003. BB – LO HS 101* v Somerset (Taunton) 2003 (NL).

SCOTT, Gary Michael (Hetton CS), b Sunderland 21 Jul 1984. 6'0". RHB, OB. Durham Academy. Debut 2001 – youngest Durham f-c debutant (17y 19d). No appearances 2002-03. Registered but not contracted. HS 25 v Derbys (Chester-le-St) 2001 – on debut. BB – LO HS 100 Durham CB v Herefords (Darlington) 2002 (CGT). LO BB 2-32 Durham CB v Bucks (Beaconsfield) 2001 (CGT).

[NQ]**SHOAIB AKHTAR** (Elliott HS; Government C, Rawalpindi), b Rawalpindi, Pakistan 13 Aug 1975. 5'11½". RHB, RF. PIA 1994-95 to 1996-97. Rawalpindi 1994-95 to 1998-99. ADBP 1996-97 to 1997-98. KRL 2001-02. Somerset (one match) 2001. Durham debut 2003. **Tests** (P): 29 (1997-98 to 2003-04); HS 37 and BB 6-11 v NZ (Lahore) 2001-02. **LOI** (P): 98 (1997-98 to 2003-04); HS 43 v E (Cape Town) 2003; BB 6-16 v NZ (Karachi) 2002-02. F-c Tours (P): E (Pak A) 1997; A 1999-00; SA 1997-98; NZ 1998-99; Z 1997-98, 2002-03; B 1998-99, 2001-02. HS 59* KRL v PIA (Lahore) 2001-02. Du HS 37 v Glam (Chester-le-St) 2003. 50 wkts (0+1): 69 (1996-97). BB 6-11 (*see Tests*). Du BB 4-9 v Somerset (Chester-le-St) 2003. LO HS 56 KRL v Habib Bank (Lahore) 2002-03. LO BB 6-16 (*see LOI*).

RELEASED/RETIRED
(Having made a first-class County appearance in 2003)

C.Mann left the staff having made no f-c appearances in 2003.

GOUGH, Michael Andrew (English Martyrs RCS; Hartlepool SFC), b Hartlepool 18 Dec 1979. Son of M.P.Gough (Durham 1974-77). 6'5". RHB, OB. Durham Academy graduate. Durham 1998-2003. F-c Tours (Eng A): NZ 1999-00; B 1999-00. HS 123 v CU (Cambridge) 1998. CC HS 103 v Essex (Colchester) 2002. BB 5-66 v Middx (Chester-le-St) 2001. Award: CGT 1. LO HS 132 v Wales MC (Cardiff) 2002 (Durham CGT record). LO BB 3-26 v Somerset (Chester-le-St) 2002 (NL).

HATCH, Nicholas Guy (Barnard Castle S; Hull U), b Darlington 21 Apr 1979. 6'8". RHB, RMF. Durham Academy graduate. Durham 2001-03. HS 24 v Sussex (Chester-le-St) 2001. BB 4-61 v Worcs (Chester-le-St) 2002. LO HS 20* v Yorks (Chester-le-St) 2002 (NL). LO BB 3-26 v Glam (Chester-le-St) 2001 (NL).

HUNTER, Ian David (Fyndoune Community C, Sacriston; Durham New C), b Durham City 11 Sep 1979. 6'2". RHB, RMF. Durham Academy graduate. Durham 2000-03. HS 65 v Northants (Northampton) 2002. BB 4-55 v Warwks (Birmingham) 2001. LO HS 39 v Leics (Leicester) 2002 (BHC). LO BB 4-29 v Essex (Ilford) 2000 (NL).

LAW, Danny Richard (Steyning GS), b Lambeth, London 15 Jul 1975. 6'5". RHB, RFM. Sussex 1993-96; cap 1996. Essex 1997-2000. Durham 2001-03; cap 2001. HS 115 Sx v Young A (Hove) 1995. Du HS 103 v Hants (Chester-le-St) 2001. BB 6-53 v Hants (Southampton) 2001. Hat trick (Ex) 1998. LO HS 82 Ex v Durham (Chelmsford) 1997 (SL). LO BB 3-26 Ex v Leics (Leicester) 1999 (NL).

LOVE, Martin Lloyd (Toowoomba GS; Queensland U), b Mundubbera, Queensland, Australia 30 Mar 1974. 6'1". RHB, OB. Queensland 1992-93 to date. Durham 2003; cap 2001. **Tests** (A): 5 (2002-03 to 2003); HS 100* v B (Cairns) 2003. F-c Tours (A): E 1995 (Young A); WI 2003. 1000 (1+2): most – 1364 (2001). HS 273 (Durham record) v Hants (Chester-le-St) 2003 BB 1-5 (Q). LO HS 127* Q v NSW (Brisbane) 2001-02. LO BB –

PHILLIPS, Nicholas Charles (Wm Parker S, Hastings), b Pembury, Kent 10 May 1974. 5'10½". RHB, OB. Sussex 1993-97. Durham 1998-2003; cap 2001. HS 53 Sx v Young A (Hove) 1995. CC HS 58* v Essex (Colchester) 2002. BB 6-97 (12-268 match) v Glam (Cardiff) 1999. Took 3-0 v Derbys (Darlington) 2002. Award: CGT 1. LO HS 38* Sx v Essex (Chelmsford) 1996 (SL). LO BB 4-13 v Derbys (Chester-le-St) 1999 (NL).

[NO]**PRETORIUS, D.** –*see WARWICKSHIRE*.

[NO]**SRINATH, Javagal** (Marimallaba's HS; S.J. Engineering C), b Mysore, India 31 Aug 1969. 6'3". RHB, RFM. Karnataka 1989-90 to 2000-01. Gloucestershire 1995 (cap 1995). Leicestershire 2002; cap 2002. Durham 2003. **Tests:** (I): 67 (1991-92 to 2002-03); HS 76 v NZ (Hamilton) 1998-99; BB 8-86 (13-132 match) v P (Calcutta) 1998-99. LOI (I): 229 (1991-92 to 2002-03; HS 53 v SA (Rajkot) 1996-97; BB 5-23 v B (Dhaka) 1997-98. F-c Tours (I): E 1996; A 1991-92, 1999-00; SA 1992-93, 1996-97, 2001-02; WI 2002; NZ 1993-94, 1998-99; SL 1993-94, 2001; Z 1992-93, 1998-99, 2001; B 2000-01. HS 76 (*see Tests*). UK HS 52 Le v Yorks (Scarborough) 2002. Du HS 13* v Somerset (Taunton) 2003. 50 wkts (1): 87 (1995). BB 9-76 (13-150 match) Gs v Glam (Abergavenny) 1995. Du BB 3-70 v Worcs (Stockton) 2003. Hat trick Le v Surrey (Oval) 2002. Awards: BHC 2. LO HS 53 (*see LOI*). LO BB 5-23 (*see LOI*).

THORPE, Ashley Michael (Kent Street Senior HS, Western Australia), b Kiama, NSW, Australia 2 Apr 1975. 5'11". LHB, RM. Qualified by residence. Durham 2002-03. HS 95 v Essex (Chester-le-St) 2002. BB – LO HS 76 v Northants (Northampton) 2003 (NL). LO BB 2-49 v Leics (Leicester) 2002 (NL).

WELLS, Vincent John (Sir William Nottidge S, Whitstable), b Dartford, Kent 6 Aug 1965. 6'0". RHB, RMF. Kent 1988-91. Leicestershire 1992-2002; cap 1994; captain 2000-02; benefit 2001. Durham 2003. **LOI:** 9 (1998-99); HS 39 v A (Sydney) 1998-99; BB 3-30 v A (Sydney) 1998-99. F-c Tour (Le): SA 1996-97. 1000 runs (2); most – 1331 (1996). HS 224 Le v Middx (Lord's) 1997. Du HS 106 v Derbys (Derby) 2003. BB 5-18 Le v Notts (Worksop) 1998. Du BB 4-16 v Somerset (Chester-le-St) 2003. Hat trick 1994. Awards: CGT 5; BHC 1. LO HS 201 Le v Berks (Leicester) 1996 (NWT). LO BB 6-20 v Berks (Reading) 2003 (CGT).

DURHAM 2003

RESULTS SUMMARY

	Place	Won	Lost	Tied	Drew	No Result
County Championship (2nd Division)	**6th**	5	7		4	
All First-Class Matches		5	7		6	
C & G Trophy	4th Round					
National League (2nd Division)	**7th**	7	10			1
Twenty20 Cup	**5th in North Group**					

COUNTY CHAMPIONSHIP AVERAGES
BATTING AND FIELDING

Cap		M	I	NO	HS	Runs	Avge	100	50	Ct/St
2001	M.L.Love	7	13	–	273	778	59.84	1	4	8
1998	J.J.B.Lewis	16	31	2	124	1104	38.06	1	10	3
–	G.J.Pratt	16	31	–	150	949	31.63	1	7	9
1998	P.D.Collingwood	4	7	1	68	169	28.16	–	2	4
2001	N.Peng	13	23	–	133	580	25.21	1	2	11
–	G.D.Bridge	8	13	3	50	240	24.00	–	1	7
–	M.A.Gough	11	22	–	73	523	23.77	–	3	7
–	P.Mustard	12	22	1	70*	484	23.04	–	1	41/1
–	V.J.Wells	11	20	1	106	419	22.05	1	2	9
–	L.E.Plunkett	6	11	4	40*	139	19.85	–	–	2
–	G.J.Muchall	11	22	–	74	379	17.22	–	3	4
–	Shoaib Akhtar	7	14	2	37	197	16.41	–	–	–
2001	A.Pratt	4	7	2	27	79	15.80	–	–	12
2001	N.C.Phillips	11	20	4	39	211	13.18	–	–	7
1999	S.J.Harmison	5	6	3	14*	38	12.66	–	–	2
–	J.Srinath	3	5	3	13*	24	12.00	–	–	1
–	A.M.Davies	4	7	2	21	55	11.00	–	–	–
–	D.Pretorius	4	7	3	16	32	8.00	–	–	3
1999	N.Killeen	10	18	4	26	110	7.85	–	–	2
2001	D.R.Law	5	9	1	35	53	6.62	–	–	–
–	N.G.Hatch	4	4	1	5	13	4.33	–	–	–

Also batted: J.A.Lowe (1 match) 80, 0; I.Pattison (1) 62; A.M.Thorpe (2) 35, 11, 4.

BOWLING

	O	M	R	W	Avge	Best	5wI	10wM
Shoaib Akhtar	183	40	580	34	17.05	4- 9	–	–
D.Pretorius	79	13	317	16	19.81	4- 15	–	–
V.J.Wells	145.4	33	456	22	20.72	4- 16	–	–
S.J.Harmison	161.1	55	441	19	23.21	4- 50	–	–
D.R.Law	76.3	10	256	11	23.27	4- 30	–	–
L.E.Plunkett	150	27	636	18	35.33	5- 53	1	–
N.Killeen	267	63	848	23	36.86	7- 70	1	–
A.M.Davies	110	26	389	10	38.90	2- 34	–	–
G.D.Bridge	289	59	996	25	39.84	4- 47	–	–
N.C.Phillips	326.4	50	1200	30	40.00	5-144	1	–

Also bowled:

J.Srinath	84	24	226	6	37.66	3- 70	–	–
N.G.Hatch	104.4	21	384	9	42.66	3- 66	–	–

P.D.Collingwood 61.1-7-228-4; M.A.Gough 9.4-3-35-2; G.J.Muchall 37.2-7-144-4; I.Pattison 5.4-3-7-1; G.J.Pratt 1-0-5-0.

The First-Class Averages (pp 123–138) give the records of Durham players in all first-class county matches (Durham's other opponents being India A and Durham UCCE), with the exception of S.J.Harmison and D.Pretorius whose full county figures are as above.

19

DURHAM RECORDS

FIRST-CLASS CRICKET

Highest Total	For	645-6d		v	Middlesex	Lord's	2002
	V	810-4d		by	Warwicks	Birmingham	1994
Lowest Total	For	67		v	Middlesex	Lord's	1996
	V	56		by	Somerset	Chester-le-St^2	2003
Highest Innings	For	273	M.L.Love	v	Hampshire	Chester-le-St^2	2003
	V	501*	B.C.Lara	for	Warwicks	Birmingham	1994

Highest Partnership for each Wicket

1st	334*	S.Hutton/M.A.Roseberry	v	Oxford U	Oxford	1996
2nd	258	J.J.B.Lewis/M.L.Love	v	Notts	Chester-le-St^2	2001
3rd	205	G.Fowler/S.Hutton	v	Yorkshire	Leeds	1993
4th	224	G.J.Pratt/N.Peng	v	Durham UCCE	Chester-le-St^2	2003
5th	197	N.Peng/V.J.Wells	v	Derbys	Derby	2003
6th	193	D.C.Boon/P.D.Collingwood	v	Warwicks	Birmingham	1998
7th	127	D.R.Law/J.E.Brinkley	v	Hampshire	Chester-le-St^2	2001
8th	134	A.C.Cummins/D.A.Graveney	v	Warwicks	Birmingham	1994
9th	127	D.G.C.Ligertwood/S.J.E.Brown	v	Surrey	Stockton	1996
10th	103	M.M.Betts/D.M.Cox	v	Sussex	Hove	1996

Best Bowling	For	9- 64	M.M.Betts	v	Northants	Northampton	1997
(Innings)	V	9- 36	M.S.Kasprowicz	for	Glamorgan	Cardiff	2003
Best Bowling	For	14-177	A.Walker	v	Essex	Chelmsford	1995
(Match)	V	13-110	M.S.Kasprowicz	for	Glamorgan	Chester-le-St^2	2003

Most Runs – Season	1536	W.Larkins	(av 37.46)		1992
Most Runs – Career	6247	J.J.B.Lewis	(av 33.22)		1997-2003
Most 100s – Season	4	D.M.Jones			1992
	4	W.Larkins			1992
	4	J.E.Morris			1994
Most 100s – Career	14	J.E.Morris			1994-99
Most Wkts – Season	77	S.J.E.Brown	(av 25.87)		1996
Most Wkts – Career	518	S.J.E.Brown	(av 28.30)		1992-2002
Most Career W-K Dismissals	194	M.P.Speight	(189 ct; 5 st)		1997-2001
Most Career Catches in the Field	96	P.D.Collingwood			1996-2003

LIST 'A' LIMITED-OVERS CRICKET

Highest Total	CGT	326-4		v	Herefords	Chester-le-St^2	1995
	BHC	287-5		v	Leics	Leicester	1996
	NL	281-2		v	Derbyshire	Durham	1993
Lowest Total	CGT	82		v	Worcs	Chester-le-St^1	1968
	BHC	133		v	Glos	Bristol	2001
	NL	72		v	Warwicks	Birmingham	2002
Highest Innings	CGT	132	M.A.Gough	v	Wales MC	Cardiff	2002
	BHC	145	J.E.Morris	v	Leics	Leicester	1996
	NL	131*	W.Larkins	v	Hampshire	Portsmouth	1994
Best Bowling	CGT	7-32	S.P.Davis	v	Lancashire	Chester-le-St^1	1983
	BHC	6-30	S.J.E.Brown	v	Northants	Chester-le-St^2	1997
	NL	6-31	N.Killeen	v	Derbyshire	Derby	2000

^{1} Chester-le-Street CC (Ropery Lane) ^{2} Riverside Ground

ESSEX

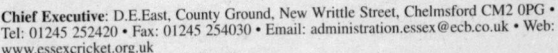

Formation of Present Club: 14 January 1876
Inaugural First-Class Match: 1894
Colours: Blue, Gold and Red
Badge: Three Seaxes above Scroll bearing 'Essex'
County Champions: (6) 1979, 1983, 1984, 1986, 1991, 1992
Gillette/NatWest/C & G Trophy Winners: (2) 1985, 1997
Benson and Hedges Cup Winners: (2) 1979, 1998
National League (Div 1) Winners: (0); best – 3rd 2003
Sunday League Winners: (3) 1981, 1984, 1985
Twenty20 Cup Winners: 5th in South Group 2003
Match Awards: CGT 51; BHC 91

Chief Executive: D.E.East, County Ground, New Writtle Street, Chelmsford CM2 0PG •
Tel: 01245 252420 • Fax: 01245 254030 • Email: administration.essex@ecb.co.uk • Web:
www.essexcricket.org.uk

First XI Coach: G.A.Gooch. **Club Captain**: N.Hussain. **First XI Captain**: R.C.Irani.
Vice-Captain: A.P.Grayson. **Overseas Players**: S.A.Brant and Danish Kaneria. **2004**
Beneficiary: Essex Academy. **Head Groundsman**: S.G.Kerrison. **Scorer**: D.J.Norris.
‡ New registration. NQ Not qualified for England.

BISHOP, Justin Edward (Bury St Edmunds County Upper S; John Snow C, Durham U), b
Bury St Edmunds, Suffolk 4 Jan 1982. 6'0". LHB, LMF. Debut 1999. Durham UCCE
2002-03. British U 2003. HS 50 DU v Notts (Nottingham) 2003 and 50 DU v Lancs
(Durham) 2003. Ex HS 23* v Worcs (Southend) 2002. BB 5-148 v Leics (Chelmsford)
2001. LO HS 16* v Hants (Colchester) 2000 (NL). LO BB 3-33 v Worcs (Worcester) 2001
(NL).

BOPARA, Ravinder Singh (Brampton Manor S; Barking Abbey Sports C), b Newham,
London 4 May 1985. 5'8". RHB, RMF. Debut 2002. HS 48 v Durham (Colchester) 2002 and
48 v Middx (Lord's) 2003. BB 1-23. LO HS 46 and BB 2-28 v P (Chelmsford) 2003.

NQ**BRANT, Scott** Andrew (St Georges C, Harare; St Johns C, Harare; St Joseph's Nudgee
C, Brisbane), b Harare, Zimbabwe 26 Jan 1983. 5'11½". RHB, LFM. Queensland 2001-02
to date. Essex debut/cap 2003. HS 23 v Lancs (Manchester) 2003. BB 6-45 v Notts
(Nottingham) 2003. LO HS 14* v Surrey (Chelmsford) 2003 (NL). LO BB 4-25 v Yorks
(Leeds) 2003 (NL).

CLARKE, Andrew John (St Martin's S, Hutton; Brentwood CHE), b Brentwood 9 Nov
1975. 6'2". LHB, RM. MCC YC. Debut 2002. HS 41 v Warwks (Chelmsford) 2003. BB
5-54 v Glam (Swansea) 2002 – on debut. LO HS 9 (CGT). LO BB 4-28 v Yorks
(Chelmsford) 2003 (NL).

COOK, Alastair Nathan (Bedford S), b Gloucester 25 Dec 1984. LHB, OB. Debut 2003.
Essex 2nd XI debut 2000 when aged 15y 235d. England U-19 capt 2003-04. HS 84 v Surrey
(Oval) 2003. BB – LO HS 27 Essex CB v Essex (Chelmsford) 2003 (CGT).

COWAN, Ashley Preston (Framlingham C), b Hitchin, Herts 7 May 1975. 6'4". RHB, RFM.
Debut 1995; cap 1997. No appearances 2003 (knee surgery). Cambridgeshire 1993. F-c
Tour: WI 1997-98. HS 94 v Leics (Leicester) 1998. 50 wkts (1): 52 (1997). BB 6-47 v Glam
(Cardiff) 1999. Hat trick 1996. Award: BHC 1. LO HS 45 v Middx (Chelmsford) 2001
(BHC). LO BB 5-14 v Middx (Southgate) 2001 (NL).

‡**NQDANISH** PARABHA SHANKER **KANERIA**, b Karachi, Pakistan 16 Dec 1980. Cousin of Anil Dalpat (Pakistan) and second Hindu to represent Pakistan. RHB, LB. Karachi 1998-99 to 2001-02. PNSC 1998-99. Habib Bank 1999-00 to date. **Tests** (P): 16 (2000-01 to 2003-04); HS 15 v A (Sharjah) 2002-03; BB 7-77 v B (Dhaka) 2001-02. Test debut was his fourth f-c match. **LOI** (P): 9 (2001-02 to 2003-04); HS 3*; BB 3-31 v NZ (Dambulla) 2003. F-c Tours (P): NZ 2003-04; SL 2001 (Pak A); K 2000 (Pak A). 50 wkts (0+1): 60 (2000-01). HS 42 Habib Bank v Allied Bank (Sheikhupura) 2001-02. BB 7-39 Karachi Whites v Gujranwala (Karachi) 2000-01. LO HS 15 PCB Whites v PCB Reds (Lahore) 2002-03. LO BB 5-24 Habib Bank v Lahore Blues (Lahore) 2001-02.

NQFLOWER, Andrew (Wainona HS, Harare), b Cape Town, South Africa 28 Apr 1968. 5'10". Elder brother of G.W.Flower (Zimbabwe). LHB, WK, occ RM. Mashonaland 1986-87 to 2001-02 (or 2002-3?). MCC 1996-99. *Wisden* 2001. Essex debut/cap 2002. S, Australia 2003-04. British passport after 2003 season. **Tests** (Z): 63 (1992-93 to 2002-03, 20 as captain); HS 232* v I (Nagpur) 2000-01. **LOI** (Z): 213 (1991-92 to 2002-03, 52 as captain); HS 145 v I (Colombo) 2002-03; scored 115 v SL (New Plymouth) on debut. F-c Tours (Z) (C=captain): E 2000C; SA 1999-00; WI 1999-00C; NZ 1995-96C, 1997-98, 2000-01; I 1992-93, 2000-01, 2001-02; P 1993-94C, 1996-97, 1998-99; SL 1996-97, 1997-98, 2001-02; B 2001-02. 1000 (2): 1244 (2003). HS 232* (*see Tests*). Ex HS 201* v Surrey (Oval) 2003. BB 1-1. Awards: BHC 2. LO HS 145 (*see LOI*). LO BB 1-21 (Mashonaland).

FOSTER, James Savin (Forest S, Snaresbrook; Collingwood C, Durham U), b Whipps Cross 15 Apr 1980. 6'0". RHB, WK. British U 2000. Essex debut 2000; cap 2001. Durham UCCE 2001. British U 2001. **ECB Contract 2002. Tests**: 7 (2001-02 to 2002-03); HS 48 v I (Bangalore) 2001-02. **LOI**: 11 (2001-02); HS 13 v I (Bombay) 2001-02. F-c Tours: A 2002-03; WI 2000-01 (Eng A); NZ 2001-02; I 2001-02. HS 103 DU v Worcs (Worcester) 2001. BB – Ex HS 85 v Notts (Nottingham) 2003. LO HS 56* v Sussex (Hove) 2001 (NL).

‡**GOUGH, Darren** (Priory CS, Lundwood), b Barnsley, Yorks 18 Sep 1970. 5'11". RHB, RF. Debut 1989; cap 1993; benefit 2001. *Wisden* 1998. **ECB contracts 2000, 2001, 2002. Tests**: 58 (1994 to 2003); HS 65 v NZ (Manchester) 1994 – on debut; BB 6-42 v SA (Leeds) 1998; hat trick v A (Sydney) 1998-99 – first for E v A since 1899. **LOI**: 121 (1994 to 2003); HS 45 v A (Melbourne) 1994-95; BB 5-44 v Z (Sydney) 1994-95 and 5-44 v A (Lord's) 1997. Took wickets with his sixth balls in both Tests and LOIs. F-c Tours: A 1994-95, 1998-99; SA 1991-92 (Y), 1992-93 (Y), 1993-94 (Eng A), 1995-96, 1999-00; NZ 1996-97; P 2000-01; SL 2000-01; Z 1996-97. HS 121 Y v Warwks (Leeds) 1996. 50 wkts (5); most – 67 (1996). BB 7-28 (10-80 match) Y v Lancs (Leeds) 1995 (not CC). CC BB 7-42 (10-96 match) Y v Somerset (Taunton) 1993. 2 hat tricks (1995, 1998-99); took 4 wkts in 5 balls Y v Kent (Leeds) 1995. Awards: CGT 2; BHC 1. LO HS 72* v Leics (Leicester) 1991 (SL). LO BB 7-27 Y v Ire (Leeds) 1997 (NWT).

GRAYSON, Adrian Paul (Bedale CS), b Ripon, Yorks 31 Mar 1971. 6'1". RHB, SLA. Yorkshire 1990-95. Essex debut/cap 1996. **LOI**: 2 (2000-01 to 2001-02); HS 6 and BB 3-40 v Z (Bulawayo) 2001-02. F-c Tour: SA 1991-92 (Y). 1000 runs (4); most – 1275 (2001). HS 189 v Glam (Chelmsford) 2001. BB 5-20 v Yorks (Scarborough) 2001. Award: BHC 1. LO HS 82* v Worcs (Chelmsford) 1997 (NWT). LO BB 4-25 Y v Glam (Cardiff) 1994 (SL).

HABIB, Aftab (Millfield S; Taunton S), b Reading, Berks 7 Feb 1972. Cousin of Zahid Sadiq (Surrey and Derbys 1988-90). 5'11". RHB, RM. Middlesex 1992 (one match). Leicestershire 1995-2001; cap 1998. Essex debut/cap 2002. **Tests**: 2 (1999); HS 19 v NZ (Lord's) 1999. F-c Tours (Eng A): WI 2000-01 (*part*); NZ 1999-00; B 1999-00. 1000 runs (2); most – 1055 (1999). HS 215 Le v Worcs (Leicester) 1996. Ex HS 151 v Notts (Nottingham) 2003. BB 1-10. Award: BHC 1. LO HS 111 Le v Durham (Chester-le-St) 1997 (BHC). LO BB 2-5 Le v Ire (Dublin) 1999.

HUSSAIN, Nasser (Forest S, Snaresbrook; Durham U), b Madras, India 28 Mar 1968. Son of J.Hussain (Madras 1966-67); brother of M.Hussain (Worcs 1985). 5'11". RHB, LB. Debut 1987; cap 1989; club captain 1999; benefit 1999. YC 1989. OBE 2002. *Wisden* 2002. **ECB contracts 2000, 2001, 2002, 2003, 2004. Tests:** 91 (1989-90 to 2003-04, 45 as captain); HS 207 v A (Birmingham) 1997. **LOI:** 88 (1989-90 to 2002-03, 56 as captain – E record); HS 115 v I (Lord's) 2002. F-c Tours (C=captain): A 1998-99, 2002-03C; SA 1999-00C; WI 1989-90, 1991-92 (Eng A), 1993-94, 1997-98; NZ 1996-97, 2001-02C; I 2001-02C; P 1990-91 (Eng A), 1995-96C (Eng A), 2000-01C; SL 1990-91 (Eng A), 2000-01C, 2003-04; Z 1996-97; B 2003-04. 1000 runs (5); most – 1854 (1995). HS 207 (*see Tests*). Ex HS 206 v Kent (Chelmsford) 2003. BB 1-38. Awards: CGT 4; BHC 4. LO HS 161* v Glam (Chelmsford) 2003 (NL).

IRANI, Ronald Charles (Smithills CS, Bolton), b Leigh, Lancs 26 Oct 1971. 6'3". RHB, RMF. Lancashire 1990-93. Essex debut/cap 1994; captain 2000 to date; benefit 2003. **Tests:** 3 (1996 to 1999); HS 41 v I (Lord's) 1996; BB 1-22. Took wicket of M.Azharuddin with his fifth ball in Test cricket. **LOI:** 31 (1996 to 2002-03); HS 53 and BB 5-26 v I (Oval) 2002. F-c Tours: NZ 1996-97, 1999-00 (Eng A); P 1995-96 (Eng A); Z 1996-97; B 1999-00 (Eng A). 1000 runs (5); most – 1196 (2000). HS 207* v Northants (Ilford) 2002. 50 wkts (1): 51 (1999). BB 6-71 v Notts (Nottingham) 2002. Awards: CGT 5; BHC 5. LO HS 124 v Durham (Chelmsford) 1996 (NWT). LO BB 5-26 (*see LOI*).

JEFFERSON, William Ingleby (Beeston Hall S, Norfolk; Oundle S; St Hild & St Bede C, Durham U), b Derby 25 Oct 1979. Son of R.I.Jefferson (Cambridge U and Surrey 1961-66); grandson of J.Jefferson (Army 1919, Comb Services 1922). 6'10". RHB, RMF. British U 2000-01. Essex debut 2000; cap 2002. Durham UCCE 2001-02. Scored 50 and 65 in first two LO innings. HS 165* v Notts (Chelmsford) 2002. LO HS 132 v Essex CB (Chelmsford) 2003 (CGT).

NQMcCOUBREY, Adrian George Agustus Mathew (Cambridge House BHS; Queens U, Belfast), b Ballymena, Co Antrim, N Ireland 3 Apr 1980. 5'10½". RHB, RFM. Ireland 1999-2000. Essex debut 2003. HS 1* and BB 3-38 Ire v Scot (Belfast) 1999 – on debut. Ex HS 1. Ex BB 1-7. LO HS 11 Ire v Berks (Finchampstead) 2001. LO BB 2-20 Ire v Wilts (Salisbury) 2001.

MIDDLEBROOK, James Daniel (Pudsey Crawshaw S), b Leeds, Yorks 13 May 1977. 6'1". RHB, OB. Yorkshire 1998-2001. Essex debut 2002; cap 2003. HS 84 Y v Essex (Chelmsford) 2001. Ex HS 82* v Leics (Southend) 2003. 50 wkts (1): 56 (2003). BB 6-82 (10-170 match) Y v Hants (Southampton) 2000 – including 4 wickets in 5 balls. Ex BB 6-123 v Kent (Chelmsford) 2003. Hat trick 2003. LO HS 46* v Yorks (Chelmsford) 2003 (NL). LO BB 4-33 v Hants (Southend) 2002.

NAPIER, Graham Richard (The Gilberd S, Colchester), b Colchester 6 Jan 1980. 5'9½". RHB, RM. Debut 1997; cap 2003. F-c Tours (Eng A): I 2003-04. HS 104 v CU (Cambridge) 2001. CC HS 89* v Sussex (Arundel) 2003. BB 5-66 v Notts (Nottingham) 2003. Award: CGT 1. LO HS 79 Essex CB v Lancs CB (Chelmsford) 2000 (NWT). LO BB 6-29 v Worcs (Chelmsford) 2001 (NL).

PALLADINO, Antonio Paul (Cardinal Pole SS; Anglia Polytechnic U), b London Hospital 29 Jun 1983. 6'0". RHB, RMF. Cambridge UCCE 2003. Essex debut 2003. HS 8 and BB 6-41 v Kent (Canterbury) 2003. LO HS 16 Essex CB v Essex (Chelmsford) 2003. LO BB 3-32 v Glam (Chelmsford) 2003 (NL).

PETTINI, Mark Lewis (Comberton Village C; Hills Road SFC, Cambridge; Cardiff U), b Brighton, Sussex 7 Aug 1983. RHB, RM. 5'10". Debut 2001. HS 78 v Warwks (Chelmsford) 2003. LO 92* v Warwks (Birmingham) 2003 (CGT).

PHILLIPS, Timothy James (Felsted S; St Hild & St Bede C, Durham U), b Cambridge 13 Mar 1981. 6'1". LHB, SLA. Essex debut 1999. No appearances 2003. Durham UCCE 2001-02. HS 75 DU v Durham (Chester-le-St) 2002. Ex HS 42 and CC BB 4-102 v Middx (Southgate) 2002. BB 4-42 v SL A (Chelmsford) 1999 – on debut. LO HS 6 (NL). LO BB 2-36 v Middx (Chelmsford) 2002 (NL).

SHARIF, Zoheb Khalid (Warwick S; Chigwell S; Coopers Co & Coborn S; Loughborough U), b Leytonstone 22 Feb 1983. LHB, LB. 5'10". Debut 2001. Loughborough UCCE 2003. HS 67 LU v Leics (Leicester) 2003. Ex HS 42 v Glos (Gloucester) 2002. BB 4-98 v Northants (Northampton) 2002. No 1-o appearances.

STEPHENSON, John Patrick (Felsted S; Durham U), b Stebbing 14 Mar 1965. 6'1". RHB, RM. Essex 1985-94 and 2002 (2nd XI captain 2002 to date); cap 1989. Hampshire 1995-2001; cap 1995; captain 1996-97; benefit 2001. Boland 1988-89. **Tests**: 1 (1989); HS 25 v A (Oval) 1989. F-c Tours: WI 1991-92 (Eng A); Z 1989-90 (Eng A). 1000 runs (5); most – 1887 (1990). HS 202* v Somerset (Bath) 1990. BB 7-44 (10-104 match) v Worcs (Worcester) 2002. Awards: CGT 1; BHC 5. LO HS 142 v Warwks (Birmingham) 1991 (BHC). LO BB 6-33 H v Worcs (Southampton) 1997 (SL).

NO Ten DOESCHATE, Ryan Neil (Fairbairn C; Cape Town U), b Port Elizabeth, South Africa 30 Jun 1980. 5'10½". RHB, RMF. Debut 2003. EU passport – Dutch ancestry. HS 31 v Sussex (Arundel) 2003. BB – LO HS – and BB 1-39 v Worcs (Worcester) 2003 (NL).

RELEASED/RETIRED
(Having made a first-class County appearance in 2003)

N.A.Denning and B.J.Hyam left the staff having made no f-c appearances in 2003.

DAKIN, J.M. – *see LEICESTERSHIRE*.

NO GRANT, Joseph Benjamin (Petersvale All-Age S, Jamaica), b White House, Jamaica 17 Dec 1967. 5'11". RHB, RFM. Jamaica 1990-91 to 1995-96. Essex 2001-03. Cambridgeshire 2001. HS 36* Jamaica v Guyana (Albion) 1994-95. Ex HS 30 v I (Chelmsford) 2002. CC HS 15 v Durham (Colchester) 2002. BB 5-38 v CU (Cambridge) 2002. CC BB 4-45 v Derbys (Derby) 2002. LO HS 14 Jamaica v Trinidad (Port-of-Spain) 1991-92. LO BB 3-10 Jamaica v Trinidad (Kingston) 1990-91.

McGARRY, Andrew Charles (King Edward VI GS, Chelmsford; SE Essex C of Arts & Technology, Southend), b Basildon 8 Nov 1981. 6'5". RHB, RFM. Essex 1999-2003. HS 11* v CU (Cambridge) 2002. CC HS 5*. BB 5-27 v CU (Cambridge) 2003. CC BB 3-29 v Worcs (Chelmsford) 2000. LO HS 1 (NL). LO BB 2-20 v Surrey (Colchester) 2000 (NL).

NO MOHAMMAD AKRAM – *see SUSSEX*.

ROBINSON, D.D.J. – *see LEICESTERSHIRE*.

SCORING OF EXTRAS 2004

The penalty for wides is now **one** run plus other runs scored in all ECB matches. For the past three seasons two runs were awarded for wides in the County and Second XI Championships. The new 20-overs Cup will carry the same penalties as the two surviving county limited-overs competitions.

COMPETITION	NO-BALL PENALTY	WIDE PENALTY
Test Matches Limited-Overs Internationals	1 + other runs scored	1 + other runs scored
County Championship Second XI Championship	2 + other runs scored	1 + other runs scored
Tourist Matches (First-Class) Tourist Matches (Limited-Overs)	1 + other runs scored	1 + other runs scored
C & G Trophy National League Twenty 20 Cup	2 + other runs scored + for foot fault free hit next ball	1 + other runs scored

ESSEX 2003

RESULTS SUMMARY

	Place	Won	Lost	Tied	Drew	No Result
County Championship (1st Division)	**7th**	3	5	1	7	
All First-Class Matches		3	5	1	8	
C & G Trophy	4th Round					
National League (1st Division)	**3rd**	8	7	1		
Twenty20 Cup	**5th in South Group**					

COUNTY CHAMPIONSHIP AVERAGES
BATTING AND FIELDING

Cap		M	I	NO	HS	Runs	Avge	100	50	Ct/St
1989	N.Hussain	5	9	1	206	453	56.62	1	2	2
–	A.N.Cook	3	6	1	84	239	47.80	–	3	3
2002	A.Flower	16	28	3	201*	1153	46.12	2	6	17
–	M.L.Pettini	3	5	1	78	172	43.00	–	2	3
–	R.S.Bopara	4	7	3	48	163	40.75	–	–	3
1989	J.P.Stephenson	3	5	1	75*	137	34.25	–	2	–
2003	G.R.Napier	15	24	8	89*	480	30.00	–	2	3
2002	A.Habib	12	20	–	151	599	29.95	1	4	9
1997	D.D.J.Robinson	10	19	2	83	503	29.58	–	3	5
–	A.J.Clarke	3	4	1	41	87	29.00	–	–	1
2002	W.I.Jefferson	13	26	3	62	656	28.52	–	5	10
2001	J.S.Foster	16	25	–	85	648	25.92	–	4	45/2
1994	R.C.Irani	12	18	–	87	450	25.00	–	4	4
2003	J.M.Dakin	10	17	1	59	390	24.37	–	2	2
1996	A.P.Grayson	9	16	2	71	287	20.50	–	2	5
2003	J.D.Middlebrook	15	24	1	82*	468	20.34	–	2	6
–	R.N.ten Doeschate	2	4	–	31	48	12.00	–	–	1
2003	S.A.Brant	10	14	6	23	37	4.62	–	–	3
–	Mohammad Akram	4	6	1	10	19	3.80	–	–	–
–	J.B.Grant	3	4	1	3	11	3.66	–	–	1

Also batted: J.E.Bishop (1 match) 21; A.G.A.M.McCoubrey (2) 1, 0, 0*; A.C.McGarry (1) 4*; A.P.Palladino (3) 5, 7*, 8; Z.K.Sharif (1) 0 (1 ct).

BOWLING

	O	M	R	W	Avge	Best	5wI	10wM
J.M.Dakin	330.3	74	1049	39	26.89	5- 86	1	
Mohammad Akram	145	31	560	20	28.00	8- 49	2	1
S.A.Brant	325.5	70	1060	36	29.44	6- 45	1	
J.D.Middlebrook	559.3	79	1889	52	36.32	6-123	3	
G.R.Napier	379.3	60	1506	33	45.63	5- 66	1	
Also bowled:								
J.B.Grant	39.2	3	181	7	25.85	3- 61	–	
R.C.Irani	87	28	223	8	27.87	4- 59	–	
A.J.Clarke	59	13	205	7	29.28	4- 34	–	
A.P.Palladino	75	21	215	7	30.71	6- 41	1	
A.P.Grayson	133	22	432	8	54.00	4- 47	–	

J.E.Bishop 29-4-101-1; R.S.Bopara 30-3-122-2; A.N.Cook 2-0-11-0; A.Flower 8.3-0-24-1; A.Habib 2.4-0-10-1; A.G.A.M.McCoubrey 24.1-3-142-3; A.C.McGarry 25.3-3-89-0; D.D.J.Robinson 5.5-0-40-1; Z.K.Sharif 17-1-103-3; J.P.Stephenson 42-8-162-3; R.N.ten Doeschate 24-3-122-0.

The First-Class Averages (pp 123–138) give the records of Essex players in all first-class county matches (Essex's other opponents being Cambridge UCCE), with the exception of: J.E.Bishop, N.Hussain, A.P.Palladino and Z.K.Sharif whose full county figures are as above.

ESSEX RECORDS

FIRST-CLASS CRICKET

Highest Total	For 761-6d		v	Leics	Chelmsford	1990
	V 803-4d		by	Kent	Brentwood	1934
Lowest Total	For 30		v	Yorkshire	Leyton	1901
	V 14		by	Surrey	Chelmsford	1983
Highest Innings	For 343*	P.A.Perrin	v	Derbyshire	Chesterfield	1904
	V 332	W.H.Ashdown	for	Kent	Brentwood	1934

Highest Partnership for each Wicket

1st	316	G.A.Gooch/P.J.Prichard	v	Kent	Chelmsford	1994
2nd	403	G.A.Gooch/P.J.Prichard	v	Leics	Chelmsford ·	1990
3rd	347*	M.E.Waugh/N.Hussain	v	Lancashire	Ilford	1992
4th	314	Salim Malik/N.Hussain	v	Surrey	The Oval	1991
5th	316	N.Hussain/M.A.Garnham	v	Leics	Leicester	1991
6th	206	J.W.H.T.Douglas/J.O'Connor	v	Glos	Cheltenham	1923
	206	B.R.Knight/R.A.G.Luckin	v	Middlesex	Brentwood	1962
7th	261	J.W.H.T.Douglas/J.Freeman	v	Lancashire	Leyton	1914
8th	263	D.R.Wilcox/R.M.Taylor	v	Warwicks	Southend	1946
9th	251	J.W.H.T.Douglas/S.N.Hare	v	Derbyshire	Leyton	1921
10th	218	F.H.Vigar/T.P.B.Smith	v	Derbyshire	Chesterfield	1947

Best Bowling	For 10- 32	H.Pickett	v	Leics	Leyton	1895
(Innings)	V 10- 40	E.G.Dennett	for	Glos	Bristol	1906
Best Bowling	For 17-119	W.Mead	v	Hampshire	Southampton	1895
(Match)	V 17- 56	C.W.L.Parker	for	Glos	Gloucester	1925

Most Runs – Season	2559	G.A.Gooch	(av 67.34)	1984
Most Runs – Career	30701	G.A.Gooch	(av 51.77)	1973-97
Most 100s – Season	9	J.O'Connor		1929, 1934
	9	D.J.Insole		1955
Most 100s – Career	94	G.A.Gooch		1973-97
Most Wkts – Season	172	T.P.B.Smith	(av 27.13)	1947
Most Wkts – Career	1610	T.P.B.Smith	(av 26.68)	1929-51
Most Career W-K Dismissals	1231	B.Taylor	(1040 ct; 191 st)	1949-73
Most Career Catches in the Field	519	K.W.R.Fletcher		1962-88

LIST 'A' LIMITED-OVERS CRICKET

Highest Total	CGT	386-5		v	Wiltshire	Chelmsford	1988
	BHC	388-7		v	Scotland	Chelmsford	1992
	NL	310-5		v	Glamorgan	Southend	1983
Lowest Total	CGT	57		v	Lancashire	Lord's	1996
	BHC	61		v	Lancashire	Chelmsford	1992
	NL	69		v	Derbyshire	Chesterfield	1974
Highest Innings	CGT	144	G.A.Gooch	v	Hampshire	Chelmsford	1990
	BHC	198*	G.A.Gooch	v	Sussex	Hove	1982
	NL	176	G.A.Gooch	v	Glamorgan	Southend	1983
Best Bowling	CGT	5- 8	J.K.Lever	v	Middlesex	Westcliff	1972
		5- 8	G.A.Gooch	v	Cheshire	Chester	1995
	BHC	5-13	J.K.Lever	v	Middlesex	Lord's	1985
	NL	8-26	K.D.Boyce	v	Lancashire	Manchester	1971

26

GLAMORGAN

Formation of Present Club: 6 July 1888
Inaugural First-Class Match: 1921
Colours: Blue and Gold
Badge: Gold Daffodil
County Champions: (3) 1948, 1969, 1997
Gillette/NatWest/C & G Trophy Winners: (0); best – finalist 1977
Benson and Hedges Cup Winners: (0); best – finalist 2000
National League (Div 1) Winners: (1) 2002
Sunday League Winners: (1) 1993
Twenty20 Cup Winners: 6th in Midlands/Wales/West Group 2003
Match Awards: CGT 44; BHC 56

Chief Executive: M.J.Fatkin, Sophia Gardens, Cardiff, CF1 9XR • Tel: 029 2040 9380 • Fax: 029 2040 9390 • Email: glam@ecb.co.uk • Web: www.glamorgancricket.com

First XI Coach: J.Derrick. **Captain**: R.D.B.Croft. **Vice-Captain**: No appointment. **Overseas Player**: M.T.G Elliott and M.S.Kasprowicz. **2004 Beneficiary**: Sophia Gardens Development Appeal. **Head Groundsman**: L.A.Smith. **Scorer**: G.N.Lewis. ‡ New registration. NQ Not qualified for England.

CHERRY, Daniel David (Tonbridge S; U of Wales, Swansea), b Newport, Gwent 7 Feb 1980. 5'9". LHB, RM. Debut 1998. No f-c appearances 2000-01. HS 47 v Glos (Cheltenham) 2002. BB – No l-o appearances.

COSKER, Dean Andrew (Millfield S), b Weymouth, Dorset 7 Jan 1978. 5'11". RHB, SLA. Debut 1996; cap 2000. F-c Tours (Eng A): SA 1998-99, SL 1997-98; Z 1998-99, K 1997-98. HS 49 v Sussex (Cardiff) 1999. BB 6-140 v Lancs (Colwyn Bay) 1998. LO HS 27* v Somerset (Taunton) 1999 (NL). LO BB 5-54 v Essex (Chelmsford) 2003 (NL).

CROFT, Robert Damien Bale (St John Lloyd Catholic CS, Llanelli; Neath Tertiary C; W Glam IHE), b Morriston 25 May 1970. 5'10½". RHB, OB. Debut 1989; cap 1992; benefit 2000; captain 2003 (part) to date. **Tests**: 21 (1996 to 2001); HS 37* v SA (Manchester) 1998; BB 5-95 v NZ (Christchurch) 1996-97. **LOI**: 50 (1996 to 2001); HS 32 v SL (Perth) 1998-99; BB 3-51 v SA (Oval) 1998. F-c Tours: A 1998-99; SA 1993-94 (Eng A), 1995-96 (Gm); WI 1991-92 (Eng A), 1997-98; NZ 1996-97; SL 2000-01, 2002-03; Z 1990-91 (Gm), 1994-95 (Gm), 1996-97. HS 143 v Somerset (Taunton) 1995. 50 wkts (6); most – 76 (1996). BB 8-66 (14-169 match) v Warwks (Swansea) 1992. Awards: CGT 1; BHC 2. LO HS 119 v Surrey (Oval) 2002 (CGT). LO BB 6-20 v Worcs (Cardiff) 1994 (SL).

DALE, Adrian (Chepstow CS; Swansea U), b Germiston, SA 24 Oct 1968 (to UK at 6 mths). 5'11½". RHB, RM. Debut 1989; cap 1992; benefit 2002. F-c Tours (Gm): SA 1993-94 (Eng A), 1995-96; Z 1990-91, 1994-95. 1000 runs (4); most – 1472 (1993). HS 214* v Middx (Cardiff) 1993. BB 6-18 v Warwks (Cardiff) 1993. Awards: CGT 2; BHC 3. LO HS 110 v Lincs (Swansea) 1994 (NWT). LO BB 6-22 v Durham (Colwyn Bay) 1993 (SL).

DAVIES, Andrew Philip (Dwr-y-Felin CS; Christ C, Brecon), b Neath 7 Nov 1976. 5'11". LHB, RMF. Debut 1995. Wales (MC). No appearances 2000. HS 40 v Essex (Cardiff) 2001. BB 5-79 v Worcs (Cardiff) 2002. LO HS 24 v Sussex (Hove) 2001 (NL). LO BB 5-19 v Lincs (Sleaford) 2002 (CGT).

NQELLIOTT, Matthew Thomas Gray (Kyabram Secondary C; La Trobe U), b Chelsea, Victoria, Australia 28 Sep 1971. 6'3". LHB, LM/SLC. Victoria 1992-93 to date. Glamorgan 2000; cap 2000. Yorkshire 2002. *Wisden* 1997. **Tests** (A): 20 (1996-97 to 1998-99); HS 199 v E (Leeds) 1997. **LOI** (A): 1 (1997); HS 1 v E (Lord's) 1997. **Tours** (A): E 1995 (Young A), 1997; SA 1996-97; WI 1998-99. 1000 runs (2+4); most – 1233 (1995-96). HS 203 v v Tasmania (Melbourne) 1995-96. UK HS 199 (*see Tests*). Gm HS 177 v Sussex (Colwyn Bay) 2000. BB 1-3 (V). Awards: CGT 2. LO HS 156 v Dorset (Bournemouth) 2000 (NWT). LO BB –

HARRISON, David Stuart (W Monmouth CS; Usk C, Pontypool), b Newport, Gwent 30 Jul 1981. Son of S.C.Harrison (Glamorgan 1971-77). 6'4". RHB, RM. Glamorgan debut 1999. HS 66 and BB 5-80 v Glos (Cardiff) 2003. LO HS 37* and LO BB 5-26 v Yorks (Leeds) 2002 (NL).

HEMP, David Lloyd (Olchfa CS; Millfield S; W Glamorgan C; Birmingham U), b Hamilton, Bermuda 8 Nov 1970. UK resident since 1976. 6'0". LHB, RM. Glamorgan 1991-96; cap 1994. Warwickshire 1997-2001; cap 1997. Wales (MC) 1992-94. F-c Tours: SA 1995-96 (Gm); I 1994-95 (Eng A); Z 1994-95 (Gm). 1000 runs (3); most – 1452 (1994). HS 186* Wa v Worcs (Birmingham) 2001. Gm HS 157 Gm v Glos (Abergavenny) 1995. BB 3-23 v SA A (Cardiff) 1996. CC BB 2-29 Wa v Glos (Birmingham) 2000. Awards: CGT 4; BHC 2. LO HS 121 v Comb U (Cardiff) 1995 (BHC). LO BB 4-32 Wa v Minor C (Lakenham) 1998 (BHC).

HUGHES, Jonathan (Coed-y-Land CS, Pontypridd), b Pontypridd 30 Jun 1981. 5'10". RHB, RM. Debut 2001. MCC YC. HS 74 v Worcs (Worcester) 2002. LO HS 51 v Derbys (Cardiff) 2003 (CGT).

JONES, Simon Philip (Coedcae CS; Millfield S), b Swansea 25 Dec 1978. Son of I.J.Jones (Glamorgan and England 1960-68). 6'3½". LHB, RF. Debut 1998; cap 2002. Unavailable 2003 (knee reconstruction). **Tests** (A): 2 (2002 to 2002-03); HS 44 and BB 2-61 v I (Lord's) 2002 – on debut. F-c Tours: A 2002-03 (*part*); I 2003-04 (Eng A – *part*). HS 46 v Yorks (Scarborough) 2001. BB 6-45 v Derbys (Cardiff) 2002. LO HS 12* and BB 1-39 v Notts (Nottingham) 1999 (NL).

NQKASPROWICZ, Michael Scott (Brisbane State HS), b South Brisbane, Australia 10 Feb 1972. 6'4". RHB, RFM. Queensland 1989-90 to date. Essex 1994; cap 1994. Leicestershire 1999; cap 1999. Glamorgan debut/cap 2002. **Tests** (A): 17 (1996-97 to 2000-01); HS 25 v I (Calcutta) 1997-98; BB 7-36 v E (Oval) 1997. **LOI** (A): 18 (1995-96 to 2003-04); HS 28* v E (Lord's) 1997; BB 3-50 v I (Cochin) 1997-98. F-c Tours (A): E 1995 (Young A), 1997; I 1997-98; P 1998-99. HS 92 Australians v India A (Nagpur) 2000-01. Gm HS 78 v Glos (Cardiff) 2003. 50 wkts (4+3); most: 77 (2003). BB 9-36 (11-77 match) v Durham (Cardiff) 2003. Also 9-45 (13-110 match) v Durham (Chester-le-St) 2003. Hat trick (Queensland 1998-99). LO HS 40 Le v Warwks (Leicester) 1999 (BHC). LO BB 5-60 Ex v Glam (Cardiff) 1994 (NWT).

MAYNARD, Matthew Peter (David Hughes S, Anglesey), b Oldham, Lancs 21 Mar 1966. 5'10½". RHB, RM. Debut 1985 v Yorks (Swansea), scoring 102 out of 117 in 87 min, reaching 100 with 3 sixes off successive balls; cap 1987; captain 1996-2000; benefit 1996. *Wisden* 1997. N Districts 1990-91 to 1991-92. Otago 1996-97 to 1997-98. YC 1988. **Tests**: 4 (1988 to 1993-94); HS 35 v WI (Kingston) 1993-94. **LOI**: 14 (1993-94 to 2000); HS 41 v P (Manchester) 1996. F-c Tours: SA 1989-90 (Eng XI), 1995-96 (Gm – captain); WI 1993-94; Z 1994-95 (Gm). 1000 runs (13); most – 1803 (1991). HS 243 v Hants (Southampton) 1991. BB 3-21 v OU (Oxford) 1987. CC BB 1-3. Awards: CGT 5; BHC 9. LO HS 151* v Durham (Darlington) 1991 (NWT) and 151* v Middx (Lord's) 1996 (BHC). LO BB 1-13 (NL).

POWELL, Michael John (Crickhowell SS; Pontypool CFE), b Abergavenny, Gwent 3 Feb 1977. 6'1". RHB, RSM. Debut 1997 scoring 200* v OU (Oxford); cap 2000. 1000 runs (3): most – 1234 (2003). HS 200* (*see above*). CC HS 198 v Durham (Chester-le-St) 2003. BB 2-39 v OU (Oxford) 1999. CC BB – . LO HS 91* v Leics (Cardiff) 2003 (NL).

SHAW, Adrian David (Llangatwg CS; Neath Tertiary C), b Neath 17 Feb 1972. 5'11". RHB, WK. Wales (MC) 1990-92. Debut 1994; cap 1999. No appearances 2002 – 2nd XI captain. HS 140 v OU (Oxford) 1999. CC HS 88* v Glos (Cardiff) 2000. BB – LO HS 48 v Glos (Swansea) 1997 (SL).

THOMAS, Ian James (Bedwas CS; Bassaleg CS; UWIC), b Newport, Gwent 9 May 1979. 5'11". LHB, OB. Debut 1998. Wales MC. HS 82 v Essex (Southend) 2000 – on CC debut. BB 1-26 (CC). LO HS 93 v Durham CB (Darlington) 2003 (CGT).

THOMAS, Stuart Darren (Graig CS, Llanelli; Neath Tertiary C), b Morriston 25 Jan 1975. 6'0". LHB, RFM. Debut v Derbys (Chesterfield) 1992, taking 5-80 when aged 17yr 217d; cap 1997. F-c Tours (Eng A): SA 1995-96 (Gm), 1998-99; NZ 1999-00; Z 1994-95 (Gm), 1998-99. HS 138 v Essex (Chelmsford) 2001. 50 wkts (5); most – 71 (1998). BB 8-50 Eng A v Zim A (Harare) 1998-99 – record Eng A analysis. CC BB 7-33 (10-83 match) v Durham (Cardiff) 2002. Award: BHC 1. LO HS 71* v Surrey (Oval) 2002 (CGT). LO BB 7-16 v Surrey (Swansea) 1998 (SL).

WALLACE, Mark Alexander (Crickhowell HS), b Abergavenny, Gwent 19 Nov 1981. 5'9". LHB, WK. Debut 1999; cap 2003. F-c Tour (ECB Acad): SL 2002-03. HS 121 v Durham (Chester-le-St) 2003. LO HS 39 v Warwks (Cardiff) 2002 (BHC).

WATKINS, Ryan Edward (Pontllanfraith CS; Cross Keys TC), b Abergavenny, Gwent 9 Jun 1983. 6'0". LHB, RM. Wales MC. Joined Glamorgan part-time staff 2002 – awaiting f-c debut.

WHARF, Alexander George (Buttershaw Upper S; Thomas Danby C), b Bradford, Yorks 4 Jun 1975. 6'5". RHB, RMF. Yorkshire 1994-97. Nottinghamshire 1998-99. Glamorgan debut 2000, scoring 100* v OU (Oxford); cap 2000. HS 101* v Northants (Northampton) 2000. 50 wkts (1): 52 (2003). BB 5-63 v Yorks (Swansea) 2001. LO HS 38* Nt v Surrey (Nottingham) 1999 (NL). LO BB 4-18 v Glos (Cardiff) 2003 (NL).

RELEASED/RETIRED
(Having made a first-class County appearance in 2003)

JAMES, Stephen Peter (Monmouth S; University C, Swansea; Hughes Hall, Cambridge), b Lydney, Glos 7 Sep 1967. 6'0". RHB. Glamorgan 1985-2003; cap 1992; captain 2001-03 (part); benefit 2001. Cambridge U 1989-90; blue 1989-90. Mashonaland 1993-94 to 1994-95. Tests: 2 (1998); HS 36 v SL (Oval) 1998. F-c Tours: SA 1995-96 (Gm); SL 1997-98; Z 1990-91 (Gm); K 1997-98. 1000 runs (9); most – 1775 (1997). HS 309* (Glamorgan record) v Sussex (Colwyn Bay) 2000. BB – Awards: CGT 3; BHC 2. LO HS 135 v Comb U (Cardiff) 1992 (BHC).

NQMAHER, James Patrick (St Augustine's C, Cairns), b Innisfail, Queensland, Australia 27 Feb 1974. LHB, RM. Queensland 1993-94 to date. Glamorgan 2001, 2003; cap 2001. LOI (A): 26 (1997-98 to 2003-04); HS 95 v SA (Pretoria) 2001-02. F-c Tour (A): WI 2002-03. 1000 (1+2): most – 1194 (2001-02). HS 217 v Essex (Cardiff) 2001. BB 3-11 Q v WA (Perth) 1995-96. LO HS 142 v Glos (Bristol) 2001 (BHC). LO BB 3-29 v Surrey (Croydon) 2003 (NL).

PARKIN, Owen Thomas (Bournemouth GS; Bath U), b Coventry, Warwks 24 Sep 1972. 6'2". RHB. RFM. Dorset 1992. Glamorgan 1994-2003. HS 24* v Essex (Chelmsford) 1998. BB 5-24 v Somerset (Cardiff) 1998. LO HS 14* v Somerset (Cardiff) 2002 (NL). LO BB 5-28 v Sussex (Hove) 1996 (SL).

GLAMORGAN 2003

RESULTS SUMMARY

	Place	Won	Lost	Tied	Drew	No Result
County Championship (2nd Division)	5th	5	5		6	
All First-Class Matches		5	6		6	
C & G Trophy	4th Round					
National League (1st Division)	5th	8	8			
Twenty20 Cup	6th in Midlands/Wales/West Group					

COUNTY CHAMPIONSHIP AVERAGES

BATTING AND FIELDING

Cap		M	I	NO	HS	Runs	Avge	100	50	Ct/St
1987	M.P.Maynard	16	28	–	142	1297	46.32	5	4	11
2000	M.J.Powell	16	29	1	198	1234	44.07	4	3	12
1994	D.L.Hemp	12	21	3	85*	607	33.72	–	5	5
2001	J.P.Maher	8	16	–	95	491	30.68	–	4	7
2003	M.A.Wallace	16	28	–	121	827	29.53	2	3	49/2
1992	R.D.B.Croft	16	28	3	122	727	29.08	1	4	8
1997	S.D.Thomas	4	7	2	69*	145	29.00	–	1	1
2000	A.G.Wharf	16	27	9	79	475	26.38	–	2	7
2002	M.S.Kasprowicz	15	26	4	78	556	25.27	–	2	7
1992	A.Dale	15	27	1	123	657	25.26	1	2	12
	J.Hughes	9	16	–	73	357	22.31	–	2	10
	I.J.Thomas	6	10	–	53	172	17.20	–	1	3
2000	D.A.Cosker	8	11	6	42	79	15.80	–	–	6
	D.S.Harrison	15	24	5	66	264	13.89	–	1	3

Also batted: A.P.Davies (3 matches) 9, 19*, 4 (1 ct); S.P.James (1 – cap 1992) 1, 14 (1 ct).

BOWLING

	O	M	R	W	Avge	Best	5wI	10wM
M.S.Kasprowicz	572.3	140	1629	77	21.15	9-36	4	2
R.D.B.Croft	711.5	189	1873	62	30.20	6-71	5	1
A.G.Wharf	432.3	72	1734	52	33.34	4-53	–	–
D.S.Harrison	349	72	1248	37	33.72	5-80	1	–
D.A.Cosker	257.5	66	672	17	39.52	3-49	–	–
Also bowled:								
S.D.Thomas	68.1	7	243	9	27.00	4-69	–	–

A.Dale 48-9-159-3; A.P.Davies 46-8-225-2; J.P.Maher 1-0-2-0; M.P.Maynard 2-0-2-0.

The First-Class Averages (pp 123–138) give the records of Glamorgan players in all first-class county matches (Glamorgan's other opponents being India A).

GLAMORGAN RECORDS

FIRST-CLASS CRICKET

Highest Total	For	718-3d		v Sussex	Colwyn Bay	2000
	V	712		by Northants	Northampton	1998
Lowest Total	For	22		v Lancashire	Liverpool	1924
	V	33		by Leics	Ebbw Vale	1965
Highest Innings	For	309*	S.P.James	v Sussex	Colwyn Bay	2000
	V	322*	M.B.Loye	for Northants	Northampton	1998

Highest Partnership for each Wicket

1st	374	M.T.G.Elliott/S.P.James	v	Sussex	Colwyn Bay	2000
2nd	252	M.P.Maynard/D.L.Hemp	v	Northants	Cardiff	2002
3rd	313	D.E.Davies/W.E.Jones	v	Essex	Brentwood	1948
4th	425*	A.Dale/I.V.A.Richards	v	Middlesex	Cardiff	1993
5th	264	M.Robinson/S.W.Montgomery	v	Hampshire	Bournemouth	1949
6th	230	W.E.Jones/B.L.Muncer	v	Worcs	Worcester	1953
7th	211	P.A.Cottey/O.D.Gibson	v	Leics	Swansea	1996
8th	202	D.Davies/J.J.Hills	v	Sussex	Eastbourne	1928
9th	203*	J.J.Hills/J.C.Clay	v	Worcs	Swansea	1929
10th	143	T.Davies/S.A.B.Daniels	v	Glos	Swansea	1982

Best Bowling	For	10- 51	J.Mercer	v Worcs	Worcester	1936
(Innings)	V	10- 18	G.Geary	for Leics	Pontypridd	1929
Best Bowling	For	17-212	J.C.Clay	v Worcs	Swansea	1937
(Match)	V	16- 96	G.Geary	for Leics	Pontypridd	1929

Most Runs – Season		2276	H.Morris	(av 55.51)	1990
Most Runs – Career		34056	A.Jones	(av 33.03)	1957-83
Most 100s – Season		10	H.Morris		1990
Most 100s – Career		52	A.Jones		1957-83
		52	H.Morris		1981-97
Most Wkts – Season		176	J.C.Clay	(av 17.34)	1937
Most Wkts – Career		2174	D.J.Shepherd	(av 20.95)	1950-72
Most Career W-K Dismissals		933	E.W.Jones	(840 ct; 93 st)	1961-83
Most Career Catches in the Field		656	P.M.Walker		1956-72

LIST 'A' LIMITED-OVERS CRICKET

Highest Total	CGT	429		v Surrey	The Oval	2002
	BHC	318-3		v Combined U	Cardiff	1995
	NL	305-6		v Worcs	Cardiff	2001
Lowest Total	CGT	76		v Northants	Northampton	1968
	BHC	68		v Lancashire	Manchester	1973
	NL	42		v Derbyshire	Swansea	1979
Highest Innings	CGT	162*	I.V.A.Richards	v Oxfordshire	Swansea	1993
	BHC	151*	M.P.Maynard	v Middlesex	Lord's	1996
	NL	155*	J.H.Kallis	v Surrey	Pontypridd	1999
Best Bowling	CGT	5-13	R.J.Shastri	v Scotland	Edinburgh	1988
	BHC	6-20	S.D.Thomas	v Combined U	Cardiff	1995
	NL	7-16	S.D.Thomas	v Surrey	Swansea	1998

GLOUCESTERSHIRE

Formation of Present Club: 1871
Inaugural First-Class Match: 1870
Colours: Blue, Gold, Brown, Silver, Green and Red
Badge: Coat of Arms of the City and County of Bristol
County Champions (since 1890): (0); best – 2nd 1930, 1931, 1947, 1959, 1969, 1986
Gillette/NatWest/C & G Trophy Winners: (4) 1973, 1999, 2000, 2003
Benson and Hedges Cup Winners: (3) 1977, 1999, 2000
National League (Div 1) Winners: (1) 2000
Sunday League Winners: (0); best – 2nd 1988
Twenty20 Cup Winners: semi-finalist 2003
Match Awards: CGT 61; BHC 72

Chief Executive: T.E.M.Richardson, County Ground, Nevil Road, Bristol BS7 9EJ • Tel: 0117 910 8000 • Fax: 0117 924 1193 • Email: info@glos@ecb.co.uk • Web: www.gloucestershire.cricinfo.com

First XI Coach: M.W.Alleyne. **Club/Limited-Overs Captain:** M.W.Alleyne. **Captain:** tba. **Vice-Captain:** tba. **Overseas Player:** Shabbir Ahmed and Shoaib Malik. **2004 Beneficiary:** R.C.Russell (testimonial). **Head Groundsman:** S.P.Williams. **Scorer:** K.T.Gerrish. ‡ New registration. ^{NQ} Not qualified for England.

‡**ADSHEAD, Stephen** John (Bridley Moor HS, Redditch), b Worcester 29 Jan 1980. 5'9". RHB, WK. Herefordshire 1999. Leicestershire 2000 (one non-CC match). Worcestershire 2003 (2 matches). HS 63 v Glam (Cardiff) 2003 – on Worcs/CC debut. LO HS 77* Shropshire v Northumb (Oswestry) 2003 (CGT).

ALLEYNE, Mark Wayne (Harrison C, Barbados; Cardinal Pole S, London E9; Haringey Cricket C), b Tottenham, London 23 May 1968. 5'10". RHB, RM. Debut 1986; cap 1990; captain 1997-2003; club/limited-overs captain/1st XI coach 2004; benefit 1999. *Wisden* 2000. MBE 2004. **LOI:** 10 (1998-99 to 2000-01); HS 53 v SA (E London) 1999-00; BB 3-27 v SL (Sydney) 1998-99. F-c Tours (Eng A) (C=captain): WI 2000-01C; NZ 1999-00C; SL 1986-87 (Gs), 1992-93 (Gs); B 1999-00C. 1000 runs (6); most – 1189 (1998). HS 256 v Northants (Northampton) 1990. 50 wkts (1): 54 (1996). BB 6-49 v Middx (Lord's) 2000. Awards: CGT 3; BHC 3. LO HS 134* v Leics (Bristol) 1992 (SL). LO BB 5-27 v Comb U (Bristol) 1988 (BHC).

AVERIS, James Maxwell Michael (Cathedral S, Bristol; Portsmouth U; St Cross C, Oxford), b Bristol 28 May 1974. 5'11". RHB, RMF. Oxford U 1997; blue 1997; rugby blue 1996-97. Gloucestershire debut 1997; cap 2001. HS 43 and BB 5-51 v Notts (Bristol) 2002. Award: BHC 1. LO HS 23* v Lancs (Manchester) 2000 (NL). LO BB 6-23 v Bucks (Ascott Park) 2003 (CGT).

BALL, Martyn Charles John (King Edmund SS; Bath CFE), b Bristol 26 Apr 1970. 5'8". RHB, OB. Debut 1988; cap 1996; benefit 2002. F-c Tours: I 2001-02; SL 1992-93 (Gs). HS 75 v Somerset (Taunton) 2003. BB 8-46 (14-169 match) v Somerset (Taunton) 1993. Award: CGT 1. LO HS 51 v SL A (Cheltenham) 1999. LO BB 5-33 v Yorks (Leeds) 2003 (NL).

BRESSINGTON, Alastair Nigel (Marling GS, Stroud; UWIC), b Downend, Bristol 28 Nov 1979. 6'1". LHB, RMF. Debut 2000. No f-c appearances 2002-03. HS 17* v Hants (Cheltenham) 2001. BB 4-36 v Glam (Bristol) 2000 – on debut. LO HS 54 Glos CB v Yorks CB (Cheltenham) 1999 (NWT). LO BB 3-21 Glos CB v Notts CB (Cheltenham) 2000 (NWT).

FISHER, Ian Douglas (Beckfoot GS, Bingley; Thomas Danby C, Leeds), b Bradford, Yorks 31 Mar 1976. 5'10½". LHB, SLA. Yorkshire 1995-96 (Y in Zim) to 2001. Gloucestershire debut 2002. F-c Tour: Z 1995-96 (Y). HS 103* v Essex (Gloucester) 2002. BB 5-30 (10-123 match) v Durham (Bristol) 2003. LO HS 20 and LO BB 3-20 Y v Somerset (Scarborough) 2000 (NL).

GIDMAN, Alex Peter Richard (Wycliffe C), b High Wycombe, Bucks 22 Jun 1981. 6'3". RHB, RM. Debut 2002. MCCYC. Appointed captain of Eng A tour to India 2003-04 but withdrew because of hand injury. HS 117 v Northants (Bristol) 2002. BB 3-33 v Middx (Cheltenham) 2002. LO HS 73 v Warwks (Birmingham) 2003 (NL). LO BB 3-26 v Warwks (Gloucester) 2003 (NL).

HANCOCK, Timothy Harold Coulter (St Edward's S, Oxford; Henley C), b Reading, Berks 20 Apr 1972. 5'10". RHB, RM. Debut 1991; cap 1998. Oxfordshire 1990. F-c Tour: SL 1992-93 (Gs). 1000 runs (1): 1227 (1998). HS 220* v Notts (Nottingham) 1998. BB 3-5 v Essex (Colchester) 1998. Awards: CGT 4. LO HS 135 v Bucks (Ascott Park) 2003 (CGT). LO BB 6-58 v Scot (Bristol) 1997 (NWT).

HARDINGES, Mark Andrew (Malvern C; Bath U), b Gloucester 5 Feb 1978. 6'1". RHB, RMF. Debut 1999. British U 2000. HS 172 v OU (Oxford) 2002. CC HS 22 v Notts (Nottingham) 2001. BB 2-16 v Essex (Bristol) 2000. Award: CGT 1. LO HS 65 v Notts (Nottingham) 2001 (NL). LO BB 4-19 v Salop (Shrewsbury) 2002 (CGT).

LEWIS, Jonathan (Churchfields S, Swindon; Swindon C), b Aylesbury, Bucks 26 Aug 1975. 6'2". RHB, RMF. Debut 1995; cap 1998. Wiltshire 1993. Northamptonshire staff 1994. F-c Tour: WI 2000-01 (Eng A). HS 62 v Worcs (Cheltenham) 1999. 50 wkts (4): most – 74 (2003). BB 8-95 v Z (Gloucester) 2000. CC BB 7-56 (10-92 match) v Notts (Bristol) 1999. Hat trick 2000. Awards: BHC 2. LO HS 33* v Somerset (Bristol) 1998 (BHC). LO BB 4-22 v Surrey (Bristol) 2002 (NL).

PEARSON, James Alexander, b Bristol 11 Sep 1983. LHB. Gloucestershire debut 2002. No appearances 2003. HS 51 v Northants (Bristol) 2002 – on debut. LO HS 7 and BB 1-29 Glos CB v Herefords (Brockhampton) 2001.

RUSSELL, Robert Charles (*'Jack'*) (Archway CS; Bristol Poly – *"briefly"*), b Stroud 15 Aug 1963. 5'8½". LHB, WK, occ OB. Debut 1981 – youngest Glos wicket-keeper (17yr 307d), setting record for most match dismissals on f-c debut – 8 v SL (Bristol); cap 1985; benefit 1994; captain 1995; testimonial 2004. Kept throughout world record total without byes – 746-9d by Northants (Bristol) 2002. *Wisden* 1989. MBE 1996. **Tests**: 54 (1988 to 1997-98); HS 128* v A (Manchester) 1989; 11 ct v SA (Jo'burg) 1995-96 (Test record); 27 dis 1995-96 series v SA (Eng record). **LOI**: 40 (1987-88 to 1998-99); HS 50 v I (Nottingham) 1990. F-c Tours: A 1990-91, 1992-93 (Eng A); SA 1995-96; WI 1989-90, 1993-94, 1997-98; NZ 1991-92, 1996-97; P 1987-88; SL 1986-87 (Gs). 1000 runs (1): 1049 (1997). HS 129* Eng XI v Boland (Paarl) 1995-96. Gs HS 124 v Notts (Nottingham) 1996. BB 1-4. Awards: CGT 1; BHC 3. LO HS 119* v Brit U (Bristol) 1998 (BHC).

ᴺᵠSHABBIR AHMED KHAN, b Khanewal, Pakistan 21 Apr 1976. 6'7". RHB, RFM. Multan 1997-98. WAPDA 1997-98 to 1999-00. Bahawalpur 1998-99. REDCO 1999-00. National Bank 2000-01 to date. **Tests**: 6 (2003 to 2003-04); HS 24* v SA (Faisalabad) 2003-04; BB 5-48 v B (Karachi) 2003 on debut. F-c Tours: WI 1999-00; NZ 2003-04; SL 2001 (Pak A). HS 50 National Bank v Allied Bank (Sheikhupura) 2000-01. BB 7-70 National Bank v Lahore Blues (Okara) 2002-03. LO HS 38 WAPDA v Faisalabad (Faisalabad) 1999-00. LO BB 5-24 WAPDA v Customs (Karachi) 1999-00.

ᴺᵠSHOAIB MALIK (Government Arabic SS, Sialkot), b Sialkot, Pakistan 1 Feb 1982. 5'6". RHB, OB. Debut (Pakistan A) 1997. Gujranwala 1997-98 to 1998-99. PIA 1998-99 to 2000-01 date. Sialkot 2001-02. Gloucestershire debut 2003. **Tests** (P): 5 (2001 to 2003-04); HS 47 and BB 4-42 v SA (Lahore) 2003-04. **LOI** (P): 63 (1999-00 to 2003-04); HS 115 v NZ (Lahore) 2001-02; BB 3-26 v E (Manchester) 2003. F-c Tour (Pak A): E 1997. HS 130* and BB 7-81 PIA v WAPDA (Faisalabad) 2000-01. Gs HS 60 v Yorks (Cheltenham) 2003. Gs BB 3-76 v Worcs (Cheltenham) 2003. Award: CGT 1. LO HS 138* PIA v Karachi Whites (Karachi) 2002-03. LO BB 5-35 PIA v Lahore Blues (Karachi) 2002-03.

SILLENCE, Roger John (Highbury SS; Salisbury Art C), b Salisbury, Wilts 29 Jun 1977. 6'3". RHB, RMF. Debut 2001 taking 5-97 v Sussex (Hove). Wiltshire 1996-2001. HS 101 v Derbys (Bristol) 2002. BB 5-63 v Durham (Bristol) 2002. LO HS (Wilts) 82 v Northants CB (Northampton) 1999 (NWT). LO BB 4-35 v WI A (Cheltenham) 2002.

SMITH, Andrew **Michael** (Queen Elizabeth GS, Wakefield; Exeter U; West of England U), b Dewsbury, Yorks 1 Oct 1967. 5'9". RHB, LMF. Debut 1991; cap 1995; benefit 2001. **Tests:** 1 (1997); HS 4* v A (Leeds) 1997. F-c Tour: P 1995-96 (Eng A – *part*). HS 61 v Yorks (Gloucester) 1998. 50 wkts (5); most – 83 (1997). BB 8-73 (10-118 match) v Middx (Lord's) 1996. Awards: CGT 1; BHC 1. LO HS 26* v Kent (Moreton-in-M) 1996 (SL). LO BB 6-39 v Hants (Southampton) 1995 (BHC).

NQ**SPEARMAN, Craig** Murray, b Auckland, New Zealand 4 Jul 1972. RHB. Auckland 1993-94 to 1995-96. Central Districts 1996-97 to date. Gloucestershire debut/cap 2002. **Tests** (NZ): 19 (1995-96 to 2000-01); HS 112 v Z (Auckland) 1995-96. **LOI** (NZ): 51 (1995-96 to 2000-01); HS 86 v Z (Harare) 2000-01. F-c Tours (NZ): SA 2000-01; WI 1995-96; I 1999-00; P 1996-97; SL 1997-98; Z 1997-98, 2000-01. 1000 (1): 1444 (2002). HS 180* (carried bat) v Glam (Cheltenham) 2002. BB 1-37 CD v Wellington (New Plymouth) 1999-00. Awards: CGT 1; BHC 1. LO HS 153 v Warwks (Gloucester) 2003 (NL).

TAYLOR, Christopher Glyn (Colston's Collegiate S), b Southmead, Bristol 27 Sep 1976. 5'7". RHB, OB. Debut 2000, scoring 104 v Middx – first to score a hundred at Lord's in a Championship match on his first-class debut. Cap 2001. HS 196 v Notts (Nottingham) 2001. BB 3-126 v Northants (Cheltenham) 2000. Award: BHC 1. LO HS 93 v Warwks (Bristol) 2002 (BHC).

WESTON, William Philip Christopher (Durham S), b Durham City 16 Jun 1973. Son of M.P.Weston (Durham; England RFU); brother of R.M.S.Weston (*see MIDDLESEX*). 6'3". LHB, LM. Worcestershire 1991-2002; cap 1995. Gloucestershire debut 2003. F-c Tours (Wo): Z 1993-94, 1996-97. 1000 runs (4); most – 1389 (1996). HS 205 Wo v Northants (Northampton) 1997. Gs HS 179 v Somerset (Taunton) 2003. BB 2-39 Wo v P (Worcester) 1992. CC BB – . Gs BB – LO HS 134 Wo v Derbys (Derby) 2001 (NL). LO BB (Wo) 1-2 (SL).

WINDOWS, Matthew Guy Newman (Clifton C; Durham U), b Bristol 5 Apr 1973. Son of A.R.Windows (Glos and CU 1960-68). 5'7". RHB, LM. Debut 1992; cap 1998. Combined U 1995. F-c Tours (Eng A): SA 1998-99; Z 1998-99. 1000 runs (3); most – 1173 (1998). HS 184 v Warwks (Cheltenham) 1996. BB (Comb U) 1-6. Gs BB – . Awards: CGT 1; BHC 2. LO HS 117 v Northants (Cheltenham) 2001 (NL). BB –

RELEASED/RETIRED
(Having made a first-class County appearance in 2003)

NQ**BUTLER, Ian** Gareth (home educated), b Otahuhu, Auckland, New Zealand 24 Nov 1981. 6'3". RHB, RFM. N Districts 2001-02 to date. Gloucestershire 2003. **Tests** (NZ): 7 (2001-02 to 2003-04); HS 26 v WI (Bridgetown) 2001-02; BB 6-46 v P (Wellington) 2003-04. **LOI** (NZ): 10 (2001-02 to 2003-04); HS 3; BB 2-32 v SL (Sharjah) 2001-02. Took wicket with his fifth ball in LOI. F-c Tours (NZ): WI 2001-02; I 2003-04. HS 26 (*see Tests*). GS HS 13 v Glam (Cardiff) 2003. BB 6-46 (*see Tests*). Gs BB 4-74 v Worcs (Worcester) 2003. LO HS 10* ND v Wellington (Wellington) 2001-02. LO BB 2-32 (*see LOI*).

NQ**HARVEY, I.J.** – *see YORKSHIRE*.

POPE, Stephen Patrick (Cheltenham Bournside CS), b Cheltenham 25 Jan 1983. 5'8". RHB, WK. Gloucestershire 2003. HS 17* v Worcs (Cheltenham) 2003. LO HS (Glos CB) 15 v Herefords (Brockhampton) 2001 (CGT).

RELEASED/RETIRED continued on p 56

GLOUCESTERSHIRE 2003

RESULTS SUMMARY

		Place	Won	Lost	Tied	Drew	No Result
County Championship (2nd Division)		3rd	5	2		9	
All First-Class Matches			5	2		9	
C & G Trophy		Winners					
National League (1st Division)		2nd	11	4			1
Twenty20 Cup		Semi-Finalist					

COUNTY CHAMPIONSHIP AVERAGES

BATTING AND FIELDING

Cap		M	I	NO	HS	Runs	Avge	100	50	Ct/St
–	J.N.Rhodes	15	27	5	151*	1293	58.77	5	7	7
1999	I.J.Harvey	6	12	3	128*	404	44.88	1	1	4
1985	R.C.Russell	11	16	4	78*	436	36.33	–	3	33/4
1998	T.H.C.Hancock	12	21	–	97	720	34.28	–	5	13
–	W.P.C.Weston	15	27	1	179	877	33.73	2	2	10
2002	C.M.Spearman	15	27	–	103	903	33.44	1	7	15
1998	M.G.N.Windows	16	29	–	150	890	30.68	1	5	11
–	A.P.R.Gidman	8	16	2	68	407	29.07	–	2	7
1996	M.C.J.Ball	10	15	3	75	304	25.33	–	2	12
–	I.D.Fisher	10	12	3	71	219	24.33	–	1	4
2001	C.G.Taylor	4	8	–	45	171	21.37	–	–	3
–	Shoaib Malik	2	4	–	60	80	20.00	–	1	–
–	R.J.Sillence	4	5	–	42	98	19.60	–	–	1
1990	M.W.Alleyne	8	13	3	32*	193	19.30	–	–	9
1998	J.Lewis	14	18	4	47	248	17.71	–	–	3
–	S.P.Pope	5	8	3	17*	65	13.00	–	–	10/1
1995	A.M.Smith	11	14	7	17*	58	8.28	–	–	1
–	I.G.Butler	4	5	–	13	20	4.00	–	–	–

Also batted: J.M.M.Averis (4 matches – cap 2001) 8, 0, 4* (1 ct); M.A.Hardinges (2) 17, 10*, 0 (1 ct).

BOWLING

	O	M	R	W	Avge	Best	5wI	10wM
I.J.Harvey	195.2	54	625	27	23.14	4- 43	–	–
A.M.Smith	329.5	91	898	38	23.63	5- 70	1	–
J.Lewis	551.2	142	1800	74	24.32	7-117	5	1
I.D.Fisher	225.1	50	767	28	27.39	5- 30	3	1
I.G.Butler	124	24	478	17	28.11	4- 74	–	–
M.C.J.Ball	378.3	99	1008	28	36.00	5-104	1	–
Also bowled:								
Shoaib Malik	66	19	146	5	29.20	3- 76	–	–
J.M.M.Averis	107.2	30	298	9	33.11	3- 84	–	–
R.J.Sillence	100.5	15	408	9	45.33	3- 55	–	–
M.W.Alleyne	133	32	460	9	51.11	3- 77	–	–
A.P.R.Gidman	104	20	441	5	88.20	2- 46	–	–

T.H.C.Hancock 5-0-22-0; M.A.Hardinges 27-9-118-3; C.G.Taylor 11-0-48-0; W.P.C.Weston 2-0-10-0.

Gloucestershire played no first-class fixtures outside the County Championship in 2003. The First-Class Averages (pp 123–138) give the records of Gloucestershire players in all first-class county matches.

GLOUCESTERSHIRE RECORDS

FIRST-CLASS CRICKET

Highest Total	For 653-6d		v	Glamorgan	Bristol	1928
	V 774-7d		by	Australians	Bristol	1948
Lowest Total	For 17		v	Australians	Cheltenham	1896
	V 12		by	Northants	Gloucester	1907
Highest Innings	For 318*	W.G.Grace	v	Yorkshire	Cheltenham	1876
	V 310*	M.E.K.Hussey	for	Northants	Bristol	2002

Highest Partnership for each Wicket

1st	395	D.M.Young/R.B.Nicholls	v	Oxford U	Oxford	1962
2nd	256	C.T.M.Pugh/T.W.Graveney	v	Derbyshire	Chesterfield	1960
3rd	336	W.R.Hammond/B.H.Lyon	v	Leics	Leicester	1933
4th	321	W.R.Hammond/W.L.Neale	v	Leics	Gloucester	1937
5th	261	W.G.Grace/W.O.Moberley	v	Yorkshire	Cheltenham	1876
6th	320	G.L.Jessop/J.H.Board	v	Sussex	Hove	1903
7th	248	W.G.Grace/E.L.Thomas	v	Sussex	Hove	1896
8th	239	W.R.Hammond/A.E.Wilson	v	Lancashire	Bristol	1938
9th	193	W.G.Grace/S.A.P.Kitcat	v	Sussex	Bristol	1896
10th	131	W.R.Gouldsworthy/J.G.Bessant	v	Somerset	Bristol	1923

Best Bowling	For 10-40	E.G.Dennett	v	Essex	Bristol	1906
(Innings)	V 10-66	A.A.Mailey	for	Australians	Cheltenham	1921
	10-66	K.Smales	for	Notts	Stroud	1956
Best Bowling	For 17-56	C.W.L.Parker	v	Essex	Gloucester	1925
(Match)	V 15-87	A.J.Conway	for	Worcs	Moreton-in-M	1914

Most Runs – Season	2860	W.R.Hammond	(av 69.75)	1933
Most Runs – Career	33664	W.R.Hammond	(av 57.05)	1920-51
Most 100s – Season	13	W.R.Hammond		1938
Most 100s – Career	113	W.R.Hammond		1920-51
Most Wkts – Season	222	T.W.J.Goddard	(av 16.80)	1937
	222	T.W.J.Goddard	(av 16.37)	1947
Most Wkts – Career	3170	C.W.L.Parker	(av 19.43)	1903-35
Most Career W-K Dismissals	1016	J.H.Board	(698 ct; 318 st)	1891-1914
	1016	R.C.Russell	(916 ct; 100 st)	1981-2002
Most Career Catches in the Field	718	C.A.Milton		1948-74

LIST 'A' LIMITED-OVERS CRICKET

Highest Total	CGT	401-7	v	Bucks	Wing	2003
	BHC	308-3	v	Ireland	Dublin	1996
	NL	344-6	v	Northants	Cheltenham	2001
Lowest Total	CGT	82	v	Notts	Bristol	1987
	BHC	62	v	Hampshire	Bristol	1975
	NL	49	v	Middlesex	Bristol	1978
Highest Innings	CGT	177	A.J.Wright	v	Scotland	Bristol	1997
	BHC	154*	M.J.Procter	v	Somerset	Taunton	1972
	NL	153	C.M.Spearman	v	Warwicks	Gloucester	2003
Best Bowling	CGT	6-21	C.A.Walsh	v	Kent	Bristol	1990
		6-21	C.A.Walsh	v	Cheshire	Bristol	1992
	BHC	6-13	M.J.Procter	v	Hampshire	Southampton	1977
	NL	6-52	J.N.Shepherd	v	Kent	Bristol	1983

HAMPSHIRE

Formation of Present Club: 12 August 1863
Inaugural First-Class Match: 1864
Colours: Blue, Gold and White
Badge: Tudor Rose and Crown
County Champions: (2) 1961, 1973
Gillette/NatWest/C & G Trophy Winners: (1) 1991
Benson and Hedges Cup Winners: (2) 1988, 1992
National League (Div 1) Winners: (0); best – 8th 1999
Sunday League Winners: (3) 1975, 1978, 1986
Twenty20 Cup Winners: 6th in South Group 2003
Match Awards: CGT 62; BHC 67

Chief Executive: N.S.Pike, The Hampshire Rose Bowl, Botley Road, West End, Southampton SO30 3XH • Tel: 023 8047 2002 • Fax: 023 8047 2122 • Email: enquiries@rosebowlplc.com • Webs: www.hampshire.cricinfo.com • www.rosebowlplc.com

First XI Manager/Coach: V.P.Terry. **2nd XI Coach/Academy Director**: T.C.Middleton. **Captain**: S.K.Warne. **Vice-Captain**: no appointment. **Overseas Players**: S.K.Warne and M.J.Clarke. **2004 Beneficiary**: Hampshire Youth Trust. **Head Groundsman**: N.Gray. **Scorer**: V.H Isaacs. ‡ New registration. ^NQ Not qualified for England.

ADAMS, James Henry Kenneth (Sherborne S; University C, London; Loughborough U), b Winchester 23 Sep 1980. 6'2". LHB, LM. British U 2002-03. Hampshire debut 2002. Loughborough UCCE 2003 – scoring 107 v Somerset (Taunton) on debut. Dorset 1998. HS 107 (*above*). H HS 60 v Derbys (Derby) 2003. BB 2-24 LU v Surrey (Oval) 2003. H BB 2-81 v Surrey (Southampton) 2002. LO HS 17 v Sussex (Hove) 2002 (NL). BB –

BENHAM, Christopher Charles (Yately CS; Loughborough U), b Frimley, Surrey 24 Mar 1983. 6'1". RHB, RM/OB. Summer Contract – awaiting f-c debut. LO HS 0 (Hants CB) (CGT).

‡BROWN, Michael James (Queen Elizabeth GS, Blackburn; Collingwood C, Durham U), b Burnley, Lancs 9 Feb 1980. 6'0". RHB, OB. Middlesex 1999-2003. Durham UCCE 2001-02. British U 2001-02. HS 98 M v Z (Shenley) 2003. CC HS 10 M v Warwks (Lord's) 2001. LO HS 18 M v Northants (Lord's) 2002 (NL).

BRUCE, James Thomas Anthony (Eton C; St Hild & St Bede C, Durham U), b Hammersmith, London 17 Dec 1979. 6'1". RHB, RMF. Durham UCCE 2001-02. Hampshire debut 2003. Cumberland 2001. HS 21* and BB 3-42 v Glam (Southampton) 2003. LO HS 6* (NL). LO BB 3-45 v Sussex (Hove) 2003 (NL).

‡BURROWS, Thomas George, b Reading, Berkshire 5 May 1985. RHB, WK. Berkshire 2001 to 2003. Staff 2004 – awaiting first-class debut. LO HS 1 (Berks).

CLAPP, Dominic Adrian (Lancing C; Worthing SFC), b Southport, Lancs 25 May 1980. 6'0". RHB, RM. Sussex 2002 (one match). Trial contract 2004. Sussex 2nd XI debut 1997 when aged 16y 347d. HS 6 Sx v Leics (Horsham) 2002. H HS 4. LO HS 43 Sx v WI A (Hove) 2002. LO BB 3-46 Sussex CB v Herefords (Colwall) 2000 (NWT).

‡^NQCLARKE, Michael John (Westfield Sports HS), b Liverpool, NSW, Australia 2 Apr 1981. RHB, SLA. New South Wales 1999-00 to date. Captained Aus U-19 in 2000 world cup in Sri Lanka. **LOI** (A): 20 (2002-03 to 2003-04); HS 75* v WI (Gros Islet) 2003; BB 4-42 v I (Bombay) 2003-04. F-c Tour (A): WI 2002-03. HS 134 NSW v Q (Brisbane) 2002-03. BB 2-25 NSW v Tasmania (Hobart) 2001-02. LO HS 101* NSW v WA (Sydney) 2001-02 (ING). LO BB 4-42 (*see LOI*).

CRAWLEY, John Paul (Manchester GS; Trinity C, Cambridge), b Maldon, Essex 21 Sep 1971. Brother of M.A.Crawley (Oxford U, Lancs and Notts 1987-94) and P.M. (Cambridge U 1992). 6'1". RHB, RM, occ WK. Lancashire 1990-2001; cap 1994; captain 1999-2001. Cambridge U 1991-93; blue 1991-92-93; captain 1992-93. Hampshire debut/cap 2002. YC 1994. **Tests**: 37 (1994 to 2002-03); HS 156* v SL (Oval) 1998. **LOI**: 13 (1994-95 to 1998-99); HS 73 v Z (Harare) 1996-97. F-c Tours: A 1994-95, 1998-99, 2002-03; SA 1993-94 (Eng A), 1995-96; WI 1995-96 (La), 1997-98, 2000-01 (Eng A); NZ 1996-97; Z 1996-97. 1000 runs (8); most − 1851 (1998). HS 286 England A v E Province (Port Elizabeth) 1993-94. CC HS 281* La v Somerset (Southport) 1994. H HS 272 v Kent (Canterbury) 2002 − on Hants debut. BB 1-90. Awards: BHC 2. LO HS 114 La v Notts (Manchester) 1995 (BHC). BB −

HAMBLIN, James Rupert Christopher (Charterhouse S; W of England U), b Pembury, Kent 16 Aug 1978. Son of C.B.Hamblin (Oxford U 1971-73). 6'0". RHB, RMF. Debut 2001. HS 96 and BB 6-93 v Derbys (Derby) 2003. LO HS 61 v Sussex (Hove) 2001 (NL). LO BB 4-29 v Middx (Southgate) 2001 (NL).

‡**HIBBERD, James**, b Southampton 19 Apr 1981. RHB, RMF. Wiltshire 2002-03. Trial contract 2004. LO HS 26 and BB 4-48 Wilts v Hants CB (Winchester) 2002 (CGT).

KENDALL, William Salwey (Bradfield C; Keble C, Oxford), b Wimbledon, Surrey 18 Dec 1973. 5'10". RHB, RM. Oxford U 1994-96; blue 1995-96. Hampshire debut 1996; cap 1999. 1000 runs (3); most − 1186 (1999). HS 201 v Sussex (Southampton) 1999. BB 3-37 OU v Derbys (Oxford) 1995. H BB 2-46 v Notts (Southampton) 1996. LO HS 110* v Middx (Southampton) 2002 (NL). LO BB 2-48 v Middx (Southampton) 2002 (BHC).

KENWAY, Derek Anthony (St George's S, Southampton; Barton Peveril C, Eastleigh), b Fareham 12 Jun 1978. 5'11". RHB, RM, occ WK. Debut 1997; cap 2001. 1000 runs (1): 1055 (1999). HS 166 v Notts (Southampton) 2001. BB 1-5. Award: CGT 1. LO HS 120* v Z (Southampton) 2003.

‡**LAMB, Gregory** Arthur, b Harare, Zimbabwe 4 Mar 1980. RHB, RM/OB. Debut CFX Academy 1998-99 to 1999-00. Mashonaland 2000-01. F-c Tour (Zim A): SL 1999-00. HS 100* CFX Academy v Manicaland (Mutare) 1999-00. BB 7-73 CFX Academy v Midlands (Kwekwe) 1999-00. LO HS 15 and BB 1-27 Zim A v SL A (Colombo) 1999-00.

‡**LATOUF, Kevin** John, b Pretoria, South Africa 7 Sep 1985. RHB, RM. Staff 2004 − awaiting first-class debut.

MASCARENHAS, Adrian Dimitri (Trinity C, Perth, Australia), b Hammersmith, London 30 Oct 1977. 6'2". Resident in Australia 1979-96. RHB, RMF. Debut 1996, taking 6-88 v Glamorgan (Southampton); took 16 wickets in first two CC matches; cap 1998. Dorset 1996. HS 104 v Worcs (Southampton) 2001. BB 6-26 v Middx (Southampton) 2001. Awards: CGT 3. LO HS 79 v Worcs (Southampton) 1999 (NL). LO BB 5-27 v Glos (Southampton) 2002 (NL).

MULLALLY, Alan David (Cannington HS, Perth, Australia; Wembley & Carlisle TC), b Southend-on-Sea, Essex 12 Jul 1969. 6'5". RHB, LFM. W Australia 1987-88 to 1989-90. Victoria 1990-91. Hampshire 1988 (1 match), 2000 to date; cap 2000. Leicestershire 1990-99; cap 1993. **Tests**: 19 (1996 to 2001); HS 24 v P (Oval) 1996; BB 5-105 v A (Brisbane) 1998-99. **LOI**: 50 (1996 to 2001); HS 20 v Z (Harare) 1996-97; BB 4-18 v A (Brisbane) 1998-99. F-c Tours: A 1998-99; SA 1999-00; NZ 1996-97; Z 1996-97. HS 75 Le v Middx (Leicester) 1996. H HS 36 v Derbys (Derby) 2001. 50 wkts (5); most − 70 (1996). BB 9-93 (14-188 match) v Derbys (Derby) 2000. Award: CGT 1. LO HS 38 Le v Kent (Leicester) 1994 (SL). LO BB 6-38 Le v NZ (Leicester) 1999.

NQ**POTHAS, Nic** (King Edward VII S; Rand Afrikaans U), b Johannesburg 18 Nov 1973. ECB qualified − EU (Greek) passport. 6'3". RHB, WK. Transvaal 1993-94 to 2000-01. Hampshire debut 2002; cap 2003. **LOI** (SA): 3 (2000-01); HS 24 v P (Singapore) 2000 − on debut. F-c Tours (SA): E 1996 (SA A); WI 2000-01 (SA A); SL 1998-99. HS 165 Gauteng v KZ-Natal (Johannesburg) 1998-99. H HS 146* v Worcs (Worcester) 2003. BB − LO HS 101 Transvaal v EP (Jo'burg) 1995-96.

PRITTIPAUL, Lawrence Roland (St John's C, Southsea; Portsmouth C), b Portsmouth 19 Oct 1979. Cousin of S.Chanderpaul (Guyana and West Indies 1991-92 to date). 6'1". RHB, RM. Debut 2000. HS 152 v Derbys (Southampton) 2000. BB 3-17 v Worcs (Southampton) 2003. LO HS 61 v Notts (Southampton) 2000 (NL). LO BB 3-33 v Glos (Southampton) 2002 (BHC).

‡**TAYLOR, Billy** Victor (Bitterne Park S, Southampton), b Southampton, Hants 11 Jan 1977. Brother of J.L.Taylor (Wiltshire 1998 to date). 6'3". LHB, RMF. Sussex 1999-2003. Wiltshire 1996-98. HS 35* Sx v Middx (Hove) 2003. BB 5-90 Sx v Warwks (Hove) 2002. Awards: CGT 1; BHC 1. LO HS 21* Sx v Notts (Cleethorpes) 1999 (NL). LO BB 5-28 Sx v Middx (Lord's) 2002 (BHC).

TOMLINSON, James Andrew (Harrow Way S, Andover; Cardiff U), b Winchester 12 Jun 1982. 6'1". LHB, LFM. Wiltshire 2001. British U 2002-03. Hampshire debut 2002. HS 23 v I (Southampton) 2002. CC HS 10 v Durham (Chester-le-St) 2003. CC BB 6-63 v Derbys (Derby) 2003. LO HS 6 (NL). LO BB 2-15 v Sussex (Southampton) 2002 (NL).

TREMLETT, Christopher Timothy (Thornden S, Chandler's Ford; Taunton's C, Southampton), b Southampton 2 Sep 1981. Son of T.M.Tremlett (Hampshire 1976-91); grandson of M.F.Tremlett (Somerset, CD and England 1947-60). 6'7". RHB, RMF. Debut 2000. F-c Tours (ECB Acad): SL 2002-03. HS 43 v Somerset (Southampton) 2003. BB 6-51 v Glam (Southampton) 2003. LO HS 30* v Glam (Southampton) 2000 (NL). LO BB 4-25 v Essex (Southend) 2002 (NL).

UDAL, Shane David (Cove CS), b Cove, Farnborough 18 Mar 1969. Grandson of G.F.U.Udal (Middx 1932 and Leics 1946); great-great-grandson of J.S.Udal (MCC 1871-75). 6'2". RHB, OB. Debut 1989; cap 1992; benefit 2002. **LOI**: 10 (1994 to 1995); HS 11* v Z (Brisbane) 1994-95; BB 2-37 v A (Sydney) 1994-95. F-c Tours: A 1994-95; P 1995-96 (Eng A). HS 117* v Warwks (Southampton) 1997. 50 wkts (7); most – 74 (1993). BB 8-50 v Sussex (Southampton) 1992. Awards: CGT 1; BHC 2. LO HS 78 v Surrey (Guildford) 1997 (SL). LO BB 5-43 v Surrey (Oval) 1998 (SL).

NQ**WARNE, Shane** Keith (Hampton HS; Mentone GS), b Upper Ferntree Gully, Melbourne, Australia 13 Sep 1969. 6'0". RHB, LBG. Victoria 1990-91 to date; captain 1997-98 to 1998-99. Hampshire 2000; cap 2000; captain 2004. *Wisden* 1993 (also one of *Five Cricketers of the Century*). **Tests** (A): 107 (1991-92 to 2002-03); HS 99 v NZ (Perth) 2001-02; BB 8-71 v E (Brisbane) 1994-95; hat trick v E (Melbourne) 1994-95. **LOI** (A): 193 (1992-93 to 2002-03, 11 as captain); HS 55 v SA (Pt Elizabeth) 1993-94; BB 5-33 v WI (Sydney) 1996-97. F-c Tours (A): E 1993, 1997; SA 1993-94, 1996-97; WI 1994-95, 1998-99; NZ 1992-93, 1999-00; I 1997-98, 2000-01; P 1994-95, 2002-03 (in SL/Sharjah); SL 1992-93, 1999-00; Z 1991-92 (Aus B), 1999-00. HS 99 (*see Tests*). H HS 69 v Kent (Portsmouth) 2000. 50 wkts (3+1); most – 75 (1993). BB 8-71 (*see Tests*). H BB 6-34 v Kent (Canterbury) 2000. Award: BHC 1. LO HS 55 (*see LOI*). LO BB 5-33 (*see LOI*).

RELEASED/RETIRED
(Having made a first-class County appearance in 2003)

C.G.van der Gucht left the staff having made no 1st XI appearances in 2003.

BRUNNSCHWEILER, Iain (King Edward VI S, Southampton), b Southampton 10 Dec 1979. 6'0". RHB, WK. Hampshire 2000-03. No appearances 2002. HS 34 v Yorks (Scarborough) 2003. LO HS 37 Hants CB v Staffs (Winchester) 2002 (CGT).

FRANCIS, J.D. – *see SOMERSET*.

GIDDINS, Edward Simon Hunter (Eastbourne C), b Eastbourne, Sussex 20 Jul 1971. 6'4½". RHB, RFM. Sussex 1991-96; cap 1994. Warwickshire 1998-2000; cap 1998. Surrey 2001-02. Hampshire 2003. MCC YC. **Tests**: 4 (1999 to 2000); HS 7 and BB 5-15 v Z (Lord's) 2000. F-c Tour: P 1995-96 (Eng A). HS 34 Sx v Essex (Hove) 1995. 50 wkts (4); most – 84 (1998). BB 6-47 Sx v Yorks (Eastbourne) 1996. H HS 10 and BB 4-88 v Worcs (Worcester) 2003 – on H debut. Awards: CGT 1; BHC 1. LO HS 13* Sy v Glos (Bristol) 2002 (NL). LO BB 5-20 Sy v Sussex (Oval) 2002 (NL).

HINDLEY, Richard James Edward (Southampton New C), b Portsmouth 25 Apr 1975. 6'3". LHB, OB. Debut 2003. HS 68* v Glam (Southampton) 2003 – on debut. BB – LO HS 38 Hants CB v Ire (Southampton) 2001 (CGT). LO BB 2-27 Hants CB v Wilts (Winchester) 2002 (CGT).

NQKATICH, Simon Mathew (Trinity C, WA; U of WA), b Middle Swan, Midland, W Australia 21 Aug 1975. 6'0". LHB, SLC. W Australia 1996-97 to 2001-02. NSW 2002-03. Durham 2000; cap 2000. Yorkshire 2002 (one match). Hampshire 2003; cap 2003. **Tests** (A): 6 (2001 to 2003-04); HS 125 v 1 (Sydney) 2003-04; BB 6-65 v Z (Sydney) 2003-04. **LOI** (A): 5 (2000-01 to 2003-04); 18* v I (Perth) 2003-04. F-c Tours (A): E 2001; SL 1999-00. 1000 (2+2): most – 1632 (1998-99). HS 228* WA v S Aus (Perth) 2000-01. UK HS 168* A v MCC (Arundel) 2001. CC HS 143* H v Yorks (Scarborough) 2003. BB 7-130 UK BB 4-21 H v Northants (Southampton) 2003. LO HS 118 WA v Vic (Perth) 2001-02. LO BB 3-21 Aus A v SA (Adelaide) 2001-02.

MORRIS, Alexander Corfield (Holgate S; Barnsley C), b Barnsley, Yorks 4 Oct 1976. Elder brother of Z.C.Morris (Hampshire 1998-99). 6'3". LHB, RMF. Yorkshire 1995-97. Yorks 2nd XI debut when 16yr 332d. Hampshire 1998-2003; cap 2001. F-c Tour: Z 1995-96 (Y). HS 65 v Sussex (Southampton) 2001. 50 wkts (2): most – 63 (2001). BB 5-39 v Durham (Chester-le-St) 2001. LO HS 48* Y v Durham (Chester-le-St) 1996 (SL). LO BB 5-32 Y v Young A (Leeds) 1995.

SMITH, Robin Arnold (Northlands BHS), b Durban, South Africa 13 Sep 1963. Younger brother of C.L.Smith (Natal, Glam, Hants and England 1977-78 to 1992) and grandson of Dr V.L.Shearer (Natal). 5'11". RHB, LB. Natal 1980-81 to 1984-85. Hampshire 1982-2003; cap 1985; benefit 1996; testimonial 2003. *Wisden* 1989. **Tests**: 62 (1988 to 1995-96); HS 175 v WI (St John's) 1993-94. **LOI**: 71 (1988 to 1995-96); HS 167* v A (Birmingham) 1993 – Eng record. F-c Tours: A 1990-91; SA 1995-96; WI 1989-90, 1993-94; NZ 1991-92; I/SL 1992-93. 1000 runs (11); most – 1577 (1989). HS 209* v Essex (Southend) 1987. BB 2-11 v Surrey (Southampton) 1985. Awards: CGT 9; BHC 5. LO HS 167* (*see LOI*). LO BB 2-13 v Berks (Southampton) 1985 (NWT).

THORBURN, Mark (Collingwood C, Durham U) b Bath Somerset 11 Aug 1978. RHB, RMF. Durham UCCE 2001-02. Hampshire 2003 – awaiting CC debut. HS 12 DU v Notts (Nottingham) 2002. H HS – BB 2-53 v OU (Oxford) 2003.

NQVAAS, Warnakulasooriya Patabendige Ushantha **Chaminda** Joseph, b Mattumagala 27 Jan 1974. LHB, LFM. Colts 1990-91 to date. Hampshire 2003. **Tests**: 71 (1994-95 to 2003-04); HS 74* v Z (Colombo) 2001-02; BB 7-71 (14-191 match) v WI (Colombo) 2001-02. **LOI**: 228 (1993-94 to 2003-04); HS 50* v P (Sharjah) 2000-01; BB 8-19 v Z (Colombo) 2001-02 – including the first of two LOI hat tricks. F-c Tours (SL): E 2002; A 1995-96; SA 1997-98, 2000-01, 2002-03; WI 2003; NZ 1994-95, 1996-97; I 1997-98; P 1995-96, 1998-99, 1999-00, 2001-02; Z 1994-95, 1999-00. HS 74* (*see Tests*). H HS 35 v Worcs (Southampton) 2003. 50 wkts (0+2); most 62 (2001-02). BB 7-71 (*see Tests*). H BB 4-82 v Derbys (Southampton) 2003 – on Hants debut. LO HS 62* Colts v SSC (Colombo) 1999-00. LO BB 8-19 (*see LOI*).

NQWASIM AKRAM (Islamia C), b Lahore, Pakistan 3 Jun 1966. 6'3". LHB, LF. PACO 1984-85 to 1985-86. Lahore 1985-86 to 1986-87. PIA 1987-88 to date. Lancashire 1988-98; cap 1989; captain 1998; benefit 1998. Hampshire 2003. *Wisden* 1992. **Tests** (P): 104 (1984-85 to 2001-02, 25 as captain); HS 257* v Z (Sheikhupura) 1996-97; BB 7-119 v NZ (Wellington) 1993-94; 2 hat tricks. **LOI** (P): 356 (1984-85 to 2002-03, 109 as captain); HS 86 v A (Melbourne) 1989-90; BB 5-15 v Z (Karachi) 1993-94; 2 hat tricks. F-c Tours (P)(C=captain): E 1987, 1992, 1996C, 2001; A 1988-89, 1989-90, 1991-92, 1992-93, 1995-96C, 1996-97C, 1999-00C; SA 1994-95, 1997-98; WI 1987-88, 1992-93C, 1999-00; NZ 1984-85, 1992-93, 1993-94, 1995-96C; I 1986-87, 1998-99C; SL 1984-85 (P U-23), 1985-86, 1994-95, 2000-01; Z 1994-95, 1997-98; B 2001-02. HS 257* (*see Tests*). UK HS 155 La v Notts (Nottingham) 1998. H HS 23 v Glam (Cardiff) 2003. 50 wkts (5); most – 82 (1992). BB 8-30 (13-147 match) La v Somerset (Southport) 1994. H BB 3-31 v Glos (Southampton) 2003. Hat trick 1988. Awards: BHC 4. LO HS 89* La v Notts (Nottingham) 1998 (BHC). LO BB 5-10 La v Leics (Leicester) 1993 (BHC).

HAMPSHIRE 2003

RESULTS SUMMARY

		Place	Won	Lost	Tied	Drew	No Result
County Championship	(2nd Division)	8th	2	6		8	
All First-Class Matches			2	6		9	
C & G Trophy		3rd Round					
National League	(2nd Division)	3rd	11	7			
Twenty20 Cup		6th in South Group					

COUNTY CHAMPIONSHIP AVERAGES

BATTING AND FIELDING

Cap		M	I	NO	HS	Runs	Avge	100	50	Ct/St
2003	S.M.Katich	13	22	3	143*	1143	60.15	4	6	15
–	J.R.C.Hamblin	4	6	2	96	219	54.75	–	2	–
2003	N.Pothas	13	20	2	146*	809	44.94	2	4	38/2
–	L.R.Prittipaul	3	5	1	56*	167	41.75	–	1	6
1985	R.A.Smith	10	15	1	92	522	37.28	–	5	9
2002	J.P.Crawley	16	27	1	93	878	33.76	–	8	5
1992	S.D.Udal	15	23	5	60*	488	27.11	–	3	5
2001	D.A.Kenway	15	26	1	115	657	26.28	2	2	13
1998	A.D.Mascarenhas	16	25	1	100*	584	24.33	1	2	7
1999	W.S.Kendall	8	12	–	69	277	23.08	–	1	6
–	J.H.K.Adams	9	18	1	60	361	21.23	–	2	6
–	J.D.Francis	6	11	–	69	211	19.18	–	1	6
–	C.T.Tremlett	10	13	2	43	199	18.09	–	–	5
–	W.P.U.C.J.Vaas	3	6	2	35	64	16.00	–	–	2
–	I.Brunnschweiler	3	4	–	34	58	14.50	–	–	6
–	Wasim Akram	5	7	1	23	55	9.16	–	–	–
–	J.T.A.Bruce	7	11	3	21*	68	8.50	–	–	2
2000	A.D.Mullally	8	10	3	14	38	5.42	–	–	2
–	E.S.H.Giddins	3	4	1	10	10	3.33	–	–	–
–	J.A.Tomlinson	7	11	5	10	19	3.16	–	–	2

Also batted (1 match each): R.J.E.Hindley 8, 68*; A.C.Morris (cap 2001) 46.

BOWLING

	O	M	R	W	Avge	Best	5wI	10wM
Wasim Akram	167.3	44	503	20	25.15	3-31	–	–
E.S.H.Giddins	98.5	18	336	13	25.84	4-88	–	–
A.D.Mascarenhas	467.1	144	1222	39	31.33	6-55	1	–
C.T.Tremlett	248.4	48	929	27	34.40	6-51	1	–
S.M.Katich	160.4	29	591	17	34.76	4-21	–	–
S.D.Udal	408.2	82	1242	34	36.52	4-69	–	–
A.D.Mullally	229.1	55	664	17	39.05	3-31	–	–
J.A.Tomlinson	150.1	18	721	16	45.06	6-63	1	–
J.T.A.Bruce	163	29	726	16	45.37	3-42	–	–
Also bowled:								
J.R.C.Hamblin	41	4	185	6	30.83	6-93	1	–
W.P.U.C.J.Vaas	94	18	310	8	38.75	4-82	–	–

R.J.E.Hindley 9-0-46-0; W.S.Kendall 8-2-34-0; D.A.Kenway 2-0-9-1; L.R.Prittipaul 28-2-131-4.

The First-Class Averages (pp 123–138) give the records of Hampshire players in all first-class county matches (Hampshire's other opponents being Oxford University), with the exception of J.H.K.Adams, J.D.Francis and J.A.Tomlinson whose full county figures are as above.

HAMPSHIRE RECORDS

FIRST-CLASS CRICKET

Highest Total	For 672-7d		v	Somerset	Taunton	1899
	V 742		by	Surrey	The Oval	1909
Lowest Total	For 15		v	Warwicks	Birmingham	1922
	V 23		by	Yorkshire	Middlesbrough	1965
Highest Innings	For 316	R.H.Moore	v	Warwicks	Bournemouth	1937
	V 303*	G.A.Hick	for	Worcs	Southampton	1997

Highest Partnership for each Wicket

1st	347	V.P.Terry/C.L.Smith	v	Warwicks	Birmingham	1987
2nd	321	G.Brown/E.I.M.Barrett	v	Glos	Southampton	1920
3rd	344	C.P.Mead/G.Brown	v	Yorkshire	Portsmouth	1927
4th	263	R.E.Marshall/D.A.Livingstone	v	Middlesex	Lord's	1970
5th	235	G.Hill/D.F.Walker	v	Sussex	Portsmouth	1937
6th	411	R.M.Poore/E.G.Wynyard	v	Somerset	Taunton	1899
7th	325	G.Brown/C.H.Abercrombie	v	Essex	Leyton	1913
8th	227	K.D.James/T.M.Tremlett	v	Somerset	Taunton	1985
9th	230	D.A.Livingstone/A.T.Castell	v	Surrey	Southampton	1962
10th	192	H.A.W.Bowell/W.H.Livsey	v	Worcs	Bournemouth	1921

Best Bowling	For 9-25	R.M.H.Cottam	v	Lancashire	Manchester	1965
(Innings)	V 10-46	W.Hickton	for	Lancashire	Manchester	1870
Best Bowling	For 16-88	J.A.Newman	v	Somerset	Weston-s-Mare	1927
(Match)	V 17-119	W.Mead	for	Essex	Southampton	1895

Most Runs – Season	2854	C.P.Mead	(av 79.27)	1928
Most Runs – Career	48892	C.P.Mead	(av 48.84)	1905-36
Most 100s – Season	12	C.P.Mead		1928
Most 100s – Career	138	C.P.Mead		1905-36
Most Wkts – Season	190	A.S.Kennedy	(av 15.61)	1922
Most Wkts – Career	2669	D.Shackleton	(av 18.23)	1948-69
Most Career W-K Dismissals	700	R.J.Parks	(630 ct/70 st)	1980-92
Most Career Catches in the Field	629	C.P.Mead		1905-36

LIST 'A' LIMITED-OVERS CRICKET

Highest Total	CGT	371-4	v	Glamorgan	Southampton	1975
	BHC	321-1	v	Minor C (S)	Amersham	1973
	NL	335-6	v	Somerset	Taunton	2003
Lowest Total	CGT	98	v	Lancashire	Manchester	1975
	BHC	50	v	Yorkshire	Leeds	1991
	NL	43	v	Essex	Basingstoke	1972
Highest Innings	CGT	177	C.G.Greenidge	v	Glamorgan	Southampton	1975
	BHC	173*	C.G.Greenidge	v	Minor C (S)	Amersham	1973
	NL	172	C.G.Greenidge	v	Surrey	Southampton	1987
Best Bowling	CGT	7-30	P.J.Sainsbury	v	Norfolk	Southampton	1965
	BHC	6-25	S.J.Renshaw	v	Surrey	Southampton	1997
	NL	6-20	T.E.Jesty	v	Glamorgan	Cardiff	1975

KENT

Formation of Present Club: 1 March 1859
Substantial Reorganisation: 6 December 1870
Inaugural First-Class Match: 1864
Colours: Maroon and White
Badge: White Horse on a Red Ground
County Champions: (6) 1906, 1909, 1910, 1913, 1970, 1978
Joint Champions: (1) 1977
Gillette/NatWest/C & G Trophy Winners: (2) 1967, 1974
Benson and Hedges Cup Winners: (3) 1973, 1976, 1978
National League (Div 1) Winners: (1) 2001
Sunday League Winners: (4) 1972, 1973, 1976, 1995
Twenty20 Cup Winners: 3rd in South Group 2003
Match Awards: CGT 55; BHC 96

Chief Executive: P.E.Millman, St Lawrence Ground, Canterbury, CT1 3NZ • Tel: 01227 456886 • Fax: 01227 762168 • Email: kent@ecb.co.uk • Web: www.kentccc.com

Coaching Co-ordinator: S.C.Willis. **Second XI Coach/Academy Director**: P.Farbrace. **Captain**: D.P.Fulton. **Vice-Captain**: No appointment. **Overseas Players**: Mohammad Sami and A.Symonds. **2004 Beneficiary**: M.M.Patel. **Head Groundsman**: M.G.Grantham. **Scorer**: J.C.Foley. ‡ New registration. ^{NQ} Not qualified for England.

CARBERRY, Michael Alexander (St John Rigby Catholic C), b Croydon, Surrey 29 Sep 1980. 6'0". LHB, OB. Surrey 2001-02. Kent debut 2003. HS 153* Sy v CU (Cambridge) 2002. K HS 137 v CU (Cambridge) 2003 – on Kent debut inc 109* before lunch 1st day. CC HS 92 v Surrey (Canterbury) 2003. BB 1-45. LO HS 79 v Worcs (Canterbury) 2003 (NL). LO BB 1-21.

‡CUSDEN, Simon Mark James (Simon Langton GS, Canterbury), b Canterbury 21 Feb 1985. RHB, RFM. Development contract – awaiting 1st XI debut. England U-19 to Australia 2002-03.

‡DENLY, Joseph Liam (Chaucer TC), b Canterbury 16 Mar 1986. RHB, LB. Development contract – awaiting first-class debut.

DENNINGTON, Matthew John (Northwood BS; UNISA), b Durban, South Africa16 Oct 1982. 6'1". RHB, RFM. Kent staff 2003 – awaiting first-class debut. LO HS 18* v Glos (Beckenham) 2003 (NL). LO BB 1-51 (Kent CB).

FERLEY, Robert Steven (King Edward VII HS; Sutton Valence S; Grey C, Durham U), b Norwich, Norfolk 4 Feb 1982. 5'8". RHB, SLA. Durham UCCE 2001-02. British U 2001-03. Kent debut 2003. Norfolk 2001. HS 78* DU v Durham (Chester-le-St) 2003. K HS 14* v Notts (Maidstone) 2003. BB 4-76 v Surrey (Oval) 2003. LO HS (Kent CB) 6 (CGT). LO BB 3-59 v Glam (Maidstone) 2003 (NL).

FULTON, David Paul (The Judd S; Kent U), b Lewisham 15 Nov 1971. 6'2". RHB, SLA, occ WK. Debut 1992; cap 1998; captain 2002 to date. 1000 (2): most – 1892 (2001). HS 208* v Somerset (Canterbury) 2001. Scored 9 hundreds in 2001, including 208*, 104* and 197 in successive innings. LB 1-37 (not CC). LO HS 82 v Yorks (Leeds) 2001 (NL). BB –

JONES, Geraint Owen (Harristown State HS, Toowoomba and MacGregor State HS, Brisbane, Australia), b Kundiawa, Papua New Guinea 14 Jul 1976. Welsh parents. 5'10". RHB, WK. Debut 2001; cap 2003. F-c Tour: SL 2003-04. HS 108* v Essex (Chelmsford) 2003. BB – LO HS 74* v Glos (Beckenham) 2003 (NL).

KEY, Robert William Trevor (Colfe's S), b East Dulwich, London 12 May 1979. 6'1". RHB, RM/OB. Debut 1998; cap 2001. **Tests**: 8 (2002 to 2003); HS 52 v A (Melbourne) 2002-03. **LOI**: 2 (2003); HS 11 v Z (Nottingham) 2003 on debut. F-c Tours: A 2002-03; SA 1998-99 (Eng A); SL 2002-03 (ECB Acad); Z 1998-99 (Eng A). 1000 (2): most – 1281 (2001). HS 174* England XI v Australia A (Hobart) 2002-03. K HS 160 v Hants (Canterbury) 2002. BB – LO HS 114 v Notts (Nottingham) 2002 (NL).

[NQ]**KHAN, Amjad** (Skolenpa Duevej, Denmark), b Copenhagen, Denmark 14 Oct 1980. 6'0". RHB, RFM. Debut 2001. Denmark 1998-2000. HS 78 v Middx (Lord's) 2003. 50 wkts (1): 63 (2002). BB 6-52 v Yorks (Canterbury) 2002. LO HS 21 v Warwks (Birmingham) 2002 (NL). LO BB 4-26 v Leics (Leicester) 2003 (NL).

LOUDON, Alexander Guy Rushworth (Wellesley House; Eton C; Collingwood C, Durham U), b Westminster, London 6 Sep 1980. Younger brother of H.J.H.Loudon (Durham UCCE 2001). 6'3". RHB, OB. Durham UCCE 2001-03; captain 2003. Kent debut 2003. HS 172 DU (record) v Durham (Chester-le-St) 2003. K HS 63 and BB 1-52 v SA A (Canterbury) 2003. CC HS 9. BB 3-86 DU v Worcs (Worcester) 2001. LO HS 53 Kent CB v Leics CB (Hinckley) 2001 (CGT). LO BB –

[NQ]**MOHAMMAD SAMI**, b Karachi, Pakistan 24 Feb 1981. RGB, RF. Customs 1999-00. Karachi 2000-01. National Bank 2000-01 to 2001-02. **Tests** (P): 12 (2000-01 to 2003-04); HS 25 v NZ (Hamilton) 2003-04; BB 5-36 v NZ (Auckland) 2000-01 on debut. **LOI** (P): 45 (2000-01 to 2003-04); HS 22 v SA (Rawalpindi) 2003-04; BB 5-10 v NZ (Lahore) 2003-04. F-c Tours (P): E 2001; SA 2002-03; NZ 2000-01, 2003-04; SL 2002-03 (v A); Z 2002-03. HS 41* National Bank v Sui Gas (Faisalabad) 2001-02. BB 8-64 (15-114 match) and K HS 16 v Notts (Maidstone) 2003. LO HS 22 (see LOI). LO BB 5-10 (see LOI).

‡[NQ]**O'BRIEN, Niall** John, b Dublin, Ireland 8 Nov 1981. LHB, WK. Staff 2004 – awaiting first-class debut. LO HS 13 Ire v Berks (Finchampstead) 2002 (CGT).

PATEL, Minal Mahesh (Dartford GS; Erith TC), b Bombay, India 7 Jul 1970. 5'9". RHB, SLA. Debut 1989; cap 1994; benefit 2004. No appearances 2003 (back injury). **Tests**: 2 (1996); HS 27 and BB 1-101 v I (Nottingham) 1996. F-c Tour: I 1994-95 (Eng A). HS 82 v Leics (Canterbury) 2002. 50 wkts (3); most – 90 (1994). BB 8-96 v Lancs (Canterbury) 1994. LO HS 27* v Somerset (Canterbury) 2001 (CGT). LO BB 3-22 v Essex (Canterbury) 1999 (NL).

SAGGERS, Martin John (Springwood HS; King's Lynn; Huddersfield U), b King's Lynn, Norfolk 23 May 1972. 6'2". RHB, RMF. Durham 1996-98. Norfolk 1995-96. Kent debut 1999; cap 2001. **Tests**: 1 (2003-04); HS 1 and BB 2-29 v B (Chittagong) 2003-04 on debut. F-c Tour: SL 2003-04. HS 61* v Lancs (Canterbury) 2001. 50 wkts (4): most – 83 (2002). BB 7-79 v Durham (Chester-le-St) 2000. Award: BHC 1. LO HS 34* Minor C v Leics (Jesmond) 1996 (BHC). LO BB 5-22 v Glos (Canterbury) 2001 (NL).

SHERIYAR, Alamgir (George Dixon S; Joseph Chamberlain SFC; Oxford Poly), b Birmingham 15 Nov 1973. 6'1". RHB, LFM. Leicestershire 1994-95. Worcestershire 1996-2002; cap 1997. Kent debut 2003. F-c Tours (Eng A): NZ 1999-00; B 1999-00. HS 21 Wo v Notts (Nottingham) 1997 and 21 Wo v Pak A (Worcester) 1997. K HS 18* v Essex (Chelmsford) 2003. 50 wkts (4); most – 92 (1999). BB 7-130 (10-172 match) Wo v Hants (Southampton) 1999. K BB 5-65 v Sussex (Hove) 2003. Hat tricks (2): 1994 (Le), 1999 (Wo). LO HS 19 Wo v Derbys (Chesterfield) 1996 (SL). LO BB 4-18 Wo v Yorks (Leeds) 1997 (SL).

SMITH, Edward Thomas (Tonbridge S; Peterhouse, Cambridge), b Pembury 19 Jul 1977. 6'2". RHB, RM. Cambridge U 1996-98, scoring 101 v Glam (Cambridge) on debut; blue 1996-97 (injured 1998). Kent debut 1996; cap 2001. British U 1998. **Tests**: 3 (2003); HS 64 v SA (Nottingham) 2003 on debut. F-c Tour (Eng A): I 2003-04. 1000 runs (4): most –1534 (2003). Scored 135, 0, 149, 113, 203 and 108 in successive f-c innings 2003. HS 213 v Warwks (Canterbury) 2003. LO HS 122 v Glam (Maidstone) 2003 (NL).

44

STIFF, David Alexander (Batley GS; Wakefield C), b Dewsbury, Yorks 20 Oct 1984. RHB, RFM. England U-19 to Australia 2002-03. Yorkshire Academy. Kent staff 2004 – awaiting first-class debut. LO HS – and BB 1-27 Yorks CB v Glos CB (Bristol) 2001 (CGT).

[NO]**SYMONDS, Andrew** (All Saints Anglican School, Mudgeeraba, Queensland), b Birmingham 9 Jun 1975. 6'1½". RHB, RMF/OB. Emigrated to Australia when 18 months old. Queensland 1994-95 to date. Gloucestershire 1995-96; cap 1996. Kent 1999, 2001; cap 1999. YC 1995. Surrendered England qualification by appearing for Australia A v WI 1996-97. **LOI** (A): 89 (1998-99 to 2003-04); HS 143* v P (Jo'burg) 2002-03; BB 4-11 v I (Sydney) 1999-00. F-c Tours (Aus A): Sc 1998; NZ 1994-95 (Aus Academy). 1000 runs (2); most – 1438 (1995). HS 254* Gs v Glam (Abergavenny) 1995 (including record 16 sixes); hit record 20 sixes in match. K HS 177 v Leics (Canterbury) 1999. BB 6-105 v Sussex (Tunbridge Wells) 2002. Awards: CGT 2; BHC 2. LO HS 143* *(see LOI)*. LO BB 6-14 Aus A v Ind A (Los Angeles) 1999.

TREDWELL, James Cullum (Southlands Community CS, New Romney), b Ashford 27 Feb 1982. 6'0". LHB, OB. Debut 2001. F-c Tour (Eng A): I 2003-04 (capt). HS 61 v Yorks (Leeds) 2002. BB 4-48 v Sussex (Hove) 2003. LO HS 71 Kent CB v Bucks (Maidstone) 2001 (CGT). LO BB 3-7 v Norfolk (Horsford) 2002 (CGT).

TROTT, Benjamin James (Court Fields Community S, Wellington; Richard Huish C, Taunton; Plymouth U), b Wellington, Somerset 14 Mar 1975. 6'5". RHB, RMF. Somerset 1997-98. Kent debut 2000. Devon 2000. HS 26 v Sussex (Tunbridge Wells) 2002. BB 6-13 (11-78 match) v Essex (Tunbridge Wells) 2003. Award: CGT 1. LO HS 3 (CGT). LO BB 5-18 v Cumb (Barrow) 2001 (CGT).

WALKER, Matthew Jonathan (King's S, Rochester), b Gravesend 2 Jan 1974. Grandson of Jack Walker (Kent 1949). 5'8". LHB, RM. Debut 1992-93 (Z tour); UK Debut 1994; cap 2000. F-c Tour: Z 1992-93 (K). 1000 (1): 1051 (2003). HS 275* v Somerset (Canterbury) 1996. BB 1-3 (FCC Select XI). K BB 1-4. Awards: BHC 3. LO HS 117 v Warwks (Canterbury) 1997 (BHC). LO BB 4-24 v Yorks (Leeds) 2001 (NL).

RELEASED/RETIRED
(Having made a first-class County appearance in 2003)

I.N.Flanagan and J.P.Hewitt left the staff having made no f-c appearances in 2003.

BANES, Matthew John (Tonbridge S; Collingwood C, Durham U), b Pembury 10 Dec 1979. 5'9". RHB, OB. Kent 1999-2003 (no appearances 2002). British U 2000-01. Durham UCCE 2001-02. HS 69 DU v Lancs (Durham) 2002. K HS 53 v NZ (Canterbury) 1999 – on debut. CC HS 5. BB 3-65 DU v Lancs (Durham) 2001. LO HS (Kent CB) 82 v Leics CB (Hinckley) 2001 (CGT). LO BB (Kent CB) 1-11 (CGT).

[NO]**BLEWETT, Gregory** Scott (Prince Alfred C), b Adelaide, Australia 28 Oct 1971. Son of R.W.Blewett (South Australia 1975-76 to 1978-79). 6'0". RHB, RM. South Australia 1991-92 to date. Yorkshire 1999; cap 1999. Nottinghamshire 2001; cap 2001. Kent 2003. **Tests** (A): 46 (1994-95 to 1999-00); HS 214 v SA (Johannesburg) 1996-97; scored 102* v E (Adelaide) on debut; first to score hundreds in his first 3 Ashes Tests; BB 2-9 v WI (St John's) 1998-99. **LOI** (A): 32 (1994-95 to 1998-99); HS 57* v WI (Melbourne) 1996-97; BB 2-6 v SL (Adelaide) 1998-99. F-c Tours (A): E 1997; SA 1996-97; WI 1994-95, 1998-99; NZ 1999-00; I 1997-98; SL 1999-00; Z 1999-00. 1000 runs (1+5); most – 1292 (2001). K HS: 71 v Warwks (Birmingham) 2003. BB 5-29 Aus XI v WI (Hobart) 1996-97. CC BB 2-16 Y v Durham (Leeds) 1999. K BB 1-6. Award: BHC 1. LO HS 131 Aus A v Z (Brisbane) 2000-01. LO BB 4-18 Y v Lancs (Manchester) 1999 (NWT).

EALHAM, M.A. – *see NOTTINGHAMSHIRE.*

RELEASED/RETIRED continued on p 56

KENT 2003

RESULTS SUMMARY

	Place	Won	Lost	Tied	Drew	No Result
County Championship (1st Division)	**4th**	6	5		5	
All First-Class Matches		6	6		6	
C & G Trophy	4th Round					
National League (1st Division)	**6th**	7	8	1		
Twenty20 Cup	**3rd in South Group**					

COUNTY CHAMPIONSHIP AVERAGES

BATTING AND FIELDING

Cap		M	I	NO	HS	Runs	Avge	100	50	Ct/St
2001	E.T.Smith	13	22	–	213	1352	61.45	7	1	9
1999	A.Symonds	10	16	2	121	659	47.07	2	4	6
2003	G.O.Jones	16	24	4	108*	886	44.30	2	6	50/5
2000	M.J.Walker	16	25	2	150	927	40.30	3	3	22
1998	D.P.Fulton	11	19	1	94*	674	37.44	–	5	4
1992	M.A.Ealham	16	24	–	101	847	35.29	1	6	18
2001	R.W.T.Key	10	17	2	140	507	33.80	1	1	9
–	G.S.Blewett	6	10	–	71	319	31.90	–	3	7
–	M.A.Carberry	12	21	1	92	607	30.35	–	5	2
–	A.Khan	7	10	–	78	236	23.60	–	1	1
–	J.C.Tredwell	11	16	2	36	263	18.78	–	–	14
2001	M.J.Saggers	13	18	5	47	229	17.61	–	–	2
–	A.Sheriyar	13	18	9	18*	88	9.77	–	–	3
–	R.S.Ferley	5	4	1	14*	24	8.00	–	–	4
–	B.J.Trott	6	8	3	12*	35	7.00	–	–	2
2003	M.Muralitharan	5	7	–	15	49	7.00	–	–	1
–	Mohammad Sami	3	4	–	16	19	4.75	–	–	–

Also batted: A.G.R.Loudon (2 matches) 8, 0, 9 (2 ct); P.D.Trego (1) 13 (1 ct).

BOWLING

	O	M	R	W	Avge	Best	5wI	10wM
M.Muralitharan	178	41	447	33	13.54	6-36	4	–
Mohammad Sami	89.1	17	357	18	19.83	8-64	2	1
M.J.Saggers	396	81	1294	54	23.96	5-42	2	–
M.A.Ealham	350.5	103	998	38	26.26	6-35	3	–
R.S.Ferley	128.2	30	429	14	30.64	4-76	–	–
A.Sheriyar	325.3	66	1042	33	31.57	5-65	1	–
A.Symonds	152	26	517	16	32.31	3-38	–	–
A.Khan	145	15	704	17	41.41	4-65	–	–
J.C.Tredwell	278.4	59	962	23	41.82	4-48	–	–
B.J.Trott	134.3	23	564	12	47.00	4-73	–	–

Also bowled: G.S.Blewett 34-7-112-2; M.A.Carberry 23-2-94-1; R.W.T.Key 0.4-0-4-0; E.T.Smith 3-1-14-0; P.D.Trego 13-0-69-2; M.J.Walker 9-0-51-0.

The First-Class Averages (pp 123–138) give the records of Kent players in all first-class county matches (Kent's other opponents being the South Africans, and Cambridge University), with the exception of:
    R.S.Ferley 6-6-1-14*-38-7.60-0-0-4ct. 149.2-30-532-16-33.25-4/76.
    R.W.T.Key 12-20-2-140-732-40.66-2-1-10ct. 0.4-0-4-0.
    A.G.R.Loudon 3-5-1-63-110-27.50-0-1-3ct. 10.3-1-52-1-52.00-1/52.
    E.T.Smith 15-25-1-213-1447-60.29-7-2-10ct. 3-1-14-0.

46

KENT RECORDS

FIRST-CLASS CRICKET

Highest Total	For 803-4d		v	Essex	Brentwood	1934
	V 676		by	Australians	Canterbury	1921
Lowest Total	For 18		v	Sussex	Gravesend	1867
	V 16		by	Warwicks	Tonbridge	1913
Highest Innings	For 332	W.H.Ashdown	v	Essex	Brentwood	1934
	V 344	W.G.Grace	for	MCC	Canterbury	1876

Highest Partnership for each Wicket

1st	300	N.R.Taylor/M.R.Benson	v	Derbyshire	Canterbury	1991
2nd	366	S.G.Hinks/N.R.Taylor	v	Middlesex	Canterbury	1990
3rd	321*	A.Hearne/J.R.Mason	v	Notts	Nottingham	1899
4th	368	P.A.de Silva/G.R.Cowdrey	v	Derbyshire	Maidstone	1995
5th	277	F.E.Woolley/L.E.G.Ames	v	New Zealand	Canterbury	1931
6th	315	P.A.de Silva/M.A.Ealham	v	Notts	Nottingham	1995
7th	248	A.P.Day/E.Humphreys	v	Somerset	Taunton	1908
8th	157	A.L.Hilder/A.C.Wright	v	Essex	Gravesend	1924
9th	171	M.A.Ealham/P.A.Strang	v	Notts	Nottingham	1997
10th	235	F.E.Woolley/A.Fielder	v	Worcs	Stourbridge	1909

Best Bowling	For	10- 30	C.Blythe	v	Northants	Northampton	1907
(Innings)	V	10- 48	C.H.G.Bland	for	Sussex	Tonbridge	1899
Best Bowling	For	17- 48	C.Blythe	v	Northants	Northampton	1907
(Match)	V	17-106	T.W.J.Goddard	for	Glos	Bristol	1939

Most Runs – Season	2894	F.E.Woolley	(av 59.06)	1928
Most Runs – Career	47868	F.E.Woolley	(av 41.77)	1906-38
Most 100s – Season	10	F.E.Woolley		1928
	10	F.E.Woolley		1934
Most 100s – Career	122	F.E.Woolley		1906-38
Most Wkts – Season	262	A.P.Freeman	(av 14.74)	1933
Most Wkts – Career	3340	A.P.Freeman	(av 17.64)	1914-36
Most Career W-K Dismissals	1253	F.H.Huish	(901 ct/352 st)	1895-1914
Most Career Catches in the Field	773	F.E.Woolley		1906-38

LIST 'A' LIMITED-OVERS CRICKET

Highest Total	CGT	384-6		v	Berkshire	Finchampstead	1994
	BHC	338-6		v	Somerset	Maidstone	1996
	NL	327-6		v	Leics	Canterbury	1993
Lowest Total	CGT	60		v	Somerset	Taunton	1979
	BHC	73		v	Middlesex	Canterbury	1979
	NL	83		v	Middlesex	Lord's	1984
Highest Innings	CGT	136*	C.L.Hooper	v	Berkshire	Finchampstead	1994
	BHC	143	C.J.Tavaré	v	Somerset	Taunton	1985
	NL	145	C.L.Hooper	v	Leics	Leicester	1996
Best Bowling	CGT	8-31	D.L.Underwood	v	Scotland	Edinburgh	1987
	BHC	6-41	T.N.Wren	v	Somerset	Canterbury	1995
	NL	6- 9	R.A.Woolmer	v	Derbyshire	Chesterfield	1979

LANCASHIRE

Formation of Present Club: 12 January 1864
Inaugural First-Class Match: 1865
Colours: Red, Green and Blue
Badge: Red Rose
County Champions (since 1890): (7) 1897, 1904, 1926, 1927, 1928, 1930, 1934
Joint Champions: (1) 1950
Gillette/NatWest/C & G Trophy Winners: (7) 1970, 1971, 1972, 1975, 1990, 1996, 1998
Benson and Hedges Cup Winners: (4) 1984, 1990, 1995, 1996
National League (Div 1) Winners: (1) 1999.
Sunday League Winners: (4) 1969, 1970, 1989, 1998
Twenty20 Cup Winners: 4th in North Group 2003
Match Awards: CGT 77; BHC 86

Chief Executive: J.Cumbes, Old Trafford, Manchester M16 0PX • Tel: 0161 282 4000 • Fax: 0161 282 4100 • Email: enquiries@lccc.co.uk • Web: www.lccc.co.uk

Cricket Manager/First XI Coach: M.Watkinson. **Captain**: W.K.Hegg. **Vice-Captain**: no appointment. **Overseas Players**: C.L.Hooper and S.G.Law. **2004 Beneficiary**: G.Chapple. **Head Groundsman**: P.Marron. **Scorer**: A.West. ‡ New registration. NQ Not qualified for England.

ANDERSON, James Michael (St Theodore RC HS and SFC, Burnley), b Burnley 30 Jul 1982. 6'2". LHB, RMF. England U-19. Debut 2002. YC 2003 **ECB contract 2004**. **Tests**: 8 (2003 to 2003-04); HS 21* v SA (Lord's) 2003; BB 5-73 v Z (Lord's) 2003 on debut. **LOI**: 27 (2002-03 to 2003-04); HS 8; BB 4-25 v Holland (E London) 2002-03. Hat trick v P (Oval) 2003 – 1st for Eng in 373 LOI. F-c Tour: SL 2003-04. HS 21* (*see Tests*). La HS 16 v Warwks (Manchester) 2002. 50 wkts (1): 50 (2002). BB 6-23 v Hants (Southampton) 2002. Hat trick (Lancs) 2003. HS LO 8 (*see LOI*). LO BB 4-25 (*see LOI*).

CHAPPLE, Glen (West Craven HS; Nelson & Colne C), b Skipton, Yorks 23 Jan 1974. 6'1". RHB, RFM. Debut 1992; cap 1994; benefit 2004. F-c Tours (Eng A): A 1996-97; WI 1995-96 (La); I 1994-95. HS 155 v Somerset (Manchester) 2001. Scored 100 off 27 balls in contrived circumstances v Glam (Manchester) 1993. 50 wkts (4); most – 55 (1994). BB 6-30 v Somerset (Blackpool) 2002. Awards: CGT 1; BHC 2. LO HS 81* v Derbys (Manchester) 2002 (CGT). LO BB 6-18 v Essex (Lord's) 1996 (NWT).

CHILTON, Mark James (Manchester GS; Durham U), b Sheffield, Yorks 2 Oct 1976. 6'3". RHB, RM. Debut 1997. Cap 2002. British U 1998. 1000 (1): 1154 (2003). HS 125 v Middx (Manchester) 2003. BB 1-1. CC BB 1-10. Awards: CGT 1; BHC 4. LO HS 103 v Somerset (Taunton) 2003 (NL). LO BB 5-26 Brit U v Sussex (Cambridge) 1997 (BHC).

‡**CORK, Dominic** Gerald (St Joseph's C, Stoke-on-Trent; Newcastle CFE), b Newcastle-under-Lyme, Staffs 7 Aug 1971. 6'2". RHB, RFM. Derbyshire 1990-2003; cap 1993; captain 1998-2003; benefit 2001. *Wisden* 1995. Staffordshire 1989-90. ECB contract 2001. **Tests**: 37 (1995 to 2002); HS 59 v NZ (Auckland) 1996-97; BB 7-43 v WI (Lord's) 1995 – on debut (record England analysis by Test match debutant); hat trick v WI (Manchester) 1995 – the first in Test history to occur in the opening over of a day's play. **LOI**: 32 (1992 to 2002-03); HS 31* v NZ (Napier) 1996-97; BB 3-27 v WI (Lord's) 1995. F-c Tours: A 1992-93 (Eng A), 1998-99; SA 1993-94 (Eng A), 1995-96; WI 1991-92 (Eng A); NZ 1996-97; I 1994-95 (Eng A); P 2000-01 (*part*). HS 200* De v Durham (Derby) 2000. 50 wkts (7); most – 90 (1995). BB 9-43 (13-93 match) De v Northants (Derby) 1995. Took 8-53 before lunch on his 20th birthday for De v Essex (Derby) 1991. 2 hat tricks: 1994 and 1995 (*see Tests*). Awards: CGT 4; BHC 4. LO HS 93 De v Derbys CB v Glam (Chesterfield) 1997 (SL).

48

CROOK, Steven Paul (Rostever C, S Aus), b Modbury, S Australia 28 May 1983. Younger brother of A.R.Crook (S Australia 1998-99), 5'11". RHB, RFM. British passport. S Australia U-17, U-19. Lancashire 2003. HS 27 and BB 1-6 v Warwks (Birmingham) 2003 – on CC debut. LO HS 1 (NL). LO BB 1-27 (NL).

CURRIE, Mark Robert (Poynton County HS; City of Westminster C), b Manchester 22 Sep 1979. 6'1". RHB, OB. Debut 2002. Cheshire 1999-2002. MCCYC. HS 97 v DU (Durham) 2003. CC HS 56 v Surrey (Manchester) 2003. LO HS 94 Cheshire v Lincs (Neston) 2002 (CGT).

FLINTOFF, Andrew (Ribbleton Hall HS), b Preston 6 Dec 1977. 6'4". RHB, RFM. Debut 1995; cap 1998. YC 1998. **ECB contracts 2000, 2002, 2003, 2004. Tests:** 29 (1998 to 2003-04); HS 142 v SA (Lord's) 2003; BB 4-50 v I (Bangalore) 2001-02. LOI: 66 (1998-99 to 2003-04); HS 84 v P (Karachi) 2000-01; BB 4-14 v B (Chittagong) 2003-04. F-c Tours (Eng): A 2002-03 (part); SA 1998-99 (Eng A), 1999-00; NZ 2001-02; I 2001-02; SL 1997-98 (Eng A), 2003-04; Z 1998-99 (Eng A); K 1997-98 (Eng A). HS 160 v Yorks (Manchester) 1999. BB 5-24 v Hants (Southampton) 1999. Awards: CGT 3; BHC 1. LO HS 143 (off 66 balls) v Essex (Chelmsford) 1999 (NL). LO BB 4-11 v Yorks (Leeds) 2002 (BHC).

HAYNES, Jamie Jonathan (St Edmunds C, Canberra; Canberra U), b Bristol 5 Jul 1974. 5'11". RHB, WK. Debut 1996. Represented Australian Capital Territory at cricket and Australian Rules football. HS 80 v SL A (Manchester) 1999. CC HS 57 v Surrey (Oval) 2001. LO HS 59* v Warwks CB (Blackpool) 2001 (CGT).

HEGG, Warren Kevin (Unsworth HS, Bury; Stand C, Whitefield), b Whitefield 23 Feb 1968. 5'8". RHB, WK. Debut 1986; cap 1989; benefit 1999; captain 2002 to date. **Tests:** 2 (1998-99); HS 15 v A (Sydney) 1998-99. F-c Tours: A 1996-97 (Eng A), 1998-99; WI 1986-87 (La), 1995-96 (La); NZ 2001-02; SL 1990-91 (Eng A); Z 1988-89 (La). HS 134 v Leics (Manchester) 1996. BB – Held 11 catches (equalling world f-c match record) v Derbys (Chesterfield) 1989. Award: BHC 1. LO HS 81 v Yorks (Manchester) 1996 (BHC).

HOGG, Kyle William (Saddleworth HS), b Birmingham 2 Jul 1983. Son of W.Hogg (Lancashire and Warwickshire 1976-83; grandson of S.Ramadhin (Trinidad, Lancashire and West Indies 1949-50 to 1965). 6'4". LHB, RFM. Debut 2001. F-c Tour (ECB Acad): SL 2002-03. HS 53 v Notts (Nottingham) 2003. BB 5-48 v Leics (Manchester) 2002. LO HS 24 v Glos (Manchester) 2002 (NL). LO BB 4-20 v Hants (Southampton) 2002 (NL).

HOOPER, Carl Llewellyn (Christchurch SS, Georgetown), b Georgetown, Guyana 15 Dec 1966. 6'1". RHB, OB. Demerara 1983-84. Guyana 1984-85 to 2002-03, scoring 130* in his final innings (captain 1996-97 to 2002-03). Kent 1992-94, 1996, 1998; cap 1992. Lancashire debut/cap 2003. **Tests** (WI): 102 (1987-88 to 2002-03, 23 as captain); HS 233 v I (Georgetown) 2001-02; BB 5-26 v SL (Kingstown) 1996-97. **LOI** (WI): 227 (1986-87 to 2002-03, 49 as captain); HS 113* v I (Gwalior) 1987-88; BB 4-34 v P (Karachi) 1991-92. F-c Tours (WI) (C=captain): E 1988, 1991, 1995; A 1988-89, 1991-92, 1992-93, 1995-96, 1996-97; SA 1998-99; NZ 1986-87; I 1987-88, 1994-95, 2002-03C; P 1990-91, 1997-98, 2001-02C (Sharjah); SL 1993-94, 2001-02C; Z 1986-87 (Young WI), 1989-90 (Young WI, 2001C). 1000 runs (8+2); most – 1579 (1994). HS 236* K v Glam (Canterbury) 1993. La HS 201 v Middx (Manchester) 2003 – scored 201, 114 and 177 in successive f-c innings. BB 7-93 K v Surrey (Oval) 1998. La BB 6-51 v Essex (Chelmsford) 2003. Awards: NWT 1; BHC 1. LO HS 145 v Leics (Leicester) 1996 (SL). LO BB 5-41 v Essex (Maidstone) 1993 (SL).

HORTON, Paul James (St Margaret's HS), b Sydney, Australia 20 Sep 1982. RHB, RM. Debut 2003. Staff.2004 – awaiting CC debut. HS 2* v DU (Durham) 2003. LO HS 26 Lancs CB v Oxon (Banbury) 2002 (CGT).

KEEDY, Gary (Garforth CS), b Wakefield, Yorks 27 Nov 1974. 6'0". LHB, SLA. Yorkshire 1994 (one match). Lancashire debut 1995; cap 2000. F-c Tour: WI 1995-96 (La). HS 57 v Yorks (Leeds) 2002. 50 wkts (1): 60 (2003). BB 6-56 (10-155 match) v Durham (Manchester) 2000. LO HS 10* v Essex (Manchester) 2000. LO BB 5-30 v Sussex (Manchester) 2000 (NL).

NQLAW, Stuart Grant (Craigslea State HS), b Herston, Brisbane, Australia 18 Oct 1968. 6'1". RHB, RM/LB. Queensland 1988-89 to 2003-04; captain 1994-95 to 1996-97, 1999-00 to 2001-02. Essex 1996-2001; cap 1996. Lancashire debut/cap 2002. *Wisden* 1997. **Tests** (A): 1 (1995-96); HS 54* v SL (Perth) 1995-96. **LOI** (A): 54 (1994-95 to 1998-99); HS 110 v Z (Hobart) 1994-95; BB 2-22 v P (Sydney) 1996-97. F-c Tours: E 1995 (Young A); Z 1991-92 (Aus B). 1000 runs (7+1); most – 1833 (1999). HS 263 Ex v Somerset (Chelmsford) 1999. La HS 236* v Warwks (Manchester) 2003. BB 3-29 Q v Tasmania (Brisbane) 1995-96. CC BB 3-27 Ex v Worcs (Chelmsford) 1997. La BB 1-24. Awards: CGT 5; BHC 1. LO HS 163 Young A v Surrey (Oval) 1995. LO BB 5-26 Q v SL (Cairns) 1995-96.

LOYE, Malachy Bernhard (Moulton S), b Northampton 27 Sep 1972. 6'2". RHB, OB. Northamptonshire 1991-2002; cap 1994. Lancashire debut 2003 – scoring 126 v Surrey (Oval) and 113 v Notts (Manchester) in his first two innings; cap 2003. F-c Tours (Eng A): SA 1993-94, 1998-99; Z 1994-95 (Nh), 1998-99. 1000 runs (4); most – 1198 (1998). HS 322* Nh v Glam (Northampton) 1998 – record Northants score until 2002. La HS 144 v Sussex (Manchester) 2003 – scored 137, 102 and 144 in successive f-c innings. BB 1-8. Awards: CGT 2; BHC 1. LO HS 124* Nh v Northants (Northampton) 2001 (CGT).

MAHMOOD, Sajid Iqbal (North C, Bolton), b Bolton 21 Dec 1981. RHB, RF. Debut 2002. F-c Tour (Eng A): I 2003-04. HS 34 and CC BB 2-40 v Kent (Canterbury) 2003. BB 5-37 v DU (Durham) 2003. LO HS 11 Lancs CB v Cheshire (Chester) 2001 (CGT). LO BB 3-28 v Ind A (Blackpool) 2003.

MARTIN, Peter James (Danum S, Doncaster), b Accrington 15 Nov 1968. 6'4". RHB, RFM. Debut 1989; cap 1994; benefit 2002. **Tests**: 8 (1995 to 1997); HS 29 v WI (Lord's) 1995; BB 4-60 v SA (Durban) 1995-96. **LOI**: 20 (1995 to 1998-99); HS 6; BB 4-44 v WI (Oval) 1995 – on debut. F-c Tour: SA 1995-96. HS 133 v Durham (Gateshead) 1992. 50 wkts (4); most – 58 (1997). BB 8-32 (13-79 match) v Middx (Uxbridge) 1997. Awards: CGT 2. LO HS 35* v Worcs (Manchester) 1996 (SL). LO BB 5-16 v Warwks CB (Blackpool) 2001 (CGT).

NEWBY, Oliver James (Ribblesdale HS), b Blackburn 26 Aug 1984. RHB, RFM. Debut 2003. Staff 2004 – awaiting CC debut. HS – and BB 1-41 v DU (Durham) 2003. LO HS 3* Lancs CB v Ind A (Blackpool) 2003.

REES, Timothy Martyn (Canon Slade S and SFC, Bolton), b Loughborough, Leics 4 Sep 1984. 6'1". RHB, OB. Debut 2002. No appearances 2003. HS 16 v Somerset (Taunton) 2002 – on debut. LO HS 7* (NL).

SCHOFIELD, Christopher Paul (Wardle HS), b Birch Hill, Rochdale 6 Oct 1978. 6'2". LHB, LB. Debut 1998; cap 2002. **ECB contract 2000.** **Tests**: 2 (2000); HS 57 v Z (Nottingham) 2000. F-c Tours (Eng A): WI 2000-01; NZ 1999-00; B 1999-00. HS 91 v Warwks (Manchester) 2002. BB 6-120 Eng A v Bangladesh (Chittagong) 1999-00. CC BB 5-48 v CU (Cambridge) 2000. CC BB 5-66 v Durham (Manchester) 1999. LO HS 69* v Ind A (Blackpool) 2003. LO BB 5-31 v Derbys (Manchester) 2001 (NL).

SUTCLIFFE, Iain John (Leeds GS; Queen's C, Oxford), b Leeds, Yorks 20 Dec 1974. 6'2". LHB, occ OB. Oxford U 1994-96; blue 1995-96; boxing blue 1993-94. Leicestershire 1995-2002; cap 1997. Lancashire debut/cap 2003. F-c tour (Le): SA 1996-97. 1000 (2); most – 1088 (2002). HS 203 Le v Glam (Cardiff) 2001. La HS 109 v Essex (Manchester) 2003. BB 2-21 OU v CU (Lord's) 1996. CC BB (Le) 1-7. La BB 1-11. Awards: CGT 1; BHC 1. LO HS 105* Le v Notts (Nottingham) 1998 (BHC).

SWANN, Alec James (Risade S; Sponne S, Towcester), b Northampton 26 Oct 1976. Son of R.Swann (Northumberland 1969-72; Bedfordshire 1988-95); elder brother of G.P.Swann (*see NORTHAMPTONSHIRE*). 6'1". RHB, RM/OB. Northamptonshire 1996-2001. Lancashire debut/cap 2002. Bedfordshire 1994. 1000 (1): 1073 (2002). HS 154 Nh v Notts (Northampton) 1999. La HS 137 v DU (Durham) 2003. BB 2-30 Nh v Glos (Northampton) 2000. La BB – LO HS 83* Nh v Glos (Bristol) 2001 (BHC). BB –

PLAYING STAFF continued on p 56

LANCASHIRE 2003

RESULTS SUMMARY

	Place	Won	Lost	Tied	Drew	No Result
County Championship (1st Division)	**2nd**	6	2		8	
All First-Class Matches		6	2		9	
C & G Trophy	Semi-Finalist					
National League (2nd Division)	**1st**	14	3			1
Twenty20 Cup	**4th in North Group**					

COUNTY CHAMPIONSHIP AVERAGES

BATTING AND FIELDING

Cap		M	I	NO	HS	Runs	Avge	100	50	Ct/St
1998	A.Flintoff	5	6	1	154	519	103.80	2	2	7
2002	S.G.Law	16	24	4	236*	1820	91.00	7	6	17
2003	C.L.Hooper	13	19	2	201	1118	65.76	5	3	14
2003	M.B.Loye	15	22	1	144	1062	50.57	5	2	4
2002	M.J.Chilton	16	24	2	125	1065	48.40	6	2	12
2003	I.J.Sutcliffe	12	17	2	109	681	45.40	1	4	13
1994	G.Chapple	16	21	3	132*	679	37.72	2	3	8
–	K.W.Hogg	5	5	–	53	158	31.60	–	1	1
1989	W.K.Hegg	16	20	7	61*	404	31.07	–	1	46/3
2002	C.P.Schofield	8	11	2	66	263	29.22	–	2	8
2002	A.J.Swann	9	14	–	57	218	15.57	–	1	13
–	S.I.Mahmood	4	4	–	34	57	14.25	–	–	–
2003	J.Wood	9	8	2	30	67	11.16	–	–	2
1994	P.J.Martin	14	12	–	23	120	10.00	–	–	8
2000	G.Keedy	12	10	6	6	16	4.00	–	–	4

Also batted: J.M.Anderson (4 matches) 3*, 0*, 9* (3 ct); S.P.Crook (1) 27 (1 ct); M.R.Currie (1) 56, 13 (1 ct); J.J.Haynes (1) 12, 0 (2 ct).

BOWLING

	O	M	R	W	Avge	Best	5wI	10wM
G.Keedy	531.5	125	1532	60	25.53	6-68	5	1
J.M.Anderson	107	19	411	15	27.40	5-61	1	–
C.L.Hooper	348.2	83	870	30	29.00	6-51	2	–
P.J.Martin	432.1	99	1295	41	31.58	5-54	1	–
J.Wood	222.4	32	854	27	31.62	3-17	–	–
G.Chapple	494.2	90	1744	49	35.59	6-98	2	–
C.P.Schofield	151.1	26	562	11	51.09	3-14	–	–

Also bowled:

A.Flintoff	50	13	135	5	27.00	2-47	–	–
K.W.Hogg	97	22	370	7	52.85	2-66	–	–
S.I.Mahmood	71	9	331	6	55.16	2-40	–	–

M.J.Chilton 39-8-94-0; S.P.Crook 13.1-1-58-2; S.G.Law 7-0-29-0; M.B.Loye 4-0-16-1; I.J.Sutcliffe 4-1-11-1; A.J.Swann 4-0-18-0.

The First-Class Averages (pp 123–138) give the records of Lancashire players in all first-class county matches (Lancashire's other opponents being Durham UCCE), with the exception of J.M.Anderson and A.Flintoff whose full county figures are as above.

LANCASHIRE RECORDS

FIRST-CLASS CRICKET

Highest Total	For 863		v	Surrey	The Oval	1990
	V 707-9d		by	Surrey	The Oval	1990
Lowest Total	For 25		v	Derbyshire	Manchester	1871
	V 22		by	Glamorgan	Liverpool	1924
Highest Innings	For 424	A.C.MacLaren	v	Somerset	Taunton	1895
	V 315*	T.W.Hayward	for	Surrey	The Oval	1898

Highest Partnership for each Wicket

1st	368	A.C.MacLaren/R.H.Spooner	v	Glos	Liverpool	1903
2nd	371	F.B.Watson/G.E.Tyldesley	v	Surrey	Manchester	1928
3rd	364	M.A.Atherton/N.H.Fairbrother	v	Surrey	The Oval	1990
4th	358	S.P.Titchard/G.D.Lloyd	v	Essex	Chelmsford	1996
5th	360	S.G.Law/C.L.Hooper	v	Warwicks	Birmingham	2003
6th	278	J.Iddon/H.R.W.Butterworth	v	Sussex	Manchester	1932
7th	248	G.D.Lloyd/I.D.Austin	v	Yorkshire	Leeds	1997
8th	158	J.Lyon/R.M.Ratcliffe	v	Warwicks	Manchester	1979
9th	142	L.O.S.Poidevin/A.Kermode	v	Sussex	Eastbourne	1907
10th	173	J.Briggs/R.Pilling	v	Surrey	Liverpool	1885

Best Bowling	For	10-46	W.Hickton	v	Hampshire	Manchester	1870
(Innings)	V	10-40	G.O.B.Allen	for	Middlesex	Lord's	1929
Best Bowling	For	17-91	H.Dean	v	Yorkshire	Liverpool	1913
(Match)	V	16-65	G.Giffen	for	Australians	Manchester	1886

Most Runs – Season	2633	J.T.Tyldesley	(av 56.02)	1901
Most Runs – Career	34222	G.E.Tyldesley	(av 45.20)	1909-36
Most 100s – Season	11	C.Hallows		1928
Most 100s – Career	90	G.E.Tyldesley		1909-36
Most Wkts – Season	198	E.A.McDonald	(av 18.55)	1925
Most Wkts – Career	1816	J.B.Statham	(av 15.12)	1950-68
Most Career W-K Dismissals	922†	G.Duckworth	(634 ct/288 st)	1923-38
Most Career Catches in the Field	556	K.J.Grieves		1949-64

† *W.K.Hegg (1987-2003) has the second-highest aggregate with 846 dismissals (762 ct; 84 st)*

LIST 'A' LIMITED-OVERS CRICKET

Highest Total	CGT	381-3		v	Herts	Radlett	1999
	BHC	353-7		v	Notts	Manchester	1995
	NL	310-7		v	Somerset	Taunton	2003
Lowest Total	CGT	59		v	Worcs	Worcester	1963
	BHC	82		v	Yorkshire	Bradford	1972
	NL	68		v	Yorkshire	Leeds	2000
		68		v	Surrey	The Oval	2002
Highest Innings	CGT	135*	A.Flintoff	v	Surrey	The Oval	2000
	BHC	136	G.Fowler	v	Sussex	Manchester	1991
	NL	143	A.Flintoff	v	Essex	Chelmsford	1999
Best Bowling	CGT	6-18	G.Chapple	v	Essex	Lord's	1996
	BHC	6-10	C.E.H.Croft	v	Scotland	Manchester	1982
	NL	6-25	G.Chapple	v	Yorkshire	Leeds	1998

52

LEICESTERSHIRE

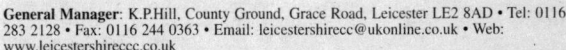

Formation of Present Club: 25 March 1879
Inaugural First-Class Match: 1894
Colours: Dark Green and Scarlet
Badge: Gold Running Fox on Green Ground
County Champions: (3) 1975, 1996, 1998
Gillette/NatWest/C & G Trophy Winners: (0); best – finalist 1992, 2001
Benson and Hedges Cup Winners: (3) 1972, 1975, 1985
National League (Div 1) Winners: (0); best – 2nd 2001
Sunday League Champions: (2) 1974, 1977
Twenty20 Cup Winners: semi-finalist 2003
Match Awards: CGT 49; BHC 79

General Manager: K.P.Hill, County Ground, Grace Road, Leicester LE2 8AD • Tel: 0116 283 2128 • Fax: 0116 244 0363 • Email: leicestershirecc@ukonline.co.uk • Web: www.leicestershireccc.co.uk

Director of Cricket: J.Whittaker. **Head Coach/Academy Director**: P.Whitticase. **Captain**: P.A.J.DeFreitas. **Vice-Captain**: *tba*. **Overseas Players**: B.J.Hodge and G.J-P.Kruger. **2004 Beneficiary**: P.A.J.DeFreitas. **Groundsmen**: A. Ward and A.Whiteman. **Scorer**: G.A.York. ‡ New registration. ᴺᵠ Not qualified for England.

BRANDY, Damien Gareth (St John's, Epping; Harlow C), b Highgate, London 14 Sep 1981. 6'1". RHB, RMF. Debut 2002. HS 52 v Kent (Canterbury) 2003. BB 2-11 v LU (Leicester) 2003. CC BB 2-86 v Surrey (Oval) 2002. LO HS 35 v Somerset (Leicester) 2002 (NL).

BRIGNULL, David Stephen (Lancaster BSS; Wyggeston & Queen Elizabeth I SFC), b Forest Gate, London 27 Nov 1981. 6'4". RHB, RMF. Debut 2003. HS 46 v Middx (Leicester) 2003. BB 2-30 v Kent (Canterbury) 2003 – on debut. LO HS (Leics CB) 9* (NWT). BB 3-40 v Worcs (Oakham) 2003 (NL).

DAGNALL, Charles Edward (Bridgewater HS, Worsley; UMIST), b Bury, Lancs 10 Jul 1976. 6'3". RHB, RMF. Warwickshire 1999-2001. Leicestershire debut 2002. HS 23* v Surrey (Oval) 2003. BB 6-50 Wa v Derbys (Derby) 2001. Le BB 5-66 v Essex (Leicester) 2003. Award: BHC 1. LO HS 28 v Worcs (Worcester) 2002 (NL). LO BB 4-34 Wa v Derbys (Birmingham) 2000 (NL).

DAKIN, Jonathan Michael (King Edward VII S, Johannesburg) b Hitchin, Herts 28 Feb 1973. 6'4". LHB, RM. Leicestershire 1993-2001; cap 2000. Essex 2002-03; cap 2003. F-c Tour (Le): SA 1996-97. HS 190 v Northants (Northampton) 1997. BB 5-86 Ex v Middx (Lord's) 2003. Awards: CGT 1; BHC 1. LO HS 179 v Wales MC (Swansea) 2001 (CGT). LO BB 5-30 v Kent (Leicester) 1999 (NL).

DeFREITAS, Phillip Anthony Jason (Willesden HS, London), b Scotts Head, Dominica 18 Feb 1966. 6'0". RHB, RFM. UK resident since 1976. Leicestershire 1985-88; cap 1986; captain 2003 to date; benefit 2004. Lancashire 1989-93; cap 1989. Boland 1993-94 and 1995-96. Derbyshire 1994-99; cap 1994; captain 1997 (*part*). Wisden 1991. MCC YC. **Tests**: 44 (1986-87 to 1995-96); HS 88 v A (Adelaide) 1994-95; BB 7-70 v SL (Lord's) 1991. **LOI**: 103 (1986-87 to 1997); HS 67 v SL (Faisalabad) 1995-96; BB 4-35 v A (Adelaide) 1986-87. F-c Tours: A 1986-87, 1990-91, 1994-95; WI 1989-90; NZ 1987-88, 1991-92; P 1987-88; I 1992-93; Z 1988-89 (La). HS 123* v Lancs (Leicester) 2000. 50 wkts (14); most – 94 (1986). Took his 1000th f-c wicket 1999. BB 7-21 La v Middx (Lord's) 1989. Le BB 7-44 (13-86 match) v Essex (Southend) 1986. Hat trick 1990. Awards: CGT 6; BHC 4. LO HS 90 v Glos (Bristol) 2003 (NL). LO BB 5-13 La v Cumb (Kendal) 1989 (NWT).

‡FERRABY, Nicholas John (Oakham S), b Market Harborough 31 May 1983. RHB, RM. Staff 2004 – awaiting first-class debut. LO HS 1 (Leics CB) (CGT).

NQHODGE, Bradley John (St Bede's C, Mentone; Deakin U), b Sandringham, Victoria, Australia 29 Dec 1974. 5'8". RHB, OB. Victoria 1993-94 to date. Australia A debut 1999-2000. Durham 2002. Leicestershire debut/cap 2003. F-c Tours (A Academy): Z 1998-99. 1000 (1+1); most 1495 (2003). HS 302* (*less record*) v Notts (Nottingham) 2003. BB 4-17 Aus A v WI (Hobart) 2000-01. Le BB 3-35 v LU (Leicester) 2003. CC BB 1-12. LO HS 164 Aus A v SA A (Perth) 2002-03. LO BB 5-28 Aus A v SA A (Canberra) 2002-03.

NQKRUGER, Garnett John-Peter (Gelvan HS; Russel Road C), b Port Elizabeth, South Africa 5 Jan 1977. RHB, RMF. E Province 1997-98 to 2002-03. Gauteng 2003-04. F-c Tour (SA A): WI 2000-01. HS 58 SA A v Windward Is (Kingstown) 2000-01. BB 7-64 EP v Border (East London) 1999-00. LO HS 20* EP v WP (Cape Town) 2002-03. LO BB 6-23 EP v North West (Port Elizabeth) 1999-00.

‡**LIDDLE, Christopher**, b Middlesbrough, Yorks 1 Feb 1984. RHB, SLA. Staff 2004 – awaiting first-class debut.

MADDY, Darren Lee (Wreake Valley C), b Leicester 23 May 1974. 5'9". RHB, RM/OB. Debut 1994; cap 1996. **Tests**: 3 (1999 to 1999-00); HS 24 v SA (Durban) 1999-00. **LOI**: 8 (1998 to 1999-00); HS 53 v Z (Harare) 1999-00. F-c Tours (Eng A): to 1996-97 (Le), 1998-99, 1999-00 (Eng); SL 1997-98; Z 1998-99; K 1997-98. 1000 runs (4); most – 1187 (2002). HS 229* v LU (Leicester) 2003. CC HS 162 v Durham (Darlington) 1998. BB 5-37 v Hants (Southampton) 2002. Awards: CGT 1; BHC 8 (*inc 5 in 1998*). LO HS 151 v Minor C (Leicester) 1998 (BHC). LO BB 4-16 v Somerset (Taunton) 2000 (NL).

MASTERS, David Daniel (Fort Luton HS; Mid Kent CHE), b Chatham, Kent 22 Apr 1978. Son of K.D.Masters (Kent 1981-85, Surrey 1986). 6'4". RHB, RMF. Kent 2000-02. Leicestershire debut 2003. HS 119 v Sussex (Hove) 2003. BB 6-27 K v Durham (Tunbridge Wells) 2000. Le BB 5-53 v Warwks (Leicester) 2003. LO HS 27 v Kent (Canterbury) 2003 (NL). LO BB 5-20 K v Durham (Maidstone) 2002 (NL).

MAUNDERS, John Kenneth (Ashford HS; Spelthorne C), b Ashford, Middx 4 Apr 1981. 5'10". LHB, RM. Middlesex 1999 (*one non-CC match*); 2nd XI debut aged 16y 19d. Leicestershire debut 2003. HS 171 v Surrey (Leicester) 2003. BB – LO HS 49 M v Glam (Cardiff) 2001 (NL).

NEW, Thomas James (Quarrydale S), b Sutton in Ashfield, Notts 18 Jan 1985. 5'10". LHB, WK. Leicestershire summer contract since 2001 – awaiting f-c debut. LO HS (Leics CB) 6 (CGT).

NIXON, Paul Andrew (Ullswater HS, Penrith), b Carlisle, Cumberland 21 Oct 1970. 6'0". LHB, WK. Leicestershire 1989-99, 2003; cap 1994. Kent 2000-02; cap 2000. Cumberland 1987. MCC YC. F-c Tours: SA 1996-97 (Le); I 1994-95 (Eng A); P 2000-01; SL 2000-01 (*no f-c*). 1000 runs (1): 1046 (1994). HS 134* K v Hants (Canterbury) 2000. Le HS 131 v Hants (Southampton) 1994. BB – Awards: CGT 1; BHC 3. LO HS 101 v SL A (Galle) 1998-99. LO BB –

‡**ROBINSON, Darren** David John (Tabor HS, Braintree; Chelmsford CFE), b Braintree, Essex 2 Mar 1973. 5'10½". RHB, RMF. Essex 1993-2003; cap 1997. 1000 (1): 1474 (2002). HS 200 Ex v NZ (Chelmsford) 1999. CC HS 175 Ex v Glos (Gloucester) 2002. BB 1-7 (Ex). Awards: BHC 2. LO HS 137* Ex v Sussex (Hove) 1998 (BHC). LO BB 1-7 (Ex – SL).

SADLER, John Leonard (St Thomas A'Beckett S, Sandal), b Dewsbury, Yorks 19 Nov 1981. 5'11". LHB, LB. Yorkshire 2nd XI 2000-02. Leicestershire debut 2003. HS 145 v Surrey (Leicester) 2003 and 145 v Sussex (Hove) 2003. BB – LO HS 35 v Surrey (Oval) 2003 (NL).

SNAPE, Jeremy Nicholas (Denstone C; Durham U), b Stoke-on-Trent, Staffs 27 Apr 1973. 5'8½". RHB, OB. Northamptonshire 1992-97. Combined U 1994. Gloucestershire 1999-2002; cap 1999. Leicestershire debut 2003. **LOI**: 10 (2001-02 to 2002-03); HS 38 v I (Madras) 2001-02; BB 3-43 v Z (Bulawayo) 2001-02. F-c Tour: Z 1994-95 (Nh). HS 131 Gs v Sussex (Cheltenham) 2001. Le HS 54 v Middx (Leicester) 2003. BB 5-65 Nh v Durham (Northampton) 1995. Le BB 3-108 v Surrey (Leicester) 2003. Awards: BHC 3. LO HS 104* Gs v Notts (Nottingham) 2001 (NL). LO BB 5-32 Nh v Leics (Northampton) 1997 (BHC).

STEVENS, Darren Ian (Hinckley C), b Leicester 30 Apr 1976. 5'11". RHB, RM. Debut 1997; cap 2002. F-c Tours (ECB Acad): SL 2002-03. HS 149 v Essex (Southend) 2003. BB 1-5 (*twice*). Award: CGT 1. LO HS 133 v Northumb (Jesmond) 2000 (NWT). LO BB 2-15 v ECB Acad v SL A (Colombo) 2002-03.

WALKER, George William (Norwich S), b Norwich, Norfolk 12 May 1984. 5'10". LHB, SLA. Debut 2002. Norfolk 2000-01. HS 37* v Kent (Canterbury) 2002 – on debut. BB 1-92.

RELEASED/RETIRED

(Registered players who made a first-class County appearance in 2003)

AMIN, Rupesh Mahesh (Riddlesdown HS; John Ruskin C; Croydon C), b Clapham, S London 20 Aug 1977. 6'0". RHB, SLA. Surrey 1997-2002. Leicestershire 2003. HS 12 Sy v Leics (Oval) 1998. BB 4-87 Sy v Somerset (Oval) 1999. LO HS (Sy) 0* (NL). LO BB 2-43 Sy v Lancs (Oval) 1997 (SL).

CUNLIFFE, Robert John (Banbury S; Banbury TC), b Oxford 8 Nov 1973. 5'10". RHB, RM. Gloucestershire 1994-2001. Oxfordshire 1991. Leicestershire 2002-03. HS 190* v OU (Bristol) 1995. CC HS 108 v Northants (Northampton) 1999. Le HS 30 v Surrey (Oval) 2002. BB – Awards: BHC 3. LO HS 137* Gs v Surrey (Oval) 1996 (BHC).

DRAKES, Vasbert Conneil (St Lucy SS), b St James, Barbados 5 Aug 1969. 6'2". RHB, RFM. Barbados 1991-92 to 1997-98, 2002-03. Sussex 1996-97; cap 1996. Border 1996-97 to date. Nottinghamshire 1999; cap 1999. Warwickshire 2001; cap 2001. Leicestershire 2003. **Tests** (WI): 12 (2002-03 to 2003-04); HS 67 v SA (Durban) 2003-04; BB 5-93 v A (Georgetown) 2002-03. **LOI** (WI): 34 (1994-95 to 2003-04); HS 25 v SL (Cape Town) 2002-03; BB 5-33 v K (Kimberley) 2002-03. F-c Tour (WI): E 1995; SA 2003-04; Z 2003-04; B 2002-03. HS 180* Barbados v Leeward Is (Anguilla) 1994-95. UK HS 145* Sx v Essex (Chelmsford) 1996. Le HS 18 v Kent (Leicester) 2003. 50 wkts (2+2); most – 80 (1999). BB 8-59 Border v Natal (Durban) 1996-97. UK BB 6-39 (12-110 match) Nt v Warwks (Nottingham) 1999. Le BB 3-58 v Notts (Nottingham) 2003. LO HS 104 Border v Boland (Paarl) 1996-97 (SBC). LO BB 5-19 v Ire (Hove) 1996 (BHC). Took 4 wkts in 4 balls v Derbys (Nottingham) 1999 (NL).

GROVE, Jamie Oliver (Bury St Edmunds County Upper S), b Bury St Edmunds, Suffolk 3 Jul 1979. 6'1". RHB, RMF. Essex 1998-99. Somerset 2000-01. Leicestershire 2002-03. HS 33 Ex v Surrey (Chelmsford) 1998. Le HS 6. BB 5-90 Sm v Leics (Leicester) 2000 – on Somerset debut. Le BB 1-21 (not CC). LO HS 13 v Kent (Leicester) 2002 (NL). LO BB 4-36 Sm v Cambs (March) 2001 (CGT).

MALCOLM, Devon Eugene (St Elizabeth THS; Richmond C, Sheffield; Derby CHE), b Kingston, Jamaica 22 Feb 1963. Qualified for England 1987. 6'2". RHB, RF. Derbyshire 1984-97; cap 1989; benefit 1997. Northamptonshire 1998-2000; cap 1999. Leicestershire 2001-03; cap 2001. *Wisden* 1994. **Tests**: 40 (1989 to 1997); HS 29 v A (Sydney) 1994-95; BB 9-57 (10-138 match) v SA (Oval) 1994. **LOI**: 10 (1990 to 1993-94); HS 4; BB 3-40 v I (Gwalior) 1992-93. F-c Tours: A 1990-91, 1994-95; SA 1995-96; WI 1989-90, 1991-92 (Eng A), 1993-94; I 1992-93; SL 1992-93. HS 51 De v Surrey (Derby) 1989. Le HS 50 v Somerset (Taunton) 2001. 50 wkts (9); most – 82 (1996). BB 9-57 (*see Tests*). CC BB 8-63 v Surrey (Leicester) 2001. Awards: CGT 1; BHC 3. LO HS 42 De v Surrey (Oval) 1996 (SL). LO BB 7-35 De v Northants (Derby) 1997 (NWT).

[NO]**SEHWAG, Virender**, b Delhi, India 20 Oct 1978. RHB, OB. Delhi 1997-98 to date. Leicestershire 2003; cap 2003. **Tests** (I): 20 (2001-02 to 2003-04); HS 195 v A (Melbourne) 2003-04; BB 1-17. **LOI** (I): 85 (1998-99 to 2003-04); HS 130 v NZ (Hyderabad) 2003-04; BB 3-25 v SA (Colombo) 2002-03. F-c Tours (I): E 2002; A 2003-04; SA 2001-02; NZ 2002-03. 1000 (0+1): 1008 (1999-00). HS 274 N Zone v S Zone (Agartala) 1999-2000. UK HS 142 and UK BB 2-52 Indians v Essex (Chelmsford) 2002. Le HS 137 v Notts (Leicester) 2003. Le BB – BB 4-32 N Zone v S Zone (Bombay) 1998-99. LO HS 130 (*see LOI*). LO BB 4-17 Delhi v Services (Delhi) 1998-99.

55

WARD, Trevor Robert (Hextable CS, nr Swanley), b Farningham, Kent 18 Jan 1968. 5'11". RHB, OB. Kent 1986-99; cap 1989; benefit 1999. Leicestershire 2000-03; cap 2001. F-c Tour: Z 1992-93 (K). 1000 runs (6); most – 1648 (1992). HS 235* K v Middx (Canterbury) 1991. Le HS 168 v Essex (Southend) 2003. BB 2-10 K v Yorks (Canterbury) 1996. Le BB 1-32. Awards: CGT 1; BHC 2. LO HS 131 K v Notts (Nottingham) 1993 (SL). LO BB 3-20 K v Glam (Canterbury) 1989 (SL).

WHILEY, Matthew Jeffrey Allen (Harry Carlton CS, East Leake), b Clifton, Nottingham 6 May 1980. 6'5½". RHB, LMF. Nottinghamshire 1998-2000. Leicestershire 2001-03. HS 16 v Warwks (Birmingham) 2003. BB 3-60 v Kent (Leicester) 2002. LO HS 14* v Somerset (Bath) 2002 (NL). LO BB 2-20 v Notts (Leicester) 2002 (BHC).

WRIGHT, L.J. – *see* SUSSEX.

GLOUCESTERSHIRE RELEASED/RETIRED (continued from p 34)

[NO]**RHODES, Jonathan Neil** (*'Jonty'*) (Maritzburg C; Natal U), b Pietermaritzburg, South Africa 27 Jul 1969. Elder brother of C.B.Rhodes (E Province B and Natal B 1990-91 to 1993-94). 5'8". RHB, RM, outstanding fielder. Natal/KwaZulu-Natal 1988-89 to 2002-03 scoring 108 v WP (Durban) on debut. Gloucestershire 2003. *Wisden* 1998. **Tests** (SA): 52 (1992-93 to 2000-01); HS 117 v E (Lord's) 1998. **LOI** (SA): 245 (1991-92 to 2002-03); HS 121 v P (Nairobi) 1996-97; 105 ct – including 5 v WI (Bombay) 1993-94 *(world record)*. F-c Tours (I): E 1994, 1998; A 1993-94, 1997-98, 2001-02; WI 1991-92, 2000-01; NZ 1994-95, 1998-99; I 1993-94, 1996-97; P 1994-95, 1997-98; SL 1993-94, 2000; Z 1995-96, 1999-00, 2001-02. 1000 (1): 1293 (2003). HS 172 KZ-Natal v GW (Kimberley) 2001-02. Gs HS 151* v Hants (Southampton) 2003. BB 1-13. LO HS 121 (*see LOI*). LO BB 1-2.

KENT RELEASED/RETIRED (continued from p 45)

[NO]**MURALITHARAN, Muthiah** (St Anthony's C, Kandy), b Kandy, Sri Lanka 17 Apr 1972. 5'5". RHB, OB. Central Province 1989-90 to date. Tamil Union 1991-92 to date. Lancashire 1999 (taking 7-44 and 7-73 v Warwks at Southport on debut); 2001; cap 1999. Kent 2003. *Wisden* 1998. **Tests** (SL): 85 (1992-93 to 2003-04); HS 67 v I (Kandy) 2001-02; BB 9-51 (13-115 match) v Z (Kandy) 2001-02. **LOI** (SL): 224 (1993-94 to 2003-04); HS 19 v P (Dambulla) 2003; BB 7-30 v I (Sharjah) 2000-01. F-c Tours (SL): E 1991, 1998; A 1995-96; SA 1992-93 (SL U-24), 1994-95, 1997-98, 2000-01, 2002-03; WI 1996-97, 2003; NZ 1994-95, 1996-97; I 1993-94, 1997-98; P 1995-96, 1999-00; Z 1994-95, 1999-00. HS 67 (*see Tests*). 50 wkts (2+4); most – 97 (2001-02). Took 66 wkts in 7 CC matches 1999). BB 9-51 (13-115 match) (*see Tests*). K HS 15 and BB 6-36 v Notts (Nottingham) 2003. Award: BHC 1. LO HS 19 (*see LOI*). LO BB 7-30 (*see LOI*).

TREGO, Peter David (Wyvern CS, W-s-M), b Weston-super-Mare, Somerset 12 Jun 1981. 6'0". RHB, RMF. Somerset 2000-02; 2nd XI debut 1997 when aged 16y 20d. Kent 2003. HS 140 Sm v WI A (Taunton) 2002. CC HS 62 Sm v Yorks (Taunton) 2003. K HS 13 and BB 1-26 v Warwks (Canterbury) 2003. BB 4-84 Sm v Yorks (Scarborough) 2003. K BB 1-26. LO HS 31* and BB 4-39 v Leics (Canterbury) 2003 (NL).

LANCASHIRE PLAYING STAFF (continued from p 50)

WOOD, John (Crofton HS; Wakefield District C; Leeds Poly), b Crofton, Yorks 22 Jul 1970. 6'3". RHB, RFM. GW (LO only) 1990-91. Durham 1992-2000; cap 1998. Lancashire debut 2001; cap 2003. HS 64 v Yorks (Leeds) 2002. 50 wkts (1): 62 (1998). BB 7-58 Du v Yorks (Leeds) 1999. La BB 4-17 v Hants (Southampton) 2002. LO HS 28* Du v Leics (Leicester) 2000 (BHC) and 28* Du v Notts (Nottingham) 2000 (NL). LO BB 5-49 v Glos (Manchester) 2002 (NL).

YATES, Gary (Manchester GS), b Ashton-under-Lyne 20 Sep 1967. 6'0". RHB, OB. Debut 1990; cap 1994. Lancashire 2nd XI captain/coach 2002 to date. No f-c appearances 2003. HS 134* v Northants (Manchester) 1993. BB 6-64 v Kent (Manchester) 1994. LO HS 38 v Essex (Chelmsford) 1996 (SL). LO BB 4-34 v Warwks (Birmingham) 1994 (SL).

RELEASED/RETIRED – None

LEICESTERSHIRE 2003

	Place	Won	Lost	Tied	Drew	No Result
County Championship (1st Division)	**9th**	1	6		9	
All First-Class Matches		2	6		9	
C & G Trophy	Quarter-Finalist					
National League (1st Division)	**7th**	7	9			
Twenty20 Cup	**Semi-Finalist**					

COUNTY CHAMPIONSHIP AVERAGES

BATTING AND FIELDING

Cap		M	I	NO	HS	Runs	Avge	100	50	Ct/St
2003	B.J.Hodge	15	25	1	302*	1293	53.87	4	3	10
2003	V.Sehwag	6	10	–	137	478	47.80	2	1	4
–	J.L.Sadler	6	10	1	145	410	45.55	2	1	5
–	J.K.Maunders	12	22	2	171	777	38.85	2	3	3
1996	D.L.Maddy	16	28	2	98	881	33.88	–	6	14
2002	D.I.Stevens	11	19	–	149	615	32.36	1	6	12
1994	P.A.Nixon	16	27	4	113*	676	29.39	1	3	46/2
2001	T.R.Ward	8	14	–	168	409	29.21	1	1	4
–	J.N.Snape	15	23	6	54	494	29.05	–	2	8
1986	P.A.J.DeFreitas	15	25	2	103	493	21.43	1	2	6
–	D.G.Brandy	5	9	2	52	148	21.14	–	1	1
–	C.E.Dagnall	10	11	5	23*	103	17.16	–	–	–
–	D.S.Brignull	3	4	–	46	58	14.50	–	–	–
–	D.D.Masters	16	23	3	119	269	13.45	1	–	4
–	V.C.Drakes	5	7	1	18	57	9.50	–	–	1
–	M.J.A.Whiley	5	6	2	16	29	7.25	–	–	1
2001	D.E.Malcolm	3	4	–	14	27	6.75	–	–	–
–	R.M.Amin	5	7	2	11	30	6.00	–	–	–

Also batted: R.J.Cunliffe (1 match) 0; G.W.Walker (2) 4*, 21 (1 ct); L.J.Wright (1) 0, 11*.

BOWLING

	O	M	R	W	Avge	Best	5wI	10wM
P.A.J.DeFreitas	528.3	151	1401	58	24.15	7- 51	4	1
D.L.Maddy	297.1	59	1002	36	27.83	5- 49	1	–
C.E.Dagnall	295.5	70	1005	28	35.89	5- 66	1	–
V.C.Drakes	143.1	33	463	11	42.09	3- 58	–	–
D.D.Masters	399.5	78	1476	34	43.41	5- 53	1	–
J.N.Snape	157.3	21	622	10	62.20	3-108	–	–
Also bowled:								
D.S.Brignull	68.4	14	235	7	33.57	2- 30	–	–
D.E.Malcolm	62	15	230	6	38.33	3- 31	–	–
R.M.Amin	146.1	24	601	8	75.12	2- 41	–	–
M.J.A.Whiley	117.3	14	562	7	80.28	2- 76	–	–

D.G.Brandy 7-1-47-0; B.J.Hodge 49-5-239-4; J.K.Maunders 9-1-38-0; J.L.Sadler 0.5-0-20-0; V.Sehwag 34.2-4-153-0; D.I.Stevens 23-5-71-1; G.W.Walker 29-3-111-1; L.J.Wright 19-0-95-0.

The First-Class Averages (pp 123–138) give the records of Leicestershire players in all first-class county matches (their other opponents being Loughborough UCCE).

LEICESTERSHIRE RECORDS

FIRST-CLASS CRICKET

Highest Total	For	701-4d		v	Worcs	Worcester	1906
	V	761-6d		by	Essex	Chelmsford	1990
Lowest Total	For	25		v	Kent	Leicester	1912
	V	24		by	Glamorgan	Leicester	1971
		24		by	Oxford U	Oxford	1985
Highest Innings	For	302*	B.J.Hodge	v	Notts	Nottingham	2003
	V	341	G.H.Hirst	for	Yorkshire	Leicester	1905

Highest Partnership for each Wicket

1st	390	B.Dudleston/J.F.Steele	v	Derbyshire	Leicester	1979
2nd	289*	J.C.Balderstone/D.I.Gower	v	Essex	Leicester	1981
3rd	436*	D.L.Maddy/B.J.Hodge	v	L'boro UCCE	Leicester	2003
4th	290*	P.Willey/T.J.Boon	v	Warwicks	Leicester	1984
5th	322	B.F.Smith/P.V.Simmons	v	Notts	Worksop	1998
6th	284	P.V.Simmons/P.A.Nixon	v	Durham	Chester-le-St	1996
7th	219*	J.D.R.Benson/P.Whitticase	v	Hampshire	Bournemouth	1991
8th	172	P.A.Nixon/D.J.Millns	v	Lancashire	Manchester	1996
9th	160	W.W.Odell/R.T.Crawford	v	Worcs	Leicester	1902
10th	228	R.Illingworth/K.Higgs	v	Northants	Leicester	1977

Best Bowling	For	10- 18	G.Geary	v	Glamorgan	Pontypridd	1929
(Innings)	V	10- 32	H.Pickett	for	Essex	Leyton	1895
Best Bowling	For	16- 96	G.Geary	v	Glamorgan	Pontypridd	1929
(Match)	V	16-102	C.Blythe	for	Kent	Leicester	1909

Most Runs – Season	2446	L.G.Berry	(av 52.04)	1937
Most Runs – Career	30143	L.G.Berry	(av 30.32)	1924-51
Most 100s – Season	7	L.G.Berry		1937
	7	W.Watson		1959
	7	B.F.Davison		1982
Most 100s – Career	45	L.G.Berry		1924-51
Most Wkts – Season	170	J.E.Walsh	(av 18.96)	1948
Most Wkts – Career	2130	W.E.Astill	(av 23.19)	1906-39
Most Career W-K Dismissals	903	R.W.Tolchard	(794 ct/109 st)	1965-83
Most Career Catches in the Field	427	M.R.Hallam		1950-70

LIST 'A' LIMITED-OVERS CRICKET

Highest Total	CGT	406-5		v	Berkshire	Leicester	1996
	BHC	382-6		v	Minor C	Leicester	1998
	NL	344-4		v	Durham	Chester-le-St	1996
Lowest Total	CGT	56		v	Northants	Leicester	1964
	BHC	56		v	Minor C	Wellington	1982
	NL	36		v	Sussex	Leicester	1973
Highest Innings	CGT	201	V.J.Wells	v	Berkshire	Leicester	1996
	BHC	158*	B.F.Davison	v	Warwicks	Coventry	1972
	NL	152	B.Dudleston	v	Lancashire	Manchester	1975
Best Bowling	CGT	6-20	K.Higgs	v	Staffs	Longton	1975
	BHC	6-25	V.J.Wells	v	Minor C	Leicester	1998
	NL	6-17	K.Higgs	v	Glamorgan	Leicester	1973

MIDDLESEX

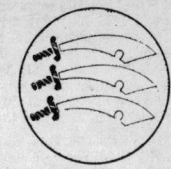

Formation of Present Club: 2 February 1864
Inaugural First-Class Match: 1864
Colours: Blue
Badge: Three Seaxes
County Champions (since 1890): (10) 1903, 1920, 1921,
1947, 1976, 1980, 1982, 1985, 1990, 1993
Joint Champions: (2) 1949, 1977
Gillette/NatWest/C & G Trophy Winners: (4) 1977, 1980,
1984, 1988
Benson and Hedges Cup Winners: (2) 1983, 1986
National League (Div 1) Winners: (0); best – 4th (Div 2)
2000, 2003
Sunday League Winners: (1) 1992
Twenty20 Cup Winners: 4th in South Group 2003
Match Awards: CGT 60; BHC 62

Secretary: V.J.Codrington, Lord's Cricket Ground, London NW8 8QN ● Tel: 020 7289
1300 ● Fax: 020 7289 5831 ● Email: enquiries.middx@ecb.co.uk ● Web:
www.middlesexccc.com

Head Coach: J.E.Emburey. **Assistant Coach**: J.C.Pooley. **Captain**: A.J.Strauss.
Vice-Captain: O.A.Shah. **Overseas Players**: N.Hayward and L.Klusener. **2004**
Beneficiary: None. **Head Groundsman**: M.Hunt. **Scorer**: M.J.Smith. ‡ New registration.
NQ Not qualified for England.

‡**BETTS, Melvyn** Morris (Fyndoune CS, Sacriston), b Sacriston, Co Durham 26 Mar 1975.
5'10". RHB, RFM. Durham 1993-2000; cap 1998. Warwickshire 2001-03; cap 2001. F-c
Tour (Eng A): Z 1998-99. HS 73 Wa v Lancs (Birmingham) 2003. BB 9-64 (Durham record;
13-143 match) v Northants (Northampton) 1997. Award: BHC 1. LO HS 21 Du v Hants
(Chester-le-St) 1997 (SL). LO BB 4-22 Wa v Somerset (Taunton) 2001 (BHC).

BLOOMFIELD, Timothy Francis (Halliford S, Shepperton), b Ashford 31 May 1973. 6'2".
RHB, RMF. Debut 1997; cap 2001. Berkshire 1996. HS 31* v Northants (Northampton)
2002. 50 wkts (1): 50 (2001). BB 5-36 v Glam (Cardiff) 1999. Award: CGT 1. LO HS 15 v
Warwks (Lord's) 1998 (SL) and 15 v Somerset (Taunton) 2003 (NL). LO BB 4-17 v
Somerset (Southgate) 2000 (NWT).

COMPTON, Nicholas Richard Denis (Harrow S), b Durban, South Africa 26 Jun 1983.
6'1". Grandson of D.C.S.Compton (Middlesex, England, Holkar, Europeans, Commonwealth and Cavaliers 1936-64); great-nephew of L.H.Compton (Middlesex 1938-56). RHB,
OB. Middlesex staff 2002 – awaiting f-c debut. LO HS 86* v Lancs (Shenley) 2002 (NL).

COOK, Simon James (Matthew Arnold S), b Oxford 15 Jan 1977. 6'4". RHB, RM. Debut
1999; cap 2003. HS 93* v Notts (Lord's) 2001. BB 8-63 v Northants (Northampton) 2002.
LO HS 67* v Durham (Lord's) 2003 (NL). LO BB 4-30 v Derbys (Lord's) 2003 (NL).

DALRYMPLE, James William Murray (Radley C; St Peter's C, Oxford), b Nairobi, Kenya
21 Jan 1981. 5'11". RHB, OB. Oxford UCCE 2001-02; captain 2002; blue 2001-02. British
U 2001-02. Middlesex debut 2001. HS 236* and BB 5-49 OU v CU (Cambridge) 2003. M
HS 33* v Leics (Southgate) 2003. M BB 2-5 v Notts (Lord's) 2003. LO HS 52 v Derbys
(Derby) 2002 (NL). LO BB 4-14 v Essex (Southgate) 2001 (NL).

‡**DUNCAN, Benjamin** James (St Paul's S, Hammersmith), b Isleworth 21 Nov 1983. RHB.
Staff 2004 – awaiting first-class debut.

‡**NQHAYWARD**, Mornantau ('*Nantie*') (Daniel Pienaar THS), b Uitenhage, South Africa 6 Mar 1977. 6'1". RHB, RF. E Province 1995-96 to date. Worcestershire 2003. **Tests** (SA): 14 (1999-00 to 2002-03); HS 14 v A (Melbourne) 2001-02; BB 5-56 v P (Durban) 2002-03. **LOI** (SA): 21 (1998 to 2001-02); HS 4; BB 4-31 v I (Sharjah) 1999-00. F-c Tours (SA): A 2001-02; I 1999-00; SL 2000-01. HS 55* EP v Boland (Pt Elizabeth) 1997-98. CC HS 28 Wo v Durham (Stockton) 2003. 50 wkts (1): 67 (2003). BB 6-31 EP v Easterns (Pt Elizabeth) 1999-00. CC BB 5-46 Wo v Somerset (Worcester) 2003. LO HS 19* EP v WP (Cape Town) 1996-97. LO BB 5-37 EP v KZ-Natal (Durban) 1998-99.

‡**HUTCHISON, Paul** Michael (Crawshaw HS, Pudsey), b Leeds, Yorks 9 Jun 1977. 6'3". LHB, LFM. Yorkshire 1995-96 (Y in 2im) to 2001; cap 1998. Sussex 2002-03. F-c Tours (Eng A): SL 1997-98; Z 1995-96 (Y); K 1997-98. HS 30 Y v Essex (Scarborough) 1998. 50 wkts (1): 59 (1998). BB 7-31 Y v Sussex (Hove) 1998. Award: CGT 1. LO HS 20 Sx v Northants (Northampton) 2003 (NL). LO BB 4-29 Sx v Scot (Edinburgh) 2003 (NL).

HUTTON, Benjamin Leonard (Radley C; Durham U), b Johannesburg, South Africa 29 Jan 1977. Elder son of R.A.Hutton (Yorkshire, Transvaal & England 1962 to 1975-76); grandson of Sir Leonard (Yorkshire and England 1934-60). 6'2". LHB, RMF. Durham U 1998-99. Middlesex debut 1999; cap 2003. HS 139 v Derbys (Southgate) 2001. BB 4-37 v SL (Shenley) 2002. CC BB 2-9 v Glam (Southgate) 2000. LO HS 77 v Durham (Chester-le-St) 2001 (NL). LO BB 5-45 v Derbys (Southgate) 2001 (NL).

NQJOYCE, Edmund Christopher (Presentation C, Bray, Co Wicklow; Trinity C, Dublin), b Dublin, Ireland 22 Sep 1978. 5'11". LHB, RM. Ireland 1997 to date. Middlesex debut 1999; cap 2002. 1000 (2): most 1267 (2002). HS 129 v Glam (Cardiff) 2002 and 129 v Derbys (Lord's) 2002. BB 1-20. CC BB 1-23. Award: CGT 1. LO HS 77 v Durham (Lord's) 2003 (NL). LO BB 2-10 v Notts (Nottingham) 2003 (NL).

NQKEEGAN, Chad Blake (Durban HS), b Sandton, near Johannesburg, South Africa 30 Jul 1979. 6'1". RHB, RF. Debut 2001; cap 2003. MCC YC. HS 36* v Kent (Lord's) 2003. 50 wkts (1): 63 (2003). BB 6-114 v Leics (Southgate) 2003. LO HS 50 v Notts (Lord's) 2003 (NL). LO BB 5-17 v Hants (Southgate) 2001 (NL).

‡**NQKLUSENER, Lance** (Durban HS), b Durban, South Africa 4 Sep 1971. LHB, RM/OB. Natal/KwaZulu-Natal 1993-94 to date. Nottinghamshire 2002. *Wisden* 1999. **Tests** (SA): 48 (1996-97 to 2001-02); HS 174 v E (Pt Elizabeth) 1999-00; BB 8-64 v I (Calcutta) 1996-97 – on debut. **LOI** (SA): 159 (1995-96 to 2003-04); HS 103* v NZ (Auckland) 1998-99; BB 6-49 v SL (Lahore) 1997-98. F-c Tours (SA): E 1998; A 1997-98, 2001-02; WI 2000-01; NZ 1998-99; I 1996-97, 1999-00; P 1997-98; SL 1998-99, 2000; Z 1999-00, 2001-02. HS 174 (see *Tests*). BB 8-34 Natal v WP (Durban) 1995-96. Award: BHC 1. LO HS 142* SA v Northants (Northampton) 1998. LO BB 6-49 (*see LOI*).

NQKOENIG, Sven Gaetan (Hilton C; Cape Town U), b Durban, South Africa 9 Dec 1973. ECB qualified – EU (Italian) passport. 5'10". LHB, OB. Western Province 1993-94 to 1996-97. Transvaal/Gauteng 1997-98 to 2000-01. Middlesex debut/cap 2002. F-c Tour (SA A): E 1996. 1000 (2): most 1251 (2002). HS 155 Gauteng v GW (Kimberley) 2000-01. M HS 166* v OU (Oxford) 2003. CC HS 113 v Essex (Southgate) 2002. BB (Gauteng) 1-0. M BB 1-19. LO HS 116 v Essex (Chelmsford) 2002 (CGT).

‡**NQMORGAN, Eoin** Joseph Gerard, b Dublin, Ireland 10 Sep 1986. LHB, RM. Summer contract 2004. Ireland U-19 in 2003-04 youth world cup. LO HS – (Ire – CGT).

NASH, David Charles (Sunbury Manor S; Malvern C), b Chertsey, Surrey 19 Jan 1978. 5'8". RHB, occ LB, WK. Debut 1997; cap 2000. F-c Tour: SL 1997-98 (Eng A). HS 114 v Somerset (Lord's) 1998. BB 1-8. LO HS 67 v Sussex (Lord's) 2002 (BHC).

PEPLOE, Christopher Thomas (Twyford C of E HS; Surrey U, Roehampton), b Hammersmith, London 26 Apr 1981. 6'4". LHB, SLA. MCC YC. Debut 2003. HS 13 v Sussex (Hove) 2003. BB 1-58 (not CC). LO HS – LO BB 1-32 (Middx CB) (CGT).

‡**RANKIN, William** Boyd, b Londonderry, Co Derry, N Ireland 5 Jul 1984. RHB, RMF. Brother of R.J.Rankin (Ire U-19). Summer contract 2004. Ire U-19 in 2003-04 world cup.

60

RICHARDS, Mali Alexander (St Joseph's Acad, Antigua; Cheltenham C), b Taunton, Somerset 2 Sep 1983. 5'11". LHB, RM. Son of Sir I.V.A.Richards (Leeward Is, Somerset, Queensland, Glamorgan and West Indies 1971-72 to 1993), nephew of D. and M.Richards (Leeward Is). Summer contract 2003. Awaiting f-c debut. LO HS 1 Antigua & Barbuda v Guyana (Gros Inlet) 2002 (RSB).

SAVILL, Thomas Edward (Bilborough C; Homerton C, Cambridge), b Sheffield, Yorks 16 May 1983. 6'6". RHB, RFM. Cambridge UCCE 2002-03. Nottinghamshire 2002 – no CC appearance. Middlesex summer contract 2003 – no 1st XI appearances. HS 18* CU v Essex (Cambridge) 2002. BB 3-86 CU v Essex (Cambridge) 2003. LO HS 35* Notts CB v Oxon (Oxford) 2001 (CGT). LO BB 1-45 (Notts CB – CGT).

‡SCOTT, Ben James Matthew (Whitton S, Richmond; Richmond C), b Isleworth, Middx 4 Aug 1981. 5'8". RHB, WK. Surrey 2003. HS 58* Sy v Essex (Oval) 2003. LO HS 11 Middx CB v Cumb (Southgate) 1999 (NWT).

SHAH, Owais Alam (Isleworth & Syon S), b Karachi, Pakistan 22 Oct 1978. 6'0". RHB, OB. Debut 1996; cap 2000. YC 2001. **LOI**: 15 (2001 to 2002-03); HS 62 v P (Lord's) 2001. F-c Tours (Eng A): A 1996-97; SL 1997-98. 1000 (3); most 1206 (2003). HS 203 v Derbys (Southgate) 2001. BB 3-33 v Glos (Bristol) 1999. Award: BHC 1. LO HS 134 v Sussex (Arundel) 1999 (NL). LO BB 2-2 v Glam (Cardiff) 1998 (BHC).

STRAUSS, Andrew John (Radley C; Durham U), b Johannesburg, South Africa 2 Mar 1977. 5'11". LHB, LM. Debut 1998; cap 2001; captain 2002 (*part*) to date. Oxfordshire 1996. **LOI**: 1 (2003-04); HS 3 v SL (Dambulla) 2003-04. 1000 (3); most – 1529 (2003). HS 176 v Durham (Lord's) 2001. BB 1-27. Award: CGT 1. LO HS 127 v Lancs (Manchester) 2003 (NL).

WEEKES, Paul Nicholas (Homerton House SS, Hackney), b Hackney, London 8 Jul 1969. 5'10". LHB, OB. Debut 1990; cap 1993; benefit 2002. F-c Tour: I 1994-95 (Eng A). MCC YC. 1000 runs (1): 1218 (1996). HS 171* v Somerset (Uxbridge) 1996. BB 8-39 v Glam (Lord's) 1996. Awards: CGT 2; BHC 4. LO HS 143* v Cornwall (St Austell) 1995 (NWT). LO BB 4-17 v Kent (Lord's) 2001 (BHC).

‡WHELAN, Christopher David, b Liverpool, Lancs 8 May 1986. RHB, RMF. Summer contract 2004.

RELEASED/RETIRED
(Having made a first-class County appearance in 2003)

A.J.Coleman, D.R.Holt and P.C.R.Tufnell left the staff having made no f-c appearances in 2003.

NQABDUL RAZZAQ (Furqan Model HS, Shahdara, Lahore), b Lahore, Pakistan 2 Dec 1979. 5'11". RHB, RFM. F-c debut (Lahore City) 1996-97. Middlesex 2002-03; cap 2002. **Tests** (P): 27 (1999-00 to 2003-04); HS 134 v B (Dhaka) 2001-02; BB 4-24 v WI (Sharjah) 2001-02. Hat trick v SL (Galle) 1999-00. **LOI** (P): 154 (1996-97 to 2003-04); HS 112 v SA (Pt Elizabeth) 2002-03; BB 6-35 v B (Dhaka) 2001-02. F-c Tours: E 1997 (Pak A), 2001; A 1999-00; SA 2002-03; WI 1999-00; NZ 2003-04; SL 1999-00; B 2001-02. HS 203* v Glam (Cardiff) 2002. BB 7-51 Lahore City v Karachi Whites (Thatta) 1996-97 – on debut. M BB 7-133 v Essex (Southgate) 2002. LO HS 112 (*see LOI*). LO BB 6-35 (*see LOI*).

ALLEYNE, D. – *see NOTTINGHAMSHIRE.*

BROWN, M.J. – *see HAMPSHIRE.*

NQDAWES, Joseph Henry (St Paul's S, Bald Hills; South Bank I, Brisbane), b Herston, Queensland, Australia 29 Aug 1970. 6'2". RHB, RFM. Queensland 1997-98 to date. MCC 2001. Middlesex 2003; cap 2003. HS 32* v Essex (Chelmsford) 2003. BB 7-67 Q v S Aus (Brisbane) 2002-03. M BB 5-46 v Notts (Nottingham) 2003. LO HS 2 (NL). LO BB 3-26 Q v Tasmania (Hobart) 2001-02.

RELEASED/RETIRED continued on p 67

MIDDLESEX 2003

RESULTS SUMMARY

	Place	Won	Lost	Tied	Drew	No Result
County Championship (1st Division)	**6th**	3	3		10	
All First-Class Matches		3	3		12	
C & G Trophy	Quarter-Finalist					
National League (2nd Division)	**4th**	10	7			1
Twenty20 Cup	**4th in South Group**					

COUNTY CHAMPIONSHIP AVERAGES
BATTING AND FIELDING

Cap		M	I	NO	HS	Runs	Avge	100	50	Ct/St
2001	A.J.Strauss	16	29	2	155	1401	51.88	4	7	6
2000	D.C.Nash	16	24	7	113	713	41.94	2	2	40/3
2003	B.L.Hutton	16	27	5	107	913	41.50	4	1	15
2002	S.G.Koenig	15	26	2	96	974	40.58	–	7	3
2000	O.A.Shah	16	27	1	147	964	37.07	2	4	11
2002	E.C.Joyce	16	27	3	117	881	36.70	3	2	7
2002	Abdul Razzaq	8	11	–	81	328	29.81	–	3	2
1993	P.N.Weekes	16	26	3	75	633	27.52	–	4	18
2003	A.A.Noffke	7	7	1	40	134	22.33	–	–	2
2003	C.B.Keegan	16	19	3	36*	244	15.25	–	–	5
2003	S.J.Cook	10	15	2	65	190	14.61	–	1	5
2003	J.H.Dawes	9	12	5	32*	97	13.85	–	–	3
	J.W.M.Dalrymple	6	10	1	33*	121	13.44	–	–	3
2001	T.F.Bloomfield	3	4	1	9*	19	6.33	–	–	1

Also batted: B.W.Gannon (1) 1*; Imran Tahir (3) 0, 29, 1*; C.T.Peploe (1) 0*, 13 (1 ct); R.M.S.Weston (1 – cap 2001) 31, 6.

BOWLING

	O	M	R	W	Avge	Best	5wI	10wM
J.H.Dawes	304.4	47	1008	32	31.50	5- 46	1	–
C.B.Keegan	563.5	113	1898	60	31.63	6-114	3	–
S.J.Cook	281.2	62	929	27	34.40	4- 42	–	–
A.A.Noffke	245.4	52	754	21	35.90	5- 52	1	–
P.N.Weekes	373.1	59	1157	28	41.32	4- 70	–	–
Abdul Razzaq	202.4	28	761	16	47.56	3- 69	–	–

Also bowled:

	O	M	R	W	Avge	Best	5wI	10wM
T.F.Bloomfield	54.4	4	257	6	42.83	4- 57	–	–
B.L.Hutton	67	8	307	5	61.40	2- 43	–	–
J.W.M.Dalrymple	128	16	437	6	72.83	2- 5	–	–

B.W.Gannon 23-4-102-0; Imran Tahir 59-13-196-1; E.C.Joyce 49-5-198-2; S.G.Koenig 5-0-19-1; D.C.Nash 5-0-25-0; C.T.Peploe 34-4-120-0; O.A.Shah 9-0-41-0; A.J.Strauss 6-0-42-1.

The First-Class Averages (pp 123–138) give the records of Middlesex players in all first-class county matches (Middlesex's other opponents being the Zimbabweans and Oxford UCCE), with the exception of J.W.M.Dalrymple whose full county figures are as above.

MIDDLESEX RECORDS

FIRST-CLASS CRICKET

Highest Total	For	642-3d		v	Hampshire	Southampton	1923
	V	734-5d		by	Lancashire	Manchester	2003
Lowest Total	For	20		v	MCC	Lord's	1864
	V	31		by	Glos	Bristol	1924
Highest Innings	For	331*	J.D.B.Robertson	v	Worcs	Worcester	1949
	V	316*	J.B.Hobbs	for	Surrey	Lord's	1926

Highest Partnership for each Wicket

1st	372	M.W.Gatting/J.L.Langer	v	Essex	Southgate	1998
2nd	380	F.A.Tarrant/J.W.Hearne	v	Lancashire	Lord's	1914
3rd	424*	W.J.Edrich/D.C.S.Compton	v	Somerset	Lord's	1948
4th	325	J.W.Hearne/E.H.Hendren	v	Hampshire	Lord's	1919
5th	338	R.S.Lucas/T.C.O'Brien	v	Sussex	Hove	1895
6th	270	J.D.Carr/P.N.Weekes	v	Glos	Lord's	1994
7th	271*	E.H.Hendren/F.T.Mann	v	Notts	Nottingham	1925
8th	182*	M.H.C.Doll/H.R.Murrell	v	Notts	Lord's	1913
9th	160*	E.H.Hendren/T.J.Durston	v	Essex	Leyton	1927
10th	230	R.W.Nicholls/W.Roche	v	Kent	Lord's	1899

Best Bowling	For	10- 40	G.O.B.Allen	v	Lancashire	Lord's	1929
(Innings)	V	9- 38	R.C.R-Glasgow†	for	Somerset	Lord's	1924
Best Bowling	For	16-114	G.Burton	v	Yorkshire	Sheffield	1888
(Match)		16-114	J.T.Hearne	v	Lancashire	Manchester	1898
	V	16-109	C.W.L.Parker	for	Glos	Cheltenham	1930

Most Runs – Season	2669	E.H.Hendren	(av 83.41)	1923
Most Runs – Career	40302	E.H.Hendren	(av 48.81)	1907-37
Most 100s – Season	13	D.C.S.Compton		1947
Most 100s – Career	119	E.H.Hendren		1907-37
Most Wkts – Season	158	F.J.Titmus	(av 14.63)	1955
Most Wkts – Career	2361	F.J.Titmus	(av 21.27)	1949-82
Most Career W-K Dismissals	1223	J.T.Murray	(1024 ct/199 st)	1952-75
Most Career Catches in the Field	561	E.H.Hendren		1907-37

LIST 'A' LIMITED-OVERS CRICKET

Highest Total	CGT	304-7		v	Surrey	The Oval	1995
		304-8		v	Cornwall	St Austell	1995
	BHC	325-5		v	Leics	Leicester	1992
	NL	337-5		v	Somerset	Southgate	2003
Lowest Total	CGT	41		v	Essex	Westcliff	1972
	BHC	73		v	Essex	Lord's	1985
	NL	23		v	Yorkshire	Leeds	1974
Highest Innings	CGT	158	G.D.Barlow	v	Lancashire	Lord's	1984
	BHC	143*	M.W.Gatting	v	Sussex	Hove	1985
	NL	147*	M.R.Ramprakash	v	Worcs	Lord's	1990
Best Bowling	CGT	6-15	W.W.Daniel	v	Sussex	Hove	1980
	BHC	7-12	W.W.Daniel	v	Minor C (E)	Ipswich	1978
	NL	6- 6	R.W.Hooker	v	Surrey	Lord's	1969

† R.C.Robertson-Glasgow

NORTHAMPTONSHIRE

Formation of Present Club: 31 July 1878
Inaugural First-Class Match: 1905
Colours: Maroon
Badge: Tudor Rose
County Champions: (0); best – 2nd 1912, 1957, 1965, 1976
Gillette/NatWest/C & G Trophy Winners: (2) 1976, 1992
Benson and Hedges Cup Winners: (1) 1980
National League (Div 1) Winners: (0); best – 3rd 2000
Sunday League Winners: (0); best – 3rd 1991
Twenty20 Cup Winners: 4th in Midlands/Wales/West Group 2003
Match Awards: CGT 55; BHC 62

Chief Executive: S.P.Coverdale (M.Tagg from April 5); County Ground, Wantage Road, Northampton, NN1 4TJ • Tel: 01604 514455 • Fax: 01604 514488 • Email: post@nccc.co.uk • Web: www.nccc.co.uk

Director of Cricket/First XI Coach: K.P.Wessels. **Captain**: D.J.G.Sales. **Vice-Captain**: none. **Overseas Players**: J.Louw and M.van Jaarsveld. **2004 Beneficiary**: none. **Head Groundsman**: P.Marshall. **Scorer**: A.C.Kingston. ‡ New registration. NQ Not qualified for England.

‡**AFZAAL, Usman** (Manvers Pierrepont CS; S Notts C), b Rawalpindi, Pakistan 9 Jun 1977. 6'0". LHB, SLA. Debut 1995; cap 2000. **Tests**: 3 (2001); HS 54 v A (Oval) 2001; BB 1-49. F-c Tours: SA 1996-97 (Nt); WI 2000-01 (Eng A); NZ 2001-02. 1000 runs (3): most – 1275 (2002). HS 161* v Ind A (Nottingham) 2003. CC HS 151* v Worcs (Nottingham) 2000. BB 4-101 v Glos (Northampton) 1998. Award: CGT 1. LO HS 105 Nt v Somerset (Taunton) 2003 (NL). LO BB 3-8 v Ire (Clontarf) 2002 (CGT).

ANDERSON, Ricaldo Sherman Glenroy (Alperton HS; Barnet C; North West London C; London Cricket C), b Hammersmith, London 22 Sep 1976. 5'10". RHB, RFM. Essex 1999-2001. Northamptonshire debut 2002. HS 67* Ex v Sussex (Chelmsford) 2000. Nh HS 51 v Essex (Northampton) 2002. 50 wkts (1): 50 (1999). BB 6-34 (11-111 match) Ex v Northants (Ilford) 2000. Nh BB 4-97 v Derbys (Derby) 2002. LO HS 22 Ex v Sussex (Hove) 2001 (NL) and 12 v Derbys (Derby) 2002 (NL). LO BB 3-28 v Glos (Northampton) 2002 (BHC).

BAILEY, Tobin Michael Barnaby (Bedford S; Loughborough U), b Kettering 28 Aug 1976. 5'10". RHB, WK. Debut 1996; cap 2003. British U 1998. Bedfordshire 1994-96. HS 101* v Somerset (Taunton) 2003. BB – LO HS 52 Brit U v Glos (Bristol) 1997.

NQ**BROPHY, Gerard** Louis (Christian Brothers C, Boksburg; Witwatersrand TC), b Welkom, South Africa 26 Nov 1975. 5'11". British/EU passport. RHB, WK. Transvaal 1996-97 to 1998-99. Free State 1999-00 to 2000-01. Northamptonshire debut 2002. HS 185 SA Academy v Zim President's XI (Harare) 1998-99. Nh HS 152* v Glos (Gloucester) 2003. LO HS 54 v Essex (Northampton) 2002 (NL).

BROWN, Jason Fred (St Margaret Ward HS & SFC), b Newcastle-under-Lyme, Staffs 10 Oct 1974. 6'0". RHB, OB. Debut 1996; cap 2000. Staffordshire 1994-95. F-c Tours: WI 2000-01 (*part*) (Eng A); SL 2000-01 (*no f-c*). HS 38 v Hants (Northampton) 2003. 50 wkts (2): most – 66 (2003). BB 7-69 v Durham (Chester-le-St) 2003. LO HS 16 v Lancs (Manchester) 2002 (SL). LO BB 4-26 v Leics (Northampton) 1997 (SL).

CAWDRON, Michael John (Cheltenham C), b Luton, Beds 7 Oct 1974. 6'2". LHB, RM. Gloucestershire staff 1994-2001; debut 1999 – taking 15 wickets in first four innings. Northamptonshire debut 2003. HS 42 Gs v Hants (Bristol) 1999 – on debut. Nh HS 24 v Hants (Northampton) 2003 – on Northants debut. BB 6-25 (10-74 match) FCC Select XI v NZ A (Milton Keynes) 2000. Nh BB 6-87 v Durham (Chester-le-St) 2003. LO HS 50 Gs v Essex (Cheltenham) 1995 (SL). LO BB 4-17 Gs v Warwks (Cheltenham) 1999 (NL).

COOK, Jeffrey William (James Cook HS, Kogarah, NSW), b Sydney, Australia 2 Feb 1972. 6'4". LHB, RM. UK resident since 1993 – England qualified 2000. Debut 2000; cap 2003. NSW U-19. HS 137 v Glos (Cheltenham) 2000. BB 5-31 v Durham (Northampton) 2003. Awards: CGT 1; BHC 1. LO HS 130 Northants CB v Wilts (Northampton) 1999 (NWT). LO BB 4-35 v Glos (Bristol) 2002 (NL).

‡**COVERDALE, Paul** Stephen (Wellingborough S), b Harrogate, Yorks 24 Jul 1983. Son of S.P.Coverdale (Yorkshire, Cambridge U and Northamptonshire 1973-80, 1987; Northants Secretary-Manager/Chief Executive 1985-2004). RHB, RM. Emerging player contract 2004 – awaiting f-c debut. LO HS 19 Northants CB v Leics CB (Barwell) 2001.

GREENIDGE, Carl Gary (Lodge S and St Michael S, Barbados; Heathcote S, Chingford; W Hatch HS; City of Westminster C), b Basingstoke, Hants 20 Apr 1978. Son of C.Gordon Greenidge (Hampshire, Barbados and West Indies 1970-92). 5'10". RHB, RMF. MCC YC. Surrey 1999-2000. Northamptonshire debut 2002. HS 46 v Derbys (Derby) 2002. 50 wkts (1): 53 (2002). BB 6-40 v Durham (Chester-le-St) 2002. LO HS 20 v Sussex (Northampton) 2002 (NL). LO BB 3-22 v Derbys (Northampton) 2002 (NL).

HUGGINS, Thomas Benjamin (Kimbolton S; De Montfort U), b Peterborough 8 Mar 1983. 6'3". RHB, OB. Debut 2003. Emerging player contract. Cambridgeshire 2001. HS 40 v CU (Cambridge) 2003 – on debut. LO HS 2 (Cambs) (CGT).

[NQ]**JAQUES, Philip** Anthony (Fig Tree HS, Wollongong; Australian C of PE, Homebush), b Wollongong, NSW, Australia 3 May 1979. 6'1". LHB, SLC. British passport (English parents). NSW 2000-01 to 2001-02, 2003-04. Northamptonshire debut/cap 2003. 1000 (1): 1409 (2003). HS 222 v Yorks (Northampton) 2003. BB – LO HS 117 v Hants (Northampton) 2003 (NL).

‡**JONES, Philip** Steffan (Stradey CS, Llanelli; Neath TC; Loughborough U; Homerton C, Cambridge), b Llanelli, Carms, Wales 9 Feb 1974. 6'2". RHB, RMF. Cambridge U 1997; blue 1997. Somerset debut 1997; cap 2001. Wales MC 1992-96. HS 105 Sm v NZ (Taunton) 1999. CC HS 63 Sm v Northants (Taunton) 2003. 50 wkts (1): 59 (2001). BB 6-67 CU v OU (Lord's) 1997. CC BB 6-110 (match 10-156) Sm v Warwks (Birmingham) 2002. LO HS 27 Sm v Northants (Northampton) 2000 (NL). LO BB 5-23 Sm v Warwks (Taunton) 1998 (SL).

‡**KING Richard** Eric (Bedford Modern S; Loughborough U), b Hitchin, Herts 3 Jan 1984. 6'0". RHB, LMF. Loughborough UCCE 2003. Northants emerging player contract 2004. HS 17 LU v Somerset (Taunton) 2003 – on debut. BB 1-108 (LU). LO HS 2 (Northants CB). LO BB 2-39 Northants CB v Yorks CB (Northampton) 2002 (CGT).

‡[NQ]**LOUW, Johann** (Fraserburg HS; Port Elizabeth U), b Cape Town, South Africa 12 Apr 1979. RHB, RMF. Griqualand West 2000-01 to date. HS 86* GW v KZ-Natal (Kimberley) 2001-02. BB 6-108 GW v Border (East London) 2002-03. LO HS 72 GW v Northerns (Kimberley) 2000-01. LO BB 5-43 GW v North West (Kimberley) 2000-01.

PANESAR, Mudhsuden Singh (*'Monty'*) (Stopsley HS; Bedford Modern S; Loughborough U), b Luton, Beds 25 Apr 1982. 6'0". LHB, SLA. Bedfordshire 1998-99. Debut 2001. F-c Tours (ECB Acad): SL 2002-03. HS 28 v CU (Cambridge) 2003. BB 5-77 ECB Acad v SL Acad XI (Colombo) 2002-03. CC HS 10 and Nh BB 4-11 (8-131 match) v Leics (Northampton) 2001 – on debut. LO HS 16* v Essex (Colchester) 2002 (NL). LO BB 5-20 ECB Acad v SL Acad XI (Colombo) 2002-03.

PHILLIPS, Ben James (Langley Park S and SFC, Beckenham), b Lewisham, London 30 Sep 1974. 6'6". RHB, RFM. Kent 1996-99. Northamptonshire debut 2002 (one non-CC match). HS 100* K v Lancs (Manchester) 1997. Nh HS 48* v Hants (Northampton) 2003. BB 5-47 K v Sussex (Horsham) 1997. Nh BB 4-45 v Worcs (Worcester) 2003. Award: CGT 1. LO HS 46 K v Glam (Cardiff) 1996 (SL). LO BB 4-25 K v Northants (Canterbury) 2000 (NL).

POWELL, Mark John (Campion S, Bugbrooke; Loughborough U), b Northampton 4 Nov 1980. 5'11". RHB, OB. Debut 2000. HS 108* v Glam (Cardiff) 2002. BB – LO HS 70 v Derbys (Derby) 2003 (NL).

ROBERTS, Timothy William (Bishop's Stopford S, Kettering; Durham U), b Kettering 4 Mar 1978. Younger brother of A.R.Roberts (Northants 1987-98). 5'7". RHB, OB. British U 1999. Bedfordshire 2000. Lancashire debut 2001. HS 83 v Somerset (Northampton) 2003 – on Northants debut. BB – LO HS 131 v Notts (Nottingham) 2003 (NL). LO BB –

SALES, David John Grimwood (Caterham S; Cumnor House S), b Carshalton, Surrey 3 Dec 1977. 6'0". RHB, RM. Debut 1996 v Worcs (Kidderminster) scoring 0 and 210* – record Championship score on f-c debut; youngest (18yr 237d) to score 200 in a Championship match; cap 1999; captain 2004. Wellington 2001-02. F-c Tours (Eng A): NZ 1999-00; SL 1997-98; K 1997-98; B 1999-00. Sustained severe knee injury prior to start of England A tour of WI 2000-01 – no f-c appearances 2001. 1000 runs (1): 1291 (1999). HS 303* v Essex (Northampton) 1999 – youngest Englishman (21y 240d) to score a f-c 300. BB 4-25 v SL A (Northampton) 1999. CC BB 2-7 v Yorks (Scarborough) 1999. Award: BHC 1. LO HS 133* v Notts (Northampton) 2003 (NL). LO BB –

SHANTRY, Adam John (Priory S; Shrewsbury SFC), b Bristol 13 Nov 1982. 6'2½". Son of B.K.Shantry (Gloucestershire 1978-79). LHB, LFM. Debut 2003. Emerging player contract. Shropshire 2001. HS 38* and BB 3-8 (3 wkts in 5 balls) v Somerset (Northampton) 2003 – on CC debut. LO HS 15 and LO BB 2-21 Northants CB v Yorks CB (Northampton) 2002 (CGT).

SWANN, Graeme Peter (Sponne SS, Towcester), b Northampton 24 Mar 1979. Son of R.Swann (Northumberland 1969-72; Bedfordshire 1988-95); younger brother of A.J.Swann (see LANCASHIRE). 6'0". RHB, OB. Debut 1998; cap 1999. Bedfordshire 1996. **LOI**: 1 (1999-00); dnb v SA (Bloemfontein) 1999-00. F-c Tours (Eng A): SA 1998-99, 1999-00 (Eng); WI 2000-01 (part); Z 1998-99. HS 183 v Glos (Bristol) 2002 – including 114 before lunch on third day. 50 wkts (1): 57 (1999). BB 7-33 v Derbys (Northampton) 2003. LO HS 83 v Leics (Northampton) 2001 (NL). LO BB 5-35 v Durham (Chester-le-St) 1999 (NL).

[NO]**VAN JAARSFELD, Martin** (Warmbaths S; Pretoria U), b Klerksdorp, South Africa 18 Jun 1974. 6'2". RHB, OB. N Transvaal/Northerns 1994-95 to date. **Tests** (SA): 4 (2002-03 to 2003-04); HS 73 v WI (Johannesburg) 2003-04. **LOI** (SA): 9 (2002-03 to 2003); HS 45 v E (Birmingham) 2003; BB 1-0. Took wickets with his first and third balls in LOI. F-c Tours (SA A): SL 1998-99; Z 1998-99 (SA Acad). 1000 (0+1): 1268 (2001-02). HS 238* Northerns v GW (Kimberley) 1999-00. BB 1-1. LO HS 123 NT v EP (Pretoria) 1996-97. LO BB 1-0 (see LOI).

WHITE, Robert Allan (Stowe S; Durham U; Loughborough U), b Chelmsford, Essex 15 Oct 1979. 5'11". RHB, LB. Debut 2000. Loughborough UCCE 2003. British U 2003. HS 277 and BB 2-30 v Glos (Northampton) 2002 – highest maiden f-c hundred in UK; included 107 before lunch on first day. LO HS 22 v Somerset (Bath) 2003 (NL). LO BB 2-18 v Sussex (Northampton) 2002 (NL).

RELEASED/RETIRED

(Having made a first-class County appearance in 2003)

T.M.Baker, D.M.Cousins and J.R.Wade left the staff having made no f-c appearances in 2003.

BLAIN, John Angus Rae (Penicuik HS; Jewel & Esk Valley C), b Edinburgh, Scotland 4 Jan 1979. 6'1". RHB, RMF. Scotland 1996-99. Northamptonshire 1997-2003. **LOI** (Scot): 5 (1999); HS 9 and BB 4-37 v B (Edinburgh) 1999. HS 34 v Surrey (Northampton) 2001. BB 6-42 v Kent (Canterbury) 2001. Award: BHC 1. LO HS 11 Nh v Worcs (Kidderminster) 2001 (BHC). LO BB 5-24 Nh v Derbys (Derby) 1997 (SL).

[NO]**HUSSEY, Michael** Edward Killeen (Prindiville Catholic C; Curtin U), b Morley, Perth, Australia 27 May 1975. Elder brother of D.J.Hussey (see NOTTINGHAMSHIRE). 5'11". LHB, RM. W Australia 1994-95 to date. Northamptonshire debut/cap 2001; captain 2002 to date. **LOI**: 1 (2003-04); HS 17* v I (Perth) 2003-04. F-c Tour (Aus A): Sc/Ire 1998. 1000 runs (3); most – y 2055 (2001). HS 331* (Northants record) in 651 minutes v Somerset (Taunton) 2003. Also scored 329* v Essex (Northampton) 2001 and 310 v Glos (Bristol) 2002. BB 2-21 WA v Q (Perth) 1998-99. Nh BB 1-5. Awards: BHC 3. LO HS 123 v Scot (Northampton) 2003 (NL). LO BB 3-52 WA v Vic (Melbourne) 1999-00 (MM).

66

^{NQ}**NEL, Andre** (Dr E.G.Jansen S, Boksburg), b Germiston, South Africa 15 Jul 1977. 6'4". RHB, RFM. Easterns 1996-97 to date. **Tests** (SA): 8 (2001-02 to 2003-04); HS 7; BB 5-87 v WI (Cape Town) 2003-04. **LOI** (SA): 18 (2000-01 to 2003-04); HS 3*; BB 4-39 v P (Rawalpindi) 2003-04. F-c Tours (SA): A 2002-03 (SA A – *part*); WI 2000-01; P 2003-04; Z 2001-02. HS 44 Easterns v FS (Benoni) 2000-01. Nh HS 42 v Glam (Cardiff) 2003. BB 6-25 Easterns v Gauteng (Jo'burg) 2001-02. Nh BB 5-47 v Glos (Gloucester) 2003. LO HS 17* Easterns v EP (Benoni) 1997-98. LO BB 6-27 Easterns v GW (Benoni) 2000-01.

PAYNTER, David Edward (St Bede's GS), b Truro, Cornwall 25 Jan 1981. 6'2". Great-grandson of E.Paynter (Lancashire and England 1926 to 1950-51). RHB, OB. Northampton-shire 2002-03. HS 146 v CU (Cambridge) 2003. CC HS 50 v Glos (Northampton) 2003. BB – LO HS 104 Northants CB v Northants (Northampton) 2001 (CGT). LO BB 2-56 v Scot (Northampton) 2003 (NL).

PENBERTHY, Anthony Leonard (Camborne CS), b Troon, Cornwall 1 Sep 1969. 6'1". LHB, RM. Northamptonshire 1989-2003; cap 1994; benefit 2002. Cornwall 1987-89. F-c Tours (Nh): SA 1991-92; Z 1994-95. HS 132* v Glam (Northampton) 2001. BB 5-37 v Glam (Swansea) 1993. Took wicket of M.A.Taylor (A) with his first ball in f-c cricket. Awards: CGT 1; BHC 1. LO HS 81* v Surrey (Northampton) 1997 (SL). LO BB 5-29 v Glos (Bristol) 2000 (NL).

^{NQ}**WRIGHT, Damien** Geoffrey (Terrigal HS, NSW), b Casino, NSW, Australia 25 Jul 1975. 6'1". RHB, RMF. Tasmania 1997-98 to date. Scotland 2001 (CGT). Northamptonshire 2003. F-c Tours (Aus A): SA 2002-03). HS 63 Tasmania v WA (Hobart) 2001-02. Nh HS 46 and BB 3-38 v Hants (Northampton) 2003 – on CC debut. BB 6-39 Tasmania v NSW (Hobart) 2002-03. LO HS 55 Scotland v Middx CB (Southgate) 2001 (CGT). LO BB 4-23 Tasmania v 2001-02. Withdrew from 2004 overseas player contract with Derbyshire because of a knee injury.

MIDDLESEX RELEASED/RETIRED (continued from p 61)

GANNON, Benjamin Ward (Dragon S, Oxford; Abingdon S; Cheltenham & Gloucester CHE), b Oxford 5 Sep 1975. 6'3". RHB, RMF. Gloucestershire 1999-2002. Middlesex 2003 (one match). Herefordshire 1996. HS 28 Gs v Essex (Colchester) 2000. M HS 1*. BB 6-80 Gs v Glam (Cardiff) 1999 – on debut. M BB – LO HS (Gs) 2. LO BB 2-29 Gs v SL A (Cheltenham) 1999.

HUNT, T.A. – *see SOMERSET*.

^{NQ}**IMRAN TAHIR**, Muhammad (Government HS, M.A.O. C, Lahore), b Lahore, Pakistan 4 Jun 1979. 5'11". RHB, LB. Lahore 1996-97, 1997-98, 2000-01. WAPDA 1997-98, 1998-99. REDCO 1999-00. Sui Gas 2001-02. Middlesex 2003. HS 48 REDCO v KRL (Rawalpindi) 1999-00. M HS 29 v Kent (Canterbury) 2003. BB 8-76 REDCO v Karachi Blues (Lahore) 1999-00. M BB 1-128. LO HS 0*. LO BB 3-22 WAPDA v Faisalabad (Faisalabad) 1997-98.

^{NQ}**NOFFKE, Ashley** Allan b Nambour, Queensland, Australia 30 Apr 1977. RHB, RFM. Debut 1998-99 for Australian Academy. Queensland 1999-00 to date. Middlesex 2002-03; cap 2003. F-c Tours (A): E 2001 (*part*); WI 2003; Z 1998-99 (A Academy). HS 76 v Worcs (Worcester) 2002. BB 8-24 (12-108 match) v Derbys (Derby) 2002. LO HS 58 v Sussex (Lord's) 2002 (BHC). LO BB 4-32 Q v Tasmania (Hobart) 2001-02.

WESTON, Robin Michael Swann (Durham S; Loughborough U), b Durham City 7 Jun 1975. Brother of W.P.C.Weston (*see GLOUCESTERSHIRE*). 5'10". RHB, LB. Durham 1995-97. Derbyshire 1998-99 (scored 72, 129*, 22, 124 and 156 in consecutive CC innings 1999). Middlesex 2000-03; cap 2001. Minor C debut 1991 when aged 15yr 355d (Durham record). HS 156 De v Somerset (Derby) 1999. M HS 135* v Hants (Southgate) 2001. BB (De) 1-15. LO HS 80* v Derbys (Southgate) 2001 (NL).

NORTHAMPTONSHIRE 2003

RESULTS SUMMARY

	Place	Won	Lost	Tied	Drew	No Result
County Championship (2nd Division)	2nd	10	2		4	
All First-Class Matches		10	3		4	
C & G Trophy	3rd Round					
National League (2nd Division)	2nd	12	5			1
Twenty20 Cup	4th in Midlands/Wales/West Group					

COUNTY CHAMPIONSHIP AVERAGES
BATTING AND FIELDING

Cap		M	I	NO	HS	Runs	Avge	100	50	Ct/St
2001	M.E.K.Hussey	14	21	2	331*	1697	89.31	6	5	17
2003	P.A.Jaques	16	25	1	222	1409	58.70	5	6	9
1999	D.J.G.Sales	16	23	2	200*	942	44.85	2	4	13
	G.L.Brophy	6	10	3	152*	289	41.28	1	1	11
	T.W.Roberts	7	10	–	83	263	26.30	–	2	3
2003	J.W.Cook	14	22	2	85	517	25.85	–	3	3
	A.Nel	13	13	3	42	258	25.80	–	–	4
2003	T.M.B.Bailey	14	19	3	101*	384	24.00	1	–	29/6
1999	G.P.Swann	9	13	1	69	256	21.33	–	2	9
	M.J.Powell	15	23	2	60	427	20.33	–	3	29
	B.J.Phillips	7	8	2	48*	119	19.83	–	–	1
	R.A.White	3	6	–	55	110	18.33	–	1	1
2000	J.F.Brown	13	12	6	38	91	15.16	–	–	2
	M.J.Cawdron	6	6	–	24	63	10.50	–	–	1
	C.G.Greenidge	7	6	2	13	32	8.00	–	–	2
	M.S.Panesar	5	6	3	6*	15	5.00	–	–	3

Also batted: R.S.G.Anderson (1 match) 13; J.A.R.Blain (3) 1*, 5; D.E.Paynter (2) 50, 2, 5; A.L.Penberthy (1 – cap 1994) 32*; A.J.Shantry (2) 38*, 0 (1 ct); D.G.Wright (2) 46, 27 (1 ct).

BOWLING

	O	M	R	W	Avge	Best	5wI	10wM
B.J.Phillips	149	47	400	21	19.04	4-45	–	–
J.F.Brown	617	180	1469	65	22.60	7-69	4	–
G.P.Swann	238.2	37	759	33	23.00	7-33	3	–
M.J.Cawdron	142.3	31	504	20	25.20	6-87	1	–
J.W.Cook	162.3	46	479	19	25.21	5-31	1	–
A.Nel	422.3	99	1292	36	35.88	5-47	1	–
J.A.R.Blain	62.2	3	366	10	36.60	5-84	1	–
M.S.Panesar	131.2	24	447	11	40.63	3-92	–	–
C.G.Greenidge	205.3	23	927	20	46.35	3-33	–	–
Also bowled:								
A.J.Shantry	31.4	9	113	6	18.83	3- 8	–	–
D.G.Wright	73.5	19	194	7	27.71	3-38	–	–

R.S.G.Anderson 10-1-67-0; T.M.B.Bailey 1-0-3-0; M.E.K.Hussey 14-2-52-1; P.A.Jaques 4-0-25-0; D.E.Paynter 6-1-26-0; A.L.Penberthy 2-1-4-0; M.J.Powell 2-0-12-0; T.W.Roberts 4-0-4-0; D.J.G.Sales 1-0-4-0; R.A.White 7-0-61-1.

The First-Class Averages (pp 123–138) give the records of Northamptonshire players in all first-class county matches (Northamptonshire's other opponents being Cambridge UCCE), with the exception of R.A.White whose full county figures are as above.

NORTHAMPTONSHIRE RECORDS

FIRST-CLASS CRICKET

Highest Total	For	781-7d		v	Notts	Northampton	1995
	V	673-8d		by	Yorkshire	Leeds	2003
Lowest Total	For	12		v	Glos	Gloucester	1907
	V	33		by	Lancashire	Northampton	1977
Highest Innings	For	331*	M.E.K.Hussey	v	Somerset	Taunton	2003
	V	333	K.S.Duleepsinhji	for	Sussex	Hove	1930

Highest Partnership for each Wicket

1st	375	R.A.White/M.J.Powell	v	Glos	Northampton	2002
2nd	344	G.Cook/R.J.Boyd-Moss	v	Lancashire	Northampton	1986
3rd	393	A.Fordham/A.J.Lamb	v	Yorkshire	Leeds	1990
4th	370	R.T.Virgin/P.Willey	v	Somerset	Northampton	1976
5th	401	M.B.Loye/D.Ripley	v	Glamorgan	Northampton	1998
6th	376	R.Subba Row/A.Lightfoot	v	Surrey	The Oval	1958
7th	293	D.J.G.Sales/D.Ripley	v	Essex	Northampton	1999
8th	164	D.Ripley/N.G.B.Cook	v	Lancashire	Manchester	1987
9th	156	R.Subba Row/S.Starkie	v	Lancashire	Northampton	1955
10th	148	B.W.Bellamy/J.V.Murdin	v	Glamorgan	Northampton	1925

Best Bowling	For	10-127	V.W.C.Jupp	v	Kent	Tunbridge W	1932
(Innings)	V	10- 30	C.Blythe	for	Kent	Northampton	1907
Best Bowling	For	15- 31	G.E.Tribe	v	Yorkshire	Northampton	1958
(Match)	V	17- 48	C.Blythe	for	Kent	Northampton	1907

Most Runs – Season	2198	D.Brookes	(av 51.11)		1952
Most Runs – Career	28980	D.Brookes	(av 36.13)		1934-59
Most 100s – Season	8	R.A.Haywood			1921
Most 100s – Career	67	D.Brookes			1934-59
Most Wkts – Season	175	G.E.Tribe	(av 18.70)		1955
Most Wkts – Career	1097	E.W.Clark	(av 21.31)		1922-47
Most Career W-K Dismissals	810	K.V.Andrew	(653 ct/157 st)		1953-66
Most Career Catches in the Field	469	D.S.Steele			1963-84

LIST 'A' LIMITED-OVERS CRICKET

Highest Total	CGT	360-2		v	Staffs	Northampton	1990
	BHC	304-6		v	Scotland	Northampton	1995
	NL	319-7		v	Scotland	Northampton	2003
Lowest Total	CGT	62		v	Leics	Leicester	1974
	BHC	85		v	Sussex	Northampton	1978
	NL	41		v	Middlesex	Northampton	1972
Highest Innings	CGT	145	R.J.Bailey	v	Staffs	Stone	1991
	BHC	134	R.J.Bailey	v	Glos	Northampton	1987
	NL	172*	W.Larkins	v	Warwicks	Luton	1983
Best Bowling	CGT	7-37	N.A.Mallender	v	Worcs	Northampton	1984
	BHC	5-14	F.A.Rose	v	Minor C	Luton	1998
	NL	7-39	A.Hodgson	v	Somerset	Northampton	1976

NOTTINGHAMSHIRE

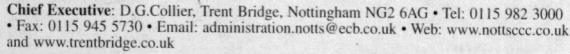

Formation of Present Club: March/April 1841
Substantial Reorganisation: 11 December 1866
Inaugural First-Class Match: 1864
Colours: Green and Gold
Badge: Badge of City of Nottingham
County Champions (since 1890): (4) 1907, 1929, 1981, 1987
Gillette/NatWest/C & G Trophy Winners: (1) 1987
Benson and Hedges Cup Winners: (1) 1989
National League (Div 1) Winners: (0); best – 5th 2001
Sunday League Winners: (1) 1991
Twenty20 Cup Winners: 6th in North Group 2003
Match Awards: CGT 45; BHC 76

Chief Executive: D.G.Collier, Trent Bridge, Nottingham NG2 6AG • Tel: 0115 982 3000 • Fax: 0115 945 5730 • Email: administration.notts@ecb.co.uk • Web: www.nottsccc.co.uk and www.trentbridge.co.uk

First XI Coach: M.Newell. **Captain**: J.E.R.Gallian. **Vice-Captain**: P.J.Franks. **Overseas Players**: S.C.G.MacGill and D.R.Martyn (Reserve: D.J.Hussey). **2004 Beneficiary**: P.Johnson (testimonial). **Head Groundsman**: S.Birks. **Scorer**: G.Stringfellow. ‡ New registration. NQ Not qualified for England.

‡**ALLEYNE, David** (Enfield GS; Hertford Regional C; City & Islington C), b York 17 Apr 1976. 5'11". RHB, WK. Middlesex 2001-02. HS 49* M v Derbys (Derby) 2002. LO HS 58 M v Notts (Nottingham) 2000 (NL).

BICKNELL, Darren John (Robert Haining County SS; Guildford TC), b Guildford, Surrey 24 Jun 1967. Elder brother of M.P.Bicknell (see SURREY). 6'4". LHB, SLA. Surrey 1987-99; cap 1990; benefit 1999. Nottinghamshire debut/cap 2000. F-c Tours (Eng A): WI 1991-92; P 1990-91; SL 1989-90. 1000 runs (7); most – 1888 (1991). HS 235* Sy v Notts (Nottingham) 1994. Nt HS 180* v Warwks (Birmingham) 2000 – sharing unbroken 1st wkt stand of 406 with G.E.Welton. BB 3-7 Sy v Sussex (Guildford) 1996. Awards: CGT 1; BHC 6. LO HS 135* Sy v Yorks (Oval) 1989 (NWT). LO BB (Sy) 1-11 (SL).

CLOUGH, Gareth David (Pudsey Grangefield S), b Leeds, Yorks 23 May 1978. 6'0". RHB, RM. Yorkshire 1998. Nottinghamshire debut 2001. HS 55 v Ind A (Nottingham) 2003. CC HS 33 Y v Glam (Cardiff) 1998 – on debut. BB 3-69 v Glos (Nottingham) 2001. LO HS 42* v Durham (Nottingham) 2003 (NL). LO BB 4-32 v Sussex (Horsham) 2003 (NL).

‡**EALHAM, Mark** Alan (Stour Valley SS, Chartham), b Willesborough, Ashford, Kent 27 Aug 1969. Son of A.G.E.Ealham (Kent 1966-82). 5'9". RHB,-RMF. Kent 1989-2003; cap 1992; benefit 2003. **Tests**: 8 (1996 to 1998); HS 53* v A (Birmingham) 1997; BB 4-21 v I (Nottingham) 1996. **LOI**: 64 (1996 to 2001); HS 45 v WI (Bridgetown) 1997-98; BB 5-15 v Z (Kimberley) 1999-00 – Eng record. F-c Tours: A 1996-97 (Eng A); SA 1999-00 (*part*); SL 1997-98; Z 1992-93 (K); K 1997-98. 1000 runs (1): 1055 (1997). HS 153* K v Northants (Canterbury) 2001. BB 8-36 (10-74 match) K v Warwks (Birmingham) 1996. Awards: CGT 2; BHC 6. LO HS 112 K v Derbys (Maidstone) 1995 (off 44 balls – SL record). LO BB 6-53 K v Hants (Basingstoke) 1993 (SL).

FRANKS, Paul John (Southwell Minster CS), b Mansfield 3 Feb 1979. 6'2". LHB, RMF. Debut 1996; cap 1999. Canterbury 2002-03. YC 2000. **LOI**: 1 (2000); HS 4 v WI (Nottingham) 2000. F-c Tours (Eng A): SA 1998-99; WI 2000-01; NZ 1999-00; B 1999-00. HS 123* v Leics (Leicester) 2003. 50 wkts (2); most – 63 (1999). BB 7-56 v Middx (Lord's) 2000. Hat trick 1997. Awards: CGT 2. LO HS 84* v Lincs (Lincoln) 2003 (CGT). LO BB 6-27 v Durham (Chester-le-St) 2000 (NL).

GALLIAN, Jason Edward Riche (Pittwater House S, Sydney; Keble C, Oxford), b Manly, Sydney, Australia 25 Jun 1971. Qualified for England 1994. 6'0". RHB, RM. Lancashire 1990-97, taking wicket of D.A.Hagan (OU) with his first ball; cap 1994. Oxford U 1992-93; blue 1992-93; captain 1993. Nottinghamshire debut/cap 1998; captain 1998 (part) to date. Captained Australia YC v England YC 1989-90, scoring 158* in 1st 'Test'. **Tests**: 3 (1995 to 1995-96); HS 28 v SA (Pt Elizabeth) 1995-96. F-c Tours: A 1996-97 (Eng A); I 1995-96 (La); SA 1995-96 (part); I 1994-95 (Eng A); P 1995-96 (Eng A). 1000 runs (4); most – 1156 (1996). HS 312 La v Derbys (Manchester) 1996 (record score at Old Trafford). Nt HS 171 v Glam (Colwyn Bay) 2002. BB 6-115 La v Surrey (Southport) 1996. Nt BB 2-28 v Warwks (Nottingham) 1999. Awards: CGT 2; BHC 2. LO HS 134 La v Notts (Manchester) 1995 (BHC). LO BB 5-15 La v Minor C (Leek) 1995 (BHC).

HARRIS, Andrew James (Hadfield CS; Glossopdale Community C), b Ashton-under-Lyne, Lancs 26 Jun 1973. 6'1". RHB, RM. Derbyshire 1994-99; cap 1996. Nottinghamshire debut/cap 2000. F-c Tour: A 1996-97 (Eng A). HS 41* v Northants (Northampton) 2002. 50 wkts (2); most – 72 (1996). BB 7-54 (11-122 match) v Northants (Nottingham) 2002. Award: CGT 1. LO HS 16* v Kent (Tunbridge Wells) 2002 (NL). LO BB 5-35 v Hants (Nottingham) 2000 (NL).

HODGKINSON, Richard (West Notts C), b Mansfield 9 Dec 1983. RHB, RFM. Nottinghamshire staff 2003 – awaiting first-class debut. LO HS – and BB 2-36 Notts CB v Oxon (Oxford) 2001.

‡**NQHUSSEY, David** John, b Morley, Perth, Australia 15 Jul 1977. Younger brother of M.E.K.Hussey (see *NORTHAMPTONSHIRE*). RHB, OB. Victoria 2002-03 to date. HS 62 Vic v Q (Brisbane) 2002-03. BB 1-6 (Vic). LO HS 118 Sussex CB v Essex CB (Chelmsford) 2001 (CGT). LO BB 3-48 Sussex CB v Glos (Horsham) 2001 (CGT).

LOGAN, Richard James (Wolverhampton GS), b Stone, Staffs 28 Jan 1980. 6'1". RHB, RMF. Northamptonshire 1999-2000. Nottinghamshire debut 2001. HS 37* v Hants (Nottingham) 2001. BB 6-93 v Derbys (Nottingham) 2001. Award: CGT 1. LO HS 24 v Northants (Northampton) 2001 (NL). LO BB 5-24 v Suffolk (Mildenhall) 2001 (CGT).

NQMacGILL, Stuart Charles Glyndwr (Christ Church GS, Perth), b Mount Lawley, W Australia 25 Feb 1971. Grandson of C.W.T. (WA 1938-39), son of T.M.D. (WA 1968-69). 6'0". RHB, LBG. W Australia 1993-94. NSW 1996-97 to date. Somerset 1997 (unregistered – 1 non-CC match). Devon 1997 to 1998 (NWT only). Nottinghamshire debut/cap 2002. **Tests** (A): 30 (1997-98 to 2003-04); HS 43 v E (Melbourne) 1998-99; BB 7-50 (12-107 match) v E (Sydney) 1998-99. **LOI** (A): 3 (1999-00); HS 1 and BB 4-19 v P (Sydney) 1999-00 – on debut. F-c Tours (A): SA 2001-02; WI 1998-99, 2002-03; P 1998-99. HS 53 NSW v S Aus (Sydney) 2001-02. Nt HS 27 v Essex (Nottingham) 2003. 50 wkts (0+2): 60 (2002-03). BB 8-111 (14-165 match) v Middx (Nottingham) 2002. LO HS 18 NSW v Vic (Melbourne) 1998-99. LO BB 5-40 NSW v ACT (Canberra) 1998-99.

McMAHON, Paul Joseph (Trinity RC CS, Nottingham; Wadham C, Oxford), b Wigan, Lancs 12 Mar 1983. 6'2". RHB, OB. Debut 2002. Oxford UCCE 2003. HS 30 v Middlesex (Lord's) 2003. BB 4-59 v Essex (Chelmsford) 2003. LO HS 0 and LO BB – (NL).

‡**NQMARTYN, Damien** Richard (Girrawheen HS), b Darwin, Australia 21 Oct 1971. 5'10". RHB, RMF, occ WK. W Australia 1990-91 to date. Leicestershire 1991 (unregistered – 1 non-CC match). Yorkshire 2003 (2 matches). **Tests**: 39 (1992-93 to 2003-04); HS 133 v SA (Johannesburg) 2001-02; BB 1-0. **LOI**: 143 (1992-93 to 2003-04); HS 144* Z (Perth) 2000-01; BB 2-21 v Z (Harare) 1999-00. F-c Tours (A): E 1993, 2001; SA 2001-02; WI 2 (Tours); NZ 1992-93, 1999-00; I 2000-01; P 2002-03 (in SL/Sharjah); SL 1992-93; Sc/Ire 1998 (Aus A). HS 238 v Glos (Leeds) 2003. BB 4-30 WA v Q (Brisbane) 1998-99 (Sheffield Shield Final). LO HS 144* (see *LOI*). LO BB 3-3 WA v V (Perth) 1992-93 (MM).

NOON, Wayne Michael (Caistor S), b Grimsby, Lincs 5 Feb 1971. 5'9". RHB, WK. Northamptonshire 1989-93. Nottinghamshire 1994; cap 1995; benefit 2003. Canterbury 1994-95. Worcs 2nd XI debut when aged 15yr 199d. F-c Tours: A 1991-92 (Nh), 1996-97 (Nt). HS 83 v Northants (Northampton) 1997. BB – LO HS 46 v Warwks (Birmingham) 1998 (BHC).

PATEL, Samit Rohit (Worksop C), b Leicester 30 Nov 1984. 5'8". RHB, SLA. Debut 2002. Notts 2nd XI debut 1999 when aged 14yr 274d. HS 55 v Lancs (Nottingham) 2003 – on CC debut. BB – LO HS 44 v Somerset (Nottingham) 2003 (NL). LO BB 2-14 v Yorks (Leeds) 2002 (NL).

NQPIETERSEN, Kevin Peter (Maritzburg C; Natal U), b Pietermaritzburg, South Africa 27 Jun 1980. British passport (English mother) – qualifies for England Sep 2004. 6'4". RHB, OB. Natal/KwaZulu-Natal 1997-98 to 1999-00. Nottinghamshire debut 2001; cap 2002. F-c Tour (Eng A): I 2003-04. 1000 (2): most – 1546 (2003). HS 254* v Middx (Nottingham) 2002. BB 4-31 v DU (Nottingham) 2003. CC BB 3-95 v Warwks (Birmingham) 2003. LO HS 147 v Somerset (Taunton) 2002 (NL). LO BB 3-39 v Warwks (Nottingham) 2001 (NL).

READ, Christopher Mark Wells (Torquay GS; Bath U), b Paignton, Devon 10 Aug 1978. 5'8". RHB, WK. Gloucestershire (L-O) 1997. Nottinghamshire debut 1998; cap 1999. Devon 1995-97. **Tests**: 8 (1999 to 2003-04); HS 38* v B (Chittagong) 2003-04. **LOI**: 23 (1999-00 to 2003-04); HS 30* v SA (Manchester) 2003. F-c Tours: SA 1998-99 (Eng A), 1999-00; WI 2000-01 (Eng A); SL 1997-98 (Eng A), 2002-03 (ECB Acad), 2003-04; Z 1998-99 (Eng A); B 2003-04; K 1997-98 (Eng A). HS 160 v Warwks (Nottingham) 1999. BB – LO HS 119* v Northants (Northampton) 2003 (NL).

SHAFAYAT, Bilal Mustapha (Greenwood Dale; Nottingham Bluecoat SFC), b Nottingham 10 Jul 1984. 5'7". RHB, RMF. Debut 2001, scoring 72 and 24 v Middx (Nottingham). Captained Eng U-19 tour of Australia 2002-03. F-c Tour (Eng A): I 2003-04. HS 105 and BB 1-22 v DU (Nottingham) 2003. CC HS 104 v Worcs (Nottingham) 2002. LO HS 66 v Somerset (Taunton) 2002 (NL). LO BB 4-35 v Somerset (Nottingham) 2002 (NL).

SHRECK, Charles Edward (Truro S), b Truro, Cornwall 6 Jan 1978. 6'7". RHB, RFM. Cornwall 1997-2002. Nottinghamshire debut 2003. Award: CGT 1. HS 19 v Essex (Chelmsford) 2003. BB 5-100 v Leics (Nottingham) 2003. LO HS 9 Cornwall v Cumb (Netherfield) 1999 (CGT). LO BB 5-19 Cornwall v Worcs (Truro) 2002 (CGT). Took 5-35 v Worcs (Nottingham) 2002 (NL) – on 1st XI debut.

‡SIDEBOTTOM, Ryan Jay (King James's GS, Almondbury), b Huddersfield, Yorks 15 Jan 1978. Son of A.Sidebottom (Yorks, OFS and England 1973-91). 6'3". LHB, LFM. Yorkshire 1997-2003; cap 2000. **Tests**: 1 (2001); HS 4 v P (Lord's) 2001; **LOI**: 2 (2001-02); HS 2*; BB 1-42 (twice). F-c Tour (Eng A): WI 2000-01. HS 54 Y v Glam (Cardiff) 1998. BB 7-97 Y v Derbys (Leeds) 2003. LO HS 30* Y v Glam (Leeds) 2002 (NL). LO BB 6-40 Y v Glam (Cardiff) 1998 (SL).

‡SINGH, Anurag (King Edward's, Birmingham; Gonville & Caius C, Cambridge), b Kanpur, India 9 Sep 1975. 5'11½". RHB, OB. Warwickshire 1995-2000. Cambridge U 1996-98; blue 1996-97-98; captain 1997-98. British U 1998 (captain). Worcestershire 2001-03. 1000 (2); most – 1167 (2002). HS 187 Wo v Glos (Bristol) 2002. BB – Awards: CGT 1; BHC 1. LO HS 123 Brit U v Somerset (Taunton) 1996 (BHC).

NQSMITH, Gregory James (Pretoria BHS; Pretoria Technikon), b Pretoria, South Africa 30 Oct 1971. ECB qualified – British passport. 6'4". RHB, LFM. N Transvaal/Northerns 1993-94 to date. Nottinghamshire debut/cap 2001. F-c Tour (SA A): E 1996. 50 wkts (2): most – 51 (2003). HS 68 NT v WP (Pretoria) 1995-96. Nt HS 44* v Sussex (Nottingham) 2001. BB 8-53 (11-74 match) v Essex (Nottingham) 2002. Awards: BHC 2. LO HS 16* v Leics (Leicester) 2002 (NL). LO BB 5-11 NT v GW (Kimberley) 1995-96.

SMITH, Will Rew (Bedford S; Collingwood C, Durham), b Luton, Beds 28 Sep 1982. 5'9". RHB. OB. Debut 2002 – awaiting CC debut. Notts 2nd XI debut 1999 when aged 16y 309d. Durham UCCE 2003. HS 38* v WI A (Nottingham) 2002 – on debut. LO HS 16 v Durham (Nottingham) 2002 (NL).

WARREN, Russell John (Kingsthorpe Upper S), b Northampton 10 Sep 1971. 6'1". RHB, OB. Northamptonshire 1992-2002; cap 1995. Nottinghamshire staff 2003. 1000 (1): 1303 (2001). HS 201* Nh v Glam (Northampton) 1996. Award: CGT 1. Nt HS 123 v Middx (Lord's) 2003. BB – LO HS 100* Nh v Ire (Northampton) 1994 (NWT).

(Having made a first-class County appearance in 2003)

D.S.Lucas left the staff having made no f-c appearances in 2003.

AFZAAL, U. – *see NORTHAMPTONSHIRE.*

ATRI, Vikram (Fernwood CS, Nottingham; Bilborough C; Loughborough U), b Hull, Yorks 9 Mar 1983. 5'7". RHB, OB. Nottinghamshire 2002-03. Notts 2nd XI debut 1999 when aged 16y 175d. Loughborough UCCE 2003. HS 98 v WI A (Nottingham) 2002. CC HS 5. LO HS 0 (CGT).

NQCAIRNS, Christopher Lance (Christchurch BHS), b Picton, New Zealand 13 Jun 1970. Son of B.L.Cairns (CD, Otago, ND and NZ 1971-86). 6'2". RHB, RFM. Nottinghamshire 1988-89, 1992-93 and 1995-96; cap 1990; limited-overs captain 2003. N Districts 1988-89. Canterbury 1990-91 to date (*occasionally*). *Wisden* 1999. **Tests** (NZ): 56 (1989-90 to 2003-04); HS 126 v I (Hamilton) 1998-99; BB 7-27 v WI (Hamilton) 1999-00. **LOI** (NZ): 180 (1990-91 to 2003-04, 7 as captain); HS 115 v I (Christchurch) 1998-99; BB 5-42 v A (Napier) 1997-98. F-c Tours (NZ): E 1999; A 1989-90, 1993-94, 1997-98, 2001-02; WI 1995-96 (part); I 1995-96, 1999-00; P 1996-97; SL 1997-98; Z 1997-98, 2000-01. 1000 runs (1): 1171 (1995). HS 126 (*see Tests*). Nt HS 115 v Middx (Lord's) 1995. 50 wkts (3); most – 56 (1992). BB 8-47 (15-83 match) v Sussex (Arundel) 1995. Awards: CGT 2; BHC 1. LO HS 143 Canterbury v Auckland (Christchurch) 1994-95. LO BB 6-37 Canterbury v Wellington (Christchurch) 1996-97.

NQELWORTHY, Steven (Chaplin HS, Gwelo; Sandown HS, Jo'burg; Witwatersrand U), b Bulawayo, Rhodesia 23 Feb 1965. 6'4". RHB, RFM. Transvaal B 1987-88. N Transvaal/ Northerns 1988-89 to date. Lancashire 1995-96 to 1996. Nottinghamshire 2003. **Tests** (SA): 4 (1998 to 2002-03); HS 48 v E (Nottingham) 1998 – on debut; BB 4-66 (8-159 match) v NZ (Wellington) 1998-99. **LOI** (SA): 39 (1997-98 to 2002-03); HS 23 v SL (Northampton) 1999; BB 3-17 v I (Sharjah) 1999-00. F-c Tours (SA): E 1998; A 2001-02; WI 1995-96 (La); NZ 1998-99; Z 1994-95 (SA A). HS 89 Northerns v Boland (Pretoria) 1997-98. UK HS 88 La v Yorks (Manchester) 1996 (non CC match). CC HS 52 Nt v Surrey (Nottingham) 2003. 50 wkts (0+1): 52 (2001-02). BB 7-65 NT v Natal (Durban) 1994-95. CC BB 5-71 Nt v Lancs (Manchester) 2003. LO HS 116* N Transvaal v GW (Pretoria) 1994-95. LO BB 4-14 La v Glos (Manchester) 1996 (BHC).

MALIK, M.N. – *see WORCESTERSHIRE.*

RANDALL, Stephen John (W Bridgford S), b Nottingham 9 Jun 1980. 5'10". RHB, OB. Debut 1999. HS 28 v Glos (Bristol) 2001. BB 2-64 v Derbys (Nottingham) 2001. LO HS 25 v Worcs (Nottingham) 2002 (NL). LO BB 3-44 v Glos (Cheltenham) 2001 (NL).

THOMAS, Aaron Courtney, b Edmonton, Middx 8 May 1985. RHB, WK. Nottinghamshire 2003 (1 non-CC match). HS – . LO HS 7* (Notts CB – CGT).

NQVETTORI, Daniel Luca (St Paul's Collegiate, Hamilton), b Epsom, Auckland, New Zealand 27 Jan 1979. 6'3". LHB, SLA. N Districts to date. **Tests** (NZ): 50 (1996-97 to 2003-04); HS 137* v P (Hamilton) 2003-04; BB 7-87 (12-149 match) v A (Auckland) 1999-00. **LOI** (NZ): 125 (1996-97 to 2003-04); HS 30 v A (Melbourne) 2001-02; BB 4-14 v SL (Dambulla) 2003. F-c Tours (NZ): E 1999; A 1997-98, 2001-02; SA 1997-98 (NZ Acad); WI 2001-02; I 1999-00, 2003-04; P 2001-02; SL 1997-98, 2002-03; Z 1997-98, 2000-01. HS 137* (*see Tests*). Nt HS 10 v Ind A (Nottingham) 2003. CC HS 0. BB 7-87 (*see Tests*). Nt BB 4-74 v Kent (Maidstone) 2003. LO HS 75 ND v CD (Napier) 2000-01 (SC). LO BB 4-14 (*see LOI*).

WELTON, Guy Edward (Healing CS; Grimsby TC; Nottingham Trent U), b Grimsby, Lincs 4 May 1978. 6'1". RHB, OB. Debut 1997. MCC YC. HS 200* v Warwks (Birmingham) 2000 – sharing unbroken 1st wkt stand of 406 with D.J.Bicknell. BB – Awards: BHC 2. LO HS 104* v Durham (Nottingham) 1999 (NL).

NOTTINGHAMSHIRE 2003

RESULTS SUMMARY

	Place	Won	Lost	Tied	Drew	No Result
County Championship (1st Division)	8th	2	8		6	
All First-Class Matches		3	9		6	
C & G Trophy	4th Round					
National League (2nd Division)	5th	9	9			
Twenty20 Cup	6th in North Group					

COUNTY CHAMPIONSHIP AVERAGES

BATTING AND FIELDING

Cap		M	I	NO	HS	Runs	Avge	100	50	Ct/St
2002	K.P.Pietersen	15	29	–	221	1488	51.31	4	10	16
–	R.J.Warren	9	18	2	123	734	45.87	3	2	9/2
1999	P.J.Franks	14	25	8	123*	729	42.88	2	1	9
1998	J.E.R.Gallian	12	23	2	116	876	41.71	3	5	15
2000	D.J.Bicknell	14	27	1	81	822	31.61	–	7	4
1993	C.L.Cairns	13	23	2	104	645	30.71	1	4	7
1999	C.M.W.Read	12	22	2	93	525	26.25	–	3	26/3
–	G.E.Welton	11	22	–	99	547	24.86	–	5	6
–	S.Elworthy	4	7	–	52	159	22.71	–	1	3
2000	U.Afzaal	7	13	–	72	264	20.30	–	1	2
–	B.M.Shafayat	11	21	–	97	422	20.09	–	3	3
1995	W.M.Noon	2	4	1	25	38	12.66	–	–	7
–	R.J.Logan	2	4	2	13*	23	11.50	–	–	–
2001	G.J.Smith	12	20	3	42	168	9.88	–	–	4
–	P.J.McMahon	2	4	–	30	38	9.50	–	–	2
2002	S.C.G.MacGill	11	18	6	27	112	9.33	–	–	2
–	C.E.Shreck	9	14	6	19	51	6.37	–	–	1
–	V.Atri	2	4	–	5	15	3.75	–	–	1
2000	A.J.Harris	8	11	1	16*	37	3.70	–	–	1

Also batted: G.D.Clough (2 matches) 0, 1*, 16 (1 ct); M.N.Malik (2) 30*, 15, 10; S.R.Patel (1) 9, 55 (1 ct); D.L.Vettori (1) 0, 0 (2 ct).

BOWLING

	O	M	R	W	Avge	Best	5wI	10wM
G.J.Smith	346.1	75	1205	50	24.10	5- 42	3	–
S.Elworthy	134.1	17	534	16	33.37	5- 71	1	–
S.C.G.MacGill	412.2	73	1408	42	33.52	6-117	2	–
C.E.Shreck	191.1	40	745	21	35.47	5-100	1	–
P.J.Franks	265.2	45	1070	25	42.80	4- 62	–	–
C.L.Cairns	184	31	755	15	50.33	3- 59	–	–
A.J.Harris	189.5	26	806	10	80.60	2- 98	–	–

Also bowled:

	O	M	R	W	Avge	Best	5wI	10wM
P.J.McMahon	40	9	142	5	28.40	4- 59		
D.L.Vettori	34.3	2	198	5	39.60	4- 74		
K.P.Pietersen	86.3	10	383	6	63.83	3- 95		

G.D.Clough 20-0-96-1; J.E.R.Gallian 29-6-91-1; R.J.Logan 14-1-94-0; M.N.Malik 57-7-227-3; S.R.Patel 8-5-10-0; B.M.Shafayat 9-0-71-0.

The First-Class Averages (pp 123–138) give the records of Nottinghamshire players in all first-class county matches (Nottinghamshire's other opponents being India A and Durham UCCE), with the exception of W.R.Smith, whose only first-class appearances were for Durham UCCE, and V.Atri and P.J.McMahon whose full county figures are as above.

NOTTINGHAMSHIRE RECORDS

FIRST-CLASS CRICKET

Highest Total	For 739-7d		v	Leics	Nottingham	1903
	V 781-7d		by	Northants	Northampton	1995
Lowest Total	For 13		v	Yorkshire	Nottingham	1901
	V 16		by	Derbyshire	Nottingham	1879
	16		by	Surrey	The Oval	1880
Highest Innings	For 312*	W.W.Keeton	v	Middlesex	The Oval	1939
	V 345	C.G.Macartney	for	Australians	Nottingham	1921

Highest Partnership for each Wicket

1st	406*	D.J.Bicknell/G.E.Welton	v	Warwicks	Birmingham	2000
2nd	398	A.Shrewsbury/W.Gunn	v	Sussex	Nottingham	1890
3rd	369	W.Gunn/J.R.Gunn	v	Leics	Nottingham	1903
4th	361	A.O.Jones/J.R.Gunn	v	Essex	Leyton	1905
5th	266	A.Shrewsbury/W.Gunn	v	Sussex	Hove	1884
6th	372*	K.P.Pietersen/J.E.Morris	v	Derbyshire	Derby	2001
7th	301	C.C.Lewis/B.N.French	v	Durham	Chester-le-St	1993
8th	220	G.F.H.Heane/R.Winrow	v	Somerset	Nottingham	1935
9th	170	J.C.Adams/K.P.Evans	v	Somerset	Taunton	1994
10th	152	E.B.Alletson/W.Riley	v	Sussex	Hove	1911
	152	U.Afzaal/A.J.Harris	v	Worcs	Nottingham	2000

Best Bowling	For	10-66	K.Smales	v	Glos	Stroud	1956
(Innings)	V	10-10	H.Verity	for	Yorkshire	Leeds	1932
Best Bowling	For	17-89	F.C.Matthews	v	Northants	Nottingham	1923
(Match)	V	17-89	W.G.Grace	for	Glos	Cheltenham	1877

Most Runs – Season		2620	W.W.Whysall	(av 53.46)	1929
Most Runs – Career		31592	G.Gunn	(av 35.69)	1902-32
Most 100s – Season		9	W.W.Whysall		1928
		9	M.J.Harris		1971
		9	B.C.Broad		1990
Most 100s – Career		65	J.Hardstaff jr		1930-55
Most Wkts – Season		181	B.Dooland	(av 14.96)	1954
Most Wkts – Career		1653	T.G.Wass	(av 20.34)	1896-1920
Most Career W-K Dismissals		957	T.W.Oates	(733 ct/224 st)	1897-1925
Most Career Catches in the Field		466	A.O.Jones		1892-1914

LIST 'A' LIMITED-OVERS CRICKET

Highest Total	CGT	344-6		v	Northumb	Jesmond	1994
	BHC	296-6		v	Kent	Nottingham	1989
	NL	329-6		v	Derbyshire	Nottingham	1993
Lowest Total	CGT	123		v	Yorkshire	Scarborough	1969
	BHC	74		v	Leics	Leicester	1987
	NL	66		v	Yorkshire	Bradford	1969
Highest Innings	CGT	149*	D.W.Randall	v	Devon	Torquay	1988
	BHC	130*	C.E.B.Rice	v	Scotland	Glasgow	1982
	NL	167*	P.Johnson	v	Kent	Nottingham	1993
Best Bowling	CGT	6-10	K.P.Evans	v	Northumb	Jesmond	1994
	BHC	6-22	M.K.Bore	v	Leics	Leicester	1980
		6-22	C.E.B.Rice	v	Northants	Northampton	1981
	NL	6-12	R.J.Hadlee	v	Lancashire	Nottingham	1980

SOMERSET

Formation of Present Club: 18 August 1875
Inaugural First-Class Match: 1882
Colours: Black, White and Maroon
Badge: Somerset Dragon
County Champions: (0); best – 2nd (Div 1) 2001
Gillette/NatWest/C & G Trophy Winners: (3) 1979, 1983, 2001
Benson and Hedges Cup Winners: (2) 1981, 1982
National League (Div 1) Winners: (0); best – 4th 2001
Sunday League Winners: (1) 1979
Twenty20 Cup Winners: 5th in Midlands/Wales/West Group 2003
Match Awards: CGT 63; BHC 70

Chief Executive: P.W.Anderson, County Ground, Taunton TA1 1JT • Tel: 01823 272946 • Fax: 01823 332395 • Email: somerset@ecb.co.uk • Web: www.somerset.cricinfo.com

First XI Coach: K.J.Shine. **Captain**: M.Burns. **Vice-Captain**: M.E.Trescothick. **Overseas Players**: N.A.M.McLean and R.T.Ponting (Reserve: J.Cox). **2004 Beneficiary**: K.A.Parsons. **Head Groundsman**: P.W.Frost. **Scorer**: G.A.Stickley. ‡ New registration. NQ Not qualified for England.

ANDREW, Gareth Mark (Ansford Community S; Richard Huish C), b Yeovil 27 Dec 1983. 6'0". LHB, RMF. Debut 2003. Somerset 2nd XI debut 1999 when aged 15y 247d. HS 11 v Yorks (Leeds) 2003. BB 3-14 v Derbys (Taunton) 2003. LO HS 23 v Hants (Southampton) 2003 (NL). LO BB 3-38 v Durham (Chester-le-St) 2003 (NL).

BLACKWELL, Ian David (Brookfield Community S), b Chesterfield, Derbys 10 Jun 1978. 6'2". LHB, SLA. Derbyshire 1997-99. Somerset debut 2000; cap 2001. **LOI**: 18 (2002-03 to 2003-04); HS 82 v I (Colombo) 2002-03; BB 3-26 v A (Adelaide) 2002-03. 1000 (1): 1160 (2003). HS 247* v Derbys (Taunton) 2003 – off 156 balls and including 204 off 98 balls in reduced post-lunch session. BB 5-49 v Hants (Southampton) 2002. Awards: CGT 1; BHC 1. LO HS 111 v Sussex (Hove) 2003 (NL). LO BB 4-24 v Kent (Taunton) 2002 (NL)

BOWLER, Peter Duncan (Scots C, Sydney, Aus; Daramalan C, Canberra, Aus; Nottingham Trent U), b Plymouth, Devon 30 Jul 1963. 6'1". RHB, OB, occ WK. Leicestershire 1986 – first to score hundred on f-c debut for Leics (100* and 62 v Hants). Tasmania 1986-87. Derbyshire 1988-94; cap 1989; scored 155* v CU (Cambridge) on debut – first instance of hundreds on debut for two counties. Somerset debut/cap 1995; captain 1997-98; benefit 2000. 1000 runs (9) inc 2000 (1): 2044 (1992). HS 241* De v Hants (Portsmouth) 1992. Sm HS 207 v Surrey (Taunton) 1996. BB 3-25 v Northants (Taunton) 1998. Awards: BHC 4. LO HS 138* De v Somerset (Derby) 1993 (SL). LO BB 3-31 De v Glos (Cheltenham) 1991 (SL).

BURNS, Michael (Walney CS), b Barrow-in-Furness, Lancs 6 Feb 1969. 6'0". RHB, RM, WK. Cumberland 1988-90. Warwickshire 1992-96. Somerset debut 1997; cap 1999; captain 2003 to date. Scored earliest hundred in UK f-c matches (160 v OU (Taunton) on 7 Apr 2000). 1000 (2): most – 1133*(2003). HS 221 v Yorks (Bath) 2001. BB 6-54 v Leics (Taunton) 2001. Awards: CGT 1; BHC 1. LO HS 115* v Middx (Taunton) 1997 (SL). LO BB 4-39 v Glos (Taunton) 1997 (SL).

76

CADDICK, Andrew Richard (Papanui HS), b Christchurch, NZ 21 Nov 1968. Son of English emigrants – qualified for England 1992. 6'5". RHB, RFM. Debut 1991; cap 1992; benefit 1999. Represented NZ in 1987-88 Youth World Cup. *Wisden* 2000. **ECB contracts 2000, 2001, 2002, 2003. Tests**: 62 (1993 to 2002-03); HS 49* v A (Birmingham) 2001; BB 7-46 v SA (Durban) 1999-00. **LOI**: 54 (1993 to 2002-03); HS 36 v A (Oval) 2001; BB 4-19 v SA (Jo'burg) 1999-00. F-c Tours: A 1992-93 (Eng A), 2002-03; SA 1999-00; WI 1993-94, 1997-98; NZ 1996-97, 2001-02; P 2000-01; SL 2000-01; Z 1996-97. HS 92 v Worcs (Worcester) 1995. 50 wkts (8) inc 100 (1): 105 (1998). BB 9-32 (12-120 match) v Lancs (Taunton) 1993. Awards: CGT 2. LO HS 39 v Hants (Taunton) 1996 (SL). LO BB 6-30 v Glos (Taunton) 1992 (NWT).

COX, Jamie (Wynyard HS; Deakin U), b Burnie, Tasmania, Australia 15 Oct 1969. 6'0". RHB, OB. Tasmania 1987-88 to date; captain 2000-01 to date. Somerset debut/cap 1999; captain 1999-2002. F-c Tours: Z 1991-92 (Aus B), 1995-96 (Tas). 1000 runs (3+2); most – 1617 (1999). HS 245 Tas v NSW (Hobart) 1999-00. Sm HS 216 v Hants (Southampton) 1999. BB 3-46 v Middx (Taunton) 1999. Awards: CGT 2. LO HS 130 v Middx (Taunton) 2003 (NL). LO BB 3-28 v Durham (Taunton) 1999 (NL).

DURSTON, Wesley John (Millfield S; University L, Worcester), b Taunton 6 Oct 1980. 5'10". RHB, OB. Debut 2002. HS 55 v WI A (Taunton) 2002 – on debut. CC HS 6. BB 1-16. LO HS 51* v Middx (Southgate) 2003 (NL). LO BB 1-32 Somerset CB v Staffs (Walsall) 2000 (CGT).

DUTCH, Keith Philip (Nower Hill HS; Weald C), b Harrow, Middlesex 21 Mar 1973. 5'10". RHB, OB. Middlesex 1993-2000. Somerset debut/cap 2001. MCC YC. HS 118 v Essex (Taunton) 2001. BB 6-62 M v Essex (Chelmsford) 2000. Sm BB 4-32 v Essex (Chelmsford) 2001. Award: CGT 1. LO HS 93 v Z (Taunton) 2003 (NL). LO BB 6-40 v Northants (Northampton) 2001 (NL).

EDWARDS, Neil James (Cape Cornwall CS; Richard Huish C), b Treliske, Cornwall 14 Oct 1983. 6'3". LHB, RM. Debut 2002. HS 160 v Hants (Taunton) 2003. BB –

‡**FRANCIS, John** Daniel (King Edward VI S, Southampton; Durham U; Loughborough U), b Bromley, Kent 13 Nov 1980. Younger brother of S.R.G.Francis. 5'11". LHB, SLA. Hampshire 2001-03. British U 2002-03. Loughborough UCCE 2003. HS 82 and BB 1-1 H v Leics (Leicester) 2002. LO HS 103* H v Northants (Southampton) 2002 (NL).

FRANCIS, Simon Richard George (Yardley Court, Tonbridge; King Edward VI S, Southampton; Durham U), b Bromley, Kent 15 Aug 1978. Elder brother of J.D.Francis. 6'2". RHB, RMF. Hampshire 1997-2000. British U 1998-99. Somerset debut 2002. F-c Tour (Eng A): I 2003-04. HS 44 v Yorks (Taunton) 2002. BB 5-73 v Warwks (Taunton) 2002. Hat trick 2003. LO HS 33* v Derbys (Taunton) 2003 (NL). LO BB 4-60 v Worcs (Worcester) 2002 (NL).

GAZZARD, Carl Matthew (Mounts Bay CS, Penzance; Richard Huish C), b Penzance, Cornwall 15 Apr 1982. 6'0". RHB, WK. Debut 2002. Cornwall 1998 to date. HS 41 v Northants (Taunton) 2003. LO HS 81 v Scot (Taunton) 2003 (NL).

‡**HUNT, Thomas** Aaron ('*Thos*') (Acton HS; St Clement Danes S), b Melbourne, Australia 19 Jan 1982. 6'2". Resident in UK since 1985 (English parents). LHB, RMF. Middlesex 2002-03 – awaiting CC debut. HS 3 (M) MB 3-43 M v CU (Cambridge) 2002 – on debut. LO HS 0 (M – NL). LO BB 1-24 (M – NL).

HILDRETH James Charles (Millfield S), b Milton Keynes, Bucks 9 Sep 1984. 5'10", RHB, RMF. Debut 2003. HS 9 v Derbys (Taunton) 2003. LO HS 30 v Lancs (Taunton) 2003 (NL). LO BB 1-44 (Somerset CB – CGT).

JOHNSON, Richard Leonard (Sunbury Manor S; S Pelthorne C), b Chertsey, Surrey 29 Dec 1974. 6'2". RHB, RFM. Middlesex 1992-2000; cap 1995. Somerset debut/cap 2001. **Tests**: 3 (2003 to 2003-04); HS 26 v SL (Galle) 2003-04; BB 6-33 v Z (Chester-le-St) 2003 on debut, including wickets with his third and fourth balls. Hit first ball in Test cricket for four. **LOI**: 10 (2003 to 2003-04); HS 10 v SA (Manchester) 2003; BB 3-22 v B (Dhaka) 2003-04. Took wicket with his second ball in LOI. F-c Tours: I 1994-95 (Eng A – part), 2001-02; SL 2003-04, B 2003-04; His Glos (Bristol) 2003 (100 off 75 balls). 50 wkts (4); most – 62 (2001). BB 10-45 M v Derbys (Derby) 1994 (second youngest to take all ten wickets in any f-c match). Sm BB 7-43 (10-75 match) v Hants (Bath) 2002. Award: CGT 1. LO HS 53 v Derbys (Derby) 2003 (NL). LO BB 5-50 M v Kent (Lord's) 1997 (NWT).

LARAMAN, Aaron William (Enfield GS), b Enfield, Middx 10 Jan 1979. 6'5". RHB, RFM. Middlesex 1998-2002. Somerset debut 2003. HS 148* v Glos (Taunton) 2003. BB 4-33 M v CU (Cambridge) 2000. CC BB 4-55 M v Northants (Northampton) 2002. Sm BB 3-20 v Glam (Taunton) 2003. LO HS 33 v Lancs (Taunton) 2003 (NL). LO BB 6-42 M v Glam (Cardiff) 2000 (NL).

NQMcLEAN, Nixon Alexei McNamara (Crapan SS, St Vincent), b Stubbs, St Vincent 20 Jul 1973. 6'4". LHB, RFM. Windward Is 1991-92 to 2000-01. Hampshire 1998-99; cap 1998. KwaZulu-Natal 2001-02 to date. Somerset debut/cap 2003. **Tests** (WI): 19 (1995-96 to 2000-01); HS 46 v P (Georgetown) 1999-00; BB 3-53 v SA (Cape Town) 1998-99. **LOI** (WI): 45 (1996-97 to 2002-03); HS 50* v Z (Canterbury) 2000; BB 3-21 v Z (Perth) 2000-01. F-c Tours (WI): E 2000; A 1996-97, 2000-01; SA 1997-98 (WI A), 1998-99. HS 76 v Glos (Taunton) 2003. 50 wkts (2): most – 65 (2003). BB 7-28 WI v FS (Bloemfontein) 1998-99. UK BB 6-101 H v Leics (Leicester) 1998. Sm BB 5-43 v Glam (Taunton) 2003. LO HS 50* (see LOI). LO BB 5-26 WI Select XI v P (St John's) 1999-00.

MUNDAY, Michael Kenneth (Truro S, Cornwall; Corpus Christi C, Oxford), b Nottingham 22 Oct 1984. 5'7½". RHB, LB. Oxford U 2003; blue 2003. Awaiting Somerset debut. Cornwall 2001-03. HS 0* (OU). BB 5-83 OU v CU (Cambridge) 2003. LO HS – and BB 1-39 Cornwall v Sussex (Truro) 2001 (CGT).

PARSONS, Keith Alan (The Castle S, Taunton; Richard Huish C), b Taunton 2 May 1973. Identical twin brother of K.J.Parsons (Somerset staff 1992-94). 6'1". RHB, RM. Debut 1992; cap 1999; benefit 2004. HS 193* v WI (Taunton) 2000. CC HS 139 v Northants (Taunton) 2001. BB 5-13 v Lancs (Taunton) 2000. Awards: CGT 2. LO HS 121 v Worcs (Taunton) 2002 (CGT). LO BB 4-43 v Surrey (Taunton) 1999 (NWT).

PARSONS, Michael (Ladymead Community S, Taunton; Richard Huish C), b Taunton 26 Nov 1984. 5'11". RHB, RMF. Somerset 1st XI debut 2002 – awaiting f-c debut. LO HS 0 (thrice). LO BB 3-70 Somerset CB v Cornwall (Camborne) 2002.

‡NQPONTING, Ricky** Thomas (Brooks HS), b Launceston, Australia 19 Dec 1974. 5'10". RHB, OB. Tasmania 1992-93 to date. Awarded Somerset cap with contract 2004. **Tests** (A): 75 (1995-96 to 2003-04); HS 257 v I (Melbourne) 2003-04; BB 1-0. **LOI** (A) : 194 (1994-95 to 2003-04, 63 as captain); HS 145 v Z (Delhi) 1997-98; BB 1-12. F-c Tours (A): E 1995 (Young Aus), 1997, 2001; SA 2001-02; WI 1994-95, 1998-99, 2002-03; NZ ; I 1996-97, 1997-98, 2000-01; P 1998-99, 2002-03 (in SL/Sharjah); SL 1999-00; Z 1995-96 (Tas), 1999-00. HS 257 (see Tests). BB 2-10 A v Bombay (Bombay) 2000-01. LO HS 145 (see LOI). LO BB 3-34 Tasmania v WA (Hobart) 1996-97 (MM).

NQSUPPIAH, Arul Vivasvan (Exeter U), b Kuala Lumpur, Malaysia 30 Aug 1983. Son of R.Suppiah (Kuala Lumpur). Brother of R.V.Suppiah (Malaysia – vice-captain). 6'0". RHB, SLA. Somerset debut 2002. Malaysia 1999-2001. HS 21 v Lancs (Taunton) 2002. BB 3-46 v WI A (Taunton) 2002. CC BB 1-44. LO HS 70 Somerset CB v Cornwall (Camborne) 2002 (CGT). LO BB 2-36 v Leics (Leicester) 2002 (NL).

TRESCOTHICK, Marcus Edward (Sir Bernard Lovell S), b Keynsham 25 Dec 1975. 6'2". LHB, RM. Debut 1993; cap 1999; joint captain 2002. **ECB contracts 2001, 2002, 2003, 2004. Tests**: 43 (2000 to 2003-04); HS 219 v SA (Oval) 2003; BB 1-34. **LOI**: 75 (2000 to 2003-04, 2 as captain); HS 137 v P.(Lord's) 2001; BB 2-7 v Z (Manchester) 2000. F-c Tours: A 2002-03; NZ 1999-00 (Eng A), 2001-02; I 2001-02; P 2000-01; SL 2000-01, 2003-04; B 1999-00 (Eng A), 2003-04. HS 219 (*see Tests*). Sm HS 190 v Middx (Taunton) 1999. BB 4-36 (inc hat trick) v Young A (Taunton) 1995. CCC BB 4-82 v Yorks (Leeds) 1998. Hat trick 1995. Awards: CGT 4; BHC 3. LO HS 137 (*see LOI*). LO BB 4-50 v Northants (Northampton) 2000 (NL).

TURNER, Robert Julian (Millfield S; Magdalene C, Cambridge), b Malvern, Worcs 25 Nov 1967. 6'1½". RHB, WK. Brother of S.J.Turner (Somerset 1984-85). Cambridge U 1988-91; blue 1988-89-90-91; captain 1991. Somerset debut 1991; cap 1994; benefit 2002. Cambridgeshire 1990. F-c Tours (Eng A): NZ 1999-00; B 1999-00. Held 7 catches in an innings v Northants (Taunton) 2001. 1000 runs (2); most – 1217 (1999). HS 144 v Kent (Taunton) 1997. BB – Award: BHC 1. LO HS 70 v Glam (Cardiff) 1996 (BHC).

WEBLEY, Thomas (King's C, Taunton; Anglia PU, Cambridge), b Bristol 2 Mar 1983. 6'1". LHB, SL. Cambridge UCCE 2003. Somerset debut 2003. Somerset 2nd XI debut 1999 when aged 16y 49d. HS 104 CU v Northants (Cambridge) 2003. Sm HS 59 v Hants (Taunton) 2003. BB 2-57 CU v Kent (Cambridge) 2003. Sm BB – LO HS (Somerset CB) 8 (CGT).

WOOD, Matthew James (Exmouth Community C; Exeter U), b Exeter, Devon 30 Sep 1980. 5'11". RHB, OB. Debut 2001. 2nd XI debut 1997 when aged 16y 345d. Devon 1998-2000. HS 196 v Kent (Taunton) 2002. BB – LO HS 88* v Durham (Taunton) 2002 (NL).

RELEASED/RETIRED continued on p 85

COUNTY CAPS AWARDED IN 2003

Derbyshire	–
Durham	–
Essex	S.A.Brant, J.M.Dakin, J.D.Middlebrook, G.R.Napier
Glamorgan	M.A.Wallace
Gloucestershire	–
Hampshire	S.M.Katich, N.Pothas
Kent	G.O.Jones, M.Muralitharan
Lancashire	C.L.Hooper, M.B.Loye, I.J.Sutcliffe, J.Wood
Leicestershire	B.J.Hodge, V.Sehwag
Middlesex	S.J.Cook, J.H.Dawes, B.L.Hutton, C.B.Keegan, A.A.Noffke
Northamptonshire	T.M.B.Bailey, J.W.Cook, P.A.Jaques
Nottinghamshire	–
Somerset	N.A.M.McLean
Surrey	J.Ormond
Sussex	T.R.Ambrose, Mushtaq Ahmed, M.J.Prior
Warwickshire	–
Worcestershire (colours)	S.J.Adshead, A.J.Hall, M.A.Harrity, M.Hayward, J.M.Kemp, S.A.Khalid, S.C.Moore, D.H.Wigley
Yorkshire	S.P.Kirby, M.J.Lumb

SOMERSET 2003

RESULTS SUMMARY

	Place	Won	Lost	Tied	Drew	No Result
County Championship (2nd Division)	**7th**	4	8		4	
All First-Class Matches		4	8		6	
C & G Trophy	4th Round					
National League (2nd Division)	**9th**	5	12			1
Twenty20 Cup	**5th in Midlands/Wales/West Group**					

COUNTY CHAMPIONSHIP AVERAGES

BATTING AND FIELDING

Cap		M	I	NO	HS	Runs	Avge	100	50	Ct/St
2001	I.D.Blackwell	13	24	2	247*	1066	48.45	3	1	6
–	A.W.Laraman	11	17	4	148*	556	42.76	1	3	4
1999	J.Cox	14	26	2	160	999	41.62	3	4	10
–	N.J.Edwards	5	9	–	160	360	40.00	1	1	1
1999	M.E.Trescothick	4	6	–	70	237	39.50	–	3	8
1999	M.Burns	16	29	2	106	897	33.22	1	7	14
1995	P.D.Bowler	8	13	1	92	372	31.00	–	4	11
1994	R.J.Turner	15	25	8	81*	502	29.52	–	3	61/4
2001	P.S.Jones	7	12	2	63	273	27.30	–	2	2
2001	R.L.Johnson	9	14	3	118	290	26.36	1	–	4
–	J.D.C.Bryant	12	21	1	73	483	24.15	–	2	8
–	M.J.Wood	11	21	1	100	472	23.60	1	2	1
–	T.Webley	6	11	1	59	208	20.80	–	1	3
2003	N.A.M.McLean	16	23	4	76	318	16.73	–	1	2
2001	K.P.Dutch	7	10	–	61	161	16.10	–	1	9
–	S.R.G.Francis	9	13	2	44	133	12.09	–	–	1
–	G.M.Andrew	5	8	3	11	36	7.20	–	–	1

Also batted: A.R.Caddick (1 match – cap 1992) 1; W.J.Durston (1) 4, 6 (2 ct); C.M.Gazzard (2) 2, 4, 41 (3 ct); G.M.Gilder (2) 12, 0*, 7*; J.C.Hildreth (1) 9, 0; P.C.L.Holloway (1 – cap 1997) 30, 11; K.A.Parsons (1 – cap 1999) 4, 6 (1 ct); A.V.Suppiah (1) 16.

BOWLING

	O	M	R	W	Avge	Best	5wI	10wM
G.M.Andrew	57	10	225	10	22.50	3-14	–	–
R.L.Johnson	310.1	70	918	34	27.00	5-64	1	–
N.A.M.McLean	521.3	113	1732	62	27.93	5-43	3	–
A.W.Laraman	252.5	55	846	24	35.25	3-20	–	–
S.R.G.Francis	302.1	66	1091	30	36.36	4-94	–	–
M.Burns	153.5	29	514	13	39.53	3-35	–	–
I.D.Blackwell	416	91	1223	30	40.76	5-96	1	–
P.S.Jones	181.3	24	824	20	41.20	5-42	1	–
Also bowled:								
A.R.Caddick	38	8	110	7	15.71	4-66	–	–
K.P.Dutch	126.1	25	428	8	53.50	3-56	–	–

P.D.Bowler 1-0-2-0; J.D.C.Bryant 1-0-8-0; J.Cox 1-0-8-0; W.J.Durston 8-1-23-1; N.J.Edwards 18.5-1-71-0; G.M.Gilder 4-0-32-0; K.A.Parsons 14.4-3-63-2; A.V.Suppiah 11-1-44-1; T.Webley 6-1-26-0; M.J.Wood 1.1-0-6-0.

The First-Class Averages (pp 123–138) give the records of Somerset players in all first-class county matches (Somerset's other opponents being the South Africans and Loughborough UCCE), with the exception of M.E.Trescothick and T.Webley whose full county figures are as above, and:

R.L.Johnson 10-14-3-118-290-26.36-1-0-5. 330.1-74-977-36-27.13-5/64-1-0.

SOMERSET RECORDS

FIRST-CLASS CRICKET

Highest Total	For 705-9d		v	Hampshire	Taunton	2003
	V 811		by	Surrey	The Oval	1899
Lowest Total	For 25		v	Glos	Bristol	1947
	V 22		by	Glos	Bristol	1920
Highest Innings	For 322	I.V.A.Richards	v	Warwicks	Taunton	1985
	V 424	A.C.MacLaren	for	Lancashire	Taunton	1895

Highest Partnership for each Wicket

1st	346	H.T.Hewett/L.C.H.Palairet	v	Yorkshire	Taunton	1892
2nd	290	J.C.W.MacBryan/M.D.Lyon	v	Derbyshire	Burton upon T	1924
3rd	319	P.M.Roebuck/M.D.Crowe	v	Leics	Taunton	1984
4th	310	P.W.Denning/I.T.Botham	v	Glos	Taunton	1980
5th	235	J.C.White/C.C.C.Case	v	Glos	Taunton	1927
6th	265	W.E.Alley/K.E.Palmer	v	Northants	Northampton	1961
7th	279	R.J.Harden/G.D.Rose	v	Sussex	Taunton	1997
8th	172	I.V.A.Richards/I.T.Botham	v	Leics	Leicester	1983
	172	A.R.K.Pierson/P.S.Jones	v	N Zealanders	Taunton	1999
9th	183	C.H.M.Greetham/H.W.Stephenson	v	Leics	Weston-s-Mare	1963
	183	C.J.Tavaré/N.A.Mallender	v	Sussex	Hove	1990
10th	163	I.D.Blackwell/N.A.M.McLean	v	Derbyshire	Taunton	2003

Best Bowling (Innings)	For	10- 49	E.J.Tyler	v	Surrey	Taunton	1895
	V	10- 35	A.Drake	for	Yorkshire	Weston-s-Mare	1914
Best Bowling (Match)	For	16- 83	J.C.White	v	Worcs	Bath	1919
	V	17-137	W.Brearley	for	Lancashire	Manchester	1905

Most Runs – Season	2761	W.E.Alley	(av 58.74)	1961
Most Runs – Career	21142	H.Gimblett	(av 36.96)	1935-54
Most 100s – Season	11	S.J.Cook		1991
Most 100s – Career	49	H.Gimblett		1935-54
Most Wkts – Season	169	A.W.Wellard	(av 19.24)	1938
Most Wkts – Career	2166	J.C.White	(av 18.02)	1909-37
Most Career W-K Dismissals	1007	H.W.Stephenson	(698 ct/309 st)	1948-64
Most Career Catches in the Field	381	J.C.White		1909-37

LIST 'A' LIMITED-OVERS CRICKET

Highest Total	CGT	413-4		v	Devon	Torquay	1990
	BHC	349-7		v	Ireland	Taunton	1997
	NL	377-9		v	Sussex	Hove	2003
Lowest Total	CGT	58		v	Middlesex	Southgate	2000
	BHC	98		v	Middlesex	Lord's	1982
	NL	58		v	Essex	Chelmsford	1977
Highest Innings	CGT	162*	C.J.Tavaré	v	Devon	Torquay	1990
	BHC	177	S.J.Cook	v	Sussex	Hove	1990
	NL	175*	I.T.Botham	v	Northants	Wellingborough	1986
Best Bowling	CGT	7-15	R.P.Lefebvre	v	Devon	Torquay	1990
	BHC	7-24	Mushtaq Ahmed	v	Ireland	Taunton	1997
	NL	6-24	I.V.A.Richards	v	Lancashire	Manchester	1983

SURREY

Formation of Present Club: 22 August 1845
Inaugural First-Class Match: 1864
Colours: Chocolate
Badge: Prince of Wales' Feathers
County Champions (since 1890): (18) 1890, 1891, 1892, 1894, 1895, 1899, 1914, 1952, 1953, 1954, 1955, 1956, 1957, 1958, 1971, 1999, 2000, 2002
Joint Champions: (1) 1950
Gillette/NatWest/C & G Trophy Winners: (1) 1982
Benson and Hedges Cup Winners: (3) 1974, 1997, 2001
National League (Div 1) Winners: (1) 2003
Sunday League Winners: (1) 1996
Twenty20 Cup Winners: (1) 2003
Match Awards: CGT 57; BHC 76

Chief Executive: P.C.J.Sheldon, Kennington Oval, London, SE11 5SS • Tel: 020 7582 6660 • Fax: 020 7735 7769 • E-mail: enquiries@surreyccc.com • Web: www.surreycricket.com

First XI Coach: S.J.Rixon. **Captain**: J.N.Batty. **Vice-Captain**: *tba*. **Overseas Players**: Azhar Mahmood and Saqlain Mushtaq. **2004 Beneficiary**: A.J.Hollioake. **Head Groundsman**: W.H.Gordon. **Scorer**: K.R.Booth. ‡ New registration. NQ Not qualified for England.

NQAZHAR MAHMOOD SAGAR (F.G. No. 1 HS, Islamabad), b Multan, Pakistan 28 Feb 1975. 5'11". RHB, RFM. Islamabad 1993-94 to 1997-98, 2001-02. United Bank 1996-97. Rawalpindi 1998-99. PIA 1999-00 to 2001-02. **Tests** (P): 21 (1997-98 to 2001); HS 136 v SA (Johannesburg) 1997-98; BB 4-50 v E (Lord's) 2001. Scored 128* and 50* v SA (Rawalpindi) 1997-98 on debut. **LOI** (P): 134 (1996-97 to 2003-04); HS 67 v I (Adelaide) 1999-00; BB 6-18 v WI (Sharjah) 1999-00. F-c Tours (P): E 2001; A 1999-00; SA 1997-98; I 1998-99; SL 2000-01; Z 1997-98. HS 136 (*see Tests*). Sy HS 98 v Notts (Nottingham) 2003. 50 wkts (0+1): 59 (1996-97). BB 8-61 v Lancs (Oval) 2002. LO HS 100* P v Aus A (Perth) 1999-00. LO BB 6-18 (*see LOI*).

BATTY, Jonathan Neil (Wheatley Park S, Oxon; Repton S; Durham U; Keble C, Oxford), b Chesterfield, Derbys 18 Apr 1974. 5'10". RHB, WK. Minor C 1994. Comb U 1995. Oxford U 1996; blue 1996. Surrey debut 1997; cap 2001; captain 2004. Oxfordshire 1993-96. HS 168* v Essex (Chelmsford) 2003. BB 1-21. LO HS 55* v Somerset (Taunton) 2003 (CGT).

BENNING, James Graham Edward (Beacon S; Chesham S; Caterham S), b Mill Hill, N London 4 May 1983. 6'0". RHB, RM. Debut 2003. Buckinghamshire 2000-01. HS 47 and BB 1-39 v Essex (Oval) 2003. LO HS 25 and BB 4-43 v Leics (Oval) 2003 (NL).

BICKNELL, Martin Paul (Robert Haining County SS), b Guildford 14 Jan 1969. Younger brother of D.J.Bicknell (*see NOTTINGHAMSHIRE*). 6'3". RHB, RFM. Debut 1986; cap 1989; benefit 1997. *Wisden* 2000. **Tests**: 4 (1993 to 2003); HS 15 v SA (Leeds) 2003; BB 4-84 v SA (Oval) 2003. **LOI**: 7 (1990-91); HS 31* v A (Perth) 1990-91; BB 3-55 v NZ (Christchurch) 1990-91. F-c Tours: A 1990-91; SA 1993-94 (Eng A); Z 1989-90 (Eng A). HS 141 v Essex (Chelmsford) 2003. 50 wkts (11); most – 72 (2001). BB 9-45 v CU (Oval) 1988. CC BB 9-47 (16-119 match) v Leics (Guildford) 2000. Begins 2004 season with 982 f-c wickets. Awards: BHC 3. LO HS 66* v Northants (Oval) 1991 (NWT). LO BB 7-30 v Glam (Oval) 1999 (NL).

BROWN, Alistair Duncan (Caterham S), b Beckenham, Kent 11 Feb 1970. 5'10". RHB, occ LB. Debut 1992; cap 1994; benefit 2002. **LOI**: 16 (1996 to 2001); HS 118 v I (Manchester) 1996. 1000 runs (6); most – 1382 (1993). HS 295* v Leics (Oakham) 2000 – record score (all levels) in Rutland. BB 1-11. Awards: CGT 1; BHC 4. LO HS 268 v Glam (Oval) 2002 (CGT) – world record 1-o score (160 balls, 12 sixes, 30 fours). LO BB 3-39 v Notts (Nottingham) 2000 (NL).

BUTCHER, Mark Alan (Trinity S; Archbishop Tenison's S, Croydon), b Croydon 23 Aug 1972. Son of A.R.Butcher (Surrey, Glamorgan and England 1972-92); brother of G.P.Butcher (Glamorgan 1994-98; Surrey 1999-2001). 5'11". LHB, RM/OB. Debut 1992; cap 1996. **ECB contracts 2002, 2003, 2004. Tests**: 62 (1997 to 2003-04, 1 as captain); HS 173* v I (Leeds) 2001; BB 4-42 v A (Birmingham) 2001. F-c Tours: A 1996-97 (Eng A), 1998-99, 2002-03; SA 1999-00; WI 1997-98; NZ 2001-02; I 2001-02; SL 2003-04; B 2003-04. 1000 runs (7); most – 1604 (1996). HS 259 v Leics (Leicester) 1999. BB 5-86 v Lancs (Manchester) 2000. Awards: CGT 2; BHC 3. LO HS 104 v Yorks (Oval) 2003 (NL). LO BB 3-23 v Sussex (Oval) 1992 (SL).

CLARKE, Rikki (Broadwater SS; Godalming C), b Orsett, Essex 29 Sep 1981. 6'4". RHB, RFM. Debut 2002 – scoring 107* v CU (Cambridge). YC 2002. **Tests**: 2 (2003-04); HS 55 and BB 2-7 v B (Chittagong) 2003-04. **LOI**: 11 (2003 to 2003-04); HS 37 v SA (Birmingham) 2003; BB 2-28 v B (Dhaka) 2003-04. F-c Tours: SL 2002-03 (ECB Acad); B 2003-04. HS 153* v Somerset (Taunton) 2002. BB 4-21 v Leics (Leicester) 2003. LO HS 98* v Derbys (Derby) 2002 (NL). LO BB 3-48 v Glos (Oval) 2003 (NL).

NO**DERNBACH, Jade** Winston (St John the Baptist S), b Johannesburg, South Africa 3 Mar 1986. 6'1½". RHB, RMF. EU (Italian) passport. UK resident since 1998. Debut 2003 when aged 17 – awaiting CC debut. 'Sir Jack Hobbs Fair Play Award' 2003. HS 3 and BB 1-74 v Ind A (Oval) 2003.

‡**HODD, Andrew** John (Bexhill C), b Chichester, Sussex 12 Jan 1984. RHB, WK. Sussex 2003 (1 match) – awaiting CC debut. HS – Sx v Z (Hove) 2003. LO HS 3 (Sx).

HOLLIOAKE, Adam John (St Joseph's C, Sydney; St Patrick's C, Ballarat; St George's C, Weybridge; Surrey Tutorial C), b Melbourne, Australia 5 Sep 1971. Elder brother of the late B.C.Hollioake (Surrey and England 1996-2001). 5'11". RHB, RMF. Debut 1993, scoring 13 and 123 v Derbys (Ilkeston); cap 1995; captain 1997-2003; benefit 2004. Qualified for England 1992. *Wisden* 2002. Retires after 2004 season. **Tests**: 4 (1997 to 1997-98); HS 45 and BB 2-31 v A (Nottingham) 1997 – on debut. **LOI**: 35 (1996 to 1999, 14 as captain); HS 83* v SA (Dhaka) 1998-99; BB 4-23 v P (Birmingham) 1996 – on debut. F-c Tours: A 1996-97 (Eng A – captain); WI 1997-98. 1000 runs (2); most – 1522 (1996). HS 208 v Leics (Oval) 2002. BB 5-62 v Glam (Swansea) 1998. Awards: CGT 2; BHC 1. LO HS 117* v Sussex (Hove) 2002 (CGT). LO BB 6-17 v Kent (Canterbury) 2003 (NL).

MURTAGH, Timothy James (John Fisher S; St Mary's C), b Lambeth 2 Aug 1981. Nephew of A.J.Murtagh (Hampshire and E Province 1973-7). 6'0". LHB, RFM. British U 2000-03. Surrey debut 2001. HS 22* and BB 6-86 Brit U v P (Nottingham) 2001. Sy HS 22 and Sy BB 5-39 v Leics (Oval) 2002. LO HS 14* v Essex (Chelmsford) 2002 (NL). LO BB 4-31 v Warwks (Croydon) 2001 (NL).

NEWMAN, Scott Alexander (Trinity S, Croydon; Coulsdon C; Brighton U), b Epsom 3 Nov 1979. 6'2". LHB, RM. Debut 2002 – scoring 99 v Hants (Oval) 2002. F-c Tour (Eng A): I 2003-04. HS 183 v Leics (Oval) 2002. BB – LO HS 49 Surrey CB v Lincs (Bourne) 2001 (CGT).

ORMOND, James (St Thomas More S, Nuneaton), b Walsgrave, Coventry, Warwks 20 Aug 1977. 6'3". RHB, RFM. Leicestershire 1995-2001; cap 1999. Surrey debut 2002; cap 2003. **Tests**: 2 (2001 to 2001-02); HS 18 v A (Oval) 2001; BB 1-70. F-c Tours: NZ 2001-02; I 2001-02; SL 1997-98 (Eng A); K 1997-98 (Eng A). HS 50* Le v Warwks (Leicester) 1999. Sy HS 47 v Middx (Guildford) 2003. 50 wkts (3); most – 52 (1999). BB 6-33 (9-62 match) Le v Somerset (Leicester) 1998. Sy BB 6-34 v LU (Oval) 2003. Sy CC BB 5-45 v Notts (Nottingham) 2003. Hat trick (4 wkts in 6 balls) 2003. Awards: BHC 2. LO HS 18* Le v Somerset (Lord's) 2001 (CGT). LO BB 4-12 Le v Middx (Leicester) 1998 (SL).

RAMPRAKASH, Mark Ravin (Gayton HS; Harrow Weald SFC), b Bushey, Herts 5 Sep 1969. 5'9". RHB, RM. Middlesex 1987-2000; cap 1990; captain 1997-99. Surrey debut 2001 – scoring 146 v Kent (Oval); cap 2002. YC 1991. **ECB contract 2000. Tests**: 52 (1991 to 2001-02); HS 154 v WI (Bridgetown) 1997-98; BB 1-2. **LOI**: 18 (1991 to 2001-02); HS 51 v WI (Pt-of-Spain) 1997-98; BB 3-28 v Z (Harare) 2001-02. F-c Tours: A 1994-95 (*part*), 1998-99; SA 1995-96; WI 1991-92 (Eng A), 1993-94, 1997-98; NZ 1991-92, 2001-02; I 1994-95 (Eng A), 2001-02; P 1990-91 (Eng A). 1000 runs (13) inc 2000 (1): 2258 (1995). HS 279* v Notts (Croydon) 2003. BB 3-32 v Glam (Lord's) 1998. Sy BB – . Awards: CGT 3; BHC 4. LO HS 147* M v Worcs (Lord's) 1990 (SL). LO BB 5-38 M v Leics (Lord's) 1993 (SL).

SAKER, Neil Clifford (Raynes Park HS; Nescot C), b Tooting, London 20 Sep 1984. 6'4". RHB, RFM. Debut 2003. HS 5. BB 1-71.

SALISBURY, Ian David Kenneth (Moulton CS), b Northampton 21 Jan 1970. 5'11". RHB, LBG. Sussex 1989-96; cap 1991. Surrey debut 1997; cap 1998. MCC YC. YC 1992. *Wisden* 1992. **Tests**: 15 (1992 to 2000-01); HS 50 v P (Manchester) 1992; BB 4-163 v WI (Georgetown) 1993-94. **LOI**: 4 (1992-93 to 1993-94); HS 5; BB 3-41 v WI (Pt-of-Spain) 1993-94. F-c Tours: WI 1991-92 (Eng A), 1993-94; I 1992-93; 1994-95 (Eng A); P 1990-91 (Eng A), 1995-96 (Eng A), 2000-01; SL 1990-91 (Eng A). HS 101* v Leics (Oval) 2003. 50 wkts (6); most – 87 (1992). BB 8-60 (12-91 match) v Somerset (Oval) 2000. Awards: CGT 1; BHC 2. LO HS 48* Sx v Glam (Swansea) 1995 (SL). LO BB 5-30 Sx v Leics (Leicester) 1992 (SL).

SAMPSON, Philip James (Pretoria BHS, SA), b Manchester 6 Sep 1980. 6'1". RHB, RFM. Debut 2002. Buckinghamshire 1999. HS 42 v CU (Cambridge) 2002 – on debut. CC HS 32* v Essex (Oval) 2003. BB 3-52 v Leics (Oval) 2002. LO HS 16 v Middx (Croydon) 2002 (NL). LO BB 3-42 v Kent (Oval) 2002 (BHC).

[NO]**SAQLAIN MUSHTAQ** (Govt Muslim League HS, M.A.O. College, Lahore), b Lahore, Pakistan 29 Dec 1976. Brother of Sibtain Mushtaq (Lahore 1988-89). 5'11". RHB, OB. Islamabad 1994-95 to 2001-02. Surrey debut 1997; cap 1998. *Wisden* 1999. **Tests** (P): 48 (1995-96 to 2003); HS 101* v NZ (Christchurch) 2000-01; BB 8-164 v E (Lahore) 2000-01 (all eight wickets to fall). **LOI** (P): 169 (1995-96 to 2003-04); HS 37* v A (Brisbane) 1999-00; BB 5-20 v E (Rawalpindi) 2000-01, 2 hat tricks. F-c Tours (P): E 1996, 2001; A 1995-96, 1996-97, 1999-00; SA 1997-98, 2002-03; WI 1999-00; NZ 2000-01; I 1998-99, SL 1996-97; Z 1997-98, 2002-03; B 1998-99, 2001-02. HS 101* (*see Tests*). Sy HS 69 v Middx (Lord's) 2003. 50 wkts (5+1); most – 66 (2000). BB 8-65 (11-107 match) v Derbys (Oval) 1988. Took 7-11 (including 7-5 in 34 balls) v Derbys (Oval) 2000. Three hat tricks, all for Surrey 1997 and 1999 (2). Awards: CGT 2. LO HS 38* v Yorks (Leeds) 2001 (NL). LO BB 5-20 (*see LOI*).

SHAHID, Nadeem (Ipswich S), b Karachi, Pakistan 23 Apr 1969. 6'0". RHB, LB. Essex 1989-94. Surrey debut 1995; cap 1998. Suffolk 1988. 1000 runs (1): 1003 (1990). HS 150 v Sussex (Oval) 2002. BB 3-91 Ex v Surrey (Oval) 1990. Sy BB 3-93 v SA A (Oval) 1996. LO HS 109* v Notts (Nottingham) 2000 (NL). LO BB 3-30 v Bucks (Oval) 1998 (NWT).

THORPE, Graham Paul (Weydon CS; Farnham SFC), b Farnham 1 Aug 1969. 5'10". LHB, RM. Debut 1988; cap 1991; benefit 2000. *Wisden* 1997. **ECB contracts 2001, 2002. Tests**: 83 (1993 to 2003-04); HS 200* v NZ (Christchurch) 2001-02; scored 114* v A (Nottingham) 1993 on debut. **LOI**: 82 (1993 to 2002, 3 as captain); HS 89 v Z (Brisbane) 1994-95 and 89 v H (Peshawar) 1995-96; BB 2-15 v I (Manchester) 1996. F-c Tours: A 1992-93 (Eng A), 1994-95, 1998-99 (*part*); SA 1995-96; WI 1991-92 (Eng A), 1993-94, 1997-98; NZ 1996-97, 2001-02; I 2001-02 (*part*); P 1990-91 (Eng A), 2000-01; SL 1990-91 (Eng A), 2000-01, 2003-04; Z 1989-90 (Eng A), 1996-97; B 2003-04. 1000 runs (9); most – 1895 (1992). HS 223* Eng XI v S Aus (Adelaide) 1998-99. Sy HS 222 v Glam (Oval) 1997. BB 4-40 v A (Oval) 1993. CC BB 2-14 v Derbys (Oval) 1996. Awards: CGT 4; BHC 1. LO HS 145* v Lancs (Oval) 1994 (NWT). LO BB 3-21 v Somerset (Oval) 1991 (SL).

TUDOR, Alex Jeremy (St Mark's S, Hammersmith; City of Westminster C), b West Brompton, London 23 Oct 1977. 6'5". RHB, RF. Debut 1995; cap 1999. YC 1999. **Tests**: 10 (1998-99 to 2002-03); HS 99* v NZ (Birmingham) 1999 - record score by an England 'night-watchman'; BB 5-44 v A (Nottingham) 2001. **LOI**: 3 (2002); HS 6; BB 2-30 v I (Oval) 2002. F-c Tours: A 1998-99, 2002-03; SA 1999-00; WI 2000-01 (Eng A). HS 116 v Essex (Oval) 2001. BB 7-48 v Lancs (Oval) 2000. LO HS 29* v Essex (Oval) 1995 (SL). LO BB 4-26 v Hants (Oval) 2000 (NL).

RELEASED/RETIRED
(Having made a first-class County appearance in 2003)

ROSE, Franklyn Albert (Ocho Rios SS; Holmwood THS), b St Ann's Bay, Jamaica 1 Feb 1972. RHB, RF. 6'5". Jamaica 1992-93 to date. Northamptonshire 1998. Gauteng 2001-02 to date. Surrey 2003 (1 match). **Tests** (WI): 19 (1996-97 to 2000); HS 69 v Z (Kingston) 1999-00; BB 7-84 v SA (Durban) 1998-99. **LOI** (WI): 27 (1996-97 to 2000); HS 30 v Z (Canterbury) 2000; BB 5-23 v P (Kingstown) 1999-00. F-c Tours (WI): E 2000; A 1996-97; SA 1998-99; NZ 1999-00; P 1997-98. HS 96 Jamaica v Leeward Is (Anguilla) 1996-97. CC HS 36 Sy and Sy BB 3-101 v Kent (Canterbury) 2003. 50 wkts (1+1): most – 71 (1996-97). BB 7-39 (11-90 match) Nh v Worcs (Worcester) 1998. Award: BHC 1. LO HS 37 Jamaica v USA (Discovery Bay) 2000-01. LO BB 5-14 Nh v Minor C (Luton) 1998.

SCOTT, B.J.M. – *see MIDDLESEX.*

STEWART, Alec James (Tiffin S), b Merton 8 Apr 1963. Son of M.J.Stewart (Surrey and England 1954-72). 5'11". RHB, WK. Debut 1981; cap 1985; captain 1992-97; benefit 1994; testimonial 2003. *Wisden* 1992. MBE 1998. OBE 2003. **ECB contracts 2000, 2001, 2003. Tests**: 133 – Eng record (1989-90 to 2003, 15 as captain); HS 190 v P (Birmingham) 1992. **LOI**: 170 – Eng record (1989-90 to 2002-03, 41 as captain); HS 116 v I (Sharjah) 1997-98. F-c Tours (C=captain): A 1990-91, 1994-95, 1998-99C, 2002-03; SA 1995-96, 1999-00; WI 1989-90, 1993-94, 1997-98; NZ 1991-92, 1996-97; I 1992-93; P 2000-01; SL 1992-93C, 2000-01; Z 1996-97. 1000 runs (8); most – 1665 (1986). HS 271* v Yorks (Oval) 1997. BB 1-7. Held 11 catches (equalling world f-c match record) v Leics (Leicester) 1989. Awards: CGT 5; BHC 6. LO HS 167* v Somerset (Oval) 1994 (BHC).

TODD, Matthew Julian (Halliford S), b Chertsey 25 May 1983. 6'3". RHB, OB. Surrey 2003 (1 non-CC match). HS 6* and BB 1-92 v Ind A (Oval) 2003.

WARD, I.J. – *see SUSSEX.*

SOMERSET RELEASED/RETIRED (continued from p 79)
(Registered players who made a first-class County appearance in 2003)

M.P.L.Bulbeck left the staff having made no f-c appearances in 2003.

BRYANT, J.D.C. – *see DERBYSHIRE.*

GILDER, Gary Michael (Northwood BHS; Natal TC); b Salisbury, Rhodesia 6 Jul 1974. 5'11". RHB, LFM. Natal/Kwa-Zulu Natal 1994-57 to 2001-02. RHB, LFM. Somerset 2003. F-c Tours (SA A): E 1996; SL 1998-99. HS 39 KZ-Natal v Gauteng (Johannesburg) 1998-99. Sm HS 12 v Northants (Northampton) 2003. BB 8-22 SA A v Worcs (Worcester) 1996. Sm BB 1-56. LO HS 36 KZ-Natal v Easterns (Benoni) 2000-01. LO BB 6-25 Natal v North West (Fochville) 1997-98.

HOLLOWAY, Piran Christopher Laity (Millfield S; Taunton S; Loughborough U), b Helston, Cornwall 1 Oct 1970. 5'8". LHB, WK. Warwickshire 1988-93. Somerset 1994-2003; cap 1997. Cornwall 2002. Awards: CGT 1; BHC 1. HS 168 v Middx (Uxbridge) 1996. BB – LO HS 117 v Glos (Taunton) 1997 (SL).

JONES, P.S. – *see NORTHAMPTONSHIRE.*

SURREY 2003

RESULTS SUMMARY

	Place	Won	Lost	Tied	Drew	No Result
County Championship (1st Division)	3rd	6	3		7	
All First-Class Matches		6	3		9	
C & G Trophy	Quarter-Finalist					
National League (1st Division)	1st	12	3			1
Twenty20 Cup	Winners					

COUNTY CHAMPIONSHIP AVERAGES

BATTING AND FIELDING

Cap		M	I	NO	HS	Runs	Avge	100	50	Ct/St
2002	M.R.Ramprakash	14	22	4	279*	1239	68.83	5	2	7
1996	M.A.Butcher	6	8	–	144	527	65.87	2	2	10
1985	A.J.Stewart	6	8	1	98	451	64.42	–	5	20
1991	G.P.Thorpe	11	18	2	156	880	55.00	1	7	8
2001	J.N.Batty	10	19	4	168*	794	52.93	2	4	25/2
–	R.Clarke	9	14	2	139	513	42.75	2	1	9
–	Azhar Mahmood	10	13	2	98	441	40.09	–	4	17
1989	M.P.Bicknell	11	11	3	141	318	39.75	1	–	1
2000	I.J.Ward	15	24	1	158	856	37.21	3	2	8
1998	I.D.K.Salisbury	14	18	4	101*	455	32.50	1	1	6
1998	Saqlain Mushtaq	14	15	2	69	421	32.38	–	4	4
1995	A.J.Hollioake	13	18	–	122	567	31.50	1	3	10
1999	A.J.Tudor	6	7	1	55	177	29.50	–	1	1
1994	A.D.Brown	12	19	2	74	481	28.29	–	5	10
2003	J.Ormond	12	14	5	47	198	22.00	–	–	2
1998	N.Shahid	2	4	–	67	72	18.00	–	1	–
–	T.J.Murtagh	5	8	4	21	61	15.25	–	–	–

Also batted (1 match each): J.G.E.Benning 18, 47; S.A.Newman 9, 0 (2 ct); F.A.Rose 1, 36; N.C.Saker 1, 0; P.J.Sampson 3, 32*; B.J.M.Scott 58*, 5 (6 ct).

BOWLING

	O	M	R	W	Avge	Best	5wI	10wM
M.P.Bicknell	326.4	83	1023	39	26.23	5- 42	3	–
Azhar Mahmood	262.2	48	994	34	29.23	5- 78	1	–
J.Ormond	366.1	65	1363	44	30.97	5- 45	2	–
Saqlain Mushtaq	471	100	1363	41	33.26	5- 46	3	–
I.D.K.Salisbury	371.1	60	1224	33	37.09	4-116	–	–
T.J.Murtagh	115	13	475	11	43.18	4-130	–	–
R.Clarke	130.1	19	607	12	50.58	4- 21	–	–
A.J.Tudor	144	24	532	10	53.20	3- 56	–	–

Also bowled: J.G.E.Benning 8-1-39-1; A.D.Brown 9.4-3-22-1; M.A.Butcher 12-1-44-3; A.J.Hollioake 68.2-8-265-4; M.R.Ramprakash 8-4-9-0; F.A.Rose 28-8-101-3; N.C.Saker 20.1-1-103-1; P.J.Sampson 19.5-1-101-4; A.J.Stewart 2.3-0-23-0; G.P.Thorpe 11-1-73-1; I.J.Ward 16.3-0-76-0.

The First-Class Averages (pp 123–138) give the records of Surrey players in all first-class county matches (Surrey's other opponents being India A and Loughborough UCCE), with the exception of A.J.Stewart whose full county figures are as above, and:

M.P.Bicknell 12-12-4-141-421-52.62-2-0-2ct. 351.4-88-1111-40-27.77-5/42-3-0.
M.A.Butcher 7-9-0-144-572-63.55-2-2-10ct. 14-1-46-3-15.33-2/20.
T.J.Murtagh 6-9-4-21-73-14.60-0-0-0ct. 132.5-13-556-11-50.54-4/130.
G.P.Thorpe 12-19-2-156-895-52.64-1-7-8ct. 11-1-73-1-73.00-1/73.

86

SURREY RECORDS

FIRST-CLASS CRICKET

Highest Total	For 811		v	Somerset	The Oval	1899
	V 863		by	Lancashire	The Oval	1990
Lowest Total	For 14		v	Essex	Chelmsford	1983
	V 16		by	MCC	Lord's	1872
Highest Innings	For 357*	R.Abel	v	Somerset	The Oval	1899
	V 366	N.H.Fairbrother	for	Lancashire	The Oval	1990

Highest Partnership for each Wicket

1st	428	J.B.Hobbs/A.Sandham	v	Oxford U	The Oval	1926
2nd	371	J.B.Hobbs/E.G.Hayes	v	Hampshire	The Oval	1909
3rd	413	D.J.Bicknell/D.M.Ward	v	Kent	Canterbury	1990
4th	448	R.Abel/T.W.Hayward	v	Yorkshire	The Oval	1899
5th	308	J.N.Crawford/F.C.Holland	v	Somerset	The Oval	1908
6th	298	A.Sandham/H.S.Harrison	v	Sussex	The Oval	1913
7th	262	C.J.Richards/K.T.Medlycott	v	Kent	The Oval	1987
8th	205	I.A.Greig/M.P.Bicknell	v	Lancashire	The Oval	1990
9th	168	E.R.T.Holmes/E.W.J.Brooks	v	Hampshire	The Oval	1936
10th	173	A.Ducat/A.Sandham	v	Essex	Leyton	1921

Best Bowling	For	10-43	T.Rushby	v	Somerset	Taunton	1921
(Innings)	V	10-28	W.P.Howell	for	Australians	The Oval	1899
Best Bowling	For	16-83	G.A.R.Lock	v	Kent	Blackheath	1956
(Match)	V	15-57	W.P.Howell	for	Australians	The Oval	1899

Most Runs – Season	3246	T.W.Hayward	(av 72.13)	1906
Most Runs – Career	43554	J.B.Hobbs	(av 49.72)	1905-34
Most 100s – Season	13	T.W.Hayward		1906
	13	J.B.Hobbs		1925
Most 100s – Career	144	J.B.Hobbs		1905-34
Most Wkts – Season	252	T.Richardson	(av 13.94)	1895
Most Wkts – Career	1775	T.Richardson	(av 17.87)	1892-1904
Most Career W-K Dismissals	1221	H.Strudwick	(1035 ct/186 st)	1902-27
Most Career Catches in the Field	605	M.J.Stewart		1954-72

LIST 'A' LIMITED-OVERS CRICKET

Highest Total	CGT	438-5		v	Glamorgan	The Oval	2002
	BHC	361-8		v	Notts	The Oval	2001
	NL	375-4		v	Yorkshire	Scarborough	1994
Lowest Total	CGT	74		v	Kent	The Oval	1967
	BHC	89		v	Notts	Nottingham	1984
	NL	64		v	Worcs	Worcester	1978
Highest Innings	CGT	268	A.D.Brown	v	Glamorgan	The Oval	2002
	BHC	167*	A.J.Stewart	v	Somerset	The Oval	1994
	NL	203	A.D.Brown	v	Hampshire	Guildford	1997
Best Bowling	CGT	7-33	R.D.Jackman	v	Yorkshire	Harrogate	1970
	BHC	5-15	S.G.Kenlock	v	Ireland	The Oval	1995
	NL	7-30	M.P.Bicknell	v	Glamorgan	The Oval	1999

SUSSEX

Formation of Present Club: 1 March 1839
Substantial Reorganisation: August 1857
Inaugural First-Class Match: 1864
Colours: Dark Blue, Light Blue and Gold
Badge: County Arms of Six Martlets
County Champions: (1) 2003
Gillette/NatWest/C & G Trophy Winners: (4) 1963, 1964, 1978, 1986
Benson and Hedges Cup Winners: (0); best – semi-finalist 1982, 1999
National League (Div 1) Winners: (0); best – 9th 2000
Sunday League Winners: (1) 1982
Twenty20 Cup Winners: 2nd in South Group 2003
Match Awards: CGT 60; BHC 64

Chief Executive: H.H.Griffiths, County Ground, Eaton Road, Hove BN3 3AN • Tel: 01273 827100 • Fax: 01273 771549 • Email: info@sussexcricket.co.uk • Web: www.sussexcricket.co.uk

First XI Coach: P.Moores. **Captain**: C.J.Adams. **Vice-Captain**: R.J.Kirtley. **Overseas Players**: M.W.Goodwin and Mushtaq Ahmed. **2004 Beneficiary**: K.Greenfield (testimonial). **Head Groundsman**: D.J.Traill. **Scorer**: J.F.Hartridge. ‡ New registration. NQ Not qualified for England.

ADAMS, Christopher John (Repton S), b Whitwell, Derbyshire 6 May 1970. 6'0". RHB, RM/OB. Derbyshire 1988-97; cap 1992. Sussex debut/cap 1998; captain 1998 to date; benefit 2003. **Tests**: 5 (1999-00); HS 31 v SA (Cape Town) 1999-00; BB 1-42. **LOI**: 5 (1998 to 1999-00); HS 42 v SA (Cape Town) 1999-00. F-c Tour: SA 1999-00. 1000 runs (5); most – 1742 (1996). HS 239 De v Hants (Southampton) 1996. Sx HS 217 v Lancs (Manchester) 2002. BB 4-28 v Durham (Chester-le-St) 2001. Awards: CGT 4; BHC 6. LO HS 163 v Middx (Arundel) 1999 (NL). LO BB 5-16 v Middx (Hove) 1998 (SL).

NQAMBROSE, Timothy Raymond (Merewether HS, NSW; TAFE C), b Newcastle, NSW, Australia 1 Dec 1982. ECB qualified – British/EU passport. 5'7". RHB, WK. Debut 2001; cap 2003. HS 149 v Yorks (Leeds) 2002. BB – Award: CGT 1. LO HS 95 v Bucks (Beaconsfield) 2002 (CGT).

COTTEY, Phillip Anthony (Bishopston CS, Swansea), b Swansea, Glamorgan 2 Jun 1966. 5'4". RHB, OB. Glamorgan 1986-98; cap 1992. Sussex debut/cap 1999. E Transvaal 1991-92. F-c Tours (Gm): SA 1995-96; Z 1990-91, 1994-95. 1000 runs (8); most – 1543 (1996). HS 203 and BB 4-49 Gm v Leics (Swansea) 1996. Sx HS 188 v Warwks (Hove) 2003. Sx BB – . LO HS 96 Gm v Sussex (Hove) 1998 (BHC). LO BB 4-56 Gm v Essex (Chelmsford) 1996 (SL).

NQDAVIS, Mark Jeffrey Gronow (Grey HS; Pretoria U), b Port Elizabeth, South Africa 10 Oct 1971. ECB qualified – British/EU passport. 6'2". RHB, OB. N Transvaal/Northerns 1990-91 to date. MCC 1999 and 2000. Sussex debut 2001; cap 2002. HS 168 v Middx (Hove) 2003. BB 8-37 (12-84 match) NT B v W Transvaal (Potchefstroom) 1994-95. Sx BB 6-97 v Surrey (Hove) 2002. Award: BHC 1. LO HS 37 v Hants (Hove) 2003 (NL). LO BB 4-14 v Lancs (Manchester) 2003 (NL).

[NQ]**GOODWIN, Murray** William (Newton Moore HS, Bunbury, WA), b Salisbury, Rhodesia 11 Dec 1972. Younger brother of D.G.Goodwin (Zimbabwe 1986-97 to 1989-90). 5'9". Emigrated to Australia in Nov 1986. Gained Australian citizenship in Sep 1997. RHB, LB. W Australia 1994-95 to 1996-97, 2000-01 to date. Mashonaland 1997-98 to 1998-99. Sussex debut/cap 2001. Holland 1997. **Tests** (Z): 19 (1997-98 to 2000); HS 166* v P (Bulawayo) 1997-98. **LOI** (Z): 71 (1997-98 to 2000); HS 112* v WI (Chester-le-St) 2000; BB 1-12. F-c Tours (Z): E 2000, SA 1999-00; WI 1999-00; NZ 1997-98; P 1998-99; SL 1997-98. 1000 (3); most – 1654 (2001). HS 335* (Sussex record) v Leics (Hove) 2003. BB 2-23 Z v Lahore City (Lahore) 1998-99. Sx BB – . Awards: BHC 2. LO HS 167 WA v NSW (Perth) 2000-01 (MC) – Australian l-o record. LO BB 1-9 Mashonaland v Eng A (Harare) 1998-99.

GREEN, Jeremy Arthur Graham (Lancing C), b Cuckfield 17 Sep 1984. 6'2". RHB, RMF. Non-contracted player awaiting f-c debut. LO HS 7 v WI A (Hove) 2002.

HOPKINSON, Carl Daniel (Brighton C), b Brighton 14 Sep 1981. 5'11". RHB, RM. Debut 2002. HS 33 and BB 1-35 v Warwks (Hove) 2002 – on debut. LO HS 67* and BB 3-19 v Scot (Edinburgh) 2003 (NL).

INNES, Kevin John (Weston Favell Upper S), b Wellingborough, Northants 24 Sep 1975. 5'10". RHB, RM. Northamptonshire 2nd XI debut 1990 (aged 14yr 8m – Nh record). Northamptonshire 1994-2001. Sussex debut 2002. HS 103* v Notts (Horsham) 2003 – when a nominated substitute for R.J.Kirtley. BB 4-41 v Surrey (Hove) 2002. LO HS 55 Nh v Worcs (Worcester) 2000 (NL). LO BB 5-41 v Middx (Lord's) 2003 (NL).

KIRTLEY, Robert **James** (Clifton C), b Eastbourne 10 Jan 1975. 6'0". RHB, RFM. Debut 1995; cap 1998. Mashonaland 1996-97. **Tests**: 4 (2003 to 2003-04); HS 12 v SL (Colombo) 2003-04; BB 6-34 v SA (Nottingham) 2003 on debut. **LOI**: 10 (2001-02 to 2003-04); HS 1 (*twice*); BB 2-33 v Z (Harare) 2001-02 on debut, and 2-33 v B (Dhaka) 2003-04. F-c Tours: NZ 1999-00 (Eng A); SL 2003-04; B 1999-00 (Eng A). HS 59 v Durham (Eastbourne) 1998. 50 wkts (6); most – 75 (2001). BB 7-21 v Hants (Southampton) 1999. Took 5-53 (7-88 match) for Mashonaland v Eng XI (Harare) 1996-97. Award: CGT 1. LO HS 30* v Middx (Lord's) 2003 (CGT). LO BB 5-33 v Essex (Chelmsford) 2002 (BHC).

LEWRY, Jason David (Durrington HS, Worthing), b Worthing 2 Apr 1971. 6'2". LHB, LFM. Debut 1994; cap 1996; benefit 2002. F-c Tour: Z 1998-99 (Eng A). HS 70 v Essex (Colchester) 2003. 50 wkts (4); most – 62 (1998). BB 8-106 v Leics (Hove) 2003. 2 hat tricks (1998, 2001). LO HS 16 v Lancs (Manchester) 2001 (CGT). LO BB 4-29 v Somerset (Bath) 1995 (SL).

MARTIN-JENKINS, Robin Simon Christopher (Radley C; Durham U), b Guildford, Surrey 28 Oct 1975. Son of C.D.A.Martin-Jenkins (*Times* Chief Cricket Correspondent/ BBC Commentator). 6'5". RHB, RFM. Debut 1995; cap 2000. British U 1996. 1000 (1): 1008 (2002). HS 205* v Somerset (Taunton) 2002. BB 7-51 v Leics (Horsham) 2002. Award: BHC 1. LO HS 68* v Northants (Hove) 2003 (NL). LO BB 4-22 v Kent (Canterbury) 2002 (BHC).

‡[NQ]**MOHAMMAD AKRAM** AWAN, b Islamabad, Pakistan 10 Sep 1972. 6'2". RHB, RFM. Rawalpindi 1992-93 to 1998-99, 2001-02 to date. Allied Bank 1996-97 to 2000-01. Northamptonshire 1997. Essex 2003. **Tests** (P): 9 (1995-96 to 2001-02); HS 10* and BB 5-138 v A (Perth) 1999-00. **LOI** (P): 23 (1995-96 to 2000-01; HS 7*; BB 2-28 v I (Toronto) 1997. F-c Tours (P): E 1996; A 1995-96. HS 28 v Durham (Northampton) 1997. BB 8-49 Ex (10-142 match) v Surrey (Oval) 2003. LO HS 33 Allied Bank v Faisalabad (Faisalabad) 1998-99. LO BB 4-19 Nh v Surrey (Northampton) 1997 (SL)

MONTGOMERIE, Richard Robert (Rugby S; Worcester C, Oxford), b Rugby, Warwks 3 Jul 1971. 5'10½". RHB, OB. Oxford U 1991-94; blue 1991-92-93-94; captain 1994; half blues for rackets and real tennis. Northamptonshire 1991-98; cap 1995. Sussex debut/cap 1999. F-c Tour: Z 1994-95 (Nh). 1000 runs (4); most – 1704 (2001). HS 196 v Hants (Hove) 2002. BB 1-0. Award: CGT 1. LO HS 129* v Z (Hastings) 2000.

[NO]**MUSHTAQ AHMED** (Mahmoodia HS, Sahiwal), b Sahiwal, Pakistan 28 Jun 1970. 5'5". RHB, LBG. Multan 1986-87, 1988-89, 1990-91. United Bank 1987-88 to 1996-97. Islamabad 1994-95. Lahore 1996-97, 2000-01. Peshawar 1998-99. National Bank 1999-00 to date. REDCO 1999-00. Somerset 1993-95, 1997-98; cap 1993. Surrey 2002 (2 matches). Sussex debut/cap 2003. *Wisden* 1996. **Tests** (P): 52 (1989-90 to 2003-04); HS 59 v SA (Rawalpindi) 1997-98; BB 7-56 (10-171 match) v NZ (Christchurch) 1995-96. **LOI** (P): 144 (1988-89 to 2003-04); HS 34* v SA (Colombo) 2000-01; BB 5-36 v I (Toronto) 1996-97. F-c Tours (P): E 1992, 1996; A 1989-90, 1991-92, 1992-93, 1995-96, 1996-97, 1999-00; SA 1997-98; WI 1992-93, 1999-00; NZ 1992-93, 1993-94, 1995-96, 2000-01; I 1998-99; SL 1994-95, 1996-97, 2000-01; Z 1997-98. HS 90 Sm v Sussex (Taunton) 1993. Sx HS 60 v Lancs (Hove) 2003. 50 wkts (5+2) inc 100 (1): 103 (2003). BB 9-93 Multan v Peshawar (Sahiwal) 1990-91. Sx BB 7-85 (11-140 match) v Warwks (Hove) 2003. Awards: NWT 2; BHC 2. LO HS 41 Sm v Durham (Taunton) 1998 (SL). LO BB 7-24 Sm v Ire (Taunton) 1997 (BHC).

NASH, Christopher David (Collyers SFC; Loughborough U), b Cuckfield 19 May 1983. 5'11". RHB, OB. Sussex debut 2002 – no appearances 2003. Loughborough UCCE 2003. HS 60 LU v Leics (Leicester) 2003. BB 1-46 (LU). Sx HS 0* and BB 1-81 v Warwks (Birmingham) 2002 – on debut.

PRIOR, Matthew James (Brighton C), b Johannesburg, South Africa 24 Feb 82. 6'2". RHB, WK. Debut 2001; cap 2003. F-c Tour (Eng A): I 2003-04. 1000 (1): 1006 (2003). HS 153* v Essex (Colchester) 2003. LO HS 73 v Essex (Horsham) 2002 (SL).

TURK, Neil Richard Keith (Sackville S, E Grinstead; Exeter U), b Cuckfield 28 Apr 1983. 6'0". LHB, RM. Awaiting f-c debut. LO HS 36 v Essex (Chelmsford) 2002 (NL). LO BB –

[‡NO]**VOROS, Jason** Alexander, b Canberra, Australia 31 Dec 1976. LHB, LFM. Hungarian passport – EU qualified 1 May 2004. Awaiting f-c debut. LO HS 11* ACT v Q (Brisbane) 1998-99 (MM). LO BB 3-28 ACT v Tasmania (Canberra) 1998-99 (MM).

[‡]**WARD, Ian** James (Millfield S), b Plymouth, Devon 30 Sep 1972. 5'8½". LHB, RM. Surrey 1992, 1996-2003; cap 2001. **Tests**: 5 (2001); HS 39 v P (Lord's) 2001 – on debut. F-c Tours (Eng A): WI 2000-01; NZ 1999-00; B 1999-00. 1000 runs (2): most 1759 (2002) – including 114, 112, 156 and 118 in successive innings. HS 168* Sy v Kent (Canterbury) 2002. BB 1-1 (Sy – *twice*). Award: CGT 1. LO HS 108 Sy v Staffs (Stone) 2003 (CGT). LO BB 2-27 Sy v Sussex (Hove) 2002 (BHC).

[‡]**WRIGHT, Luke** James (Belvoir HS; Ratcliffe C; Loughborough U), b Grantham, Lincs 7 Mar 1985. 5'11". Younger brother of A.S.Wright (Leicestershire 2001-02). RHB, RM. Leicestershire 2003 (one f-c match). HS 11* and BB – Le v Sussex (Hove) 2003 – on debut. LO HS 16 Leics CB v Kent CB (Hinckley) 2001 (CGT). LO BB –

YARDY, Michael Howard (William Parker S, Hastings), b Pembury, Kent 27 Nov 1980. 6'0". LHB, LM. Debut 2000. HS 93 v Surrey (Oval) 2002. BB 1-13. LO HS 59 v Middx (Hove) 2001 (BHC). LO BB 3-30 v Warwks (Hove) 2002 (BHC).

RELEASED/RETIRED
(Having made a first-class County appearance in 2003)

S.Rashid left the staff having made no f-c appearances in 2003.

HODD, A.D. – *see SURREY.*

HUTCHISON, P.M. – *see MIDDLESEX.*

TAYLOR, B.V. – *see HAMPSHIRE.*

[NO]**ZUIDERENT** Bastiaan (*'Bas'*) (Erasmiaans Gymnasium, Rotterdam; Amsterdam U), b Utrecht, Holland 3 Mar 1977. 6'3". RHB, OB. Debut 2001. Holland 1994 to date. **LOI** (H): 13 (1995-96 to 2002-03); HS 54 v E (Peshawar) 1995-96. HS 122 v Notts (Hove) 2001. Award: BHC 1. LO HS 102* v Hants (Southampton) 2001 (BHC).

SUSSEX 2003

RESULTS SUMMARY

	Place	Won	Lost	Tied	Drew	No Result
County Championship (1st Division)	**1st**	10	4		2	
All First-Class Matches		10	4		3	
C & G Trophy	4th Round					
National League (2nd Division)	**8th**	6	12			
Twenty20 Cup	**2nd in South Group**					

COUNTY CHAMPIONSHIP AVERAGES
BATTING AND FIELDING

Cap		M	I	NO	HS	Runs	Avge	100	50	Ct/St
2001	M.W.Goodwin	16	28	3	335*	1496	59.84	4	5	10
2003	M.J.Prior	16	24	3	153*	1006	47.90	4	3	28
1999	P.A.Cottey	15	25	–	188	1149	45.96	3	7	8
2003	T.R.Ambrose	15	26	3	93*	931	40.47	–	9	29/7
2000	R.S.C.Martin-Jenkins	16	25	3	121*	811	36.86	1	5	7
1998	C.J.Adams	16	27	–	190	966	35.77	4	2	18
1998	R.J.Kirtley	11	13	7	40*	207	34.50	–	–	3
1999	R.R.Montgomerie	16	28	2	105	884	34.00	1	7	22
2003	Mushtaq Ahmed	16	19	2	60	456	26.82	–	3	3
2002	M.J.G.Davis	10	12	2	168	259	25.90	1	–	4
	K.J.Innes	7	11	3	103*	182	22.75	1	–	1
	B.V.Taylor	7	7	4	35*	55	18.33	–	–	–
1996	J.D.Lewry	11	15	3	70	215	17.91	–	1	4

Also batted: P.M.Hutchison (4 matches) 18, 5, 0; M.H.Yardy (2) 0, 69, 47 (3 ct).

BOWLING

	O	M	R	W	Avge	Best	5wI	10wM
Mushtaq Ahmed	836.3	163	2539	103	24.65	7- 85	10	5
J.D.Lewry	315.2	71	1020	41	24.87	8-106	3	1
R.J.Kirtley	430.2	95	1403	49	28.63	6- 26	2	–
B.V.Taylor	214.1	60	617	21	29.38	4- 42	–	–
R.S.C.Martin-Jenkins	364	82	1258	31	40.58	3- 9	–	–
M.J.G.Davis	220	42	703	14	50.21	3- 44	–	–

Also bowled:
K.J.Innes   74   11   297   7   42.42   2- 18   –   –
C.J.Adams 1-0-1-0; P.A.Cottey 13-1-59-0; M.W.Goodwin 3-0-17-0; P.M.Hutchison 77-12-311-3; R.R.Montgomerie 3-0-9-1; M.H.Yardy 27-3-89-0.

The First-Class Averages (pp 123–138) give the records of Sussex players in all first-class county matches (Sussex's other opponents being the Zimbabweans), with the exception of C.D.Nash whose only first-class appearances were for Loughborough UCCE, and R.J.Kirtley whose full county figures are as above.

SUSSEX RECORDS

FIRST-CLASS CRICKET

Highest Total	For 705-8d		v	Surrey	Hastings	1902
	V 726		by	Notts	Nottingham	1895
Lowest Total	For 19		v	Surrey	Godalming	1830
	19		v	Notts	Hove	1873
	V 18		by	Kent	Gravesend	1867
Highest Innings	For 335*	M.W.Goodwin	v	Leics	Hove	2003
	V 322	E.Paynter	for	Lancashire	Hove	1937

Highest Partnership for each Wicket

1st	490	E.H.Bowley/J.G.Langridge	v	Middlesex	Hove	1933
2nd	385	E.H.Bowley/M.W.Tate	v	Northants	Hove	1921
3rd	298	K.S.Ranjitsinhji/E.H.Killick	v	Lancashire	Hove	1901
4th	326*	J.Langridge/G.Cox	v	Yorkshire	Leeds	1949
5th	297	J.H.Parks/H.W.Parks	v	Hampshire	Portsmouth	1937
6th	255	K.S.Duleepsinhji/M.W.Tate	v	Northants	Hove	1930
7th	344	K.S.Ranjitsinhji/W.Newham	v	Essex	Leyton	1902
8th	291	R.S.C.Martin-Jenkins/M.J.G.Davis	v	Somerset	Taunton	2002
9th	178	H.W.Parks/A.F.Wensley	v	Derbyshire	Horsham	1930
10th	156	G.R.Cox/H.R.Butt	v	Cambridge U	Cambridge	1908

Best Bowling	For 10- 48	C.H.G.Bland	v	Kent	Tonbridge	1899
(Innings)	V 9- 11	A.P.Freeman	for	Kent	Hove	1922
Best Bowling	For 17-106	G.R.Cox	v	Warwicks	Horsham	1926
(Match)	V 17- 67	A.P.Freeman	for	Kent	Hove	1922

Most Runs – Season	2850	J.G.Langridge	(av 64.77)		1949
Most Runs – Career	34152	J.G.Langridge	(av 37.69)		1928-55
Most 100s – Season	12	J.G.Langridge			1949
Most 100s – Career	76	J.G.Langridge			1928-55
Most Wkts – Season	198	M.W.Tate	(av 13.47)		1925
Most Wkts – Career	2211	M.W.Tate	(av 17.41)		1912-37
Most Career W-K Dismissals	1176	H.R.Butt	(911 ct/265 st)		1890-1912
Most Career Catches in the Field	779	J.G.Langridge			1928-55

LIST 'A' LIMITED-OVERS CRICKET

Highest Total	CGT	384-9		v	Ireland	Belfast	1996
	BHC	316-3		v	Essex	Chelmsford	2000
	NL	312-8		v	Hampshire	Portsmouth	1993
Lowest Total	CGT	49		v	Derbyshire	Chesterfield	1969
	BHC	61		v	Middlesex	Hove	1978
	NL	59		v	Glamorgan	Hove	1996
Highest Innings	CGT	158	R.K.Rao	v	Derbyshire	Derby	1997
	BHC	157*	M.G.Bevan	v	Essex	Chelmsford	2000
	NL	163	C.J.Adams	v	Middlesex	Arundel	1999
Best Bowling	CGT	6- 9	A.I.C.Dodemaide	v	Ireland	Downpatrick	1990
	BHC	5- 8	Imran Khan	v	Northants	Northampton	1978
	NL	7-41	A.N.Jones	v	Notts	Nottingham	1986

WARWICKSHIRE

Formation of Present Club: 8 April 1882
Substantial Reorganisation: 19 January 1884
Inaugural First-Class Match: 1894
Colours: Dark Blue, Gold and Silver
Badge: Bear and Ragged Staff
County Champions: (5) 1911, 1951, 1972, 1994, 1995
Gillette/NatWest/C & G Trophy Winners: (5) 1966, 1968, 1989, 1993, 1995
Benson and Hedges Cup Winners: (2) 1994, 2002
National League (Div 1) Winners: (0); best – 3rd 2001, 2002
Sunday League Winners: (3) 1980, 1994, 1997
Twenty20 Cup Winners: finalist 2003
Match Awards: CGT 73; BHC 69

Chief Executive: D.L.Amiss MBE, County Ground, Edgbaston, Birmingham, B5 7QU • Tel: 0121 446 4422 • Fax: 0121 446 4544 • Email: info@thebears.co.uk • Web: www.thebears.co.uk

Director of Coaching/First XI Coach: R.J.Inverarity. **Captain**: N.V.Knight. **Vice-Captain**: D.R.Brown. **Overseas Players**: G.B.Hogg and H.H.Streak (Reserve: D.Pretorius). **2004 Beneficiary**: N.V.Knight. **Head Groundsman**: S.J.Rouse. **Scorer**: D.E.Wainwright. ‡ New registration. ᴺᑫ Not qualified for England.

ALI, Moeen Munir, b Birmingham 18 Jun 1987. Brother of Kadeer Ali and cousin of Kabir Ali of Worcestershire. 6'0". LHB, OB. Warwickshire staff 2003 when aged 15. Awaiting 1st XI debut.

BELL, Ian Ronald (Princethorpe C), b Walsgrave-on-Sowe 11 Apr 1982. 5'9". RHB, RM. Debut 1999; cap 2001. F-c Tour (Eng A): WI 2000-01 (*part*;) SL 2002-03 (ECB Acad). HS 135 v Derbys (Derby) 2001. BB 4-12 v Ind A (Birmingham) 2003. CC BB 3-79 v Notts (Birmingham) 2003. Awards: BHC 2. LO HS 125 v Essex (Chelmsford) 2003 (NL).

BROWN, Douglas Robert (Alloa Academy; W London IHE), b Stirling, Scotland 29 Oct 1969. 6'2". RHB, RFM. Scotland 1989. Warwickshire debut 1991-92 (SA tour); cap 1995. Wellington 1995-96. **LOI**: 9 (1997-98); HS 21 v WI (Bridgetown) 1997-98; BB 2-28 v WI (Sharjah) 1997-98. F-c Tours (Eng A): SA 1991-92, 1994-95; SL 1997-98 (Eng A). 1000 (1): 1028 (2003). HS 203 v Sussex (Hove) 2000. 50 wkts (3); most – 81 (1997). BB 8-89 (11-154 match) F-C Counties XI v Pak A (Chelmsford) 1997. Wa BB 7-66 v Durham (Chester-le-St) 1999. Awards: CGT 1; BHC 1. LO HS 108 v Essex (Birmingham) 2003 (CGT). LO BB 5-31 v Worcs (Worcester) 1997 (BHC).

ᴺᑫ**CARTER, Neil** Miller (Hottentots Holland HS; Cape Technicon), b Cape Town, South Africa 29 Jan 1975. ECB qualified – British passport. 6'2". LHB, LFM. Boland 1999-00 to 2000-01. Warwickshire debut 2001. HS 103 v Sussex (Hove) 2002 – completed maiden hundred off 67 balls. BB 6-63 Boland v GW (Kimberley) 2000-01. Wa BB 5-75 v Surrey (Birmingham) 2003. Award: CGT 1. LO HS 75 v Leics (Birmingham) 2003 (NL). LO BB 5-31 v Durham (Birmingham) 2002 (NL).

CLIFFORD, Jeffrey Ian (*not I.J.*) (Park Hall SFC), b Birmingham 12 Oct 1982. 5'6". RHB, WK. Debut 2002. No appearances 2003. HS 7. LO HS 5* (CGT).

FROST, Tony (James Brinkley HS; Stoke-on-Trent C), b Stoke-on-Trent, Staffs 17 Nov 1975. 5'11". RHB, WK. Debut 1997; cap 1999. HS 111* v OU (Oxford) 1998. CC HS 103 v Yorks (Birmingham) 2002. BB – LO HS 47 v Beds (Luton) (CGT).

GILES, Ashley Fraser (George Abbot S, Guildford), b Chertsey, Surrey 19 Mar 1973. 6'3". RHB, SLA. Debut 1993; cap 1996. **ECB contracts 2001, 2002, 2003, 2004. Tests**: 30 (1998 to 2003-04): HS 52 v Z (Lord's) 2003; BB 5-67 v I (Ahmedabad) 2001-02. **LOI**: 35 (1997 to 2003-04): HS 21* v NZ (Dunedin) 2001-02; BB 5-57 v I (Delhi) 2001-02. F-c Tours: A 1996-97 (Eng A), 2002-03 (*part*); NZ 2001-02; I 2001-02; P 2000-01; SL 1997-98 (Eng A), 2000-01, 2003-04; B 2003-04; K 1997-98 (Eng A). HS 128* v Sussex (Hove) 2000. 50 wkts (2); most – 64 (1996). BB 8-90 (12-135 match) v Northants (Northampton) 2000. Awards: CGT 2; BHC 1. LO HS 107 v Derbys (Birmingham) 2000 (NWT). LO BB 5-21 v Norfolk (Birmingham) 1997 (NWT).

‡NQHOGG, George Bradley, b Narrogin, W Australia 6 Feb 1971. LHB, SLC. W Australia 1993-94 to date. **Tests** (A): 4 (1996-97 to 2003-04): HS 17* v WI (Port-of-Spain) 2002-03; BB 2-40 v WI (Georgetown) 2002-03. **LOI** (A): 41 (1996-97 to 2003-04); HS 71* v E (Melbourne) 2002-03; BB 3-31 v B (Cairns) 2003. F-c Tours (A): WI 2002-03; I 1996-97. HS 111* WA v NSW (Sydney) 1995-96. BB 5-53 WA v NSW (Sydney) 1999-00. LO HS 71* (*see LOI*). LO BB 4-50 WA v Tasmania (Hobart) 2001-02 (IC).

JONES, Huw Rhys (Trinity S; Warwick S; Brookes U, Oxford), b Oxford 23 Nov 1980. 5'11". RHB, LB. Oxford UCCE 2001-03. Warwickshire summer contract – awaiting county f-c debut. HS 97 OU v Worcs (Oxford) 2002. LO HS 72 Warwks CB v Leics (Coventry) 2002 (CGT).

KNIGHT, Nicholas Verity (Felsted S; Loughborough U), b Watford, Herts 28 Nov 1969. 6'0". LHB, occ RM. Essex 1991-94; cap 1994. Warwickshire debut 1994-95 (SA tour); cap 1995; captain 2004; benefit 2004. **Tests**: 17 (1995 to 2001); HS 113 v P (Leeds) 1996. **LOI**: 100 (1996 to 2002-03); HS 125* v P (Nottingham) 1996. F-c Tours: SA 1994-95 (Wa), 1999-00 (*part*); NZ 1996-97; I 1994-95 (Eng A); SL 1997-98 (Eng A – captain); P 1995-96 (Eng A); Z 1996-97; K 1997-98 (Eng A – captain). 1000 runs (4); most – 1520 (1996). HS 255* (carried bat) v Hants (Birmingham) 2002. BB 1-61. Awards: CGT 4; BHC 4. LO HS 151 v Somerset (Birmingham) 1995 (NWT). LO BB 1-14 (SL).

MEES, Thomas (Worcester RGS; King Edward VII C, Stourbridge; Brookes U, Oxford), b Wolverhampton, Staffs 8 Jun 1981. 6'3". RHB, RMF. Oxford UCCE 2001-03. Herefordshire 1999. Warwickshire summer contract – awaiting 1st XI debut. HS 36* OU v Hants (Oxford) 2003. BB 6-64 OU v Middx (Oxford) 2001. Award: CGT 1. LO HS (Wa CB) 4* (CGT). LO BB 3-19 Warwks CB v Cambs (March) 2001 (CGT).

OSTLER, Dominic Piers (Princethorpe C; Solihull TC), b Solihull 15 Jul 1970. 6'3". RHB, occ RM. Debut 1990; cap 1991; benefit 1999. F-c Tours: SA 1992-93 (Wa); P 1995-96 (Eng A). 1000 runs (6); most – 1284 (1991). HS 225 v Yorks (Birmingham) 2002. BB 1-46. Awards: CGT 2; BHC 1. LO HS 134* v Glos (Birmingham) 2001 (NL). LO BB 1-4 (NWT).

PENNEY, Trevor Lionel (Prince Edward S, Salisbury), b Salisbury, Rhodesia 12 Jun 1968. 6'0". RHB, RM. Qualified for England 1992. Boland 1991-92. Warwickshire debut 1991-92 (SA tour); UK debut v CU (Cambridge) 1992, scoring 102*; cap 1994; benefit 2003. No f-c appearances 2002. Mashonaland 1993-94; 1997-98 to date. F-c Tours (Wa): SA 1991-92, 1992-93, 1994-95; Z 1993-94. 1000 runs (2); most – 1295 (1996). HS 151 v Middx (Lord's) 1992. BB 3-18 Mashonaland v Mashonaland U-24 (Harare) 1993-94. Wa BB 1-40 (Z tour). CC BB – . Awards: CGT 3. LO HS 90 v Cornwall (St Austell) 1996 (NWT). LO BB 1-8 (NWT).

PIPER, Keith John (Haringey Cricket C), b Leicester 18 Dec 1969. 5'6". RHB, WK. Warwickshire debut 1989; cap 1992; benefit 2001. F-c Tours (Wa): SA 1991-92, 1992-93, 1994-95; I 1994-95 (Eng A); P 1995-96 (Eng A); Z 1993-94. HS 116* v Durham (Birmingham) 1994. BB 1-57. LO HS 38* v Leics (Birmingham) 1999 (NL).

POWELL, Michael James (Lawrence Sheriff S, Rugby), b Bolton, Lancs 5 Apr 1975. 5'11". RHB, RM. Debut 1996; cap 1999; captain 2001-03. Griqualand West 2001-02. F-c Tour (Eng A): WI 2000-01. 1000 runs (1): 1046 (2000). HS 236 v OU (Oxford) 2001. CC HS 145 v Northants (Northampton) 2002. BB 2-16 v OU (Oxford) 1998. CC BB 2-29 v Somerset (Taunton) 2002. Award: BHC 1. LO HS 101* v Northants (Birmingham) 2002 (BHC). LO BB 5-40 v Kent (Canterbury) 2002 (CGT).

NQPRETORIUS, Dewald (Dr Viljoen HS), b Pretoria, South Africa 6 Dec 1977. 6'3". RHB, RF. Free State 1997-98 to date. Durham 2003. **Tests** (SA): 4 (2001-02 to 2003); HS 9; BB 4-115 v E (Birmingham) 2003. F-c Tours (SA): E 2003; Sc/Ire 1999 (SA A). HS 43 FS v WP (Bloemfontein) 1998-99. UK HS 16 Du v Glos (Chester-le-St) 2003. BB 6-49 SA A v Ind A (Bloemfontein) 2001-02. UK BB 4-15 Du v Yorks (Leeds) 2003. LO HS 7*. LO BB 4-31 Du v Somerset (Taunton) 2003 (NL).

RICHARDSON, Alan (Alleyne's HS; Stafford CFE; Durham U), b Newcastle-under-Lyme, Staffs 6 May 1975. 6'2". RHB, RMF. Derbyshire 1995 (one match). Warwickshire debut 1999, cap 2002. Staffordshire 1996-98. HS 91 v Hants (Birmingham) 2002 – adding 214 for 10th wicket with N.V.Knight. BB 8-46 v Sussex (Birmingham) 2002. LO HS 18 v Surrey (Oval) (NL). LO BB 5-35 v Staffs (Stone) 2002 (CGT).

SPIRES, James Ashley S. ('*Jamie*') (Solihull S), b Solihull 12 Nov 1979. 6'0". RHB, SLA. Debut 2001. No appearances 2003. HS 37* v Sussex (Hove) 2002. BB 5-165 v Yorks (Birmingham) 2002. LO HS – and BB (Warwks CB) 1-33 (CGT).

NQSTREAK, Heath Hilton (Falcon C), b Bulawayo, Rhodesia 16 Mar 1974. 6'1". Son of D.H.Streak (Rhodesia 1976-77 to 1978-79). RHB, RFM. Debut for Zimbabwe B v Kent xz(Harare) 1992-93. Matabeleland 1993-94 to date. Hampshire 1995. **Tests** (Z): 57 (1993-94 to 2003-04, 19 as captain); HS 127* v WI (Harare) 2003-04; BB 6-87 v E (Lord's) 2003. **LOI** (Z): 180 (1993-94 to 2003-04, 65 as captain; HS 79* v NZ (Auckland) 2000-01; BB 5-32 v I (Bulawayo) 1996-97. F-c Tours (Z) (C=captain): E 1993, 2000, 2003C; A 1994-95, 2003-04C; WI 1999-00; NZ 1995-96, 1997-98, 2000-01C; I 2000-01C, 2001-02; P 1993-94, 1998-99; SL 1996-97, 1997-98, 2001-02; B 2001-02. HS 131 and BB 7-69 Matabeleland v Mashonaland CD (Bulawayo) 1995-96. CC HS 38 H v Worcs (Southampton) 1995. 50 wkts (1): 53 (1995). CC BB 4-40 H v Leics (Basingstoke) 1995. LO HS 79* (*see LOI*). LO BB 5-32 (*see LOI*).

TAHIR, Naqaash (Moseley S; Spring Hill C), b Birmingham 14 Nov 1983. 5'10", RHB, RFM. Staff 2001 – awaiting 1st XI debut.

‡TAYLOR, Stephen Andrew (Charlton SS, Wellington), b Shrewsbury, Shropshire 17 Dec 1985. 6'3". RHB, RM. Staff 2004 – awaiting 1st XI debut.

NQTROTT, Ian Jonathan Leonard (Rondebosch BHC; Stellenbosch U), b Cape Town, South Africa 22 Apr 1981. 6'0". Step brother of K.C.Jackson (WP and Boland 1988-89 to 2001-02). RHB, RM. Boland 2002-01. W Province 2001-02. EU/British passport. Warwickshire debut 2003 scoring 134. HS 134 v Sussex (Birmingham) 2003 – on UK debut. BB 7-39 v Kent (Canterbury) 2003. LO HS 108* Boland v North West (Paarl) 2000-01. LO BB 2-32 Boland v EP (Paarl) 1999-00.

TROUGHTON, Jamie Oliver ('*Jim*') (Trinity S; Leamington Spa; Birmingham U), b Camden, London 2 Mar 1979. Great-grandson of H.T.Crichton (Warwicks 1908). 5'11". LHB, SLA. Debut 2001, cap 2002. **LOI**: 6 (2003); HS 20 v P (Lord's) 2003. F-c Tour (ECB Acad): SL 2002-03. 1000 (1): 1067 (2002). HS 131* v Hants (Southampton) 2002. BB – Awards: CGT 2. LO HS 115* and BB 4-23 Warwks CB v Cumb (Millom) 2001 (CGT).

WAGG, Graham Grant (Ashlawn S, Rugby), b Rugby, 28 Apr 1983. 6'0". RHB, LM. Debut 2002 – scoring 42* and 51 v Somerset (Birmingham). HS 74 v Ind A (Birmingham) 2003. CC HS 51 (*see above*). BB 4-43 v Somerset (Birmingham) 2002 – on debut. LO HS 32 V Essex (Chelmsford) 2003 (NL). LO BB 4-50 v Kent (Birmingham) 2002 (NL).

WAGH, Mark Anant (King Edward's S, Birmingham; Keble C, Oxford), b Birmingham 20 Oct 1976. 6'2". RHB, OB. Oxford U 1996-98; blue 1996-97-98; captain 1997. Warwickshire debut 1997; cap 2000. Mashonaland A 1998-99. F-c Tour (Eng A): I 2003-04. 1000 runs (3): 1277 (2001). HS 315 v Middx (Lord's) 2001. BB 7-222 v Lancs (Birmingham) 2003. LO HS 84 v Worcs (Birmingham) 2002 (NL). LO BB 3-35 v Beds (Luton) 2003 (CGT).

WARREN, Nick Alexander (Wheelers Lane S; Solihull SFC), b Moseley, Birmingham 26 Jun 1982. 5'11". RHB, RMF. No appearances 2003. 2nd XI debut 1998 when aged 16y 76d. HS 11 and BB 2-48 v WI A (Birmingham) 2002. LO HS 2 and LO BB 3-34 v Kent (Canterbury) 2002 (NL).

WESTWOOD, Ian James (Wheelers Lane S; Solihull SFC), b Birmingham 13 Jul 1982. 5'7½". LHB, OB. Debut 2003 – awaiting CC debut. HS 19 and BB – v Ind A (Birmingham) 2003 – only f-c match. LO HS 55 and BB 1-28 Warwks CB v Cambs (March) 2001 (CGT).

RELEASED/RETIRED
(Having made a first-class County appearance in 2003)

BETTS, M.M. – *see MIDDLESEX*.

NQ**CLARK, Michael** Wayne, b Perth, Australia 31 Mar 1978. Son of W.M.Clark (WA and Australia 1974-75 to 1984-85). RHB, LMF. W Australia 2001-02 to date. Warwickshire 2003 (1 match – injured back). HS 26 WA v Tasmania (Perth) 2002-03. Wa HS 2* and BB 2-71 v Notts (Nottingham) 2003. BB 5-47 WA v S Aus (Perth) 2002-03. LO HS 27 WA v NSW (Perth) 2002-03. LO BB 3-34 WA v NSW (Coffs Harbour) 2002-03.

NQ**COLLYMORE, Corey** Dalanelo (Alexandra SS), b Boscobelle, Barbados 21 Dec 1977. 6'0". RHB, RFM. Barbados 1998-99 to date. Warwickshire 2003. **Tests** (WI): 7 (1998-99 to 2003-04); HS 16* v Z (Bulawayo) 2003-04; BB 7-57 v SL (Kingston) 2003. **LOI** (WI): 51 (1900 to 2003-04); HS 13* v I (Toronto) 1999; BB 5-51 v SL (Colombo) 2001-02. F-c Tours (WI): E 2000; SA 2003-04; Z 2002, 2003-04; K 2000-01. HS 20 Barbados v WI B (Bridgetown) 2002-03. Wa HS 11* and BB 3-42 v Middx (Birmingham) 2003. BB 7-57 (*see Tests*). LO HS 13* (*see LOI*). LO BB 5-51 (*see LOI*).

NQ**OBUYA, Collins** Omondi, b Nairobi, Kenya 27 Jul 1981. RHB, LBG. Kenya 1999-00 to date. U of WI Vice-Chancellor's XI (1 match) 2002-03. Warwickshire 2003. **LOI** (K): 28 (2001 to 2002-03); HS 29 v I (Durban) 2002-03; BB 5-24 v SL (Nairobi) 2002-03. F-c Tours (K): SA 2001-02; SL 2001-02. HS 55 and Wa BB 3-91 v Notts (Birmingham) 2003 – on Warwks debut. BB 5-97 Kenya v Zim A (Nairobi) 2001-02. LO HS 29 (*see LOI*). LO BB 5-24 (*see LOI*).

SHEIKH, Mohammad Avez (Broadway S), b Birmingham 2 Jul 1973. 6'0". LHB, RM. Warwickshire 1997-2003. HS 58* v Northants (Northampton) 2000. BB 4-36 v Hants (Birmingham) 2001. LO HS 36 v Hants (Southampton) 2000 (NL). LO BB 4-17 v Yorks (Birmingham) 2001 (NL).

SMITH, Neil Michael Knight (Warwick S), b Birmingham 27 Jul 1967. Son of M.J.K. Smith (Leics, Warwks and England 1951-75). 6'0". RHB, OB. Warwickshire 1987-2003; cap 1993; captain 1999-2000; benefit 2002. MCC YC. **LOI**: 7 (1995-96 to 1996); HS 31 v H (Peshawar) 1995-96; BB 3-29 v UAE (Peshawar) 1995-96. F-c Tours (Wa): SA 1991-92, 1994-95; Z 1993-94. 1000 runs (1): 1002 (1998). HS 161 v Yorks (Leeds) 1989. BB 7-42 v Lancs (Birmingham) 1994. Awards: CGT 1; BHC 2. LO HS 125 v Kent (Canterbury) 1997 (BHC). LO BB 6-33 v Sussex (Birmingham) 1995 (SL).

NQ**WAQAR YOUNIS** (Government C, Vehari), b Vehari, Pakistan 16 Nov 1969. 6'0". RHB, RF. Multan 1987-88 to 1990-91, 1997-98. United Bank 1988-89 to 1996-97. Rawalpindi 1998-99. Redco 1999-00. Lahore 2000-01. National Bank 2001-02. Surrey 1990-91 and 1993; cap 1990. Glamorgan 1997-98; cap 1997. Warwickshire 2003. *Wisden* 1991. **Tests** (P): 87 (1989-90 to 2002-03, 17 as captain); HS 45 v SA (Rawalpindi) 1997-98; BB 7-76 v NZ (Faisalabad) 1990-91. **LOI** (P): 262 (1989-90 to 2002-03, 62 as captain); HS 37 v A (Sydney) 1999-00; BB 7-36 v E (Leeds) 2001. F-c Tours (P (C=captain): E 1992, 1996, 2001C; A 1989-90, 1995-96, SA 1997-98, 2002-03C; WI 1992-93, 1999-00; NZ 1992-93, 1993-94, 1995-96, 2000-01; I 1998-99; SL 1994-95, 2000-01; Z 2002-03C. HS 64 National Bank v Pakistan Customs (Gujranwala) 2001-02. CC HS 61 v Leics (Birmingham) 2003. 50 wkts (4+1) inc 100 (1): 113 (1991). BB 8-17 Gm v Sussex (Swansea) 1997. Wa BB 5-40 v Middx (Birmingham) 2003. Hat trick 1997. Awards: NWT 3. HS LO 45 Gm v Sussex (Hove) 1998 (BHC). BB LO 6-26 (*see LOI*).

WARWICKSHIRE 2003

RESULTS SUMMARY

	Place	Won	Lost	Tied	Drew	No Result
County Championship (1st Division)	5th	4	5	1	6	
All First-Class Matches		4	5	1	7	
C & G Trophy	Quarter-Finalist					
National League (1st Division)	4th	8	8			
Twenty20 Cup	Finalist					

COUNTY CHAMPIONSHIP AVERAGES

BATTING AND FIELDING

Cap		M	I	NO	HS	Runs	Avge	100	50	Ct/St
–	C.O.Obuya	2	4	2	55	95	47.50	–	1	1
1995	D.R.Brown	16	26	4	140*	1028	46.72	3	7	10
2000	M.A.Wagh	16	30	3	138	1228	45.48	3	7	15
1995	N.V.Knight	14	26	3	146	1012	44.00	3	5	11
2002	J.O.Troughton	12	20	2	129*	748	41.55	3	2	5
–	I.J.L.Trott	9	17	–	134	685	40.29	2	4	4
1996	A.F.Giles	6	10	1	96	338	37.55	–	2	–
–	Waqar Younis	8	13	5	61	268	33.50	–	2	1
1999	M.J.Powell	11	21	–	110	686	32.66	1	5	2
–	M.A.Sheikh	5	7	3	57*	129	32.25	–	1	2
2001	M.M.Betts	9	13	2	73	327	29.72	–	2	2
2001	I.R.Bell	16	29	2	107	779	28.85	1	4	4
1999	T.Frost	12	20	1	84	401	21.10	–	3	31/2
–	N.M.Carter	4	6	–	38	118	19.66	–	–	1
1992	K.J.Piper	4	7	–	42	137	19.57	–	–	12/1
1993	N.M.K.Smith	6	8	–	57	138	17.25	–	1	2
1991	D.P.Ostler	4	7	–	58	109	15.57	–	1	2
2002	A.Richardson	14	19	5	47	158	11.28	–	–	1
–	C.D.Collymore	5	8	3	11*	25	5.00	–	–	2

Also batted (1 match each): M.W.Clark 2*, 2; T.L.Penney (cap 1994) 19, 2 (1 ct); G.G.Wagg 11, 4.

BOWLING

	O	M	R	W	Avge	Best	5wI	10wM
Waqar Younis	244.2	39	917	39	23.51	5- 40	3	–
D.R.Brown	377.5	81	1274	36	35.38	5- 72	2	–
M.A.Wagh	193.3	28	730	20	36.50	7-222	–	–
M.M.Betts	214.2	24	885	24	36.87	5- 43	1	–
M.A.Sheikh	151	37	454	12	37.83	4- 60	–	–
A.Richardson	453	104	1314	33	39.81	4- 37	–	–
A.F.Giles	198.5	36	577	13	44.38	5-115	1	–

Also bowled:

I.J.L.Trott	37.1	3	168	7	24.00	7- 39	–	–
N.M.Carter	103	13	443	8	55.37	5- 75	1	–
C.D.Collymore	138	24	475	8	59.37	3- 42	–	–
I.R.Bell	78.3	10	346	5	69.20	3- 79	–	–

M.W.Clark 33-7-110-3; N.V.Knight 6-3-39-0; C.O.Obuya 36-2-180-3; D.P.Ostler 2-0-33-0; M.J.Powell 6-0-28-0; N.M.K.Smith 90.3-9-408-4; J.O.Troughton 13-0-85-0; G.G.Wagg 31-2-189-3.

The First-Class Averages (pp 123–138) give the records of Warwickshire's players in all first-class county matches (Warwickshire's other opponents being India A), with the exception of T.Mees whose only first-class appearances were for Oxford UCCE and British Universities, and A.F.Giles whose full county figures are as above.

WARWICKSHIRE RECORDS

FIRST-CLASS CRICKET

Highest Total	For 810-4d		v	Durham	Birmingham	1994
	V 887		by	Yorkshire	Birmingham	1896
Lowest Total	For 16		v	Kent	Tonbridge	1913
	V 15		by	Hampshire	Birmingham	1922
Highest Innings	For 501*	B.C.Lara	v	Durham	Birmingham	1994
	V 322	I.V.A.Richards	for	Somerset	Taunton	1985

Highest Partnership for each Wicket

1st	377*	N.F.Horner/K.Ibadulla	v	Surrey	The Oval	1960
2nd	465*	J.A.Jameson/R.B.Kanhai	v	Glos	Birmingham	1974
3rd	327	S.P.Kinneir/W.G.Quaife	v	Lancashire	Birmingham	1901
4th	470	A.I.Kallicharran/G.W.Humpage	v	Lancashire	Southport	1982
5th	322*	B.C.Lara/K.J.Piper	v	Durham	Birmingham	1994
6th	220	H.E.Dollery/J.Buckingham	v	Derbyshire	Derby	1938
7th	289	D.Brown/A.F.Giles	v	Sussex	Hove	2000
8th	228	A.J.W.Croom/R.E.S.Wyatt	v	Worcs	Dudley	1925
9th	154	G.W.Stephens/A.J.W.Croom	v	Derbyshire	Birmingham	1925
10th	214	N.V.Knight/A.Richardson	v	Hampshire	Birmingham	2002

Best Bowling	For	10-41	J.D.Bannister	v	Comb Servs	Birmingham	1959
(Innings)	V	10-36	H.Verity	for	Yorkshire	Leeds	1931
Best Bowling	For	15-76	S.Hargreave	v	Surrey	The Oval	1903
(Match)	V	17-92	A.P.Freeman	for	Kent	Folkestone	1932

Most Runs – Season	2417	M.J.K.Smith	(av 60.42)	1959
Most Runs – Career	35146	D.L.Amiss	(av 41.64)	1960-87
Most 100s – Season	9	A.I.Kallicharran		1984
	9	B.C.Lara		1994
Most 100s – Career	78	D.L.Amiss		1960-87
Most Wkts – Season	180	W.E.Hollies	(av 15.13)	1946
Most Wkts – Career	2201	W.E.Hollies	(av 20.45)	1932-57
Most Career W-K Dismissals	800	E.J.Smith	(662 ct/138 st)	1904-30
Most Career Catches in the Field	422	M.J.K.Smith		1956-75

LIST 'A' LIMITED-OVERS CRICKET

Highest Total	CGT	392-5		v	Oxfordshire	Birmingham	1984
	BHC	369-8		v	Minor C	Jesmond	1996
	NL	307-5		v	Essex	Chelmsford	2003
Lowest Total	CGT	98		v	Leics	Leicester	1998
	BHC	91		v	Glos	Bristol	2002
	NL	59		v	Yorks	Leeds	2001
Highest Innings	CGT	206	A.I.Kallicharran	v	Oxfordshire	Birmingham	1984
	BHC	137*	T.A.Lloyd	v	Lancashire	Birmingham	1985
	NL	134*	D.P.Ostler	v	Glos	Birmingham	2001
Best Bowling	CGT	6-32	K.Ibadulla	v	Hampshire	Birmingham	1965
		6-32	A.I.Kallicharran	v	Oxfordshire	Birmingham	1984
	BHC	7-32	R.G.D.Willis	v	Yorkshire	Birmingham	1981
	NL	6-15	A.A.Donald	v	Yorkshire	Birmingham	1995

WORCESTERSHIRE

Formation of Present Club: 11 March 1865
Inaugural First-Class Match: 1899
Colours: Dark Green and Black
Badge: Shield Argent a Fess between three Pears Sable
County Championships: (5) 1964, 1965, 1974, 1988, 1989
Gillette/NatWest/C & G Trophy Winners: (1) 1994
Benson and Hedges Cup Winners: (1) 1991
National League (Div 1) Winners: (0); best – 2nd 1999, 2002
Sunday League Winners: (3) 1971, 1987, 1988
Twenty20 Cup Winners: 3rd in Midlands/Wales/West Group
Match Awards: CGT 50; BHC 72

Chief Executive: M.S.Newton, County Ground, New Road, Worcester, WR2 4QQ • Tel: 01905 748474 • Fax: 01905 748005 • Email: admin@wccc.co.uk • Web: www.wccc.co.uk

Director of Cricket/First XI Coach: T.M.Moody. **Captain**: B.F.Smith. **Vice-Captain**: S.J.Rhodes. **Overseas Players**: A.J.Bichel and A.J.Hall. **2004 Beneficiary**: T.M.Moody (testimonial). **Head Groundsman**: T.Packwood. **Scorer**: N.D.Smith. ‡ New registration. NQ Not qualified for England.

Worcestershire revised their capping policy in 2002 and now award players with their County Colours when they make their Championship debut.

ALI, Kabir (Moseley CS and SFC), b Moseley, Birmingham 24 Nov 1980. 6'0". Cousin of Kadeer Ali. RHB, RMF. Debut 1999. F-c Tour: SL 2002-03 (ECB Acad). **Tests**: 1 (2003); HS 9 and BB 3-80 v SA (Leeds) on debut. **LOI**: 1 (2003); dnb v Z (Leeds) 2003. HS 84* v Durham (Stockton) 2003. 50 wkts (2); most – 71 (2002). BB 8-53 (*before lunch first day*) v Yorks (Scarborough) 2003. Award: BHC 1. LO HS 92 v Essex (Worcester) 2003 (NL). LO BB 5-36 v Yorks (Leeds) 2002 (NL).

ALI, Kadeer (Handsworth GS), b Moseley, Birmingham 7 Mar 1983. 6'1". Brother of M.M.Ali (*see* WARWICKSHIRE), cousin of Kabir Ali. RHB, LB. Debut 2000. No f-c appearances 2002. F-c Tour (Eng A): I 2003-04. HS 99 v Yorks (Worcester) 2003. BB – LO HS 66 Worcs CB v Sussex CB (Kidderminster) 2002 (CGT). LO BB 1-4 (CGT).

BATTY, Gareth Jon (Bingley GS), b Bradford, Yorks 13 Oct 1977. Younger brother of J.D.Batty (Yorkshire and Somerset 1989-96). 5'11". RHB, OB. Yorkshire 1997. Surrey 1999-2001. Worcestershire debut 2002. **Tests**: 4 (2003-04); HS 38 v SL (Kandy) 2003-04; BB 3-55 v SL (Galle) 2003-04. Took wicket with third ball in Test cricket. **LOI**: 3 (2002-03 to 2003-04); HS 3; BB 1-35. F-c Tours: SL 2002-03 (ECB Acad); SL 2003-04; B 2003-04. HS 74 v Derbys (Worcester) 2002. 50 wkts (2); most – 60 (2003). BB 6-71 v Essex (Southend) 2002. LO HS 83* Sy v Yorks (Oval) 2001 (NL). LO BB 4-36 Sy v Kent (Canterbury) 2001 (NL) and 4-36 v Notts (Nottingham) 2002 (NL).

NQ BICHEL, Andrew John (Laidley HS; Ipswich C, Queensland), b Laidley, Queensland, Australia 27 Aug 1970. RHB, RFM. 5'11". Queensland 1992-93 to date. Worcestershire 2001-02; cap 2001. **Tests** (A): 19 (1996-97 to 2003-04); HS 71 v WI (Bridgetown) 2002-03; BB 5-60 v WI (Melbourne) 2000-01. **LOI** (A): 67 (1996-97 to 2003-04); HS 64 v NZ (Pt Elizabeth) 2002-03; BB 7-20 v E (Pt Elizabeth) 2002-03. F-c Tours: A: E 1997; SA 1996-97, 2001-02; WI 1998-99, 2002-03; P 2002-03 (in Sharjah); Scot 1998 (Aus A). HS 110 (off 110 balls) Q v Vic (Brisbane) 1997-98. Wo HS 78* v Durham (Worcester) 2002. 50 wkts (1+1); most – 66 (2001). BB 9-93 (10-131 match) v Yorks (Worcester) 2002. Awards: BHC 3. LO HS 100 v Glam (Cardiff) 2001 (BHC). LO BB 7-20 (*see* LOI).

‡DAVIES, Steven Michael, b Bromsgrove 17 Jun 1986. LHB, WK. Staff 2004 – awaiting first-class debut. LO HS 13 Worcs CB v Worcs (Worcester) 2003 (CGT).

FARROW, Jonathan Colin (Kingsway HS; Wilmslow SFS; University C, Worcester), b Stockport, Cheshire 22 Feb 1984. 6'3". RHB, RFM. Cheshire 2002. Worcestershire staff 2003 – awaiting first-class debut. LO HS – . LO BB 2-81 Cheshire v Lincs (Neston) 2002 (CGT).

NO HALL, Andrew James (Hoerskool Alberton), b Alberton, Johannesburg, South Africa 31 Jul 1975. RHB, RFM. Transvaal/Gauteng 1995-96 to 2001-02. Easterns 2001-02 to date. Suffolk 2002. **Tests** (SA): 10 (2001-02 to 2003-04); HS 99* v E (Leeds) 2003; B 3-1 v SL (Jo'burg) 2002-03. **LOI** (SA): 43 (1998-99 to 2003-04); HS 81 v SL (Galle) 2000-01; BB 3-32 v B (Dhaka) 2002-03. F-c Tour (SA): E 2003. HS 153 Easterns v North West (Benoni) 2001-02. Wo HS 104 v Somerset (Bath) 2003. BB 6-77 Easterns v WP (Port Elizabeth) 2002-03. Wo BB 3-10 v Durham (Stockton) 2003. Award: CGT 1. LO HS 129* Gauteng v Border (E London) 1999-00. LO BB 4-33 Suffolk v Northants (Bury St Edmunds) 2002 (CGT).

NO HARRITY, Mark Andrew (Taperoo HS), b Semaphore, S Australia 9 Mar 1974. British passport (English father). 6'4". RHB, LFM. S Australia 1993-94 to date. Worcestershire debut 2003. HS 19 S Aus v Vic (Melbourne) 2001-02. Wo HS 16 v Z (Worcester) 2003. CC HS 5*. BB 5-65 S Aus v Tasmania (Hobart) 2002-02. Wo BB 4-39 v Durham (Worcester) 2003. LO HS 15 v Glos (Worcester) 2003 (NL). LO BB 5-42 S Aus v Vic (Adelaide) 1997-98.

HICK, Graeme Ashley (Prince Edward HS, Salisbury), b Salisbury, Rhodesia 23 May 1966. 6'3". RHB, OB. Zimbabwe 1983-84 to 1985-86. Worcestershire debut 1984; cap 1986; benefit 1999; captain 2000-02. N Districts 1987-88 to 1988-89. Queensland 1990-91. *Wisden* 1986. **ECB contract 2000. Tests**: 65 (1991 to 2000-01); HS 178 v I (Bombay) 1992-93; BB 4-126 v NZ (Wellington) 1991-92. Took wicket with third ball in Test cricket. **LOI**: 120 (1991 to 2000-01); HS 126* v SL (Adelaide) 1998-99; BB 5-33 v Z (Harare) 1999-00. F-c Tours: E 1985 (Z); A 1994-95, 1998-99 (*part*); SA 1995-96, 1999-00 (*part*); WI 1993-94; NZ 1991-92; I 1992-93; P 2000-01; SL 1983-84 (Z), 1992-93, 2000-01; Z 1990-91 (Wo), 1996-97 (Wo). Scored runs (17+1) inc 2000 (3); most – 2713 (1988); youngest to score 2000 (1986). Scored 1019 runs before June 1988, including a record 410 runs in April. Fewest innings for 10,000 runs in county cricket (179). Youngest (24) to score 50 f-c hundreds. Second-youngest (32) to score 100 f-c hundreds. Scored 645 runs without being dismissed (UK record) in 1990. Wo 405* (Worcs record and then second highest in UK f-c matches) v Somerset (Taunton) 1988. BB 5-18 v Leics (Worcester) 1995. Awards: CGT 5; BHC 11. LO HS 172* v Devon (Worcester) 1987 (NWT). LO BB 5-19 E v Pak A (Lahore) 1998-99.

KHALID, Shaftab Ahmad (Dormers Wells HS; W Thames C; Middlesex U), b Lahore, Pakistan 6 Oct 1982. 5'11". RHB, OB. Debut 2003. F-c Tour (Eng A): I 2003-04. HS 13 v Glam (Worcester) 2003 – on CC debut. BB 4-131 v Northants (Northampton) 2003. LO HS 3* (NL). LO BB 2-40 v Essex (Worcester) 2003 (NL).

LEATHERDALE, David Anthony (Pudsey Grangefield S), b Bradford, Yorks 26 Nov 1967. 5'10½". RHB, RM. Debut 1988; cap 1994; benefit 2003. F-c Tours (Wo): Z 1993-94, 1996-97. 1000 runs (1): 1001 (1998). HS 157 v Somerset (Worcester) 1991. BB 5-20 v Glos (Worcester) 1998. Awards: CGT 1; BHC 1. LO HS 80 v Yorks (Worcester) 2003 (CGT). LO BB 5-9 v Durham (Chester-le-St) 2002 (NL).

‡**MALIK** Muhammad **Nadeem**, (Wilford Meadows CS; Bilborough C), b Nottingham 6 Oct 1982. 6'5". RHB, RFM. Nottinghamshire 2001-03. Notts 2nd XI debut 1999 when aged 16y 337d. HS 30* Nt v Essex (Nottingham) 2003. BB 5-57 Nt v Derbys (Nottingham) 2001. LO HS 11 Nt v Worcs (Nottingham) 2002 (NL). LO BB 2-34 Nt v Yorks (Nottingham) 2001 (NL).

NO MASON, Matthew Sean (Mazenod C, Lesmurdie, WA), b Claremont, Perth, Australia 20 Mar 1974. ECB qualified – British passport. 6'5". RHB, RFM. W Australia 1996-97 to 1997-98. Worcestershire debut 2002. HS 52 v Glam (Cardiff) 2003. 50 wkts (1): 53 (2003). BB 6-68 v Durham (Worcester) 2003. LO HS 20* v Leics (Worcester) 2003 (NL). LO BB 4-34 v Surrey (Guildford) 2003 (NL).

MITCHELL, Daryl Keith Henry (Prince Henry's HS; University C, Worcester), b Badsey, near Evesham 25 Nov 1983. 5'10". RHB, RM. Worcestershire staff 2003 – awaiting 1st XI debut.

MOORE, Stephen Colin (St Stithian's C, Jo'burg; Exeter U), b Johannesburg, South Africa 4 Nov 1980. 6'1". RHB, RM. Debut 2003. HS 28* v Glam (Cardiff) 2003 – on debut. LO HS 12 v Leics (Worcester) 2003 (NL). LO BB –

PETERS, Stephen David (Coopers Coborn & Co S), b Harold Wood, Essex 10 Dec 1978. 5'11". RHB, occ LB. Essex 1996-2001, scoring 110 and 12* v CU (Cambridge) on debut. Worcestershire debut 2002. 1000 (1): 1177 (2003). HS 165 v Somerset (Bath) 2003. BB (Ex) 1-19 (not CC). Award: CGT 1. LO HS 82 v Leics (Oakham) 2003 (NL).

PIPE, David **James** (Queensbury S, Bradford), b Bradford, Yorks 16 Dec 1977. 5'11". RHB, WK. Debut 1998. HS 104* v Hants (Southampton) 2003. LO HS 56 Worcs CB v Kent CB (Kidderminster) 2000 (NWT). Held 8 catches v Herts (Hertford) 2001 (CGT) to equal 1-o record.

RHODES, Steven John (Lapage Middle S; Carlton-Bolling S, Bradford), b Bradford, Yorks 17 Jun 1964. Son of W.E. (Notts 1961-64). 5'7". RHB, WK. Yorkshire 1981-84. Worcestershire debut 1985; cap 1986; benefit 1996. *Wisden* 1994. **Tests**: 11 (1994 to 1994-95); HS 65* v SA (Leeds) 1994. **LOI**: 9 (1989 to 1994-95); HS 56 v SA (Manchester) 1994. F-c Tours: A 1994-95; SA 1993-94 (Eng A); WI 1991-92 (Eng A); SL 1985-86 (Eng B). 1990-91 (Eng A); Z 1989-90 (Eng A), 1990-91 (Wo), 1993-94 (Wo), 1996-97 (Wo – captain). 1000 runs (2); most – 1018 (1995). HS 124 v Notts (Nottingham) 2002. BB – Awards: CGT 1; BHC 2. LO HS 105 v Lancs (Manchester) 1991 (RAC).

SMITH, Benjamin Francis (Kibworth HS), b Corby, Northants 3 Apr 1972. 5'9". RHB, RM. Leicestershire 1990-2001; cap 1995. Central Districts 2001-02. Worcestershire debut 2002; captain 2003 to date. F-c Tour (Eng A): SA 1996-97. 1000 runs (5); most – 1289 (2003). HS 204 Le v Surrey (Oval) 1998. Wo HS 137 v OU (Oxford) 2002 – on Worcs debut. BB (Le) 1-5. Wo BB 1-45. Award: CGT 1. LO HS 115 Le v Somerset (Weston-s-M) 1995 (SL). LO BB 1-2 (CGT).

SOLANKI, Vikram Singh (Regis S, Wolverhampton), b Udaipur, India 1 Apr 1976. 6'0". RHB, OB. Debut 1995; cap 1998. F-c Tours (Eng A): SA 1999-00 (Eng – *part*); WI 2000-01; NZ 1999-00; Z 1996-97 (Wo), 1998-99; B 1999-00. **LOI**: 21 (1999-00 to 2003-04); HS 50 v SA (Oval) 2003. 1000 runs (2); most – 1339 (1999). HS 185 Eng A v Bangladesh (Chittagong) 1999-00. Wo HS 171 v Glos (Cheltenham) 1999. BB 5-69 v Middx (Lord's) 1996. Awards: CGT 2; BHC 1. LO HS 164* v Worcs CB (Worcester) 2003 (CGT). LO BB 2-40 Eng A v Zim Academy (Harare) 1998-99.

WIGLEY, David Harry (St Mary's RCS, Menstom, Ilkley; Loughborough U), b Bradford, Yorks 26 Oct 1981. 6'4". RHB, RFM. Yorkshire 2002 (one match). Loughborough UCCE 2003. Worcestershire debut 2003. HS 15 Y v Surrey (Guildford) 2002 – on debut – and 15 plus BB 2-56 v Yorks (Worcester) 2003 – on Worcs debut. LO HS 1 (NL). LO BB 1-58 (NL).

‡**WHITNEY, Jonathan** David, b Bridgnorth, Shropshire 7 Apr 1985. RHB, RFM. Staff 2004 – awaiting first-class debut.

RELEASED/RETIRED
(Having made a first-class County appearance in 2003)

C.S.Guest and D.K.Taylor left the staff having made no f-c appearances in 2003.

ADSHEAD, S.J. – *see* GLOUCESTERSHIRE.

^NQ^HAYWARD, M. – *see* MIDDLESEX.

RELEASED/RETIRED continued on p 107

WORCESTERSHIRE 2003

RESULTS SUMMARY

	Place	Won	Lost	Tied	Drew	No Result
County Championship (2nd Division)	1st	10	1		5	
All First-Class Matches		10	1	1	6	
C & G Trophy	Finalist					
National League (1st Division)	9th	4	12			
Twenty20 Cup	3rd in Midlands/Wales/West Group					

COUNTY CHAMPIONSHIP AVERAGES

BATTING AND FIELDING

Cap		M	I	NO	HS	Runs	Avge	100	50	Ct/St
2002[c]	B.F.Smith	16	26	2	110	1155	48.12	2	10	3
2002[c]	D.J.Pipe	3	6	2	104*	163	40.75	1	–	14/1
2002[c]	S.D.Peters	16	27	1	165	1009	38.80	2	7	11
2002[c]	Kadeer Ali	6	11	–	99	375	34.09	–	3	2
2003[c]	S.J.Adshead	2	4	1	63	102	34.00	–	1	7/1
1986	G.A.Hick	13	23	3	155	670	33.50	1	3	19
2003[c]	S.C.Moore	2	4	1	28*	97	32.33	–	–	2
2003[c]	A.J.Hall	6	7	–	104	222	31.71	1	1	2
2002[c]	Kabir Ali	12	16	4	84*	371	30.91	–	2	2
2002[c]	A.Singh	14	24	1	105	628	27.30	1	3	6
2003[c]	J.M.Kemp	6	11	–	90	290	26.36	–	1	9
1986	S.J.Rhodes	11	14	2	81*	309	25.75	–	2	38/2
1998	V.S.Solanki	13	20	1	79	464	24.42	–	3	18
1994	D.A.Leatherdale	4	7	–	61	164	23.42	–	2	2
2002[c]	G.J.Batty	16	25	3	60	497	22.59	–	3	14
2002[c]	M.S.Mason	13	18	3	52	237	15.80	–	1	2
2003[c]	M.Hayward	16	21	5	28	123	7.68	–	–	5
2003[c]	M.A.Harrity	5	5	3	5*	14	7.00	–	–	–

Also batted: S.A.Khalid (4 matches – 2003[c]) 13, 8 (1 ct); D.H.Wigley (1 – 2003[c]) 15, 8.

BOWLING

	O	M	R	W	Avge	Best	5wI	10wM
A.J.Hall	110	29	297	17	17.47	3- 10	–	–
M.S.Mason	385.3	101	1038	49	21.18	6- 68	2	–
J.M.Kemp	102.1	17	319	14	22.78	5- 48	1	–
M.Hayward	427.3	83	1533	67	22.88	5- 46	2	–
Kabir Ali	336.2	57	1279	54	23.68	8- 53	2	–
G.J.Batty	515.2	121	1436	53	27.09	6- 88	1	–

Also bowled:

S.A.Khalid	77	13	275	8	34.37	4-131	–	–
M.A.Harrity	120.5	29	423	9	47.00	4- 39	–	–

G.A.Hick 21-5-63-0; D.A.Leatherdale 39-6-142-4; V.S.Solanki 2-1-9-0; D.H.Wigley 29.1-9-95-3.

The First-Class Averages (pp 123–138) give the records of Worcestershire's players in all first-class county matches (Worcestershire's other opponents being the Zimbabweans and Oxford UCCE), with the exception of D.H.Wigley whose full county figures are as above, and:

Kabir Ali 13-18-4-84*-371-26.50-0-2-2ct. 379.2-67-1416-62-22.83-8/53-3-0.
A.J.Hall 7-9-0-104-324-36.00-1-2-4ct. 149-41-393-19-20.68-3/10.

2003[c] Awarded County Colours – a system which replaced capping in 2002.

WORCESTERSHIRE RECORDS

FIRST-CLASS CRICKET

Highest Total	For 670-7d		v	Somerset	Worcester	1995
	V 701-4d		by	Leics	Worcester	1906
Lowest Total	For 24		v	Yorkshire	Huddersfield	1903
	V 30		by	Hampshire	Worcester	1903
Highest Innings	For 405*	G.A.Hick	v	Somerset	Taunton	1988
	V 331*	J.D.B.Robertson	for	Middlesex	Worcester	1949

Highest Partnership for each Wicket

1st	309	F.L.Bowley/H.K.Foster	v	Derbyshire	Derby	1901
2nd	300	W.P.C.Weston/G.A.Hick	v	Indians	Worcester	1996
3rd	438*	G.A.Hick/T.M.Moody	v	Hampshire	Southampton	1997
4th	281	J.A.Ormrod/Younis Ahmed	v	Notts	Nottingham	1979
5th	393	E.G.Arnold/W.B.Burns	v	Warwicks	Birmingham	1909
6th	265	G.A.Hick/S.J.Rhodes	v	Somerset	Taunton	1988
7th	256	D.A.Leatherdale/S.J.Rhodes	v	Notts	Nottingham	2002
8th	184	S.J.Rhodes/S.R.Lampitt	v	Derbyshire	Kidderminster	1991
9th	181	J.A.Cuffe/R.D.Burrows	v	Glos	Worcester	1907
10th	119	W.B.Burns/G.A.Wilson	v	Somerset	Worcester	1906

Best Bowling	For	9- 23	C.F.Root	v	Lancashire	Worcester	1931
(Innings)	V	10- 51	J.Mercer	for	Glamorgan	Worcester	1936
Best Bowling	For	15- 87	A.J.Conway	v	Glos	Moreton-in-M	1914
(Match)	V	17-212	J.C.Clay	for	Glamorgan	Swansea	1937

Most Runs – Season		2654	H.H.I.Gibbons	(av 52.03)	1934
Most Runs – Career		34490	D.Kenyon	(av 34.18)	1946-67
Most 100s – Season		10	G.M.Turner		1970
		10	G.A.Hick		1988
Most 100s – Career		87	G.A.Hick		1984-2001
Most Wkts – Season		207	C.F.Root	(av 17.52)	1925
Most Wkts – Career		2143	R.T.D.Perks	(av 23.73)	1930-55
Most Career W-K Dismissals		1026	S.J.Rhodes	(931 ct/95 st)	1985-2003
Most Career Catches in the Field		412	D.W.Richardson		1952-67

LIST 'A' LIMITED-OVERS CRICKET

Highest Total	CGT	404-3		v	Devon	Worcester	1987
	BHC	314-5		v	Lancashire	Manchester	1980
	NL	307-4		v	Derbyshire	Worcester	1975
Lowest Total	CGT	98		v	Durham	Chester-le-St	1968
	BHC	70		v	Glos	Worcester	2002
	NL	86		v	Yorkshire	Leeds	1969
Highest Innings	CGT	180*	T.M.Moody	v	Surrey	The Oval	1994
	BHC	143*	G.M.Turner	v	Warwicks	Birmingham	1976
	NL	160	T.M.Moody	v	Kent	Worcester	1991
Best Bowling	CGT	7-19	N.V.Radford	v	Beds	Bedford	1991
	BHC	6- 8	N.Gifford	v	Minor C (S)	High Wycombe	1979
	NL	6-26	A.P.Pridgeon	v	Surrey	Worcester	1978

YORKSHIRE

Formation of Present Club: 8 January 1863 .
Substantial Reorganisation: 10 December 1891
Inaugural First-Class Match: 1864
Colours: Dark Blue, Light Blue and Gold
Badge: White Rose
County Championships (since 1890): (30) 1893, 1896, 1898, 1900, 1901, 1902, 1905, 1908, 1912, 1919, 1922, 1923, 1924, 1925, 1931, 1932, 1933, 1935, 1937, 1938, 1939, 1946, 1959, 1960, 1962, 1963, 1966, 1967, 1968, 2001
Joint Champions: (1) 1949
Gillette/NatWest/C & G Trophy Winners: (3) 1965, 1969, 2002
Benson and Hedges Cup Winners: (1) 1987
National League (Div 1) Winners: (0); best – 2nd 2000
Sunday League Winners: (1) 1983
Twenty20 Cup Winners: 2nd in North Group 2003
Match Awards: CGT 46; BHC 80

Chief Executive: C.J.Graves, Headingley Cricket Ground, Leeds, LS6 3BU • Tel: 0113 278 7394 • Fax: 0113 278 4099 • Email: cricket@yorkshireccc.org.uk • Web: www.yorkshireccc.org.uk

First XI Coach: D.Byas. **Captain**: C.White. **Vice-Captain**: M.J.Wood. **Overseas Players**: I.J.Harvey and D.S.Lehmann. **2004 Beneficiary**: C.E.W.Silverwood. **Head Groundsman**: A.W.Fogarty. **Scorer**: J.T.Potter. ‡ New registration. ^NQ Not qualified for England.

BLAKEY, Richard John (Rastrick GS), b Huddersfield 15 Jan 1967. 5'9". RHB, WK. Debut 1985; cap 1987; benefit 1998. YC 1987. **Tests**: 2 (1992-93); HS 6. **LOI**: 3 (1992 to 1992-93); HS 25 v P (Lord's) 1992 – on debut. F-c Tours: SA 1991-92 (Y); WI 1986-87 (Y); I 1992-93 (Eng A); P 1990-91 (Eng A); SL 1990-91 (Eng A); Z 1989-90 (Eng A). 1000 runs (6); most – 1361 (1987). HS 223* v Northants (Leeds) 2003. BB 1-68. Awards: BHC 2. LO HS 130* v Kent (Scarborough) 1991 (SL).

BRESNAN, Timothy Thomas (Castleford HS and TC; Pontefract New C), b Pontefract 28 Feb 1985. 6'0". RHB, RMF. Debut 2003. HS 52 and BB 3-88 v Ind A (Leeds) 2003. CC HS 19 and BB 2-63 v Derbys (Derby) 2003. LO HS 61 v Leics (Leeds) 2003 (NL). BB 3-29 v Essex (Leeds) 2003 (NL).

CRAVEN, Victor John (Harrogate GS), b Harrogate 31 Jul 1980. 6'0". LHB, RM. Debut 2000. HS 72 v Hants (Southampton) 2002. BB 2-25 v Hants (Scarborough) 2003. LO HS 59 v Durham (Leeds) 2002 (NL). BB 4-22 v Kent (Scarborough) 2003 (NL).

DAWSON, Richard Kevin James (Batley GS; Exeter U), b Doncaster 4 Aug 1980. 6'3". RHB, OB. British U 2000. Yorkshire debut 2001. Devon 1999-2000. **Tests**: 7 (2000-02 to 2002-03); HS 19* v A (Perth) 2002-03; BB 4-134 v I (Chandigarh) 2001-02 – on debut. F-c Tours: A 2002-03; NZ 2001-02; I 2001-02; SL 2002-03 (ECB Acad). HS 87 v Kent (Canterbury) 2002. BB 6-82 v Glam (Scarborough) 2001. LO HS 41 v Leics (Scarborough) 2002 (NL). LO BB 4-13 v Derbys (Derby) 2002 (BHC).

‡GALE, Andrew William (Whitcliffe Mount S; Heckmondwike GS), b Dewsbury 28 Nov 1983. LHB, LB. England U-19 to Australia 2002-03. Yorkshire Academy. Staff 2004 – awaiting first-class debut. LO HS 17 Yorks CB v Northumb (Jesmond) 2002 (CGT).

GRAY, Andrew Kenneth Donovan, b Armadale, W Australia 19 May 1974. RHB, OB. Debut 2001. HS 104 v Somerset (Taunton) 2003. BB 4-128 v Surrey (Oval) 2001. LO HS 30* v Leics (Leicester) 2003 (NL). LO BB 4-34 v Kent (Leeds) 2002 (NL).

GUY, Simon Mark (Wickersley CS), b Rotherham 17 Nov 1978. 5'7". RHB, WK. Debut 2000. No 1st appearances 2002. HS 42 v Somerset (Taunton) 2000. BB – LO HS 13 v WI A (Leeds) 2002.

‡**NOHARVEY, Ian** Joseph (Wonthaggi TC), b Wonthaggi, Victoria, Australia 10 Apr 1972. 5'10". RHB, RMF. Victoria 1993-94 to date. Gloucestershire 1999-2003/cap 1999. **LOI** (A): 68 (1997-98 to 2003-04); HS 48* v WI (Kingston) 2003; BB 4-16 v B (Darwin) 2003. F-c Tour: NZ 1994-95 (Aus Academy). HS 136 Vic v S Aus (Melbourne) 1995-96. UK HS 130* Gs v Middx (Lord's) 2001. BB 8-101 Aus A v SA A (Adelaide) 2002-03. UK BB 6-19 (10-32 match) Gs v Sussex (Hove) 2000. Hat trick (Victoria 2001-02). Awards: CGT 3; BHC 4. LO HS 96 Gs v Essex (Chelmsford) 2003 (NL). LO BB 5-19 Gs v Northants (Bristol) 2000 (NL).

HOGGARD, Matthew James (Grangefield S, Pudsey), b Leeds 31 Dec 1976. 6'2". RHB, RFM. Debut 1996; cap 2000. Free State 1998-99 to 1999-00. **ECB contracts 2001, 2002, 2003.** Tests: 22 (2000 to 2003-04); HS 32 v I (Nottingham) 2002; BB 7-63 v NZ (Christchurch) 2001-02. **LOI**: 20 (2001-02 to 2002-03); HS 5; BB 5-49 v Z (Harare) 2001-02. F-c Tours: A 2002-03; NZ 2001-02; I 2001-02; P 2000-01; SL 2000-01, 2003-04; B 2003-04. HS 32 (*see Tests*). Y HS 21* v Hants (Leeds) 2002 and 21* v Northants (Northampton) 2003. 50 wkts (1): 50 (2000). BB 7-49 v Somerset (Leeds) 2003. LO HS 7* (*twice*). LO BB 5-28 v Leics (Leicester) 2000 (NL).

KIRBY, Steven Paul (Elton HS; Bury C), b Ainsworth, nr Bolton, Lancs 4 Oct 1977. 6'3½". RHB, RF. Leicestershire staff 1998 – no f-c appearances. Debut 2001, sub for M.J.Hoggard (England duty) taking 7-50; cap 2003. F-c Tour (Eng A): I 2003-04 (*part*). HS 57 v Hants (Leeds) 2002. 50 wkts (1): 67 (2003). BB 8-80 (13-154 match) v Somerset (Taunton) 2003. LO HS 15 v Leics (Leicester) 2003 (NL). LO BB 3-27 v Worcs (Scarborough) 2003 (NL).

‡**LAWSON, Mark** Anthony Kenneth, b Leeds 24 Oct 1985. RHB, LB. Staff 2004 – awaiting 1st XI debut.

NQLEHMANN, Darren Scott (Gawler HS), b Gawler, S Australia 5 Feb 1970. 5'10. LHB, SLA. S Australia 1987-88 to 1989-90, 1993-94 to date; captain 1998-99 to date. Victoria 1990-91 to 1992-93. Yorkshire 1997-98, 2000, 2002; cap 1997; captain 2002. *Wisden* 2000. **Tests** (A): 15 (1997-98 to 2003-04); HS 177 v B (Cairns) 2003; BB 3-61 v Z (Perth) 2003-04. **LOI** (A): 100 (1996-97 to 2003); HS 119 v SL (Perth) 2002-03; BB 3-16 v B (Cairns) 2003. F-c Tours (A): E 1991 (Vic); SA 2001-02; WI 2002-03; I 1997-98; P 1998-99. 1000 runs (4+5); most – 1575 (1997). HS 255 S Aus v Queensland (Adelaide) 1996-97. Y HS 252 v Lancs (Leeds) 2001. BB 4-42 v Kent (Maidstone) 1998. Awards: CGT 1; BHC 5. LO HS 191 v Notts (Scarborough) 2001 (NL). LO BB 4-26 v Devon (Exmouth) 2002 (CGT).

LUMB, Michael John (St Stithians C, Jo'burg), b Johannesburg, South Africa 12 Feb 1980. Son of R.G.Lumb (Yorkshire 1970-84); nephew of A.J.S.Smith (SAU and Natal 1971-72 to 1983-84). 6'0". LHB, RM. Debut 2000; ECB qualified and CC debut 2001; cap 2003. F-c Tour (Eng A): I 2003-04. 1000 (1): 1038 (2003). HS 124 v Surrey (Guildford) 2002. BB 2-10 v Kent (Canterbury) 2001. LO HS 92 v Glam (Colwyn Bay) 2003 (NL).

McGRATH, Anthony (Yorkshire Martyrs Collegiate S), b Bradford 6 Oct 1975. 6'2". RHB, RM. Debut 1995; cap 1999; captain 2003. **Tests**: 4 (2003); HS 81 v Z (Chester-le-St) 2003; BB 3-16 v Z (Lord's) 2003 on debut. **LOI**: 10 (2003); HS 52 v SA (Manchester) 2003; BB 1-15. F-c Tours (Eng A): A 1996-97; P 1995-96; Z 1995-96 (Y). HS 165 v Lancs (Leeds) 2002. BB 4-49 v Hants (Southampton) 2002. Awards: CGT 2; BHC 1. LO HS 109* v Minor C (Leeds) 1997 (BHC). LO BB 4-41 v Surrey (Leeds) 2003 (NL).

‡**PYRAH, Richard** Michael (Ossett S; Wakefield C), b Dewsbury 1 Nov 1982. RHB, RM. Staff 2004 – awaiting first-class debut. LO HS 27 (Yorks CB) v Northants CB (Northampton) 2001 (CGT) and 27 v Northumb (Jesmond) 2002 (CGT). LO BB 5-50 Yorks CB v Somerset (Scarborough) 2002 (CGT).

‡**SAYERS, Joseph John** (St Mary's RC CS, Menston; Worcester C, Oxford) b Leeds 5 Nov 1983. 6'0". LHB, OB. Oxford U 2002-03; blue 2002-03. Awaiting Yorkshire f-c debut. HS 122 OU v Hants (Oxford) 2003. BB – LO HS 62 v Glos (Leeds) 2003 (NL).

SILVERWOOD, Christopher Eric Wilfred (Garforth CS), b Pontefract 5 Mar 1975. 6'1". RHB, RFM. Debut 1993; cap 1996; benefit 2004. YC 1996. **Tests**: 6 (1996-97 to 2002-03); HS 10 v A (Perth) 2002-03; BB 5-91 v SA (Cape Town) 1999-00. **LOI**: 7 (1996-97 to 2001-02); HS 12 v NZ (Auckland) 1996-97; BB 3-43 v Z (Bulawayo) 2001-02. F-c Tours: A 2002-03 (part); SA 1999-00 (part); WI 1997-98, 2000-01 (Eng A); NZ 1996-97; Z 1995-96 (Y), 1996-97. HS 70 v Essex (Chelmsford) 2001. 50 wkts (2); most – 59 (1999). BB 7-93 (12-148 match) v Kent (Leeds) 1997. Awards: CGT 1; BHC 2. LO HS 61 v Northants (Northampton) 2002 (CGT). LO BB 5-28 v Scot (Leeds) 1996 (BHC).

TAYLOR, Christopher Robert (Benton Park HS, Rawdon), b Leeds 21 Feb 1981. 6'4". RHB, RMF. Debut 2001. HS 52* v Surrey (Leeds) 2002. LO HS 28 v Glos (Leeds) 2003 (NL).

THORNICROFT, Nicholas David (Easingwold S), b York 23 Jan 1985. 5'11". LHB, RMF. Debut 2002. HS 4* and BB 2-51 v Lancs (Manchester) 2002 – on debut. LO HS 0* (NL). LO BB 5-42 v Glos (Leeds) 2003 (NL).

VAUGHAN, Michael Paul (Silverdale CS, Sheffield), b Manchester, Lancs 29 Oct 1974. 6'2". RHB, OB. Debut 1993; cap 1995. *Wisden* 2002. **ECB contracts 2000, 2001, 2002, 2003, 2004. Tests**: 40 (1999-00 to 2003-04, 9 as captain); HS 197 and BB 2-71 v I (Nottingham) 2002. Scored Eng record 1,481 runs (avge 61.70) with six hundreds in 2002. **LOI**: 39 (2000-01 to 2003-04, 13 as captain); HS 83 v SA (Birmingham) 2003; BB 4-22 v SL (Manchester) 2002. F-c Tours (C=captain): A 1996-97 (Eng A), 2002-03; SA 1998-99C (Eng A), 1999-00; NZ 2001-02; I 1994-95 (Eng A), 2001-02; P 2000-01; SL 2000-01, 2003-04C; Z 1995-96 (Y), 1998-99C (Eng A); B 2003-04C. 1000 runs (4); most – 1244 (1995). HS 197 (*see Tests*). Y HS 183 v Glam (Cardiff) 1996. BB 4-39 v OU (Oxford) 1994. CC BB 4-47 v Somerset (Leeds) 2001. Awards: CGT 2; BHC 2. LO HS 125* v Somerset (Taunton) 2001 (BHC). LO BB 4-22 (*see LOI*).

WHITE, Craig (Flora Hill HS, Bendigo, Australia; Bendigo HS), b Morley 16 Dec 1969. 6'0". RHB, RFM. Debut 1990; cap 1993; benefit 2004; captain 2004. Victoria 1990-91 (2 matches). **ECB contracts 2000, 2001. Tests**: 30 (1994 to 2002-03); HS 121 v I (Ahmedabad) 2001-02; BB 5-32 v WI (Oval) 2000. **LOI**: 51 (1994-95 to 2002-03); HS 57* v A (Melbourne) 2002-03; BB 5-21 v Z (Bulawayo) 1999-00. F-c Tours: A 1994-95, 1996-97 (Eng A), 2002-03; SA 1991-92 (Y), 1992-93 (Y); NZ 1996-97, 2001-02; I 2001-02; P 1995-96 (Eng A), 2000-01; SL 2000-01; Z 1996-97 (part). HS 186 v Lancs (Manchester) 2001. BB 8-55 v Glos (Gloucester) 1998 – inc hat trick. Hat trick 1998. Awards: CGT 4; BHC 4. LO HS 148 v Leics (Leicester) 1997 (SL). LO BB 5-19 v Somerset (Scarborough) 2002 (NL).

WOOD, Matthew James (Shelley HS & SFC), b Huddersfield 6 Apr 1977. 5'9". RHB, OB. Debut 1997; cap 2001. 1000 runs (3): most – 1432 (2003). HS 207 v Somerset (Taunton) 2003. BB 1-4. Awards: CGT 1; BHC 1. LO HS 118* and BB 3-45 v Cambs (March) 2003 (CGT).

RELEASED/RETIRED
(Having made a first-class County appearance in 2003)

NQELLIOT, M.T.G – *see* GLAMORGAN.

FELLOWS, Gary Matthew (N Halifax GS), b Halifax 30 Jul 1978. 5'9". RHB, RM. Matabeleland 1996-97. Yorkshire 1998-2003. HS 109 v Lancs (Manchester) 2002. BB 3-23 v Essex (Chelmsford) 2001. Award: CGT 1. LO HS 80 * v Surrey (Leeds) 2001 (CGT). LO BB 4-19 v Durham (Leeds) 2002 (NL).

NQFLEMING, Stephen Paul (Cashmere HS, Canterbury; Christchurch C), b Christchurch, New Zealand 1 Apr 1973. 6'3". LHB. Canterbury 1991-92 to 1999-00. Wellington 2000-01 to date. Middlesex 2001; cap 2001. Yorkshire 2003. **Tests** (NZ): 79 (1993-94 to 2003-04, 55 as captain); HS 274* v SL (Colombo) 2002-03. **LOI** (NZ): 212 (1993-94 to 2003-04, 152 as captain); HS 134* v SA (Johannesburg) 2002-03; BB 1-8. F-c Tours (NZ) (C=captain): E 1994, 1999C; A 1997-98C, 2001-02C; SA 1993-94 (Cant), 1994-95, 2000-01C; WI 1995-96; 1999-96, 1999-00C, 2003-04C; P 1996-97; SL 1997-98C, 2002-03C; Z 1997-98C, 2000-01C. 1000 (1): 1091 (2001). HS 274* (see Tests). CC HS 151 M v Notts (Nottingham) 2001. Y HS 98 v Somerset (Taunton) 2003 – on Yorks debut. BB – LO HS 139* Y v Warwks (Leeds) 2003 (NL). LO BB (NZ) 1-3.

GOUGH, D. – see ESSEX.

HAMILTON, G.M. – see DURHAM.

NQMARTYN, D.R. – see NOTTINGHAMSHIRE.

RICHARDSON, Scott Andrew (Hulme GS, Oldham; Manchester GS), b Oldham, Lancs 5 Sep 1977. 6'2". RHB, RM. Yorkshire 2000-03. HS 69 v Kent (Leeds) 2001. LO HS 7 v WI A (Leeds) 2002.

SIDEBOTTOM, R. – see NOTTINGHAMSHIRE.

SWANEPOEL, Pieter Johannes (Paarl Gymnasium), b Paarl, South Africa 30 Mar 1977. 6'3". RHB, RMF. Yorkshire 2003. HS 17 and BB 2-40 v Durham (Leeds) 2003 on debut. LO HS 28* Yorks CB v Glos CB (Bristol) 2001 (CGT). LO BB 3-9 Yorks CB v Lancs CB (Nelson) 2001 (CGT).

NQYUVRAJ SINGH b Chandigarh, India 12 Dec 1981. LHB, SLA/LM. Punjab 1996-97, 1998-99 to 2001-02. Yorkshire 2003. **Tests** (I): 1 (2003-04); HS 20 v NZ (Chandigarh) 2003-04. **LOI** (I): 89 (2000-01 to 2003-04); HS 139 v A (Sydney) 20003-04; BB 4-6 v Namibia (Pretoria) 2002-03. F-c Tour (I): SA 2001-02 (Ind A). HS 209 N Zone v S Zone (Faridabad) 2001-02. Y HS 56 v Durham (Leeds) 2003. BB 3-25 Punjab v Jammu & Kashmir (Jammu) 2001-02 Y BB 1-8. LO HS 139 (see LOI). LO BB 4-6 (see LOI).

WORCESTERSHIRE RELEASED/RETIRED (continued from p 101)

NQKEMP, Justin Miles (Queens C; Port Elizabeth U), b Queenstown, South Africa 2 Oct 1977. Son of J.W.Kemp (Border 1975-76 to 1976-77); grandson of J.M.Kemp (Border 1947-48). RHB, RMF. E Province 1996-97 to date. **Tests** (SA): 3 (2000-01); HS 16 v WI (St John's) 2000-01; BB 3-33 v SL (Pretoria) 2000-01 on debut. **LOI** (SA) : 14 (2000-01 to 2001-02); HS 46 v WI (Port-of-Spain) 2000-01; BB 3-20 v I (Durban) 2001-02. F-c Tours (SA): WI 2000 (SA A), 2000-01; Z 1998-99 (SA Acad). HS 188 EP v North West (Port Elizabeth) 2000-01. Wo HS 90 v Hants (Southampton) 2003. BB 6-56 EP v Border (Port Elizabeth) 2000-01. Wo BB 5-48 v Glam (Cardiff) 2003 – on Worcs debut. LO HS 95* EP v Boland (Port Elizabeth) 2000-01. LO BB 6-20 EP v FS (Port Elizabeth) 2000-01.

LIPTROT, Christopher George (The Deanery HS), b Wigan, Lancs 13 Feb 1980. 6'2". LHB, RFM. Worcestershire 1999-2003. HS 61 v Warwks (Birmingham) 1999. BB 6-44 v Warwks (Worcester) 2000. LO HS 15* and LO BB 3-44 v Kent (Canterbury) 2000 (NL).

SINGH, A. – see NOTTINGHAMSHIRE.

YORKSHIRE 2003

RESULTS SUMMARY

	Place	Won	Lost	Tied	Drew	No Result
County Championship (2nd Division)	4th	4	5		7	
All First-Class Matches		4	5		8	
C & G Trophy	4th Round					
National League (1st Division)	8th	5	11			
Twenty20 Cup	2nd in North Group					

COUNTY CHAMPIONSHIP AVERAGES

BATTING AND FIELDING

Cap		M	I	NO	HS	Runs	Avge	100	50	Ct/St
1995	M.P.Vaughan	3	6	2	103	263	65.75	1	1	1
2001	M.J.Wood	16	31	6	207	1339	53.56	5	2	8
1993	C.White	9	14	2	173*	592	49.33	2	3	4
1999	A.McGrath	10	18	3	127*	649	43.26	1	5	5
2003	M.J.Lumb	16	25	2	115*	917	39.86	2	5	7
–	S.P.Fleming	7	14	2	98	469	39.08	–	3	13
–	A.K.D.Gray	8	11	1	104	366	36.50	1	1	11
1987	R.J.Blakey	12	17	2	223*	447	29.80	1	–	30/1
–	R.K.J.Dawson	12	18	2	77	467	29.18	–	2	11
–	V.J.Craven	5	9	1	47	208	26.00	–	–	1
2000	M.J.Hoggard	6	7	5	21*	49	24.50	–	–	2
1993	D.Gough	7	10	1	83	199	22.11	–	2	1
–	G.M.Fellows	5	6	–	53	114	19.00	–	1	3
–	S.A.Richardson	3	6	–	50	103	17.16	–	1	3
–	Yuvraj Singh	7	12	2	56	145	14.50	–	1	12
2000	R.J.Sidebottom	9	11	2	28	122	13.55	–	–	4
1996	C.E.W.Silverwood	12	18	4	53	152	10.85	–	1	2
–	S.M.Guy	6	8	–	26	73	9.12	–	–	16/2
2003	S.P.Kirby	14	18	4	33	113	8.07	–	–	5

Also batted: T.T.Bresnan (3 matches) 7, 3, 19 (1 ct); G.M.Hamilton (1 – cap 1998) 68 (1 ct); D.R.Martyn (2) 87*, 238, 17 (2 ct); P.J.Swanepoel (1) 17, 2 (1 ct); C.R.Taylor (2) 16, 40, 14 (1 ct).

BOWLING

	O	M	R	W	Avge	Best	5wI	10wM
R.J.Sidebottom	222.2	37	710	35	20.28	7- 97	2	
C.E.W.Silverwood	351.4	73	1177	48	24.52	5- 63	2	
S.P.Kirby	463	80	1769	67	26.40	8- 80	5	2
A.McGrath	117.1	20	347	13	26.69	3- 26		
M.J.Hoggard	192.3	44	547	18	30.38	7- 49	1	
D.Gough	218.1	46	651	19	34.26	3- 40		
R.K.J.Dawson	241.5	47	840	17	49.41	3-119		
A.K.D.Gray	207.2	43	628	12	52.33	3- 43		

Also bowled:

	O	M	R	W	Avge	Best	5wI	10wM
V.J.Craven	72	18	239	8	29.87	2- 25		

T.T.Bresnan 58-12-171-4; G.M.Fellows 14-1-27-1; M.J.Lumb 12-0-66-1; P.J.Swanepoel 34-11-70-3; M.P.Vaughan 1-0-5-0; C.White 21-3-64-0; M.J.Wood 2-0-4-1; Yuvraj Singh 34.3-5-130-3.

The First-Class Averages (pp 123–138) give the records of Yorkshire players in all first-class county matches (Yorkshire's other opponents being India A), with the exception of D.Gough, M.J.Hoggard, A.McGrath and M.P.Vaughan whose full county figures are as above.

YORKSHIRE RECORDS

FIRST-CLASS CRICKET

Highest Total	For 887		v	Warwicks	Birmingham	1896
	V 681-7d		by	Leics	Bradford	1996
Lowest Total	For 23		v	Hampshire	Middlesbrough	1965
	V 13		by	Notts	Nottingham	1901
Highest Innings	For 341	G.H.Hirst	v	Leics	Leicester	1905
	V 318*	W.G.Grace	for	Glos	Cheltenham	1876

Highest Partnership for each Wicket

1st	555	P.Holmes/H.Sutcliffe	v	Essex	Leyton	1932
2nd	346	W.Barber/M.Leyland	v	Middlesex	Sheffield	1932
3rd	323*	H.Sutcliffe/M.Leyland	v	Glamorgan	Huddersfield	1928
4th	330	M.J.Wood/D.R.Martyn	v	Glos	Leeds	2003
5th	340	E.Wainwright/G.H.Hirst	v	Surrey	The Oval	1899
6th	276	M.Leyland/E.Robinson	v	Glamorgan	Swansea	1926
7th	254	W.Rhodes/D.C.F.Burton	v	Hampshire	Dewsbury	1919
8th	292	R.Peel/Lord Hawke	v	Warwicks	Birmingham	1896
9th	192	G.H.Hirst/S.Haigh	v	Surrey	Bradford	1898
10th	149	G.Boycott/G.B.Stevenson	v	Warwicks	Birmingham	1982

Best Bowling	For	10-10	H.Verity	v	Notts	Leeds	1932
(Innings)	V	10-37	C.V.Grimmett	for	Australians	Sheffield	1930
Best Bowling	For	17-91	H.Verity	v	Essex	Leyton	1933
(Match)	V	17-91	H.Dean	for	Lancashire	Liverpool	1913

Most Runs – Season	2883	H.Sutcliffe	(av 80.08)		1932
Most Runs – Career	38561	H.Sutcliffe	(av 50.20)		1919-45
Most 100s – Season	12	H.Sutcliffe			1932
Most 100s – Career	112	H.Sutcliffe			1919-45
Most Wkts – Season	240	W.Rhodes	(av 12.72)		1900
Most Wkts – Career	3608	W.Rhodes	(av 16.00)		1898-1930
Most Career W-K Dismissals	1186	D.Hunter	(863 ct/323 st)		1888-1909
Most Career Catches in the Field	665	J.Tunnicliffe			1891-1907

LIST 'A' LIMITED-OVERS CRICKET

Highest Total	CGT	345-5		v	Notts	Leeds	1996
	BHC	317-5		v	Scotland	Leeds	1986
	NL	352-6		v	Notts	Scarborough	2001
Lowest Total	CGT	76		v	Surrey	Harrogate	1970
	BHC	81		v	Lancs	Leeds	2002
	NL	54		v	Essex	Leeds	2003
Highest Innings	CGT	146	G.Boycott	v	Surrey	Lord's	1965
	BHC	142	G.Boycott	v	Worcs	Worcester	1980
	NL	191	D.S.Lehmann	v	Notts	Scarborough	2001
Best Bowling	CGT	7-27	D.Gough	v	Ireland	Leeds	1997
	BHC	6-27	A.G.Nicholson	v	Minor C (N)	Middlesbrough	1972
	NL	7-15	R.A.Hutton	v	Worcs	Leeds	1969

ECB FIRST-CLASS UMPIRES 2004

No new appointments

BENSON, Mark Richard (Sutton Valence S), b Shoreham, Sussex 6 Jul 1958. LHB, OB. Kent 1980-95; cap 1981; captain 1991-96 (did not play in 1996); benefit 1991. **Tests:** 1 (1986); HS 30 v I (Birmingham) 1986. **LOI:** 1 (1986; HS 24). 1000 runs (11); most – 1725 (1987). HS 257 K v Hants (Southampton) 1991. BB 2-55 K v Surrey (Dartford) 1986. F-c career: 292 matches; 18387 runs @ 40.23, 48 hundreds; 5 wickets @ 98.60; 140 ct. Appointed 2000.

BURGESS, Graham Iefvion (Millfield S), b Glastonbury, Somerset 5 May 1943. RHB, RM. Somerset 1966-79; cap f968; testimonial 1977. HS 129 Sm v Glos (Taunton) 1973. BB 7-43 (13-75 match) Sm v OU (Oxford) 1975. F-c career: 252 matches; 7129 runs @ 18.90, 2 hundreds; 474 wickets @ 28.57. Appointed 1991.

CLARKSON, Anthony (Harrogate GS), b Killinghall, Harrogate, Yorks 5 Sep 1939. RHB, OB. Yorkshire 1963. Somerset 1966-71; cap 1968. Devon. 1000 runs (2); most – 1246 (1970). HS 131 Sm v Northants (Northampton) 1969. BB 3-51 Sm v Essex (Yeovil) 1967. F-c career: 110 matches; 4458 runs @ 25.18, 2 hundreds; 13 wickets @ 28.23. Appointed 1996.

CONSTANT, David John, b Bradford-on-Avon, Wilts 9 Nov 1941. LHB, SLA. Kent 1961-63. Leicestershire 1965-68. HS 80 Le v Glos (Bristol) 1966. BB 1-28. F-c career: 61 matches; 1517 runs @ 19.20; 1 wicket @ 36.00. Appointed 1969. Umpired 36 Tests (1971 to 1988) and 33 LOI (1972 to 2001). Represented Gloucestershire at bowls 1984-86.

COWLEY, Nigel Geoffrey (Dutchy Manor S, Mere), b Shaftesbury, Dorset 1 Mar 1953. RHB, OB. Dorset 1972. Hampshire 1974-89; cap 1978; benefit 1988. Glamorgan 1990. 1000 runs (1): 1042 (1984). HS 109* H v Somerset (Taunton) 1977. BB 6-48 H v Leics (Southampton) 1982. F-c career: 271 matches; 7309 runs @ 23.35, 2 hundreds; 437 wickets @ 34.04. Appointed 2000.

DUDLESTON, Barry (Stockport S), b Bebington, Cheshire 16 Jul 1945. RHB, SLA. Leicestershire 1966-80; cap 1969; benefit 1980. Gloucestershire 1981-83. Rhodesia 1976-77 to 1979-80. 1000 runs (8); most – 1374 (1970). HS 202 Le v Derbys (Leicester) 1979. BB 4-6 Le v Surrey (Leicester) 1972. F-c career: 295 matches; 14747 runs @ 32.48, 32 hundreds; 47 wickets @ 29.04. Appointed 1984. Umpired 2 Tests (1991 to 1992) and 4 LOI (1992 to 2001).

EVANS, Jeffery Howard, b Llanelli, Carms 7 Aug 1954. No f-c appearances. Appointed 2001.

GOULD, Ian James (Westgate SS, Slough), b Taplow, Bucks 19 Aug 1957. LHB, WK. Middlesex 1975 to 1980-81, 1996; cap 1977. Auckland 1979-80. Sussex 1981-90; cap 1981; captain 1987; benefit 1990. MCC YC. **LOI:** 18 (1982-83 to 1983; HS 42). Tours: A 1982-83; P 1980-81 (Int); Z 1980-81 (M). HS 128 M v Worcs (Worcester) 1978. BB 3-10 Sx v Surrey (Oval) 1989. Middlesex coach 1991-2000. Reappeared in one match (v OU) 1996. F-c career: 298 matches; 8756 runs @ 26.05, 4 hundreds; 7 wickets @ 52.14; 603 dismissals (536 ct, 67 st). Appointed 2002.

HAMPSHIRE, John Harry (Oakwood THS, Rotherham), b Thurnscoe, Yorks 10 Feb 1941. RHB, LB. Son of J. (Yorks 1937); brother of A.W. (Yorks 1975). Yorkshire 1961-81; cap 1963; benefit 1976; captain 1979-80. Leicestershire 1980-81 (tour). Derbyshire 1982-84; cap 1982. Tasmania 1967-68 to 1978-79. **Tests:** 8 (1969 to 1975); 403 runs @ 26.86, HS 107 v WI (Lord's) 1969 on debut (only England player to score hundred at Lord's on Test debut). Tours: A 1970-71; SA 1972-73 (DHR), 1974-75 (DHR); WI 1964-65 (Cav); NZ 1970-71; P 1967-68 (Cwlth XI); SL 1969-70; Z 1980-81 (Le XI). 1000 runs (15); most – 1596 (1983). HS 183* Y v Sussex (Hove) 1971. BB 7-52 Y v Glam (Cardiff) 1963. F-c career: 577 matches; 28059 runs @ 34.55, 43 hundreds; 30 wickets @ 54.56; 445 ct. Appointed 1985. Umpired 21 Tests (1989 to 2001-02) and 20 LOI (1989 to 2001). International Panel 1999 to 2001-02.

HARRIS, Michael John ('*Pasty*') (Gerrans S, nr Truro), b St Just-in-Roseland, Cornwall 25 May 1944. RHB, LB, WK. Middlesex 1964-68; cap 1967. Nottinghamshire 1969-82; cap 1970; benefit 1977. E Province 1971-72. Wellington 1975-76. 1000 runs (11); most – 2238

(1971). Equalled Notts record with 9 hundreds in 1971. HS 201* Nt v Glam (Nottingham) 1973. BB 4-16 Nt v Warwks (Nottingham) 1969. F-c career: 344 matches; 19196 runs @ 36.70, 41 hundreds; 79 wickets @ 43.78; 302 dismissals (288 ct, 14 st). Appointed 1998.

HARTLEY, Peter John (Greenhead GS; Bradford C), b Keighley, Yorks 18 Apr 1960. RHB, RMF. Warwickshire 1982. Yorkshire 1985-97; cap 1987; benefit 1996. Hampshire 1998-2000; cap 1998. Tours (Y): SA 1991-92; WI 1986-87; Z 1995-96. HS 127* Y v Lancs (Manchester) 1988. 50 wkts (7); most – 81 (1995). BB 9-41 (inc hat trick, 4 wkts in 5 balls and 5 in 9; 11-68 match) Y v Derbys (Chesterfield) 1995. Hat trick 1995. F-c career: 232 matches; 4321 runs @ 19.91, 2 hundreds; 683 wickets @ 30.21. Appointed 2003.

HOLDER, John (Combermere S), b St George, Barbados 19 Mar 1945. RHB, RFM. Hampshire 1968-72. HS 33 H v Sussex (Hove) 1971. BB 7-79 H v Glos (Gloucester) 1972. Hat trick 1972. F-c career: 47 matches; 374 runs @ 10.68; 139 wickets @ 24.56. Appointed 1983. Umpired 11 Tests (1988 to 2001) and 19 LOI (1988 to 2001).

HOLDER, Vanburn Alonza (Richmond SM), b Deans Village, St Michael, Barbados 8 Oct 1945. RHB, RFM. Barbados 1966-67 to 1977-78. Worcestershire 1968-80; cap 1970; benefit 1979. Shropshire 1981. **Tests** (WI): 40 (1969 to 1978-79); 682 runs @ 14.20, HS 42 v NZ (P-o-S) 1971-72; 109 wkts @ 33.27, BB 6-28 v A (P-o-S) 1977-78. **LOI** (WI): 12. Tours (WI): E 1969, 1973, 1976; A 1975-76; I 1974-75, 1978-79; P 1973-74 (RW), 1974-75; SL 1974-75, 1978-79. HS 122 Barbados v Trinidad (Bridgetown) 1973-74. BB 7-40 Wo v Glam (Cardiff) 1974. F-c career: 311 matches; 3559 runs @ 13.03, 1 hundred; 947 wickets @ 24.48. Appointed 1992.

JESTY, Trevor Edward (Privet County SS, Gosport), b Gosport, Hants 2 Jun 1948. RHB, RM. Hampshire 1966-84; cap 1971; benefit 1982. Surrey 1985-87; captain 1985. Lancashire 1987-88 to 1991; cap 1989. Border 1973-74. GW 1974-75 to 1980-81. Canterbury 1979-80. *Wisden* 1983. **LOI**: 10. Tours: WI 1987-88 (La.), 1982-83 (Int); Z 1988-89 (La). 1000 runs (10); most – 1645 (1982). HS 248 H v CU (Cambridge) 1984. Scored 122* La v OU (Oxford) 1991 in his final f-c innings. 50 wkts (2); most – 52 (1981). BB 7-75 H v Worcs (Southampton) 1976. F-c career: 490 matches; 21916 runs @ 32.71, 35 hundreds; 585 wickets @ 27.47. Appointed 1994.

JONES, Allan Arthur (St John's C, Horsham), b Horley, Surrey 9 Dec 1947. RHB, RFM. Sussex 1966-69. Somerset 1970-75; cap 1972. Middlesex 1976-79; cap 1976. Glamorgan 1980-81. Northern Transvaal 1972-73. Orange Free State 1976-77. HS 33 M v Kent (Canterbury) 1978. BB 9-51 Sm v Sussex (Hove) 1972. F-c career: 214 matches; 799 runs @ 5.39; 549 wickets @ 28.07. Appointed 1985. Umpired 1 LOI (1996).

KITCHEN, Mervyn John (Backwell SM, Nailsea), b Nailsea, Somerset 1 Aug 1940. LHB, RM. Somerset 1960-79; cap 1966; testimonial 1973. Tour: Rhodesia 1972-73 (Int W). 1000 runs (7); most – 1730 (1968). HS 189 Sm v Pakistanis (Taunton) 1967. BB 1-4. F-c career: 354 matches; 15230 runs @ 26.25, 17 hundreds; 2 wickets @ 54.50. Appointed 1982. Umpired 20 Tests (1990 to 2000) and 28 LOI (1983 to 2001). International Panel 1995 to 1999.

LEADBEATER, Barrie (Harehills SS), b Harehills, Leeds, Yorks 14 Aug 1943. RHB, RM. Yorkshire 1966-79; cap 1969; joint benefit with G.A.Cope 1980. Tour: WI 1969-70 (DN). HS 140* Y v Hants (Portsmouth) 1976. BB 1-1. F-c career: 147 matches; 5373 runs @ 25.34, 1 hundred; 1 wicket @ 5.00. Appointed 1981. Umpired 5 LOI (1983 to 2000).

LLONG, Nigel James (Ashford North S), b Ashford, Kent 11 Feb 1969. LHB, OB. Kent 1990-98; cap 1993. Tour: Z 1992-93 (K). HS 130 K v Hants (Canterbury) 1996. BB 5-21 K v Middx (Canterbury) 1996. F-c career: 68 matches; 3024 runs @ 31.17, 6 hundreds; 35 wickets @ 35.97. Appointed 2002.

LLOYDS, Jeremy William (Blundells S), b Penang, Malaya 17 Nov 1954. LHB, OB. Somerset 1979-84; cap 1982. Gloucestershire 1985-91; cap 1985. Orange Free State 1983-84 to 1987-88, Tour (Glos): SL 1986-87. 1000 runs (3); most – 1295 (1986). HS 132* Sm v Northants (Northampton) 1982. BB 7-88 Sm v Essex (Chelmsford) 1982. F-c career: 267 matches; 10679 runs @ 31.04, 10 hundreds; 333 wickets @ 38.86; 229 ct. Appointed 1998. Umpired 2 LOI (2000 to 2001).

MALLENDER, Neil Alan (Beverley GS), b Kirk Sandall, Yorks 13 Aug 1961. RHB, RFM. Northamptonshire 1980-86 and 1995-96; cap 1984. Somerset 1987-94; cap 1987; benefit 1994. Otago 1983-84 to 1992-93; captain 1990-91 to 1992-93. **Tests:** 2 (1992); 8 runs @ 2.66, HS 4; 10 wkts @ 21.50, BB 5-50 v P (Leeds) 1992 – on debut. Tour: Z 1994-95 (Nh). HS 100* Otago v CD (Palmerston N) 1991-92. UK HS 87* Sm v Sussex (Hove) 1990. 50 wkts (6); most – 56 (1983). BB 7-27 Otago v Auckland (Auckland) 1984-85. UK BB 7-41 Nh v Derbys (Northampton) 1982. F-c career: 345 matches; 4709 runs @ 17.18, 1 hundred; 937 wickets @ 26.31; 111 ct. Appointed 1999. Umpired 1 Test (2003-04) and 22 LOI (2001 to 2003-04), including 2002-03 World Cup. **Elite Panel 2004.**

PALMER, Roy (Southbroom SM, Devizes), b Devizes, Wilts 12 Jul 1942. RHB, RFM. Younger brother of K.E.Palmer, MBE (Somerset and England 1955-69). Somerset 1965-70. HS 84 Sm v Leics (Taunton) 1967. BB 6-45 Sm v Middx (Lord's) 1967. F-c career: 74 matches; 1037 runs @ 13.29; 172 wickets @ 31.62. Appointed 1980. Umpired 2 Tests (1992 to 1993) and 8 LOI (1983 to 1995).

SHARP, George (Elwick Road SS, Hartlepool), b West Hartlepool, Co Durham 12 Mar 1950. RHB, WK, occ LM. Northamptonshire 1968-85; cap 1973; benefit 1982. HS 98 Nh v Yorks (Northampton) 1983. BB 1-47. F-c career: 306 matches; 6254 runs @ 19.85; 1 wicket @ 70.00; 655 dismissals (565 ct, 90 st). Appointed 1992. Umpired 15 Tests (1996 to 2001-02) and 31 LOI (1995-96 to 2001-02). International Panel 1996 to 2001-02.

SHEPHERD, David Robert (Barnstaple GS; St Luke's C, Exeter), b Bideford, Devon 27 Dec 1940. RHB, RM. Gloucestershire 1965-79; cap 1969; joint benefit with J.Davey 1978. Scored 108 on debut (v OU). Devon 1959-64. 1000 runs (2); most – 1079 (1970). HS 153 Gs v Middx (Bristol) 1968. BB 1-1. F-c career: 282 matches; 10672 runs @ 24.47, 12 hundreds; 2 wickets @ 53.00. Appointed 1981. Umpired 78 Tests (1985 to 2003-04) and a record 145 LOI (1983 to 2003-04), including 1987-88, 1991-92, 1995-96, 1999 and 2002-03 World Cups (3 finals). International Panel 1994 to 2001-02. **Elite Panel 2001-02 to date.**

STEELE, John Frederick (Endon SS), b Brown Edge, Staffs 23 Jul 1946. RHB, SLA. Brother of D.S. (Northants, Derbys and England 1963-84). Leicestershire 1970-83; cap 1971; benefit 1983. Glamorgan 1984-86; cap 1984. Natal 1973-74 to 1977-78. Staffordshire 1965-69. Tour: SA 1974-75 (DHR). 1000 runs (6); most – 1347 (1972). HS 195 Le v Derbys (Leicester) 1971. BB 7-29 Natal B v GW (Umzinto) 1973-74 and 7-29 Le v Glos (Leicester) 1980. F-c career: 379 matches; 15054 runs @ 28.95, 21 hundreds; 584 wickets @ 27.04; 413 ct. Appointed 1997.

WHITEHEAD, Alan Geoffrey Thomas, b Butleigh, Somerset 28 Oct 1940. LHB, SLA. Somerset 1957-61. HS 15 Sm v Hants (Southampton) 1959 and 15 Sm v Leics (Leicester) 1960. BB 6-74 Sm v Sussex (Eastbourne) 1959. F-c career: 38 matches; 137 runs @ 5.70; 67 wickets @ 34.41. Appointed 1970. Umpired 5 Tests (1982 to 1987) and 14 LOI (1979 to 2001).

WILLEY, Peter (Seaham SS), b Sedgefield, Co Durham 6 Dec 1949. RHB, OB. Northamptonshire 1966-83; cap 1971; benefit 1981. Leicestershire 1984-91; cap 1984; captain 1987. E Province 1982-83 to 1984-85. Northumberland 1992. **Tests:** 26 (1976 to 1986); 1184 runs @ 26.90, HS 102* v WI (St John's) 1980-81; 7 wkts @ 65.14, BB 2-73 v WI (Lord's) 1980. **LOI:** 26. Tours: A 1979-80; SA 1972-73 (DHR), 1981-82 (SAB); WI 1980-81, 1985-86; I 1979-80; SL 1977-78 (DHR). 1000 runs (10); most – 1783 (1982). HS 227 Nh v Somerset (Northampton) 1976. 50 wkts (3); most – 52 (1979). BB 7-37 Nh v OU (Oxford) 1975. F-c career: 559 matches; 24361 runs @ 30.56, 44 hundreds; 756 wickets @ 30.95. Appointed 1993. Umpired 25 Tests (1995-96 to 2003-04) and 34 LOI (1996 to 2003), including 1999 and 2002-03 World Cups. International Panel 1996 to 2001-02 and 2003-04.

RESERVE FIRST-CLASS LIST: R.J.Bailey, N.L.Bainton, S.A.Garratt, R.K.Illingworth, R.A.Kettleborough, R.T.Robinson.

Test Match and LOI statistics to 18 February 2004 inclusive. See page 9 for key to abbreviations.

INTERNATIONAL UMPIRES AND REFEREES 2004

ELITE PANEL OF UMPIRES 2004

The Elite Panel of ICC Umpires and Referees was introduced in April 2002 to raise standards and guarantee impartial adjudication. Two umpires from this panel stand in Test matches while one officiates with a home umpire from the Supplementary International Panel in limited-overs internationals.

Full Names	Birthdate	Birthplace	Tests	Debut	LOI	Debut
ALIM Sarwar DAR	06.06.68	Jhang, Pakistan	4	2003-04	33	1999-00
BOWDEN, Brent Fraser	11.04.63	Auckland, N Zealand	11	1999-00	45	1994-95
BUCKNOR, Stephen Anthony	31.05.46	Montego Bay, Jamaica	86	1988-89	118	1988-89
DE SILVA, Ellawalakankanamage Asoka Ranjith	28.03.56	Kalutara, Sri Lanka	28	1999-00	46	1999-00
HAIR, Darrell Bruce	30.09.52	Mudgee, Australia	51	1991-92	99	1991-92
HARPER, Daryl John	23.10.61	Adelaide, Australia	37	1998-99	80	1993-94
KOERTZEN, Rudolf Eric ('Rudi')	26.03.49	Knysna, S Africa	46	1992-93	113	1992-93
MALLENDER, Neil Alan	13.08.61	Kirk Sandall, England	1	2003-04	22	2001
SHEPHERD, David Robert	27.12.40	Bideford, England	78	1985	145	1983
TAUFEL, Simon James Arthur	21.01.71	Sydney, Australia	11	2000-01	59	1998-99

ELITE PANEL OF REFEREES 2004

Full Names	Birthdate	Birthplace	Tests	Debut	LOI	Debut
BROAD, Brian Christopher	29.09.57	Bristol, England	2	2003-04	5	2003-04
CROWE, Jeffey John	14.09.58	Auckland, N Zealand				
HURST, Alan George	15.07.50	Melbourne, Australia				
LLOYD, Clive Hubert	31.08.44	Georgetown, Guyana	30	1992-93	92	1992-93
MADUGALLE, Ranjan Senerath	22.04.59	Kandy, Sri Lanka	58	1993-94	149	1993-94
MAHANAMA, Roshan Siriwardena	31.05.66	Colombo, Sri Lanka				
PROCTER, Michael John	15.09.46	Durban, S Africa	20	2001-02	48	2001-02
VISWANATH, Gundappa Ranganath	12.02.49	Bhadravati, India	15	1999-00	63	1998-99

INTERNATIONAL PANEL OF UMPIRES 2004

Nominated by their respective cricket boards, members from this panel officiate in home LOIs and supplement the Elite panel for Test matches. Specialist third umpires have been selected to undertake adjudication involving television replays.

			Third Umpire
Australia	S.J.Davis	P.D.Parker	R.L.Parry
Bangladesh	Akhtaruddin Sahin	Mahbubur Rahman	Showkatur Rahman
England	P.Willey	–	J.W.Lloyds
India	K.Hariharan	A.V.Jayaprakash	I.Sivaram
New Zealand	D.B.Cowie	A.L.Hill	G.A.Baxter
Pakistan	Nadeem Ghauri	–	Asad Rauf
South Africa	I.L.Howell	B.G.Jerling	G.B.Cuddumbey
Sri Lanka	P.T.Manuel	T.H.Wijewardena	M.G.Silva
West Indies	B.R.Doctrove	E.A.Nicholls	B.E.W.Morgan
Zimbabwe	K.C.Barbour	I.D.Robinson	

SUPPLEMENTARY PANEL OF REFEREES 2004

Australia	–	Pakistan	Sultan Rana
Bangladesh	Raquibul Hassan	South Africa	D.T.Lindsay
England	–	Sri Lanka	G.F.Labrooy
India	E.A.S.Prasanna	West Indies	–
New Zealand	J.F.M.Morrison	Zimbabwe	A.M.Ebrahim

TOURING TEAM FIRST-CLASS REGISTER 2003

ZIMBABWE

Full Names	Birthdate	Birthplace	Team	Type	F-C Debut
BLIGNAUT, Arnoldus Mauritius ('Andy')	01.08.78	Salisbury	Mashonaland	LHB/RFM	1997-98
CARLISLE, Stuart Vance	10.05.72	Salisbury	Mashonaland	RHB/RSM	1993-94
EBRAHIM, Dion Digby	07.08.80	Bulawayo	Mashonaland	RHB/RM-OB	1999-00
ERVINE, Sean Michael	06.12.82	Harare	Midlands	LHB/RM	2000-01
FLOWER, Grant William	20.12.70	Salisbury	Mashonaland	RHB/SLA	1989-90
FRIEND, Travis John	07.01.81	Kwekwe	Midlands	RHB/RMF	1999-00
HONDO, Douglas Tafadzwa	07.07.79	Bulawayo	Midlands	RHB/RFM	1999-00
MARILLIER, Douglas Anthony	24.04.78	Salisbury	Midlands	RHB/OB	1998-99
NKALA, Mluleki Luke	01.04.81	Bulawayo	Matabeleland	RHB/RMF	1999-00
PRICE, Raymond William	12.06.76	Salisbury	Midlands	LHB/SLA	1995-96
ROGERS, Barney Guy	20.08.82	Harare	Mashonaland	LHB/OB	2000-01
SIBANDA, Vusimuzi	10.10.83	Harare	CFX Academy	RHB/RM	2001-02
STREAK, Heath Hilton	16.03.74	Bulawayo	Matabeleland	RHB/RFM	1992-93
TAIBU, Tatenda	14.05.83	Harare	Mashonaland	RHB/WK	1999-00
VERMEULEN, Mark Andrew	02.03.79	Salisbury	Matabeleland	RHB/OB	1997-98

SOUTH AFRICA

Full Names	Birthdate	Birthplace	Team	Type	F-C Debut
ADAMS, Paul Regan	20.01.77	Cape Town	W Province	RHB/SLC	1995-96
BOUCHER, Mark Verdon	03.12.76	East London	Border	RHB/WK	1995-96
DIPPENAAR, Hendrik Human ('Boeta')	14.06.77	Kimberley	Free State	RHB/OB	1995-96
GIBBS, Herschelle Herman	23.02.74	Cape Town	W Province	RHB/RM	1990-91
HALL, Andrew James	31.07.75	Johannesburg	Gauteng	RHB/RFM	1995-96
KALLIS, Jacques Henry	16.10.75	Cape Town	W Province	RHB/RFM	1993-94
KIRSTEN, Gary	23.11.67	Cape Town	W Province	LHB/OB	1987-88
McKENZIE, Neil Douglas	24.11.75	Johannesburg	Northerns	RHB/RM	1994-95
NTINI, Makhaya	06.07.77	King William's Town	Border	RHB/RF	1995-96
PETERSON, Robin John	04.08.79	Port Elizabeth	E Province	LHB/SLA	1998-99
POLLOCK, Shaun Maclean	16.07.73	Port Elizabeth	KZ-Natal	RHB/RFM	1991-92
PRETORIUS, Dewald	06.12.77	Pretoria	Free State	RHB/RF	1997-98
RUDOLPH, Jacobus Andries ('Jacques')	04.05.81	Springs	Northerns	LHB/LBG	1997-98
SMITH, Graeme Craig	01.02.81	Johannesburg	W Province	LHB/OB	1999-00
TSOLEKILE, Thami Lungisa	09.10.80	Cape Town	W Province	RHB/WK	1999
WILLOUGHBY, Charl Myles	03.12.74	Cape Town	W Province	LHB/LMF	1994-95
ZONDEKI, Monde	25.07.82	King William's Town	Border	RHB/RF	2000-01

INDIA A

Full Names	Birthdate	Birthplace	Team	Type	F-C Debut
BADANI, Hemang Kamal	14.11.76	Madras	Tamil Nadu	LHB/SLA	1996-97
BALAJI, Lakshmipathy	27.09.81	Madras	Tamil Nadu	RHB/RMF	2001-02
BHANDARI, Amit	01.10.78	Delhi	Delhi	RHB/RFM	1997-98
BHARADWAJ, Raghvendrarao Vijay	15.08.75	Bangalore	Karnataka	RHB/OB	1994-95
DAS, Shiv Sunder	05.11.77	Bhubaneshwar	Orissa	RHB/RM	1993-94
GAMBHIR, Gautam	14.10.81	Delhi	Delhi	LHB/LB	1999-00
GAVASKAR, Rohan Sunil	20.02.76	Kanpur	Bengal	RHB/OB	1996-97
JAFFER, Wasim	16.02.78	Bombay	Bombay	RHB/OB	1996-97
KARTIK, Murali	11.09.76	Madras	Railways	LHB/SLA	1996-97
MISHRA, Amit	24.11.82	Delhi	Haryana	RHB/LB	2000-01
PARAB, Satyajit Sudhir	01.09.75	Baroda	Baroda	RHB/LB	1997-98
PATEL, Pathiv Ajay	09.03.85	Ahmedabad	Gujarat	LHB/WK	2001-02
PATHAN, Irfan Khan	27.10.84	Baroda	Baroda	LHB/LFM	2000-01
RAYUDU, Ambati Thirupathi	23.09.85	Guntur	Hyderabad	RHB/OB	2001-02
SALVI, Aavishkar Madhav	20.10.81	Bombay	Bombay	RHB/RM	2001-02
SRIRAM, Sridharan	21.02.76	Madras	Tamil Nadu	LHB/SLA	1993-94

114

UNIVERSITY FIRST-CLASS REGISTER 2003

‡ Represented British Universities v Zimbabweans

CAMBRIDGE († Blue 2003)

Full Names	Birthdate	Birthplace	College	Bat/Bowl	F-C Debut
AKRAM, Mohammed Adnan	17.11.83	Leytonstone	(Anglia PU)	RHB/RM	2003
AKRAM, Mohammed Arfan	17.11.83	Leytonstone	(Anglia PU)	RHB/LB	2003
†HEATH, Duncan Robert	06.11.81	Grimsby	Pembroke	RHB/RM	2002
†HEATH, John Alexander	01.06.78	Grimsby	Pembroke	RHB/RM	2002
†HEYWOOD, James John Neville	24.09.82	Eastbourne	Homerton	RHB/WK	2003
†KUMAR, Vikram Harsh	21.01.81	Beckenham	St John's	RHB/WK	2001
†McGRATH, Daniel Edwin Taylor	13.02.76	Sydney, Aus	St Edmund's	RHB/RM	2002
†MANN, Richard James	26.09.82	Ipswich	St John's	LHB/OB	2003
†MARSHALL, Simon James	20.09.82	Birkenhead	Pembroke	RHB/LB	2002
†NOBLE, David Jonathan	08.11.82	Manchester	Emmanuel	RHB/RM	2002
PALLADINO, Antonio Paul	29.06.83	London	(Anglia PU)	RHB/RMF	2003
PARK, Garry Terence	19.04.83	Empangeni, SA	(Anglia PU)	RHB/RMF	2003
†SAVILL, Thomas Edward	16.05.83	Sheffield	Homerton	RHB/RFM	2002
†SHANKAR, Adrian	07.05.82	Ascot	Queens	RHB/OB	2002
†SINGH, Anirudh	28.12.83	Sutton Coldfield	Gonville & Caius	RHB/LB	2003
WEBLEY, Thomas	02.03.83	Bristol	(Anglia PU)	LHB/SLA	2003

DURHAM

Full Names	Birthdate	Birthplace	College	Bat/Bowl	F-C Debut
‡BISHOP, Justin Edward	04.01.82	Bury St Edmunds	John Snow	LHB/LMF	1999
BROWN, David Owen	08.12.82	Burnley	Collingwood	RHB/RM	2003
DAGGETT, Lee Martin	01.10.82	Bury	John Snow	RHB/RMF	2003
DALE, Mark Adam Paul	16.03.82	Hucknall	George Stephenson	RHB/RM	2003
‡FERLEY, Robert Steven	04.02.82	Norwich	Grey	RHB/SLA	2001
HANSON, William Thomas Daniel	21.04.82	Leicester	John Snow	RHB/WK	2003
HAWK, Simon Laurence John McLeod	22.09.79	London	John Snow	RHB/RM	2003
LOUDON, Alexander Guy Rushworth	06.09.80	London	Collingwood	RHB/OB	2001
MAIDEN, Alastair Jonathan	15.09.82	Stourbridge	Collingwood	RHB/RM	2002
POLLEY, Sean Robert	27.04.81	Luanshya, Zambia	George Stephenson	RHB/RM	2003
SMITH, Will Rew	28.09.82	Luton	Collingwood	RHB/OB	2002
SOMERVILLE-HENDRIE, John William	22.06.83	Hillingdon	George Stephenson	RHB/RFM	2003
‡TAYLOR, Delroy Bertram	30.06.75	Linstead, Jamaica	Graduate Society	RHB/RM	2003

LOUGHBOROUGH UNIVERSITY

(Excluding players listed either above or in the County Register)

Full Names	Birthdate	Birthplace	Bat/Bowl	F-C Debut
‡ADAMS, James Henry Kenneth	23.09.80	Winchester	LHB/LM	2002
ANYON, James Edward	05.05.83	Lancaster	LHB/RFM	2003
ATRI, Vikram	09.03.83	Hull	RHB/OB	2002
CUMMINS, Ryan Anthony Gilbert	14.04.84	Sutton (Surrey)	RHB/RM	2003
‡FRANCIS, John Daniel	13.11.80	Bromley	LHB/SLA	2001
GODDARD, Lee James	22.10.82	Dewsbury	RHB/WK	2003
KING, Richard Eric	03.01.84	Hitchin	RHB/LMF	2003
LEWIS, Philip David	04.10.81	Liss	RHB/RFM	2003
NASH, Christopher David	19.05.83	Cuckfield	RHB/OB	2002
SHARIF, Zoheb Khalid	22.02.83	Leytonstone	LHB/LB	2001
‡WHITE, Robert Allan	15.10.79	Chelmsford	RHB/LB	2000
WIGLEY, David Harry	26.10.81	Bradford	RHB/RFM	2002

OXFORD († Blue 2003)

Full Names	Birthdate	Birthplace	College	Bat/Bowl	F-C Debut
AIREY, Stuart James	18.03.83	Cleethorpes	(Brookes U)	RHB/RMF	2003
†ALLEN, John Aubrey	19.07.74	Windsor, Aus	University	RHB	2003
ANWAR, Omar Sohail	01.07.83	Harrow	(Brookes U)	RHB	2003
†BUTCHER, Graham Robert	25.09.81	Epsom	Oriel	RHB/RM	2001
‡COWAN, Edward James McKenzie	16.06.82	Sydney, Aus	(Brookes U)	LHB/LB	2003
†DALEY, Stephen Robert	15.04.77	Atherton, Australia	Magdalen	LHB/RMF	2003
†DALRYMPLE, James William Murray	21.01.81	Nairobi, Kenya	St Peter's	RHB/OB	2001
†EVANS, Patrick Peter	25.08.81	London	Keble	RHB	2002
†FREE, Clinton Wallace	17.09.75	Sydney, Australia	Balliol	RHB/RMF	2003
†HAWINKELS, Stephen John	12.03.82	Cape Town, SA	University	RHB/RM	2001
HOWARD, William Oliver Fitzalen	13.02.81	Guildford	(Brookes U)	RHB/WK	2002
JONES, Huw Rhys	23.11.80	Oxford	(Brookes U)	RHB/LB	2001
LINLEY, Timothy Edward	23.03.82	Leeds	(Brookes U)	RHB	2003
LOWE, Stephen James	07.05.81	Welwyn Garden C	(Brookes U)	LHB/WK	2003
‡MEES, Thomas	08.06.81	Wolverhampton	(Brookes U)	RHB/RMF	2001
†McMAHON, Paul Joseph	12.03.83	Wigan	Wadham	RHB/OB	2002
†MILLAR, Neil	03.02.81	London	Christ Church	RHB/RM	2000
†MUNDAY, Michael Kenneth	22.10.84	Nottingham	Corpus Christi	RHB/LB	2003
‡SAYERS, Joseph John	05.11.83	Leeds	Worcester	LHB/OB	2002
SHARPE, Toby John	05.07.81	London	(Brookes U)	RHB/RMF	2001

BRITISH UNIVERSITIES

(Excluding players listed above)

Full Names	Birthdate	Birthplace	University	Bat/Bowl	F-C Debut
‡DAWOOD, Ismail	23.07.76	Dewsbury	Bradford/Leeds	RHB/WK	1994
‡MURTAGH, Timothy James	02.08.81	Lambeth	St Mary's	LHB/RFM	2000
‡TOMLINSON, James Andrew	12.06.82	Winchester	Cardiff	LHB/LFM	2002

SCOTLAND

NATIONAL LEAGUE REGISTER 2003

Full Names	Birthdate	Birthplace	Bat/Bowl	F-C Debut
BLAIN, John Angus Rae	04.01.79	Edinburgh	RHB/RMF	1996
BRINKLEY, James Edward	13.03.74	Helensburgh	RHB/RFM	1993-94
COETZER, Kyle James	14.04.84	Aberdeen	RHB/RMF	–
DRAVID, Rahul	11.01.73	Indore, India	RHB/OB/WK	1990-91
HAQ, Rana Majid	11.12.83	Paisley	RHB/OB	–
HOFFMAN, Paul Jacob Christopher	14.01.70	Rockhampton, Australia	RHB/RMF	–
KENT, Jon Carter	07.05.79	Cape Town, S Africa	RHB/RMF	1997-98
KNOX, Steven Thomas	16.02.74	Barrow-in-Furness	RHB/RM	–
LOCKHART, Douglas Ross	19.01.76	Glasgow	RHB/WK	1996
MacRAE, Neil John	25.03.72	Liverpool, Lancs	RHB	1999
MAIDEN, Gregor Ian	22.07.79	Glasgow	RHB/OB	1999
RIGBY, Dominic Anthony John	17.11.70	Ayr	RHB	–
SMITH, Colin John Ogilvie	27.09.72	Aberdeen	RHB/WK	1999
STANGER, Ian Michael	05.10.71	Glasgow	RHB/RMF	1997
STEINDL, Peter David	14.06.70	Bundaberg, Australia	RHB/RM	1998
THOMSON, Kevin	24.12.71	Dundee	RHB/RMF	1992
WATSON, Ryan Robert	12.11.76	Salisbury, Rhodesia	RHB/RM	–
WATTS, David Fraser	05.06.79	King's Lynn, Norfolk	RHB/RM	1999
WILLIAMSON, John Greig	20.12.68	Glasgow	RHB/RM	1994
WRIGHT, Craig McIntyre	28.04.74	Paisley	RHB/RMF	1997

THE 2003 FIRST-CLASS SEASON
STATISTICAL HIGHLIGHTS

FIRST TO INDIVIDUAL TARGETS

1000 RUNS	E.T.Smith	Kent	15 July
2000 RUNS	–	Most 1820 – S.G.Law (Lancashire)	
100 WICKETS	Mushtaq Ahmed Sussex		17 September

TEAM HIGHLIGHTS

HIGHEST INNINGS TOTALS († *County record*)

781	Lancashire v Warwickshire	Birmingham
734-5d	Lancashire v Middlesex	Manchester
705-9d†	Somerset v Hampshire	Taunton
693	Surrey v Nottinghamshire	Croydon
682-6d	South Africa v England (2nd Test)	Lord's
681-5d	Northamptonshire v Somerset	Taunton
673-8d	Yorkshire v Northants	Leeds
663-9d	Surrey v Loughborough UCCE	The Oval
647-5d	Northamptonshire v Derbyshire	Derby
646	Nottinghamshire v Warwickshire	Birmingham
636-4d	Leicestershire v Surrey	Leicester
622-8d	Northamptonshire v Gloucestershire	Gloucester
620-7d	Middlesex v Leicestershire	Southgate
619-7d	Sussex v Nottinghamshire	Horsham
614-4d	Sussex v Leicestershire	Hove
612	Sussex v Essex	Colchester
611-9d	Gloucestershire v Somerset	Taunton
604-9d	England v South Africa (5th Test)	The Oval
602-6d	Kent v Lancashire	Blackpool
600-7d	Leicestershire v Essex	Southend

HIGHEST FOURTH INNINGS TOTALS

425	Warwickshire (set 561) v Surrey	Birmingham

LOWEST FOURTH INNINGS TOTALS

56	Somerset v Durham	Chester-le-St
79	Nottinghamshire v Essex	Nottingham
89	Derbyshire v Gloucestershire	Derby
91	Worcestershire v Yorkshire	Scarborough
93	Yorkshire v Durham	Leeds
94	Zimbabwe v England (2nd Test)	Chester-le-St
96	Derbyshire v Northamptonshire	Worcester
96	Somerset v Northamptonshire	Northampton
98	Gloucestershire v Worcestershire	Worcester

MATCH AGGREGATES OF 1500 RUNS

1568-29	Middlesex (620-7d, 166-2) v Leicestershire (447, 335)	Southgate
1515-22	Lancashire (734-5d) v Middlesex (544, 237-7)	Manchester

BATSMEN'S MATCH (Qualification: 1200 runs, average 70 per wicket)

80.00 (1360-17)	Middlesex (516-6d, 222-2d) v Zimbabweans (401-4d, 221-5)	Shenley

LARGE MARGINS OF VICTORY

Inns & 343	Yorkshire (673-8d) beat Northamptonshire (184, 146)	Leeds
369 runs	Glamorgan (270, 464-8d) beat Durham (247, 118)	Chester-le-St

VICTORY AFTER FOLLOWING ON

Hampshire (185, 449) beat Glamorgan (437, 104) by 93 runs   Southampton

TIED MATCHES

Warwickshire (446-7d, forfeit) v Essex (66-0d, 380)	Birmingham
Worcestershire (262, 247) v Zimbabweans (334, 175)	Worcester

FOUR HUNDREDS IN AN INNINGS

Surrey (663-9d) v Loughborough UCCE	The Oval
Lancashire (734-5d) v Middlesex	Manchester
Lancashire (781) v Warwickshire	Birmingham

SIX FIFTIES IN AN INNINGS

Nottinghamshire (542) v Durham UCCE	Nottingham
Lancashire (503-6d) v Leicestershire	Liverpool
Somerset (705-9d) v Hampshire	Taunton
Hampshire (580) v Derbyshire	Derby

SIXTY EXTRAS IN AN INNINGS

	B	LB	W	NB		
68	18	21	–	29	Leicestershire (636-4d) v Surrey	Leicester
67	8	5	6	48	Lancashire (781) v Warwickshire	Birmingham
64	25	21	5	13	South Africa (682-6d) v England (2nd Test)	Lord's
64	16	13	5	30	Surrey (693) v Nottinghamshire	Croydon
62	12	7	1	42	Hampshire (580) v Derbyshire	Derby
61	14	27	3	17	England (472) v Zimbabwe (1st Test)	Lord's

Under ECB regulations (Test matches excluded), two extras were scored for each no-ball, in addition to any runs scored off that ball.

BATTING HIGHLIGHTS

TRIPLE HUNDREDS (*† County record*)

M.W.Goodwin	335*†	Sussex v Leicestershire	Hove
B.J.Hodge	302*†	Leicestershire v Nottinghamshire	Nottingham
M.E.K.Hussey	331*†	Northamptonshire v Somerset	Taunton

DOUBLE HUNDREDS (*† County record*)

I.D.Blackwell	247*	Somerset v Derbyshire	Taunton
R.J.Blakey	223*	Yorkshire v Northamptonshire	Leeds
J.W.M.Dalrymple	236*	Oxford U v Cambridge U	Cambridge
A.Flower	201*	Essex v Surrey	The Oval
M.W.Goodwin	210	Sussex v Essex	Colchester
B.J.Hodge	202*	Leicestershire v Loughborough UCCE	Leicester
C.L.Hooper	201	Lancashire v Middlesex	Manchester
N.Hussain	206	Essex v Kent	Chelmsford
M.E.K.Hussey	264	Northamptonshire v Gloucestershire	Gloucester

W.Jaffer		218	India A v Warwickshire	Birmingham
P.A.Jaques		222	Northamptonshire v Yorkshire	Northampton
J.H.Kallis		200	South Africans v Derbyshire	Derby
S.G.Law		236*	Lancashire v Warwickshire	Manchester
M.L.Love		273†	Durham v Hampshire	Chester-le-St
D.L.Maddy		229*	Leicestershire v Loughborough UCCE	Leicester
D.R.Martyn		238	Yorkshire v Gloucestershire	Leeds
K.P.Pietersen		221	Nottinghamshire v Warwickshire	Birmingham
M.R.Ramprakash	(2)	205	Surrey v Loughborough UCCE	The Oval
		279	Surrey v Nottinghamshire	Croydon
D.J.G.Sales		200*	Northamptonshire v Derbyshire	Derby
E.T.Smith	(2)	203	Kent v Lancashire	Blackpool
		213	Kent v Warwickshire	Canterbury
G.C.Smith	(2)	277	South Africa v England (1st Test)	Birmingham
		259	South Africa v England (2nd Test)	Lord's
M.E.Trescothick		219	England v South Africa (5th Test)	The Oval
M.J.Wood		207	Yorkshire v Somerset	Taunton

HUNDREDS IN FIVE CONSECUTIVE INNINGS

M.E.K.Hussey (Northamptonshire) 100 v Hampshire (Southampton), 331* v Somerset (Taunton), 115 v Derbyshire (Derby), 187 v Durham (Northampton), 147 v Glamorgan (Cardiff)

HUNDREDS IN FOUR CONSECUTIVE INNINGS

E.T.Smith (Kent) 149 and 113 v Nottinghamshire (Maidstone), 203 v Lancashire (Blackpool), 108 v Essex (Canterbury)

HUNDREDS IN THREE CONSECUTIVE INNINGS

C.L.Hooper (Lancashire) 201 v Middlesex (Manchester), 114 v Surrey (Manchester), 177 v Warwickshire (Birmingham)
    M.B.Loye (Lancashire) 137 v Middlesex (Manchester), 102 v Warwickshire (Birmingham), 144 v Sussex (Manchester)

HUNDRED IN EACH INNINGS OF A MATCH

C.J.Adams	140	190	Sussex v Lancashire	Hove
M.J.Powell	125	142	Glamorgan v Worcestershire	Cardiff
J.N.Rhodes	103	102	Gloucestershire v Durham	Bristol
E.T.Smith	149	113	Kent v Nottinghamshire	Maidstone
R.J.Warren	123	113*	Nottinghamshire v Middlesex	Lord's

FASTEST DOUBLE HUNDREDS

D.R.Martyn (238)	128 balls	Yorkshire v Gloucestershire	Leeds
I.D.Blackwell (247*)	134 balls	Somerset v Derbyshire	Taunton

Scored 204 off 98 balls between lunch and pre-tea end of innings

FASTEST HUNDRED (WALTER LAWRENCE TROPHY)

D.R.Martyn	65 balls	Yorkshire v Gloucestershire	Leeds
(238)			

HUNDRED BEFORE LUNCH

Day

M.A.Carberry	0*-109*	1	Kent v Cambridge UCCE	Cambridge
B.J.Hodge	67*-175*	2	Leicestershire v Loughborough UCCE	Leicester
C.L.Hooper	26*-135*	2	Lancashire v Middlesex	Manchester
W.I.Jefferson	0*-125*	1	Essex v Cambridge UCCE	Cambridge

On first day of season – April 12

S.G.Law	41*-142*	2	Lancashire v Middlesex	Manchester
N.Peng	0*-103*	1	Durham v Durham UCCE	Chester-le-St
M.J.Prior	9*-133*	2	Sussex v Nottinghamshire	Horsham

TEN OR MORE SIXES IN AN INNINGS

11	I.D.Blackwell (247*)	Somerset v Derbyshire	Taunton
11	C.L.Hooper (201)	Lancashire v Middlesex	Manchester

FOUR SIXES OFF CONSECUTIVE BALLS

Shoaib Malik (off R.K.J.Dawson)   Gloucestershire v Yorkshire   Cheltenham

200 RUNS FROM BOUNDARIES IN AN INNINGS

Runs	6s	4s			
214	1	52	M.W.Goodwin (335*)	Sussex v Leicestershire	Hove
202	3	46	B.J.Hodge (302*)	Leicestershire v Nottinghamshire	Nottingham

HUNDRED ON FIRST-CLASS DEBUT IN BRITAIN

J.D.C.Bryant   109*   Somerset v Loughborough UCCE   Taunton

CARRYING BAT THROUGH COMPLETED INNINGS († One man absent)

J.N.Batty	154*	Surrey (337) v Lancashire	Manchester
D.P.Fulton	94*	Kent (284) v Essex	Canterbury
J.E.R.Gallian	112*	Nottinghamshire (211) v Surrey	Nottingham
M.W.Goodwin	118*	Sussex (251) v Lancashire	Manchester
A.Singh	83*	Worcestershire (212) v Gloucestershire	Worcester

LONG INNINGS

Min	Balls			
651	471	M.E.K.Hussey (331*)	Northamptonshire v Somerset	Taunton

UNUSUAL DISMISSAL

TIMED OUT
A.J.Harris (0)   Nottinghamshire v Durham UCCE   Nottingham

FIRST-WICKET PARTNERSHIP OF 100 IN EACH INNINGS

104/113   N.V.Knight/I.J.L.Trott   Warwickshire v Nottinghamshire   Birmingham

OTHER NOTABLE PARTNERSHIPS († County record)

First Wicket

338	G.C.Smith/H.H.Gibbs	South Africa v England (1st Test)	Birmingham
258	M.A.Carberry/R.W.T.Key	Kent v Cambridge UCCE	Cambridge

Second Wicket

281	J.K.Maunders/B.J.Hodge	Leicestershire v Surrey	Leicester
268	M.E.K.Hussey/P.A.Jaques	Northamptonshire v Durham	Northampton
259	M.J.Chilton/M.B.Loye	Lancashire v Middlesex	Manchester
257	G.C.Smith/G.Kirsten	South Africa v England (2nd Test)	Lord's

Third Wicket

436*†	D.L.Maddy/B.J.Hodge	Leics v Loughboro' UCCE	Leicester
282	M.B.Loye/S.G.Law	Lancashire v Surrey	The Oval
268	M.E.Trescothick/G.P.Thorpe	England v South Africa (5th Test)	The Oval
267	M.W.Goodwin/C.J.Adams	Sussex v Leicestershire	Hove
263	J.W.M.Dalrymple/N.Millar	Oxford U v Cambridge U	Cambridge

Fourth Wicket

330†	M.J.Wood/D.R.Martyn	Yorkshire v Gloucestershire	Leeds
282	S.G.Law/C.L.Hooper	Lancashire v Middlesex	Manchester
278	B.J.Hodge/P.A.Nixon	Leicestershire v Nottinghamshire	Nottingham
273	K.P.Pietersen/C.L.Cairns	Nottinghamshire v Warwickshire	Birmingham
267	E.T.Smith/M.J.Walker	Kent v Warwickshire	Canterbury
264	S.G.Law/M.J.Chilton	Lancashire v Middlesex	Lord's
224†	G.J.Pratt/N.Peng	Durham v Durham UCCE	Chester-le-St

Fifth Wicket

360†	S.G.Law/C.L.Hooper	Lancashire v Warwickshire	Birmingham
247	S.G.Law/C.L.Hooper	Lancashire v Leicestershire	Leicester
197†	N.Peng/V.J.Wells	Durham v Derbyshire	Derby

Sixth Wicket

260	M.E.K.Hussey/G.L.Brophy	Northamptonshire v Gloucestershire	Gloucester
242*	M.E.K.Hussey/T.M.B.Bailey	Northamptonshire v Somerset	Taunton
228	S.G.Law/G.Chapple	Lancashire v Warwickshire	Manchester

Seventh Wicket

195	M.J.Prior/M.J.G.Davis	Sussex v Middlesex	Hove

Eighth Wicket

150	G.Kirsten/M.Zondeki	South Africa v England (4th Test)	Leeds

Ninth Wicket

141	M.J.Prior/J.D.Lewry	Sussex v Essex	Colchester

Tenth Wicket

163†	I.D.Blackwell/N.A.M.McLean	Somerset v Derbyshire	Taunton
107	M.R.Ramprakash/Saqlain Mushtaq	Surrey v Nottinghamshire	Croydon
106	M.J.G.Davis/B.V.Taylor	Sussex v Middlesex	Hove

BOWLING HIGHLIGHTS

EIGHT OR MORE WICKETS IN AN INNINGS

P.R.Adams	9- 79	South Africans v Kent	Canterbury
Kabir Ali	8- 58	Worcestershire v Derbyshire	Worcester
(2)	8- 53	Worcestershire v Yorkshire	Scarborough
Before lunch on the first day			
M.S.Kasprowicz (2)	9- 36	Glamorgan v Durham	Cardiff
	9- 45	Glamorgan v Durham	Chester-le-St
S.P.Kirby	8- 80	Yorkshire v Somerset	Taunton
J.D.Lewry	8-106	Sussex v Leicestershire	Hove
Mohammad Akram	8- 49	Essex v Surrey	The Oval
Mohammad Sami	8- 64	Kent v Nottinghamshire	Maidstone

TEN OR MORE WICKETS IN A MATCH

P.R.Adams	11-140	South Africans v Kent	Canterbury
D.G.Cork (2)	10- 67	Derbyshire v Hampshire	Southampton
	10-127	Derbyshire v Somerset	Taunton
R.D.B.Croft	10-147	Glamorgan v Northamptonshire	Cardiff
P.A.J.DeFreitas	10-113	Leicestershire v Nottinghamshire	Nottingham
N.R.C.Dumelow	10-160	Derbyshire v Northamptonshire	Northampton
I.D.Fisher	10-123	Gloucestershire v Durham	Bristol

M.S.Kasprowicz (2)		11- 77	Glamorgan v Durham	Cardiff
		13-110	Glamorgan v Durham	Chester-le-St
G.Keedy		10-167	Lancashire v Sussex	Manchester
S.P.Kirby	(2)	13-154	Yorkshire v Somerset	Taunton
		10-183	Yorkshire v Gloucestershire	Cheltenham
J.Lewis		11-183	Gloucestershire v Derbyshire	Bristol
J.D.Lewry		10-124	Sussex v Essex	Arundel
Mohammad Akram		10-142	Essex v Surrey	The Oval
Mohammad Sami		15-114	Kent v Nottinghamshire	Maidstone
Mushtaq Ahmed (5)		12-244	Sussex v Nottinghamshire	Horsham
		11-140	Sussex v Warwickshire	Hove
		10-189	Sussex v Leicestershire	Leicester
		11-173	Sussex v Lancashire	Hove
		10-225	Sussex v Middlesex	Hove
M.Ntini		10-220	South Africa v England (2nd Test)	Lord's

OUTSTANDING BOWLING SPELLS

| Mohammad Sami | 8 in 38 balls | Kent v Nottinghamshire | Maidstone |
| M.Muralitharan | 6 in 12 balls | Kent v Nottinghamshire | Nottingham |

BOWLED UNCHANGED THROUGHOUT INNINGS

S.A.Brant (8.5-3-45-6)/J.M.Dakin (8-2-22-4) Essex v Nottinghamshire (79) Nottingham

HAT TRICKS

J.M.Anderson	Lancashire v Essex	Manchester
S.R.G.Francis	Somerset v Loughborough UCCE	Taunton
J.D.Middlebrook	Essex v Kent	Canterbury

200 RUNS CONCEDED IN AN INNINGS

| M.A.Wagh | 39.5-2-222-7 | Warwickshire v Lancashire | Birmingham |
| I.D.Blackwell | 53-4-206-3 | Somerset v Northamptonshire | Taunton |

60 OVERS IN AN INNINGS

| J.F.Brown | 62.2-24-100-3 | Northamptonshire v Glamorgan | Cardiff |

WICKET-KEEPING HIGHLIGHTS

SIX OR MORE DISMISSALS IN AN INNINGS

R.J.Blakey	6 ct	Yorkshire v Glamorgan	Leeds
G.O.Jones	6 ct	Kent v Essex	Canterbury
R.J.Turner	6 ct	Somerset v Derbyshire	Taunton

NINE OR MORE DISMISSALS IN A MATCH

| R.J.Turner | 8 ct, 1 st | Somerset v Derbyshire | Taunton |

NO BYES CONCEDED IN TOTAL OF 550 OR MORE

612	J.S.Foster	Essex v Sussex	Colchester
600-7d	J.S.Foster	Essex v Leicestershire	Southend
599	J.N.Batty	Surrey v Lancashire	The Oval
568	D.C.Nash	Middlesex v Surrey	Lord's

FIELDING HIGHLIGHTS

SIX OR MORE CATCHES IN A MATCH

| M.J.Powell | 6 ct | NorthamptonshirevDurham | Northampton |

2003 FIRST-CLASS AVERAGES

These averages involve the 496 cricketers who appeared in the 178 first-class matches played by 29 teams in the British Isles during the 2003 season.

Cap denotes the season in which the player was awarded a 1st XI cap by the county he represented in 2003. For Worcestershire players, 2003[c] denotes he was awarded his county colours.

Team abbreviations: BU – British Universities; CU – Cambridge University/Cambridge UCCE; De – Derbyshire; Du – Durham; DU – Durham UCCE; E – England; Ex – Essex; Gm – Glamorgan; Gs – Gloucestershire; H – Hampshire; IA – India A; K – Kent; La – Lancashire; LU – Loughborough UCCE; M – Middlesex; Nh – Northamptonshire; Nt – Nottinghamshire; OU – Oxford University/Oxford UCCE; SA – South Africa(ns); Sm – Somerset; Sy – Surrey; Sx – Sussex; Wa – Warwickshire; Wo – Worcestershire; Y – Yorkshire; Z – Zimbabwe(ans).

† Left-handed batsman.

BATTING AND FIELDING

	Cap	M	I	NO	HS	Runs	Avge	100	50	Ct/St
Abdul Razzaq (M)	2002	8	11	–	81	328	29.81	–	3	2
Adams, C.J.(Sx)	1998	16	27	–	190	966	35.77	4	2	18
†Adams, J.H.K.(LU/H/BU)		13	26	1	107	661	26.44	1	3	6
Adams, P.R.(SA)		6	5	2	22*	64	21.33	–	–	7
Adnan, M.H.(De)		2	4	1	84	189	63.00	–	2	1
Adshead, S.J.(Wo)	2003[c]	2	4	1	63	102	34.00	–	1	7/1
†Afzaal, U.(Nt)	2000	9	15	1	161*	477	34.07	1	2	3
Airey, S.J.(OU)		3	4	1	46*	100	33.33	–	–	1
Akram, M.Adnan (CU)		3	4	–	98	162	40.50	–	1	–
Akram, M.Arfan (CU)		3	5	1	110	191	47.75	1	–	3
Ali, Kabir (Wo/E)	2002[c]	14	20	4	84*	381	23.81	–	2	2
Ali, Kadeer (Wo)	2002[c]	8	14	–	99	426	30.42	–	3	2
Ali, S.M.B.(De)		10	17	3	101	101	7.21	–	1	1
Allen, J.A.(OU)		2	2	–	0	0	0.00	–	–	–
Alleyne, M.W.(Gs)	1990	8	13	3	32*	193	19.30	–	–	9
Ambrose, T.R.(Sx)	2003	15	26	3	93*	931	40.47	–	9	29/7
Amin, R.M.(Le)		5	7	2	11	30	6.00	–	–	–
†Anderson, J.M.(La/E)	2003	11	13	12	21*	55	55.00	–	–	5
Anderson, R.S.G.(Nh)		2	2	–	13	13	6.50	–	–	–
†Andrew, G.M.(Sm)		4	5	–	11	36	7.20	–	–	–
Anwar, O.S.(OU)		3	4	–	99	128	32.00	–	1	–
†Anyon, J.E.(LU)		3	3	–	21	21	7.00	–	–	2
Atri, V.(LU/Nt)		5	10	2	82*	240	30.00	–	2	3
Averis, J.M.M.(Gs)	2001	4	3	1	8	12	6.00	–	–	1
Azhar Mahmood (Sy)		11	14	2	98	445	37.08	–	4	17
†Badani, H.K.(IA)		5	7	2	133	248	49.60	1	1	5
Bailey, T.M.B.(Nh)	2003	14	19	3	101*	384	24.00	1	–	29/6
Balaji, L.(IA)		6	4	–	14	29	7.25	–	–	1
Ball, M.C.J.(Gs)	1996	10	15	3	75	304	25.33	–	2	12
Banes, M.J.(K)		1	2	–	24	39	19.50	–	–	1
Bassano, C.W.G.(De)	2002	12	22	3	53*	277	14.57	–	2	7
Batty, G.J.(Wo)	2002[c]	18	28	4	60	529	22.04	–	3	14
Batty, J.N.(Sy)	2001	12	22	5	168*	968	56.94	3	4	32/2
Bell, I.R.(Wa)	2001	17	30	2	107	854	30.50	1	5	5
Benning, J.G.E.(Sy)		2	3	–	47	87	29.00	–	–	1
Betts, M.M.(Wa)	2001	10	14	2	73	348	29.00	–	2	2
Bhandari, A.(IA)		7	4	3	5*	12	12.00	–	–	1
Bharadwaj, R.V.(IA)		3	3	1	12*	20	10.00	–	–	2
†Bicknell, D.J.(Nt)	2000	16	29	1	81	936	33.42	–	9	4
Bicknell, M.P.(Sy/E)	1989	14	15	4	141	440	40.00	2	–	4

F-C	Cap	M	I	NO	HS	Runs	Avge	100	50	Ct/St
†Bishop, J.E.(DU/BU/Ex)	–	5	6	–	50	125	20.83	–	2	1
†Blackwell, I.D.(Sm)	2001	15	26	3	247*	1160	50.43	3	2	7
Blain, J.A.R.(Nh)	–	4	2	1	5	6	6.00	–	–	–
Blakey, R.J.(Y)	1987	13	19	2	223*	468	27.52	1	–	32/1
Blewett, G.S.(K)	–	7	12	–	71	377	31.41	–	3	7
†Blignaut, A.M.(Z)	–	5	8	1	42	114	16.28	–	–	2
Bloomfield, T.F.(M)	2001	5	4	1	9*	19	6.33	–	–	2
Bopara, R.S.(Ex)	–	4	7	3	48	163	40.75	–	–	3
Boucher, M.V.(SA)	–	8	11	1	89	360	36.00	–	3	21/1
Bowler, P.D.(Sm)	1995	9	15	1	92	477	34.07	–	5	11
Brandy, D.G.(Le)	–	6	9	2	52	148	21.14	–	1	2
Brant, S.A.(Ex)	2003	11	14	6	23	37	4.62	–	–	3
Bresnan, T.T.(Y)	–	4	4	–	52	81	20.25	–	1	1
Bridge, G.D.(Du)	–	8	13	3	50	240	24.00	–	1	7
Brignull, D.S.(Le)	–	3	4	–	46	58	14.50	–	–	–
Brophy, G.L.(Nh)	–	7	12	5	152*	436	62.28	2	1	14
Brown, A.D.(Sy)	1994	14	21	2	74	484	25.47	–	5	12
Brown, D.O.(DU)	–	3	6	–	59	223	37.16	–	2	1
Brown, D.R.(Wa)	1995	16	26	4	140*	1028	46.72	3	7	10
Brown, J.F.(Nh)	2000	14	12	6	38	91	15.16	–	–	2
Brown, M.J.(M)	–	1	1	–	98	98	98.00	–	1	2
Bruce, J.T.A.(H)	–	8	11	3	21*	68	8.50	–	–	3
Brunnschweiler, I.(H)	–	4	4	–	34	58	14.50	–	–	11
Bryant, J.D.C.(Sm)	–	14	24	2	109*	658	29.90	1	2	8
Burns, M.(Sm)	1999	18	32	3	118*	1133	39.06	2	8	15
Butcher, G.R.(OU)	–	2	3	–	7	14	4.66	–	–	–
†Butcher, M.A.(Sy/E)	1996	14	20	1	144	1162	61.15	4	5	17
Butler, I.G.(Gs)	–	4	5	–	13	20	4.00	–	–	1
Caddick, A.R.(Sm)	1992	1	1	–	1	1	1.00	–	–	–
Cairns, C.L.(Nt)	1993	13	23	2	104	645	30.71	1	4	7
†Carberry, M.A.(K)	–	14	24	1	137	824	35.82	1	6	2
Carlisle, S.V.(Z)	–	6	9	–	157	469	52.11	2	1	2
†Carter, N.M.(Wa)	–	5	7	–	38	118	16.85	–	–	1
†Cawdron, M.J.(Nh)	–	6	6	–	24	63	10.50	–	–	1
Chapple, G.(La)	1994	16	21	3	132*	679	37.72	2	3	8
†Cherry, D.D.(Gm)	–	1	1	–	9	9	9.00	–	–	1
Chilton, M.J.(La)	2002	17	25	2	125	1154	50.17	6	3	15
Clapp, D.A.(H)	–	1	1	–	4	4	4.00	–	–	–
Clark, M.W.(Wa)	–	1	2	1	2*	4	4.00	–	–	–
†Clarke, A.J.(Ex)	–	3	4	1	41	87	29.00	–	–	1
Clarke, R.(Sy)	–	11	16	2	139	551	39.35	2	1	10
Clough, G.(Nt)	–	3	4	1	55	72	24.00	–	1	1
Collingwood, P.D.(Du)	1998	4	7	1	68	169	28.16	–	2	4
Collymore, C.D.(Wa)	–	5	8	3	11*	25	5.00	–	–	2
†Cook, A.N.(Ex)	–	3	6	1	84	239	47.80	–	3	3
†Cook, J.W.(Nh)	2003	14	22	2	85	517	25.85	–	3	3
Cook, S.J.(M)	2003	12	17	3	65	211	15.07	–	1	5
Cork, D.G.(De)	1993	16	29	3	92	593	22.80	–	3	11
Cosker, D.A.(Gm)	2000	9	12	6	42	80	13.33	–	–	7
Cottey, P.A.(Sx)	1999	15	25	–	188	1149	45.96	3	7	8
†Cowan, E.D.M.(OU/BU)	–	4	7	2	137*	370	74.00	1	1	1
Cox, J.(Sm)	1999	15	27	3	160	1087	45.29	3	5	10
†Craven, V.J.(Y)	–	6	11	1	47	281	28.10	–	–	–
Crawley, J.P.(H)	2002	16	27	1	93	878	33.76	–	8	5
Croft, R.D.B.(Gm)	1992	17	29	4	122	739	29.56	1	4	9
Crook, S.P.(La)	–	2	1	–	27	27	27.00	–	–	1
Cummins, R.A.G.(LU)	–	3	3	2	2*	3	3.00	–	–	–
Cunliffe, R.J.(Le)	–	1	1	–	0	0	0.00	–	–	–

124

F-C	Cap	M	I	NO	HS	Runs	Avge	100	50	Ct/St
Currie, M.R.(La)	–	2	3	–	97	166	55.33	–	2	3
Daggett, L.M.(DU)	–	3	5	3	3*	10	5.00	–	–	–
Dagnall, C.E.(Le)	–	10	11	5	23*	103	17.16	–	–	–
†Dakin, J.M.(Ex)	2003	11	19	2	59	411	24.17	–	2	2
Dale, A.(Gm)	1992	15	27	1	123	657	25.26	1	2	12
Dale, M.A.P.(DU)	–	1	2	–	8	13	6.50	–	–	–
†Daley, S.R.(OU)	–	1	–	–	0	0	0.00	–	–	–
Dalrymple, J.W.M.(OU/M)	–	7	11	2	236*	357	39.66	1	–	6
Das, S.S.(IA)	–	7	10	–	125	428	42.80	1	3	8
Davies, A.M.(Du)	–	5	8	3	21	64	12.80	–	–	4
†Davies, A.P.(Gm)	–	3	3	1	19*	32	16.00	–	–	1
Davis, M.J.G.(Sx)	2002	11	12	2	168	259	25.90	1	–	4
Dawes, J.H.(M)	2003	10	12	5	32*	97	13.85	–	–	3
Dawood, I.(BU)	–	1	2	–	12	17	8.50	–	–	4
Dawson, R.K.J.(Y)	–	12	18	2	77	467	29.18	–	2	11
†Dean, K.J.(De)	1998	16	24	3	30*	148	7.04	–	–	4
DeFreitas, P.A.J.(Le)	1986	16	25	2	103	493	21.43	1	2	6
Dernbach, J.(Sy)	–	1	1	–	3	3	3.00	–	–	–
Dippenaar, H.H.(SA)	–	7	11	1	92	339	33.90	–	3	4
†Di Venuto, M.J.(De)	2000	16	31	–	150	1520	49.03	5	8	25
Drakes, V.C.(Le)	–	5	7	1	18	57	9.50	–	–	1
Dumelow, N.R.C.(De)	–	10	17	3	75	347	24.78	–	3	2
Durston, W.J.(Sm)	–	2	4	1	30*	48	16.00	–	–	4
Dutch, K.P.(Sm)	2001	7	10	–	61	161	16.10	–	1	9
Ealham, M.A.(K)	1992	17	25	–	101	911	36.44	1	7	18
Ebrahim, D.D.(Z)	–	6	11	1	68	271	27.10	–	3	4
†Edwards, N.J.(Sm)	–	5	9	–	160	360	40.00	1	1	1
Elworthy, S.(Nt)	–	5	8	–	52	179	22.37	–	1	3
†Ervine, S.M.(Z)	–	5	8	2	57*	161	26.83	–	1	5
Evans, P.P.(OU)	–	1	1	–	14	14	14.00	–	–	4
Fellows, G.M.(Y)	–	6	8	–	53	142	17.75	–	1	1
Ferley, R.S.(DU/BU/K)	–	10	14	4	78*	262	26.20	–	2	5
†Fisher, I.D.(Gs)	–	10	12	3	71	219	24.33	–	1	4
†Fleming, S.P.(Y)	–	7	14	2	98	469	39.08	–	3	13
Flintoff, A.(La/E)	1998	10	14	1	154	942	72.46	3	5	7
†Flower, A.(Ex)	2002	17	29	3	201*	1244	47.84	2	7	17
Flower, G.P.(Z)	–	6	10	1	130	399	44.33	1	2	7
Foster, J.S.(Ex)	2001	17	26	–	85	689	26.50	–	4	49/2
†Francis, J.D.(LU/BU/H)	–	10	19	–	65	369	19.42	–	2	6
Francis, S.R.G.(Sm)	–	10	13	2	44	133	12.09	–	–	2
†Franks, P.J.(Nt)	1999	16	26	8	123*	729	40.50	2	1	9
Free, C.W.(OU)	–	1	–	–	–	–	–	–	–	–
Friend, T.J.(Z)	–	4	6	1	65*	151	30.20	–	1	1
†Frost, T.(Wa)	1999	13	21	1	84	477	23.85	–	4	33/2
Fulton, D.P.(K)	1998	11	19	1	94*	674	37.44	–	5	4
Gait, A.I.(De)	–	13	25	–	110	664	26.56	1	4	10
Gallian, J.E.R.(Nt)	1998	13	24	3	126*	1002	47.71	4	5	16
†Gambhir, G.(IA)	–	4	6	1	130*	277	55.40	1	1	2
Gannon, B.W.(M)	–	1	1	1	1*	1	–	–	–	–
†Gavaskar, R.S.(IA)	–	3	3	1	139*	216	108.00	1	1	1
Gazzard, C.M.(Sm)	–	3	5	1	41	109	27.25	–	–	5
Gibbs, H.H.(SA)	–	8	14	–	183	590	42.14	2	1	6
Giddins, E.S.H.(H)	–	3	4	1	10	10	3.33	–	–	–
Gidman, A.P.R.(Gs)	–	8	16	2	68	407	29.07	–	2	7
Gilder, G.M.(Sm)	–	3	3	2	12	19	19.00	–	–	1
Giles, A.F.(Wa/E)	–	12	18	1	96	556	32.70	–	4	2
Goddard, L.J.(LU)	–	3	5	2	23*	48	16.00	–	–	2
Goodwin, M.W.(Sx)	2001	17	29	3	335*	1545	59.42	4	5	12

125

F-C	Cap	M	I	NO	HS	Runs	Avge	100	50	Ct/St
Gough, D.(Y)	1993	9	13	1	83	248	20.66	–	2	2
Gough, M.A.(Du)	–	13	25	–	73	584	23.36	–	4	8
Grant, J.B.(Ex)	–	3	4	1	4	11	3.66	–	–	1
Gray, A.K.D.(Y)	–	9	13	2	104	415	37.72	1	1	12
Grayson, A.P.(Ex)	1996	10	18	2	90	388	24.25	–	3	5
Greenidge, C.G.(Nh)	–	8	6	2	13	32	8.00	–	–	2
Grove, J.O.(Le)	–	1	–	–	–	–	–	–	–	–
†Gunter, N.E.L.(De)	–	3	2	2	20*	29	–	–	–	–
Guy, S.M.(Y)	–	6	8	–	26	73	9.12	–	–	16/2
Habib, A.(Ex)	2002	13	22	1	151	738	35.14	2	4	9
Hall, A.J.(Wo/SA)	2003ᶜ	11	16	2	104	445	31.78	1	3	11
Hamblin, J.R.C.(H)	–	5	8	2	96	273	45.50	–	2	1
†Hamilton, G.M.(Y)	1998	1	1	–	68	68	68.00	–	1	1
Hancock, T.H.C.(Gs)	1998	12	21	–	97	720	34.28	–	5	13
Hanson, W.T.D.(DU)	–	3	4	2	9*	13	6.50	–	–	5/3
Hardinges, M.A.(Gs)	–	2	3	1	17	27	13.50	–	–	1
Harmison, S.J.(Du/E)	1999	11	14	5	14*	78	8.66	–	–	2
Harris, A.J.(Nt)	2000	10	12	1	16*	37	3.36	–	–	2
Harrison, D.S.(Gm)	–	16	25	5	66	271	13.55	–	1	3
Harrity, M.A.(Wo)	2003ᶜ	7	9	6	16	30	10.00	–	–	1
Harvey, I.J.(Gs)	1999	6	12	3	128*	404	44.88	1	1	4
Hatch, N.G.(Du)	–	5	5	2	5	16	5.33	–	–	1
†Havell, P.M.R.(De)	–	4	6	5	7*	10	10.00	–	–	2
Hawinkels, S.J.(OU)	–	1	1	–	49	49	49.00	–	–	–
Hawk, S.L.J.M.(DU)	–	2	4	–	59	81	20.25	–	1	–
Haynes, J.J.(La)	–	2	3	–	13	25	8.33	–	–	3
Hayward, M.(Wo)	2003ᶜ	16	21	5	28	123	7.68	–	–	5
Heath, D.R.(CU)	–	4	7	–	32	104	14.85	–	–	4
Heath, J.A.(CU)	–	1	2	–	6	8	4.00	–	–	–
Hegg, W.K.(La)	1989	16	20	7	61*	404	31.07	–	1	46/3
†Hemp, D.L.(Gm)	1994	12	21	3	85*	607	33.72	–	5	5
Hewson, D.R.(De)	–	9	16	–	57	222	13.87	–	1	4
Heywood, J.J.N.(CU)	–	2	2	–	8	11	5.50	–	–	3
Hick, G.A.(Wo)	1986	13	23	3	155	670	33.50	1	3	19
Hildreth, J.C.(Sm)	–	1	2	–	9	9	4.50	–	–	–
†Hindley, R.J.E.(H)	–	1	2	1	68*	76	76.00	–	1	–
Hodd, A.J.(Sx)	–	1	–	–	–	–	–	–	–	2
Hodge, B.J.(Le)	2003	16	26	2	302*	1495	62.29	5	3	12
†Hogg, K.W.(La)	–	5	5	–	53	158	31.60	–	1	1
Hoggard, M.J.(Y/E)	2000	7	8	5	21*	68	22.66	–	–	3
Hollioake, A.J.(Sy)	1995	14	19	1	122	688	38.22	2	3	11
†Holloway, P.C.L.(Sm)	1997	2	3	–	96	137	45.66	–	1	–
Hondo, D.T.(Z)	–	4	7	3	24*	41	10.25	–	–	2
Hooper, C.L.(La)	2003	14	20	2	201	1219	67.72	6	3	15
Hopkinson, C.D.(Sx)	–	1	1	1	7*	7	–	–	–	–
Horton, P.J.(La)	–	1	1	1	2*	2	–	–	–	1
Howard, W.O.F.(OU)	–	2	3	–	72	97	32.33	–	1	–/2
Huggins, T.B.(Nh)	–	1	2	–	40	40	20.00	–	–	–
Hughes, J.(Gm)	–	10	17	–	73	372	21.88	–	2	10
†Hunt, T.A.(M)	–	1	–	–	–	–	–	–	–	–
Hunter, I.D.(Du)	–	2	2	–	47	91	45.50	–	–	1
Hussain, N.(Ex/E)	1989	11	19	2	206	783	46.05	2	3	3
Hussey, M.E.K.(Nh)	2001	14	21	2	331*	1697	89.31	6	5	17
†Hutchison, P.M.(Sx)	–	5	5	3	18	23	7.66	–	–	–
†Hutton, B.L.(M)	2003	18	30	6	107	961	40.04	4	1	17
Imran Tahir (M)	–	3	3	1	29	30	15.00	–	–	1
Innes, K.J.(Sx)	–	8	12	4	103*	188	23.50	1	–	1
Irani, R.C.(Ex)	1994	13	20	1	102*	597	31.42	1	4	4

F-C	Cap	M	I	NO	HS	Runs	Avge	100	50	Ct/St
Jaffer, W.(IA)	–	6	9	–	218	522	58.00	1	3	2
James, S.P.(Gm)	1992	1	2	–	14	15	7.50	–	–	1
†Jaques, P.A.(Nh)	2003	16	25	1	222	1409	58.70	5	6	9
Jefferson, W.I.(Ex)	2002	14	27	4	125*	781	33.95	1	5	12
Johnson, R.L.(Sm/E)	2001	11	15	3	118	314	26.16	1	–	5
Jones, G.O.(K)	2003	18	27	5	108*	985	44.77	2	7	54/5
Jones, H.R.(OU)	–	3	4	–	35	84	21.00	–	–	1
Jones, P.S.(Sm)	2001	8	12	2	63	273	27.30	–	2	2
†Joyce, E.C.(M)	2002	18	30	4	117	1023	39.34	3	4	7
Kaif, M.(De)	–	8	15	–	87	332	22.13	–	1	5
Kallis, J.H.(SA)	–	5	9	–	200	471	52.33	1	2	6
†Kartik, M.(IA)	–	4	3	–	50	79	26.33	–	1	1
Kasprowicz, M.S.(Gm)	2002	15	26	4	78	556	25.27	–	2	7
†Katich, S.M.(H)	2003	13	22	3	143*	1143	60.15	4	6	15
†Keedy, G.(La)	2000	13	10	6	6	16	4.00	–	–	4
Keegan, C.B.(M)	2003	17	20	3	36*	270	15.88	–	–	5
Kemp, J.M.(Wo)	2003c	6	11	–	90	290	26.36	–	1	9
Kendall, W.S.(H)	1999	9	13	–	114	391	30.07	1	1	6
Kenway, D.A.(H)	2001	16	28	1	115	760	28.14	2	3	14
Key, R.W.T.(K/E)	2001	14	22	2	140	754	37.70	2	1	13
Khalid, S.A.(Wo)	2003c	5	2	–	13	21	10.50	–	–	1
Khan, A.(K)	–	8	10	–	78	236	23.60	–	1	1
Khan, R.M.(De)	–	9	16	–	76	336	21.00	–	2	3
Killeen, N.(Du)	1999	11	18	4	26	110	7.85	–	–	2
King, R.E.(LU)	–	3	5	–	17	19	3.80	–	–	–
Kirby, S.P.(Y)	2003	14	18	4	33	113	8.07	–	–	5
†Kirsten, G.(SA)	–	7	12	2	130	713	71.30	2	4	5
Kirtley, R.J.(Sx/E)	1998	13	17	7	40*	223	22.30	–	–	5
†Knight, N.V.(Wa)	1995	14	26	3	146	1012	44.00	3	5	11
†Koenig, S.G.(M)	2002	16	27	3	166*	1140	47.50	1	7	3
Krikken, K.M.(De)	1992	1	2	–	14	15	7.50	–	–	1
Kumar, V.H.(CU)	–	4	6	2	62*	172	43.00	–	2	3
Laraman, A.W.(Sm)	–	13	18	5	148*	597	45.92	1	3	5
Law, D.R.(Du)	2001	6	10	1	74	127	14.11	–	1	1
Law, S.G.(La)	2002	16	24	4	236*	1820	91.00	7	6	17
Leatherdale, D.A.(Wo)	1994	4	7	–	61	164	23.42	–	2	2
Lewis, J.(Gs)	1998	14	18	4	47	248	17.71	–	–	3
Lewis, J.J.B.(Du)	1998	18	34	2	124	1188	37.12	1	11	5
Lewis, P.D.(LU)	–	2	3	1	10*	14	7.00	–	–	–
†Lewry, J.D.(Sx)	1996	12	15	3	70	215	17.91	–	1	4
Linley, T.E.(OU)	–	1	1	–	7	7	7.00	–	–	–
†Liptrot, C.G.(Wo)	2002c	1	2	–	–	–	–	–	–	2
Logan, R.J.(Nt)	–	3	4	–	13*	23	11.50	–	–	–
Loudon, A.G.R.(DU/K)	–	6	11	1	172	427	42.70	1	1	4
Love, M.L.(Du)	2001	7	13	–	273	778	59.84	1	4	8
Lowe, J.A.(Du)	–	1	2	–	80	80	40.00	–	1	–
†Lowe, S.J.(OU)	–	2	3	–	38	59	19.66	–	–	5/2
Loye, M.B.(La)	2003	15	22	1	144	1062	50.57	5	2	4
†Lumb, M.J.(Y)	2003	17	27	2	115*	1038	41.52	2	7	7
†Lungley, T.(De)	–	5	8	1	29	80	11.42	–	–	2
McCoubrey, A.G.A.M.(Ex)	–	2	3	1	1	1	0.50	–	–	–
McGarry, A.C.(Ex)	–	2	2	2	4*	6	–	–	–	–
MacGill, S.C.G.(Nt)	2002	11	18	6	27	112	9.33	–	–	2
McGrath, A.(Y/E)	1999	14	23	3	127*	850	42.50	1	7	8
McGrath, D.E.T.(CU)	–	1	2	–	4	5	2.50	–	–	–
McKenzie, N.D.(SA)	–	6	11	3	105*	470	58.75	1	3	2
†McLean, N.A.M.(Sm)	2003	17	23	4	76	318	16.73	–	1	2
McMahon, P.J.(OU/Nt)	–	6	9	–	30	93	10.33	–	–	3

F-C	Cap	M	I	NO	HS	Runs	Avge	100	50	Ct/St
Maddy, D.L.(Le)	1996	17	29	3	229*	1110	42.69	1	6	15
†Maher, J.P.(Gm)	2001	8	16	–	95	491	30.68	–	4	7
Mahmood, S.I.(La)	–	5	5	1	34	62	15.50	–	–	1
Maiden, A.J.(DU)	–	3	6	–	53	144	24.00	–	2	2
Malcolm, D.E.(Le)	–	4	4	–	14	27	6.75	–	–	–
Malik, M.N.(Nt)	–	2	3	1	30*	55	27.50	–	–	–
†Mann, R.J.(CU)	–	3	5	–	63	181	36.20	–	2	2
Marillier, D.A.(Z)	–	2	2	–	1	1	0.50	–	–	4
Marshall, S.J.(CU)	–	4	7	3	126*	229	57.25	1	1	2
Martin, P.J.(La)	1994	14	12	–	23	120	10.00	–	–	8
Martin–Jenkins, R.S.C.(Sx)	2000	16	25	3	121*	811	36.86	1	5	7
Martyn, D.R.(Y)	–	2	3	1	238	342	171.00	1	1	2
Mascarenhas, A.D.(H)	1998	17	26	2	100*	600	25.00	1	2	7
Mason, M.S.(Wo)	2002ᶜ	15	20	4	52	250	15.62	–	1	2
Masters, D.D.(Le)	–	17	23	3	119	269	13.45	1	–	4
†Maunders, J.K.(Le)	–	12	22	2	171	777	38.85	2	3	3
Maynard, M.P.(Gm)	1987	16	28	–	142	1297	46.32	5	4	11
Mees, T.(OU/BU)	–	4	6	2	36*	82	20.50	–	–	–
Middlebrook, J.D.(Ex)	2003	16	25	1	82*	484	20.16	–	2	7
Millar, N.(OU)	–	1	1	–	108	108	108.00	1	–	–
Mishra, A.(IA)	–	6	5	1	52*	89	22.25	–	1	1
Mohammad Akram (Ex)	–	4	6	1	10	19	3.80	–	–	–
Mohammad Sami (K)	–	3	4	–	16	19	4.75	–	–	–
Montgomerie, R.R.(Sx)	1999	17	29	2	105	908	33.62	1	7	24
Moore, S.C.(Wo)	2003ᶜ	2	4	1	28*	97	32.33	–	–	2
†Morris, A.C.(H)	2001	2	3	–	46	67	22.33	–	–	2
Muchall, G.J.(Du)	–	13	25	1	121	620	25.83	2	3	5
Mullally, A.D.(H)	2000	8	10	3	14	38	5.42	–	–	2
Munday, M.K.(OU)	–	4	3	2	0*	0	0.00	–	–	2
Muralitharan, M.(K)	2003	5	7	–	15	49	7.00	–	–	1
†Murtagh, T.J.(Sy/BU)	–	7	11	4	21	95	13.57	–	–	–
Mushtaq Ahmed (Sx)	2003	16	19	2	60	456	26.82	–	3	3
†Mustard, P.(Du)	–	13	23	1	70*	486	22.09	–	1	42/3
Napier, G.R.(Ex)	2003	15	24	8	89*	480	30.00	–	2	3
Nash, C.D.(LU)	–	3	6	–	60	229	38.16	–	2	1
Nash, D.C.(M)	2000	17	26	7	113	752	39.57	2	2	42/3
Nel, A.(Nh)	–	13	13	3	42	258	25.80	–	4	4
Newby, O.J.(La)	–	1	–	–	–	–	–	–	–	–
†Newman, S.A.(Sy)	–	2	4	1	27	42	14.00	–	–	2
†Nixon, P.A.(Le)	1994	17	27	4	113*	676	29.39	1	3	50/2
Nkala, M.L.(Z)	–	2	1	–	0	0	0.00	–	–	1
Noble, D.J.(CU)	–	1	2	1	8*	9	9.00	–	–	–
Noffke, A.A.(M)	2003	7	7	1	40	134	22.33	–	–	2
Noon, W.M.(Nt)	–	2	4	1	25	38	12.66	–	–	7
Ntini, M.(SA)	–	6	7	3	32*	64	16.00	–	–	–
Obuya, C.O.(Wa)	–	3	5	3	55	131	65.50	–	2	2
Ormond, J.(Sy)	2003	13	15	5	47	226	22.60	–	–	2
Ostler, D.P.(Wa)	1991	5	8	–	58	119	14.87	–	1	3
Palladino, A.P.(CU/Ex)	–	6	5	3	8	24	12.00	–	–	2
†Panesar, M.S.(Nh)	–	6	7	3	28	43	10.75	–	–	3
Parab, S.S.(IA)	–	2	3	–	90	94	31.33	–	1	–
Park, G.T.(CU)	–	3	4	–	68	132	33.00	–	1	–
Parkin, O.T.(Gm)	–	1	1	–	2	2	2.00	–	–	1
Parsons, K.A.(Sm)	1999	2	4	–	6	13	3.25	–	–	1
†Patel, P.A.(IA)	–	7	7	3	129	238	59.50	1	–	15/3
Patel, S.R.(Nt)	–	1	2	–	55	64	32.00	–	1	1
†Pathan, I.K.(IA)	–	5	4	2	6	8	4.00	–	–	2
Pattison, I.(Du)	–	1	1	–	62	62	62.00	–	1	–

128

F-C	Cap	M	I	NO	HS	Runs	Avge	100	50	Ct/St
Paynter, D.E.(Nh)	–	3	5	1	146	236	59.00	1	1	–
†Penberthy, A.L.(Nh)	1994	23	31	1	45	93	46.50	–	–	–
Peng, N.(Du)	2001	15	25	–	158	743	29.72	2	2	12
Penney, T.L.(Wa)	1994	1	2	–	19	21	10.50	–	–	1
†Peploe, C.T.(M)	–	2	2	1	13	13	13.00	–	–	2
Peters, S.D.(Wo)	2002ᶜ	18	30	1	165	1177	40.58	2	9	15
†Peterson, R.J.(SA)	–	5	5	2	33	78	26.00	–	–	2
Pettini, M.L.(Ex)	–	3	5	1	78	172	43.00	–	2	3
Phillips, B.J.(Nh)	–	7	8	2	48*	119	19.83	–	–	1
Phillips, N.C.(Du)	2001	13	22	5	39	239	14.05	–	–	9
Pietersen, K.P.(Nt)	2002	16	30	–	221	1546	51.53	4	11	17
Pipe, D.J.(Wo)	2002ᶜ	5	9	3	104*	184	30.66	1	–	20/2
Piper, K.J.(Wa)	1992	4	7	–	42	137	19.57	–	–	12/1
Plunkett, L.E.(Du)	–	7	12	5	40*	164	23.42	–	–	2
Polley, S.R.(DU)	–	3	6	1	41	105	21.00	–	–	2
Pollock, S.M.(SA)	–	5	7	3	66*	241	60.25	–	2	6
Pope, S.P.(Gs)	–	5	8	3	17*	65	13.00	–	–	10/1
Pothas, N.(H)	2003	13	20	2	146*	809	44.94	2	4	38/2
Powell, M.J.(Gm)	2000	17	30	1	198	1234	42.55	4	3	14
Powell, M.J.(Nh)	–	16	25	2	64	494	21.47	–	4	32
Powell, M.J.(Wa)	1999	12	22	–	110	754	34.27	1	6	4
†Pratt, A.(Du)	2001	5	9	3	27	93	15.50	–	–	15
†Pratt, G.J.(Du)	–	18	33	1	150	1055	32.96	1	8	11
Pretorius, D.(Du/SA)	–	10	10	3	16	49	7.00	–	–	4
Price, R.W.(Z)	–	5	7	2	26	68	13.60	–	–	1
Prior, M.J.(Sx)	2003	16	24	3	153*	1006	47.90	4	3	28
Prittipaul, L.R.(H)	–	4	6	2	69*	236	59.00	–	2	7
Ramprakash, M.R.(Sy)	2002	15	23	4	279*	1444	76.00	6	2	7
Rayudu, A.T.(IA)	–	5	7	4	101*	262	87.33	1	1	1
Read, C.M.W.(Nt)	1999	13	23	3	94*	619	30.95	–	4	32/3
Rhodes, J.N.(Gs)	–	15	27	5	151*	1293	58.77	5	7	7
Rhodes, S.J.(Wo)	1986	11	14	2	81*	309	25.75	–	2	38/2
Richardson, A.(Wa)	2002	14	19	5	47	158	11.28	–	–	4
Richardson, S.A.(Y)	–	3	6	–	50	103	17.16	–	1	3
Roberts, T.W.(Nh)	–	7	10	–	83	263	26.30	–	2	7
Robinson, D.D.J.(Ex)	1997	11	20	2	89	592	32.88	–	4	7
†Rogers, B.G.(Z)	–	3	4	–	6	11	2.75	–	–	–
Rose, F.A.(Sy)	–	1	2	–	36	37	18.50	–	–	–
†Rudolph, J.A.(SA)	–	8	13	–	92	389	29.92	–	4	6
†Russell, R.C.(Gs)	1985	11	16	4	78*	436	36.33	–	3	33/4
†Sadler, J.L.(Le)	–	7	11	1	145	434	43.40	2	1	5
Saggers, M.J.(K)	2001	15	20	5	47	240	16.00	–	–	3
Saker, N.C.(Sy)	–	2	3	–	5	6	2.00	–	–	–
Sales, D.J.G.(Nh)	1999	16	23	2	200*	942	44.85	2	4	13
Salisbury, I.D.K.(Sy)	1998	14	18	4	101*	455	32.50	1	1	6
Salvi, A.M.(IA)	–	4	3	–	0	0	0.00	–	–	1
Sampson, P.J.(Sy)	–	1	2	1	32*	35	35.00	–	–	–
Saqlain Mushtaq (Sy)	1998	14	15	2	69	421	32.38	–	4	4
Savill, T.E.(CU)	–	4	4	1	10	22	7.33	–	–	2
†Sayers, J.J.(OU)	–	4	6	1	122	243	48.60	1	1	1
†Schofield, C.P.(La)	2002	9	12	2	66	310	31.00	–	2	9
Scott, B.J.M.(Sy)	–	2	3	1	58*	79	39.50	–	1	6
Sehwag, V.(Le)	2003	6	10	–	137	478	47.80	2	1	4
†Selwood, S.A.(De)	–	9	17	1	88	333	20.81	–	2	3
Shafayat, B.M.(Nt)	–	13	23	–	105	533	23.17	1	3	3
Shah, O.A.(M)	2000	18	30	2	147	1206	43.07	3	6	11
Shahid Afridi (De)	–	3	6	–	67	92	15.33	–	1	–
Shahid, N.(Sy)	1998	4	6	–	67	76	12.66	–	1	2

F-C	Cap	M	I	NO	HS	Runs	Avge	100	50	Ct/St
Shankar, A.(CU)	–	4	5	–	40	120	24.00	–	–	1
†Shantry, A.J.(Nh)	–	3	3	2	38*	55	55.00	–	–	1
†Sharif, Z.K.(LU/Ex)	–	4	7	1	67	199	33.16	–	2	1
Sharpe, T.J.(OU)	–	2	2	1	10*	15	15.00	–	–	–
Shaw, A.D.(Gm)	–	1	1	–	33	33	33.00	–	–	–
†Sheikh, M.A.(Wa)	–	6	8	3	57*	171	34.20	–	1	2
Sheriyar, A.(K)	–	15	20	9	18*	97	8.81	–	–	3
Shoaib Akhtar (Du)	–	7	14	2	37	197	16.41	–	–	–
Shoaib Malik (Gs)	–	2	4	–	60	80	20.00	–	1	–
Shreck, C.E.(Nt)	–	11	15	6	19	51	5.66	–	–	1
Sibanda, V.(Z)	–	1	1	–	0	0	0.00	–	–	1
†Sidebottom, R.J.(Y)	2000	9	11	2	28	122	13.55	–	–	4
Sillence, R.J.(Gs)	–	4	5	–	42	98	19.60	–	–	1
Silverwood, C.E.W.(Y)	1996	12	18	4	53	152	10.85	–	1	2
Singh, A.(Wo)	2002c	16	27	1	105	754	29.00	1	4	6
Singh, A.(CU)	–	1	2	–	22	22	11.00	–	–	–
Smith, A.M.(Gs)	1995	11	14	7	17*	58	8.28	–	–	1
Smith, B.F.(Wo)	2002c	18	29	2	110	1289	47.74	2	12	4
Smith, E.T.(K/E)	2001	18	30	1	213	1534	52.89	7	3	15
†Smith, G.C.(SA)	–	8	13	1	277	980	81.66	3	2	6
Smith, G.J.(Nt)	2001	13	21	3	42	172	9.55	–	–	4
Smith, N.M.K.(Wa)	1993	6	8	–	57	138	17.25	–	1	2
Smith, R.A.(H)	1985	10	15	1	92	522	37.28	–	5	9
Smith, W.R.(DU)	–	3	6	–	31	87	14.50	–	–	2
Snape, J.N.(Le)	–	16	23	6	54	494	29.05	–	2	8
Solanki, V.S.(Wo)	1998	15	23	1	79	584	26.54	–	4	24
Somerville–Hendrie, J.W.(DU)	–	2	1	1	1*	1	–	–	–	–
Spearman, C.M.(Gs)	2002	15	27	–	103	903	33.44	1	7	15
Srinath, J.(Du)	–	3	5	3	13*	24	12.00	–	–	1
†Sriram, S.(IA)	–	3	4	1	115	322	107.33	2	1	–
Stephenson, J.P.(Ex)	1989	3	5	1	75*	137	34.25	–	2	–
Stevens, D.I.(Le)	2002	11	19	–	149	615	32.36	1	6	12
Stewart, A.J.(Sy)	1985	13	18	1	98	727	42.76	–	7	36/1
†Strauss, A.J.(M)	2001	18	33	3	155	1529	50.96	4	8	6
Streak, H.H.(Z)	–	5	7	–	51	127	18.14	–	1	1
†Stubbings, S.D.(De)	2001	4	7	–	103	350	50.00	1	2	1
Suppiah, A.V.(Sm)	–	1	1	–	16	16	16.00	–	–	–
†Sutcliffe, I.J.(La)	2003	12	17	2	109	681	45.40	1	4	13
Sutton, L.D.(De)	2002	16	30	5	127	982	39.28	2	2	26/2
Swanepoel,P.J.(Y)	–	2	3	–	17	20	6.66	–	–	1
Swann, A.J.(La)	2002	10	15	–	137	355	23.66	1	1	14
Swann, G.P.(Nh)	1999	9	13	1	69	256	21.33	–	2	9
Symonds, A.(K)	1999	10	16	2	121	659	47.07	2	4	6
Taibu, T.(Z)	–	6	10	2	57	254	31.75	–	1	17/2
†Taylor, B.V.(Sx)	–	8	7	4	35*	55	18.33	–	–	–
Taylor, C.G.(Gs)	2001	4	8	–	45	171	21.37	–	–	3
Taylor, C.R.(Y)	–	3	5	–	40	87	17.40	–	–	1
Taylor, D.B.(DU/BU)	–	2	4	–	82	126	31.50	–	1	–
Ten Doeschate, R.N.(Ex)	–	2	4	–	31	48	12.00	–	–	1
Thomas, A.C.(Nt)	–	1	–	–	–	–	–	–	–	1
†Thomas, I.J.(Gm)	–	7	11	–	53	182	16.54	–	1	8
†Thomas, S.D.(Gm)	1997	5	8	2	69*	145	24.16	–	1	1
Thorburn, M.(H)	–	1	–	–	–	–	–	–	–	–
Thornicroft, N.D.(Y)	–	1	1	1	1*	1	–	–	–	–
†Thorpe, A.M.(Du)	–	2	3	–	35	50	16.66	–	–	1
†Thorpe, G.P.(Sy/E)	1991	13	20	2	156	1019	56.61	2	9	7
Todd, M.J.(Sy)	–	1	1	1	6*	6	–	–	–	–
†Tomlinson, J.A.(BU/H)	–	8	13	5	10	27	3.37	–	–	2

130

F-C	Cap	M	I	NO	HS	Runs	Avge	100	50	Ct/St
†Tredwell, J.C.(K)	–	13	19	3	36	267	16.68	–	–	15
Trego, P.D.(K)	–	1	1	–	13	13	13.00	–	–	1
Tremlett, C.T.(H)	–	10	13	2	43	199	18.09	–	–	5
†Trescothick, M.E.(Sm/E)	1999	11	18	2	219	826	51.62	1	7	17
Trott, B.J.(K)	–	7	10	4	12*	37	6.16	–	–	2
Trott, I.J.L.(Wa)	–	10	18	–	134	763	42.38	2	5	4
†Troughton, J.O.(Wa)	2002	12	20	2	129*	748	41.55	3	2	5
Tsolekile, T.L.(SA)	–	2	1	–	90	90	90.00	–	1	2
Tudor, A.J.(Sy)	1999	6	7	1	55	177	29.50	–	1	–
Turner, R.J.(Sm)	1994	16	26	9	139*	641	37.70	1	3	65/5
Udal, S.D.(H)	1992	16	24	6	60*	488	27.11	–	3	5
†Vaas, W.P.U.C.J.(H)	–	3	6	2	35	64	16.00	–	–	2
Vaughan, M.P.(Y/E)	1995	10	18	2	156	609	38.06	2	1	3
Vermeulen, M.A.(Z)	–	6	11	1	198	451	45.10	1	3	4
†Vettori, D.L.(Nt)	–	2	3	–	10	10	3.33	–	–	1
Wagg, G.G.(Wa)	–	2	3	–	74	89	29.66	–	1	–
Wagh, M.A.(Wa)	2000	16	30	3	138	1228	45.48	3	7	15
†Walker, G.W.(Le)	–	2	1	2	21	25	25.00	–	–	1
†Walker, M.J.(K)	2000	17	27	3	150	1051	43.79	3	4	22
†Wallace, M.A.(Gm)	2003	17	29	–	121	856	29.51	2	3	49/2
Waqar Younis (Wa)	–	8	13	5	61	268	33.50	–	2	1
†Ward, I.J.(Sy)	2000	15	24	1	158	856	37.21	3	2	8
Ward, T.R.(Le)	2001	9	15	–	168	443	29.53	1	1	7
Warren, R.J.(Nt)	–	9	18	2	123	734	45.87	3	2	9/2
†Wasim Akram (H)	–	5	7	1	23	55	9.16	–	–	–
†Webley, T.(CU/Sm)	–	9	16	2	104	428	30.57	1	2	3
†Weekes, P.N.(M)	1993	18	29	5	102*	760	31.66	1	4	20
Welch, G.(De)	2001	15	27	6	54	429	20.42	–	2	3
Wells, V.J.(Du)	–	12	21	1	106	420	21.00	1	2	11
Welton, G.E.(Nt)	–	12	23	–	99	572	24.86	–	5	6
Weston, R.M.S.(M)	2001	2	4	–	129	207	51.75	1	–	–
†Weston, W.P.C.(Gs)	–	15	27	1	179	877	33.73	2	2	10
†Westwood, I.J.(Wa)	–	1	1	–	19	19	19.00	–	–	–
Wharf, A.G.(Gm)	2000	16	27	9	79	475	26.38	–	2	7
†Wharton, L.J.(De)	–	6	9	5	30	46	11.50	–	–	4
Whiley, M.J.A.(Le)	–	5	6	2	16	29	7.25	–	–	1
White, C.(Y)	1993	10	16	3	173*	644	49.53	2	3	4
White, R.A.(LU/Nh/BU)	–	7	14	–	76	261	18.64	–	2	4
Wigley, D.H.(LU/Wo)	2003c	2	4	–	15	38	9.50	–	–	–
†Willoughby, C.M.(SA)	–	1	1	–				–	–	1
Windows, M.G.N.(Gs)	1998	16	29	–	150	890	30.68	1	5	11
Wood, J.(La)	2003	9	8	2	30	67	11.16	–	–	2
Wood, M.J.(Sm)	–	12	23	1	100	536	24.36	1	3	1
Wood, M.J.(Y)	2001	17	33	6	207	1432	53.03	5	3	8
Wright, D.G.(Nh)	–	2	2	–	46	73	36.50	–	–	1
Wright, L.J.(Le)	–	1	2	1	11*	11	11.00	–	–	–
†Yardy, M.H.(Sx)	–	3	4	–	69	134	33.50	–	1	4
†Yuvraj Singh (Y)	–	7	12	2	56	145	14.50	–	1	12
Zondeki, M.(SA)	–	4	3	1	59	78	39.00	–	1	1
Zuiderent, B.(Sx)	–	1	1	–	50	50	50.00	–	1	1

BOWLING

See BATTING and FIELDING section for details of matches, caps and teams

	Cat	O	M	R	W	Avge	Best	5wI	10wM
Abdul Razzaq	RFM	202.4	28	761	16	47.56	3-69	–	–
Adams, C.J.	RM/OB	1	0	1	0			–	–
Adams, J.H.K.	LM	13	1	44	2	22.00	2-24	–	–

F-C	Cat	O	M	R	W	Avge	Best	5wI	10wM
Adams, P.R.	SLC	130.3	21	425	15	28.33	9- 79	1	1
Afzaal, U.	SLA	4	2	14	0			–	–
Airey, S.J.	RMF	53.1	8	218	4	54.50	2- 32	–	–
Akram, M.Adnan	RM	37	1	160	3	53.33	2- 85	–	–
Akram, M.Arfan	LB	16	0	83	4	20.75	3- 41	–	–
Ali, Kabir	RMF	415.2	72	1552	67	23.16	8- 53	3	–
Ali, S.M.B.	LFM	221	36	1060	28	37.85	4- 79	–	–
Alleyne, M.W.	RM	133	32	460	9	51.11	3- 77	–	–
Amin, R.M.	SLA	146.1	24	601	8	75.12	2- 41	–	–
Anderson, J.M.	RFM	332.5	72	1232	41	30.04	5- 61	3	–
Anderson, R.S.G.	RMF	30	4	147	2	73.50	2- 33	–	–
Andrew, G.M.	RMF	78	13	310	10	31.00	3- 14	–	–
Anyon, J.E.	RFM	75	11	375	3	125.00	2- 59	–	–
Averis, J.M.M.	RMF	107.2	30	298	9	33.11	3- 84	–	–
Azhar Mahmood	RMF	283.5	52	1097	35	31.34	5- 78	1	–
Badani, H.K.	SLA	1	1	0	0			–	–
Bailey, T.M.B.	(WK)	1	0	3	0			–	–
Balaji, L.	RFM	137	32	430	12	35.83	3- 58	–	–
Ball, M.C.J.	OB	378.3	99	1008	28	36.00	5-104	1	–
Batty, G.J.	OB	574.4	142	1575	60	26.25	6- 88	1	–
Bell, I.R.	RM	96.3	15	407	9	45.22	4- 12	–	–
Benning, J.G.E.	RM	13	1	81	1	81.00	1- 39	–	–
Betts, M.M.	RFM	240.2	30	970	26	37.30	5- 43	1	–
Bhandari, A.	RFM	119.2	23	424	16	26.50	6- 38	2	–
Bharadwaj, R.V.	OB	3	0	13	0			–	–
Bicknell, D.J.	SLA	0.3	0	4	0			–	–
Bicknell, M.P.	RFM	444.4	110	1391	50	27.82	5- 42	3	–
Bishop, J.E.	LMF	87.1	10	369	11	33.54	4-111	–	–
Blackwell, I.D.	SLA	466.4	111	1336	36	37.11	5- 65	2	–
Blain, J.A.R.	RMF	87.1	7	449	13	34.53	5- 84	1	–
Blewett, G.S.	RM	43	10	150	2	75.00	1- 6	–	–
Blignaut, A.M.	RFM	130.5	21	487	15	32.46	4- 89	–	–
Bloomfield, T.F.	RMF	107.4	14	428	8	53.50	4- 57	–	–
Bopara, R.S.	RMF	30	3	122	2	61.00	1- 23	–	–
Bowler, P.D.	OB	4	0	8	0				
Brandy, D.G.	RMF	8.3	1	58	2	29.00	2- 11	–	–
Brant, S.A.	LFM	344.5	77	1117	37	30.18	6- 45	1	–
Bresnan, T.T.	RMF	79.1	16	259	7	37.00	3- 88	–	–
Bridge, G.D.	SLA	289	59	996	25	39.84	4- 47	–	–
Brignull, D.S.	RMF	68.4	14	235	7	33.57	2- 30	–	–
Brown, A.D.	LB	11.4	3	29	1	29.00	1- 11	–	–
Brown, D.O.	RM	13	1	90	1	90.00	1- 38	–	–
Brown, D.R.	RFM	377.5	81	1274	36	35.38	5- 72	2	–
Brown, J.F.	OB	647	188	1565	66	23.71	7- 69	4	–
Bruce, J.T.A.	RMF	196	39	829	19	43.63	3- 42	–	–
Bryant, J.D.C.	RM	1	0	8	0			–	–
Burns, M.	RM	153.5	29	514	13	39.53	3- 35	–	–
Butcher, M.A.	RM	44.5	4	175	8	21.87	4- 60	–	–
Butler, I.G.	RFM	124	24	478	17	28.11	4- 74	–	–
Caddick, A.R.	RFM	38	8	110	7	15.71	4- 66	–	–
Cairns, C.L.	RFM	184	31	755	15	50.33	3- 59	–	–
Carberry, M.A.	OB	23	2	94	1	94.00	1- 45	–	–
Carter, N.M.	LFM	126	20	522	8	65.25	5- 75	1	–
Cawdron, M.J.	RM	142.3	31	504	20	25.20	6- 87	1	–
Chapple, G.	RFM	494.2	90	1744	49	35.59	6- 98	2	–
Chilton, M.J.	RM	43	9	109	1	109.00	1- 2	–	–
Clark, M.W.	LMF	33	7	110	3	36.66	2- 71	–	–
Clarke, A.J.	RM	59	13	205	7	29.28	4- 34	–	–

132

F-C	Cat	O	M	R	W	Avge	Best	5wI	10wM
Clarke, R.	RFM	164.1	22	709	17	41.70	4- 21	–	–
Clough, G.D.	RM	25	0	119	1	119.00	1- 76	–	–
Collingwood, P.D.	RMF	61.1	7	228	4	57.00	3- 38	–	–
Collymore, C.D.	RFM	138	24	475	8	59.37	3- 42	–	–
Cook, A.N.	OB	2	0	11	0				
Cook, J.W.	RM	162.3	46	479	19	25.21	5- 31	1	–
Cook, S.J.	RM	332.2	78	1048	27	38.81	4- 42	–	–
Cork, D.G.	RFM	444.1	99	1363	50	27.26	6- 28	3	2
Cosker, D.A.	SLA	264.5	67	695	17	40.88	3- 49	–	–
Cottey, P.A.	OB	13	1	59	0				
Cowan, E.J.M.	LB	1	0	3	0				
Cox, J.	OB	2	0	15	0				
Craven, V.J.	RM	75	18	253	8	31.62	2- 25	–	–
Croft, R.D.B.	OB	731.5	192	1928	65	29.66	6- 71	5	1
Crook, S.P.	RFM	37.1	4	155	2	77.50	1- 6	–	–
Cummins, R.A.G.	RM	62	11	357	2	178.50	2-108	–	–
Daggett, L.M.	RMF	76	13	317	3	105.66	2- 95	–	–
Dagnall, C.E.	RM	295.5	70	1005	28	35.89	5- 66	1	–
Dakin, J.M.	RM	352.3	79	1099	40	27.47	5- 86	1	–
Dale, A.	RMF	48	9	159	3	53.00	3- 29	–	–
Dale, M.A.P.	RM	4	0	32	0				
Daley, S.R.	RMF	9	1	31	0				
Dalrymple, J.W.M.	OB	172.1	27	529	12	44.08	5- 49	1	–
Davies, A.M.	RM	149	35	509	11	46.27	2- 34	–	–
Davies, A.P.	RMF	46	8	225	2	112.50	1- 22	–	–
Davis, M.J.G.	OB	237	46	761	15	50.73	3- 44	–	–
Dawes, J.H.	RFM	331.4	58	1071	34	31.50	5- 46	1	–
Dawson, R.K.J.	OB	241.5	47	840	17	49.41	3-119	–	–
Dean, K.J.	LMF	445.3	108	1593	41	38.85	4- 39	–	–
DeFreitas, P.A.J.	RFM	540.3	154	1443	60	24.05	7- 51	4	1
Dernbach, J.	RMF	13	3	74	1	74.00	1- 74	–	–
Di Venuto, M.J.	RM/LB	6	0	23	0				
Drakes, V.C.	RFM	143.1	33	463	11	42.09	3- 58	–	–
Dumelow, N.R.C.	OB	214.5	43	776	18	43.11	5- 78	2	1
Durston, W.J.	OB	40	8	125	3	41.66	1- 16	–	–
Dutch, K.P.	OB	126.1	25	428	8	53.50	3- 56	–	–
Ealham, M.A.	RMF	357.5	106	1013	38	26.65	6- 35	3	–
Edwards, N.J.	RM	18.5	1	71	0				
Elworthy, S.	RFM	160.1	22	627	20	31.35	5- 71	1	–
Ervine, S.M.	RM	79	16	343	4	85.75	2- 95	–	–
Fellows, G.M.	RM	19	2	48	2	24.00	1- 20	–	–
Ferley, R.S.	SLA	259	44	1032	24	43.00	4- 76	–	–
Fisher, I.D.	SLA	225.1	50	767	28	27.39	5- 30	3	1
Flintoff, A.	RFM	232	57	727	15	48.46	2- 47	–	–
Flower, A.	(WK)	10.3	0	29	2	14.50	1- 5	–	–
Flower, G.W.	SLA	40.5	7	129	6	21.50	3- 25	–	–
Francis, S.R.G.	RMF	328.1	72	1179	35	33.68	4- 47	–	–
Franks, P.J.	RMF	296	49	1177	28	42.03	4- 62	–	–
Free, C.W.	RMF	15	1	55	1	55.00	1- 32	–	–
Friend, T.J.	RMF	67	6	357	6	59.50	2- 42	–	–
Gallian, J.E.R.	RM	31	6	94	1	94.00	1- 7	–	–
Gambhir, G.	LB	1	0	3	0				
Gannon, B.W.	RMF	23	4	102	0				
Gavaskar, R.S.	SLA	6	3	10	0				
Giddins, E.S.H.	RFM	98.5	18	336	13	25.84	4- 88	–	–
Gidman, A.P.R.	RM	104	20	441	5	88.20	2- 46	–	–
Gilder, G.M.	LFM	29	2	133	1	133.00	1- 56	–	–
Giles, A.F.	SLA	374.5	62	1146	22	52.09	5-115	1	–

F-C	Cat	O	M	R	W	Avge	Best	5wI	10wM
Goodwin, M.W.	RM/LB	3	0	17	0			–	–
Gough, D.	RF	271.1	55	866	20	43.30	3- 40	–	–
Gough, M.A.	OB	28.4	5	109	3	36.33	2- 23	–	–
Grant, J.B.	RFM	39.2	3	181	7	25.85	3- 61	–	–
Gray, A.K.D.	OB	233.2	51	692	13	53.23	3- 43	–	–
Grayson, A.P.	SLA	147	29	453	9	50.33	4- 47	–	–
Greenidge, C.G.	RMF	230.4	25	1039	22	47.22	3- 33	–	–
Grove, J.O.	RMF	20	3	64	1	64.00	1- 21	–	–
Gunter, N.E.L.	RFM	45.1	5	234	4	58.50	2- 48	–	–
Habib, A.	RM	2.4	0	10	1	10.00	1- 10	–	–
Hall, A.J.	RFM	293.4	70	823	35	23.51	3- 10	–	–
Hamblin, J.R.C.	RMF	68	13	262	7	37.42	6- 93	1	–
Hancock, T.H.C.	RM	5	0	22	0			–	–
Hardinges, M.A.	RMF	27	9	118	3	39.33	1- 28	–	–
Harmison, S.J.	RF	349.2	97	1002	37	27.08	4- 33	–	–
Harris, A.J.	RM	208.5	31	850	15	56.66	4- 23	–	–
Harrison, D.S.	RM	366	84	1284	40	32.10	5- 80	1	–
Harrity, M.A.	LFM	166.5	37	549	11	49.90	4- 39	–	–
Harvey, I.J.	RM	195.2	54	625	27	23.14	4- 43	–	–
Hatch, N.G.	RM	149.4	28	484	13	37.23	3- 66	–	–
Havell, P.M.R.	RFM	106.4	18	498	14	35.57	4-129	–	–
Hayward, M.	RF	427.3	83	1533	67	22.88	5- 66	2	–
Heath, D.R.	RM	37	5	146	1	146.00	1- 27	–	–
Heath, J.A.	RM	21	1	83	2	41.50	2- 83	–	–
Hewson, D.R.	RM	4	0	14	0				
Hick, G.A.	OB	21	5	63	0				
Hindley, R.J.E.	OB	9	0	46	0				
Hodge, B.J.	OB	68	12	274	7	39.14	3- 35	–	–
Hogg, K.W.	RFM	97	22	370	7	52.85	2- 66	–	–
Hoggard, M.J.	RFM	225.3	57	606	21	28.85	7- 49	1	–
Hollioake, A.J.	RM	80.2	11	300	5	60.00	2- 32	–	–
Hondo, D.T.	RMF	94	23	312	15	20.80	5- 26	1	–
Hooper, C.L.	OB	366.2	86	912	30	30.40	6- 51	2	–
Hopkinson, C.D.	RM	2	0	8	0				
Hunt, T.A.	RMF	22	4	96	3	32.00	2- 28	–	–
Hunter, I.D.	RMF	51	6	191	3	63.66	2- 55	–	–
Hussey, M.E.K.	RM	14	2	52	1	52.00	1- 5	–	–
Hutchison, P.M.	LFM	99.5	17	405	7	57.85	4- 94	–	–
Hutton, B.L.	RMF	83	14	363	5	72.60	2- 43	–	–
Imran Tahir	LBG	59	13	196	1	196.00	1-128	–	–
Innes, K.J.	RM	98	18	354	9	39.33	2- 18	–	–
Irani, R.C.	RMF	100	33	245	9	27.22	4- 59	–	–
Jaques, P.A.	SLC	4	0	25	0				
Johnson, R.L.	RFM	364.1	85	1077	42	25.64	6- 33	2	–
Jones, P.S.	RMF	204.3	27	930	22	42.27	5- 42	1	–
Joyce, E.C.	RM	56	7	219	2	109.50	1- 23	–	–
Kaif, M.	OB	4	0	21	1	21.00	1- 21	–	–
Kallis, J.H.	RFM	131.3	29	412	15	27.46	6- 54	1	–
Kartik, M.	SLA	135.5	27	400	10	40.00	4-112	–	–
Kasprowicz, M.S.	RFM	572.3	140	1629	77	21.15	9- 36	4	2
Katich, S.M.	SLC	160.4	29	591	17	34.76	4- 21	–	–
Keedy, G.	SLA	555.5	126	1593	60	26.55	6- 68	5	1
Keegan, C.B.	RFM	585.4	121	1925	63	30.55	6-114	3	–
Kemp, J.M.	RFM	102.1	17	319	14	22.78	5- 48	1	–
Kendall, W.S.	RM	9	2	53	0				
Kenway, D.A.	RM	2	0	9	1	9.00	1- 9	–	–
Key, R.W.T.	RM/OB	0.4	0	4	0				
Khalid, S.A.	OB	90.5	14	334	10	33.40	4-131	–	–

134

F-C	Cat	O	M	R	W	Avge	Best	5wI	10wM
Khan, A.	RFM	165	16	797	17	46.88	4- 65	–	–
Khan, R.M.	OB	3	1	13	0			–	–
Killeen, N.	RFM	290	70	946	26	36.38	7- 70	1	–
King, R.E.	LMF	58.3	7	313	1	313.00	1-108	–	–
Kirby, S.P.	RFM	463	80	1769	67	26.40	8- 80	5	2
Kirtley, R.J.	RFM	529.1	127	1662	62	26.80	6- 26	3	–
Knight, N.V.	RM	6	3	39	0				
Koenig, S.G.	OB	5	0	19	1	19.00	1- 19	–	–
Laraman, A.W.	RFM	279.5	58	979	24	40.79	3- 20	–	–
Law, D.R.	RFM	103.3	15	353	12	29.41	4- 30	–	–
Law, S.G.	RM/LB	7	0	29	0				
Leatherdale, D.A.	RM	39	6	142	4	35.50	2- 18	–	–
Lewis, J.	RMF	551.2	142	1800	74	24.32	7-117	5	1
Lewis, P.D.	RFM	37	4	173	3	57.66	2- 96	–	–
Lewry, J.D.	LFM	337.2	73	1118	42	26.61	8-106	3	1
Linley, T.E.	RMF	10	2	63	0				
Liptrot, C.G.	RFM	20	8	47	3	15.66	3- 47	–	–
Logan, R.J.	RMF	28	2	173	0				
Loudon, A.G.R.	OB	48.1	2	276	2	138.00	1- 52	–	–
Loye, M.B.	OB	4	0	16	1	16.00	1- 8	–	–
Lumb, M.J.	RM	13	0	73	1	73.00	1- 29	–	–
Lungley, T.	RMF	66.2	6	350	7	50.00	4-101	–	–
McCoubrey, A.G.A.M.	RFM	24.1	3	142	3	47.33	1- 7	–	–
McGarry, A.C.	RFM	53.3	14	145	5	29.00	5- 27	1	–
MacGill, S.C.G.	LBG	412.2	73	1408	42	33.52	6-117	2	–
McGrath, A.	RM	134.1	21	403	17	23.70	3- 16	–	–
McGrath, D.E.T.	RM	20	7	90	2	45.00	2- 90	–	–
McLean, N.A.M.	RFM	551.3	115	1872	65	28.80	5- 43	3	–
McMahon, P.J.	OB	203.4	51	595	18	33.05	4- 59	–	–
Maddy, D.L.	RM/OB	297.1	59	1002	36	27.83	5- 49	1	–
Maher, J.P.	RM	1	0	2	0				
Mahmood, S.I.	RMF	109	16	444	15	29.60	5- 37	1	–
Malcolm, D.E.	RF	94	22	358	14	25.57	5- 40	1	–
Malik, M.N.	RFM	57	7	227	3	75.66	2- 58	–	–
Marillier, D.A.	OB	17	4	65	2	32.50	2- 10	–	–
Marshall, S.J.	LB	130	11	482	1	482.00	1- 76	–	–
Martin, P.J.	RFM	432.1	99	1295	41	31.58	5- 54	1	–
Martin-Jenkins, R.S.C.	RFM	364	82	1258	31	40.58	3- 9	–	–
Mascarenhas, A.D.	RMF	489.1	150	1287	40	32.17	6- 55	1	–
Mason, M.S.	RFM	439.3	128	1144	53	21.58	6- 68	2	–
Masters, D.D.	RMF	425.3	85	1581	37	42.72	5- 53	1	–
Maunders, J.K.	RM	9	1	38	0				
Maynard, M.P.	RM	2	0	2	0				
Mees, T.	RMF	107	14	425	5	85.00	2- 68	–	–
Middlebrook, J.D.	OB	593	87	1979	56	35.33	6-123	1	–
Millar, N.	RM	2	0	11	0				
Mishra, A.	LB	134	22	468	13	36.00	5-183	1	–
Mohammad Akram	RFM	145	31	560	20	28.00	8- 49	2	1
Mohammad Sami	RF	89.1	17	357	18	19.83	8- 64	2	1
Montgomerie, R.R.	OB	3	0	9	1	9.00	1- 9	–	–
Muchall, G.J.	RM	52.2	8	216	5	43.20	3- 26	–	–
Mullally, A.D.	LFM	229.1	55	664	17	39.05	3- 31	–	–
Munday, M.K.	LB	80	8	305	14	21.78	5- 83	1	–
Muralitharan, M.	OB	178	41	447	33	13.54	6- 36	4	–
Murtagh, T.J.	RFM	146.5	17	615	12	51.25	4-130	–	–
Mushtaq Ahmed	LBG	836.3	163	2539	103	24.65	7- 85	10	5
Napier, G.R.	RM	379.3	60	1506	33	45.63	5- 66	1	–
Nash, C.D.	OB	45.4	4	239	1	239.00	1- 46	–	–

135

F-C

	Cat	O	M	R	W	Avge	Best	5wI	10wM
Nash, D.C.	(WK)	5	0	25	0				
Nel, A.	RFM	422.3	99	1292	36	35.88	5- 47	1	–
Newby, O.J.	RFM	29	7	82	1	82.00	1- 41	–	–
Newman, S.A.	RM	1	0	5	0				
Nkala, M.L.	RMF	46	13	182	0				
Noble, D.J.	RMF	11	2	49	0				
Noffke, A.A.	RFM	245.4	52	754	21	35.90	5- 52	1	–
Ntini, M.	RF	222.2	40	910	24	37.91	5- 75	2	1
Obuya, C.O.	LB	54	2	276	4	69.00	3- 91	–	–
Ormond, J.	RFM	392.1	74	1428	51	28.00	6- 34	3	–
Ostler, D.P.	RM	2	0	33	0				
Palladino, A.P.	RMF	162	31	594	11	54.00	6- 41	1	–
Panesar, M.S.	SLA	161.2	30	557	13	42.84	3- 92	–	–
Park, G.T.	RMF	50	1	261	0				
Parkin, O.T.	RFM	12	5	22	1	22.00	1- 19	–	–
Parsons, K.A.	RM	32.4	5	123	4	30.75	2- 63	–	–
Patel, S.R.	SLA	8	5	10	0				
Pathan, I.K.	LMF	124	28	394	9	43.77	4- 60	–	–
Pattison, I.	RM	5.4	3	7	1	7.00	1- 7	–	–
Paynter, D.E.	OB	6	1	26	0				
Penberthy, A.L.	RM	17	5	54	0				
Peploe, C.T.	SLA	65	9	239	2	119.50	1- 58	–	–
Peterson, R.J.	SLA	116.2	28	381	7	54.42	3- 58	–	–
Phillips, B.J.	RFM	149	47	400	21	19.04	4- 45	–	–
Phillips, N.C.	OB	408.4	63	1513	38	39.81	5-144	1	–
Pietersen, K.P.	OB	108.4	18	428	11	38.90	4- 31	–	–
Plunkett, L.E.	RMF	164	34	672	19	35.36	5- 53	1	–
Polley, S.R.	RM	30	1	160	1	160.00	1- 54	–	–
Pollock, S.M.	RFM	198	61	480	22	21.81	6- 39	1	–
Powell, M.J.(Nh)	OB	2	0	12	0				
Powell, M.J.(Wa)	RM	9	0	42	0				
Pratt, G.J.	(WK)	1	0	5	0				
Pretorius, D.	RFM	206	31	863	26	33.19	4- 15	–	–
Price, R.W.	SLA	156.3	34	431	8	53.87	2- 47	–	–
Prittipaul, L.R.	RM/OB	42	6	178	5	35.60	3- 17	–	–
Ramprakash, M.R.	RM	18	6	40	0				
Rayudu, A.T.	OB	3	0	13	0				
Richardson, A.	RMF	453	104	1314	33	39.81	4- 37	–	–
Roberts, T.W.	OB	4	0	4	0				
Robinson, D.D.J.	RMF	8.5	0	62	1	62.00	1- 7	–	–
Rogers, B.G.	OB	3	0	8	0				
Rose, F.A.	RFM	28	8	101	3	33.66	3-101	–	–
Rudolph, J.A.	LB	24	5	82	1	82.00	1- 1	–	–
Sadler, J.L.	LB	7.5	1	40	0				
Saggers, M.J.	RMF	450	97	1441	58	24.84	5- 42	2	–
Saker, N.C.	RFM	35.1	2	179	1	179.00	1- 71	–	–
Sales, D.J.G.	RM	1	0	4	0				
Salisbury, I.D.K.	LBG	371.1	60	1224	33	37.09	4-116	–	–
Salvi, A.M.	RM	87	25	267	9	29.66	4- 92	–	–
Sampson, P.J.	RFM	19.5	1	101	4	25.25	2- 16	–	–
Saqlain Mushtaq	OB	471	100	1364	41	33.26	5- 46	3	–
Savill, T.E.	RFM	97.4	8	460	8	57.50	3- 86	–	–
Schofield, C.P.	LB	187.1	37	636	15	42.40	4- 64	–	–
Sehwag, V.	OB	34.2	4	153	0				
Selwood, S.A.	SLA	7	0	28	0				
Shafayat, B.M.	RMF	16	2	96	1	96.00	1- 22	–	–
Shah, O.A.	OB	11	0	55	0				
Shahid Afridi	LBG	54.4	15	147	4	36.75	2- 29	–	–

F-C	Cat	O	M	R	W	Avge	Best	5wI	10wM
Shahid, N.	LB	18	3	75	1	75.00	1- 33	–	–
Shantry, A.J.	LFM	46.4	13	153	7	21.85	3- 8	–	–
Sharif, Z.K.	LB	69	6	345	5	69.00	3-103	–	–
Sharpe, T.J.	RMF	38	9	126	1	126.00	1- 27	–	–
Sheikh, M.A.	RM	181.5	43	553	15	36.86	4- 60	–	–
Sheriyar, A.	LFM	374.3	76	1257	38	33.07	5- 65	1	–
Shoaib Akhtar	RF	183	40	580	34	17.05	4- 9	–	–
Shoaib Malik	OB	66	19	146	5	29.20	3- 76	–	–
Shreck, C.E.	RMF	227.1	46	878	23	38.17	5-100	1	–
Sibanda, V.	RM	5	1	34	0			–	–
Sidebottom, R.J.	LFM	222.2	37	710	35	20.28	7- 97	2	–
Sillence, R.J.	RMF	100.5	15	408	9	45.33	3- 55	–	–
Silverwood, C.E.W.	RFM	351.4	73	1177	48	24.52	5- 63	2	–
Singh, A. (CU)	LB	4	0	19	0			–	–
Smith, A.M.	LMF	329.5	91	898	38	23.63	5- 70	1	–
Smith, E.T.	RM	3	1	14	0			–	–
Smith, G.J.	LFM	356.1	78	1227	51	24.05	5- 42	3	–
Smith, N.M.K.	OB	90.3	9	408	4	102.00	2-111	–	–
Snape, J.N.	OB	177.3	25	669	11	60.81	3-108	–	–
Solanki, V.S.	OB	2	1	9	0			–	–
Somerville-Hendrie, J.W.	RFM	45.4	4	213	4	53.25	3-124	–	–
Srinath, J.	RFM	84	24	226	6	37.66	3- 70	–	–
Sriram, S.	SLA	11	2	43	0			–	–
Stephenson, J.P.	RM	42	8	162	3	54.00	2- 55	–	–
Stevens, D.I.	RM	23	5	71	1	71.00	1- 5	–	–
Stewart, A.J.	(WK)	2.3	0	23	0			–	–
Strauss, A.J.	LM	6	0	42	1	42.00	1- 27	–	–
Streak, H.H.	RFM	123.3	38	263	12	21.91	4- 64	–	–
Suppiah, A.V.	SLA	11	1	44	1	44.00	1- 44	–	–
Sutcliffe, I.J.	OB	4	1	11	1	11.00	1- 11	–	–
Swanepoel, P.J.	RMF	51	16	129	3	43.00	2- 40	–	–
Swann, A.J.	RM/OB	5	0	22	0			–	–
Swann, G.P.	OB	238.2	37	759	33	23.00	7- 33	3	–
Symonds, A.	RMF/OB	152	26	517	16	32.31	3- 38	–	–
Taylor, B.V.	RMF	244.1	69	681	23	29.60	4- 42	–	–
Taylor, C.G.	OB	11	0	48	0			–	–
Ten Doeschate, R.N.	RFM	24	3	122	0			–	–
Thomas, S.D.	RFM	82.1	8	293	13	22.53	4- 47	–	–
Thorburn, M.	RMF	31	6	120	3	40.00	2- 53	–	–
Thornicroft, N.D.	RMF	14	2	57	0			–	–
Thorpe, G.P.	RM	11	1	73	1	73.00	1- 73	–	–
Todd, M.J.	OB	14	0	92	1	92.00	1- 92	–	–
Tomlinson, J.A.	LFM	171.5	22	794	17	46.70	6- 63	1	–
Tredwell, J.C.	OB	329.4	73	1125	28	40.17	4- 48	–	–
Trego, P.D.	RM	13	0	69	2	34.50	1- 26	–	–
Tremlett, C.T.	RMF	248.4	48	929	27	34.40	6- 51	1	–
Trott, B.J.	RFM	150.3	27	649	13	49.92	4- 73	–	–
Trott, I.J.L.	RM	49.1	4	215	7	30.71	7- 39	1	–
Troughton, J.O.	SLA	13	0	85	0			–	–
Tudor, A.J.	RF	144	24	532	10	53.20	3- 56	–	–
Udal, S.D.	OB	436.4	87	1350	42	32.14	4- 50	–	–
Vaas, W.P.U.C.J.	LMF	94	18	310	8	38.75	4- 82	–	–
Vaughan, M.P.	OB	20	2	68	1	68.00	1- 26	–	–
Vettori, D.L.	SLA	48.3	2	302	6	50.33	4- 74	–	–
Wagg, G.G.	LM	40	4	250	5	50.00	2- 61	–	–
Wagh, M.A.	OB	193.3	28	730	20	36.50	7-222	1	–
Walker, G.W.	SLA	29	3	111	1	111.00	1- 92	–	–
Walker, M.J.	RM	17	2	75	1	75.00	1- 24	–	–

F-C	Cat	O	M	R	W	Avge	Best	5wI	10wM
Waqar Younis	RFM	244.2	39	917	39	23.51	5- 40	3	–
Ward, I.J.	RM	16.3	0	76	0				
Wasim Akram	LFM	167.3	44	503	20	25.15	3- 31	–	–
Webley, T.	SLA	82	8	344	6	57.33	2- 57	–	–
Weekes, P.N.	OB	451.1	85	1355	35	38.71	4- 55	–	–
Welch, G.	RM	483.3	121	1476	53	27.84	6-102	2	–
Wells, V.J.	RMF	164.4	36	515	22	23.40	4- 16	–	–
Weston, W.P.C.	LB	2	0	10	0				
Westwood, I.J.	OB	8	0	57	0				
Wharf, A.G.	RMF	432.3	72	1734	52	33.34	4- 53	–	–
Wharton, L.J.	SLA	115	24	364	9	40.44	4- 50	–	–
Whiley, M.J.A.	LMF	117.3	14	562	7	80.28	2- 76	–	–
White, C.	RFM	21	3	64	0				
White, R.A.	LB	18	0	123	1	123.00	1- 35	–	–
Wigley, D.H.	RFM	61.1	12	280	4	70.00	2- 56	–	–
Willoughby, C.M.	LMF	79	23	220	8	27.50	3- 31	–	–
Wood, J.	RFM	222.4	32	854	27	31.62	3- 17	–	–
Wood, M.J. (Sm)	OB	5.1	0	32	0				
Wood, M.J. (Y)	OB	8	0	22	2	11.00	1- 4	–	–
Wright, D.G.	RMF	73.5	19	194	7	27.71	3- 38	–	–
Wright, L.J.	RMF	19	0	95	0				
Yardy, M.H.	LM	32	3	99	0				
Yuvraj Singh	SLA	34.3	5	130	3	43.33	1- 8	–	–
Zondeki, M.	RF	63.5	8	281	9	31.22	5- 64	1	–

COUNTY BENEFITS AWARDED IN 2004

Derbyshire	–
Durham	J.J.B.Lewis
Essex	Essex Academy
Glamorgan	Sophia Gardens Development Appeal
Gloucestershire	R.C.Russell
Hampshire	Hampshire Youth Trust
Kent	M.M.Patel
Lancashire	G.Chapple
Leicestershire	P.A.J.DeFreitas
Middlesex	–
Northamptonshire	–
Nottinghamshire	P.Johnson (*Testimonial*)
Somerset	K.A.Parsons
Surrey	A.J.Hollioake
Sussex	K.Greenfield (*Testimonial*)
Warwickshire	N.V.Knight
Worcestershire	T.M.Moody (*Testimonial*)
Yorkshire	C.E.W.Silverwood

COUNTY CHAMPIONSHIP 2003
FRIZZELL FINAL TABLES

DIVISION 1

	P	W	L	T	D	Bonus Points Bat	Points Bowl	Deduct Points	Total Points
1 SUSSEX (6)	16	10	4	–	2	62	47	–	257.00
2 Lancashire (4)	16	6	2	–	8	64	43	–	223.00
3 Surrey (1)	16	6	3	–	7	63	44	–	219.00
4 Kent (3)	16	6	5	–	5	47	47	–	198.00
5 Warwickshire (2)	16	4	5	1	6	50	37	2.50	171.50
6 Middlesex (-)	16	3	3	–	10	46	41	–	169.00
7 Essex (-)	16	3	5	1	7	34	45	–	156.00
8 Northamptonshire (-)	16	2	8	–	6	36	45	1.00	132.00
9 Leicestershire (5)	16	1	6	–	9	36	40	0.50	125.50

DIVISION 2

	P	W	L	T	D	Bonus Points Bat	Points Bowl	Deduct Points	Total Points
1 WORCESTERSHIRE (4)	16	10	1	–	5	42	44	0.25	245.75
2 Northamptonshire (7)	16	10	2	–	4	45	44	8.00	237.00†
3 Gloucestershire (8)	16	5	2	–	9	38	46	–	190.00
4 Yorkshire (-)	16	4	5	–	7	54	47	1.50	183.50
5 Glamorgan (-)	16	5	5	–	6	45	45	1.00	183.00
6 Durham (9)	16	5	7	–	4	31	45	0.75	159.25
7 Somerset (-)	16	4	8	–	4	41	44	–	157.00
8 Hampshire (-)	16	2	6	–	8	36	44	–	140.00
9 Derbyshire (-)	16	2	11	–	3	30	44	–	114.00

2002 final positions for that division are shown in brackets.
† Eight points deducted for a sub-standard pitch.

SCORING OF CHAMPIONSHIP POINTS 2003

(a) For a win, 14 points, plus any points scored in the first innings.

(b) In a tie, each side to score seven points, plus any points scored in the first innings.

(c) In a drawn match, each side to score four points, plus any points scored in the first innings (see also paragraph (f) below).

(d) If the scores are equal in a drawn match, the side batting in the fourth innings to score seven points plus any points scored in the first innings, and the opposing side to score four points plus any points scored in the first innings.

(e) **First Innings Points** (awarded only for performances **in the first 130 overs** of each first innings and retained whatever the result of the match).
   • A maximum of five batting points to be available as under:-
   200 to 249 runs – 1 point; 250 to 299 runs – 2 points; 300 to 349 runs – 3 points;
   350 to 399 runs – 4 points; 400 runs or over – 5 points.
   • A maximum of three bowling points to be available as under:-
   3 to 5 wickets taken – 1 point; 6 to 8 wickets taken – 2 points; 9 to 10 wickets taken – 3 points.

(f) If play starts when fewer than eight hours' playing time remains (in which event a one innings match shall be played as provided for in First-Class Playing Condition 18), no first innings points shall be scored. The side winning on the one innings to score 14 points. In a tie, each side to score seven points. In a drawn match, each side to score four points. If the scores are equal in a drawn match, the side batting in the second innings to score seven points and the opposing side to score four points.

(g) If a match is abandoned without a ball being bowled, each side to score four points.

(h) The side which has the highest aggregate of points gained at the end of the season shall be the Champion County of their respective Division. Should any sides in the Championship table be equal on points, the following tie-breakers will be applied in the order stated: most wins, least losses, team achieving most points in contests between level on points, most wickets taken, most runs scored. At the end of the season, the top three teams from the Second Division will be promoted and the bottom three teams from the First Division will be relegated.

COUNTY CHAMPIONS

The English County Championship was not officially constituted until December 1889. Prior to that date there was no generally accepted method of awarding the title; although the 'least matches lost' method existed, it was not consistently applied. Rules governing playing qualifications were agreed in 1873 and the first unofficial points system 15 years later.

Research has produced a list of champions dating back to 1826, but at least seven different versions exist for the period from 1864 to 1889 (see *The Wisden Book of Cricket Records*). Only from 1890 can any authorised list of county champions commence.

That first official Championship was contested between eight counties: Gloucestershire, Kent, Lancashire, Middlesex, Nottinghamshire, Surrey, Sussex and Yorkshire. The remaining counties were admitted in the following seasons: 1891 – Somerset, 1895 – Derbyshire, Essex, Hampshire, Leicestershire and Warwickshire, 1899 – Worcestershire, 1905 – Northamptonshire, 1921 – Glamorgan, and 1992 – Durham.

The Championship pennant was introduced by the 1951 champions, Warwickshire, and the Lord's Taverners' Trophy was first presented in 1973. The first sponsors, Schweppes (1977 to 1983), were succeeded by Britannic Assurance (1984 to 1998), PPP Healthcare (1999-2000), CricInfo (2001) and Frizzell (2002 to date). Based on their previous season's positions, the 18 counties were separated into two divisions in 2001.

1890	Surrey	1930	Lancashire	1970	Kent
1891	Surrey	1931	Yorkshire	1971	Surrey
1892	Surrey	1932	Yorkshire	1972	Warwickshire
1893	Yorkshire	1933	Yorkshire	1973	Hampshire
1894	Surrey	1934	Lancashire	1974	Worcestershire
1895	Surrey	1935	Yorkshire	1975	Leicestershire
1896	Yorkshire	1936	Derbyshire	1976	Middlesex
1897	Lancashire	1937	Yorkshire	1977	Kent
1898	Yorkshire	1938	Yorkshire		Middlesex
1899	Surrey	1939	Yorkshire	1978	Kent
1900	Yorkshire	1946	Yorkshire	1979	Essex
1901	Yorkshire	1947	Middlesex	1980	Middlesex
1902	Yorkshire	1948	Glamorgan	1981	Nottinghamshire
1903	Middlesex	1949	Middlesex	1982	Middlesex
1904	Lancashire		Yorkshire	1983	Essex
1905	Yorkshire	1950	Lancashire	1984	Essex
1906	Kent		Surrey	1985	Middlesex
1907	Nottinghamshire	1951	Warwickshire	1986	Essex
1908	Yorkshire	1952	Surrey	1987	Nottinghamshire
1909	Kent	1953	Surrey	1988	Worcestershire
1910	Kent	1954	Surrey	1989	Worcestershire
1911	Warwickshire	1955	Surrey	1990	Middlesex
1912	Yorkshire	1956	Surrey	1991	Essex
1913	Kent	1957	Surrey	1992	Essex
1914	Surrey	1958	Surrey	1993	Middlesex
1919	Yorkshire	1959	Yorkshire	1994	Warwickshire
1920	Middlesex	1960	Yorkshire	1995	Warwickshire
1921	Middlesex	1961	Hampshire	1996	Leicestershire
1922	Yorkshire	1962	Yorkshire	1997	Glamorgan
1923	Yorkshire	1963	Yorkshire	1998	Leicestershire
1924	Yorkshire	1964	Worcestershire	1999	Surrey
1925	Yorkshire	1965	Worcestershire	2000	Surrey
1926	Lancashire	1966	Yorkshire	2001	Yorkshire
1927	Lancashire	1967	Yorkshire	2002	Surrey
1928	Lancashire	1968	Yorkshire	2003	Sussex
1929	Nottinghamshire	1969	Glamorgan		

COUNTY CHAMPIONSHIP RESULTS 2003

DIVISION 1

	ESSEX	KENT	LANCS	LEICS	MIDDX	NOTTS	SURREY	SUSSEX	WARWKS
ESSEX	–	Chelms Drawn	Chelms Drawn	S'end Drawn	Chelms Drawn	Chelms Ex 9w	Chelms Sy 258	Colch'r Sx I/120	Chelms Wa 9w
KENT	Cant K 55	–	Cant La 75	Cant Drawn	Cant Drawn	Maid K 287	Cant K I/155	Tun W Sx 191	Cant K I/70
LANCS	Man Drawn	B'pool Drawn	–	L'pool La 10w	Man Drawn	Man Drawn	Man La 8w	Man La I/19	Man Drawn
LEICS	Leics Drawn	Leics Le 10w	Leics La 7w	–	Leics Drawn	Leics Drawn	Leics Drawn	Leics Sx 5w	Leics Drawn
MIDDX	Lord's Drawn	Lord's K 8w	Lord's Drawn	S'gate M 8w	–	Lord's Drawn	Lord's Drawn	Lord's M 3w	S'gate Drawn
NOTTS	N'ham Ex 268	N'ham K 9w	N'ham Nt 233	N'ham Drawn	N'ham M 4w	–	N'ham Sy I/6	N'ham Drawn	N'ham Nt 3w
SURREY	Oval Ex 8w	Oval Sy 186	Oval Drawn	Oval Drawn	Guild Sy I/211	Croydon Drawn	–	Oval Sy 113	Oval Drawn
SUSSEX	Arundel Sx 6w	Hove Sx 133	Hove Sx 252	Hove Sx I/55	Hove Sx 7w	Horsham Sx 10w	Hove Drawn	–	Hove Sx I/59
WARWKS	B'ham Tied	B'ham Drawn	B'ham La I/145	B'ham Wa 8w	B'ham Wa 31	B'ham Drawn	B'ham Sy 135	B'ham Wa 234	–

DIVISION 2

	DERBYS	DURHAM	GLAM	GLOS	HANTS	N'HANTS	SOM'T	WORCS	YORKS
DERBYS	–	Derby Drawn	Derby Drawn	Derby Gs 5w	Derby H 10w	Derby Nh I/231	Derby Drawn	Derby Wo 9w	Derby Y 10w
DURHAM	C-le-St Du 30	–	C-le-St Gm 369	C-le-St Drawn	C-le-St Du I/115	C-le-St Nh 8w	C-le-St Du 318	Stockton Drawn	C-le-St Du 3w
GLAM	Swansea Gm I/70	Cardiff Gm 8w	–	Cardiff Gs 6w	Cardiff Drawn	Cardiff Nh 20	Cardiff Gm 110	Cardiff Drawn	Col Bay Drawn
GLOS	Bristol Gs 20	Bristol Gs 126	Bristol Drawn	–	Bristol Drawn	Bristol Nh I/54	Glos Gs 8	Chelt Drawn	Chelt Drawn
HANTS	So'ton De I/43	So'ton Drawn	So'ton H 93	So'ton Drawn	–	So'ton Nh 5w	So'ton Sm 6w	So'ton Wo 101	So'ton Drawn
N'HANTS	No'ton Nh 180	No'ton Nh I/85	No'ton Gm 55	No'ton Drawn	No'ton Nh 7w	–	No'ton Nh I/61	No'ton Nh 92	No'ton Drawn
SOM'T	Taunton Sm 27	Taunton Sm 6w	Taunton Sm I/143	Taunton Drawn	Taunton Drawn	Taunton Drawn	–	Bath Wo 9w	Taunton Y 10w
WORCS	Worcs Wo I/42	Worcs Wo 31	Worcs Wo 14	Worcs Wo 111	Worcs Drawn	Worcs Drawn	Worcs Wo 8w	–	Worcs Wo 71
YORKS	Leeds De 166	Leeds Du 167	Leeds Drawn	Leeds Drawn	Scar Drawn	Leeds Y I/343	Leeds Y 9w	Scar Wo 5w	–

COUNTY CHAMPIONSHIP RESULTS 2004

KEEP YOUR OWN RECORD (see page 141)

DIVISION 1

	GLOS	KENT	LANCS	MIDDX	N'HANTS	SURREY	SUSSEX	WARWKS	WORCS
GLOS	–	Bristol	Chelt	Glos	Bristol	Bristol	Bristol	Bristol	Chelt
KENT	Cant	–	Tun W	Cant	Cant	Cant	Cant	Beck'm	Cant
LANCS	Man	Man	–	Man	L'pool	Man	Man	Man	Man
MIDDX	Lord's	S'gate	Lord's	–	Lord's	Lord's	Lord's	Lord's	Lord's
N'HANTS	No'ton	No'ton	No'ton	No'ton	–	No'ton	No'ton	No'ton	No'ton
SURREY	Oval	Oval	Croydon	Oval	Oval	–	Oval	Guild	Oval
SUSSEX	Arundel	Hove	Hove	Hove	Hove	Hove	–	Horsham	Hove
WARWKS	B'ham	B'ham	Strafford	B'ham	B'ham	B'ham	B'ham	–	B'ham
WORCS	Worcs	Worcs	Worcs	Worcs	Worcs	Worcs	Worcs	Worcs	–

DIVISION 2

	DERBYS	DURHAM	ESSEX	GLAM	HANTS	LEICS	NOTTS	SOM'T	YORKS
DERBYS	–	Derby	Derby	Derby	Derby	Derby	Derby	Derby	Derby
DURHAM	C-le-St	–	C-le-St	C-le-St	C-le-St	C-le-St	C-le-St	C-le-St	C-le-St
ESSEX	Chelms	Chelms	–	Chelms	Chelms	Chelms	S'end	Chelms	Chelms
GLAM	Cardiff	Cardiff	Cardiff	–	Cardiff	Cardiff	Cardiff	Swansea	Col Bay
HANTS	So'ton	So'ton	So'ton	So'ton	–	So'ton	So'ton	So'ton	So'ton
LEICS	Oakham	Leics	Leics	Leics	Leics	–	Leics	Leics	Leics
NOTTS	N'ham	N'ham	N'ham	N'ham	N'ham	N'ham	–	N'ham	N'ham
SOM'T	Taunton	Taunton	Taunton	Taunton	Taunton	Taunton	Bath	–	Taunton
YORKS	Leeds	Scar	Leeds	Leeds	Leeds	Leeds	Leeds	Scar	–

UNIVERSITY MATCH RESULTS

Played: 158. Wins: Cambridge 56; Oxford 50. Drawn: 52. Abandoned: 1

In 2001, for the very first time, Cambridge hosted the University Match, cricket's oldest surviving first-class fixture after the ECB's re-organisation of university cricket around six centres of excellence had removed it from Lord's. Dating from 1827 it has, wartime interruptions apart, been played annually since 1838. With the exception of five matches played in the area of Oxford (1829, 1843, 1846, 1848 and 1850), all the previous fixtures had been staged at Lord's. Last season's contest was the first to be played over four days. In 2003, Oxford (with Brookes), Cambridge (with Anglia) and Durham were joined by Loughborough in playing three first-class matches against counties. The other two centres – Cardiff (with UWIC and Glamorgan), Leeds (with Bradford and Leeds Metropolitan) – also play three counties apiece but without first-class status.

1827	Drawn	1876	Cambridge	1921	Cambridge	1968	Drawn
1829	Oxford	1877	Oxford	1922	Cambridge	1969	Drawn
1836	Oxford	1878	Cambridge	1923	Oxford	1970	Drawn
1838	Oxford	1879	Cambridge	1924	Cambridge	1971	Drawn
1839	Cambridge	1880	Cambridge	1925	Drawn	1972	Cambridge
1840	Cambridge	1881	Oxford	1926	Cambridge	1973	Drawn
1841	Cambridge	1882	Cambridge	1927	Cambridge	1974	Drawn
1842	Cambridge	1883	Cambridge	1928	Drawn	1975	Drawn
1843	Cambridge	1884	Oxford	1929	Drawn	1976	Oxford
1844	Drawn	1885	Cambridge	1930	Cambridge	1977	Drawn
1845	Cambridge	1886	Oxford	1931	Oxford	1978	Drawn
1846	Oxford	1887	Oxford	1932	Drawn	1979	Cambridge
1847	Cambridge	1888	Drawn	1933	Drawn	1980	Drawn
1848	Oxford	1889	Cambridge	1934	Drawn	1981	Drawn
1849	Cambridge	1890	Cambridge	1935	Cambridge	1982	Cambridge
1850	Oxford	1891	Cambridge	1936	Cambridge	1983	Drawn
1851	Cambridge	1892	Oxford	1937	Oxford	1984	Oxford
1852	Oxford	1893	Cambridge	1938	Drawn	1985	Drawn
1853	Oxford	1894	Oxford	1939	Oxford	1986	Cambridge
1854	Oxford	1895	Cambridge	1946	Oxford	1987	Drawn
1855	Oxford	1896	Oxford	1947	Drawn	1988	Abandoned
1856	Cambridge	1897	Cambridge	1948	Oxford	1989	Drawn
1857	Oxford	1898	Oxford	1949	Cambridge	1990	Drawn
1858	Oxford	1899	Drawn	1950	Drawn	1991	Drawn
1859	Cambridge	1900	Drawn	1951	Oxford	1992	Cambridge
1860	Cambridge	1901	Drawn	1952	Drawn	1993	Oxford
1861	Cambridge	1902	Cambridge	1953	Cambridge	1994	Drawn
1862	Cambridge	1903	Oxford	1954	Drawn	1995	Oxford
1863	Oxford	1904	Drawn	1955	Drawn	1996	Drawn
1864	Oxford	1905	Cambridge	1956	Drawn	1997	Drawn
1865	Oxford	1906	Cambridge	1957	Cambridge	1998	Cambridge
1866	Oxford	1907	Cambridge	1958	Cambridge	1999	Drawn
1867	Cambridge	1908	Oxford	1959	Oxford	2000	Drawn
1868	Cambridge	1909	Drawn	1960	Drawn	2001	Drawn
1869	Cambridge	1910	Oxford	1961	Drawn	2002	Drawn
1870	Cambridge	1911	Oxford	1962	Drawn	2003	Oxford
1871	Oxford	1912	Cambridge	1963	Drawn		
1872	Cambridge	1913	Cambridge	1964	Drawn		
1873	Oxford	1914	Oxford	1965	Drawn		
1874	Oxford	1919	Oxford	1966	Oxford		
1875	Oxford	1920	Drawn	1967	Drawn		

CAMBRIDGE UNIVERSITY RECORDS

ALL FIRST-CLASS MATCHES

Highest Total	For 703-9d		v	Sussex	Hove	1890
	V 730-3		by	W Indians	Cambridge	1950
Lowest Total	For 30		v	Yorkshire	Cambridge	1928
	V 32		by	Oxford U	Lord's	1878
Highest Innings	For 254*	K.S.Duleepsinhji	v	Middlesex	Cambridge	1927
	V 304*	E.de C.Weekes	for	W Indians	Cambridge	1950
Highest Partnership						
(2nd wicket)	429*	J.G.Dewes/G.H.G.Doggart	v	Essex	Cambridge	1949
Best Innings Bowling	10-69	S.M.J.Woods	v	Thornton's XI	Cambridge	1890
Best Match Bowling	15-88	S.M.J.Woods	v	Thornton's XI	Cambridge	1890
Most Runs – Season	1581	D.S.Sheppard		(av 79.05)		1952
Most Runs – Career	4310	J.M.Brearley		(av 38.48)		1961-68
Most 100s – Season	7	D.S.Sheppard				1952
Most 100s – Career	14	D.S.Sheppard				1950-52
Most Wkts – Season	80	O.S.Wheatley		(av 17.63)		1958
Most Wkts – Career	208	G.Goonesena		(av 21.82)		1954-57

UNIVERSITY MATCH RECORDS

Highest Total	604		Oxford	2002
Lowest Total	39		Lord's	1858
Highest Innings	211	G.Goonesena	Lord's	1957
Best Innings Bowling	8-44	G.E.Jeffery	Lord's	1873
Best Match Bowling	13-73	A.G.Steel	Lord's	1878

Hat Tricks: F.C.Cobden (1870), A.G.Steel (1879), P.H.Morton (1880), J.F.Ireland (1911), R.G.H.Lowe (1926).

OXFORD UNIVERSITY RECORDS

ALL FIRST-CLASS MATCHES

Highest Total	For 651		v	Sussex	Hove	1895
	V 679-7d		by	Australians	Oxford	1938
Lowest Total	For 12		v	MCC	Oxford	1877
	V 24		by	MCC	Oxford	1846
Highest Innings	For 281	K.J.Key	v	Middlesex	Chiswick Park	1887
	V 338	W.W.Read	for	Surrey	The Oval	1888
Highest Partnership						
(7th wicket)	340	K.J.Key/H.Philipson	v	Middlesex	Chiswick Park	1887
Best Innings Bowling	10-38	S.E.Butler	v	Cambridge U	Lord's	1871
Best Match Bowling	15-65	B.J.T.Bosanquet	v	Sussex	Oxford	1900
Most Runs – Season	1307	Nawab of Pataudi sr		(av 93.35)		1931
Most Runs – Career	3319	N.S.Mitchell-Innes		(av 47.41)		1934-37
Most 100s – Season	6	Nawab of Pataudi sr				1931
Most 100s – Career	9	A.M.Crawley				1927-30
	9	Nawab of Pataudi sr				1928-31
	9	N.S.Mitchell-Innes				1934-37
	9	M.P.Donnelly				1946-47
Most Wkts – Season	70	I.A.R.Peebles		(av 18.15)		1930
Most Wkts – Career	182	R.H.B.Bettington		(av 19.38)		1920-23

UNIVERSITY MATCH RECORDS

Highest Total	522-7d		Cambridge	2003
Lowest Total	32		Lord's	1878
Highest Innings	238*	Nawab of Pataudi sr	Lord's	1931
Best Innings Bowling	10-38	S.E.Butler	Lord's	1871
Best Match Bowling	15-95	S.E.Butler	Lord's	1871

Match Doubles: P.R.le Couteur (160 and 11-66 in 1910); G.J.Toogood (149 and 10-93 in 1985)

CHELTENHAM & GLOUCESTER TROPHY 2003 RESULTS CHART

THIRD ROUND 7 May	FOURTH ROUND 28 May	QUARTER-FINALS 10, 11 June	SEMI-FINALS 7, 9 August	FINAL 30 August
Buckinghamshire†				
GLOUCESTERSHIRE	GLOUCESTERSHIRE			
Cornwall†		GLOUCESTERSHIRE		
KENT	Kent†			
Bedfordshire†			GLOUCESTERSHIRE†	
WARWICKSHIRE	WARWICKSHIRE†			
Essex CB†		Warwickshire† (£11,500)		
ESSEX	Essex			
Kent CB†				GLOUCESTERSHIRE (£53,000)
DERBYSHIRE	DERBYSHIRE			
Durham CB†		DERBYSHIRE†		
GLAMORGAN	Glamorgan†			
Staffordshire†			Derbyshire (£16,500)	
SURREY	SURREY			
Scotland†		Surrey† (£11,500)		
SOMERSET	Somerset†			
Northamptonshire†				
MIDDLESEX	MIDDLESEX†			
Hampshire†		Middlesex† (£11,500)		
SUSSEX	Sussex			
Devon†			Lancashire (£16,500)	
LANCASHIRE	LANCASHIRE			
Berkshire†		LANCASHIRE†		
DURHAM	Durham†			
Lincolnshire†			WORCESTERSHIRE†	
NOTTINGHAMSHIRE	Nottinghamshire			
Northumberland†		Leicestershire† (£11,500)		
LEICESTERSHIRE	LEICESTERSHIRE†			
Cambridgeshire†				Worcestershire (£27,000)
YORKSHIRE	Yorkshire			
Worcestershire CB†		WORCESTERSHIRE		
WORCESTERSHIRE	WORCESTERSHIRE†			

† Home team. Winning teams are in capitals. Prize-money shown in brackets.

2003 C & G TROPHY FINAL

GLOUCESTERSHIRE v WORCESTERSHIRE

At Lord's, London on 30 August
Result: **GLOUCESTERSHIRE won by seven wickets**
Toss: Gloucestershire. Award: I.J.Harvey.

WORCESTERSHIRE		Runs	Balls	4/6	Fall
V.S.Solanki	run out	40	51	7	1- 64
A.Singh	c Ball b Harvey	28	55	4	3- 72
G.A.Hick	c Windows b Harvey	0	4	–	2- 65
* B.F.Smith	run out	12	13	1	4- 92
A.J.Hall	lbw b Gidman	11	29	1	6- 99
D.A.Leatherdale	c Ball b Gidman	2	8	–	5- 96
G.J.Batty	lbw b Lewis	20	41	1	7-133
† S.J.Rhodes	c Ball b Lewis	15	43	1	8-134
Kabir Ali	not out	5	21	–	
M.S.Mason	st Russell b Ball	0	6	–	9-136
M.Hayward	c sub (C.G.Taylor) b Ball	4	9	–	10-149
Extras	(LB 6, W 4, NB 2)	12			
Total	(46.3 overs; 190 minutes)	**149**			

GLOUCESTERSHIRE		Runs	Balls	4/6	Fall
C.M.Spearman	c Smith b Ali	10	6	2	1- 30
W.P.C.Weston	c Hall b Mason	46	50	8	2-108
I.J.Harvey	st sub (D.J.Pipe) b Batty	61	36	12	3-132
A.P.R.Gidman	not out	12	21	2	
J.N.Rhodes	not out	7	12	1	
* M.W.Alleyne					
† R.C.Russell					
M.G.N.Windows					
M.C.J.Ball					
J.Lewis					
A.M.Smith					
Extras	(B 4, LB 3, W 3, NB 4)	14			
Total	(20.3 overs; 3 wickets; 91 minutes)	**150**			

WORCS	O	M	R	W	GLOS	O	M	R	W
Smith	5	0	24	0	Kabir Ali	4	0	25	1
Lewis	10	2	28	2	Hayward	3	0	20	0
Harvey	10	1	37	2	Mason	7	0	38	1
Alleyne	7	0	21	0	Hall	3	0	33	0
Gidman	7	1	12	2	Batty	3.3	0	27	1
Ball	7.3	0	21	2					

Scores after 15 overs: Worcestershire 62-0; Gloucestershire 130-2.

Umpires: M.R.Benson and J.H.Hampshire.

CHELTENHAM & GLOUCESTER TROPHY

PRINCIPAL RECORDS 1963-2003
(Including Gillette Cup and NatWest Trophy Matches)

Highest Total		438-5	Surrey v Glamorgan	The Oval	2002
Highest Total in a Final		322-5	Warwicks v Sussex	Lord's	1993
Highest Total Batting Second		429	Glamorgan v Surrey	The Oval	2002
Highest Total to Win Batting Second		329-5	Sussex v Derbyshire	Derby	1997
Lowest Total		39	Ireland v Sussex	Hove	1985
Lowest Total in a Final		57	Essex v Lancashire	Lord's	1996
Lowest Total to Win Batting First		Worcs v Durham	Chester-le-St	1968

Highest Score		268	A.D.Brown	Surrey v Glamorgan	The Oval	2002
Fastest Hundred		36 balls	G.D.Rose	Somerset v Devon	Torquay	1990
Most Hundreds		8	R.A.Smith	Hampshire		1985-03
Most Runs		2547	(av 48.98)	G.A.Gooch	Essex	1973-96

Highest Partnership for each Wicket

1st	311	A.J.Wright/N.J.Trainor	Glos v Scotland	Bristol	1997
2nd	286	I.S.Anderson/A.Hill	Derbys v Cornwall	Derby	1986
3rd	309*	T.S.Curtis/T.M.Moody	Worcs v Surrey	The Oval	1994
4th	234*	D.Lloyd/C.H.Lloyd	Lancashire v Glos	Manchester	1978
5th	166	M.A.Lynch/G.R.J.Roope	Surrey v Durham	The Oval	1982
6th	226	N.J.Llong/M.V.Fleming	Kent v Cheshire	Bowdon	1999
7th	170	D.R.Brown/A.F.Giles	Warwicks v Essex	Birmingham	2003
8th	112	A.L.Penberthy/J.E.Emburey	Northants v Lancs	Manchester	1996
9th	87	M.A.Nash/A.E.Cordle	Glamorgan v Lincs	Swansea	1974
10th	81	S.Turner/R.E.East	Essex v Yorkshire	Leeds	1982

Best Bowling		8-21	M.A.Holding	Derbys v Sussex	Hove	1988
		8-31	D.L.Underwood	Kent v Scotland	Edinburgh	1987
Most Wickets		88	(av 14.35)	A.A.Donald	Warwks/Worcs	1987-02

Most Wicket-Keeping Dismissals in an Innings

8 (8ct)		D.J.Pipe	Worcs v Herts	Hertford	2001

Most Match Wins: 86 – Lancashire.   **Most Cup/Trophy Wins: 7 – Lancashire**

GILLETTE CUP WINNERS

1963	Sussex	1970	Lancashire	1977	Middlesex
1964	Sussex	1971	Lancashire	1978	Sussex
1965	Yorkshire	1972	Lancashire	1979	Somerset
1966	Warwickshire	1973	Gloucestershire	1980	Middlesex
1967	Kent	1974	Kent		
1968	Warwickshire	1975	Lancashire		
1969	Yorkshire	1976	Northamptonshire		

NATWEST TROPHY WINNERS

1981	Derbyshire	1988	Middlesex	1995	Warwickshire
1982	Surrey	1989	Warwickshire	1996	Lancashire
1983	Somerset	1990	Lancashire	1997	Essex
1984	Middlesex	1991	Hampshire	1998	Lancashire
1985	Essex	1992	Northamptonshire	1999	Gloucestershire
1986	Sussex	1993	Warwickshire	2000	Gloucestershire
1987	Nottinghamshire	1994	Worcestershire		

CHELTENHAM & GLOUCESTER TROPHY WINNERS

2001	Somerset	2002	Yorkshire	2003	Gloucestershire

ECB NATIONAL LEAGUE 2003

FIRST DIVISION

		P	W	L	T	NR	Pts	NRR
1	SURREY (-)	16	12	3	–	1	50	2.99
2	Gloucestershire (-)	16	11	4	–	1	46	4.48
3	Essex (-)	16	8	7	1	–	34	3.80
4	Warwickshire (3)	16	8	8	–	–	32	–0.57
5	Glamorgan (1)	16	8	8	–	–	32	–0.94
6	Kent (5)	16	7	8	1	–	30	3.51
7	Leicestershire (6)	16	7	9	–	–	28	–3.82
8	Yorkshire (4)	16	5	11	–	–	20	–6.95
9	Worcestershire (2)	16	4	12	–	–	16	–1.16

SECOND DIVISION

		P	W	L	T	NR	Pts	NRR
1	LANCASHIRE (5)	18	14	3	–	1	58	5.81
2	Northamptonshire (6)	18	12	5	–	1	50	10.99
3	Hampshire (7)	18	11	7	–	–	44	4.79
4	Middlesex (9)	18	10	7	–	1	42	–0.27
5	Nottinghamshire (-)	18	9	9	–	–	36	–0.61
6	Derbyshire (4)	18	8	8	–	2	36	–0.36
7	Durham (3)	18	7	10	–	1	30	4.24
8	Sussex (8)	18	6	12	–	–	24	–8.16
9	Somerset (-)	18	5	12	–	1	22	–4.12
10	Scotland (-)	18	4	13	–	1	18	–14.03

Win = 4 points. Tie (T)/No Result (NR) = 2 points. Positions of counties finishing equal on points are decided by most wins or, if equal, by higher net run-rate (NRR – overall run-rate in all matches, i.e. total runs scored x 100 divided by balls received, minus the run-rate of its opponents in those same matches). Horizontal rules segregate the counties relegated and promoted for the 2004 competition.

2002 final positions for that division are shown in brackets.

HIGHEST BATTING AGGREGATE– Div I   717   (av 51.21) C.M.Spearman   Gloucestershire
           – Div 2   820   (av 54.66) M.E.K.Hussey   Northamptonshire
HIGHEST BOWLING AGGREGATE – Div I   33   (av 16.24) G.R.Napier   Essex
           – Div 2   34   (av 17.20)A.D.Mascarenhas   Hampshire

SUNDAY LEAGUE CHAMPIONS

1969	Lancashire	1979	Somerset	1989	Lancashire
1970	Lancashire	1980	Warwickshire	1990	Derbyshire
1971	Worcestershire	1981	Essex	1991	Nottinghamshire
1972	Kent	1982	Sussex	1992	Middlesex
1973	Kent	1983	Yorkshire	1993	Glamorgan
1974	Leicestershire	1984	Essex	1994	Warwickshire
1975	Hampshire	1985	Essex	1995	Kent
1976	Kent	1986	Hampshire	1996	Surrey
1977	Leicestershire	1987	Worcestershire	1997	Warwickshire
1978	Hampshire	1988	Worcestershire	1998	Lancashire

NATIONAL LEAGUE CHAMPIONS

1999	Lancashire	2002	Glamorgan
2000	Gloucestershire	2003	Surrey
2001	Kent		

NATIONAL (SUNDAY) LEAGUE 1969-2003
PRINCIPAL RECORDS

Highest Total		377-9	Somerset v Sussex	Hove	2003
Highest Total Batting Second		317-6	Surrey v Notts	The Oval	1993
Lowest Total		23	Middlesex v Yorks	Leeds	1974
Largest Victory (Runs)		220	Somerset v Glamorgan	Neath	1990
Highest Scores	203	A.D.Brown	Surrey v Hampshire	Guildford	1997
	191	D.S.Lehmann	Yorks v Notts	Scarborough	2001
	176	G.A.Gooch	Essex v Glamorgan	Southend	1983
	175*	I.T.Botham	Somerset v Northants	Wellingborough	1986
Fastest Hundred	44 balls	M.A.Ealham	Kent v Derbyshire	Maidstone	1995
Most Sixes (Inns)	13	I.T.Botham	Somerset v Northants	Wellingborough	1986

Highest Partnership for each Wicket

1st	239	G.A.Gooch/B.R.Hardie	Essex v Notts	Nottingham	1985
2nd	273	G.A.Gooch/K.S.McEwan	Essex v Notts	Nottingham	1983
3rd	228*	M.W.Goodwin/C.J.Adams	Sussex v Middlesex	Hove	2003
4th	219	C.G.Greenidge/C.L.Smith	Hampshire v Surrey	Southampton	1987
5th	220*	C.C.Lewis/P.A.Nixon	Leics v Kent	Canterbury	1999
6th	142	N.R.D.Compton/B.L.Hutton	Middx v Lancs	Shenley	2002
7th	164	J.N.Snape/M.A.Hardinges	Glos v Notts	Nottingham	2001
8th	116*	N.D.Burns/P.A.J.DeFreitas	Leics v Northants	Leicester	2001
9th	105	D.G.Moir/R.W.Taylor	Derbyshire v Kent	Derby	1984
10th	82	G.Chapple/P.J.Martin	Lancashire v Worcs	Manchester	1996

Best Bowling

	8-26	K.D.Boyce	Essex v Lancashire	Manchester	1971
	7-15	R.A.Hutton	Yorkshire v Worcs	Leeds	1969
	7-16	S.D.Thomas	Glamorgan v Surrey	Swansea	1998
	7-30	M.P.Bicknell	Surrey v Glamorgan	The Oval	1999
	7-39	A.Hodgson	Northants v Somerset	Northampton	1976
	7-41	A.N.Jones	Sussex v Notts	Nottingham	1986
Four Wkts in Four Balls		A.Ward	Derbyshire v Sussex	Derby	1970
		V.C.Drakes	Notts v Derbys	Nottingham	1999

Most Economical Analysis

8-8-0-0		B.A.Langford	Somerset v Essex	Yeovil	1969

Most Economical Analysis

9-0-99-1		M.R.Strong	Northants v Glos	Cheltenham	2001

Most Wicket-Keeping Dismissals in an Innings

7 (6ct, 1st)		R.W.Taylor	Derbyshire v Lancs	Manchester	1975

Most Catches in an Innings

5		J.M.Rice	Hampshire v Warwicks	Southampton	1978

NATWEST CHALLENGE 2003
Manchester 17 June (floodlit)
Toss: England. **PAKISTAN** beat **England** by two wickets. England 204-9 (50 overs) (Shoaib Malik 3-26). Pakistan 208-8 (49.2 overs) (Mohammad Hafeez 69, J.M.Anderson 3-59. R.Clarke dismissed Imran Nazir with his first ball in LOIs). Award: Mohammad Hafeez.

The Oval 20 June
Toss: Pakistan. **ENGLAND** beat **Pakistan** by seven wickets. Pakistan 185 (44 overs) (Yousuf Youhana 75*, J.M.Anderson 4-27 including the first hat trick for England – in 373 LOIs. He also took wickets with the first and last balls of the innings). England 189-3 (22 overs) (M.E.Trescothick 86). Award: M.E.Trescothick.

Lord's 22 June
Toss: England. **ENGLAND** beat **Pakistan** by four wickets. Pakistan 229-7 (50 overs) (Abdul Razzaq 64, Younis Khan 63, A.Flintoff 4-32). England 231-6 (48.3 overs) (M.E.Trescothick 108*, Mohammad Hafeez 3-31). Match and Series Award: M.E.Trescothick.
ENGLAND won series 2-1

149

NATWEST TRIANGULAR SERIES 2003

Nottingham 26 June

Toss: Zimbabwe. **ZIMBABWE** beat **England** by four wickets. England 191-8 (50 overs) (A. Flintoff 53). Zimbabwe 195-6 (48 overs) (G.W.Flower 96*, R.L.Johnson 3-32). Award: G.W.Flower.

The Oval 28 June

Toss: South Africa. **ENGLAND** beat **South Africa** by six wickets. South Africa 264-6 (50 overs) (J.H.Kallis 107, M.V.Boucher 55, A.Flintoff 3-46). England 265-4 (45.5 overs) (M.E.Trescothick 114* and V.S.Solanki 106 shared record England LOI first-wicket partnership of 200). Award: V.S.Solanki.

Canterbury 29 June

Toss: Zimbabwe. **SOUTH AFRICA** beat **Zimbabwe** by 46 runs. South Africa 272-5 (50 overs) (J.H.Kallis 125*, A.J.Hall 56). Zimbabwe 226-9 (50 overs) (T.J.Friend 82, A.J.Hall 3-38). Award: J.H.Kallis.

Leeds 1 July

Toss: Zimbabwe. **England** v **Zimbabwe** – match reduced to 25-overs and abandoned (rain). England 81-4 (16.3 overs) (M.P.Vaughan 35*). No award.

Manchester 3 July (floodlit)

Toss: England. **SOUTH AFRICA** beat **England** by seven wickets. England 223-7 (50 overs) (M.E.Trescothick 60, A.McGrath 52, M.Ntini 3-38). South Africa 227-3 (47.3 overs) (J.H.Kallis 82*, J.A.Rudolph 71*). Award: J.H.Kallis.

Cardiff 5 July

Toss: South Africa. **SOUTH AFRICA** beat **Zimbabwe** by nine wickets. Zimbabwe 174-8 (50 overs) (H.H.Streak 54, J.H.Kallis 3-47). South Africa 175-1 (34.2 overs) (H.H.Gibbs 93*, G.C.Smith 58). Award: H.H.Gibbs.

Bristol 6 July

Toss: England. **ENGLAND** beat **Zimbabwe** by six wickets. Zimbabwe 92 (24.5 overs) (D.Gough 4-26, A.Flintoff 3-13). England 95-4 (17.5 overs) (A.Flintoff 47*, H.H.Streak 4-21). Award: A.Flintoff.

Birmingham 8 July (floodlit)

Toss: South Africa. **ENGLAND** beat **South Africa** by four wickets. South Africa 198-9 (50 overs) (J.M.Anderson 4-38). England 199-6 (39 overs) (M.P.Vaughan 83, A.Flintoff 54). Award: A.Flintoff.

Southampton 10 July

Toss: Zimbabwe. **SOUTH AFRICA** beat **Zimbabwe** by seven wickets. Zimbabwe 173-8 (50 overs) (H.H.Streak 50*, M.Ntini 4-45). South Africa 174-3 (35.2 overs) (G.C.Smith 69, J.A.Rudolph 69*). Award: M.Ntini.

	Played	Won	Lost	No Result	Points	NRR
South Africa	6	4	2	–	23	0.48
England	6	3	2	1	22	0.83
Zimbabwe	6	1	4	1	9	–1.37

Final – Lord's 12 July

Toss: England. **ENGLAND** beat **South Africa** by seven wickets. South Africa 107 (32.1 overs) (J.M.Anderson 3-50). England 111-3 (20.2 overs) (V.S.Solanki 50). Award: D.Gough. Series Award: A.Flintoff.

TWENTY20 CUP 2003

GROUP TABLES

MIDLANDS/WALES/WEST	P	W	L	T	NR	Pts	NRR
1 GLOUCESTERSHIRE	5	5	–	–	–	10	2.18
2 WARWICKSHIRE	5	4	1	–	–	8	1.07
3 Worcestershire	5	2	3	–	–	4	–0.45
4 Northamptonshire	5	2	3	–	–	4	–0.24
5 Somerset	5	1	4	–	–	2	–1.41
6 Glamorgan	5	1	4	–	–	2	–1.09

NORTH	P	W	L	T	NR	Pts	NRR
1 LEICESTERSHIRE	5	5	–	–	–	10	0.86
2 Yorkshire	5	3	2	–	–	6	0.45
3 Derbyshire	5	3	2	–	–	6	0.60
4 Lancashire	5	2	3	–	–	4	–0.12
5 Durham	5	1	4	–	–	2	–1.02
6 Nottinghamshire	5	1	4	–	–	2	–0.88

SOUTH	P	W	L	T	NR	Pts	NRR
1 SURREY	5	5	–	–	–	10	1.06
2 Sussex	5	3	2	–	–	6	0.61
3 Kent	5	2	3	–	–	4	0.25
4 Middlesex	5	2	3	–	–	4	0.19
5 Essex	5	2	3	–	–	4	–0.81
6 Hampshire	5	1	4	–	–	2	–1.32

SEMI-FINALS

Played at Trent Bridge, Nottingham, on 19 July

WARWICKSHIRE beat Leicestershire by seven wickets. Toss: Leicestershire. Leicestershire 162-7 (20 overs; B.J.Hodge 66, Waqar Younis 3-21). Warwickshire 166-3 (19.2 overs; T.L.Penney 43*).

SURREY beat Gloucestershire by five runs. Toss: Surrey. Surrey 147-9 (20 overs; I.J.Ward 49, M.A.Hardinges 3-37). Gloucestershire 142-6 (20 overs; A.P.R.Gidman 61, Azhar Mahmood 3-28).

LEADING AVERAGES

BATTING (Qualification: Avge 50)		M	I	NO	HS	Runs	Avge	100	50	SR
M.E.K.Hussey	Northamptonshire	5	5	1	88	279	69.75	–	3	122.36
M.J.Di Venuto	Derbyshire	5	5	2	67	198	66.00	–	2	122.22
I.J.Harvey	Gloucestershire	6	6	2	100*	248	62.00	1	1	171.03
S.M.Katich	Hampshire	5	5	2	59*	179	59.66	–	2	111.87
S.C.Moore	Worcestershire	5	5	–	39*	116	58.00	–	–	118.36
A.Flower	Essex	5	5	–	83	266	53.20	–	2	147.77
B.J.Hodge	Leicestershire	6	6	–	97	301	50.16	–	3	138.07

BOWLING (Qualification: 10 wkts)		O	M	R	W	Avge	BB	4w	R/Over
J.Ormond	Surrey	20	–	111	11	10.09	5-26	2	5.55
Azhar Mahmood	Surrey	18.5	–	123	12	10.25	4-20	1	6.53
D.R.Hewson	Derbyshire	19	–	109	10	10.90	4-18	1	5.73
J.F.Brown	Northamptonshire	17.5	–	122	11	11.09	5-27	1	6.84
A.J.Hollioake	Surrey	25.1	–	197	16	12.31	5-21	2	7.82
I.J.Harvey	Gloucestershire	23.5	–	153	10	15.30	3-28	–	6.41
C.O.Obuya	Warwickshire	20	–	177	10	17.70	5-24	1	8.85

TWENTY20 CUP FINAL

SURREY v WARWICKSHIRE

At Trent Bridge, Nottingham, on 19 July
Result: **SURREY won by nine wickets**
Toss: Warwickshire. Award: J Ormond.

WARWICKSHIRE		Runs	Balls	4/6	Fall
N.M.Carter	b Ormond	8	12	–/1	1- 16
* N.V.Knight	b Ormond	8	6	1	2- 20
I.R.Bell	c Clarke b Mahmood	5	11	–	4- 32
J.O.Troughton	c Brown b Ormond	1	3	–	3- 22
T.L.Penney	b Hollioake	33	21	2/2	6- 63
D.R.Brown	c Batty b Ormond	0	3	–	5- 33
† T.Frost	c Ormond b Saqlain	31	35	1	8-112
G.G.Wagg	b Hollioake	5	6	–	7- 83
C.O.Obuya	c Ward b Saqlain	17	11	1/1	9-115
N.M.K.Smith	run out	1	2	–	10-115
Waqar Younis	not out	0	1		
Extras	(W 2, NB 4)	6			
Total	(18.1 overs)	**115**			

SURREY		Runs	Balls	4/6	Fall
I.J.Ward	c Waqar b Wagg	50	28	8/1	1-100
A.D.Brown	not out	55	34	6/3	
M.R.Ramprakash	not out	4	5	1	
R.Clarke					
* A.J.Hollioake					
Azhar Mahmood					
G.P.Thorpe					
† J.N.Batty					
I.D.K.Salisbury					
Saqlain Mushtaq					
J.Ormond					
Extras	(LB 4, W 2, NB 4)	10			
Total	(10.5 overs; 1 wicket)	**119**			

SURREY	O	M	R	W	WARWICKS	O	M	R	W
Ormond	4	0	11	4	Carter	2	0	20	0
Azhar Mahmood	3	0	22	1	Waqar Younis	4	0	29	0
Saqlain Mushtaq	4	0	35	2	Brown	2	0	24	0
Clarke	4	0	20	0	Obuya	1	0	18	0
Hollioake	3.1	0	27	2	Wagg	1	0	20	1
					Knight	0.5	0	4	0

Umpires: B.Dudleston and J.W.Holder.

BENSON AND HEDGES CUP

PRINCIPAL RECORDS 1972-2002

Highest Total	388-7		Essex v Scotland	Chelmsford	1992
Highest Total Batting Second	318-5		Lancashire v Leics	Manchester	1995
Lowest Total	50		Hampshire v Yorks	Leeds	1991
Largest Victory (Runs)	172		Essex v Scotland	Chelmsford	1992
Highest Score	198*	G.A.Gooch	Essex v Sussex	Hove	1982
Fastest Hundred	62 min	M.A.Nash	Glamorgan v Hants	Swansea	1976

Highest Partnership for each Wicket

1st	252	V.P.Terry/C.L.Smith	Hants v Combined U	Southampton	1990
2nd	285*	C.G.Greenidge/D.R.Turner	Hants v Minor C (S)	Amersham	1973
3rd	271	C.J.Adams/M.G.Bevan	Sussex v Essex	Chelmsford	2000
4th	207	R.C.Russell/A.J.Wright	Glos v British U	Bristol	1998
5th	160	A.J.Lamb/D.J.Capel	Northants v Leics	Northampton	1986
6th	167*	M.G.Bevan/R.J.Blakey	Yorkshire v Lancs	Manchester	1996
7th	149*	J.D.Love/C.M.Old	Yorks v Scotland	Bradford	1981
8th	112	D.C.Nash/A.A.Noffke	Middlesex v Sussex	Lord's	2002
9th	83	P.G.Newman/M.A.Holding	Derbyshire v Notts	Nottingham	1985
10th	80*	D.L.Bairstow/M.Johnson	Yorkshire v Derbys	Derby	1981

Best Bowling	7-12	W.W.Daniel	Middx v Minor C (E)	Ipswich	1978
	7-22	J.R.Thomson	Middx v Hampshire	Lord's	1981
	7-24	Mushtaq Ahmed	Somerset v Ireland	Taunton	1997
	7-32	R.G.D.Willis	Warwicks v Yorks	Birmingham	1981
Four Wickets in Four Balls		S.M.Pollock	Warwicks v Leics	Birmingham	1996

Most Wicket-Keeping Dismissals in an Innings					
	8 (8ct)	D.J.S.Taylor	Somerset v Combined U	Taunton	1982
Most Catches in an Innings					
	5	V.J.Marks	Combined U v Kent	Oxford	1976

BENSON AND HEDGES CUP WINNERS

1972	Leicestershire	1983	Middlesex	1994	Warwickshire
1973	Kent	1984	Lancashire	1995	Lancashire
1974	Surrey	1985	Leicestershire	1996	Lancashire
1975	Leicestershire	1986	Middlesex	1997	Surrey
1976	Kent	1987	Yorkshire	1998	Essex
1977	Gloucestershire	1988	Hampshire	1999	Gloucestershire
1978	Kent	1989	Nottinghamshire	2000	Gloucestershire
1979	Essex	1990	Lancashire	2001	Surrey
1980	Northamptonshire	1991	Worcestershire	2002	Warwickshire
1981	Somerset	1992	Hampshire		
1982	Somerset	1993	Derbyshire		

MINOR COUNTIES CHAMPIONSHIP

FINAL TABLES 2003

	P	W	L	D	Bonus Points Bat	Bonus Points Bowl	Total Points
EASTERN DIVISION							
LINCOLNSHIRE	6	5	–	1	21	22	127†
Staffordshire	6	3	1	2	20	20	96
Bedfordshire	6	3	1	2	16	15	87
Cambridgeshire	6	3	3	–	12	19	79
Suffolk	6	2	1	3	13	19	76
Cumberland	6	2	3	1	13	24	73
Norfolk	6	2	3	1	17	19	72
Hertfordshire	6	1	2	3	8	23	59
Northumberland	6	–	3	3	13	19	44
Buckinghamshire	6	–	4	2	6	18	32
WESTERN DIVISION							
DEVON	6	3	–	3	20	20	100
Berkshire	6	3	1	2	17	21	94
Cornwall	6	2	–	4	17	22	89
Wiltshire	6	3	2	1	16	20	88
Shropshire	6	2	–	4	18	20	86
Cheshire	6	2	2	1	16	20	80
Herefordshire	6	1	1	4	16	20	68†
Wales MC	6	1	4	1	9	16	45
Dorset	6	–	4	2	10	22	40
Oxfordshire	6	–	4	2	10	20	38

† Two points deducted for a slow over rate.

CHAMPIONSHIP FINAL

At Cleethorpes Sports Ground on 7, 8, 9 September. Toss: Devon. **LINCOLNSHIRE beat DEVON by eight wickets.** Devon 371-3 (70 overs; M.P.Hunt 94*, R.J.Foan 84, C.M.Mole 57*, Extras 60 inc 24 penalties) and 97 (E.J.Wilson 4-24, S.J.Airey 4-25). Lincolnshire 270-6 closed (70 overs; M.P.Dowman 65, O.E.Burford 58, S.Webb 56*, I.E.Bishop 4-88) and 202-2 (P.R.Pollard 85*, M.P.Dowman 70*).

MCCA KNOCK-OUT TROPHY FINAL

At Lord's, London, on 2 September. Toss: Cambridgeshire. **CAMBRIDGESHIRE beat SHROPSHIRE by three wickets.** Shropshire 266-9 closed (50 overs; S.J.Adshead 59, M.A.Downes 56, Ajaz Akhtar 3-61). Cambridgeshire 267-7 (47.5 overs; M.D.R.Sutcliff 99, A.M.Shimmons 3-61).

MINOR COUNTIES RECORDS

Highest Total	621		Surrey II v Devon	The Oval	1928
Lowest Total	14		Cheshire v Staffs	Stoke	1909
Highest Score	282	E.Garnett	Berkshire v Wiltshire	Reading	1908
Most Runs – Season	1212	A.F.Brazier	Surrey II		1949
Record Partnership:					
2nd wkt	388*	T.H.Clark/A.F.Brazier	Surrey II v Sussex II	The Oval	1949
Best Bowling – Innings	10-11	S.Turner	Cambs v Cumberland	Penrith	1987
– Match	18-100	N.W.Harding	Kent II v Wiltshire	Swindon	1937
Most Wickets – Season	119	S.F.Barnes	Staffordshire		1906

MINOR COUNTIES CHAMPIONS

1895	Norfolk	1931	Leicestershire II	1972	Bedfordshire
	Durham	1932	Buckinghamshire	1973	Shropshire
	Worcestershire	1933	Undecided	1974	Oxfordshire
1896	Worcestershire	1934	Lancashire II	1975	Hertfordshire
1897	Worcestershire	1935	Middlesex II	1976	Durham
1898	Worcestershire	1936	Hertfordshire	1977	Suffolk
1899	Northamptonshire	1937	Lancashire II	1978	Devon
	Buckinghamshire	1938	Buckinghamshire	1979	Suffolk
1900	Glamorgan	1939	Surrey II	1980	Durham
	Durham	1946	Suffolk	1981	Durham
	Northamptonshire	1947	Yorkshire II	1982	Oxfordshire
1901	Durham	1948	Lancashire II	1983	Hertfordshire
1902	Wiltshire	1949	Lancashire II	1984	Durham
1903	Northamptonshire	1950	Surrey II	1985	Cheshire
1904	Northamptonshire	1951	Kent II	1986	Cumberland
1905	Norfolk	1952	Buckinghamshire	1987	Buckinghamshire
1906	Staffordshire	1953	Berkshire	1988	Cheshire
1907	Lancashire II	1954	Surrey II	1989	Oxfordshire
1908	Staffordshire	1955	Surrey II	1990	Hertfordshire
1909	Wiltshire	1956	Kent II	1991	Staffordshire
1910	Norfolk	1957	Yorkshire II	1992	Staffordshire
1911	Staffordshire	1958	Yorkshire II	1993	Staffordshire
1912	In abeyance	1959	Warwickshire II	1994	Devon
1913	Norfolk	1960	Lancashire II	1995	Devon
1920	Staffordshire	1961	Somerset II	1996	Devon
1921	Staffordshire	1962	Warwickshire II	1997	Devon
1922	Buckinghamshire	1963	Cambridgeshire	1998	Staffordshire
1923	Buckinghamshire	1964	Lancashire II	1999	Cumberland
1924	Berkshire	1965	Somerset II	2000	Dorset
1925	Buckinghamshire	1966	Lincolnshire	2001	Cheshire
1926	Durham	1967	Cheshire		Lincolnshire
1927	Staffordshire	1968	Yorkshire II	2002	Herefordshire
1928	Berkshire	1969	Buckinghamshire		Norfolk
1929	Oxfordshire	1970	Bedfordshire	2003	Lincolnshire
1930	Durham	1971	Yorkshire II		

LEADING CHAMPIONSHIP BATTING AVERAGES
(Qualifications: 8 innings; average 33.00)

		M	I	NO	HS	Runs	Avge	100	50
K.J.Barnett	Staffordshire	6	10	2	198*	689	86.12	3	2
A.A.Metcalfe	Cumberland	5	10	2	172	680	85.00	2	4
P.R.Pollard	Lincolnshire	7	12	3	184	702	78.00	2	4
D.M.Ward	Hertfordshire	6	11	2	150*	678	75.33	1	5
M.P.Dowman	Lincolnshire	7	11	1	179	690	69.00	2	4
S.C.Goldsmith	Norfolk	6	10	1	118	599	66.55	2	3
D.J.Roberts	Cornwall	6	9	2	112*	465	66.42	2	2
G.F.Archer	Staffordshire	6	10	2	201*	502	62.75	1	2
P.J.Prichard	Berkshire	5	9	1	101	496	62.00	1	5
J.A.Knott	Bedfordshire	6	11	2	158	535	59.44	1	5
C.W.Boroughs	Herefordshire	6	11	4	134	410	58.57	2	1
R.W.J.Howitt	Berkshire	6	12	3	170*	507	56.33	2	—
R.I.Dawson	Devon	7	12	1	140*	614	55.81	2	2
G.D.Lloyd	Cumberland	6	11	1	130	541	54.10	1	3
J.R.Wood	Berkshire	6	11	1	158	503	50.30	1	3
D.J.M.Mercer	Bedfordshire	5	9	1	116	395	49.37	1	2
A.T.Heather	Northumberland	5	9	—	106	444	49.33	2	2
B.Parker	Northumberland	6	11	1	175	491	49.10	1	3
K.Pearson	Herefordshire	5	8	1	84	337	48.14	—	1

		M	I	NO	HS	Runs	Avge	100	50
M.P.Hunt	Devon	5	9	1	94*	384	48.00	–	3
D.B.Pennett	Cheshire	5	8	5	50*	136	45.33	–	1
G.P.Rees	Wales MC	4	8	1	104*	317	45.28	1	1
P.F.Shaw	Staffordshire	6	10	1	200*	398	44.22	2	–
C.M.Mole	Devon	4	8	2	136*	264	44.00	1	1
C.Amos	Norfolk	6	10	–	107	438	43.80	1	3
R.P.Harvey	Staffordshire	5	8	3	51	218	43.60	–	1
C.Jones	Cambridgeshire	6	12	3	162*	391	43.44	1	1
C.D.Crowe	Berkshire	5	9	4	54	217	43.40	–	1
N.A.Din	Cheshire	4	8	–	160	347	43.37	2	–
M.O.Wilkinson	Norfolk	6	9	2	82	302	43.14	–	3
M.C.Dobson	Lincolnshire	7	11	2	161*	385	42.77	1	1
M.D.R.Sutcliff	Cambridgeshire	4	8	–	118	332	41.50	1	1
A.J.Hall	Cheshire	6	11	1	175	414	41.40	1	2
C.J.Rogers	Norfolk	6	10	1	68*	368	40.88	–	1
S.T.Knox	Cumberland	4	1	1	108	286	40.85	1	1
G.R.Treagus	Dorset	5	10	1	152	364	40.44	1	1
S.J.Renshaw	Cheshire	5	9	2	69*	283	40.42	–	2
P.J.Caley	Suffolk	6	9	3	67*	241	40.16	–	1
A.J.Pugh	Devon	4	8	–	76	321	40.12	–	3
R.J.Rowe	Wiltshire	6	9	–	128	355	39.44	1	2
S.Webb	Lincolnshire	5	8	3	60*	195	39.00	–	2
I.S.Morton	Suffolk	5	8	2	91*	232	38.66	–	2
R.D.Hughes	Herefordshire	6	11	2	103*	346	38.44	1	3
J.Clarke	Lincolnshire	5	9	1	118	303	37.87	1	2
R.J.Foan	Devon	7	12	–	130	453	37.75	1	2
S.Chapman	Northumberland	5	9	1	107	302	37.75	1	1
D.G.Court	Devon	7	11	3	75	298	37.25	–	3
N.J.Thurgood	Dorset	5	10	1	79	329	36.55	–	3
A.R.Roberts	Bedfordshire	6	10	1	79	326	36.22	–	2
T.J.Mason	Shropshire	6	8	2	85*	211	35.16	–	2
K.Patel	Bedfordshire	6	12	1	77	383	34.81	–	4
Ajaz Akhtar	Cambridgeshire	6	11	1	100*	347	34.70	1	1
Baqar Rizvi	Wiltshire	6	9	–	89	310	34.44	–	4
P.D.Atkins	Buckinghamshire	6	11	1	83	341	34.10	–	1
R.M.Lewis	Wales MC	4	8	1	57	234	33.42	–	2
R.M.Eason	Oxfordshire	5	10	–	90	333	33.30	–	2

LEADING CHAMPIONSHIP BOWLING AVERAGES
(Qualification: 20 wickets)

		O	M	R	W	Avge	BB	5w	10w
T.G.Sharp	Cornwall	134.5	35	352	23	15.30	6- 26	1	–
I.E.Bishop	Devon	262.3	73	708	36	19.66	8- 99	2	1
C.D.Crowe	Berkshire	223.2	56	657	33	19.90	6- 93	3	–
J.E.Anyon	Cumberland	105	17	430	21	20.47	6- 31	1	1
T.J.Mason	Shropshire	258.3	86	676	32	21.12	6- 66	2	–
R.K.Illingworth	Wiltshire	204.1	63	428	20	21.40	5- 46	2	–
M.P.Dowman	Lincolnshire	160.1	40	524	24	21.83	4- 43	–	–
R.C.Driver	Cornwall	168	49	481	22	21.86	5- 49	2	–
T.M.Smith	Suffolk	164.1	45	467	21	22.23	5- 46	2	–
M.A.Sharp	Cumberland	229	81	529	23	23.00	4- 40	–	–
A.R.Roberts	Bedfordshire	201.5	47	589	25	23.56	5- 48	2	1
D.Follett	Staffordshire	264.2	47	932	39	23.89	8- 87	3	1
E.J.Wilson	Lincolnshire	204.5	31	721	30	24.03	4- 24	–	–
M.J.Rawnsley	Herefordshire	192.2	61	486	20	24.30	6- 79	2	–
C.Brown	Norfolk	307	95	905	36	25.13	6-147	2	–
M.W.Patterson	Bedfordshire	192	40	636	23	27.65	5- 34	2	–
M.J.McCague	Herefordshire	213.1	31	790	28	28.21	7- 68	2	–
M.P.Eccles	Norfolk	130.2	18	592	20	29.60	4- 53	–	–
G.Bulpitt	Staffordshire	256	61	698	20	34.90	4- 45	–	–

SECOND XI CHAMPIONSHIP 2003
FINAL TABLE

	P	W	L	D	Bonus Points Bat	Bowl	Total Points	Avge
1 YORKSHIRE (3)	10	7	1	2	29	32	167	16.70
2 Kent (1)	10	6	-	4	31	34	165	16.50
3 Hampshire (8)	10	5	3	2	24	34	136	13.60
4 Northamptonshire (6)	12	5	2	5	30	43	163	13.58
5 Durham (9)	11	5	4	2	36	35	149	13.55
6 Surrey (11)	13	4	4	5	45	39	160	12.31
7 Somerset (15)	10	3	3	4	31	31	120	12.00
8 Lancashire (7)	14	5	4	5	38	36	164	11.71
9 Nottinghamshire (13)	11	3	4	4	30	39	127	11.55
10 Gloucestershire (16)	10	2	2	6	31	32	115	11.50
11 Leicestershire (17)	10	2	1	7	31	27	114	11.40
12 Warwickshire (5)	12	4	4	4	31	33	136	11.33
13 Essex (18)	10	2	3	5	30	33	111	11.10
14 Sussex (14)	12	2	6	4	28	41	113	9.42
15 Middlesex (10)	10	-	3	7	23	35	86	8.60
16 Glamorgan (4)	11	1	5	5	21	37	92	8.36
17 Worcestershire (12)	10	-	4	6	32	24	80	8.00
18 Derbyshire (2)	10	-	3	7	31	19	78	7.80

Win = 14 points, plus any first-innings points.
Draw = 4 points, plus any first-innings points.
2002 final positions are shown in brackets.

ECB SECOND XI AWARDS 2003

No awards were made.

SECOND XI CHAMPIONS

1959	Gloucestershire	1974	Middlesex	1989	Middlesex
1960	Northamptonshire	1975	Surrey	1990	Sussex
1961	Kent	1976	Kent	1991	Yorkshire
1962	Worcestershire	1977	Yorkshire	1992	Surrey
1963	Worcestershire	1978	Sussex	1993	Middlesex
1964	Lancashire	1979	Warwickshire	1994	Somerset
1965	Glamorgan	1980	Glamorgan	1995	Hampshire
1966	Surrey	1981	Hampshire	1996	Warwickshire
1967	Hampshire	1982	Worcestershire	1997	Lancashire
1968	Surrey	1983	Leicestershire	1998	Northamptonshire
1969	Kent	1984	Yorkshire	1999	Middlesex
1970	Kent	1985	Nottinghamshire	2000	Middlesex
1971	Hampshire	1986	Lancashire	2001	Hampshire
1972	Nottinghamshire	1987	Kent/Yorkshire	2002	Kent
1973	Essex	1988	Surrey	2003	Yorkshire

YOUNG CRICKETER OF THE YEAR

This annual award, made by The Cricket Writers' Club (founded 1946), is currently restricted to players qualified for England, Andrew Symonds meeting that requirement at the time of his award, and under the age of 23 on 1st May. In 1986 their ballot resulted in a dead heat. To 10 March 2004 their selections have gained a tally of 1,811 England Test caps (shown in brackets).

1950	R.Tattersall (16)	1978	D.I.Gower (117)
1951	P.B.H.May (66)	1979	P.W.G.Parker (1)
1952	F.S.Trueman (67)	1980	G.R.Dilley (41)
1953	M.C.Cowdrey (114)	1981	M.W.Gatting (79)
1954	P.J.Loader (13)	1982	N.G.Cowans (19)
1955	K.F.Barrington (82)	1983	N.A.Foster (29)
1956	B.Taylor	1984	R.J.Bailey (4)
1957	M.J.Stewart (8)	1985	D.V.Lawrence (5)
1958	A.C.D.Ingleby-Mackenzie	1986 {	A.A.Metcalfe
1959	G.Pullar (28)		J.J.Whitaker (1)
1960	D.A.Allen (39)	1987	R.J.Blakey (2)
1961	P.H.Parfitt (37)	1988	M.P.Maynard (4)
1962	P.J.Sharpe (12)	1989	N.Hussain (91)
1963	G.Boycott (108)	1990	M.A.Atherton (115)
1964	J.M.Brearley (39)	1991	M.R.Ramprakash (52)
1965	A.P.E.Knott (95)	1992	I.D.K.Salisbury (15)
1966	D.L.Underwood (86)	1993	M.N.Lathwell (2)
1967	A.W.Greig (58)	1994	J.P.Crawley (37)
1968	R.M.H.Cottam (4)	1995	A.Symonds
1969	A.Ward (5)	1996	C.E.W.Silverwood (6)
1970	C.M.Old (46)	1997	B.C.Hollioake (2)
1971	J.Whitehouse	1998	A.Flintoff (29)
1972	D.R.Owen-Thomas	1999	A.J.Tudor (10)
1973	M.Hendrick (30)	2000	P.J.Franks
1974	P.H.Edmonds (51)	2001	O.A.Shah
1975	A.Kennedy	2002	R.Clarke (2)
1976	G.Miller (34)	2003	J.M.Anderson (8)
1977	I.T.Botham (102)		

THE PROFESSIONAL CRICKETER'S ASSOCIATION
PLAYER OF THE YEAR

Introduced in 1970, this annual award is decided by the PCA membership. Mushtaq Ahmed, their choice for 2003, contributed 103 wickets to Sussex's first Championship title.

1970 {	M.J.Procter	1987	R.J.Hadlee
	J.D.Bond	1988	G.A.Hick
1971	L.R.Gibbs	1989	S.J.Cook
1972	A.M.E.Roberts	1990	G.A.Gooch
1973	P.G.Lee	1991	Waqar Younis
1974	B.Stead	1992	C.A.Walsh
1975	Zaheer Abbas	1993	S.L.Watkin
1976	P.G.Lee	1994	B.C.Lara
1977	M.J.Procter	1995	D.G.Cork
1978	J.K.Lever	1996	P.V.Simmons
1979	J.K.Lever	1997	S.P.James
1980	R.D.Jackman	1998	M.B.Loye
1981	R.J.Hadlee	1999	S.G.Law
1982	M.D.Marshall	2000	M.E.Trescothick
1983	K.S.McEwan	2001	D.P.Fulton
1984	R.J.Hadlee	2002	M.P.Vaughan
1985	N.V.Radford	2003	Mushtaq Ahmed
1986	C.A.Walsh		

FIRST-CLASS CAREER RECORDS

Compiled by **PHILIP BAILEY**

The following career records are for all players who appeared in first-class or limited-overs cricket during the 2003 season and are complete to the end of that season. Some players who did not appear in 2003 but may do so in 2004 are also included.

BATTING AND FIELDING

'1000' denotes instances of scoring 1000 runs in a season. Where these have been achieved outside the British Isles they are shown after a plus sign.

	M	I	NO	HS	Runs	Avge	100	50	1000	Ct/St
Abdul Razzaq	76	114	16	203*	3151	32.15	7	16	–	18
Adams, C.J.	257	422	29	239	14750	37.53	37	70	5	299
Adams, J.H.K.	16	31	2	107	749	25.82	1	3	–	9
Adams, P.R.	95	95	41	61*	845	15.64	–	1	–	54
Adnan, M.H.	51	81	14	130	3095	46.19	4	24	–	26
Adshead, S.J.	3	5	1	63	102	25.50	–	1	–	7/2
Afzaal, U.	131	226	20	161*	6692	32.48	13	37	3	63
Airey, S.J.	3	4	1	46*	100	33.33	–	–	–	1
Akram, M.Adnan	3	4	–	98	162	40.50	–	1	–	–
Akram, M.Arfan	3	5	1	110	191	47.75	1	–	–	3
Ali, Kabir	48	66	14	84*	1085	20.86	–	5	–	10
Ali, Kadeer	17	29	–	99	504	17.37	–	3	–	5
Ali, S.M.B.	80	106	25	92	1137	14.03	–	4	–	25
Allen, J.A.	2	2	–	0	0	0.00	–	–	–	–
Alleyne, D.	5	7	1	49*	148	24.66	–	–	–	12
Alleyne, M.W.	322	529	51	256	14705	30.76	22	69	6	267/3
Ambrose, T.R.	30	51	4	149	1821	38.74	2	12	–	41/7
Amin, R.M.	20	25	10	12	65	4.33	–	–	–	6
Anderson, J.M.	24	29	20	21*	113	12.55	–	–	–	7
Anderson, R.S.G.	39	51	5	67*	650	14.13	–	2	–	7
Andrew, G.M.	4	5	–	11	36	7.20	–	–	–	2
Anwar, O.S.	3	4	–	99	128	32.00	–	1	–	–
Anyon, J.E.	3	3	–	21	21	7.00	–	–	–	2
Atri, V.	6	11	2	98	338	37.55	–	3	–	5
Averis, J.M.M.	43	59	12	43	512	10.89	–	–	–	10
Azhar Mahmood	94	146	19	136	3579	28.18	4	19	–	74
Badani, H.K.	75	103	13	164	4118	45.75	10	28	–	61
Bailey, T.M.B.	49	66	10	101*	1235	22.05	1	5	–	94/14
Balaji, L.	33	32	11	37	224	10.66	–	–	–	9
Ball, M.C.J.	172	264	49	75	4253	19.78	–	15	–	207
Banes, M.J.	11	18	1	69	388	22.82	–	3	–	4
Bassano, C.W.G.	36	65	6	186*	1889	32.01	3	12	1	26
Batty, G.J.	42	67	10	74	1207	21.17	–	6	–	29
Batty, J.N.	94	135	22	168*	3351	29.65	6	13	–	234/32
Bell, I.R.	49	83	6	135	2627	34.11	4	15	–	25
Benning, J.G.E.	2	3	–	47	87	29.00	–	–	–	–
Betts, M.M.	99	146	33	73	1656	14.65	–	5	–	34
Bhandari, A.	53	55	20	72	548	15.65	–	1	–	24
Bharadwaj, R.V.	84	128	14	207*	5191	45.53	13	25	0+1	88
Bichel, A.J.	110	142	13	110	2738	21.22	1	11	–	63
Bicknell, D.J.	272	478	39	235*	16778	38.21	39	76	7	98
Bicknell, M.P.	267	322	80	141	5790	23.92	3	22	–	93
Bishop, J.E.	21	28	4	50	285	11.87	–	2	–	3

F-C	M	I	NO	HS	Runs	Avge	100	50	1000	Ct/St
Blackwell, I.D.	83	128	7	247*	4112	33.98	11	14	1	34
Blain, J.A.R.	20	22	8	34	150	10.71	–	–	–	5
Blakey, R.J.	348	554	87	223*	14674	31.42	13	86	6	778/57
Blewett, G.S.	207	370	25	268	15878	46.02	42	78	1+5	167
Blignaut, A.M.	32	46	3	130	996	23.16	1	4	–	23
Bloomfield, T.F.	57	61	25	31*	298	8.27	–	–	–	8
Bopara, R.S.	8	14	4	48	328	32.80	–	–	–	9
Botha, A.G.	44	70	10	94	1206	20.10	–	5	–	36
Boucher, M.V.	112	159	25	134	4805	35.85	7	28	–	387/20
Bowler, P.D.	302	515	53	241*	18533	40.11	42	98	9	221/1
Brandy, D.G.	8	12	2	52	176	17.60	–	1	–	3
Brant, S.A.	16	18	8	23	72	7.20	–	–	–	7
Breese, G.R.	42	65	11	124	1553	28.75	1	12	–	29
Bresnan, T.T.	4	4	–	52	81	20.25	–	1	–	1
Bressington, A.N.	6	6	3	17*	42	14.00	–	–	–	3
Bridge, G.D.	26	43	7	50	560	15.55	–	1	–	17
Brignull, D.S.	3	4	–	46	58	14.50	–	–	–	–
Brophy, G.L.	34	58	11	185	1712	36.42	4	7	–	92/5
Brown, A.D.	184	288	28	295*	11051	42.50	32	45	6	192/1
Brown, D.O.	3	6	–	59	223	37.16	–	2	–	1
Brown, D.R.	162	248	33	203	6510	30.27	6	38	1	103
Brown, J.F.	62	73	33	38	294	7.35	–	–	–	13
Brown, M.J.	12	20	4	98	494	30.87	–	4	–	12
Bruce, J.T.A.	14	17	6	21*	95	8.63	–	–	–	4
Brunnschweiler, I.	6	8	1	34	91	13.00	–	–	–	20
Bryant, J.D.C.	62	113	14	234*	3596	36.32	7	17	–	48
Burns, M.	129	209	11	221	6431	32.47	7	45	2	121/7
Butcher, G.R.	3	5	–	10	30	6.00	–	–	–	–
Butcher, M.A.	212	363	26	259	13400	39.76	27	72	7	202
Butler, I.G.	19	24	7	26	161	9.47	–	–	–	5
Caddick, A.R.	203	273	51	92	3156	14.21	–	5	–	70
Cairns, C.L.	205	322	38	126	9997	35.20	12	66	1	78
Carberry, M.A.	22	38	2	153*	1358	37.72	2	7	–	10
Carlisle, S.V.	79	135	12	219*	4310	35.04	6	24	–	56
Carter, N.M.	29	38	8	103	567	18.90	1	1	–	9
Cawdron, M.J.	24	32	4	42	396	14.14	–	–	–	4
Chapple, G.	162	220	51	155	3957	23.41	4	15	–	54
Cherry, D.D.	7	10	–	47	149	14.90	–	–	–	4
Chilton, M.J.	80	129	8	125	3879	32.05	10	15	1	71
Clapp, D.A.	2	2	–	6	10	5.00	–	–	–	–
Clark, M.W.	16	22	10	26	138	11.50	–	–	–	10
Clarke, A.J.	5	8	2	41	129	21.50	–	–	–	2
Clarke, M.J.	33	60	3	134	2113	37.07	7	9	–	27
Clarke, R.	23	36	4	153*	1337	41.78	4	6	–	23
Clifford, J.I.	4	6	0	7	20	3.33	–	–	–	15/1
Clough, G.D.	9	13	1	55	133	11.08	–	1	–	3
Collingwood, P.D.	95	164	11	190	4899	32.01	8	28	1	96
Collymore, C.D.	38	47	19	20	212	7.57	–	–	–	17
Cook, A.N.	3	6	1	84	239	47.80	–	3	–	3
Cook, J.W.	49	79	7	137	2156	29.94	2	12	–	16
Cook, S.J.	54	72	11	93*	1096	17.96	–	3	–	17
Cork, D.G.	223	334	44	200*	7305	25.18	5	42	–	156
Cosker, D.A.	102	121	35	49	947	11.01	–	–	–	70
Cottey, P.A.	266	431	51	203	14057	36.99	30	73	8	175
Cowan, A.P.	100	149	28	94	2178	18.00	–	9	–	48
Cowan, E.J.M.	4	7	2	137*	370	74.00	1	1	–	1

F-C	M	I	NO	HS	Runs	Avge	100	50	1000	Ct/St
Cox, J.	234	414	29	245	16824	43.69	47	73	3+2	106
Craven, V.J.	27	47	5	72	1004	23.90	–	5	–	16
Crawley, J.P.	274	450	45	286	18850	46.54	42	107	8	181
Croft, R.D.B.	283	415	79	143	8666	25.79	4	41	–	143
Crook, S.P.	2	1	–	27	27	27.00	–	–	–	1
Cummins, R.A.G.	3	3	2	2*	3	3.00	–	–	–	–
Cunliffe, R.J.	68	114	7	190*	2542	23.75	3	10	–	53
Currie, M.R.	3	5	1	97	216	54.00	–	2	–	3
Daggett, L.M.	3	5	3	3*	10	5.00	–	–	–	–
Dagnall, C.E.	20	20	8	23*	148	12.33	–	–	–	1
Dakin, J.M.	74	110	11	190	2727	27.54	5	13	–	21
Dale, A.	244	400	32	214*	12345	33.54	23	58	4	104
Dale, M.A.P.	1	2	–	8	13	6.50	–	–	–	–
Daley, S.R.	1	–	–	–	–	–	–	–	–	–
Dalrymple, J.W.M.	20	35	4	236*	1095	35.32	3	2	–	16
Danish Kaneria	43	50	26	42	212	8.83	–	–	–	13
Das, S.S.	106	180	8	253	7207	41.90	17	37	–	113
Davies, A.M.	19	32	10	33	248	11.27	–	–	–	3
Davies, A.P.	21	25	4	40	254	12.09	–	–	–	4
Davis, M.J.G.	111	167	27	168	2686	19.18	2	7	–	62
Dawes, J.H.	54	67	24	32*	410	9.53	–	–	–	10
Dawood, I.	18	30	3	102	486	18.00	1	1	–	47/3
Dawson, R.K.J.	50	76	10	87	1374	20.81	–	4	–	24
Dean, K.J.	89	120	37	54*	942	11.34	–	2	–	17
DeFreitas, P.A.J.	355	506	47	123*	10535	22.95	10	53	–	126
Dernbach, J.	1	1	–	3	3	3.00	–	–	–	–
Dippenaar, H.H.	81	134	12	200*	5140	42.13	16	20	0+1	58
Di Venuto, M.J.	180	316	15	230	12682	42.13	27	80	4	196
Drakes, V.C.	156	243	29	180*	4486	20.96	4	16	–	52
Dumelow, N.R.C.	21	35	4	75	731	23.58	–	6	–	5
Durston, W.J.	3	6	1	55	129	25.80	–	1	–	5
Dutch, K.P.	66	94	9	118	1620	19.05	1	9	–	70
Ealham, M.A.	192	304	47	153*	8140	31.67	7	52	1	96
Ebrahim, D.D.	44	76	7	182	1926	27.91	1	13	–	29
Edwards, N.J.	6	11	–	160	418	38.00	1	1	–	2
Elliott, M.T.G.	145	267	22	203	12034	49.11	36	57	2+4	168
Elworthy, S.	138	203	27	89	3617	20.55	–	10	–	47
Ervine, S.M.	20	33	5	126	926	33.07	3	3	–	26
Evans, P.P.	2	2	–	16	30	15.00	–	–	–	6
Fellows, G.M.	48	74	6	109	1592	23.41	1	6	–	23
Ferley, R.S.	18	24	7	78*	399	23.47	–	2	–	7
Fisher, I.D.	50	70	15	103*	1332	24.21	1	7	–	13
Fleming, S.P.	164	274	26	274*	10416	42.00	20	64	1	219
Flintoff, A.	108	167	11	160	5512	35.33	12	27	–	122
Flower, A.	166	277	54	232*	12031	53.95	34	60	2	311/21
Flower, G.W.	144	253	21	243*	9199	39.65	19	51	–	135
Foster, J.S.	55	83	8	103	1958	26.10	1	10	–	131/13
Francis, J.D.	22	40	2	82	891	23.44	–	6	–	13
Francis, S.R.G.	36	51	20	44	291	9.38	–	–	–	3
Franks, P.J.	98	147	29	123*	2943	24.94	2	12	–	41
Free, C.W.	1	–	–	–	–	–	–	–	–	–
Friend, T.J.	33	48	8	121	1310	32.75	2	5	–	26
Frost, T.	51	77	8	111*	1697	24.59	2	8	–	116/9
Fulton, D.P.	153	269	17	208*	9217	36.57	20	39	2	222
Gait, A.I.	49	93	1	175	2584	28.08	4	17	–	43
Gallian, J.E.R.	170	298	29	312	10213	37.96	26	47	4	144

F-C	M	I	NO	HS	Runs	Avge	100	50	1000	Ct/St
Gambhir, G.	42	66	4	233*	3532	56.96	11	13	–	21
Gannon, B.W.	32	37	17	28	188	9.40	–	–	–	8
Gavaskar, R.S.	74	113	17	212*	4434	46.18	13	20	–	49
Gazzard, C.M.	4	7	1	41	140	23.33	–	–	–	8/1
Gibbs, H.H.	135	228	9	228	9725	44.40	25	41	–	96
Giddins, E.S.H.	147	175	74	34	534	5.28	–	–	–	22
Gidman, A.P.R.	18	33	3	117	965	32.16	1	6	–	12
Gilder, G.M.	51	51	13	39	408	10.73	–	–	–	19
Giles, A.F.	139	190	37	128*	4130	26.99	3	18	–	60
Goddard, L.J.	3	5	2	23*	48	16.00	–	–	–	2
Goodwin, M.W.	122	214	16	335*	9155	46.23	27	37	3	83
Gough, D.	202	273	51	121	3627	16.33	1	14	–	43
Gough, M.A.	67	119	3	123	2952	25.44	2	15	–	57
Grant, J.B.	29	35	14	36*	165	7.85	–	–	–	7
Gray, A.K.D.	16	23	3	104	612	30.60	1	2	–	14
Grayson, A.P.	175	288	25	189	8290	31.52	15	41	4	121
Greenidge, C.G.	28	30	4	46	221	8.50	–	–	–	12
Grove, J.O.	25	31	9	33	204	9.27	–	–	–	2
Gunter, N.E.L.	5	5	2	20*	47	15.66	–	–	–	3
Guy, S.M.	13	19	3	42	221	13.81	–	–	–	37/4
Habib, A.	131	197	27	215	7388	43.45	19	38	2	68
Hall, A.J.	63	92	15	153	2630	34.15	3	19	–	43
Hamblin, J.R.C.	11	18	2	96	440	27.50	–	3	–	5
Hamilton, G.M.	81	108	20	125	2321	26.37	1	15	–	28
Hancock, T.H.C.	171	300	19	220*	7863	27.98	7	47	1	109
Hanson, W.T.D.	3	4	2	9*	13	6.50	–	–	–	5/3
Hardinges, M.A.	10	11	1	172	259	25.90	1	–	–	3
Harmison, S.J.	86	123	32	36	760	8.35	–	–	–	16
Harris, A.J.	90	126	32	41*	812	8.63	–	–	–	28
Harrison, D.S.	20	30	5	66	327	13.08	–	1	–	3
Harrity, M.A.	80	100	52	19	251	5.22	–	–	–	26
Harvey, I.J.	116	196	18	136	5816	32.67	9	33	–	84
Hatch, N.G.	18	25	12	24	157	12.07	–	–	–	4
Havell, P.M.R.	5	6	5	7*	10	10.00	–	–	–	2
Hawinkels, S.J.	4	7	–	78	243	34.71	–	1	–	1
Hawk, S.L.J.M.	2	4	–	59	81	20.25	–	1	–	–
Haynes, J.J.	16	24	4	80	443	22.15	–	3	–	35/2
Hayward, M.	83	85	30	55*	720	13.09	–	1	–	25
Heath, D.R.	8	14	1	75	192	14.76	–	1	–	6
Heath, J.A.	3	4	–	35	44	11.00	–	–	–	–
Hegg, W.K.	321	466	90	134	10388	27.62	7	51	–	793/84
Hemp, D.L.	185	309	29	186*	9577	34.20	18	51	3	118
Hewson, D.R.	71	130	8	168	2787	22.84	3	15	–	34
Heywood, J.J.N.	2	2	–	8	11	5.50	–	–	–	3
Hick, G.A.	453	748	72	405*	35916	53.13	122	136	17+1	571
Hildreth, J.C.	1	2	–	9	9	4.50	–	–	–	–
Hindley, R.J.E.	1	2	1	68*	76	76.00	–	1	–	–
Hodd, A.J.	1									2
Hodge, B.J.	118	212	20	302*	8147	42.43	23	32	1+1	68
Hogg, G.B.	69	104	23	111*	2474	30.54	2	15	–	38
Hogg, K.W.	15	18	1	53	358	21.05	–	3	–	7
Hoggard, M.J.	81	100	35	32	465	7.15	–	–	–	18
Hollioake, A.J.	162	244	20	208	8964	40.01	17	53	2	151
Holloway, P.C.L.	128	216	28	168	5923	31.50	9	32	–	86/1
Hondo, D.T.	16	25	10	51*	210	14.00	–	1	–	10
Hooper, C.L.	326	514	49	236*	22341	48.04	67	100	8+2	356

F-C	M	I	NO	HS	Runs	Avge	100	50	1000	Ct/St
Hopkinson, C.D.	2	3	1	33	49	24.50	–	–	–	2
Horton, P.J.	1	1	1	2*	2	–	–	–	–	1
Howard, W.O.F.	3	5	–	72	98	19.60	–	1	–	1/2
Huggins, T.B.	1	2	–	40	40	20.00	–	–	–	–
Hughes, J.	18	29	1	74	684	24.42	–	3	–	12
Hunt, T.A.	3	1	–	3	3	3.00	–	–	–	–
Hunter, I.D.	21	32	4	65	577	20.60	–	2	–	6
Hussain, N.	321	523	51	207	19872	42.10	50	101	5	337
Hussey, D.J.	3	4	0	62	88	22.00	–	1	–	2
Hussey, M.E.K.	136	241	18	331*	11807	52.94	31	49	3	137
Hutchison, P.M.	52	53	27	30	252	9.69	–	–	–	9
Hutton, B.L.	62	102	11	139	2794	30.70	8	10	–	69
Imran Tahir	30	34	9	48	338	13.52	–	–	–	17
Innes, K.J.	42	66	17	103*	1188	24.24	1	3	–	14
Irani, R.C.	186	305	36	207*	10035	37.30	19	54	5	68
Jaffer, W.	88	145	17	314*	6485	50.66	15	37	0+2	92
James, S.P.	245	424	33	309*	15890	40.63	47	58	9	173
Jaques, P.A.	18	29	1	222	1495	53.39	5	6	1	11
Jefferson, W.I.	34	64	8	165*	1802	32.17	3	8	–	32
Johnson, R.L.	126	179	25	118	2736	17.76	1	6	–	52
Jones, G.O.	23	32	6	108*	1152	44.30	2	8	–	60/5
Jones, H.R.	8	14	1	97	304	23.38	–	2	–	6
Jones, P.S.	69	84	23	105	1105	18.11	1	3	–	16
Jones, S.P.	42	49	13	46	397	11.02	–	–	–	8
Joyce, E.C.	48	76	9	129	2810	41.94	9	11	2	38
Kaif, M.	53	85	9	136	2931	38.56	5	17	–	30
Kallis, J.H.	150	239	31	200	10373	49.87	26	60	1	122
Kartik, M.	71	80	7	79	1380	18.90	–	9	–	39
Kasprowicz, M.S.	192	258	54	92	3739	18.32	–	11	–	74
Katich, S.M.	100	175	26	228*	7304	49.02	21	36	2+2	104
Keedy, G.	107	121	63	57	679	11.70	–	1	–	29
Keegan, C.B.	33	40	5	36*	373	10.65	–	–	–	9
Kemp, J.M.	53	87	9	188	2493	31.96	3	12	–	54
Kendall, W.S.	132	216	24	201	6584	34.29	10	32	3	111
Kenway, D.A.	78	138	14	166	3810	30.72	6	19	1	73/1
Key, R.W.T.	110	189	8	174*	6089	33.64	15	27	2	72
Khalid, S.A.	5	2	–	13	21	10.50	–	–	–	1
Khan, A.	25	29	5	78	449	18.70	–	2	–	6
Khan, R.M.	15	25	1	91	510	21.25	–	3	–	5
Killeen, N.	71	104	21	48	917	11.04	–	–	–	19
King, R.E.	3	5	–	17	19	3.80	–	–	–	–
Kirby, S.P.	34	45	9	57	303	8.41	–	1	–	9
Kirsten, G.	210	368	39	275	15707	47.74	42	75	–	170
Kirtley, R.J.	117	163	48	59	1338	11.63	–	2	–	38
Klusener, L.	111	154	32	174	4214	34.54	6	22	–	65
Knight, N.V.	190	319	33	255*	12556	43.90	32	58	4	252
Koenig, S.G.	109	187	10	166*	7033	39.73	12	39	2	54
Krikken, K.M.	214	323	60	104	5725	21.76	1	25	–	526/31
Kruger, G.J-P.	38	51	15	58	412	11.44	–	1	–	9
Kumar, V.H.	12	20	3	86*	485	28.52	–	4	–	8/1
Lamb, G.A.	16	23	3	100*	491	24.55	1	2	–	9
Laraman, A.W.	27	32	8	148*	956	39.83	1	4	–	10
Law, D.R.	108	170	8	115	3298	20.35	2	15	–	55
Law, S.G.	284	469	51	263	21179	50.66	63	100	7+1	318
Leatherdale, D.A.	214	346	41	157	10003	32.79	14	54	1	151
Lehmann, D.S.	221	375	26	255	19891	56.99	64	89	4+5	117

F-C	M	I	NO	HS	Runs	Avge	100	50	1000	Ct/St
Lewis, J.	116	170	35	62	1727	12.79	–	3	–	28
Lewis, J.J.B.	169	301	24	210*	9214	33.26	15	57	4	97
Lewis, P.D.	2	3	1	10*	14	7.00	–	–	–	–
Lewry, J.D.	113	156	35	70	1271	10.50	–	1	–	26
Linley, T.E.	1	1	–	7	7	7.00	–	–	–	–
Liptrot, C.G.	30	36	11	61	303	12.12	–	1	–	11
Logan, R.J.	34	48	9	37*	380	9.74	–	–	–	11
Loudon, A.G.R.	11	18	1	172	523	30.76	1	1	–	10
Louw, J.	16	28	3	86*	531	21.24	–	3	–	12
Love, M.L.	148	255	23	273	11588	49.94	27	54	1+3	177
Lowe, J.A.	1	2	–	80	80	40.00	–	1	–	–
Lowe, S.J.	2	3	–	38	59	19.66	–	–	–	5/2
Loye, M.B.	166	265	23	322*	9411	38.88	26	37	4	79
Lumb, M.J.	38	66	5	124	2101	34.44	4	13	1	15
Lungley, T.	19	32	5	47	356	13.18	–	–	–	6
McCoubrey, A.G.A.M.	4	5	2	1*	2	0.66	–	–	–	–
McGarry, A.C.	15	18	13	11*	28	5.60	–	–	–	3
MacGill, S.C.G.	106	139	33	53	993	9.36	–	1	–	56
McGrath, A.	130	222	16	165	6370	30.92	10	31	–	78
McGrath, D.E.T.	2	3	–	4	5	1.66	–	–	–	–
McKenzie, N.D.	97	163	16	175	5869	39.92	13	33	–	77
McLean, N.A.M.	121	189	27	76	2228	13.75	–	3	–	34
McMahon, P.J.	8	12	–	30	108	9.00	–	–	–	3
Maddy, D.L.	171	276	18	229*	8575	33.23	17	41	4	171
Maher, J.P.	131	231	27	217	8633	42.31	18	41	1+2	135/2
Mahmood, S.I.	6	6	1	34	80	16.00	–	–	–	2
Maiden, A.J.	4	7	–	53	144	20.57	–	2	–	2
Malcolm, D.E.	304	366	113	51	1985	7.84	–	2	–	45
Malik, M.N.	14	16	7	30*	99	11.00	–	–	–	1
Mann, R.J.	3	5	–	63	181	36.20	–	2	–	2
Marillier, D.A.	32	55	4	163	1989	39.00	6	12	–	28
Marshall, S.J.	8	14	3	126*	411	37.36	1	2	–	3
Martin, P.J.	207	239	59	133	3535	19.63	2	7	–	55
Martin–Jenkins, R.S.C.	85	137	17	205*	3755	31.29	3	20	1	23
Martyn, D.R.	164	276	39	238	11794	49.76	35	61	–	135/2
Mascarenhas, A.D.	103	154	15	104	3278	23.58	3	15	–	41
Mason, M.S.	25	33	7	52	367	14.11	–	2	–	4
Masters, D.D.	45	53	12	119	465	11.34	1	1	–	13
Maunders, J.K.	13	24	2	171	790	35.90	2	3	–	4
Maynard, M.P.	379	617	57	243	23873	42.63	56	127	13	357/7
Mees, T.	8	12	2	36*	110	11.00	–	–	–	1
Middlebrook, J.D.	57	84	8	84	1386	18.23	–	4	–	28
Millar, N.	9	13	1	108	398	33.16	1	2	–	3
Mishra, A.	33	42	5	84	522	14.10	–	2	–	19
Mohammad Akram	80	105	26	28	585	7.40	–	–	–	24
Mohammad Sami	34	45	27	41*	230	12.77	–	–	–	10
Montgomerie, R.R.	181	317	29	196	10442	36.25	24	53	4	177
Moore, S.C.	2	4	1	28*	97	32.33	–	–	–	2
Morris, A.C.	62	81	12	65	1392	20.17	–	7	–	34
Muchall, G.J.	31	56	1	127	1492	27.12	3	8	–	20
Mullally, A.D.	220	248	65	75	1548	8.45	–	2	–	43
Munday, M.K.	4	3	2	0*	0	0.00	–	–	–	2
Muralitharan, M.	160	193	57	67	1472	10.82	–	1	–	84
Murtagh, T.J.	15	22	9	22*	181	13.92	–	–	–	3
Mushtaq Ahmed	227	285	36	90	3829	15.37	–	15	–	98
Mustard, P.	14	24	1	75	561	24.39	–	2	–	44/3

F-C	M	I	NO	HS	Runs	Avge	100	50	1000	Ct/St
Napier, G.R.	40	61	12	104	1323	27.00	1	5	–	19
Nash, C.D.	4	8	1	60	229	32.71	–	2	–	2
Nash, D.C.	103	145	29	114	3754	32.36	6	17	–	213/17
Nel, A.	53	58	24	44	606	17.82	–	–	–	18
Newby, O.J.	1	–	–	–	–	–	–	–	–	–
Newman, S.A.	5	9	1	183	364	45.50	1	1	–	5
Nixon, P.A.	253	366	81	134*	9158	32.13	14	39	1	669/52
Nkala, M.L.	32	45	7	168	885	23.28	1	3	–	13
Noble, D.J.	5	8	3	21	70	14.00	–	–	–	–
Noffke, A.A.	47	51	9	76	967	23.02	–	3	–	19
Noon, W.M.	92	145	23	83	2527	20.71	–	12	–	195/20
Ntini, M.	88	95	34	34*	560	9.18	–	–	–	21
Obuya, C.O.	14	22	4	55	405	22.50	–	1	–	5
Ormond, J.	93	109	27	50*	1223	14.91	–	1	–	20
Ostler, D.P.	205	336	25	225	10856	34.90	16	67	6	259
Palladino, A.P.	6	5	3	8	24	12.00	–	–	–	2
Panesar, M.S.	16	19	9	28	69	6.90	–	–	–	6
Parab, S.S.	40	65	4	141	2581	42.31	8	13	–	26
Park, G.T.	3	4	–	68	132	33.00	–	1	–	–
Parkin, O.T.	41	48	20	24*	228	8.14	–	–	–	12
Parsons, K.A.	109	178	17	193*	4298	26.69	5	23	–	99
Patel, M.M.	160	214	44	82	2925	17.20	–	11	–	88
Patel, P.A.	27	34	7	129	748	27.70	1	3	–	59/8
Patel, S.R.	2	3	–	55	99	33.00	–	1	–	1
Pathan, I.K.	29	34	9	54	423	16.92	–	1	–	9
Pattison, I.	4	7	–	62	123	17.57	–	1	–	2
Paynter, D.E.	5	9	2	146	268	38.28	1	1	–	2
Pearson, J.A.	3	6	1	51	114	22.80	–	1	–	2
Penberthy, A.L.	181	270	30	132*	7212	30.05	10	40	–	108
Peng, N.	48	83	2	158	2033	25.09	4	8	–	29
Penney, T.L.	158	248	45	151	7975	39.28	15	36	2	94/2
Peploe, C.T.	2	2	1	13	13	13.00	–	–	–	1
Peters, S.D.	90	148	16	165	4089	30.97	6	22	1	67
Peterson, R.J.	44	67	8	130	1354	22.94	2	4	–	19
Pettini, M.L.	7	13	1	78	371	30.91	–	4	–	6
Phillips, B.J.	35	48	6	100*	720	17.14	1	2	–	9
Phillips, N.C.	77	118	27	58*	1410	15.49	–	4	–	44
Phillips, T.J.	17	25	3	75	388	17.63	–	1	–	7
Pietersen, K.P.	53	86	9	254*	3945	51.23	12	19	2	53
Pipe, D.J.	16	25	3	104*	435	19.77	1	1	–	38/5
Piper, K.J.	199	275	44	116*	4618	19.99	2	14	–	502/34
Plunkett, L.E.	7	12	5	40*	164	23.42	–	–	–	2
Polley, S.R.	3	6	1	41	105	21.00	–	–	–	2
Pollock, S.M.	145	207	42	150*	5724	34.69	6	30	–	110
Ponting, R.T.	157	261	36	233	12576	55.89	46	50	–	159
Pope, S.P.	5	8	3	17*	65	13.00	–	–	–	10/1
Pothas, N.	115	179	28	165	5295	35.06	9	26	–	305/28
Powell, M.J. (Gm)	103	170	16	200*	6096	39.58	15	28	3	60
Powell, M.J. (Nh)	20	32	3	108*	785	27.06	2	4	–	38
Powell, M.J. (Wa)	102	169	5	236	5246	31.98	9	31	1	76
Pratt, A.	48	80	11	93	1356	19.65	–	4	–	117/10
Pratt, G.J.	38	67	1	150	1893	28.68	1	12	1	25
Pretorius, D.	49	56	14	43	383	9.11	–	–	–	12
Price, R.W.	47	80	12	82	892	13.11	–	4	–	12
Prior, M.J.	48	75	8	153*	2180	32.53	5	9	1	106/4
Prittipaul, L.R.	18	27	2	152	744	29.76	1	4	–	15

F-C	M	I	NO	HS	Runs	Avge	100	50	1000	Ct/St
Ramprakash, M.R.	340	560	70	279*	23223	47.39	66	110	13	194
Rayudu, A.T.	21	34	6	210	1347	48.10	4	6	–	11
Read, C.M.W.	115	179	27	160	4102	26.98	2	20	–	321/14
Rees, T.M.	1	1	–	16	16	16.00	–	–	–	1
Rhodes, J.N.	164	263	31	172	9546	41.14	22	52	1	127
Rhodes, S.J.	423	597	157	124	14406	32.74	12	70	2	1095/120
Richardson, A.	57	58	23	91	366	10.45	–	1	–	16
Richardson, S.A.	13	23	2	69	377	17.95	–	3	–	11
Roberts, T.W.	12	17	–	83	373	21.94	–	2	–	9
Robinson, D.D.J.	136	240	13	200	7149	31.49	15	33	1	111
Rogers, B.G.	22	37	2	141	1358	38.80	2	10	–	16
Rose, F.A.	94	130	21	96	1426	13.08	–	2	–*	24
Rudolph, J.A.	49	86	4	222*	3362	41.00	10	15	–	39
Russell, R.C.	463	688	144	129*	16831	30.93	11	89	1	1191/128
Sadler, J.L.	7	11	1	145	434	43.40	2	1	–	5
Saggers, M.J.	74	94	26	61*	717	10.54	–	1	–	16
Saker, N.C.	2	3	–	5	6	2.00	–	–	–	–
Sales, D.J.G.	106	164	12	303*	5317	34.98	11	23	1	79
Salisbury, I.D.K.	275	354	72	101*	5656	20.05	2	19	–	177
Salvi, A.M.	20	26	15	21*	120	10.90	–	–	–	6
Sampson, P.J.	3	5	2	42	78	26.00	–	–	–	–
Saqlain Mushtaq	159	221	53	101*	2862	17.03	1	12	–	58
Savill, T.E.	8	10	3	18*	80	11.42	–	–	–	4
Sayers, J.J.	8	14	1	122	395	30.38	1	2	–	2
Schofield, C.P.	65	89	14	91	2144	28.58	–	17	–	40
Scott, B.J.M.	2	3	1	58*	79	39.50	–	1	–	6
Scott, G.M.	1	2	0	25	33	16.50	–	–	–	1
Sehwag, V.	60	92	3	274	4669	52.46	16	20	0+1	63
Selwood, S.A.	21	40	1	99	833	21.35	–	4	–	5
Shabbir Ahmed	52	73	14	50	631	10.69	–	1	–	11
Shafayat, B.M.	23	42	1	105	1214	29.60	2	7	–	8
Shah, O.A.	113	186	13	203	6281	36.30	15	30	3	72
Shahid Afridi	69	116	3	164	3420	30.26	7	17	–	46
Shahid, N.	145	229	26	150	6344	31.25	9	34	1	151
Shankar, A.	8	12	–	143	287	23.91	1	–	–	5
Shantry, A.J.	3	3	2	38*	55	55.00	–	–	–	1
Sharif, Z.K.	7	10	1	67	258	28.66	–	2	–	2
Sharpe, T.J.	7	10	5	10*	27	5.40	–	–	–	2
Shaw, A.D.	77	103	16	140	1906	21.90	1	9	–	180/14
Sheikh, M.A.	20	27	7	58*	572	28.60	–	2	–	3
Sheriyar, A.	142	154	59	21	780	8.21	–	–	–	22
Shoaib Akhtar	95	129	43	59*	976	11.34	–	1	–	30
Shoaib Malik	42	60	7	130*	1260	23.77	1	4	–	23
Shreck, C.E.	11	15	6	19	51	5.66	–	–	–	1
Sibanda, V.	11	21	1	82	391	19.55	–	1	–	4
Sidebottom, R.J.	60	79	24	54	624	11.34	–	1	–	23
Sillence, R.J.	10	14	–	101	271	19.35	1	–	–	3
Silverwood, C.E.W.	135	180	36	70	2175	15.10	–	6	–	28
Singh, A. (Wo)	95	157	6	187	4804	31.81	9	21	2	37
Singh, A. (CU)	1	2	–	22	22	11.00	–	–	–	–
Smith, A.M.	154	204	61	61	1744	12.19	–	4	–	30
Smith, B.F.	232	359	42	204	12738	40.18	30	62	5	113
Smith, E.T.	114	193	10	213	7334	40.07	18	32	4	42
Smith, G.C.	41	67	4	277	3361	53.34	10	10	–	61
Smith, G.J.	113	145	50	68	1260	13.26	–	2	–	23
Smith, N.M.K.	205	289	34	161	6783	26.60	4	35	1	73

166

F-C	M	I	NO	HS	Runs	Avge	100	50	1000	Ct/St
Smith, R.A.	426	717	87	209*	26155	41.51	61	131	11	233
Smith, W.R.	4	7	1	38*	125	20.83	–	–	–	2
Snape, J.N.	106	157	29	131	3734	29.17	3	21	–	70
Solanki, V.S.	157	258	19	185	8410	35.18	14	46	2	200
Somerville-Hendrie, J.W.	2	1	1	1*	1	–	–	–	–	–
Spearman, C.M.	127	229	13	180*	7858	36.37	16	42	1	123
Spires, J.A.S	7	7	3	37*	70	17.50	–	–	–	3
Srinath, J.	147	191	34	76	2276	14.49	–	7	–	62
Sriram, S.	76	113	11	288	6261	61.38	24	19	0+3	41
Stephenson, J.P.	297	503	54	202*	14546	32.39	25	76	5	181
Stevens, D.I.	67	112	5	149	2853	26.66	3	18	–	51
Stewart, A.J.	447	734	81	271*	26165	40.06	48	148	8	721/32
Strauss, A.J.	81	139	9	176	5438	41.83	11	27	3	41
Streak, H.H.	117	175	30	131	3586	24.73	3	18	–	39
Stubbings, S.D.	56	102	5	135*	2954	30.45	6	13	1	19
Suppiah, A.V.	3	5	–	21	43	8.60	–	–	–	1
Sutcliffe, I.J.	133	209	18	203	6416	33.59	10	33	2	71
Sutton, L.D.	54	98	13	140*	2518	29.62	4	8	–	95/4
Swanepoel, P.J.	2	3	–	17	20	6.66	–	–	–	1
Swann, A.J.	72	116	4	154	3193	28.50	8	14	1	54
Swann, G.P.	94	139	8	183	3494	26.67	4	15	–	62
Symonds, A.	163	273	25	254*	10295	41.51	28	44	2	111
Taibu, T.	34	52	8	114*	1086	24.68	1	4	–	81/8
Taylor, B.V.	28	32	11	35*	183	8.71	–	–	–	2
Taylor, C.G.	43	79	5	196	2257	30.50	5	6	–	32
Taylor, C.R.	11	20	1	52*	297	15.63	–	2	–	6
Taylor, D.B.	3	6	–	82	206	34.33	–	2	–	1
Ten Doeschate, R.N.	2	4	–	31	48	12.00	–	–	–	1
Thomas, A.C.	1	–	–	–	–	–	–	–	–	1
Thomas, I.J.	26	43	4	82	835	21.41	–	5	–	17
Thomas, S.D.	148	201	39	138	3204	19.77	1	14	–	48
Thorburn, M.	6	5	1	12	35	8.75	–	–	–	1
Thornicroft, N.D.	4	7	4	4*	10	3.33	–	–	–	–
Thorpe, A.M.	9	16	–	95	321	20.06	–	2	–	5
Thorpe, G.P.	303	505	68	223*	19644	44.95	45	107	9	269
Todd, M.J.	1	1	1	6*	6	–	–	–	–	–
Tomlinson, J.A.	14	23	10	23	61	4.69	–	–	–	4
Tredwell, J.C.	18	26	3	61	438	19.04	–	2	–	23
Trego, P.D.	15	22	3	140	534	28.10	1	1	–	6
Tremlett, C.T.	31	41	12	43	507	17.48	–	–	–	11
Trescothick, M.E.	157	267	13	219	8803	34.65	13	52	–	166
Trott, B.J.	29	30	10	26	122	6.10	–	–	–	7
Trott, I.J.L.	27	50	3	134	1563	33.25	2	12	–	17
Troughton, J.O.	29	50	6	131*	2007	45.61	7	8	1	15
Tsolekile, T.L.	38	47	7	95	1013	25.32	–	5	–	115/12
Tudor, A.J.	90	118	26	116	2023	21.98	1	6	–	24
Turner, R.J.	225	349	64	144	8896	31.21	10	45	2	620/45
Udal, S.D.	216	310	58	117*	5781	22.94	1	25	–	97
Vaas, W.P.U.C.J.	115	145	30	74*	2258	19.63	–	10	–	31
Van Jaarsveld, M.	81	133	13	238*	5386	44.88	16	22	0+1	92
Vaughan, M.P.	193	339	19	197	12182	38.06	32	48	4	87
Vermeulen, M.A.	39	73	3	198	3037	43.38	8	11	–	37
Vettori, D.L.	80	111	16	112	1827	19.23	1	9	–	37
Wagg, G.G.	7	11	2	74	250	27.77	–	2	–	1
Wagh, M.A.	108	178	16	315	6302	38.90	16	27	3	53
Walker, G.W.	3	4	2	37*	69	34.50	–	–	–	2

167

F-C	M	I	NO	HS	Runs	Avge	100	50	1000	Ct/St
Walker, M.J.	116	192	21	275*	5263	30.77	10	18	1	81
Wallace, M.A.	52	83	10	121	2020	27.67	3	9	–	160/6
Waqar Younis	225	279	61	64	2906	13.33	–	6	–	58
Ward, I.J.	112	189	16	168*	6923	40.01	17	38	2	64
Ward, T.R.	248	425	22	235*	13876	34.43	29	77	6	226
Warne, S.K.	200	267	34	99	4103	17.60	–	15	–	156
Warren, N.A.	1	2	1	11	13	13.00	–	–	–	–
Warren, R.J.	119	198	23	201*	6501	37.14	13	33	1	115/5
Wasim Akram	257	355	40	257*	7161	22.73	7	24	–	97
Webley, T.	9	16	2	104	428	30.57	1	2	–	3
Weekes, P.N.	196	305	41	171*	8869	33.59	16	41	1	189
Welch, G.	123	188	31	84*	3295	20.98	–	14	–	44
Wells, V.J.	196	306	22	224	9314	32.79	18	46	2	134
Welton, G.E.	73	133	5	200*	3299	25.77	2	19	–	43
Weston, R.M.S.	62	104	6	156	2841	28.98	7	9	–	37
Weston, W.P.C.	185	326	32	205	10009	34.04	19	49	4	99
Westwood, I.J.	1	1	–	19	19	19.00	–	–	–	–
Wharf, A.G.	62	89	17	101*	1389	19.29	2	5	–	29
Wharton, L.J.	38	59	30	30	173	5.96	–	–	–	14
Whiley, M.J.A.	18	24	6	16	72	4.00	–	–	–	3
White, C.	227	359	47	186	9952	31.89	16	48	–	144
White, R.A.	13	25	1	277	854	35.58	1	5	–	7
Wigley, D.H.	3	6	1	15	57	11.40	–	–	–	–
Willoughby, C.M.	75	86	34	17*	213	4.09	–	–	–	14
Windows, M.G.N.	145	258	17	184	8248	34.22	16	44	3	84
Wood, J.	113	161	23	64	1714	12.42	–	3	–	27
Wood, M.J. (Sm)	34	63	1	196	2036	32.83	5	12	–	8
Wood, M.J. (Y)	89	156	16	207	4660	33.28	14	16	3	63
Wright, D.G.	42	61	13	63	1002	20.87	–	4	–	19
Wright, L.J.	1	2	1	11*	11	11.00	–	–	–	–
Yardy, M.H.	34	58	7	93	1486	29.13	–	8	–	24
Yates, G.	82	107	36	134*	1789	25.19	3	5	–	38
Yuvraj Singh	35	57	4	209	2204	41.58	7	11	–	41
Zondeki, M.	17	25	9	59	199	12.43	–	1	–	3
Zuiderent, B.	19	30	1	122	679	23.41	1	4	–	19

BOWLING

'50wS' denotes instances of taking 50 or more wickets in a season. Where these have been achieved outside the British Isles they are shown after a plus sign.

	Runs	Wkts	Avge	Best	5wI	10wM	50wS
Abdul Razzaq	7181	232	30.95	7- 51	8	2	–
Adams, C.J.	1855	41	45.24	4- 28	–	–	–
Adams, J.H.K.	146	4	36.50	2- 24	–	–	–
Adams, P.R.	9571	315	30.38	9- 79	13	2	–
Adnan, M.H.	20	0					
Afzaal, U.	3347	66	50.71	4-101	–	–	–
Airey, J.	218	4	54.50	2- 32	–	–	–
Akram, M.Adnan	160	3	53.33	2- 85	–	–	–
Akram, M.Arfan	83	4	20.75	3- 41	–	–	–
Ali, Kabir	4643	177	26.23	8- 53	9	2	2
Ali, Kadeer	57	0					
Ali, S.M.B.	8121	254	31.97	6- 37	11	2	0+1
Alleyne, M.W.	13345	403	33.11	6- 49	8	–	1
Ambrose, T.R.	1	0					
Amin, R.M.	1709	35	48.82	4- 87	–	–	–

F-C	Runs	Wkts	Avge	Best	5wI	10wM	50wS
Anderson, J.M.	2346	91	25.78	6- 23	6	–	1
Anderson, R.S.G.	3398	120	28.31	6- 34	8	1	1
Andrew, G.M.	310	10	31.00	3- 14	–	–	–
Anyon, J.E.	375	3	125.00	2- 59	–	–	–
Averis, J.M.M.	4309	98	43.96	5- 51	3	–	–
Azhar Mahmood	8080	331	24.41	8- 61	13	3	0+1
Badani, H.K.	391	6	65.16	1- 6	–	–	–
Bailey, T.M.B.	3	0					
Balaji, L.	2955	120	24.62	6- 26	9	3	–
Ball, M.C.J.	12743	345	36.93	8- 46	12	1	–
Banes, M.J.	175	3	58.33	3- 65	–	–	–
Bassano, C.W.G.	11	0					
Batty, G.J.	3738	133	28.10	6- 71	4	–	2
Batty, J.N.	61	1	61.00	1- 21	–	–	–
Bell, I.R.	556	13	42.76	4- 12	–	–	–
Benning, J.G.E.	81	1	81.00	1- 39	–	–	–
Betts, M.M.	9220	308	29.93	9- 64	13	2	–
Bhandari, A.	4983	188	26.50	7- 92	10	1	0+1
Bharadwaj, R.V.	1986	57	34.84	6- 24	2	–	–
Bichel, A.J.	11040	454	24.31	9- 93	22	4	1+1
Bicknell, D.J.	793	23	34.47	3- 7	–	–	–
Bicknell, M.P.	24139	982	24.58	9- 45	40	4	11
Bishop, J.E.	1934	49	39.46	5-148	1	–	–
Blackwell, I.D.	5418	129	42.00	5- 49	5	–	–
Blain, J.A.R.	2313	49	47.20	6- 42	2	–	–
Blakey, R.J.	68	1	68.00	1- 68	–	–	–
Blewett, G.S.	5480	130	42.15	5- 29	1	–	–
Blignaut, A.M.	2754	84	32.78	5- 73	3	–	–
Bloomfield, T.F.	5236	156	33.56	5- 36	6	–	1
Bopara, R.S.	196	3	65.33	1- 23	–	–	–
Botha, A.G.	3516	117	30.05	8- 53	2	1	–
Boucher, M.V.	20	0					
Bowler, P.D.	2049	34	60.26	3- 25	–	–	–
Brandy, D.G.	172	4	43.00	2- 11	–	–	–
Brant, S.A.	1342	48	27.95	6- 45	1	–	–
Breese, G.R.	2994	131	22.85	7- 60	7	2	–
Bresnan, T.T.	259	7	37.00	3- 88	–	–	–
Bressington, A.N.	446	16	27.87	4- 36	–	–	–
Bridge, G.D.	2280	65	35.07	6- 84	1	–	–
Brignull, D.S.	235	7	33.57	2- 30	–	–	–
Brown, A.D.	461	2	230.50	1- 11	–	–	–
Brown, D.O.	90	1	90.00	1- 38	–	–	–
Brown, D.R.	12326	437	28.20	8- 89	17	4	3
Brown, J.F.	7136	248	28.77	7- 69	13	3	2
Bruce, J.T.A.	1218	24	50.75	3- 42	–	–	–
Bryant, J.D.C.	37	1	37.00	1- 22	–	–	–
Burns, M.	2588	62	41.74	6- 54	1	–	–
Butcher, M.A.	4190	124	33.79	5- 86	1	–	–
Butler, I.G.	1948	73	26.68	5- 44	1	–	–
Caddick, A.R.	22296	897	24.85	9- 32	61	15	8
Cairns, C.L.	17248	614	28.09	8- 47	29	6	3
Carberry, M.A.	94	1	94.00	1- 45	–	–	–
Carlisle, S.V.	4	0					
Carter, N.M.	2885	77	37.46	6- 63	4	–	–
Cawdron, M.J.	1802	73	24.68	6- 25	6	1	–
Chapple, G.	14063	487	28.87	6- 30	20	1	4

F-C	Runs	Wkts	Avge	Best	5wI	10wM	50wS
Cherry, D.D.	0	0					
Chilton, M.J.	506	6	84.33	1- 1	–	–	–
Clark, M.W.	1313	48	27.35	5- 47	1	–	–
Clarke, A.J.	318	14	22.71	5- 54	1	–	–
Clarke, M.J.	231	4	57.75	2- 25	–	–	–
Clarke, R.	1335	32	41.71	4- 21	–	–	–
Clough, G.D.	544	9	60.44	3- 69	–	–	–
Collingwood, P.D.	2629	65	40.44	4- 31	–	–	–
Collymore, C.D.	2993	125	23.94	7- 57	7	–	–
Cook, A.N.	11	0					
Cook, J.W.	1084	29	37.37	5- 31	1	–	–
Cook, S.J.	4338	133	32.61	8- 63	2	–	–
Cork, D.G.	18933	722	26.22	9- 43	28	5	7
Cosker, D.A.	8898	240	37.07	6-140	2	–	–
Cottey, P.A.	954	16	59.62	4- 49	–	–	–
Cowan, A.P.	8773	270	32.49	6- 47	8	–	1
Cowan, E.J.M.	3	0					
Cox, J.	338	4	84.50	3- 46	–	–	–
Craven, V.J.	393	9	43.66	2- 25	–	–	–
Crawley, J.P.	201	1	201.00	1- 90	–	–	–
Croft, R.D.B.	28031	781	35.89	8- 66	36	6	6
Crook, S.P.	155	2	77.50	1- 6	–	–	–
Cummins, R.A.G.	357	2	178.50	2-108	–	–	–
Cunliffe, R.J.	3	0					
Daggett, L.M.	317	3	105.66	2- 95	–	–	–
Dagnall, C.E.	1823	58	31.43	6- 50	2	–	–
Dakin, J.M.	5082	154	33.00	5- 86	1	–	–
Dale, A.	8232	217	37.93	6- 18	4	–	–
Dale, M.A.P.	32	0					
Daley, S.R.	31	0					
Dalrymple, J.W.M.	1574	28	56.21	5- 49	1	–	–
Danish Kaneria	4447	211	21.07	7- 39	18	2	0+1
Das, S.S.	140	4	35.00	1- 0	–	–	–
Davies, A.M.	1451	47	30.87	5- 61	1	–	–
Davies, A.P.	1589	42	37.83	5- 79	1	–	–
Davis, M.J.G.	7529	208	36.19	8- 37	5	1	–
Dawes, J.H.	5058	209	24.20	7- 67	8	2	–
Dawson, R.K.J.	4542	105	43.25	6- 82	4	–	–
Dean, K.J.	8269	332	24.90	8- 52	14	4	2
DeFreitas, P.A.J.	33339	1205	27.66	7- 21	61	6	14
Dernbach, J.	74	1	74.00	1- 74	–	–	–
Dippenaar, H.H.	12	0					
Di Venuto, M.J.	430	5	86.00	1- 0	–	–	–
Drakes, V.C.	15290	591	25.87	8- 59	27	3	2+2
Dumelow, N.R.C.	1644	32	51.37	5- 78	2	1	–
Durston, W.J.	190	4	47.50	1- 16	–	–	–
Dutch, K.P.	3739	96	38.94	6- 62	1	–	–
Ealham, M.A.	12133	425	28.54	8- 36	19	1	–
Ebrahim, D.D.	78	3	26.00	1- 2	–	–	–
Edwards, N.J.	71	0					
Elliott, M.T.G.	640	10	64.00	1- 3	–	–	–
Elworthy, S.	13687	494	27.70	7- 65	18	4	0+1
Ervine, S.M.	1483	30	49.43	6- 82	2	–	–
Fellows, G.M.	1228	32	38.37	3- 23	–	–	–
Ferley, R.S.	1672	39	42.87	4- 76	–	–	–
Fisher, I.D.	3876	103	37.63	5- 30	6	1	–

F-C	Runs	Wkts	Avge	Best	5wI	10wM	50wS
Fleming, S.P.	129	0					
Flintoff, A.	4725	124	38.10	5- 24	1	–	–
Flower, A.	250	6	41.66	1- 1	–	–	–
Flower, G.W.	4735	136	34.81	7- 31	3	–	–
Foster, J.S.	6	0					
Francis, J.D.	35	2	17.50	1- 1	–	–	–
Francis, S.R.G.	3358	88	38.15	5- 73	1	–	–
Franks, P.J.	8545	293	29.16	7- 56	9	–	2
Free, C.W.	55	1	55.00	1- 32	–	–	–
Friend, T.J.	2702	62	43.58	5- 31	1	–	–
Frost, T.	15	0					
Fulton, D.P.	112	1	112.00	1- 37	–	–	–
Gallian, J.E.R.	3919	95	41.25	6-115	1	–	–
Gambhir, G.	156	5	31.20	3- 12	–	–	–
Gannon, B.W.	2832	85	33.31	6- 80	3	–	–
Gavaskar, R.S.	1287	30	42.90	5- 3	1	–	–
Gibbs, H.H.	74	3	24.66	2- 14	–	–	–
Giddins, E.S.H.	13562	478	28.37	6- 47	22	2	4
Gidman, A.P.R.	883	15	58.86	3- 33	–	–	–
Gilder, G.M.	4032	151	26.70	8- 22	6	2	–
Giles, A.F.	11986	414	28.95	8- 90	20	3	2
Goodwin, M.W.	355	7	50.71	2- 23	–	–	–
Gough, D.	19578	727	26.92	7- 28	27	3	5
Gough, M.A.	1350	30	45.00	5- 66	1	–	–
Grant, J.B.	2247	63	35.66	5- 38	1	–	–
Gray, A.K.D.	1270	28	45.35	4-128	–	–	–
Grayson, A.P.	5871	136	43.16	5- 20	1	–	–
Greenidge, C.G.	3057	87	35.13	6- 40	4	–	1
Grove, J.O.	2089	43	48.58	5- 90	1	–	–
Gunter, N.E.L.	387	12	32.25	4- 14	–	–	–
Guy, S.M.	8	0					
Habib, A.	62	1	62.00	1- 10	–	–	–
Hall, A.J.	4634	200	23.17	6- 77	9	1	–
Hamblin, J.R.C.	723	14	51.64	6- 93	1	–	–
Hamilton, G.M.	6067	239	25.38	7- 50	9	2	1
Hancock, T.H.C.	1680	44	38.18	3- 5	–	–	–
Hardinges, M.A.	617	13	47.46	2- 16	–	–	–
Harmison, S.J.	8323	264	31.52	6-111	5	–	2
Harris, A.J.	9315	291	32.01	7- 54	12	3	2
Harrison, D.S.	1525	44	34.65	5- 80	1	–	–
Harrity, M.A.	8109	208	38.98	5- 65	2	–	–
Harvey, I.J.	9053	338	26.78	8-101	14	2	–
Hatch, N.G.	1795	48	37.39	4- 61	–	–	–
Havell, P.M.R.	514	14	36.71	4-129	–	–	–
Hawinkels, S.J.	133	2	66.50	1- 44	–	–	–
Hayward, M.	8334	304	27.41	6- 31	9	2	1
Heath, D.R.	376	7	53.71	3- 28	–	–	–
Heath, J.A.	114	2	57.00	2- 83	–	–	–
Hegg, W.K.	7	0					
Hemp, D.L.	778	17	45.76	3- 23	–	–	–
Hewson, D.R.	91	1	91.00	1- 7	–	–	–
Hick, G.A.	10268	231	44.45	5- 18	5	1	–
Hindley, R.J.E.	46	0					
Hodge, B.J.	1956	47	41.61	4- 17	–	–	–
Hogg, G.B.	4358	102	42.72	5- 53	4	–	–
Hogg, K.W.	1137	31	36.67	5- 48	1	–	–

F-C	Runs	Wkts	Avge	Best	5wI	10wM	50wS
Hoggard, M.J.	7633	290	26.32	7- 49	11	–	1
Hollioake, A.J.	4637	113	41.03	5- 62	1	–	–
Holloway, P.C.L.	69	0					
Hondo, D.T.	1171	38	30.81	5- 26	1	–	–
Hooper, C.L.	19000	540	35.18	7- 93	18	–	–
Hopkinson, C.D.	43	1	43.00	1- 35	–	–	–
Hunt, T.A.	285	7	40.71	3- 43	–	–	–
Hunter, I.D.	1894	45	42.08	4- 55	–	–	–
Hussain, N.	323	2	161.50	1- 38	–	–	–
Hussey, D.J.	6	1	6.00	1- 6	–	–	–
Hussey, M.E.K.	321	6	53.50	2- 21	–	–	–
Hutchison, P.M.	4356	168	25.92	7- 31	7	1	1
Hutton, B.L.	1201	23	52.21	4- 37	–	–	–
Imran Tahir	2791	101	27.63	8- 76	6	2	–
Innes, K.J.	2305	76	30.32	4- 41	–	–	–
Irani, R.C.	10007	339	29.51	6- 71	9	–	1
Jaffer, W.	59	2	29.50	2- 18	–	–	–
James, S.P.	3	0					
Jaques, P.A.	25	0					
Johnson, R.L.	11258	426	26.42	10- 45	16	3	4
Jones, G.O.	4	0					
Jones, P.S.	6913	188	36.77	6- 67	5	1	1
Jones, S.P.	3738	101	37.00	6- 45	4	–	–
Joyce, E.C.	395	3	131.66	1- 20	–	–	–
Kaif, M.	524	17	30.82	3- 4	–	–	–
Kallis, J.H.	7945	279	28.47	6- 54	7	–	–
Kartik, M.	5874	229	25.65	9- 70	15	2	–
Kasprowicz, M.S.	20258	779	26.00	9- 36	44	6	4+3
Katich, S.M.	2098	56	37.46	7-130	2	–	–
Keedy, G.	10038	291	34.49	6- 56	12	3	1
Keegan, C.B.	3368	100	33.68	6-114	3	–	1
Kemp, J.M.	3173	127	24.98	6- 56	4	–	–
Kendall, W.S.	692	13	53.23	3- 37	–	–	–
Kenway, D.A.	159	4	39.75	1- 5	–	–	–
Key, R.W.T.	44	0					
Khalid, S.A.	334	10	33.40	4-131	–	–	–
Khan, A.	2847	81	35.14	6- 52	4	–	1
Khan, R.M.	28	0					
Killeen, N.	5949	202	29.45	7- 70	7	–	1
King, R.E.	313	1	313.00	1-108	–	–	–
Kirby, S.P.	4011	151	26.56	8- 80	9	3	1
Kirsten, G.	835	20	41.75	6- 68	1	–	–
Kirtley, R.J.	11698	465	25.15	7- 21	27	4	6
Klusener, L.	8224	307	26.78	8- 34	11	3	–
Knight, N.V.	230	1	230.00	1- 61	–	–	–
Koenig, S.G.	86	2	43.00	1- 0	–	–	–
Krikken, K.M.	121	1	121.00	1- 54	–	–	–
Kruger, G.J.P.	3509	118	29.73	7- 64	2	1	–
Lamb, G.A.	559	26	21.50	7- 73	1	–	–
Laraman, A.W.	1974	57	34.63	4- 33	–	–	–
Law, D.R.	7000	213	32.86	6- 53	8	–	–
Law, S.G.	4092	82	49.90	5- 39	1	–	–
Leatherdale, D.A.	4111	131	31.38	5- 20	2	–	–
Lehmann, D.S.	2671	66	40.46	4- 42	–	–	–
Lewis, J.	11087	412	26.91	8- 95	20	3	4
Lewis, J.J.B.	121	1	121.00	1- 73	–	–	–

F-C	Runs	Wkts	Avge	Best	5wI	10wM	50wS
Lewis, P.D.	173	3	57.66	2- 96	–	–	–
Lewry, J.D.	10834	405	26.75	8-106	24	4	4
Linley, T.E.	63	0					
Liptrot, C.G.	2212	69	32.05	6- 44	2	–	–
Logan, R.J.	3370	97	34.74	6- 93	4	–	–
Loudon, A.G.R.	552	9	61.33	3- 86	–	–	–
Louw, J.	1436	47	30.55	6-108	1	–	–
Love, M.L.	5	1	5.00	1- 5	–	–	–
Loye, M.B.	60	1	60.00	1- 8	–	–	–
Lumb, M.J.	99	3	33.00	2- 10	–	–	–
Lungley, T.	1334	42	31.76	4-101	–	–	–
McCoubrey, A.G.A.M.	279	8	34.87	3- 38	–	–	–
McGarry, A.C.	1386	27	51.33	5- 27	1	–	–
MacGill, S.C.G.	13631	478	28.51	8-111	30	5	0+2
McGrath, A.	1482	53	27.96	4- 49	–	–	–
McGrath, D.E.T.	238	8	29.75	3- 49	–	–	–
McKenzie, N.D.	263	5	52.60	1- 6	–	–	–
McLean, N.A.M.	11274	411	27.43	7- 28	14	1	2
McMahon, P.J.	698	20	34.90	4- 59	–	–	–
Maddy, D.L.	3916	134	29.22	5- 37	4	–	–
Maher, J.P.	504	10	50.40	3- 11	–	–	–
Mahmood, S.I.	450	15	30.00	5- 37	1	–	–
Malcolm, D.E.	31973	1054	30.33	9- 57	46	9	9
Malik, M.N.	1203	35	34.37	5- 57	2	–	–
Marillier, D.A.	1506	40	37.65	4- 44	–	–	–
Marshall, S.J.	1139	11	103.54	6-128	1	–	–
Martin, P.J.	16358	596	27.44	8- 32	17	1	4
Martin-Jenkins, R.S.C.	6565	199	32.98	7- 51	4	–	–
Martyn, D.R.	1465	36	40.69	4- 30	–	–	–
Mascarenhas, A.D.	6821	216	31.57	6- 26	6	–	–
Mason, M.S.	2006	79	25.39	6- 68	3	–	1
Masters, D.D.	3885	115	33.78	6- 27	4	–	–
Maunders, J.K.	38	0					
Maynard, M.P.	868	6	144.66	3- 21	–	–	–
Mees, T.	917	20	45.85	6- 64	1	–	–
Middlebrook, J.D.	5173	143	36.17	6- 82	4	1	1
Millar, N.	376	4	94.00	2- 50	–	–	–
Mishra, A.	3592	138	26.02	6- 86	10	1	–
Mohammad Akram	7310	279	26.20	8- 49	14	1	–
Mohammad Sami	3527	131	26.92	8- 64	8	1	–
Montgomerie, R.R.	108	2	54.00	1- 0	–	–	–
Morris, A.C.	4119	156	26.40	5- 39	5	1	2
Muchall, G.J.	410	9	45.55	3- 26	–	–	–
Mullally, A.D.	19242	690	27.88	9- 93	30	4	5
Munday, M.K.	305	14	21.78	5- 83	1	–	–
Muralitharan, M.	17619	900	19.57	9- 51	79	23	2+4
Murtagh, T.J.	1159	37	31.32	6- 86	2	–	–
Mushtaq Ahmed	25605	991	25.83	9- 93	70	21	5+2
Napier, G.R.	2783	70	39.75	5- 66	1	–	–
Nash, C.D.	410	3	136.66	1- 46	–	–	–
Nash, D.C.	44	1	44.00	1- 8	–	–	–
Nel, A.	4403	184	23.92	6- 25	8	–	–
Newby, O.J.	82	1	82.00	1- 41	–	–	–
Newman, S.A.	5	0					
Nixon, P.A.	22	0					
Nkala, M.L.	2422	55	44.03	4- 46	–	–	–

F-C	Runs	Wkts	Avge	Best	5wI	10wM	50wS
Noble, D.J.	529	9	58.77	3-66	–	–	–
Noffke, A.A.	5000	176	28.40	8-24	9	1	–
Noon, W.M.	34	0					
Ntini, M.	8195	271	30.23	6-37	7	1	–
Obuya, C.O.	1253	34	36.85	5-97	1	–	–
Ormond, J.	9139	329	27.77	6-33	18	1	3
Ostler, D.P.	295	1	295.00	1-46	–	–	–
Palladino, A.P.	594	11	54.00	6-41	1	–	–
Panesar, M.S.	1678	51	32.90	5-77	1	–	–
Parab, S.S.	165	1	165.00	1-57	–	–	–
Park, G.T.	261	0					
Parkin, O.T.	3014	108	27.90	5-24	2	–	–
Parsons, K.A.	3675	88	41.76	5-13	2	–	–
Patel, M.M.	14484	470	30.81	8-96	23	9	3
Patel, P.A.	9	0					
Patel, S.R.	10	0					
Pathan, I.K.	2742	87	31.51	6-31	3	1	–
Pattison, I.	166	5	33.20	3-41	–	–	–
Paynter, D.E.	26	0					
Penberthy, A.L.	9051	231	39.18	5-37	4	–	–
Peng, N.	2	0					
Penney, T.L.	184	6	30.66	3-18	–	–	–
Peploe, C.T.	239	2	119.50	1-58	–	–	–
Peters, S.D.	19	1	19.00	1-19	–	–	–
Peterson, R.J.	4206	128	32.85	6-67	6	1	–
Phillips, B.J.	2355	90	26.16	5-47	2	–	–
Phillips, N.C.	7074	162	43.66	6-97	5	1	–
Phillips, T.J.	1704	32	53.25	4-42	–	–	–
Pietersen, K.P.	2183	48	45.47	4-31	–	–	–
Piper, K.J.	60	1	60.00	1-57	–	–	–
Plunkett, L.E.	672	19	35.36	5-53	1	–	–
Polley, S.R.	160	1	160.00	1-54	–	–	–
Pollock, S.M.	11600	530	21.88	7-33	21	2	0+1
Ponting, R.T.	691	13	53.15	2-10	–	–	–
Pothas, N.	5	0					
Powell, M.J. (Gm)	132	2	66.00	2-39	–	–	–
Powell, M.J. (Nh)	12	0					
Powell, M.J. (Wa)	576	10	57.60	2-16	–	–	–
Pratt, G.J.	17	0					
Pretorius, D.	4654	186	25.02	6-49	7	–	–
Price, R.W.	5422	167	32.46	8-35	10	2	–
Prittipaul, L.R.	372	8	46.50	3-17	–	–	–
Ramprakash, M.R.	2104	32	65.75	3-32	–	–	–
Rayudu, A.T.	254	8	31.75	4-43	–	–	–
Read, C.M.W.	25	0					
Rhodes, J.N.	83	1	83.00	1-13	–	–	–
Rhodes, S.J.	30	0					
Richardson, A.	4887	160	30.54	8-46	4	1	–
Roberts, T.W.	10	0					
Robinson, D.D.J.	215	1	215.00	1- 7	–	–	–
Rogers, B.G.	1039	26	39.96	4-34	–	–	–
Rose, F.A.	7849	296	26.51	7-39	14	2	1+1
Rudolph, J.A.	1152	36	32.00	5-87	2	–	–
Russell, R.C.	68	1	68.00	1- 4	–	–	–
Sadler, J.L.	40	0					
Saggers, M.J.	6887	301	22.88	7-79	15	–	4

F-C	Runs	Wkts	Avge	Best	5wI	10wM	50wS
Saker, N.C.	179	1	179.00	1- 71	–	–	–
Sales, D.J.G.	167	9	18.55	4- 25	–	–	–
Salisbury, I.D.K.	24504	760	32.24	8- 60	34	6	6
Salvi, A.M.	1505	74	20.33	5- 39	5	1	–
Sampson, P.J.	261	11	23.72	3- 52	–	–	–
Saqlain Mushtaq	16213	717	22.61	8- 65	54	14	5+1
Savill, T.E.	882	16	55.12	3- 86	–	–	–
Sayers, J.J.	12	0					
Schofield, C.P.	5262	170	30.95	6-120	4	–	–
Scott, G.M.	11	0					
Sehwag, V.	2035	50	40.70	4- 32	–	–	–
Selwood, S.A.	95	2	47.50	1- 8	–	–	–
Shabbir Ahmed	5097	226	22.55	7- 70	13	–	0+1
Shafayat, B.M.	148	1	148.00	1- 22	–	–	–
Shah, O.A.	682	17	40.11	3- 33	–	–	–
Shahid Afridi	4049	144	28.11	6-101	5	–	–
Shahid, N.	2146	45	47.68	3- 91	–	–	–
Shantry, A.J.	153	7	21.85	3- 8	–	–	–
Sharif, Z.K.	532	9	59.11	4- 98	–	–	–
Sharpe, T.J.	676	10	67.60	3- 70	–	–	–
Shaw, A.D.	7	0					
Sheikh, M.A.	1391	36	38.63	4- 36	–	–	–
Sheriyar, A.	14132	480	29.44	7-130	22	3	4
Shoaib Akhtar	8749	326	26.83	6- 11	19	–	0+1
Shoaib Malik	3121	128	24.38	7- 81	5	1	–
Shreck, C.E.	878	23	38.17	5-100	1	–	–
Sibanda, V.	280	10	28.00	4- 30	–	–	–
Sidebottom, R.J.	4429	179	24.74	7- 97	8	1	–
Sillence, R.J.	957	27	35.44	5- 63	2	–	–
Silverwood, C.E.W.	11719	439	26.69	7- 93	20	1	2
Singh, A. (Wo)	111	0					
Singh, A. (CU)	19	0					
Smith, A.M.	13031	525	24.82	8- 73	22	5	5
Smith, B.F.	350	3	116.66	1- 5	–	–	–
Smith, E.T.	59	0					
Smith, G.C.	120	2	60.00	1- 9	–	–	–
Smith, G.J.	9758	355	27.48	8- 53	13	2	2
Smith, N.M.K.	13968	374	37.34	7- 42	18	–	–
Smith, R.A.	993	14	70.92	2- 11	–	–	–
Snape, J.N.	5228	108	48.40	5- 65	1	–	–
Solanki, V.S.	3309	72	45.95	5- 69	3	1	–
Somerville-Hendrie, J.W.	213	4	53.25	3-124	–	–	–
Spearman, C.M.	55	1	55.00	1- 37	–	–	–
Spires, J.A.S.	768	20	38.40	5-165	1	–	–
Srinath, J.	14027	533	26.31	9- 76	23	3	1
Sriram, S.	3100	73	42.46	4- 26	–	–	–
Stephenson, J.P.	12497	383	32.62	7- 44	11	1	–
Stevens, D.I.	333	3	111.00	1- 5	–	–	–
Stewart, A.J.	446	3	148.66	1- 7	–	–	–
Strauss, A.J.	58	1	58.00	1- 27	–	–	–
Streak, H.H.	9443	343	27.53	7- 69	9	–	1
Stubbings, S.D.	77	0					
Suppiah, A.V.	99	4	24.75	3- 46	–	–	–
Sutcliffe, I.J.	329	9	36.55	2- 21	–	–	–
Swanepoel, P.J.	129	3	43.00	2- 40	–	–	–
Swann, A.J.	308	5	61.60	2- 30	–	–	–

F-C	Runs	Wkts	Avge	Best	5wI	10wM	50wS
Swann, G.P.	7791	254	30.67	7- 33	12	2	1
Symonds, A.	5650	150	37.66	6-105	1	–	–
Taibu, T.	124	1	124.00	1- 58	–	–	–
Taylor, B.V.	2493	71	35.11	5- 90	1	–	–
Taylor, C.G.	220	3	73.33	3-126	–	–	–
Taylor, D.B.	100	2	50.00	1- 35	–	–	–
Ten Doeschate, R.N.	122	0					
Thomas, I.J.	32	1	32.00	1- 26	–	–	–
Thomas, S.D.	14160	461	30.71	8- 50	18	1	5
Thorburn, M.	523	12	43.58	2- 53	–	–	–
Thornicroft, N.D.	305	4	76.25	2- 51	–	–	–
Thorpe, A.M.	32	0					
Thorpe, G.P.	1378	26	53.00	4- 40	–	–	–
Todd, M.J.	92	1	92.00	1- 92	–	–	–
Tomlinson, J.A.	1542	29	53.17	6- 63	1	–	–
Tredwell, J.C.	1606	40	40.15	4- 48	–	–	–
Trego, P.D.	1272	29	43.86	4- 84	–	–	–
Tremlett, C.T.	2667	95	28.07	6- 51	3	–	–
Trescothick, M.E.	1438	36	39.94	4- 36	–	–	–
Trott, B.J.	2461	78	31.55	6- 13	4	1	–
Trott, I.J.L.	435	11	39.54	7- 39	1	–	–
Troughton, J.O.	199	0					
Tudor, A.J.	7751	274	28.28	7- 48	13	–	–
Turner, R.J.	58	0					
Udal, S.D.	20455	604	33.86	8- 50	29	4	7
Van Jaarsveld, M.	298	6	49.66	1- 1	–	–	–
Vaas, W.P.U.C.J.	10202	404	25.25	7- 71	16	2	0+2
Vaughan, M.P.	4978	113	44.05	4- 39	–	–	–
Vermeulen, M.A.	392	13	30.15	3- 26	–	–	–
Vettori, D.L.	8157	263	31.01	7- 87	16	1	–
Wagg, G.G.	593	17	34.88	4- 43	–	–	–
Wagh, M.A.	3533	78	45.29	7-222	2	–	–
Walker, G.W.	161	1	161.00	1- 92	–	–	–
Walker, M.J.	563	9	62.55	1- 3	–	–	–
Waqar Younis	21143	951	22.23	8- 17	63	14	4+1
Ward, I.J.	197	3	65.66	1- 1	–	–	–
Ward, T.R.	694	9	77.11	2- 10	–	–	–
Warne, S.K.	22220	850	26.14	8- 71	40	6	3+1
Warren, N.A.	90	2	45.00	2- 48	–	–	–
Warren, R.J.	0	0					
Wasim Akram	22549	1042	21.64	8- 30	70	16	5
Webley, T.	344	6	57.33	2- 57	–	–	–
Weekes, P.N.	10490	259	40.50	8- 39	4	–	–
Welch, G.	10752	336	32.00	6- 30	11	1	3
Wells, V.J.	7920	302	26.22	5- 18	5	–	–
Welton, G.E.	5	0					
Weston, R.M.S.	104	2	52.00	1- 15	–	–	–
Weston, W.P.C.	650	4	162.50	2- 39	–	–	–
Westwood, I.J.	57	0					
Wharf, A.G.	5391	161	33.48	5- 63	2	–	1
Wharton, L.J.	2167	54	40.12	6- 62	3	–	–
Whiley, M.J.A.	1797	27	66.55	3- 60	–	–	–
White, C.	10821	379	28.55	8- 55	11	–	–
White, R.A.	221	6	36.83	2- 30	–	–	–
Wigley, D.H.	396	5	79.20	2- 56	–	–	–
Willoughby, C.M.	6442	269	23.94	6- 44	9	2	0+1

F-C	Runs	Wkts	Avge	Best	5wI	10wM	50wS
Windows, M.G.N.	131	2	65.50	1- 6	–	–	–
Wood, J.	10544	314	33.57	7-58	11	–	1
Wood, M.J. (Sm)	62	0					
Wood, M.J. (Y)	38	2	19.00	1- 4	–	–	–
Wright, D.G.	4021	115	34.96	6-39	1	–	–
Wright, L.J.	95	0					
Yardy, M.H.	475	3	158.33	1-13	–	–	–
Yates, G.	7025	184	38.17	6-64	5	–	–
Yuvraj Singh	359	9	39.88	3-25	–	–	–
Zondeki, M.	1308	41	31.90	5-64	1	–	–

STOP PRESS

ICC UNDER-19 WORLD CUP

Pakistan beat West Indies to win the 2004 ICC Under-19 World Cup played in Bangladesh. Previous Under-19 world champions were Australia (1988 and 2002), England (1998) and India (2000).

Semi-Finals at Bangabandhu National Stadium, Dhaka.
On 29 February 2004 (day/night). Pakistan beat India (won toss) by five wickets. India 169 (47.3 overs). Pakistan 171-5 (44.5 overs) (Tariq Mahmood 45*, Fawad Alam 43*). Match award: Tariq Mahmood.

On 2 March 2004 (day/night). West Indies (won toss) beat England by 94 runs. West Indies 249-6 (50 overs) (D.Ramdin 72, Zamal Khan 60*, A.B.Fudadin 51, X.M.Marshall 45, A.J.Harrison 3-28). England 155 (39.1 overs) (T.T.Bresnan 41, R.Rampaul 3-27). Match award: Dinesh Ramdin.

Final at Bangabandhu National Stadium, Dhaka.
On 5 March 2004 (day/night). Pakistan beat West Indies by 25 runs. Pakistan 230-9 (50 overs) (Asif Iqbal 54, Salman Qadir 42), R.Bachan 3-34). West Indies 205 (47.1 overs) (Tariq Mahmood 3-34). Match award: Asif Iqbal.

ICC SIX NATIONS CHALLENGE

The USA qualified for the 12th place in September's ICC Champions Trophy by finishing 0.028 ahead of Scotland on net run-rate in the ICC Six Nations Challenge staged in Sharjah and Dubai in February and March. Both countries finished level on points (six) with Namibia, Holland and the UAE. Canada lost all its five matches.

ICC Champions Trophy Groupings
Pool 1: Australia, New Zealand and USA. Pool 2: South Africa, West Indies and Bangladesh. Pool 3: Pakistan, India and Kenya. Pool 4: Sri Lanka, India and Zimbabwe.

10.30am STARTS TO TESTS IN ENGLAND

Six of this season's Test matches will start at 10.30am following an agreement between the ECB and Channel 4 television. The exception is the Second Test against New Zealand at Headingley, Leeds. Broadcast by Sky Sports, it will begin at 11.00am.

LEADING CURRENT PLAYERS

These are the leading career batting/bowling averages and wicket-keeping/fielding aggregates among players currently registered for first-class county cricket at the time of going to press (3 March 2004). All figures are to the end of the 2003 English season.

BATTING
(Qualification: 100 innings)

	Runs	Avge
D.S.Lehmann	19891	56.99
R.T.Ponting	12576	55.89
A.Flower	12031	53.95
G.A.Hick	35916	53.13
S.G.Law	21179	50.66
M.T.G.Elliott	12034	49.11
D.R.Martyn	11452	48.73
C.L.Hooper	22341	48.04
M.R.Ramprakash	23223	47.39
J.P.Crawley	18850	46.54
M.W.Goodwin	9155	46.23
G.P.Thorpe	19644	44.95
H.H.Gibbs	9725	44.40
N.V.Knight	12556	43.90
J.Cox	16824	43.69
A.Habib	7388	43.45
M.P.Maynard	23873	42.63
A.D.Brown	11051	42.50
B.J.Hodge	8147	42.43
M.J.Di Venuto	12682	42.13
N.Hussain	19872	42.10
A.J.Strauss	5438	41.83
A.Symonds	10295	41.51
B.F.Smith	12738	40.18
P.D.Bowler	18533	40.11
E.T.Smith	7334	40.07
A.J.Hollioake	8964	40.0178
I.J.Ward	6923	40.0173
M.A.Butcher	13400	39.76
S.G.Koenig	7033	39.73
M.J.Powell (Gm)	6096	39.58
T.L.Penney	7975	39.28
M.A.Wagh	6302	38.90
M.B.Loye	9411	38.88
D.J.Bicknell	16778	38.21
M.P.Vaughan	12182	38.06

BOWLING
(Qualification: 100 wickets)

	Wkts	Avge
Danish Kaneria	211	21.07
Shabbir Ahmed	226	22.55
Saqlain Mushtaq	717	22.61
M.J.Saggers	301	22.88
A.J.Hall	200	23.17
A.J.Bichel	454	24.31
Shoaib Malik	128	24.38
Azhar Mahmood	331	24.41
M.P.Bicknell	982	24.58
R.J.Sidebottom	179	24.74
A.M.Smith	525	24.82
A.R.Caddick	897	24.85
K.J.Dean	332	24.90
D.Pretorius	186	25.02
R.J.Kirtley	465	25.15
G.M.Hamilton	239	25.38
Mushtaq Ahmed	991	25.83
P.M.Hutchison	168	25.92
M.S.Kasprowicz	779	26.00
S.K.Warne	850	26.14
Mohammad Akram	279	26.20
D.G.Cork	722	26.22
Kabir Ali	177	26.23
M.J.Hoggard	290	26.32
R.L.Johnson	426	26.42
S.P.Kirby	151	26.56
C.E.W.Silverwood	439	26.69
J.D.Lewry	405	26.75
I.J.Harvey	338	26.78
Shoaib Akhtar	326	26.83
J.Lewis	412	26.91
Mohammad Sami	131	26.923
D.Gough	727	26.928

WICKET-KEEPING

	Total	Ct	St
R.C.Russell	1319	1191	128
S.J.Rhodes	1215	1095	120
W.K.Hegg	877	793	84
R.J.Blakey	835	778	57
P.A.Nixon	721	669	52
R.J.Turner	665	620	45
K.J.Piper	536	502	34

FIELDING

G.A.Hick	571
C.L.Hooper	356
M.P.Maynard	357
N.Hussain	337
S.G.Law	318
C.J.Adams	299
G.P.Thorpe	269
M.W.Alleyne	267
D.P.Ostler	259
N.V.Knight	252

LIMITED-OVERS CAREER RECORDS

Compiled by **PHILIP BAILEY**

The following career records, to the end of the 2003 season, include all players currently registered with first-class counties. These records are restricted to performances in limited-overs matches of 'List A' status as defined by the Association of Cricket Statisticians and Historians. The following matches qualify for List A status and are included in the figures that follow: Limited-Overs Internationals; Other international matches (e.g. Commonwealth Games, 'A' team internationals); Premier domestic limited-overs tournaments in Test status countries; Official tourist matches against the main first-class teams.

The following matches do NOT qualify for inclusion: World Cup warm-up games; Tourist matches against first-class teams outside the major domestic competitions (e.g. Universities, Minor Counties, etc.); Festival, pre-season friendly games and Twenty20 Cup matches.

	M	Runs	Avge	HS	100	50	Wkts	Avge	Best	Ct/St
Adams, C.J.	291	9253	40.76	163	18	58	32	37.93	5-16	143
Adams, J.H.K.	3	28	9.33	17	–	–	0	–	–	2
Adnan, M.H.	21	581	36.31	101*	1	3	–	–	–	7
Adshead, S.J.	8	154	30.80	77*	–	1	–	–	–	9/3
Afzaal, U.	95	2509	35.33	105	1	20	33	26.48	3- 8	26
Ali, Kabir	77	397	13.23	92	–	1	112	22.47	5-36	17
Ali, Kadeer	14	365	28.07	66	–	3	1	25.00	1- 4	4
Ali, S.M.B.	33	85	9.44	19	–	–	36	33.08	4-34	5
Alleyne, D.	30	256	11.13	58	–	1	–	–	–	22/6
Alleyne, M.W.	405	7991	27.94	134*	9	33	379	29.74	5-27	168/1
Ambrose, T.R.	39	904	25.11	95	–	5	–	–	–	38/3
Anderson, J.M.	32	37	5.28	8	–	–	57	22.26	4-25	5
Anderson, R.S.G.	30	127	7.47	22	–	–	27	41.07	3-28	1
Andrew, G.M.	12	53	8.83	23	–	–	12	26.66	3-38	5
Averis, J.M.M.	109	288	10.28	23*	–	–	166	23.83	6-23	14
Azhar Mahmood	198	2391	19.76	100*	1	7	197	33.77	6-18	63
Bailey, T.M.B.	64	593	22.80	52	–	1	–	–	–	61/28
Ball, M.C.J.	238	1519	13.56	51	–	1	230	32.01	5-33	115
Bassano, C.W.G.	45	1282	34.64	126*	4	5	–	–	–	8
Batty, G.J.	72	912	19.00	83*	–	4	55	35.43	4-36	26
Batty, J.N.	98	761	14.63	55*	–	1	–	–	–	99/16
Bell, I.R.	47	1469	36.72	125	1	11	9	35.22	5-41	12
Benham, C.C.	1	0	0.00	0	–	–	–	–	–	–
Benning, J.G.E.	5	84	16.80	25	–	–	7	18.14	4-43	3
Betts, M.M.	76	304	10.13	21	–	–	89	30.76	4-22	12
Bichel, A.J.	144	1407	22.69	100	1	3	195	25.89	7-20	4
Bicknell, D.J.	231	7422	37.86	135*	10	51	3	27.33	1-11	55
Bicknell, M.P.	322	1479	15.73	66*	–	2	414	25.06	7-30	76
Bishop, J.E.	23	58	5.80	16*	–	–	26	28.61	3-33	4
Blackwell, I.D.	137	2965	25.78	111	1	18	105	33.54	4-24	39
Blain, J.A.R.	26	56	8.00	11	–	–	40	27.65	5-24	5
Blakey, R.J.	378	7591	31.11	130*	3	37	–	–	–	367/59
Bloomfield, T.F.	58	85	7.72	15	–	–	56	34.19	4-17	11
Bopara, R.S.	12	147	14.70	46	–	1	3	45.00	2-28	1
Botha, A.G.	44	408	17.73	60*	–	1	35	30.71	3-16	20
Bowler, P.D.	322	9350	32.02	138*	7	72	13	40.84	3-31	119/2
Brandy, D.G.	3	50	25.00	35	–	–	–	–	–	–
Brant, S.A.	20	22	11.00	14*	–	–	31	24.70	4-25	8
Breese, G.R.	19	217	18.08	44*	–	1	17	28.76	3-24	7
Bresnan, T.T.	38	306	20.40	61	–	1	36	30.05	3-29	12
Bressington, A.N.	9	144	24.00	54	–	1	8	37.50	3-21	5
Bridge, G.D.	37	284	16.70	50*	–	1	43	27.88	4-20	6
Brignull, D.S.	12	31	7.75	9*	–	–	16	26.00	3-40	6
Brinkley, J.E.	59	340	11.72	67	–	1	52	35.69	3-50	7
Brophy, G.L.	36	484	19.36	54	–	2	–	–	–	33/7

Brown, A.D.	306	8903	31.68	268	16	38	10	34.90	3-39	100
Brown, D.R.	238	3827	22.77	108	1	20	275	26.58	5-31	60
Brown, J.F.	77	64	5.81	16	–	–	69	37.00	4-26	18
Brown, M.J.	1	18	18.00	18	–	–	–	–	–	–
Bruce, J.T.A.	4	6	6.00	6*	–	–	4	25.00	3-45	–
Bryant, J.D.C.	57	1588	34.52	105*	1	12	–	–	–	13
Burns, M.	196	4175	25.77	115*	2	27	57	30.08	4-39	84/14
Burrows, T.G.	1	1	1.00	1	–	–	–	–	–	1
Butcher, M.A.	152	3078	27.98	104	1	17	49	45.10	3-23	48
Caddick, A.R.	220	710	10.44	39	–	–	286	26.18	6-30	33
Carberry, M.A.	20	236	13.88	79	–	1	1	21.00	1-21	5
Carter, N.M.	54	431	13.90	75	–	1	74	26.06	5-31	6
Cawdron, M.J.	78	382	14.69	50	–	1	92	28.70	4-17	8
Chapple, G.	203	1235	15.83	81*	–	6	225	29.30	6-18	41
Chilton, M.J.	92	2216	28.77	103	3	10	31	25.32	5-26	26
Clapp, D.A.	3	57	19.00	43	–	–	3	15.33	3-46	–
Clarke, A.J.	34	33	3.66	9	–	–	44	24.27	4-28	8
Clarke, M.J.	41	1268	46.96	101*	1	9	8	27.75	3-57	15
Clarke, R.	44	811	23.85	98*	–	4	28	40.46	3-48	23
Clifford, J.I.	5	9	4.50	5*	–	–	–	–	–	7/1
Clough, G.D.	42	317	19.81	42*	–	–	41	35.36	4-32	15
Coetzer, A.J.	5	56	14.00	30	–	–	–	–	–	3
Collingwood, P.D.	170	4200	30.21	118*	2	25	94	34.63	4-31	80
Compton, N.R.D.	5	129	64.50	86*	–	1	0	–	–	1
Cook, A.N.	3	52	26.00	27	–	–	–	–	–	2
Cook, J.W.	75	1568	25.70	130	2	6	46	26.28	4-35	21
Cook, S.J.	87	801	16.02	67*	–	2	91	32.92	4-30	12
Cork, D.G.	225	3246	21.07	93	–	17	285	27.26	6-21	90
Cosker, D.A.	108	261	8.15	27*	–	–	118	30.84	5-54	32
Cottey, P.A.	269	4794	24.21	96	–	26	21	37.76	4-56	89
Coverdale, P.S.	3	33	11.00	19	–	–	–	–	–	2
Cowan, A.P.	135	976	13.94	45	–	–	167	27.59	5-14	45
Cox, J.	175	5206	31.93	130	5	35	4	36.00	3-28	60
Craven, V.J.	29	468	18.00	59	–	2	9	23.55	4-22	10
Crawley, J.P.	241	6648	31.35	114	6	41	0	–	–	69/4
Croft, R.D.B.	324	4882	23.24	119	2	23	338	31.64	6-20	79
Crook, S.P.	3	1	1.00	1	–	–	1	83.00	1-27	1
Currie, M.R.	6	145	29.00	94	–	1	–	–	–	1
Dagnall, C.E.	44	167	11.13	28	–	–	60	23.46	4-34	5
Dakin, J.M.	173	2512	20.25	179	2	2	146	29.08	5-30	33
Dale, A.	299	6501	28.51	110	2	32	252	31.09	6-22	66
Dalrymple, J.W.M.	32	469	23.45	52	–	1	28	29.96	4-14	13
Danish Kaneria	52	69	5.75	15	–	–	90	21.66	5-24	13
Davies, A.M.	46	148	8.70	31*	–	–	48	27.79	4-13	7
Davies, A.P.	54	111	12.33	24	–	–	77	24.55	5-19	8
Davies, S.M.	2	13	13.00	13	–	–	–	–	–	–
Davis, M.J.G.	132	760	16.52	37	–	–	119	37.61	4-14	30
Dawson, R.K.J.	45	200	7.69	41	–	–	49	26.34	4-13	15
Dean, K.J.	107	221	10.04	16*	–	–	125	28.86	5-32	20
DeFreitas, P.A.J.	467	5115	18.80	90	–	13	534	27.61	5-13	100
Denning, N.A.	6	3	3.00	2	–	–	6	41.50	3-22	–
Dennington, M.J.	3	29	29.00	18*	–	–	1	102.00	1-51	–
Di Venuto, M.	190	5624	32.88	173*	7	31	5	34.60	1-10	70
Dumelow, N.R.C.	35	466	17.25	52	–	1	34	34.44	3-24	1
Durston, W.J.	12	221	27.62	51*	–	2	3	69.00	1-32	1
Dutch, K.P.	151	2097	20.76	93	–	8	149	27.85	6-40	62
Ealham, M.A.	342	5482	24.80	112	1	24	378	27.91	6-53	85
Elliott, M.T.G.	91	2905	37.24	156	9	13	0	–	–	34
Farrow, J.C.	2	–	–	–	–	–	2	54.50	2-81	–

Name	M	Runs	Avg	HS	100	50	Wkts	Avg	BB	Ct/St
Ferley, R.S.	3	6	6.00	6	–	–	6	17.00	3-59	–
Ferraby, N.J.	2	1	0.50	1	–	–	0	–	–	–
Fisher, I.D.	32	78	6.50	20	–	–	35	24.68	3-20	7
Flintoff, A.	188	4250	27.77	143	3	23	160	23.13	4-11	78
Flower, A.	326	10849	38.60	145	10	85	1	103.00	1-21	239/48
Foster, J.S.	49	621	20.70	56*	–	2	–	–	–	62/13
Francis, J.D.	27	818	40.90	103*	1	6	–	–	–	4
Francis, S.R.G.	37	169	15.36	33*	–	–	33	41.96	4-60	11
Franks, P.J.	108	1124	21.61	84*	–	3	139	26.89	6-27	18
Frost, T.	41	224	14.93	47	–	–	–	–	–	33/7
Fulton, D.P.	78	1405	19.78	82	–	5	0	–	–	41
Gait, A.I.	30	725	26.85	138*	1	2	–	–	–	8
Gale, A.W.	3	35	11.66	17	–	–	–	–	–	1
Gallian, J.E.R.	181	5070	31.29	134	7	29	55	32.87	5-15	57
Gazzard, C.M.	16	376	25.06	81	–	3	–	–	–	18/1
Gibbs, H.H.	224	6701	34.36	153	15	33	2	28.50	1-16	99
Gidman, A.P.R.	35	725	29.00	73	–	2	13	37.00	3-26	14
Giles, A.F.	185	1813	21.08	107	1	5	234	24.38	5-21	56
Goodwin, M.W.	195	5826	34.27	167	10	34	7	43.71	1- 9	55
Gough, D.	316	1645	12.95	72*	–	1	455	24.09	7-27	53
Gray, A.K.D.	23	126	12.60	30*	–	–	20	31.75	4-34	4
Grayson, A.P.	232	3164	20.02	82*	–	9	205	32.51	4-25	65
Green, J.A.G.	1	7	7.00	7	–	–	–	–	–	1
Greenidge, C.G.	42	66	6.00	20	–	–	43	37.09	3-22	13
Gunter, N.E.L.	6	10	3.33	5	–	–	0	–	–	2
Guy, S.M.	3	14	7.00	13	–	–	–	–	–	3
Habib, A.	149	2813	26.53	111	1	12	2	12.50	2- 5	52
Hall, A.J.	132	2829	32.51	129*	3	14	119	30.36	4-33	36
Hamblin, J.R.C.	40	547	17.09	61	–	2	28	31.07	4-29	12
Hamilton, G.M.	111	1312	22.62	76	–	4	128	24.42	5-16	17
Hancock, T.H.C.	203	3996	21.95	135	2	17	47	24.72	6-58	65
Haq, R.M.	20	135	27.00	55*	–	1	14	48.21	4-36	1
Hardinges, M.A.	31	281	12.21	65	–	1	23	39.39	4-19	11
Harmison, S.J.	57	57	4.07	11*	–	–	62	34.87	4-43	10
Harris, A.J.	109	150	6.25	16*	–	–	138	30.09	5-35	25
Harrison, D.S.	17	138	17.25	37*	–	–	16	35.75	5-26	3
Harrity, M.A.	52	30	6.00	15	–	–	76	26.01	5-42	10
Harvey, I.J.	223	4290	24.79	96	–	21	359	20.33	5-19	63
Havell, P.M.R.	2						0			–
Haynes, J.J.	13	126	21.00	59*	–	1	–	–	–	18/3
Hayward, M.	95	140	9.33	19*	–	–	131	28.01	5-37	19
Hegg, W.K.	380	3061	20.40	81	–	5	–	–	–	432/57
Hemp, D.L.	192	3960	25.71	121	5	19	8	20.87	4-32	70
Hewson, D.R.	64	1145	22.01	69	–	5	17	24.00	4-25	19
Hibberd, J.	2	26	26.00	26	–	–	4	12.00	4-48	–
Hick, G.A.	569	19833	42.19	172*	37	129	225	29.47	5-19	258
Hildreth, J.C.	10	124	13.77	30	–	–	1	44.00	1-44	4
Hindley, R.J.E.	4	50	25.00	38	–	–	3	30.66	2-27	2
Hodd, A.J.	2	4	2.00	3	–	–	–	–	–	3
Hodge, B.J.	109	3502	36.10	164	5	20	25	33.16	5-28	43
Hodgkinson, R.	1						2	18.00	2-36	–
Hoffmann, P.J.C.	21	101	14.42	33	–	–	19	39.73	3-40	3
Hogg, G.B.	104	1179	26.20	71*	–	4	87	31.00	4-50	44
Hogg, K.W.	38	150	12.50	24	–	–	46	22.86	4-20	8
Hoggard, M.J.	96	52	3.46	7*	–	–	146	22.13	5-28	12
Hollioake, A.J.	269	5620	27.96	117*	2	27	343	22.83	6-17	85
Holloway, P.C.L.	133	2751	27.51	117	3	17	–	–	–	53/8
Hooper, C.L.	442	13061	40.31	145	15	83	387	34.10	5-41	237
Hopkinson, C.D.	21	245	16.33	67*	–	1	9	43.55	3-19	13

Name	M	Runs	Avg	HS	100	50	Wkts	Avg	Best	Ct/St
Horton, P.J.	2	49	24.50	26	–	–	–	–	–	–
Huggins, T.B.	1	2	2.00	2	–	–	–	–	–	–
Hughes, J.	4	91	22.75	51	–	1	–	–	–	1
Hunt, T.A.	4	0	0.00	0	–	–	2	56.00	1-24	1
Hussain, N.	361	10583	36.49	161*	10	71	–	–	–	159
Hussey, D.J.	6	265	88.33	118*	1	–	6	26.83	3-48	7
Hutchison, P.M.	50	97	8.81	20	–	–	67	21.65	4-29	7
Hutton, B.L.	70	924	21.00	77	–	5	28	34.96	5-45	30
Innes, K.J.	82	789	21.32	55	–	2	79	31.84	5-41	25
Irani, R.C.	262	5874	28.65	124	3	35	309	25.22	5-26	65
Jaques, P.A.	24	896	40.72	117	2	6	–	–	–	4
Jefferson, W.I.	34	1160	35.15	132	3	7	–	–	–	20
Johnson, R.L.	153	999	12.64	53	–	1	175	31.61	5-50	18
Jones, G.O.	32	564	23.50	74*	–	2	–	–	–	31/8
Jones, H.R.	3	88	29.33	72	–	1	–	–	–	–
Jones, P.S.	119	374	12.89	27	–	–	171	27.63	5-23	22
Jones, S.P.	5	17	17.00	12*	–	–	1	175.00	1-39	–
Joyce, E.C.	60	1425	29.68	77	–	9	2	31.00	2-10	22
Kasprowicz, M.S.	167	909	14.90	40	–	–	208	28.37	5-60	32
Keedy, G.	16	13	6.50	10*	–	–	16	33.50	5-30	1
Keegan, C.B.	55	400	17.39	50	–	1	81	25.14	5-17	9
Kendall, W.S.	122	1951	21.43	110*	1	5	4	53.50	2-48	57
Kenway, D.A.	91	2348	28.28	120*	2	14	–	–	–	47/7
Key, R.W.T.	97	2647	31.14	114	1	19	–	–	–	16
Khan, A.	19	70	6.36	21	–	–	20	33.30	4-26	4
Khan, R.M.	3	36	12.00	29	–	–	–	–	–	1
Khalid, S.A.	4	4	4.00	3*	–	–	3	45.66	2-40	–
Killeen, N.	146	514	9.51	32	–	–	207	23.87	6-31	25
King, R.E.	2	2	1.00	2	–	–	2	33.00	2-39	1
Kirby, S.P.	20	35	3.88	15	–	–	19	43.68	3-27	4
Kirtley, R.J.	139	305	10.51	30*	–	–	209	22.84	5-33	43
Klusener, L.	214	4744	40.89	142*	3	26	235	29.85	6-49	52
Knight, N.V.	359	11262	37.04	151	22	61	2	44.50	1-14	158
Knox, S.T.	18	377	23.56	108*	1	–	–	–	–	6
Koenig, S.G.	49	900	19.14	116	2	1	–	–	–	8
Kruger, G.J.P.	44	34	8.50	20*	–	–	62	25.06	6-23	6
Lamb, G.A.	5	37	9.25	15	–	–	1	37.00	1-27	–
Laraman, A.W.	27	177	11.80	33	–	–	34	25.32	6-42	7
Law, S.G.	318	9368	33.81	163	19	42	89	35.33	5-26	128
Leatherdale, D.A.	290	4435	21.63	80	–	19	152	22.67	5- 9	116
Lehmann, D.S.	300	10569	45.16	191	17	72	117	25.47	4-26	88
Lewis, J.	109	424	12.11	33*	–	–	122	31.26	4-22	22
Lewis, J.J.B.	201	4007	28.41	102	1	20	0	–	–	34
Lewry, J.D.	66	182	7.28	16	–	–	82	28.81	4-29	12
Lockhart, D.R.	28	365	14.60	75	–	2	–	–	–	12
Logan, R.J.	42	144	9.00	24	–	–	51	32.68	5-24	13
Loudon, A.G.R.	5	85	21.25	53	–	1	0	–	–	–
Louw, J.	18	345	26.53	72	–	3	22	28.31	5-43	–
Loye, M.B.	212	6254	34.93	124*	8	40	–	–	–	54
Lumb, M.J.	51	1126	26.18	92	–	7	–	–	–	15
Lungley, T.	36	234	13.76	45	–	–	51	23.78	4-28	7
McCoubrey, A.G.A.M.	6	13	4.33	11	–	–	3	42.00	2-20	–
MacGill, S.C.G.	69	85	5.31	18	–	–	117	23.04	5-40	17
McGrath, A.	175	4311	31.01	109*	3	24	30	33.36	4-41	57
McLean, N.A.M.	158	1268	14.24	50*	–	1	201	26.74	5-26	28
McMahon, P.J.	1	0	0.00	0	–	–	0	–	–	–
MacRae, N.J.	10	160	26.66	83	–	1	–	–	–	–
Maddy, D.L.	240	5763	29.70	151	6	34	140	28.70	4-16	87
Mahmood, S.I.	11	19	6.33	11	–	–	14	25.85	3-28	1

Name	M	Runs	Avge	HS	100	50	Wkts	Avge	Best	Ct/St
Maiden, G.I.	11	98	19.60	62	–	1	7	47.57	2-27	4
Malik, M.N.	20	30	10.00	11	–	–	10	66.00	2-34	4
Martin, P.J.	247	497	13.07	35*	–	–	347	22.15	5-16	45
Martin-Jenkins, R.S.C.	123	1089	12.96	68*	–	2	136	27.88	4-22	28
Mascarenhas, A.D.	136	1985	20.05	79	–	12	183	22.30	5-27	35
Mason, M.S.	37	96	8.72	20*	–	–	50	24.58	4-34	5
Masters, D.D.	50	193	10.15	27	–	–	38	44.47	5-20	5
Maunders, J.K.	12	165	13.75	49	–	–	0	–	–	1
Maynard, M.P.	416	12833	36.04	151*	15	76	3	94.66	1-13	177/5
Mees, T.	4	4	4.00	4*	–	–	3	48.00	3-19	–
Middlebrook, J.D.	56	321	14.59	46*	–	–	44	35.02	4-33	21
Mohammad Akram	95	187	9.35	33	–	–	98	32.35	4-19	19
Mohammad Sami	53	142	8.87	20	–	–	80	26.03	4-25	14
Montgomerie, R.R.	159	4951	35.61	129*	4	35	0	–	–	39
Moore, S.C.	2	12	6.00	12	–	–	0	–	–	–
Morgan, E.J.G.	1	–	–	–	–	–	0	–	–	–
Muchall, G.J.	27	716	28.64	87	–	4	1	86.00	1-15	9
Mullally, A.D.	288	502	7.07	38	–	–	337	28.00	6-38	43
Munday, M.K.	1	–	–	–	–	–	1	39.00	1-39	–
Murtagh, T.J.	24	65	6.50	14*	–	–	32	31.34	4-31	5
Mushtaq Ahmed	320	1431	11.35	41	–	–	392	28.20	7-24	55
Mustard, P.	20	212	12.47	41	–	–	–	–	–	23/4
Napier, G.R.	86	1090	17.58	79	–	6	78	22.06	6-29	24
Nash, D.C.	105	1263	21.40	67	–	5	–	–	–	87/15
New, T.J.	3	9	4.50	6	–	–	–	–	–	–
Newby, O.J.	3	3	3.00	3*	–	–	3	54.66	2-60	1
Newman, S.A.	12	228	19.00	49	–	–	–	–	–	2
Nixon, P.A.	286	4733	23.90	101	1	21	0	–	–	299/63
Noon, W.M.	121	778	13.89	46	–	–	–	–	–	89/28
O'Brien, N.J.	1	13	13.00	13	–	–	–	–	–	–
Onions, G.	1	5	5.00	5	–	–	2	29.50	2-59	–
Ormond, J.	99	296	9.54	18*	–	–	127	25.02	4-12	20
Ostler, D.P.	272	7227	32.26	134*	3	50	1	14.00	1- 4	96
Palladino, A.P.	8	17	5.66	16	–	–	12	24.25	3-32	1
Panesar, M.S.	4	23	–	16*	–	–	6	18.00	5-20	1
Parsons, K.A.	186	3718	28.82	121	1	18	106	36.83	4-43	70
Parsons, M.	4	0	0.00	0	–	–	4	42.75	3-70	–
Patel, M.M.	77	229	9.16	27*	–	–	78	31.32	3-22	23
Patel, S.R.	8	108	27.00	44	–	–	4	25.00	2-14	1
Pattison, I.	7	73	14.60	48*	–	–	3	65.66	1-25	3
Pearson, J.A.	3	2	2.33	7	–	–	1	29.00	1-29	1
Peng, N.	66	1682	27.57	121	3	7	–	–	–	14
Penney, T.L.	259	4602	29.12	90	–	19	1	21.00	1- 8	99/2
Peploe, C.T.	1	–	–	–	–	–	1	32.00	1-32	–
Peters, S.D.	102	1672	19.21	82	–	9	–	–	–	25
Pettini, M.L.	58	535	23.26	92*	–	4	–	–	–	7
Phillips, B.J.	41	176	11.00	29	–	–	43	26.69	4-25	12
Phillips, T.J.	7	20	5.00	6	–	–	6	34.83	2-36	2
Pietersen, K.P.	68	1979	42.10	147	4	10	24	61.25	3-39	35
Pipe, D.J.	18	303	23.30	56	–	2	–	–	–	19/5
Piper, K.J.	231	970	14.26	38*	–	–	–	–	–	246/50
Plunkett, L.E.	4	4	4.00	3	–	–	9	17.88	3-38	1
Ponting, R.T.	238	8117	40.78	145	16	45	8	30.62	3-34	92
Pothas, N.	141	2475	36.39	101	1	13	–	–	–	131/25
Powell, M.J. (Gm)	120	2720	28.04	91*	–	13	–	–	–	40
Powell, M.J. (Nh)	14	246	22.36	70	–	2	–	–	–	4
Powell, M.J. (Wa)	91	1663	25.19	101*	1	5	25	29.08	5-40	43
Pratt, A.	62	728	20.80	86	–	3	–	–	–	67/20
Pratt, G.J.	43	1020	30.90	101*	1	6	–	–	–	18

Name	M	Runs	Avge	HS	100	50	Runs	Avge	Best	Ct/St
Pretorius, D.	42	36	3.60	7*	–	–	69	22.33	4-31	4
Prior, M.J.	49	434	12.05	73	–	2	–	–	–	27/5
Prittipaul, L.R.	50	450	13.63	61	–	1	19	44.26	3-33	17
Pyrah, R.M.	4	106	26.50	27	–	–	7	14.00	5-50	2
Ramprakash, M.R.	325	10434	39.82	147*	11	69	45	27.88	5-38	113
Randall, S.J.	21	122	15.25	25	–	–	15	52.06	3-44	7
Read, C.M.W.	149	2167	24.90	119*	1	4	–	–	–	166/35
Rees, T.M.	2	7	7.00	7*	–	–	–	–	–	2
Rhodes, S.J.	456	4167	19.38	105	1	5	0	–	–	509/125
Richards, M.A.	1	1	1.00	–	–	–	–	–	–	–
Richardson, A.	34	63	7.00	18	–	–	36	30.27	5-35	8
Rigby, D.A.J.	2	19	19.00	15*	–	–	–	–	–	1
Roberts, T.W.	19	469	26.05	131	1	2	0	–	–	4
Robinson, D.D.J.	159	3694	26.38	137*	3	19	1	26.00	1- 7	42
Russell, R.C.	478	6620	24.16	119*	2	25	–	–	–	465/98
Sadler, J.L.	14	154	12.83	35	–	–	–	–	–	2
Saggers, M.J.	81	202	9.61	34*	–	–	112	25.76	5-22	20
Sales, D.J.G.	148	3818	32.08	133*	2	25	0	–	–	58
Salisbury, I.D.K.	232	1387	13.08	48*	–	–	231	32.50	5-30	79
Sampson, P.J.	12	33	6.60	16	–	–	12	36.75	3-42	4
Saqlain Mushtaq	298	1224	11.88	38*	–	–	459	22.64	5-20	77
Savill, T.E.	2	50	–	35*	–	–	1	90.00	1-45	1
Sayers, J.J.	1	62	62.00	62	–	1	–	–	–	–
Schofield, C.P.	79	870	20.71	69*	–	2	82	25.03	5-31	21
Scott, B.J.M.	2	15	7.50	11	–	–	–	–	–	–
Scott, G.M.	3	130	43.33	100	1	–	4	26.75	2-32	2
Selwood, S.A.	37	869	31.03	93	–	7	2	31.50	1- 7	8
Shabbir Ahmed	68	264	10.15	38	–	–	103	25.09	5-24	16
Shafayat, B.M.	35	564	17.62	66	–	1	9	31.77	4-35	10
Shah, O.A.	162	4007	29.46	134	5	19	8	31.12	2- 2	55
Shahid, N.	169	2941	24.50	109*	2	12	5	53.40	3-30	53
Shantry, A.J.	2	19	9.50	15	–	–	2	19.00	2-21	1
Shaw, A.D.	85	759	15.48	48	–	–	–	–	–	59/17
Sheriyar, A.	112	127	7.93	19	–	–	126	27.85	4-18	7
Shoaib Akhtar	116	433	12.73	56	–	1	185	22.70	6-16	25
Shoaib Malik	94	1885	36.96	138*	4	8	118	25.83	5-35	41
Shreck, C.E.	9	14	7.00	9	–	–	18	21.94	5-19	3
Sidebottom, R.J.	102	253	11.00	30*	–	–	106	29.75	6-40	21
Sillence, R.J.	7	102	17.00	82	–	1	10	13.60	4-35	1
Silverwood, C.E.W.	169	898	14.48	61	–	4	225	23.70	5-28	26
Singh, A. (Wo)	97	2482	26.68	123	1	18	–	–	–	25
Smith, A.M.	244	499	10.61	26*	–	–	289	25.96	6-39	48
Smith, B.F.	295	7501	30.49	115	2	47	2	52.50	1- 2	99
Smith, C.J.O.	28	496	24.80	60	–	2	–	–	–	20/8
Smith, E.T.	57	1243	24.37	122	1	7	–	–	–	8
Smith, G.J.	101	131	6.23	16*	–	–	149	24.11	5-11	11
Smith, W.R.	6	41	8.20	16	–	–	–	–	–	2
Snape, J.N.	211	2790	22.32	104*	1	8	173	28.88	5-32	77
Solanki, V.S.	208	4556	27.28	164*	5	24	11	43.45	2-40	73
Spearman, C.M.	185	5052	28.38	153	5	31	0	–	–	57
Spires, J.A.S.	1	–	–	–	–	–	1	33.00	1-33	–
Stanger, I.M.	47	374	13.35	44	–	–	14	77.28	3-34	14
Steindl, P.D.	10	52	17.33	18	–	–	7	48.57	3-43	–
Stephenson, J.P.	319	7252	29.36	142	8	38	270	26.40	6-33	119
Stevens, D.I.	107	2661	28.61	133	3	16	12	34.58	2-15	44
Stiff, D.A.	1	–	–	–	–	–	1	27.00	1-27	–
Strauss, A.J.	88	2108	26.02	127	1	15	–	–	–	15
Streak, H.H.	234	2969	23.19	79*	–	9	287	29.94	5-32	59
Stubbings, S.D.	67	1139	20.33	98*	–	4	–	–	–	7

Name	M	Runs	Avg	HS	100	50	Wkts	Avg	Best	Ct/St
Suppiah, A.V.	6	125	20.83	70	–	1	3	40.66	2-36	3
Sutcliffe, I.J.	95	2618	31.16	105*	3	18	–	–	–	19
Sutton, L.D.	68	823	17.51	83	–	3	–	–	–	64/6
Swanepoel, P.J.	7	68	34.00	28*	–	–	11	21.72	3- 9	1
Swann, A.J.	50	1020	28.33	83*	–	7	0	–	–	9
Swann, G.P.	107	1434	18.86	83	–	7	103	28.16	5-35	32
Symonds, A.	256	5877	28.95	143*	1	32	159	30.05	6-14	114
Taylor, B.V.	77	126	6.63	21*	–	–	109	23.29	5-28	12
Taylor, C.G.	69	820	17.08	93	–	2	–	–	–	21/1
Taylor, C.R.	1	28	28.00	28	–	–	–	–	–	–
Ten Doeschate, R.N.	1	–	–	–	–	–	1	39.00	1-39	–
Thomas, I.J.	33	886	28.58	93	–	6	–	–	–	12
Thomas, S.D.	128	1167	15.98	71*	–	1	164	26.57	7-16	23
Thomson, K.	16	46	11.50	17	–	–	15	39.40	3-45	1
Thornicroft, N.D.	5	0	–	0*	–	–	8	18.75	5-42	1
Thorpe, G.P.	349	10611	39.89	145*	9	78	16	40.56	3-21	160
Tomlinson, J.A.	13	14	2.80	6	–	–	12	34.50	2-15	1
Tredwell, J.C.	42	361	15.04	71	–	2	38	29.21	3- 7	14
Tremlett, C.T.	47	164	8.63	30*	–	–	66	22.51	4-25	9
Trescothick, M.E.	214	6776	37.02	137	16	31	55	26.58	4-50	80
Trott, B.J.	34	12	1.71	3	–	–	48	26.20	5-18	6
Trott, I.J.L.	35	993	34.24	108*	1	8	5	20.60	2-32	12
Troughton, J.O.	44	1125	31.25	115*	2	5	8	14.37	4-23	11
Tudor, A.J.	62	340	11.33	29*	–	–	92	23.17	4-26	15
Turk, N.R.K.	3	64	21.33	36	–	–	0	–	–	–
Turner, R.J.	219	3253	26.02	70	–	9	–	–	–	222/33
Udal, S.D.	303	2088	15.58	78	–	8	341	30.42	5-43	99
Van Jaarsveld, M.	114	3495	38.40	123	5	21	4	57.75	1- 0	60
Vaughan, M.P.	209	5050	27.15	125*	1	29	67	29.46	4-22	62
Voros, J.A.	6	15	15.00	11*	–	–	9	23.44	3-28	2
Wagg, G.G.	11	117	16.71	32	–	–	14	27.64	4-50	6
Wagh, M.A.	49	935	21.25	84	–	5	10	54.90	3-35	6
Walker, M.J.	181	4199	28.95	117	3	23	18	23.61	4-24	42
Wallace, M.A.	47	406	14.00	39	–	–	–	–	–	51/12
Ward, I.J.	131	3084	27.53	108	1	19	2	90.50	2-27	26
Warne, S.K.	250	1469	12.44	55	–	1	382	24.95	5-33	101
Warren, N.A.	4	2	1.00	2	–	–	3	50.00	3-34	2
Warren, R.J.	155	2811	24.02	100*	1	13	–	–	–	126/11
Watson, R.R.	21	505	28.05	103*	1	2	10	37.40	3-11	4
Watts, D.F.	7	70	17.50	20*	–	–	–	–	–	1
Webley, T.	2	12	6.00	8	–	–	–	–	–	1
Weekes, P.N.	272	5584	27.50	143*	4	30	294	28.48	4-17	115
Welch, G.	176	1773	18.27	71	–	4	163	33.81	6-31	21
Weston, W.P.C.	148	2732	22.57	134	2	11	1	2.00	1- 2	36
Westwood, I.J.	4	78	19.50	55	–	1	2	69.50	1-28	1
Wharf, A.G.	74	422	12.41	38*	–	–	77	33.55	4-18	15
White, C.	300	5854	25.78	148	3	23	313	25.50	5-19	88
White, R.A.	10	116	11.60	22	–	–	2	18.50	2-18	2
Wigley, D.H.	3	1	0.50	1	–	–	1	137.00	1-58	–
Williamson, J.G.	45	599	14.97	77	–	3	16	48.43	3-38	8
Windows, M.G.N.	186	3975	26.85	117	3	17	0	–	–	67
Wood, J.	157	610	10.33	28*	–	–	174	30.25	5-49	21
Wood, M.J. (Sm)	30	573	22.03	88*	–	4	–	–	–	7
Wood, M.J. (Y)	91	1917	26.62	118*	3	9	3	15.00	3-45	35
Wright, C.M.	35	440	22.00	46*	–	–	48	18.91	5-23	6
Wright, L.J.	4	23	11.50	16	–	–	0	–	–	–
Yardy, M.H.	45	480	15.00	59	–	2	23	39.43	3-30	15
Yates, G.	172	661	14.36	38	–	–	159	32.16	4-34	39

LIMITED-OVERS INTERNATIONALS
CAREER RECORDS

These records, complete to 12 February 2004, include all players registered for county cricket in 2004 at the time of going to press, plus those who have appeared in LOI matches since 11 September 2002 (the start of the 2002-03 ICC Champions Trophy).

ENGLAND – BATTING AND FIELDING

	M	I	NO	HS	Runs	Avge	100	50	Ct/St
C.J.Adams	5	4	–	42	71	17.75	–	–	3
Kabir Ali	1	–	–	–	–	–	–	–	–
M.W.Alleyne	10	8	1	53	151	21.57	–	1	3
J.M.Anderson	27	11	4	8	28	4.00	–	–	3
G.J.Batty	3	2	–	3	3	1.50	–	–	2
M.P.Bicknell	7	6	2	31*	96	24.00	–	–	2
I.D.Blackwell	18	15	1	82	255	18.21	–	1	5
R.J.Blakey	3	2	–	25	25	12.50	–	–	2/1
A.D.Brown	16	16	–	118	354	22.12	1	1	6
D.R.Brown	9	8	4	21	99	24.75	–	–	1
A.R.Caddick	54	38	18	36	249	12.45	–	–	9
R.Clarke	11	5	–	37	66	13.20	–	–	10
P.D.Collingwood	42	41	12	100	996	34.34	1	5	20
D.G.Cork	32	21	3	31*	180	10.00	–	–	6
J.P.Crawley	13	12	1	73	235	21.36	–	2	1/1
R.D.B.Croft	50	36	12	32	345	14.37	–	–	11
P.A.J.DeFreitas	103	66	23	67	690	16.04	–	1	26
M.A.Ealham	64	45	4	45	716	17.46	–	–	9
A.Flintoff	66	58	9	84	1478	30.16	–	11	25
J.S.Foster	11	6	3	13	41	13.66	–	–	13/7
P.J.Franks	1	1	–	4	4	4.00	–	–	1
A.F.Giles	35	20	8	21*	159	13.25	–	–	11
D.Gough	121	72	30	45	469	11.16	–	–	17
A.P.Grayson	2	2	–	6	6	3.00	–	–	1
S.J.Harmison	6	2	1	7	9	9.00	–	–	3
G.A.Hick	120	118	15	126*	3846	37.33	5	27	64
M.J.Hoggard	20	5	2	5	10	3.33	–	–	3
A.J.Hollioake	35	30	6	83*	606	25.25	–	3	13
N.Hussain	88	87	10	115	2332	30.28	1	16	40
R.C.Irani	31	30	5	53	360	14.40	–	1	6
R.L.Johnson	10	4	1	10	16	5.33	–	–	–
R.W.T.Key	2	2	–	11	11	5.50	–	–	–
R.J.Kirtley	10	2	–	1	2	1.00	–	–	5
N.V.Knight	100	100	10	125*	3637	40.41	5	25	44
A.McGrath	10	9	2	52	143	20.42	–	1	4
D.L.Maddy	8	6	–	53	113	18.83	–	1	4
P.J.Martin	20	13	7	6	38	6.33	–	–	1
M.P.Maynard	14	12	1	41	156	14.18	–	–	4
A.D.Mullally	50	25	10	20	86	5.73	–	–	8
M.R.Ramprakash	18	18	4	51	376	26.85	–	1	8
C.M.W.Read	23	13	5	30*	154	19.25	–	–	32/2
S.J.Rhodes	9	8	2	56	107	17.83	–	1	9/2
R.C.Russell	40	31	7	50	423	17.62	–	1	41/6
I.D.K.Salisbury	4	2	1	5	7	7.00	–	–	1
O.A.Shah	15	15	2	62	283	21.76	–	2	6
R.J.Sidebottom	2	1	1	2*	2	–	–	–	–
C.E.W.Silverwood	7	4	–	12	17	4.25	–	–	–
J.N.Snape	10	7	3	38	118	29.50	–	–	5
V.S.Solanki	21	20	2	106	373	20.72	1	1	6
A.J.Strauss	1	1	–	3	3	3.00	–	–	–
G.P.Swann	1	–	–	–	–	–	–	–	–
G.P.Thorpe	82	77	13	89	2380	37.18	–	21	42

ENGLAND – BATTING AND FIELDING (continued)

	M	I	NO	HS	Runs	Avge	100	50	Ct/St
M.E.Trescothick	75	75	3	137	2700	37.50	6	15	29
J.O.Troughton	6	5	1	20	36	9.00	–	–	1
A.J.Tudor	3	2	1	6	9	9.00	–	–	1
S.D.Udal	10	6	4	11*	35	17.50	–	–	1
M.P.Vaughan	39	38	4	83	882	25.94	–	6	10
C.White	51	41	5	57*	568	15.77	–	1	12

ENGLAND – BOWLING

	O	M	R	W	Avge	Best	4wI	R/Over
M.W.Alleyne	61	1	280	10	28.00	3-27	–	4.59
J.M.Anderson	226.2	27	1041	46	22.63	4-25	4	4.59
G.J.Batty	30	–	155	2	77.50	1-35	–	5.16
M.P.Bicknell	68.5	3	347	13	26.69	3-55	–	5.04
I.D.Blackwell	101	3	438	14	31.28	3-26	–	4.33
A.D.Brown	1	–	5	–	–	–	–	5.00
D.R.Brown	54	3	305	7	43.57	2-28	–	5.64
A.R.Caddick	489.3	66	1965	69	28.47	4-19	3	4.01
R.Clarke	45.2	3	220	7	31.42	2-28	–	4.85
P.D.Collingwood	111.1	–	665	16	41.56	4-38	1	5.98
D.G.Cork	295.2	17	1368	41	33.36	3-27	–	4.63
R.D.B.Croft	411	25	1743	45	38.73	3-51	–	4.24
P.A.J.DeFreitas	952	113	3775	115	32.82	4-35	1	3.97
M.A.Ealham	537.5	32	2197	67	32.79	5-15	3	4.08
A.Flintoff	386.2	33	1625	66	24.62	4-14	3	4.20
P.J.Franks	9	–	48	–	–	–	–	5.33
A.F.Giles	260	10	1184	31	38.19	5-57	1	4.55
D.Gough	1098.1	96	4694	188	24.96	5-44	10	4.27
A.P.Grayson	15	–	60	3	20.00	3-40	–	4.00
S.J.Harmison	41.4	1	246	5	49.20	2-39	–	5.90
G.A.Hick	206	6	1026	30	34.20	5-33	1	4.98
M.J.Hoggard	162.4	9	817	27	30.25	5-49	1	5.02
A.J.Hollioake	201.2	4	1019	32	31.84	4-23	2	5.06
R.C.Irani	213.5	5	989	24	41.20	5-26	2	4.62
R.L.Johnson	67	7	239	11	21.72	3-22	–	3.56
R.J.Kirtley	85.3	4	453	9	50.33	2-33	–	5.29
A.McGrath	26	1	126	2	63.00	1-15	–	4.84
P.J.Martin	174.4	9	806	27	29.85	4-44	1	4.61
A.D.Mullally	449.5	48	1728	63	27.42	4-18	2	3.84
M.R.Ramprakash	22	–	108	4	27.00	3-28	–	4.90
I.D.K.Salisbury	31	1	177	5	35.40	3-41	–	5.71
R.J.Sidebottom	14	–	84	2	42.00	1-42	–	6.00
C.E.W.Silverwood	51	–	244	6	40.66	3-43	–	4.78
J.N.Snape	88.1	2	403	13	31.00	3-43	–	4.57
G.P.Swann	5	–	24	–	–	–	–	4.80
G.P.Thorpe	20	1	97	2	48.50	2-15	–	4.85
M.E.Trescothick	7.4	–	45	2	22.50	2- 7	–	5.86
A.J.Tudor	21.1	–	136	4	34.00	2-30	–	6.42
S.D.Udal	95	4	371	8	46.37	2-37	–	3.91
M.P.Vaughan	55.4	–	278	8	34.75	4-22	1	4.99
C.White	394	25	1725	65	26.53	5-21	2	4.37

AUSTRALIA – BATTING AND FIELDING

	M	I	NO	HS	Runs	Avge	100	50	Ct/St
A.J.Bichel	67	36	13	64	471	20.47	–	1	19
N.W.Bracken	17	1	1	7*	7	–	–	–	5
R.J.Campbell	2	2	–	38	54	27.00	–	–	4/1
M.J.Clarke	20	18	5	75*	575	44.23	–	4	8
M.J.Di Venuto	9	9	–	89	241	26.77	–	2	1
M.T.G.Elliott	1	1	–	1	1	1.00	–	–	–
A.C.Gilchrist	185	179	6	172	6280	36.30	10	36	272/38
J.N.Gillespie	65	29	12	26	182	10.70	–	–	3

AUSTRALIA – BATTING AND FIELDING (continued)

	M	I	NO	HS	Runs	Avge	100	50	Ct/St
B.J.Haddin	3	3	–	32	59	19.66	–	–	1/2
I.J.Harvey	68	49	11	48*	689	18.13	–	–	17
N.M.Hauritz	8	4	3	20*	35	35.00	–	–	2
M.L.Hayden	89	85	11	146	3128	42.27	4	20	31
G.B.Hogg	41	25	11	71*	271	19.35	–	2	12
M.E.K.Hussey	1	1	1	17*	17	–	–	–	1
M.S.Kasprowicz	18	8	6	28*	60	30.00	–	–	4
S.M.Katich	5	3	2	18*	31	31.00	–	–	–
S.G.Law	54	51	5	110	1237	26.89	1	7	12
B.Lee	81	34	10	51*	346	14.41	–	1	20
D.S.Lehmann	100	88	19	119	2714	39.33	4	14	20
S.C.G.MacGill	3	2	1	1	1	1.00	–	–	2
G.D.McGrath	185	50	27	11	94	4.08	–	–	23
J.P.Maher	26	20	3	95	438	25.76	–	1	18
D.R.Martyn	143	123	39	144*	3484	41.47	5	20	50
R.T.Ponting	194	190	25	145	6897	41.80	15	36	78
A.Symonds	89	66	12	143*	1833	33.94	1	9	42
S.K.Warne	193	106	28	55	1016	13.02	–	1	80
S.R.Watson	23	15	7	77*	288	36.00	–	1	6
B.A.Williams	22	6	4	13*	27	13.50	–	–	3

AUSTRALIA – BOWLING

	O	M	R	W	Avge	Best	4wI	R/Over
A.J.Bichel	542.5	28	2463	78	31.57	7-20	3	4.53
N.W.Bracken	142	18	552	28	19.71	4-29	1	3.88
M.J.Clarke	72	1	384	12	32.00	4-42	1	5.33
J.N.Gillespie	591.3	56	2492	99	25.17	5-22	4	4.21
I.J.Harvey	519.3	29	2451	83	29.53	4-16	4	4.71
N.M.Hauritz	60	1	308	9	34.22	4-39	1	5.13
M.L.Hayden	1	–	18	–	–	–	–	18.00
G.B.Hogg	321.1	14	1364	39	34.97	3-31	–	4.24
M.E.K.Hussey	3	–	15	–	–	–	–	5.00
M.S.Kasprowicz	154.1	5	774	24	32.25	3-50	–	5.02
S.G.Law	134.3	3	635	12	52.91	2-22	–	4.72
B.Lee	692.1	57	3222	149	21.62	5-27	9	4.65
D.S.Lehmann	216.5	2	1040	37	28.10	3-16	–	4.79
S.C.G.MacGill	30	4	105	6	17.50	4-19	1	3.50
G.D.McGrath	1630.4	218	6356	284	22.38	7-15	14	3.89
D.R.Martyn	132.2	2	704	12	58.66	2-21	–	5.32
R.T.Ponting	25	–	104	3	34.66	1-12	–	4.16
A.Symonds	462.2	11	2295	67	34.25	4-11	2	4.96
S.K.Warne	1766.4	110	7514	291	25.82	5-33	13	4.25
S.R.Watson	136.5	8	632	18	35.11	3-27	–	4.61
B.A.Williams	181.3	18	726	33	22.00	5-22	3	4.00

SOUTH AFRICA – BATTING AND FIELDING

	M	I	NO	HS	Runs	Avge	100	50	Ct/St
P.R.Adams	24	9	5	33*	66	16.50	–	–	7
D.M.Benkenstein	23	20	3	69	305	17.94	–	1	3
N.Boje	91	55	12	129	1197	27.83	2	3	26
M.V.Boucher	165	113	29	70	2075	24.70	–	14	237/11
A.C.Dawson	16	4	3	23*	40	40.00	–	–	7
H.H.Dippenaar	72	60	9	110*	2208	43.29	1	19	24
A.A.Donald	164	40	18	12	94	4.27	–	–	28
S.Elworthy	39	16	8	23	100	12.50	–	–	9
H.H.Gibbs	143	142	11	153	4582	34.97	12	18	59
A.J.Hall	43	32	7	81	586	23.44	–	2	17
M.Hayward	21	5	1	4	3	3.00	–	–	4
J.H.Kallis	190	181	34	139	6858	46.65	12	46	80
J.M.Kemp	14	6	2	46	70	17.50	–	–	6
G.Kirsten	185	185	19	188*	6798	40.95	13	45	62/1

SOUTH AFRICA – BATTING AND FIELDING (continued)

	M	I	NO	HS	Runs	Avge	100	50	Ct/St
L.Klusener	159	127	48	103*	3433	43.45	2	19	32
C.K.Langeveldt	6	1	–	3	3	3.00	–	–	–
N.D.McKenzie	59	51	10	131*	1580	38.53	2	9	19
A.Nel	18	4	2	3*	5	2.50	–	–	4
M.Ntini	90	18	8	16*	71	7.10	–	–	22
J.L.Ontong	16	10	1	32	87	9.66	–	–	8
R.J.Peterson	18	7	1	36	86	14.33	–	–	8
S.M.Pollock	208	134	48	75	2030	23.60	–	7	83
N.Pothas	3	1	–	24	24	24.00	–	–	4/1
A.G.Prince	1	1	1	14*	14	–	–	–	–
J.N.Rhodes	245	220	51	121	5935	35.11	2	33	105
J.A.Rudolph	22	18	4	81	610	43.57	–	4	7
G.C.Smith	43	42	1	99	1513	36.90	–	13	18
E.L.R.Stewart	6	6	2	23*	61	15.25	–	–	5
M.van Jaarsveld	9	6	1	45	124	24.80	–	–	3
M.N.van Wyk	1	1	–	17	17	17.00	–	–	–
C.M.Willoughby	3	2	–	0	0	0.00	–	–	–
M.Zondeki	5	2	2	3*	4	–	–	–	2

SOUTH AFRICA – BOWLING

	O	M	R	W	Avge	Best	4wI	R/Over
P.R.Adams	184.5	7	815	29	28.10	3-26	–	4.40
D.M.Benkenstein	10.5	1	44	4	11.00	3- 5	–	4.06
N.Boje	581.2	17	2616	77	33.97	5-21	3	4.50
A.C.Dawson	131.1	11	608	19	32.00	4-49	1	4.63
A.A.Donald	1426.5	101	5926	272	21.78	6-23	13	4.15
S.Elworthy	283.4	29	1235	44	28.06	3-17	–	4.35
A.J.Hall	203	11	901	28	32.17	3-32	–	4.43
M.Hayward	165.3	5	858	21	40.85	4-31	–	5.18
J.H.Kallis	1185.2	56	5590	184	30.38	5-30	4	4.71
J.M.Kemp	91	5	418	17	24.58	3-20	–	4.59
G.Kirsten	5	1	23	–	–	–	–	4.60
L.Klusener	1132.4	44	5323	182	29.24	6-49	7	4.69
C.K.Langeveldt	41.3	–	168	7	24.00	4-21	1	4.04
N.D.McKenzie	7.4	–	27	–	–	–	–	3.52
A.Nel	147.5	13	669	23	29.08	4-39	1	4.52
M.Ntini	754.2	68	3184	138	23.07	5-31	7	4.22
J.L.Ontong	84	3	345	7	49.28	3-30	–	4.10
R.J.Peterson	110	1	534	7	76.28	2-26	–	4.85
S.M.Pollock	1818.4	202	6783	295	22.99	6-35	15	3.72
J.N.Rhodes	2.2	–	4	–	–	–	–	1.71
J.A.Rudolph	4	–	26	–	–	–	–	6.50
G.C.Smith	26.1	–	160	2	80.00	1-24	–	6.11
M.van Jaarsveld	5.1	1	18	2	9.00	1- 0	–	3.48
C.M.Willoughby	28	–	148	2	74.00	2-39	–	5.28
M.Zondeki	34	3	149	4	37.25	1-17	–	4.38

WEST INDIES – BATTING AND FIELDING

	M	I	NO	HS	Runs	Avge	100	50	Ct/St
O.A.C.Banks	3	3	–	29	44	14.66	–	–	–
C.S.Baugh	5	5	2	29	65	21.66	–	–	2
D.E.Bernard	4	2	–	7	7	3.50	–	–	1
S.Chanderpaul	142	132	17	150	4173	36.28	3	27	44
P.T.Collins	23	7	3	10*	26	6.50	–	–	8
C.D.Collymore	51	21	9	13*	71	5.91	–	–	9
C.E.Cuffy	41	22	8	17*	62	4.42	–	–	5
M.Dillon	98	48	19	21*	215	7.41	–	–	18
V.C.Drakes	34	17	5	25	94	7.83	–	–	5
F.H.Edwards	2	–	–				–	–	–
D.Ganga	28	27	1	71	691	26.57	–	8	8
C.H.Gayle	88	86	4	153*	3323	40.52	8	20	37

	M	I	NO	HS	Runs	Avge	100	50	Ct/St
W.W.Hinds	83	79	6	127*	2245	30.75	4	12	26
C.L.Hooper	227	206	43	113*	5761	35.34	7	29	120
R.O.Hurley	9	4	–	6	13	3.25	–	–	5
R.D.Jacobs	133	105	29	80*	1805	23.75	–	9	144/26
B.C.Lara	229	224	24	169	8533	42.66	18	53	97
J.J.C.Lawson	6	1	–	3	3	3.00	–	–	–
N.A.M.McLean	45	34	8	50*	314	12.07	–	1	8
M.V.Nagamootoo	24	18	6	33	162	13.50	–	–	6
D.B.Powell	2	–	–	–	–	–	–	–	–
R.L.Powell	84	77	12	124	1710	26.30	1	7	39
R.Rampaul	8	3	1	24	25	12.50	–	–	2
M.N.Samuels	53	51	8	108*	1412	32.83	1	10	16
R.R.Sarwan	54	50	12	102*	1674	44.05	1	8	16
D.R.Smith	5	3	–	24	37	12.33	–	–	1
D.S.Smith	3	3	–	26	36	12.00	–	–	1
J.E.Taylor	1	–	–	–	–	–	–	–	–

WEST INDIES – BOWLING

	O	M	R	W	Avge	Best	4wI	R/Over
O.A.C.Banks	25	–	124	4	31.00	2-44	–	4.96
D.E.Bernard	4	–	28	1	28.00	1-11	–	7.00
S.Chanderpaul	118	–	606	14	43.28	3-18	–	5.13
P.T.Collins	205.5	15	946	30	31.53	3-18	–	4.59
C.D.Collymore	423.1	24	1840	57	32.28	5-51	2	4.34
C.E.Cuffy	358.5	14	1436	41	35.02	4-24	1	4.00
M.Dillon	841.2	61	3813	119	32.04	5-51	5	4.53
V.C.Drakes	273.2	22	1293	51	25.35	5-33	5	4.73
F.H.Edwards	15.5	1	82	8	10.25	6-22	1	5.18
D.Ganga	0.1	–	4	–	–	–	–	24.00
C.H.Gayle	502.2	24	2303	77	29.90	5-46	4	4.58
W.W.Hinds	66.5	–	348	13	26.76	3-35	–	5.20
C.L.Hooper	1595.3	53	6957	193	36.04	4-34	3	4.36
R.O.Hurley	63	–	313	5	62.60	1-25	–	4.96
B.C.Lara	8.1	–	61	4	15.25	2- 5	–	7.46
J.J.C.Lawson	45	–	217	9	24.11	4-57	1	4.82
N.A.M.McLean	353.2	18	1729	46	37.58	3-21	–	4.89
M.V.Nagamootoo	198.1	4	998	18	55.44	4-32	1	5.03
D.B.Powell	19	2	71	1	71.00	1-34	–	3.73
R.L.Powell	56.3	3	349	9	38.77	2- 5	–	6.17
R.Rampaul	54	5	275	4	68.75	2-56	–	5.09
M.N.Samuels	250	6	1239	34	36.44	3-25	–	4.95
R.R.Sarwan	28.4	1	187	3	62.33	1-15	–	6.52
D.R.Smith	6	–	27	–	–	–	–	4.50
J.E.Taylor	10	–	39	2	19.50	2-39	–	3.90

NEW ZEALAND – BATTING AND FIELDING

	M	I	NO	HS	Runs	Avge	100	50	Ct/St
A.R.Adams	30	24	7	45	338	19.88	–	–	3
N.J.Astle	174	171	10	122*	5540	34.40	13	32	69
S.E.Bond	27	13	6	31*	122	17.42	–	–	8
I.G.Butler	10	5	3	3	6	3.00	–	–	4
C.L.Cairns	180	164	18	115	4272	29.26	4	21	56
T.K.Canning	3	3	1	23*	36	18.00	–	–	1
C.D.Cumming	10	10	1	45*	138	15.33	–	–	4
S.P.Fleming	212	204	18	134*	5866	31.53	5	34	101
C.Z.Harris	238	205	61	130	4250	29.51	1	15	92
R.G.Hart	2	1	–	–	–	0.00	–	–	1
P.A.Hitchcock	13	6	2	10	30	7.50	–	–	4
R.A.Jones	5	5	–	63	168	33.60	–	1	–
B.B.McCullum	42	33	9	56*	451	18.79	–	2	56/2
C.D.McMillan	141	133	8	105	3369	26.95	2	19	36

	M	I	NO	HS	Runs	Avge	100	50	Ct/St
H.J.H.Marshall	10	10	2	101*	417	52.12	1	4	5
M.J.Mason	3	1	1	13*	13	–	–	–	–
K.D.Mills	27	16	5	23*	124	11.27	–	–	8
C.J.Nevin	37	36	–	74	732	20.33	–	4	16/3
J.D.P.Oram	54	43	5	81	681	17.92	–	3	13
M.S.Sinclair	38	37	2	118*	941	26.88	2	5	9
C.M.Spearman	51	50	–	86	936	18.72	–	5	15
S.B.Styris	75	62	9	141	1407	26.54	2	6	30
D.R.Tuffey	64	37	18	20*	145	7.63	–	–	17
D.L.Vettori	125	79	24	30	597	10.85	–	–	30
L.Vincent	62	60	8	60*	1133	21.78	–	4	23
M.D.J.Walker	3	1	–	10	10	10.00	–	–	2
K.P.Walmsley	2	–							
P.J.Wiseman	15	7	5	16	45	22.50	–	–	2

NEW ZEALAND – BOWLING

	O	M	R	W	Avge	Best	4wI	R/Over
A.R.Adams	239.4	11	1237	44	28.11	5-22	3	5.16
N.J.Astle	735.3	28	3412	95	35.91	4-43	1	4.63
S.E.Bond	228.2	28	968	51	18.98	6-23	5	4.23
I.G.Butler	66.3	1	377	7	53.85	2-32	–	5.66
C.L.Cairns	1139.2	69	5446	163	33.41	5-42	3	4.78
T.K.Canning	24	1	123	4	30.75	2-30	–	5.12
S.P.Fleming	4.5	–	28	1	28.00	1- 8	–	5.79
C.Z.Harris	1718.5	74	7374	199	37.05	5-42	3	4.29
P.A.Hitchcock	85	5	412	12	34.33	3-30	–	4.84
C.D.McMillan	231.3	6	1231	37	33.27	3-20	–	5.31
M.J.Mason	29	1	179	1	179.00	1-61	–	6.17
K.D.Mills	215.3	16	928	34	27.29	3-30	–	4.30
J.D.P.Oram	397.1	36	1766	59	29.93	5-26	2	4.44
C.M.Spearman	0.3	–	6	–	–	–	–	12.00
S.B.Styris	483.5	24	2340	74	31.62	6-25	3	4.83
D.R.Tuffey	499.4	55	2291	80	28.63	4-24	2	4.58
D.L.Vettori	936.5	37	4108	109	37.68	4-14	3	4.38
L.Vincent	0.2	–	3	–	–	–	–	9.00
M.D.J.Walker	22	–	119	4	29.75	4-49	1	5.40
K.P.Walmsley	20	–	117	2	58.50	1-53	–	5.85
P.J.Wiseman	75	–	368	12	30.66	4-45	1	4.90

INDIA – BATTING AND FIELDING

	M	I	NO	HS	Runs	Avge	100	50	Ct/St
A.B.Agarkar	127	80	26	95	954	17.66	–	3	41
H.K.Badani	39	35	9	100	859	33.03	1	4	13
S.V.Bahutule	8	4	1	11	23	7.66	–	–	3
L.Balaji	11	4	1	11	15	5.00	–	–	6
S.B.Bangar	15	15	2	57*	180	13.84	–	1	4
A.Bhandari	2	1	1	0*	0	0.00	–	–	–
S.S.Das	4	4	1	30	39	13.00	–	–	–
R.Dravid	224	205	25	153	7002	38.90	8	49	131/11
G.Gambhir	5	5	–	71	113	22.60	–	1	1
S.C.Ganguly	244	236	20	183	9144	42.33	22	53	86
R.S.Gavaskar	6	6	2	54	90	22.50	–	1	4
Harbhajan Singh	82	44	11	46	355	10.75	–	–	23
M.Kaif	59	49	11	111*	1170	30.78	1	6	28
A.V.Kale	1	1	–	10	10	10.00	–	–	–
M.Kartik	13	7	3	32*	74	18.50	–	–	4
Z.Khan	77	40	15	34*	292	11.68	–	–	19
A.Kumble	251	124	41	26	867	10.44	–	–	83
V.V.S.Laxman	68	66	6	131	1915	31.91	5	9	34
A.Mishra	3	–							
D.Mongia	48	42	5	159*	1028	27.78	1	3	21

LOI **INDIA – BATTING AND FIELDING (continued)**

	M	I	NO	HS	Runs	Avge	100	50	Ct/St
A.Nehra	44	15	10	24	61	12.20	–	–	6
P.A.Patel	12	8	–	28	113	14.12	–	–	10/3
I.K.Pathan	10	7	3	30	85	21.25	–	–	2
A.M.Salvi	4	3	1	4*	4	2.00	–	–	2
Sarandeep Singh	5	4	1	19	47	15.66	–	–	2
V.Sehwag	85	83	6	130	2655	34.48	6	12	30
R.S.Sodhi	18	14	3	67	280	25.45	–	2	9
J.Srinath	229	121	38	53	883	10.63	–	1	32
S.R.Tendulkar	328	319	31	186*	12921	44.86	36	66	99
J.P.Yadav	2	1	–	0	0	0.00	–	–	3
Yuvraj Singh	89	78	11	139	2071	30.91	2	13	30

INDIA – BOWLING

	O	M	R	W	Avge	Best	4wI	R/Over
A.B.Agarkar	1049.1	62	5363	193	27.78	6-42	9	5.11
H.K.Badani	30.3	–	149	3	49.66	1- 7	–	4.88
S.V.Bahutule	49	–	283	2	141.50	1-31	–	5.77
L.Balaji	94	5	485	13	37.30	4-48	1	5.15
S.B.Bangar	73.4	2	384	7	54.85	2-39	–	5.21
A.Bhandari	17.4	–	106	5	21.20	3-31	–	5.99
R.Dravid	31	1	170	4	42.50	2-43	–	5.48
S.C.Ganguly	643.1	27	3230	93	34.73	5-16	3	5.02
R.S.Gavaskar	9	–	56	1	56.00	1-56	–	6.22
Harbhajan Singh	719	33	2992	104	28.76	5-43	3	4.16
M.Kartik	113	5	567	9	63.00	3-36	–	5.01
Z.Khan	628	38	2969	118	25.16	4-19	6	4.72
A.Kumble	2236.3	104	9530	315	30.25	6-12	10	4.26
V.V.S.Laxman	7	–	40	–	–	–	–	5.71
A.Mishra	14	1	67	2	33.50	1-29	–	4.78
D.Mongia	52.3	1	280	8	35.00	3-31	–	5.33
A.Nehra	367.4	25	1727	50	34.54	6-23	2	4.69
I.K.Pathan	89.4	4	497	16	31.06	4-24	1	5.54
A.M.Salvi	28.4	3	120	4	30.00	2-15	–	4.18
Sarandeep Singh	43	1	180	3	60.00	2-34	–	4.18
V.Sehwag	297.3	7	1565	39	40.12	3-25	–	5.26
R.S.Sodhi	77	3	365	5	73.00	2-31	–	4.74
J.Srinath	1989.1	137	8847	315	28.08	5-23	10	4.44
S.R.Tendulkar	1082.5	20	5417	114	47.51	5-32	4	5.00
J.P.Yadav	6	–	36	–	–	–	–	6.00
Yuvraj Singh	181.3	8	893	24	37.20	4- 6	1	4.92

PAKISTAN – BATTING AND FIELDING

	M	I	NO	HS	Runs	Avge	100	50	Ct/St
Abdul Razzaq	154	131	31	112	2959	29.59	1	16	22
Azhar Mahmood	134	103	23	67	1435	17.93	–	3	37
Danish Kaneria	9	5	4	3*	4	4.00	–	–	–
Faisal Athar	1	1	–	9	9	9.00	–	–	–
Faisal Iqbal	17	15	2	100*	284	21.84	1	–	2
Imran Farhat	14	14	–	107	548	39.14	1	4	4
Imran Nazir	57	57	2	105*	1340	24.36	1	8	16
Inzamam-ul-Haq	307	287	42	137*	9456	38.59	8	68	93
Junaid Zia	4	2	1	2*	2	2.00	–	–	–
Kamran Akmal	12	8	2	44	167	27.83	–	–	8
Misbah-ul-Haq	11	10	2	50*	282	35.25	–	2	5
Mohammad Akram	23	9	7	7*	14	7.00	–	–	8
Mohammad Hafeez	22	22	–	69	419	19.04	–	3	9
Mohammad Sami	45	24	16	22	134	16.75	–	–	12
Mohammad Zahid	11	4	2	7*	15	7.50	–	–	1
Moin Khan	200	167	37	72*	3061	23.54	–	11	195/69
Mushtaq Ahmed	144	76	34	34*	399	9.50	–	–	16
Naved Latif	11	11	–	113	262	23.81	1	–	2

PAKISTAN – BATTING AND FIELDING (continued)

	M	I	NO	HS	Runs	Avge	100	50	Ct/St
Naved-ul-Hasan	2	1	–	13	13	13.00	–	–	–
Rashid Latif	166	117	29	79	1709	19.42	–	3	182/38
Saeed Anwar	247	244	19	194	8823	39.21	20	43	42
Salim Elahi	48	47	4	135	1579	36.72	4	9	10
Saqlain Mushtaq	169	98	39	37*	709	12.01	–	–	40
Shabbir Ahmed	19	6	1	2	8	1.60	–	–	7
Shahid Afridi	176	171	7	109	3887	23.70	3	22	65
Shoaib Akhtar	98	49	26	43	287	12.47	–	–	14
Shoaib Malik	63	50	7	115	1147	26.67	2	3	20
Taufiq Umar	17	17	1	81*	426	26.62	–	3	8
Umar Gul	15	1	–	2	2	2.00	–	–	1
Waqar Younis	262	139	45	37	969	10.30	–	–	35
Wasim Akram	356	280	55	86	3717	16.52	–	6	88
Yasir Hamid	24	24	1	127*	1020	44.34	2	7	4
Younis Khan	96	92	13	90	2508	31.74	–	19	46
Yousuf Youhana	159	151	23	141*	5461	42.66	9	35	36

PAKISTAN – BOWLING

	O	M	R	W	Avge	Best	4wI	R/Over
Abdul Razzaq	1118.5	68	4955	179	27.68	6-35	7	4.42
Azhar Mahmood	996	53	4572	120	38.10	6-18	5	4.59
Danish Kaneria	82	8	356	8	44.50	3-31	–	4.34
Faisal Iqbal	3	–	33	–	–	–	–	11.00
Imran Farhat	6.5	–	57	1	57.00	1-22	–	8.34
Imran Nazir	4.1	–	19	1	19.00	1- 3	–	4.55
Inzamam-ul-Haq	9.4	1	64	3	21.33	1- 0	–	6.61
Junaid Zia	24.1	1	127	3	42.33	3-21	–	5.25
Mohammad Akram	164.5	6	790	19	41.57	2-28	–	4.79
Mohammad Hafeez	133	7	533	21	25.38	3-17	–	4.00
Mohammad Sami	367.3	18	1759	71	24.77	5-10	4	4.78
Mohammad Zahid	85.2	8	391	10	39.10	2-20	–	4.58
Mushtaq Ahmed	1257.1	51	5361	161	33.29	5-36	4	4.26
Naved Latif	8	–	51	–	–	–	–	6.37
Naved-ul-Hasan	16	1	87	3	29.00	2-55	–	5.43
Saeed Anwar	40.2	3	191	6	31.83	2- 9	–	4.73
Salim Elahi	1	–	10	–	–	–	–	10.00
Saqlain Mushtaq	1461.4	65	6275	288	21.78	5-20	17	4.29
Shabbir Ahmed	164.2	16	701	17	41.23	3-52	–	4.26
Shahid Afridi	1118.5	43	5152	131	39.32	5-40	1	4.60
Shoaib Akhtar	762	64	3436	158	21.74	6-16	6	4.50
Shoaib Malik	449.1	15	1928	52	37.07	3-26	–	4.29
Taufiq Umar	11	–	77	1	77.00	1-49	–	7.00
Umar Gul	112.2	7	519	19	27.31	5-17	1	4.62
Waqar Younis	2116.2	145	9919	416	23.84	7-36	27	4.68
Wasim Akram	3031	236	11812	502	23.52	5-15	23	3.89
Yasir Hamid	2	–	20	–	–	–	–	10.00
Younis Khan	15	–	99	1	99.00	1-24	–	6.60

SRI LANKA – BATTING AND FIELDING

	M	I	NO	HS	Runs	Avge	100	50	Ct/St
R.P.Arnold	120	105	27	103	2810	36.02	1	19	38
M.S.Atapattu	201	198	24	132*	6567	37.74	10	45	53
U.D.U.Chandana	106	81	10	89	1179	16.60	–	3	62
P.A.de Silva	308	296	30	145	9284	34.90	11	64	95
H.D.P.K.Dharmasena	138	84	32	69*	1196	23.00	–	4	34
T.M.Dilshan	24	20	5	53	393	26.20	–	2	11
C.R.D.Fernando	55	23	13	13*	81	8.10	–	–	11
K.A.D.M.Fernando	1	–	–	–	–	–	–	–	1
K.H.R.K.Fernando	5	3	2	23*	40	40.00	–	–	3
T.C.B.Fernando	17	10	6	14*	29	7.25	–	–	3
P.W.Gunaratne	23	8	3	15*	36	7.20	–	–	3

SRI LANKA – BATTING AND FIELDING (continued)

	M	I	NO	HS	Runs	Avge	100	50	Ct/St
D.A.Gunawardana	45	45	–	132	1287	28.60	1	7	10
S.T.Jayasuriya	308	300	13	189	9172	31.95	16	54	102
D.P.M.D.Jayawardena	148	138	12	128	3760	29.84	6	18	73
H.A.P.W.Jayawardena	3	2	–	4	4	2.00	–	–	3/1
R.S.Kaluwitharana	187	179	14	102*	3709	22.47	2	23	132/74
M.D.N.Kulasekera	1	–	–	–	–	–	–	–	1
M.K.G.C.P.Lakshitha	7	2	1	4	7	7.00	–	–	1
K.S.Lokuarachchi	5	5	–	28	51	10.20	–	–	1
J.Mubarak	7	7	–	20	68	9.71	–	–	2
M.Muralitharan	224	104	41	19	374	5.93	–	–	92
H.G.D.Nayanakantha	3	2	1	2*	3	3.00	–	–	2
R.A.P.Nissanka	23	13	5	11	53	6.62	–	–	3
T.T.Samaraweera	14	11	1	33	175	17.50	–	–	2
K.C.Sangakkara	96	88	12	103*	2170	28.55	2	9	77/19
H.P.Tillekeratne	200	168	40	104	3789	29.60	2	13	89/6
W.P.U.C.J.Vaas	228	157	53	50*	1481	14.24	–	1	44
K.Weeraratne	11	5	1	14*	41	10.25	–	–	1

SRI LANKA – BOWLING

	O	M	R	W	Avge	Best	4wI	R/Over
R.P.Arnold	324.4	7	1554	35	44.40	3-47	–	4.78
M.S.Atapattu	8.3	–	41	–	–	–	–	4.82
U.D.U.Chandana	711.5	14	3303	101	32.70	4-31	3	4.64
P.A.de Silva	858	28	4177	106	39.40	4-30	2	4.86
H.D.P.K.Dharmasena	1141.2	41	4878	137	35.60	4-37	1	4.27
T.M.Dilshan	8	–	31	1	31.00	1-14	–	3.87
C.R.D.Fernando	391.3	15	2048	73	28.05	4-48	1	5.23
K.A.D.M.Fernando	7	2	13	2	6.50	2-13	–	1.85
K.H.R.K.Fernando	28	4	118	5	23.60	3-12	–	4.21
T.C.B.Fernando	116.4	7	586	15	39.06	5-67	1	5.02
P.W.Gunaratne	159.5	6	908	27	33.62	4-44	1	5.68
S.T.Jayasuriya	1881.4	28	9040	251	36.01	6-29	9	4.80
D.P.M.D.Jayawardena	88.4	1	502	7	71.71	2-56	–	5.66
M.D.N.Kulasekera	9	1	19	2	9.50	2-19	–	2.11
M.K.G.C.P.Lakshitha	50	2	254	8	31.75	2-34	–	5.08
K.S.Lokuarachchi	39	3	153	7	21.85	3-37	–	3.92
J.Mubarak	5	–	29	–	–	–	–	5.80
M.Muralitharan	2020.3	142	7646	343	22.29	7-30	16	3.78
H.G.D.Nayanakantha	15.5	2	83	2	41.50	1-26	–	5.24
R.A.P.Nissanka	166.1	6	857	27	31.74	4-12	1	5.15
T.T.Samaraweera	112	2	509	10	50.90	3-34	–	4.54
H.P.Tillekeratne	30	1	141	6	23.50	1- 3	–	4.70
W.P.U.C.J.Vaas	1855.4	188	7714	285	27.06	8-19	7	4.15
K.Weeraratne	68	5	302	6	50.33	3-46	–	4.44

ZIMBABWE – BATTING AND FIELDING

	M	I	NO	HS	Runs	Avge	100	50	Ct/St
A.M.Blignaut	46	35	7	63*	505	18.03	–	4	10
G.B.Brent	46	31	12	24	184	9.68	–	–	9
A.D.R.Campbell	188	184	14	131*	5185	30.50	7	30	77
S.V.Carlisle	105	101	8	121*	2595	27.90	3	8	36
C.K.Coventry	1	1	–	3	3	3.00	–	–	1
D.D.Ebrahim	59	53	3	121	1005	20.10	1	1	13
S.M.Ervine	39	31	7	100	643	26.79	1	1	5
C.N.Evans	53	47	5	96*	764	18.19	–	2	12
A.Flower	213	208	16	145	6786	35.34	4	55	141/32
G.W.Flower	216	209	18	142*	6472	33.88	6	39	86
T.J.Friend	51	39	5	91	548	16.11	–	3	17
M.W.Goodwin	71	70	3	112*	1818	27.13	2	8	20
T.R.Gripper	8	8	–	26	80	10.00	–	–	4
D.T.Hondo	37	16	9	15*	62	8.85	–	–	7

ZIMBABWE – BATTING AND FIELDING (continued)

	M	I	NO	HS	Runs	Avge	100	50	Ct/St
N.B.Mahwire	2	1	1	8*	8	–	–	–	1
A.Maregwede	1	1	–	–	–	0.00	–	–	–
D.A.Marillier	48	41	4	100	672	18.16	1	3	12
S.Matsikenyeri	18	16	2	44	153	10.92	–	–	2
B.A.Murphy	31	17	8	20*	72	8.00	–	–	11
W.Mwayenga	1	–	–	–	–	–	–	–	–
M.L.Nkala	35	21	3	36	157	8.72	–	–	5
H.K.Olonga	50	27	14	31	95	7.30	–	–	13
R.W.Price	23	11	4	18*	70	10.00	–	–	1
G.J.Rennie	40	37	6	76	617	19.90	–	2	16
B.G.Rogers	4	4	–	34	47	11.75	–	–	1
V.Sibanda	11	10	–	58	116	11.60	–	1	4
R.W.Sims	3	2	1	24	31	31.00	–	–	1
H.H.Streak	180	150	53	79*	2646	27.27	–	12	41
T.Taibu	51	38	12	74*	628	24.15	–	3	44/3
M.A.Vermeulen	19	19	4	79	454	30.26	–	4	5
G.J.Whittall	147	142	22	83	2705	22.54	–	11	35
C.B.Wishart	89	81	8	172*	1716	23.50	2	5	26

ZIMBABWE – BOWLING

	O	M	R	W	Avge	Best	4wI	R/Over
A.M.Blignaut	339.2	10	1759	41	42.90	4-43	1	5.18
G.B.Brent	358	17	1840	47	39.14	4-53	1	5.13
A.D.R.Campbell	84.5	3	434	12	36.16	2-20	–	5.11
D.D.Ebrahim	0.5	–	11	–	–	–	–	13.20
S.M.Ervine	249.3	8	1433	37	38.72	3-29	–	5.74
C.N.Evans	160.4	4	848	21	40.38	3-11	–	5.27
A.Flower	5	–	23	–	–	–	–	4.60
G.W.Flower	877.1	11	4076	100	40.76	4-32	2	4.64
T.J.Friend	321.4	13	1779	37	48.08	4-55	1	5.53
M.W.Goodwin	41.2	1	210	4	52.50	1-12	–	5.08
T.R.Gripper	20	5	76	2	38.00	2-28	–	3.80
D.T.Hondo	250	16	1406	39	36.05	4-37	3	5.62
N.B.Mahwire	6	1	35	1	35.00	1-35	–	5.83
D.A.Marillier	262.2	7	1235	30	41.16	4-38	1	4.70
S.Matsikenyeri	6	–	61	1	61.00	1-31	–	10.16
B.A.Murphy	237	9	1130	29	38.96	3-43	–	4.76
W.Mwayenga	9	–	74	–	–	–	–	8.22
M.L.Nkala	212.3	6	1245	18	69.16	3-12	–	5.85
H.K.Olonga	343.1	12	1977	58	34.08	6-19	4	5.76
R.W.Price	191.2	9	795	12	66.25	2-16	–	4.15
G.J.Rennie	15	–	75	2	37.50	1-17	–	5.00
B.G.Rogers	7	–	62	–	–	–	–	8.85
R.W.Sims	22	–	127	–	–	–	–	5.77
H.H.Streak	1503.1	105	6813	227	30.01	5-32	7	4.53
G.J.Whittall	676.4	17	3480	88	39.54	4-35	1	5.14
C.B.Wishart	2	–	12	–	–	–	–	6.00

BANGLADESH – BATTING AND FIELDING

	M	I	NO	HS	Runs	Avge	100	50	Ct/St
Akram Khan	44	44	2	65	976	23.23	–	5	8
Al Sahariar	29	29	1	62*	374	13.35	–	2	7
Alok Kapali	32	31	2	89*	712	24.55	–	4	9
Anwar Hossain Monir	1	1	1	–*	–	–	–	–	–
Anwar Hossain Piju	1	1	–	42	42	42.00	–	–	–
Ehsanul Haque	6	6	–	20	57	9.50	–	–	1
Fahim Muntasir	3	3	1	5	6	3.00	–	–	2
Habibul Bashar	42	42	–	74	776	18.47	–	7	7
Hannan Sarkar	16	16	–	61	270	16.87	–	2	6
Hasibul Hussain	31	25	5	21*	171	8.55	–	–	6
Jamal Ahmed	1	1	1	18*	18	–	–	–	1

	M	I	NO	HS	Runs	Avge	100	50	Ct/St
Javed Omar	28	28	3	85*	567	22.68	–	4	6
Khaled Mahmud	53	50	1	50	714	14.57	–	1	10
Khaled Masud	69	64	12	54*	870	16.73	–	3	48/13
Manjurul Islam	34	22	13	13	53	5.88	–	–	8
Manjural Rana	3	3	1	20*	46	23.00	–	–	–
Mashrafe Mortaza	12	12	2	28	72	7.20	–	–	2
Mehrab Hossain	18	18	–	101	449	24.94	1	2	6
Mohammed Ashraful	24	24	1	56	326	14.17	–	2	4
Mohammed Rafique	54	51	9	77	562	13.38	–	1	13
Mohammed Salim	1	1	–	9	9	9.00	–	–	1
Moniruzzaman	2	2	–	1	1	–.50	–	–	–
Mushfiqur Rahman	14	12	2	36*	182	18.20	–	1	–
Nafis Iqbal	2	2	–	9	13	6.50	–	–	–
Naimur Rahman	29	27	2	47	488	19.52	–	–	7
Rafiqul Islam	1	1	–	–	–	0.00	–	–	–
Rajin Saleh	8	8	–	71	269	33.62	–	2	3
Sanwar Hossain	27	27	2	52	290	11.60	–	1	11
Talha Jubair	6	5	3	4*	5	2.50	–	–	1
Tapash Baisya	26	22	6	35*	157	9.81	–	–	5
Tareq Aziz	5	4	3	7*	11	11.00	–	–	3
Tushar Imran	24	23	–	65	403	17.52	–	2	3

BANGLADESH – BOWLING

	O	M	R	W	Avge	Best	4wI	R/Over
Akram Khan	19.3	–	138	–	–	–	–	7.07
Alok Kapali	118.3	5	603	11	54.81	2-40	–	5.08
Anwar Hossain Monir	8	–	45	–	–	–	–	5.62
Ehsanul Haque	23.3	–	113	3	37.66	2-34	–	4.80
Fahim Muntasir	28.1	–	111	–	–	–	–	3.94
Habibul Bashar	29.1	–	142	1	142.00	1-31	–	4.86
Hannan Sarkar	0.3	–	13	–	–	–	–	26.00
Hasibul Hussain	223.1	13	1285	29	44.31	4-56	1	5.75
Jamal Ahmed	4	1	28	–	–	–	–	7.00
Khaled Mahmud	387	21	1997	43	46.44	3-31	–	5.16
Manjurul Islam	265.2	24	1288	24	53.66	3-37	–	4.85
Manjural Rana	15	1	73	1	73.00	1-33	–	4.86
Mashrafe Mortaza	98.2	9	520	13	40.00	2-26	–	5.28
Mehrab Hossain	5	–	42	–	–	–	–	8.40
Mohammed Ashraful	49.2	1	297	8	37.12	3-26	–	6.02
Mohammed Rafique	437.2	23	2085	43	48.48	3-56	–	4.76
Mushfiqur Rahman	123.5	12	542	11	49.27	2-29	–	4.37
Naimur Rahman	182.2	6	905	10	90.50	2-51	–	4.96
Rajin Saleh	22	–	124	4	31.00	3-48	–	5.63
Sanwar Hossain	63.5	1	327	10	32.70	3-49	–	5.12
Talha Jubair	34	2	255	6	42.50	4-65	1	7.50
Tapash Baisya	190.5	5	1094	25	43.76	4-56	1	5.73
Tareq Aziz	39.3	5	207	4	51.75	3-19	–	5.24

KENYA – BATTING AND FIELDING

	M	I	NO	HS	Runs	Avge	100	50	Ct/St
J.O.Angara	17	11	5	6	23	3.83	–	–	2
J.K.Kamande	16	12	4	32*	137	17.12	–	–	6
A.Y.Karim	34	24	6	53	228	12.66	–	1	6
A.S.Luseno	1	1	–	–	–	0.00	–	–	–
H.S.Modi	53	46	7	78*	961	24.64	–	5	8
C.O.Obuya	28	22	3	29	246	12.94	–	–	8
D.O.Obuya	23	23	2	57	227	10.80	–	1	20/4
K.O.Obuya	61	60	1	144	1412	23.93	2	8	25/13
T.M.Odoyo	61	58	7	53	1120	21.96	–	2	16
M.O.Odumbe	61	59	5	83	1409	26.09	–	11	12
P.O.Ongondo	20	18	5	36	141	10.84	–	–	1

KENYA – BATTING AND FIELDING (continued)

	M	I	NO	HS	Runs	Avge	100	50	Ct/St
B.J.Patel	22	16	1	44	278	18.53	–	–	6
R.D.Shah	42	42	–	71	1092	26.00	–	10	11
A.O.Suji	43	33	7	67	317	12.19	–	1	13
M.A.Suji	59	47	21	16*	222	8.53	–	–	10
S.O.Tikolo	63	61	2	106*	1708	28.94	1	14	20

KENYA – BOWLING

	O	M	R	W	Avge	Best	4wI	R/Over
J.O.Angara	98	8	569	14	40.64	3-30	–	5.80
J.K.Kamande	38.3	–	240	3	80.00	1-16	–	6.23
A.Y.Karim	261.2	21	1114	27	41.25	5-33	1	4.26
A.S.Luseno	4	–	26	–	–	–	–	6.50
H.S.Modi	3.1	1	27	–	–	–	–	8.53
C.O.Obuya	222	8	1125	25	45.00	5-24	1	5.06
K.O.Obuya	1	–	5	–	–	–	–	5.00
T.M.Odoyo	443.2	32	2163	57	37.94	4-28	1	4.87
M.O.Odumbe	372.5	21	1807	39	46.33	4-38	1	4.85
P.O.Ongondo	106.2	5	527	7	75.28	2-44	–	4.95
L.N.Onyango	13.3	–	130	1	130.00	1-45	–	9.62
B.J.Patel	16.1	–	108	2	54.00	1-15	–	6.67
R.D.Shah	10	–	72	–	–	–	–	7.20
A.O.Suji	176.5	8	945	15	63.00	2-24	–	5.34
M.A.Suji	453	44	1981	41	48.31	4-24	1	4.37
S.O.Tikolo	273.5	6	1418	40	35.45	3-14	–	5.17

CANADA – BATTING AND FIELDING

	M	I	NO	HS	Runs	Avge	100	50	Ct/St
A.Bagai	6	6	1	28*	56	11.20	–	–	8/2
I.S.Billcliff	6	6	–	71	147	24.50	–	1	–
D.Chumney	5	5	–	28	68	13.60	–	–	–
A.Codrington	5	5	–	16	28	5.60	–	–	–
J.M.Davison	6	6	–	111	226	37.66	1	1	1
N.A.de Groot	6	6	–	17	44	7.33	–	–	–
J.V.Harris	6	6	–	31	91	15.16	–	–	1
N.Ifill	3	2	–	9	16	8.00	–	–	1
D.Joseph	4	3	3	9*	13	–	–	–	–
I.Maraj	6	6	1	53*	98	19.60	–	1	2
A.Patel	2	1	–	25	25	25.00	–	–	–
A.M.Samad	1	1	–	12	12	12.00	–	–	–
A.F.Sattaur	3	3	–	13	20	6.66	–	–	2
B.B.Seebaran	4	3	2	4*	4	4.00	–	–	1
S.Thuraisingham	3	3	–	13	25	8.33	–	–	–

CANADA – BOWLING

	O	M	R	W	Avge	Best	4wI	R/Over
A.Codrington	25	4	129	6	21.50	5-27	1	5.16
J.M.Davison	42	5	187	10	18.70	3-15	–	4.45
N.A.de Groot	13.3	–	88	3	29.33	2-45	–	6.51
N.Ifill	12	–	88	–	–	–	–	7.33
D.Joseph	31	3	170	5	34.00	2-42	–	5.48
I.Maraj	4.3	–	22	–	–	–	–	4.88
A.Patel	10	–	73	3	24.33	3-41	–	7.30
B.B.Seebaran	18	–	130	1	130.00	1-61	–	7.22
S.Thuraisingham	18.4	1	109	4	27.25	2-53	–	5.83

HOLLAND – BATTING AND FIELDING

	M	I	NO	HS	Runs	Avge	100	50	Ct/St
T.B.M.de Leede	13	13	1	58*	243	20.25	–	1	3
J.J.Esmeijer	6	5	1	7	10	2.50	–	–	3
V.D.Grandia	1	1	–	–	–	0.00	–	–	–
J.F.Kloppenburg	6	6	–	121	165	27.50	1	–	1
R.P.Lefebvre	11	11	5	45	171	28.50	–	–	4

LOI **HOLLAND – BATTING AND FIELDING (continued)**

	M	I	NO	HS	Runs	Avge	100	50	Ct/St
H.J.C.Mol	5	4	–	23	38	9.50	–	–	2
M.A.K.Raja	5	4	1	5	9	3.00	–	–	1
E.Schiferli	8	8	–	22	90	11.25	–	–	1
R.H.Scholte	5	5	–	12	39	7.80	–	–	–
J.Smits	6	5	2	26	58	19.33	–	–	4/ 1
N.A.Statham	2	2	–	7	7	3.50	–	–	–
D.L.S.van Bunge	8	7	–	62	139	19.85	–	1	2
K-J.J.van Noortwijk	9	9	2	134*	322	46.00	1	1	–
R.F.van Oosterom	3	3	2	5*	7	7.00	–	–	2
L.P.van Troost	8	8	1	26	112	16.00	–	–	1
B.Zuiderent	13	13	1	54	133	11.08	–	1	12

HOLLAND – BOWLING

	O	M	R	W	Avge	Best	4wI	R/Over
T.B.M.de Leede	82.5	–	488	11	44.36	4-35	1	5.89
J.J.Esmeijer	38	–	208	–	–	–	–	5.47
V.D.Grandia	5	–	40	1	40.00	1-40	–	8.00
J.F.Kloppenburg	40.2	–	191	8	23.87	4-42	1	4.73
R.P.Lefebvre	89	6	346	9	38.44	2-38	–	3.88
H.J.C.Mol	13	–	89	2	44.50	1-24	–	6.84
M.A.K.Raja	35.1	1	204	8	25.50	4-42	1	5.80
E.Schiferli	60	5	327	4	81.75	2-43	–	5.45
D.L.S.van Bunge	12	–	85	5	17.00	3-16	–	7.08
L.P.van Troost	8	–	48	–	–	–	–	6.00

NAMIBIA – BATTING AND FIELDING

	M	I	NO	HS	Runs	Avge	100	50	Ct/St
A.J-B.Burger	6	6	–	85	199	33.16	–	1	–
L.J.Burger	6	6	1	5	11	2.20	–	–	6
S.F.Burger	2	2	–	6	11	5.50	–	–	1
M.Karg	3	2	–	41	45	22.50	–	–	1
D.Keulder	6	6	–	52	132	22.00	–	1	3
B.L.Kotze	5	4	1	24*	27	9.00	–	–	1
D.B.Kotze	6	6	1	27	82	16.40	–	–	3
J.L.Louw	1	–	–	–	–	–	–	–	1
B.G.Murgatroyd	6	6	–	52	90	15.00	–	1	–
G.Snyman	5	4	–	5	5	1.25	–	–	–
S.J.Swanepoel	5	5	–	23	43	8.60	–	–	–
B.O.van Rooi	3	3	2	17	26	26.00	–	–	1
M.van Schoor	5	5	1	24	58	14.50	–	–	4
R.J.van Vuuren	5	5	2	14	26	8.66	–	–	1
R.Walters	2	2	–	–	0	0.00	–	–	1

NAMIBIA – BOWLING

	O	M	R	W	Avge	Best	4wI	R/Over
A.J-B.Burger	16	–	104	3	34.66	1-18	–	6.50
L.J.Burger	55	3	297	6	49.50	3-39	–	5.40
S.F.Burger	11	–	67	–	–	–	–	6.09
B.L.Kotze	43	2	276	3	92.00	2-51	–	6.41
D.B.Kotze	47	–	256	2	128.00	1-32	–	5.44
J.L.Louw	10	–	60	1	60.00	1-60	–	6.00
G.Snyman	48	–	281	6	46.83	3-69	–	5.85
B.O.van Rooi	20	–	119	1	119.00	1-24	–	5.95
R.J.van Vuuren	50	5	298	8	37.25	5-43	1	5.96

SCOTLAND – BATTING AND FIELDING

	M	I	NO	HS	Runs	Avge	100	50	Ct/St
G.M.Hamilton	5	5	1	76	217	54.25	–	2	1

SCOTLAND – BOWLING

	O	M	R	W	Avge	Best	4wI	R/Over
G.M.Hamilton	35.4	3	149	3	49.66	2-36	–	4.18

TEST CAREER RECORDS

These records, complete to 20 January 2004, contain all players registered for county cricket in 2004 at the time of going to press, plus those who have played Test cricket since 1 October 2002 (Test No.1615 onwards).

ENGLAND – BATTING AND FIELDING

	M	I	NO	HS	Runs	Avge	100	50	Ct/St
C.J.Adams	5	8	–	31	104	13.00	–	–	6
U.Afzaal	3	6	1	54	83	16.60	–	1	–
Kabir Ali	1	2	–	9	10	5.00	–	–	–
J.M.Anderson	8	12	10	21*	45	22.50	–	–	2
G.J.Batty	4	7	1	38	136	22.66	–	–	–
M.P.Bicknell	4	7	–	15	45	6.42	–	–	2
R.J.Blakey	2	4	–	6	7	1.75	–	–	2
M.A.Butcher	62	114	4	173*	3790	34.45	8	17	55
A.R.Caddick	62	95	12	49*	861	10.37	–	–	21
R.Clarke	2	3	–	55	96	32.00	–	1	1
P.D.Collingwood	2	4	–	36	89	22.25	–	–	6
D.G.Cork	37	56	8	59	864	18.00	–	3	18
J.P.Crawley	37	61	9	156*	1800	34.61	4	9	29
R.D.B.Croft	21	34	8	37*	421	16.19	–	–	10
R.K.J.Dawson	7	13	3	19*	114	11.40	–	–	3
P.A.J.DeFreitas	44	68	5	88	934	14.82	–	4	14
M.A.Ealham	8	13	3	53*	210	21.00	–	2	4
A.Flintoff	29	47	–	142	1209	25.72	2	6	14
J.S.Foster	7	12	3	48	226	25.11	–	–	17/1
J.E.R.Gallian	3	6	–	28	74	12.33	–	–	1
A.F.Giles	30	43	6	52	641	17.32	–	2	15
D.Gough	58	86	18	65	855	12.57	–	2	13
A.Habib	2	3	–	19	26	8.66	–	–	–
G.M.Hamilton	1	2	–	0	0	0.00	–	–	–
S.J.Harmison	12	18	4	20*	90	6.42	–	–	1
W.K.Hegg	2	4	–	15	30	7.50	–	–	8
G.A.Hick	65	114	6	178	3383	31.32	6	18	90
M.J.Hoggard	22	31	14	32	137	8.05	–	–	7
A.J.Hollioake	4	6	–	45	65	10.83	–	–	4
N.Hussain	91	162	14	207	5430	36.68	13	30	59
R.C.Irani	3	5	–	41	86	17.20	–	–	2
R.L.Johnson	3	4	–	26	59	14.75	–	–	–
S.P.Jones	2	1	–	44	44	44.00	–	–	1
R.W.T.Key	8	13	–	52	244	18.76	–	1	6
R.J.Kirtley	4	7	1	12	32	5.33	–	–	3
N.V.Knight	17	30	–	113	719	23.96	1	4	26
A.McGrath	4	5	–	81	201	40.20	–	2	3
D.L.Maddy	3	4	–	24	46	11.50	–	–	4
P.J.Martin	8	13	–	29	115	8.84	–	–	6
M.P.Maynard	4	8	–	35	87	10.87	–	–	3
A.D.Mullally	19	27	4	24	127	5.52	–	–	6
J.Ormond	2	4	1	18	38	12.66	–	–	–
M.M.Patel	2	2	–	27	45	22.50	–	–	–
M.R.Ramprakash	52	92	6	154	2350	27.32	2	12	39
C.M.W.Read	8	13	3	38*	163	16.30	–	–	25/3
S.J.Rhodes	11	17	5	65*	294	24.50	–	1	46/3
R.C.Russell	54	86	16	128*	1897	27.10	2	6	153/12
M.J.Saggers	1	1	–	1	1	1.00	–	–	1
I.D.K.Salisbury	15	25	3	50	368	16.72	–	1	5
C.P.Schofield	2	3	–	57	67	22.33	–	1	–
R.J.Sidebottom	1	1	–	4	4	4.00	–	–	–
C.E.W.Silverwood	6	7	3	10	29	7.25	–	–	2
A.M.Smith	1	2	1	4*	4	4.00	–	–	–

ENGLAND – BATTING AND FIELDING (continued)

	M	I	NO	HS	Runs	Avge	100	50	Ct/St
E.T.Smith	3	5	–	64	87	17.40	–	1	5
J.P.Stephenson	1	2	–	25	36	18.00	–	–	–
A.J.Stewart	133	235	21	190	8463	39.54	15	45	263/14
G.P.Thorpe	83	151	19	200*	5552	42.06	12	33	88
M.E.Trescothick	43	81	7	219	3175	42.90	5	21	45
A.J.Tudor	10	16	4	99*	229	19.08	–	1	3
M.P.Vaughan	40	71	4	197	3118	46.53	10	8	23
I.J.Ward	5	9	1	39	129	16.12	–	–	1
C.White	30	50	7	121	1052	24.46	1	5	14

ENGLAND – BOWLING

	O	M	R	W	Avge	Best	5wl	10wM
C.J.Adams	20	5	59	1	59.00	1- 42	–	–
U.Afzaal	9	–	49	1	49.00	1- 49	–	–
Kabir Ali	36	5	136	5	27.20	3- 80	–	–
J.M.Anderson	249.5	58	906	26	34.84	5- 73	2	–
G.J.Batty	165.2	28	504	8	63.00	3- 55	–	–
M.P.Bicknell	180	39	543	14	38.78	4- 84	–	–
M.A.Butcher	150.1	27	541	15	36.06	4- 42	–	–
A.R.Caddick	2259.4	501	6999	234	29.91	7- 46	13	1
R.Clarke	29	11	60	4	15.00	2- 7	–	–
P.D.Collingwood	16	3	37	–				
D.G.Cork	1279.4	264	3906	131	29.81	7- 43	5	–
R.D.B.Croft	769.5	195	1825	49	37.24	5- 95	1	–
R.K.J.Dawson	186	20	677	11	61.54	4-134	–	–
P.A.J.DeFreitas	1639.4	367	4700	140	33.57	7- 70	4	–
M.A.Ealham	176.4	43	488	17	28.70	4- 21	–	–
A.Flintoff	820.5	195	2369	52	45.55	4- 50	–	–
J.E.R.Gallian	14	1	62	–				
A.F.Giles	1242	279	3322	83	40.02	5- 67	3	–
D.Gough	1970.1	370	6503	229	28.39	6- 42	9	–
G.M.Hamilton	15	1	63	–				
S.J.Harmison	416.3	99	1215	41	29.63	5- 35	1	–
G.A.Hick	509.3	128	1306	23	56.78	4-126	–	–
M.J.Hoggard	822.4	190	2606	79	32.98	7- 63	2	–
A.J.Hollioake	24	2	67	2	33.50	2- 31	–	–
N.Hussain	5	1	15	–				
R.C.Irani	32	10	112	3	37.33	1- 22	–	–
R.L.Johnson	91.1	25	275	16	17.18	6- 33	2	–
S.P.Jones	45	3	161	5	32.20	2- 61	–	–
R.J.Kirtley	179.5	50	561	19	29.52	6- 34	1	–
A.McGrath	17	1	56	4	14.00	3- 16	–	–
D.L.Maddy	14	1	40	–				
P.J.Martin	242	73	580	17	34.11	4- 60	–	–
A.D.Mullally	754.1	214	1812	58	31.24	5-105	1	–
J.Ormond	62	12	185	2	92.50	1- 70	–	–
M.M.Patel	46	8	180	1	180.00	1-101	–	–
M.R.Ramprakash	149.1	16	477	4	119.25	1- 2	–	–
M.J.Saggers	19.1	4	62	3	20.66	2- 29	–	–
I.D.K.Salisbury	415.2	50	1539	20	76.95	4-163	–	–
C.P.Schofield	18	2	73	–				
R.J.Sidebottom	20	2	64	–				
C.E.W.Silverwood	138	27	444	11	40.36	5- 91	1	–
A.M.Smith	23	2	89	–				
A.J.Stewart	3.2	–	13	–				
G.P.Thorpe	23	7	37	–				
M.E.Trescothick	22	2	62	1	62.00	1- 34	–	–

TEST　　　　**ENGLAND – BOWLING (continued)**

	O	M	R	W	Avge	Best	5wI	10wM
A.J.Tudor	252	51	963	28	34.39	5-44	1	–
M.P.Vaughan	119	17	400	5	80.00	2-71	–	–
C.White	659.5	119	2220	59	37.62	5-32	3	–

AUSTRALIA – BATTING AND FIELDING

	M	I	NO	HS	Runs	Avge	100	50	Ct/St
A.J.Bichel	19	22	1	71	355	16.90	–	1	16
N.W.Bracken	3	3	1	6*	9	4.50	–	–	1
M.T.G.Elliott	20	34	1	199	1171	35.48	3	4	13
A.C.Gilchrist	51	70	13	204*	3169	55.59	9	16	195/19
J.N.Gillespie	49	59	20	48*	628	16.10	–	–	13
M.L.Hayden	50	85	8	380	4488	58.28	17	14	58
G.B.Hogg	4	5	1	17*	38	9.50	–	–	–
M.S.Kasprowicz	17	23	5	25	234	13.00	–	–	6
S.M.Katich	6	9	2	125	420	60.00	1	3	5
J.L.Langer	71	118	6	250	5037	44.97	17	20	46
S.G.Law	1	1	–	54*	54	–	–	1	1
B.Lee	37	36	6	62*	593	19.76	–	2	9
D.S.Lehmann	15	22	2	177	995	49.75	3	4	8
M.L.Love	5	8	3	100*	233	46.60	1	1	7
S.C.G.MacGill	30	34	4	43	238	7.93	–	–	16
G.D.McGrath	95	104	36	39	450	6.61	–	–	29
D.R.Martyn	39	61	10	133	2339	45.86	5	15	19
R.T.Ponting	75	119	15	257	5821	55.97	20	21	88
S.K.Warne	107	146	13	99	2238	16.82	–	8	86
M.E.Waugh	128	209	17	153*	8029	41.81	20	47	181
S.R.Waugh	168	260	46	200	10927	51.06	32	50	112
B.A.Williams	3	4	2	10*	21	10.50	–	–	4

AUSTRALIA – BOWLING

	O	M	R	W	Avge	Best	5wI	10wM
A.J.Bichel	556	111	1870	58	32.24	5-60	1	–
N.W.Bracken	128	38	351	6	58.50	2-12	–	–
M.T.G.Elliott	2	1	4	–				
J.N.Gillespie	1665.3	465	4772	189	25.24	7-37	7	–
M.L.Hayden	9	–	40	–				
G.B.Hogg	129	25	452	9	50.22	2-40	–	–
M.S.Kasprowicz	556.2	121	1739	47	37.00	7-36	2	–
S.M.Katich	83.5	8	305	11	27.72	6-65	1	–
J.L.Langer	1	–	3	–				
S.G.Law	3	1	9	–				
B.Lee	1230	256	4401	139	31.66	5-47	4	–
D.S.Lehmann	79.2	23	180	7	25.71	3-61	–	–
S.C.G.MacGill	1352.3	286	4210	147	28.63	7-50	9	2
G.D.McGrath	3729	1116	9338	430	21.71	8-38	23	3
D.R.Martyn	58	15	168	2	84.00	1-0	–	–
R.T.Ponting	72.5	18	190	4	47.50	1-0	–	–
S.K.Warne	4979.2	1416	12624	491	25.71	8-71	23	6
M.E.Waugh	808.5	171	2429	59	41.16	5-40	1	–
S.R.Waugh	1300.5	332	3445	92	37.44	5-28	3	–
B.A.Williams	118	38	339	9	37.66	4-53	–	–

SOUTH AFRICA – BATTING AND FIELDING

	M	I	NO	HS	Runs	Avge	100	50	Ct/St
P.R.Adams	44	54	15	35	353	9.05	–	–	29
N.Boje	21	30	5	85	586	23.44	–	2	8
M.V.Boucher	71	96	12	125	2679	31.89	4	16	264/10
A.C.Dawson	2	1	–	10	10	10.00	–	–	–

	M	I	NO	HS	Runs	Avge	100	50	Ct/St
H.H.Dippenaar	24	36	2	177*	949	27.91	2	3	14
S.Elworthy	4	5	1	48	72	18.00	–	–	4
H.H.Gibbs	56	94	5	228	4372	49.12	13	14	44
A.J.Hall	10	14	3	99*	297	27.00	–	2	11
M.Hayward	14	14	7	14	62	8.85	–	–	2
C.W.Henderson	7	7	–	30	65	9.28	–	–	2
J.H.Kallis	75	123	20	189*	5486	53.26	15	27	71
G.Kirsten	98	170	14	275	7039	45.12	20	33	83
L.Klusener	48	68	11	174	1904	33.40	4	8	33
N.D.McKenzie	39	61	4	120	1939	34.01	2	12	37
A.Nel	8	6	–	7	11	1.83	–	–	4
M.Ntini	42	40	14	32*	285	10.96	–	–	10
R.J.Peterson	4	5	1	61	125	31.25	–	1	3
S.M.Pollock	80	112	29	111	2868	34.55	2	13	62
D.Pretorius	4	4	1	9	22	7.33	–	–	–
A.G.Prince	7	11	–	49	185	16.81	–	–	3
J.A.Rudolph	11	17	1	222*	645	40.31	2	2	7
G.C.Smith	21	34	2	277	1881	58.78	6	4	25
D.J.Terbrugge	6	6	5	4*	14	14.00	–	–	4
M.van Jaarsveld	4	5	1	73	141	35.25	–	1	5
C.M.Willoughby	2	–	–	–	–	–	–	–	–
M.Zondeki	1	2	–	59	66	33.00	–	1	–

SOUTH AFRICA – BOWLING

	O	M	R	W	Avge	Best	5wI	10wM
P.R.Adams	1427	328	4285	132	32.46	7-128	4	1
N.Boje	629.3	159	1640	53	30.94	5- 62	2	–
A.C.Dawson	42	14	117	5	23.40	2- 20	–	–
S.Elworthy	144.3	35	444	13	34.15	4- 66	–	–
A.J.Hall	241.1	48	761	24	31.70	3- 1	–	–
M.Hayward	427.3	85	1417	50	28.34	5- 56	1	–
C.W.Henderson	327	79	928	22	42.18	4-116	–	–
J.H.Kallis	1750	484	4777	158	30.23	6- 54	4	–
G.Kirsten	58.1	19	142	2	71.00	1- 0	–	–
L.Klusener	1114.5	317	2924	78	37.48	8- 64	1	–
N.D.McKenzie	9	–	54	–	–	–	–	–
A.Nel	277.1	68	879	32	27.46	5- 87	1	–
M.Ntini	1414.5	355	4494	156	28.80	6- 66	7	1
R.J.Peterson	109.5	35	313	7	44.71	3- 46	–	–
S.M.Pollock	2996.4	938	6893	326	21.14	7- 87	16	1
D.Pretorius	95	18	430	6	71.66	4-115	–	–
J.A.Rudolph	42	6	170	2	85.00	1- 1	–	–
G.C.Smith	49.5	9	152	2	76.00	1- 9	–	–
D.J.Terbrugge	146.4	40	424	20	21.20	5- 46	1	–
C.M.Willoughby	50	18	125	1	125.00	1- 47	–	–
M.Zondeki	4.5		25					

WEST INDIES – BATTING AND FIELDING

	M	I	NO	HS	Runs	Avge	100	50	Ct/St
O.A.C.Banks	5	8	3	50*	190	38.00	–	1	2
C.S.Baugh	3	6	–	24	85	14.16	–	–	2/1
D.E.Bernard	1	2	–	7	11	5.50	–	–	–
T.L.Best	1	2	1	20*	20	20.00	–	–	–
G.R.Breese	1	2	–	5	5	2.50	–	–	1
S.Chanderpaul	71	119	15	140	4546	43.71	9	29	29
P.T.Collins	19	30	6	24	165	6.87	–	–	2
C.D.Collymore	7	12	5	16*	76	10.85	–	–	–
C.E.Cuffy	15	23	9	15	58	4.14	–	–	5

	M	I	NO	HS	Runs	Avge	100	50	Ct/St
M.Dillon	38	68	3	43	546	8.40	–	–	16
V.C.Drakes	12	20	2	67	386	21.44	–	1	2
F.H.Edwards	7	12	6	18	40	6.66	–	–	2
D.Ganga	28	50	–	117	1198	23.96	2	5	19
C.H.Gayle	37	64	2	204	2232	36.00	4	12	46
R.O.Hinds	4	8	1	62	162	23.14	–	1	–
W.W.Hinds	38	68	1	165	2142	31.97	4	12	30
C.L.Hooper	102	173	15	233	5762	36.46	13	27	115
R.D.Jacobs	57	100	19	118	2221	27.41	2	13	183/9
B.C.Lara	102	180	5	375	9157	52.32	24	43	136
J.J.C.Lawson	7	10	1	14	34	3.77	–	–	1
N.A.M.McLean	19	32	2	46	368	12.26	–	–	5
D.Mohammed	1	1	–	36	36	36.00	–	–	–
M.V.Nagamootoo	5	8	1	68	185	26.42	–	1	2
D.B.Powell	4	5	–	16	19	3.80	–	–	1
M.N.Samuels	19	33	3	104	874	29.13	1	6	9
A.Sanford	9	13	2	18*	68	6.18	–	–	4
R.R.Sarwan	40	72	5	119	2641	39.41	4	18	22
D.R.Smith	2	4	1	105*	164	54.66	1	–	–
D.S.Smith	4	8	–	62	189	23.62	–	2	2
J.E.Taylor	3	4	1	9*	22	7.33	–	–	–

WEST INDIES – BOWLING

	O	M	R	W	Avge	Best	5wI	10wM
O.A.C.Banks	221.1	38	701	14	50.07	3- 35	–	–
D.E.Bernard	11	1	61	–				
T.L.Best	20	1	99	–				
G.R.Breese	31.2	3	135	2	67.50	2-108	–	–
S.Chanderpaul	241	44	725	8	90.62	1- 2	–	–
P.T.Collins	709.4	130	2218	55	40.32	6- 76	2	–
C.D.Collymore	248	50	785	28	28.03	7- 57	2	–
C.E.Cuffy	561	145	1455	43	33.83	4- 82	–	–
M.Dillon	1450.4	268	4398	131	33.57	5- 71	2	–
V.C.Drakes	436.1	65	1362	33	41.27	5- 93	1	–
F.H.Edwards	230.5	23	971	22	44.13	5- 36	2	–
D.Ganga	26	2	82	–				
C.H.Gayle	234.3	47	617	11	56.09	3- 25	–	–
R.O.Hinds	36	5	119	–				
W.W.Hinds	135.1	27	473	14	33.78	3- 79	–	–
C.L.Hooper	2298	531	5635	114	49.42	5- 26	4	–
B.C.Lara	10	1	28	–				
J.J.C.Lawson	208.3	38	711	29	24.51	7- 78	2	–
N.A.M.McLean	549.5	85	1873	44	42.56	3- 53	–	–
D.Mohammed	39	5	142	3	47.33	3-112	–	–
M.V.Nagamootoo	249	70	637	12	53.08	3-119	–	–
D.B.Powell	128.2	27	354	12	29.50	3- 36	–	–
M.N.Samuels	175	27	550	5	110.00	2- 49	–	–
A.Sanford	317.3	61	1134	27	42.00	4-132	–	–
R.R.Sarwan	138	9	501	9	55.66	2- 1	–	–
D.R.Smith	15	1	46	1	46.00	1- 42	–	–
J.E.Taylor	63.4	10	226	3	75.33	2- 38	–	–

NEW ZEALAND – BATTING AND FIELDING

	M	I	NO	HS	Runs	Avge	100	50	Ct/St
N.J.Astle	59	101	9	222	3592	39.04	9	17	53
S.E.Bond	10	10	5	17	53	10.60	–	–	4
I.G.Butler	7	9	1	26	61	7.62	–	–	4
C.L.Cairns	56	94	5	126	2864	32.17	4	20	14

	M	I	NO	HS	Runs	Avge	100	50	Ct/St
S.P.Fleming	79	137	9	274*	4926	38.48	6	34	117
R.G.Hart	11	19	3	57*	260	16.25	–	1	29/1
M.J.Horne	35	65	2	157	1788	28.38	4	5	17
R.A.Jones	1	2	–	16	23	11.50	–	–	
C.D.McMillan	48	80	10	142	2909	41.55	6	18	19
J.D.P.Oram	7	13	2	97	312	28.36	–	2	4
M.H.Richardson	28	48	3	145	2206	49.02	3	17	21
M.S.Sinclair	20	34	5	214	1100	37.93	3	1	17
C.M.Spearman	19	37	2	112	922	26.34	1	3	21
S.B.Styris	9	16	1	119	560	37.33	2	2	6
D.R.Tuffey	18	24	6	35	221	12.27	–	–	9
D.L.Vettori	50	73	12	137*	1249	20.47	1	6	27
L.Vincent	15	27	1	106	754	29.00	2	6	13
P.J.Wiseman	18	25	6	29	186	9.78	–	–	8

NEW ZEALAND – BOWLING

	O	M	R	W	Avge	Best	5wI	10wM
N.J.Astle	773.5	266	1711	36	47.52	2-22	–	–
S.E.Bond	301.3	64	1045	43	24.30	5-78	2	–
I.G.Butler	212	33	842	24	35.08	6-46	1	–
C.L.Cairns	1757.5	381	5735	197	29.11	7-27	12	1
M.J.Horne	11	7	26	–				
C.D.McMillan	399.5	98	1206	27	44.66	3-48	–	–
J.D.P.Oram	193.5	46	510	22	23.18	4-41	–	–
M.H.Richardson	10	–	17	1	17.00	1-16	–	–
M.S.Sinclair	4	–	13	–				
S.B.Styris	110	23	359	7	51.28	3-28	–	–
D.R.Tuffey	549.5	145	1667	61	27.32	6-54	2	–
D.L.Vettori	2033	531	5368	150	35.78	7-87	7	1
P.J.Wiseman	674	157	2017	45	44.82	5-82	2	–

INDIA – BATTING AND FIELDING

	M	I	NO	HS	Runs	Avge	100	50	Ct/St
A.B.Agarkar	20	31	3	109*	382	13.64	1	–	4
L.Balaji	2	1	–	4	4	4.00	–	–	
S.B.Bangar	12	18	2	100*	470	29.37	1	3	4
A.Chopra	6	12	–	60	371	30.91	–	2	8
R.Dravid	75	130	16	233	6546	57.42	16	32	94
S.C.Ganguly	72	120	12	173	4509	41.75	11	21	52
Harbhajan Singh	36	51	11	66	540	13.50	–	2	14
M.Kartik	5	5	–	43	61	12.20	–	–	1
Z.Khan	28	37	7	46	278	9.26	–	–	8
A.Kumble	81	103	19	88	1408	16.76	–	3	37
V.V.S.Laxman	50	83	10	281	3460	47.39	7	18	58
A.Nehra	16	24	10	19	76	5.42	–	–	4
P.A.Patel	13	20	6	62	382	27.28	–	1	22/6
I.K.Pathan	2	2	1	13*	14	14.00	–	–	1
V.Sehwag	20	33	–	195	1513	45.84	5	5	24
J.Srinath	67	92	21	76	1009	14.21	–	4	22
S.R.Tendulkar	111	180	18	241*	9265	57.19	32	37	71
T.Yohannan	3	4	4	8*	13	–	–	–	1
Yuvraj Singh	1	2	1	20	25	25.00	–	–	

INDIA – BOWLING

	O	M	R	W	Avge	Best	5wI	10wM
A.B.Agarkar	659.3	135	2226	51	43.64	6-41	1	–
L.Balaji	67	21	183	1	183.00	1-84	–	–
S.B.Bangar	127	35	343	7	49.00	2-23	–	–

TEST   **INDIA – BOWLING (continued)**

	O	M	R	W	Avge	Best	5wI	10wM
R.Dravid	20	4	39	1	39.00	1- 18	–	–
S.C.Ganguly	345.2	73	1162	23	50.52	3- 28	–	–
Harbhajan Singh	1607.5	352	4299	151	28.47	8- 84	11	2
M.Kartik	192.3	46	520	10	52.00	3-123	–	–
Z.Khan	869.2	184	2847	82	34.71	5- 29	3	–
A.Kumble	4311.2	1083	10812	382	28.30	10- 74	23	5
V.V.S.Laxman	42	10	100	1	100.00	1- 32	–	–
A.Nehra	547.3	116	1786	41	43.56	4- 72	–	–
I.K.Pathan	68	7	266	4	66.50	2- 80	–	–
V.Sehwag	73.3	8	262	3	87.33	1- 17	–	–
J.Srinath	2517.2	596	7196	236	30.49	8- 86	10	1
S.R.Tendulkar	441	68	1461	31	47.12	3- 10	–	–
T.Yohannan	81	17	256	5	51.20	2- 56	–	–
Yuvraj Singh	1	–	1	–			–	–

PAKISTAN – BATTING AND FIELDING

	M	I	NO	HS	Runs	Avge	100	50	Ct/St
Abdul Razzaq	27	42	4	134	1122	29.52	3	4	7
Asim Kamal	2	3	–	99	138	46.00	–	1	2
Azhar Mahmood	21	34	4	136	900	30.00	3	1	14
Danish Kaneria	16	18	8	15	53	5.30	–	–	3
Faisal Iqbal	10	18	1	83	403	23.70	–	3	7
Farhan Adil	1	2	–	25	33	16.50	–	–	–
Hasan Raza	5	7	1	68	213	35.50	–	2	1
Imran Farhat	8	14	–	128	451	32.21	1	2	10
Imran Nazir	8	13	–	131	427	32.84	2	1	4
Inzamam-ul-Haq	91	150	16	329	6680	49.85	18	35	70
Irfan Fazil	1	2	1	3	4	4.00	–	–	2
Kamran Akmal	4	7	–	56	139	19.85	–	1	13/1
Misbah-ul-Haq	5	9	–	28	120	13.33	–	–	1
Mohammad Akram	9	15	6	10*	24	2.66	–	–	4
Mohammad Hafeez	3	6	1	102*	214	42.80	1	1	1
Mohammad Sami	12	17	9	25	95	11.87	–	–	–
Mohammad Zahid	5	6	1	6*	7	1.40	–	–	–
Moin Khan	67	100	8	137	2713	29.48	4	15	124/20
Mushtaq Ahmed	52	72	16	59	656	11.71	–	2	23
Rashid Latif	37	57	9	150	1381	28.77	1	7	119/11
Salim Elahi	13	24	1	72	436	18.95	–	1	10/1
Salman Butt	1	2	–	37	49	24.50	–	–	1
Saqlain Mushtaq	48	76	14	101*	922	14.87	1	2	15
Shabbir Ahmed	6	7	2	24*	63	12.60	–	–	3
Shahid Afridi	14	25	1	141	780	32.50	2	4	8
Shoaib Akhtar	29	41	10	37	246	7.93	–	–	7
Shoaib Malik	5	7	2	47	121	24.20	–	–	1
Taufiq Umar	19	34	1	135	1518	46.00	4	9	28
Umar Gul	4	5	–	5	13	2.60	–	–	1
Waqar Younis	87	120	21	45	1010	10.20	–	–	18
Yasir Ali	1	2	2	1*	1	–	–	–	–
Yasir Hamid	7	13	2	170	589	53.54	2	2	2
Younis Khan	28	47	2	153	1680	37.33	5	9	31
Yousuf Youhana	48	78	8	204*	3458	49.40	10	20	47

PAKISTAN – BOWLING

	O	M	R	W	Avge	Best	5wI	10wM
Abdul Razzaq	650.1	128	1884	54	34.88	4-24	–	–
Azhar Mahmood	502.3	109	1402	39	35.94	4-50	–	–
Danish Kaneria	661.2	152	1839	65	28.29	7-77	5	1
Faisal Iqbal	1	–	7	–			–	–

TEST PAKISTAN – BOWLING (continued)

	O	M	R	W	Avge	Best	5wI	10wM
Hasan Raza	1	–	1	–				
Inzamam-ul-Haq	1.3	–	8	–				
Irfan Fazil	8	–	65	2	32.50	1- 30		
Mohammad Akram	246.1	36	859	17	50.52	5-138	1	–
Mohammad Hafeez	34	15	61	1	61.00	1- 14	–	–
Mohammad Sami	424	78	1396	32	43.62	5- 36	2	–
Mohammad Zahid	132	17	502	15	33.46	7- 66	1	1
Mushtaq Ahmed	2088.4	406	6100	185	32.97	7- 56	10	3
Rashid Latif	2	–	10	–				
Saqlain Mushtaq	2302	534	6002	207	28.99	8-164	13	3
Shabbir Ahmed	286.5	70	719	33	21.78	5- 48	2	–
Shahid Afridi	221.5	42	661	21	31.47	5- 52	1	–
Shoaib Akhtar	856.3	155	2762	118	23.40	6- 11	8	2
Shoaib Malik	94.1	16	291	7	41.57	4- 42	–	–
Taufiq Umar	11	2	36	–				
Umar Gul	157	28	518	19	27.26	4- 58	–	–
Waqar Younis	2704	517	8788	373	23.56	7- 76	22	5
Yasir Ali	20	5	55	2	27.50	1- 12	–	–
Younis Khan	37	7	139	1	139.00	1- 47	–	–
Yousuf Youhana	1	–	3	–				

SRI LANKA – BATTING AND FIELDING

	M	I	NO	HS	Runs	Avge	100	50	Ct/St
R.P.Arnold	43	67	4	123	1804	28.63	3	10	49
M.S.Atapattu	68	117	14	223	3907	37.93	11	12	43
U.D.U.Chandana	9	12	1	92	340	30.90	–	2	4
H.D.P.K.Dharmasena	30	49	7	62*	862	20.52	–	3	13
T.M.Dilshan	12	19	2	163*	618	36.35	2	2	21
C.R.D.Fernando	14	20	6	15	85	6.07	–	–	5
K.A.D.M.Fernando	2	3	1	51*	56	28.00	–	1	–
K.H.R.K.Fernando	2	4	–	24	38	9.50	–	–	1
S.T.Jayasuriya	83	140	13	340	5258	41.40	10	26	63
D.P.M.D.Jayawardena	54	86	7	242	3877	49.07	10	19	66
R.S.Kaluwitharana	44	69	4	132*	1760	27.07	3	8	82/22
M.K.G.C.P.Lakshitha	2	3	–	40	42	14.00	–	–	1
K.S.Lokuarachchi	3	3	1	28*	63	31.50	–	–	1
M.T.T.Mirando	1	2	–	13	24	12.00	–	–	–
J.Mubarak	2	4	–	48	118	29.50	–	–	4
M.Muralitharan	85	108	40	67	859	12.63	–	1	41
R.A.P.Nissanka	4	5	2	12*	18	6.00	–	–	–
P.D.R.L.Perera	8	9	6	11*	33	11.00	–	–	2
T.T.Samaraweera	14	16	4	142	806	67.16	3	4	7
K.C.Sangakkara	33	53	4	230	2286	46.65	4	13	88/10
H.P.Tillekeratne	80	125	24	204*	4373	43.29	11	19	120/2
W.P.U.C.J.Vaas	71	100	16	74*	1659	19.75	–	6	20

SRI LANKA – BOWLING

	O	M	R	W	Avge	Best	5wI	10wM
R.P.Arnold	221.2	45	589	11	53.54	3- 76	–	–
M.S.Atapattu	8	–	24	1	24.00	1- 9	–	–
U.D.U.Chandana	230.2	45	697	20	34.85	6-179	1	–
H.D.P.K.Dharmasena	1112.3	258	2768	67	41.31	6- 72	3	–
T.M.Dilshan	3	1	10	–				
C.R.D.Fernando	353.1	50	1340	37	36.21	5- 42	2	–
K.A.D.M.Fernando	21	2	107	1	107.00	1- 29	–	–
K.H.R.K.Fernando	39	7	108	4	27.00	3- 63	–	–
S.T.Jayasuriya	1013.1	238	2489	74	33.63	5- 43	1	–
D.P.M.D.Jayawardena	70.2	15	214	4	53.50	2- 32	–	–

TEST

	O	M	R	W	Avge	Best	5wI	10wM
M.K.G.C.P.Lakshitha	48	10	158	5	31.60	2-33	–	–
K.S.Lokuarachchi	87	18	262	5	52.40	2-47	–	–
M.T.T.Mirando	15	1	59	–				
J.Mubarak	2	–	6	–				
M.Muralitharan	4828	1308	11130	485	22.94	9-51	39	12
R.A.P.Nissanka	97.5	21	366	10	36.60	5-64	1	–
P.D.R.L.Perera	188.2	31	661	17	38.88	3-40	–	–
T.T.Samaraweera	136.4	28	409	11	37.18	4-49	–	–
H.P.Tillekeratne	12.4	4	25	–				
W.P.U.C.J.Vaas	2606.1	587	6899	229	30.12	7-71	7	2

ZIMBABWE – BATTING AND FIELDING

	M	I	NO	HS	Runs	Avge	100	50	Ct/St
A.M.Blignaut	14	26	2	92	599	24.95	–	3	11
A.D.R.Campbell	60	109	4	103	2858	27.21	2	18	60
S.V.Carlisle	33	59	4	118	1390	25.27	1	7	30
D.D.Ebrahim	18	34	1	94	835	25.30	–	7	12
S.M.Ervine	3	6	–	53	101	16.83	–	1	5
C.N.Evans	3	6	–	22	52	8.66	–	–	1
G.M.Ewing	1	2	–	2	2	1.00	–	–	
A.Flower	63	112	19	232*	4794	51.54	12	27	151/9
G.W.Flower	65	120	5	201*	3412	29.66	6	15	42
T.J.Friend	12	19	4	81	447	29.80	–	3	1
M.W.Goodwin	19	37	4	166*	1414	42.84	3	8	10
T.R.Gripper	18	35	1	112	739	21.73	1	4	13
D.T.Hondo	3	6	3	6	16	5.33	–	–	2
N.B.Mahwire	4	7	3	8*	27	6.75	–	–	1
H.Masakadza	7	14	1	119	347	26.69	1	1	–
S.Matsikenyeri	2	4	1	57	116	38.66	–	1	4
M.L.Nkala	7	9	2	47	114	16.28	–	–	3
H.K.Olonga	30	45	11	24	184	5.41	–	–	10
R.W.Price	16	28	6	36	214	9.72	–	–	3
V.Sibanda	2	4	–	18	36	9.00	–	–	1
H.H.Streak	57	94	18	127*	1746	22.97	1	9	17
T.Taibu	12	24	1	83	482	20.95	–	2	19/2
M.A.Vermeulen	7	14	–	118	408	29.14	1	2	6
G.J.Whittall	46	82	7	203*	2207	29.42	4	10	19
C.B.Wishart	25	46	1	114	1063	23.62	1	5	15

ZIMBABWE – BOWLING

	O	M	R	W	Avge	Best	5wI	10wM
A.M.Blignaut	440.2	91	1579	46	34.32	5- 73	3	–
A.D.R.Campbell	11	2	28	–				
S.M.Ervine	56	9	258	6	43.00	4-146	–	–
C.N.Evans	9	–	35	–				
G.M.Ewing	14	1	73	–				
A.Flower	0.3	–	4	–				
G.W.Flower	563	122	1537	25	61.48	4- 41	–	–
T.J.Friend	324.2	61	1070	24	44.58	5- 31	1	–
M.W.Goodwin	19.5	3	69	–				
T.R.Gripper	128.1	19	501	6	83.50	2- 91	–	–
D.T.Hondo	55	6	230	4	57.50	3- 98	–	–
N.B.Mahwire	82.5	17	359	3	119.66	2- 75	–	–
H.Masakadza	4	–	12	1	12.00	1- 9	–	–
S.Matsikenyeri	4	–	16	–				
M.L.Nkala	177	40	525	8	65.62	3- 82	–	–
H.K.Olonga	750.2	130	2620	68	38.52	5- 70	2	–
R.W.Price	801.1	189	2315	61	37.95	6- 73	5	1

TEST   **ZIMBABWE – BOWLING (continued)**

	O	M	R	W	Avge	Best	5wI	10wM
H.H.Streak	2081.5	550	5509	197	27.96	6-87	6	–
G.J.Whittall	781	208	2088	51	40.94	4-18	–	–

BANGLADESH – BATTING AND FIELDING

	M	I	NO	HS	Runs	Avge	100	50	Ct/St
Akram Khan	8	16	–	44	259	16.18	–	–	3
Al Sahariar	15	30	–	71	683	22.76	–	4	10
Alamgir Kabir	2	4	1	4	5	1.66	–	–	–
Alok Kapali	14	28	1	85	519	19.22	–	2	4
Aminul Islam	13	26	1	145	530	21.20	1	2	5
Anwar Hossain Monir	1	2	–	4	4	4.00	–	–	–
Anwar Piju Hossain	1	2	–	12	14	7.00	–	–	–
Enamul Haque	10	19	4	24*	180	12.00	–	–	1
Enamul Haque II	2	4	2	9	10	5.00	–	–	–
Habibul Bashar	26	52	1	108	1840	36.07	2	16	12
Hannan Sarkar	12	24	–	76	603	25.12	–	5	2
Javed Omar	19	38	1	119	868	23.45	1	4	6
Khaled Mahmud	12	23	1	45	266	12.09	–	–	2
Khaled Masud	23	44	5	51	653	16.74	–	1	37/3
Manjural Islam	16	31	10	21	75	3.57	–	–	4
Mashrafe Mortaza	12	22	3	29	161	8.47	–	–	4
Mehrab Hossain	9	18	–	71	241	13.38	–	1	6
Mohammed Ashraful	15	30	1	114	592	20.41	1	2	3
Mohammed Rafique	8	16	3	32	169	13.00	–	–	3
Mohammed Salim	2	4	1	26	49	16.33	–	–	3/1
Mushfiqur Rahman	4	8	2	46*	124	20.66	–	–	1
Naimur Rahman	8	15	1	48	210	15.00	–	–	4
Rafiqul Islam	1	2	–	6	7	3.50	–	–	–
Rajin Saleh	5	10	–	60	246	24.60	–	1	6
Sanwar Hossain	9	18	–	49	345	19.16	–	–	1
Talha Jubair	6	12	6	5*	21	3.50	–	–	–
Tapash Baisya	11	22	5	52*	157	9.23	–	1	2
Tushar Imran	3	6	–	28	52	8.66	–	–	1

BANGLADESH – BOWLING

	O	M	R	W	Avge	Best	5wI	10wM
Alamgir Kabir	35.3	5	182	–			–	–
Alok Kapali	175.5	15	674	6	112.33	3- 3	–	–
Aminul Islam	33	1	149	1	149.00	1- 66	–	–
Anwar Hossain Monir	21	4	95	–			–	–
Enamul Haque	371.4	88	1027	18	57.05	4-136	–	–
Enamul Haque II	67	17	201	4	50.25	2- 53	–	–
Habibul Bashar	39	1	195	–			–	–
Javed Omar	1	–	12	–			–	–
Khaled Mahmud	270	65	832	13	64.00	4- 37	–	–
Manjural Islam	455	91	1512	27	56.00	6- 81	1	–
Mashrafe Mortaza	324.4	70	1043	29	35.96	4- 60	–	–
Mehrab Hossain	2	–	5	–			–	–
Mohammed Ashraful	95	3	432	5	86.40	2- 42	–	–
Mohammed Rafique	390.5	91	997	36	27.69	6- 77	3	–
Mushfiqur Rahman	80.3	20	274	4	68.50	2- 50	–	–
Naimur Rahman	220.1	45	718	12	59.83	6-132	1	–
Rajin Saleh	21	3	61	1	61.00	1- 9	–	–
Sanwar Hossain	74	5	310	5	62.00	2-128	–	–
Talha Jubair	162.4	20	676	14	48.28	3-135	–	–
Tapash Baisya	283.2	43	1072	18	59.55	4- 72	–	–

FIRST-CLASS CRICKET RECORDS

To the end of the 2003 season

TEAM RECORDS

HIGHEST INNINGS TOTALS

1107	Victoria v New South Wales	Melbourne	1926-27
1059	Victoria v Tasmania	Melbourne	1922-23
952-6d	Sri Lanka v India	Colombo	1997-98
951-7d	Sind v Baluchistan	Karachi	1973-74
944-6d	Hyderabad v Andhra	Secunderabad	1993-94
918	New South Wales v South Australia	Sydney	1900-01
912-8d	Holkar v Mysore	Indore	1945-46
910-6d	Railways v Dera Ismail Khan	Lahore	1964-65
903-7d	England v Australia	The Oval	1938
887	Yorkshire v Warwickshire	Birmingham	1896
863	Lancashire v Surrey	The Oval	1990
860-6d	Tamil Nadu v Goa	Panjim	1988-89

Excluding penalty runs in India, there have been 30 innings totals of 800 runs or more in first-class cricket. Tamil Nadu's total of 860-6d was boosted to 912 by 52 penalty runs.

HIGHEST SECOND INNINGS TOTAL

770	New South Wales v South Australia	Adelaide	1920-21

HIGHEST FOURTH INNINGS TOTAL

654-5	England v South Africa	Durban	1938-39

HIGHEST MATCH AGGREGATE

2376	Maharashtra v Bombay	Poona	1948-49

RECORD MARGIN OF VICTORY

Innings and 851 runs: Railways v Dera Ismail Khan	Lahore	1964-65

MOST RUNS IN A DAY

721	Australians v Essex	Southend	1948

MOST HUNDREDS IN AN INNINGS

6	Holkar v Mysore	Indore	1945-46

LOWEST INNINGS TOTALS

12	†Oxford University v MCC and Ground	Oxford	1877
12	Northamptonshire v Gloucestershire	Gloucester	1907
13	Auckland v Canterbury	Auckland	1877-78
13	Nottinghamshire v Yorkshire	Nottingham	1901
14	Surrey v Essex	Chelmsford	1983
15	MCC v Surrey	Lord's	1839
15	†Victoria v MCC	Melbourne	1903-04
15	†Northamptonshire v Yorkshire	Northampton	1908
15	Hampshire v Warwickshire	Birmingham	1922

† Batted one man short

There have been 27 instances of a team being dismissed for under 20.

LOWEST MATCH AGGREGATE BY ONE TEAM

34 (16 and 18) Border v Natal   East London   1959-60

LOWEST COMPLETED MATCH AGGREGATE BY BOTH TEAMS

105   MCC v Australians   Lord's   1878

FEWEST RUNS IN AN UNINTERRUPTED DAY'S PLAY

95   Australia (80) v Pakistan (15-2)   Karachi   1956-57

TIED MATCHES

Before 1949 a match was considered to be tied if the scores were level after the fourth innings, even if the side batting last had wickets in hand when play ended. Law 22 was amended in 1948 and since then a match has been tied only when the scores are level after the fourth innings has been completed. There have been 56 tied first-class matches, five of which would not have qualified under the current law. The most recent are:

Warwickshire (446-7d & forfeit) v Essex (66-0d & 380)   Birmingham   2003
Worcestershire (262 & 247) v Zimbabweans (334 & 175)   Worcester   2003

BATTING RECORDS
HIGHEST INDIVIDUAL INNINGS

501*	B.C.Lara	Warwickshire v Durham	Birmingham	1994
499	Hanif Mohammed	Karachi v Bahawalpur	Karachi	1958-59
452*	D.G.Bradman	New South Wales v Queensland	Sydney	1929-30
443*	B.B.Nimbalkar	Maharashtra v Kathiawar	Poona	1948-49
437	W.H.Ponsford	Victoria v Queensland	Melbourne	1927-28
429	W.H.Ponsford	Victoria v Tasmania	Melbourne	1922-23
428	Aftab Baloch	Sind v Baluchistan	Karachi	1973-74
424	A.C.MacLaren	Lancashire v Somerset	Taunton	1895
405*	G.A.Hick	Worcestershire v Somerset	Taunton	1988
394	Naved Latif	Sargodha v Gujranwala	Gujranwala	2000-01
385	B.Sutcliffe	Otago v Canterbury	Christchurch	1952-53
383	C.W.Gregory	New South Wales v Queensland	Brisbane	1906-07
377	S.V.Manjrekar	Bombay v Hyderabad	Bombay	1990-91
375	B.C.Lara	West Indies v England	St John's	1993-94
369	D.G.Bradman	South Australia v Tasmania	Adelaide	1935-36
366	N.H.Fairbrother	Lancashire v Surrey	The Oval	1990
366	M.V.Sridhar	Hyderabad v Andhra	Secunderabad	1993-94
365*	C.Hill	South Australia v NSW	Adelaide	1900-01
365*	G.St A.Sobers	West Indies v Pakistan	Kingston	1957-58
364	L.Hutton	England v Australia	The Oval	1938
359*	V.M.Merchant	Bombay v Maharashtra	Bombay	1943-44
359	R.B.Simpson	New South Wales v Queensland	Brisbane	1963-64
357*	R.Abel	Surrey v Somerset	The Oval	1899
357	D.G.Bradman	South Australia v Victoria	Melbourne	1935-36
356	B.A.Richards	South Australia v W Australia	Perth	1970-71
355*	G.R.Marsh	W Australia v S Australia	Perth	1989-90
355	B.Sutcliffe	Otago v Auckland	Dunedin	1949-50
353	W.V.S.Laxman	Hyderabad v Karnataka	Bangalore	1999-00
352	W.H.Ponsford	Victoria v New South Wales	Melbourne	1926-27
350	Rashid Israr	Habib Bank v National Bank	Lahore	1976-77

There have been 140 triple hundreds in first-class cricket, W.V.Raman (313) and Arjan Kripal Singh (302*) for Tamil Nadu v Goa at Panjim in 1988-89 providing the only instance of two batsmen scoring 300 in the same innings.

MOST HUNDREDS IN SUCCESSIVE INNINGS

6	C.B.Fry	Sussex and Rest of England	1901
6	D.G.Bradman	South Australia and D.G.Bradman's XI	1938-39

6	M.J.Procter	Rhodesia		1970-71

TWO DOUBLE HUNDREDS IN A MATCH

244	202* A.E.Fagg	Kent v Essex	Colchester	1938

TRIPLE HUNDRED AND HUNDRED IN A MATCH

333	123 G.A.Gooch	England v India	Lord's	1990

DOUBLE HUNDRED AND HUNDRED IN A MATCH MOST TIMES

4	Zaheer Abbas	Gloucestershire		1976-81

TWO HUNDREDS IN A MATCH MOST TIMES

8	Zaheer Abbas	Gloucestershire and PIA	1976-82
7	W.R.Hammond	Gloucestershire, England and MCC	1927-45

MOST HUNDREDS IN A SEASON

18	D.C.S.Compton	1947	16	J.B.Hobbs	1925

100 HUNDREDS IN A CAREER

	Total		100th Hundred	
	Hundreds	*Inns*	*Season*	*Inns*
J.B.Hobbs	197	1315	1923	821
E.H.Hendren	170	1300	1928-29	740
W.R.Hammond	167	1005	1935	679
C.P.Mead	153	1340	1927	892
G.Boycott	151	1014	1977	645
H.Sutcliffe	149	1088	1932	700
F.E.Woolley	145	1532	1929	1031
L.Hutton	129	814	1951	619
G.A.Gooch	128	990	1992-93	820
W.G Grace	126	1493	1895	1113
D.C.S.Compton	123	839	1952	552
G.A.Hick	122	748	1998	574
T.W.Graveney	122	1223	1964	940
D.G.Bradman	117	338	1947-48	295
I.V.A.Richards	114	796	1988-89	658
Zaheer Abbas	108	768	1982-83	658
A.Sandham	107	1000	1935	871
M.C.Cowdrey	107	1130	1973	1035
T.W.Hayward	104	1138	1913	1076
G.M.Turner	103	792	1982	779
J.H.Edrich	103	979	1977	945
L.E.G.Ames	102	951	1950	915
G.E.Tyldesley	102	961	1934	919
D.L.Amiss	102	1139	1986	1081

MOST 400s: 2 – W.H.Ponsford
MOST 300s or more: 6 – D.G.Bradman; 4 – W.R.Hammond
MOST 200s or more: 37 – D.G.Bradman; 36 – W.R.Hammond; 22 – E.H.Hendren

MOST RUNS IN A MONTH

1294 (avge 92.42)	L.Hutton	Yorkshire	June 1949

MOST RUNS IN A SEASON

Runs			I	NO	HS	Avge	100	Season
3816	D.C.S.Compton	Middlesex	50	8	246	90.85	18	1947
3539	W.J.Edrich	Middlesex	52	8	267*	80.43	12	1947
3518	T.W.Hayward	Surrey	61	8	219	66.37	13	1906

The feat of scoring 3000 runs in a season has been achieved 28 times, the most recent instance being by W.E.Alley (3019) in 1961. The highest aggregate in a season since 1969 is 2755 by S.J.Cook in 1991.

1000 RUNS IN A SEASON MOST TIMES

28   W.G.Grace (Gloucestershire), F.E.Woolley (Kent)

HIGHEST BATTING AVERAGE IN A SEASON

(Qualification: 12 innings)

Avge			I	NO	HS	Runs	100	Season
115.66	D.G.Bradman	Australians	26	5	278	2429	13	1938
104.66	D.R.Martyn	Australians	14	5	176*	942	5	2001
102.53	G.Boycott	Yorkshire	20	5	175*	1538	6	1979
102.00	W.A.Johnston	Australians	17	16	28*	102	–	1953
101.70	G.A.Gooch	Essex	30	3	333	2746	12	1990
100.12	G.Boycott	Yorkshire	30	5	233	2503	13	1971

FASTEST HUNDRED AGAINST AUTHENTIC BOWLING

35 min	P.G.H.Fender	Surrey v Northamptonshire	Northampton	1920

FASTEST DOUBLE HUNDRED

113 min	R.J.Shastri	Bombay v Baroda	Bombay	1984-85

FASTEST TRIPLE HUNDRED

181 min	D.C.S.Compton	MCC v NE Transvaal	Benoni	1948-49

MOST SIXES IN AN INNINGS

16	A.Symonds	Gloucestershire v Glamorgan	Abergavenny	1995

MOST SIXES IN A MATCH

20	A.Symonds	Gloucestershire v Glamorgan	Abergavenny	1995

MOST SIXES IN A SEASON

80	I.T.Botham	Somerset and England		1985

MOST FOURS IN AN INNINGS

72	B.C.Lara	Warwickshire v Durham	Birmingham	1994

MOST RUNS OFF ONE OVER

36	G.St A.Sobers	Nottinghamshire v Glamorgan	Swansea	1968
36	R.J.Shastri	Bombay v Baroda	Bombay	1984-85

Both batsmen hit for six all six balls of overs bowled by M.A.Nash and Tilak Raj respectively.

MOST RUNS IN A DAY

390*	B.C.Lara	Warwickshire v Durham	Birmingham	1994

There have been 19 instances of a batsman scoring 300 or more runs in a day.

LONGEST INNINGS

1015 min R.Nayyar (271)   Himachal Pradesh v Jammu & Kashmir Chamba   1999-00

HIGHEST PARTNERSHIPS FOR EACH WICKET

First Wicket

561	Waheed Mirza/Mansoor Akhtar	Karachi W v Quetta	Karachi	1976-77
555	P.Holmes/H.Sutcliffe	Yorkshire v Essex	Leyton	1932
554	J.T.Brown/J.Tunnicliffe	Yorkshire v Derbys	Chesterfield	1898

Second Wicket

576	S.T.Jayasuriya/R.S.Mahanama	Sri Lanka v India	Colombo (RPS)	1997-98
475	Zahir Alam/L.S.Rajput	Assam v Tripura	Gauhati	1991-92
465*	J.A.Jameson/R.B.Kanhai	Warwickshire v Glos	Birmingham	1974

Third Wicket

467	A.H.Jones/M.D.Crowe	N Zealand v Sri Lanka	Wellington	1990-91
456	Khalid Irtiza/Aslam Ali	United Bank v Multan	Karachi	1975-76
451	Mudassar Nazar/Javed Miandad	Pakistan v India	Hyderabad	1982-83
445	P.E.Whitelaw/W.N.Carson	Auckland v Otago	Dunedin	1936-37
438*	G.A.Hick/T.M.Moody	Worcestershire v Hants	Southampton	1997

Fourth Wicket

577	V.S.Hazare/Gul Mahomed	Baroda v Holkar	Baroda	1946-47
574*	C.L.Walcott/F.M.M.Worrell	Barbados v Trinidad	Port-of-Spain	1945-46
502*	F.M.M.Worrell/J.D.C.Goddard	Barbados v Trinidad	Bridgetown	1943-44
470	A.I.Kallicharran/G.W.Humpage	Warwickshire v Lancs	Southport	1982

Fifth Wicket

464*	M.E.Waugh/S.R.Waugh	NSW v W Australia	Perth	1990-91
405	S.G.Barnes/D.G.Bradman	Australia v England	Sydney	1946-47
401	M.B.Loye/D.Ripley	Northants v Glamorgan	Northampton	1998

Sixth Wicket

487*	G.A.Headley/C.C.Passailaigue	Jamaica v Tennyson's	Kingston	1931-32
428	W.W.Armstrong/M.A.Noble	Australians v Sussex	Hove	1902
411	R.M.Poore/E.G.Wynyard	Hampshire v Somerset	Taunton	1899

Seventh Wicket

460	Bhupinder Singh jr/P.Dharmani	Punjab v Delhi	Delhi	1994-95
347	D.St E.Atkinson/C.C.Depeiza	W Indies v Australia	Bridgetown	1954-55
344	K.S.Ranjitsinhji/W.Newham	Sussex v Essex	Leyton	1902

Eighth Wicket

433	V.T.Trumper/A.Sims	Australians v C'bury	Christchurch	1913-14
313	Wasim Akram/Saqlain Mushtaq	Pakistan v Zimbabwe	Sheikhupura	1996-97
292	R.Peel/Lord Hawke	Yorkshire v Warwicks	Birmingham	1896

Ninth Wicket

283	J.Chapman/A.Warren	Derbys v Warwicks	Blackwell	1910
268	J.B.Commins/N.Boje	SA 'A' v Mashonaland	Harare	1994-95
251	J.W.H.T.Douglas/S.N.Hare	Essex v Derbyshire	Leyton	1921

Tenth Wicket

307	A.F.Kippax/J.E.H.Hooker	NSW v Victoria	Melbourne	1928-29
249	C.T.Sarwate/S.N.Banerjee	Indians v Surrey	The Oval	1946
235	F.E.Woolley/A.Fielder	Kent v Worcs	Stourbridge	1909

213

35000 RUNS IN A CAREER

	Career	I	NO	HS	Runs	Avge	100
J.B.Hobbs	1905-34	1315	106	316*	**61237**	50.65	197
F.E.Woolley	1906-38	1532	85	305*	**58969**	40.75	145
E.H.Hendren	1907-38	1300	166	301*	**57611**	50.80	170
C.P.Mead	1905-36	1340	185	280*	**55061**	47.67	153
W.G.Grace	1865-1908	1493	105	344	**54896**	39.55	126
W.R.Hammond	1920-51	1005	104	336*	**50551**	56.10	167
H.Sutcliffe	1919-45	1088	123	313	**50138**	51.95	149
G.Boycott	1962-86	1014	162	261*	**48426**	56.83	151
T.W.Graveney	1948-71/72	1223	159	258	**47793**	44.91	122
G.A.Gooch	1973-2000	990	75	333	**44846**	49.01	128
T.W.Hayward	1893-1914	1138	96	315*	**43551**	41.79	104
D.L.Amiss	1960-87	1139	126	262*	**43423**	42.86	102
M.C.Cowdrey	1950-76	1130	134	307	**42719**	42.89	107
A.Sandham	1911-37/38	1000	79	325	**41284**	44.82	107
L.Hutton	1934-60	814	91	364	**40140**	55.51	129
M.J.K.Smith	1951-75	1091	139	204	**39832**	41.84	69
W.Rhodes	1898-1930	1528	237	267*	**39802**	30.83	58
J.H.Edrich	1956-78	979	104	310*	**39790**	45.47	103
R.E.S.Wyatt	1923-57	1141	157	232	**39405**	40.04	85
D.C.S.Compton	1936-64	839	88	300	**38942**	51.85	123
G.E.Tyldesley	1909-36	961	106	256*	**38874**	45.46	102
J.T.Tyldesley	1895-1923	994	62	295*	**37897**	40.60	86
K.W.R.Fletcher	1962-88	1167	170	228*	**37665**	37.77	63
C.G.Greenidge	1970-92	889	75	273*	**37354**	45.88	92
J.W.Hearne	1909-36	1025	116	285*	**37252**	40.98	96
L.E.G.Ames	1926-51	951	95	295	**37248**	43.51	102
D.Kenyon	1946-67	1159	59	259	**37002**	33.63	74
W.J.Edrich	1934-58	964	92	267*	**36965**	42.39	86
J.M.Parks	1949-76	1227	172	205*	**36673**	34.76	51
M.W.Gatting	1975-98	861	123	258	**36549**	49.52	94
D.Denton	1894-1920	1163	70	221	**36479**	33.37	69
G.H.Hirst	1891-1929	1215	151	341	**36323**	34.13	60
I.V.A.Richards	1971/72-93	796	63	322	**36212**	49.40	114
A.Jones	1957-83	1168	72	204*	**36049**	32.89	56
W.G.Quaife	1894-1928	1203	185	255*	**36012**	35.37	72
G.A.Hick	1983/84-2003	748	72	405*	**35916**	53.13	122
R.E.Marshall	1945/46-72	1053	59	228*	**35725**	35.94	68
G.Gunn	1902-32	1061	82	220	**35208**	35.96	62

BOWLING RECORDS

ALL TEN WICKETS IN AN INNINGS

This feat has been achieved 78 times in first-class matches (excluding 12-a-side fixtures).
Three Times: A.P.Freeman (1929, 1930, 1931)
Twice: V.E.Walker (1859, 1865); H.Verity (1931, 1932); J.C.Laker (1956)

Instances since 1945:

W.E.Hollies	Warwickshire v Notts	Birmingham	1946
J.M.Sims	East v West	Kingston on Thames	1948
J.K.R.Graveney	Gloucestershire v Derbyshire	Chesterfield	1949
T.E.Bailey	Essex v Lancashire	Clacton	1949
R.Berry	Lancashire v Worcestershire	Blackpool	1953
S.P.Gupte	President's XI v Combined XI	Bombay	1954-55
J.C.Laker	Surrey v Australians	The Oval	1956

K.Smales	Nottinghamshire v Glos	Stroud	1956
G.A.R.Lock	Surrey v Kent	Blackheath	1956
J.C.Laker	England v Australia	Manchester	1956
P.M.Chatterjee	Bengal v Assam	Jorhat	1956-57
J.D.Bannister	Warwicks v Combined Services	Birmingham (M & B)	1959
A.J.G.Pearson	Cambridge U v Leicestershire	Loughborough	1961
N.I.Thomson	Sussex v Warwickshire	Worthing	1964
P.J.Allan	Queensland v Victoria	Melbourne	1965-66
I.J.Brayshaw	Western Australia v Victoria	Perth	1967-68
Shahid Mahmood	Karachi Whites v Khairpur	Karachi	1969-70
E.E.Hemmings	International XI v W Indians	Kingston	1982-83
P.Sunderam	Rajasthan v Vidarbha	Jodhpur	1985-86
S.T.Jefferies	Western Province v OFS	Cape Town	1987-88
Imran Adil	Bahawalpur v Faisalabad	Faisalabad	1989-90
G.P.Wickremasinghe	Sinhalese v Kalutara	Colombo	1991-92
R.L.Johnson	Middlesex v Derbyshire	Derby	1994
Naeem Akhtar	Rawalpindi B v Peshawar	Peshawar	1995-96
A.Kumble	India v Pakistan	Delhi	1998-99
D.S.Mohanty	East Zone v South Zone	Agartala	2000-01

MOST WICKETS IN A MATCH

| 19 | J.C.Laker | England v Australia | Manchester | 1956 |

MOST WICKETS IN A SEASON

Wkts		Season	Matches	Overs	Mdns	Runs	Avge
304	A.P.Freeman	1928	37	1976.1	423	5489	18.05
298	A.P.Freeman	1933	33	2039	651	4549	15.26

The feat of taking 250 wickets in a season has been achieved on 12 occasions, the last instance being by A.P.Freeman in 1933. 200 or more wickets in a season have been taken on 59 occasions, the last being by G.A.R.Lock (212 wickets, average 12.02) in 1957.

The highest aggregates of wickets taken in a season since the reduction of County Championship matches in 1969 are as follows:

Wkts		Season	Matches	Overs	Mdns	Runs	Avge
134	M.D.Marshall	1982	22	822	225	2108	15.73
131	L.R.Gibbs	1971	23	1024.1	225	2475	18.89
125	F.D.Stephenson	1988	22	819.1	196	2289	18.31
121	R.D.Jackman	1980	23	746.2	220	1864	15.40

Since 1969 there have been 50 instances of bowlers taking 100 wickets in a season.

MOST HAT TRICKS IN A CAREER

7	D.V.P.Wright
6	T.W.J.Goddard, C.W.L.Parker
5	S.Haigh, V.W.C.Jupp, A.E.G.Rhodes, F.A.Tarrant

2000 WICKETS IN A CAREER

	Career	Runs	Wkts	Avge	100w
W.Rhodes	1898-1930	69993	4187	16.71	23
A.P.Freeman	1914-36	69577	3776	18.42	17
C.W.L.Parker	1903-35	63817	3278	19.46	16
J.T.Hearne	1888-1923	54352	3061	17.75	15
T.W.J.Goddard	1922-52	59116	2979	19.84	16
W.G.Grace	1865-1908	51545	2876	17.92	10
A.S.Kennedy	1907-36	61034	2874	21.23	15
D.Shackleton	1948-69	53303	2857	18.65	20
G.A.R.Lock	1946-70/71	54709	2844	19.23	14

	Career	Runs	Wkts	Avge	100w
F.J.Titmus	1949-82	63313	**2830**	22.37	16
M.W.Tate	1912-37	50571	**2784**	18.16	13+1
G.H.Hirst	1891-1929	51282	**2739**	18.72	15
C.Blythe	1899-1914	42136	**2506**	16.81	14
D.L.Underwood	1963-87	49993	**2465**	20.28	10
W.E.Astill	1906-39	57783	**2431**	23.76	9
J.C.White	1909-37	43759	**2356**	18.57	14
W.E.Hollies	1932-57	48656	**2323**	20.94	14
F.S.Trueman	1949-69	42154	**2304**	18.29	12
J.B.Statham	1950-68	36999	**2260**	16.37	13
R.T.D.Perks	1930-55	53771	**2233**	24.07	16
J.Briggs	1879-1900	35431	**2221**	15.95	12
D.J.Shepherd	1950-72	47302	**2218**	21.32	12
E.G.Dennett	1903-26	42571	**2147**	19.82	12
T.Richardson	1892-1905	38794	**2104**	18.43	10
T.E.Bailey	1945-67	48170	**2082**	23.13	9
R.Illingworth	1951-83	42023	**2072**	20.28	10
F.E.Woolley	1906-38	41066	**2068**	19.85	8
N.Gifford	1960-88	48731	**2068**	23.56	4
G.Geary	1912-38	41339	**2063**	20.03	11
D.V.P.Wright	1932-57	49307	**2056**	23.98	10
J.A.Newman	1906-30	51111	**2032**	25.15	9
A.Shaw	1864-97	24580	**2026+1**	12.12	9
S.Haigh	1895-1913	32091	**2012**	15.94	11

ALL-ROUND RECORDS

THE 'DOUBLE'

3000 runs and 100 wickets: J.H.Parks (1937)

2000 runs and 200 wickets: G.H.Hirst (1906)

2000 runs and 100 wickets: F.E.Woolley (4), J.W.Hearne (3), W.G.Grace (2), G.H.Hirst (2), W.Rhodes (2), T.E.Bailey, D.E.Davies, G.L.Jessop, V.W.C.Jupp, J.Langridge, F.A.Tarrant, C.L.Townsend, L.F.Townsend.

1000 runs and 200 wickets: M.W.Tate (3), A.E.Trott (2), A.S.Kennedy

Most Doubles: 16 – W.Rhodes; 14 – G.H.Hirst; 10 – V.W.C.Jupp

Double in Debut Season: D.B.Close (1949) – aged 18, the youngest to achieve this feat.

The feat of scoring 1000 runs and taking 100 wickets in a season has been achieved on 305 occasions, R.J.Hadlee (1984) and F.D.Stephenson (1988) being the only players to complete the 'double' since the reduction of County Championship matches in 1969.

WICKET-KEEPING RECORDS

EIGHT DISMISSALS IN AN INNINGS

9	(8ct, 1st)	Tahir Rashid	Habib Bank v PACO	Gujranwala	1992-93
9	(7ct, 2st)	W.R.James	Matabeleland v Mashonaland CD	Bulawayo	1995-96
8	(8ct)	A.T.W.Grout	Queensland v W Australia	Brisbane	1959-60
8	(8ct)	D.E.East	Essex v Somerset	Taunton	1985
8	(8ct)	S.A.Marsh	Kent v Middlesex	Lord's	1991
8	(6ct, 2st)	T.J.Zoehrer	Australians v Surrey	The Oval	1993
8	(7ct, 1st)	D.S.Berry	Victoria v South Australia	Melbourne	1996-97
8	(7ct, 1st)	Y.S.S.Mendis	Bloomfield v Kurunegala Youth	Colombo	2000-01
8	(7ct, 1st)	S.Nath	Assam v Tripura (*on debut*)	Gauhati	2001-02

TWELVE DISMISSALS IN A MATCH

13	(11ct, 2st)	W.R.James	Matabeleland v Mashonaland CD	Bulawayo	1995-96
12	(8ct, 4st)	E.Pooley	Surrey v Sussex	The Oval	1868
12	(9ct, 3st)	D.Tallon	Queensland v NSW	Sydney	1938-39
12	(9ct, 3st)	H.B.Taber	NSW v South Australia	Adelaide	1968-69

MOST DISMISSALS IN A SEASON

128	(79ct, 49st)	L.E.G.Ames	1929

1000 DISMISSALS IN A CAREER

	Career	*Dismissals*	*Ct*	*St*
R.W.Taylor	1960-88	**1649**	1473	176
J.T.Murray	1952-75	**1527**	1270	257
H.Strudwick	1902-27	**1497**	1242	255
A.P.E.Knott	1964-85	**1344**	1211	133
R.C.Russell	1981-2003	**1319**	1191	128
F.H.Huish	1895-1914	**1310**	933	377
B.Taylor	1949-73	**1294**	1083	211
D.Hunter	1889-1909	**1253**	906	347
H.R.Butt	1890-1912	**1228**	953	275
S.J.Rhodes	1981-2003	**1215**	1095	120
J.H.Board	1891-1914/15	**1207**	852	355
H.Elliott	1920-47	**1206**	904	302
J.M.Parks	1949-76	**1181**	1088	93
R.Booth	1951-70	**1126**	948	178
L.E.G.Ames	1926-51	**1121**	703	418
D.L.Bairstow	1970-90	**1099**	961	138
G.Duckworth	1923-47	**1096**	753	343
H.W.Stephenson	1948-64	**1082**	748	334
J.G.Binks	1955-75	**1071**	895	176
T.G.Evans	1939-69	**1066**	816	250
A.Long	1960-80	**1046**	922	124
G.O.Dawkes	1937-61	**1043**	895	148
R.W.Tolchard	1965-83	**1037**	912	125
W.L.Cornford	1921-47	**1017**	675	342

FIELDING RECORDS

MOST CATCHES IN AN INNINGS

7	M.J.Stewart	Surrey v Northamptonshire	Northampton	1957
7	A.S.Brown	Gloucestershire v Nottinghamshire	Nottingham	1966

MOST CATCHES IN A MATCH

10	W.R.Hammond	Gloucestershire v Surrey	Cheltenham	1928

MOST CATCHES IN A SEASON

78	W.R.Hammond	1928	77	M.J.Stewart	1957

750 CATCHES IN A CAREER

1018	F.E.Woolley	1906-38	784	J.G.Langridge	1928-55
887	W.G.Grace	1865-1908	764	W.Rhodes	1898-1930
830	G.A.R.Lock	1946-70/71	758	C.A.Milton	1948-74
819	W.R.Hammond	1920-51	754	E.H.Hendren	1907-38
813	D.B.Close	1949-86			

1970-71 to 12 February 2004

	Opponents	Matches	E	A	SA	WI	NZ	I	P	SL	Z	B	C	EA	H	K	N	SC	UAE	Tied	NR
England	Australia	77	31	44																1	1
	South Africa	27	10		17																
	West Indies	61	26			32															3
	New Zealand	52	25				23													1	3
	India	48	23					23													2
	Pakistan	53	31						21												1
	Sri Lanka	31	18							13											
	Zimbabwe	25	16								8										1
	Bangladesh	4	4									0									
	Canada	1	1										0								
	East Africa	1	1											0							
	Holland	2	2												0						
	Kenya	1	1													0					
	Namibia	1	1														0				
	U A Emirates	1	1																0		
Australia	South Africa	56		29	24																3
	West Indies	105		47		55														3	1
	New Zealand	89		61			25														3
	India	79		49				27													3
	Pakistan	67		37					26											1	3
	Sri Lanka	50		33						15											2
	Zimbabwe	24		22							1										1
	Bangladesh	6		6								0									
	Canada	1		1									0								
	Holland	1		1											0						
	Kenya	4		4												0					
	Namibia	1		1													0				
	Scotland	1		1															0		
S Africa	West Indies	32			21	10															1
	N Zealand	34			22		9														3
	India	46			28			16													2
	Pakistan	41			28				13												
	Sri Lanka	34			18					14										1	1
	Zimbabwe	18			15						2										1
	Bangladesh	6			6							0									
	Canada	1			1								0								
	Holland	1			1										0						
	Kenya	8			8											0					
	U A Emirates	1			1														0		
W Indies	New Zealand	36				22	11														3
	India	76				46		28												1	1
	Pakistan	98				60			36											1	2
	Sri Lanka	39				23				15											1
	Zimbabwe	24				17					7										
	Bangladesh	7				5						0									2
	Canada	1				1							0								
	Kenya	6				5										1					
	Scotland	1				1													0		
N Zealand	India	72					33	35													4
	Pakistan	77					28		47											1	1
	Sri Lanka	55					28			24										1	1
	Zimbabwe	26					17				7									1	1
	Bangladesh	4					4					0									
	Canada	1					1						0								
	East Africa	1					1							0							
	Holland	1					1								0						
	Scotland	1					1												0		
	U A Emirates	1					1												0		
India	Pakistan	86						30	52												4
	Sri Lanka	76						40		29											7
	Zimbabwe	47						37			8										2

	Opponents	Matches	E	A	SA	WI	NZ	I	P	SL	Z	B	C	EA	H	K	N	SC	UAE	Tied	NR
	Bangladesh	10	–	–	–	–	–	10	–	–	–	0	–	–	–	–	–	–	–	–	–
	East Africa	1	–	–	–	–	–	1	–	–	–	–	–	0	–	–	–	–	–	–	–
	Holland	1	–	–	–	–	–	1	–	–	–	–	–	–	0	–	–	–	–	–	–
	Kenya	12	–	–	–	–	–	10	–	–	–	–	–	–	–	2	–	–	–	–	–
	Namibia	1	–	–	–	–	–	1	–	–	–	–	–	–	–	–	0	–	–	–	–
	U A Emirates	1	–	–	–	–	–	1	–	–	–	–	–	–	–	–	–	–	0	–	–
Pakistan	Sri Lanka	99	–	–	–	–	–	–	60	36	–	–	–	–	–	–	–	–	–	1	2
	Zimbabwe	32	–	–	–	–	–	–	28	–	2	–	–	–	–	–	–	–	–	1	1
	Bangladesh	16	–	–	–	–	–	–	15	–	–	1	–	–	–	–	–	–	–	–	–
	Canada	1	–	–	–	–	–	–	1	–	–	–	0	–	–	–	–	–	–	–	–
	Holland	3	–	–	–	–	–	–	3	–	–	–	–	–	0	–	–	–	–	–	–
	Kenya	4	–	–	–	–	–	–	4	–	–	–	–	–	–	0	–	–	–	–	–
	Namibia	1	–	–	–	–	–	–	1	–	–	–	–	–	–	–	0	–	–	–	–
	Scotland	1	–	–	–	–	–	–	1	–	–	–	–	–	–	–	–	0	–	–	–
	U A Emirates	2	–	–	–	–	–	–	2	–	–	–	–	–	–	–	–	–	0	–	–
Sri Lanka	Zimbabwe	29	–	–	–	–	–	–	–	22	6	–	–	–	–	–	–	–	–	–	1
	Bangladesh	10	–	–	–	–	–	–	–	10	–	0	–	–	–	–	–	–	–	–	–
	Canada	1	–	–	–	–	–	–	–	1	–	–	0	–	–	–	–	–	–	–	–
	Holland	1	–	–	–	–	–	–	–	1	–	–	–	–	0	–	–	–	–	–	–
	Kenya	5	–	–	–	–	–	–	–	4	–	–	–	–	–	1	–	–	–	–	–
Zimbabwe	Bangladesh	10	–	–	–	–	–	–	–	–	10	0	–	–	–	–	–	–	–	–	–
	Holland	1	–	–	–	–	–	–	–	–	1	–	–	–	0	–	–	–	–	–	–
	Kenya	16	–	–	–	–	–	–	–	–	13	–	–	–	–	1	–	–	–	–	2
	Namibia	1	–	–	–	–	–	–	–	–	1	–	–	–	–	–	0	–	–	–	–
Bangladesh	Canada	1	–	–	–	–	–	–	–	–	–	0	1	–	–	–	–	–	–	–	–
	Kenya	7	–	–	–	–	–	–	–	–	–	1	–	–	–	6	–	–	–	–	–
	Scotland	1	–	–	–	–	–	–	–	–	–	1	–	–	–	–	–	0	–	–	–
Kenya	Canada	1	–	–	–	–	–	–	–	–	–	–	0	–	–	1	–	–	–	–	–
Holland	U A Emirates	1	–	–	–	–	–	–	–	–	–	–	–	–	0	–	–	–	1	–	–
	Namibia	1	–	–	–	–	–	–	–	–	–	–	–	–	1	–	0	–	–	–	–
	2098		191	336	190	277	183	260	310	184	66	3	1	0	1	12	0	0	1	19	64

MERIT TABLE OF ALL L-O INTERNATIONALS
1970-71 to 12 February 2004

	Matches	Won	Lost	Tied	No Result	% Won (exc NR)
South Africa	305	190	103	4	8	63.97
Australia	561	336	204	7	14	61.42
West Indies	486	277	192	5	12	58.43
Pakistan	581	310	253	6	12	54.48
England	385	191	181	2	11	51.06
India	556	260	270	3	23	48.78
Sri Lanka	430	184	227	3	16	44.44
New Zealand	450	183	243	4	20	42.55
Zimbabwe	253	66	175	4	8	26.93
Kenya	64	12	50	–	2	19.35
Associate Members	43	3	40	–	–	6.97
Bangladesh	82	3	77	–	2	3.75

TEAM RECORDS
HIGHEST TOTALS

398-5	(50 overs)	Sri Lanka v Kenya	Kandy	1995-96
376-2	(50 overs)	India v New Zealand	Hyderabad, India	1999-00
373-6	(50 overs)	India v Sri Lanka	Taunton	1999
371-9	(50 overs)	Pakistan v Sri Lanka	Nairobi	1996-97
363-3	(50 overs)	South Africa v Zimbabwe	Bulawayo	2001-02
363-7	(55 overs)	England v Pakistan	Nottingham	1992

360-4	(50 overs)	West Indies v Sri Lanka	Karachi	1987-88
359-2	(50 overs)	Australia v India	Johannesburg	2002-03
359-5	(50 overs)	Australia v India	Sydney	2003-04
354-3	(50 overs)	South Africa v Kenya	Cape Town	2001-02
353-5	(50 overs)	India v New Zealand	Hyderabad, India	2003-04
351-3	(50 overs)	India v Kenya	Paarl	2001-02

The highest for New Zealand is 349-9 (v India, Rajkot, 1999-00), for Zimbabwe 340-2 (v Namibia, Harare, 2002-03), for Bangladesh 272-8 (v Z, Bulawayo, 2000-01), and for Kenya 347-3 (v B, Nairobi, 1997-98).

HIGHEST TOTALS BATTING SECOND

| **WINNING:** | 330-7 | (49.1 overs) | Australia v South Africa | Port Elizabeth | 2001-02 |
| **LOSING:** | 329 | (49.3 overs) | Sri Lanka v West Indies | Sharjah | 1995-96 |

HIGHEST MATCH AGGREGATE

| 664-19 | (99.4 overs) | Sri Lanka (349-9) v Pakistan (315) | Singapore | 1995-96 |

LARGEST RUNS MARGINS OF VICTORY

256 runs	Australia beat Namibia	Potschefstroom	2002-03
245 runs	Sri Lanka beat India	Sharjah	2000-01
233 runs	Pakistan v Bangladesh	Dhaka	1999-00
232 runs	Australia beat Sri Lanka	Adelaide	1984-85
224 runs	Australia beat Pakistan	Nairobi	2002
217 runs	Pakistan beat Sri Lanka	Sharjah	2001-02
209 runs	South Africa beat West Indies	Cape Town	2003-04
208 runs	South Africa beat Kenya	Cape Town	2001-02
208 runs	Australia beat India	Sydney	2003-04
206 runs	New Zealand beat Australia	Adelaide	1985-86
206 runs	Sri Lanka beat Holland	Colombo (RPS)	2002-03
202 runs	England beat India	Lord's	1975
202 runs	South Africa beat Kenya	Nairobi	1996-97
202 runs	Zimbabwe beat Kenya	Dhaka	1998-99
200 runs	India beat Bangladesh	Dhaka	2002-03

LOWEST TOTALS (Excluding reduced innings)

36	(18.4 overs)	Canada v Sri Lanka	Paarl	2002-03
38	(15.4 overs)	Zimbabwe v Sri Lanka	Colombo (SSC)	2001-02
43	(19.5 overs)	Pakistan v West Indies	Cape Town	1992-93
45	(40.3 overs)	Canada v England	Manchester	1979
45	(14.0 overs)	Namibia v Australia	Potschefstroom	2002-03
54	(26.3 overs)	India v Sri Lanka	Sharjah	2000-01
54	(23.2 overs)	West Indies v South Africa	Cape Town	2003-04
55	(28.3 overs)	Sri Lanka v West Indies	Sharjah	1986-87
63	(25.5 overs)	India v Australia	Sydney	1980-81
64	(35.5 overs)	New Zealand v Pakistan	Sharjah	1985-86
68	(31.3 overs)	Scotland v West Indies	Leicester	1999
69	(28.0 overs)	South Africa v Australia	Sydney	1993-94
70	(25.2 overs)	Australia v England	Birmingham	1977
70	(26.3 overs)	Australia v New Zealand	Adelaide	1985-86

The lowest for England is 86 (v A, Manchester, 2001), for Bangladesh 76 (v SL, Colombo (SSC), 2002, and v I, Dhaka, 2002-03), and for Kenya 84 (v A, Nairobi, 2002).

LOWEST MATCH AGGREGATE

| 73-11 | (23.2 overs) | Canada (36) v Sri Lanka (37-1) | Paarl | 2002-03 |
| 78-11 | (20 overs) | Zimbabwe (38) v Sri Lanka (40-1) | Colombo (SSC) | 2001-02 |

BATTING RECORDS
HIGHEST INDIVIDUAL INNINGS

194	Saeed Anwar	Pakistan v India	Madras	1996-97
189*	I.V.A.Richards	West Indies v England	Manchester	1984
189	S.T.Jayasuriya	Sri Lanka v India	Sharjah	2000-01
188*	G.Kirsten	South Africa v UAE	Rawalpindi	1995-96
186*	S.R.Tendulkar	India v New Zealand	Hyderabad	1999-00
183	S.C.Ganguly	India v Sri Lanka	Taunton	1999
181	I.V.A.Richards	West Indies v Sri Lanka	Karachi	1987-88
175*	Kapil Dev	India v Zimbabwe	Tunbridge Wells	1983
173	M.E.Waugh	Australia v West Indies	Melbourne	2000-01
172*	C.B.Wishart	Zimbabwe v Namibia	Harare	2002-03
172	A.C.Gilchrist	Australia v Zimbabwe	Hobart	2003-04
171*	G.M.Turner	New Zealand v East Africa	Birmingham	1975
169*	D.J.Callaghan	South Africa v New Zealand	Pretoria	1994-95
169	B.C.Lara	West Indies v Sri Lanka	Sharjah	1995-96
167*	R.A.Smith	England v Australia	Birmingham	1993
161	A.C.Hudson	South Africa v Holland	Rawalpindi	1995-96
159*	D.Mongia	India v Zimbabwe	Gauhati	2001-02
158	D.I.Gower	England v New Zealand	Brisbane	1982-83
154	A.C.Gilchrist	Australia v Sri Lanka	Melbourne	1998-99
153*	I.V.A.Richards	West Indies v Australia	Melbourne	1979-80
153*	M.Azharuddin	India v Zimbabwe	Cuttack	1997-98
153*	S.C.Ganguly	India v New Zealand	Gwalior	1999-00
153*	C.H.Gayle	West Indies v Zimbabwe	Bulawayo	2003-04
153	B.C.Lara	West Indies v Pakistan	Sharjah	1993-94
153	R.Dravid	India v New Zealand	Hyderabad	1999-00
153	H.H.Gibbs	South Africa v Bangladesh	Potchefstroom	2002-03
152*	D.L.Haynes	West Indies v India	Georgetown	1988-89
152*	C.H.Gayle	West Indies v South Africa	Johannesburg	2003-04
152	C.H.Gayle	West Indies v Kenya	Nairobi	2001-02
152	S.R.Tendulkar	India v Namibia	Pietermaritzburg	2002-03
151*	S.T.Jayasuriya	Sri Lanka v India	Bombay	1996-97
150	S.Chanderpaul	West Indies v South Africa	East London	1998-99

The highest for Bangladesh is 101 by Mehrab Hossain (v Z, Dhaka, 1998-99), and for Kenya 144 by K.O.Obuya (v B, Nairobi, 1997-98).

HUNDRED ON DEBUT

D.L.Amiss	103	England v Australia	Manchester	1972
D.L.Haynes	148	West Indies v Australia	St John's	1977-78
A.Flower	115*	Zimbabwe v Sri Lanka	New Plymouth	1991-92
Salim Elahi	102*	Pakistan v Sri Lanka	Gujranwala	1995-96

Shahid Afridi scored 102 for P v SL, Nairobi, 1996-97, in his second match having not batted in his first.

Fastest 100	37 balls	Shahid Afridi (102)	P v SL	Nairobi	1996-97
Fastest 50	17 balls	S.T.Jayasuriya (76)	SL v P	Singapore	1995-96

CARRYING BAT THROUGH COMPLETED INNINGS (ALL OUT)

G.W.Flower	84*	Zimbabwe (205) v England	Sydney	1994-95
Saeed Anwar	103*	Pakistan (219) v Zimbabwe	Harare	1994-95
N.V.Knight	125*	England (246) v Pakistan	Nottingham	1996
R.D.Jacobs	49*	West Indies (110) v Australia	Manchester	1999
D.R.Martyn	116*	Australia (191) v New Zealand	Auckland	1999-00
H.H.Gibbs	59*	South Africa (101) v Pakistan	Sharjah	1999-00
A.J.Stewart	100*	England (192) v West Indies	Nottingham	2000
Javed Omar	33*	Bangladesh (103) v Zimbabwe	Harare	2000-01

5000 RUNS IN A CAREER

		LOI	I	NO	HS	Runs	Avge	100	50
S.R.Tendulkar	I	328	319	31	186*	**12921**	44.86	36	66
Inzamam-ul-Haq	P	307	287	42	137*	9456	38.59	8	68
M.Azharuddin	I	334	308	54	153*	9378	36.92	7	58
P.A.de Silva	SL	308	296	30	145	9284	34.90	11	64
S.T.Jayasuriya	SL	308	300	13	189	9172	31.95	16	54
S.C.Ganguly	I	244	236	20	183	9144	42.33	22	53
Saeed Anwar	P	247	244	19	194	8823	39.21	20	43
D.L.Haynes	WI	238	237	28	152*	8648	41.37	17	57
B.C.Lara	WI	229	224	24	169	8533	42.66	18	53
M.E.Waugh	A	244	236	20	173	8500	39.35	18	50
S.R.Waugh	A	325	288	58	120*	7569	32.90	3	45
A.Ranatunga	SL	269	255	47	131*	7454	35.83	4	49
Javed Miandad	P	233	218	41	119*	7381	41.70	8	50
Salim Malik	P	283	256	38	102	7171	32.89	5	47
R.Dravid	I	224	205	25	153	7002	38.90	8	49
R.T.Ponting	A	194	190	25	145	6897	41.80	15	36
J.H.Kallis	SA	190	181	34	139	6858	46.65	12	46
M.G.Bevan	A	227	191	66	108*	6829	54.63	6	46
G.Kirsten	SA	185	185	19	188*	6798	40.95	13	45
A.Flower	Z	213	208	16	145	6786	35.34	4	55
I.V.A.Richards	WI	187	167	24	189*	6721	47.00	11	45
M.S.Atapattu	SL	201	198	24	132*	6567	37.74	10	45
Ijaz Ahmed	P	250	232	29	139*	6564	32.33	10	37
A.R.Border	A	273	252	39	127*	6524	30.62	3	39
G.W.Flower	Z	216	209	18	142*	6472	33.88	6	39
A.C.Gilchrist	A	185	179	6	172	6280	36.30	10	36
R.B.Richardson	WI	224	217	30	122	6248	33.41	5	44
D.M.Jones	A	164	161	25	145	6068	44.61	7	46
D.C.Boon	A	181	177	16	122	5964	37.04	5	37
J.N.Rhodes	SA	245	220	51	121	5935	35.11	2	33
S.P.Fleming	NZ	212	204	18	134*	5866	31.53	5	34
Ramiz Raja	P	198	197	15	119*	5841	32.09	9	31
C.L.Hooper	WI	227	206	43	113*	5761	35.34	7	29
W.J.Cronje	SA	188	175	31	112	5565	38.64	2	39
N.J.Astle	NZ	174	171	10	120*	5540	34.40	13	32
Yousuf Youhana	P	159	151	23	141*	5461	42.66	9	35
A.Jadeja	I	196	179	36	119	5359	37.47	6	30
A.D.R.Campbell	Z	188	184	14	131*	5185	30.50	7	30
R.S.Mahanama	SL	213	198	23	119*	5162	29.49	4	35
C.G.Greenidge	WI	128	127	14	133*	5134	45.03	11	31

The most for England is 4677 in 162 innings by A.J.Stewart, for Bangladesh 976 (44) by Akram Khan, and for Kenya 1708 (61) by S.O.Tikolo.

15 HUNDREDS

		Inns	100	E	A	SA	WI	NZ	I	P	SL	Z	B	K	N
S.R.Tendulkar	I	319	36	1	7	3	2	4	–	2	7	5	–	4	1
S.C.Ganguly	I	236	22	1	1	3	–	3	–	2	4	3	1	3	1
Saeed Anwar	P	244	20	–	1	1	2	4	4	–	7	2	–	–	–
B.C.Lara	WI	224	18	1	3	3	–	2	–	4	2	1	1	1	–
M.E.Waugh	A	236	18	1	–	2	3	3	3	1	1	3	–	1	–
D.L.Haynes	WI	237	17	2	6	–	–	2	2	4	1	–	–	–	–
S.T.Jayasuriya	SL	300	16	2	1	–	–	4	4	3	–	1	1	–	–
R.T.Ponting	A	190	15	1	–	4	1	4	1	3	1	1	–	–	–

The most for England is 8 in 122 innings by G.A.Gooch, for South Africa 13 (185) by G.Kirsten, for New Zealand 13 (171) by N.J.Astle, for Zimbabwe 7 (184) by A.D.R.Campbell, for Bangladesh 1 (18) by Mehrab Hossain, and for Kenya 2 (60) by K.O.Obuya.

HIGHEST PARTNERSHIP FOR EACH WICKET

1st	258	S.C.Ganguly/S.R.Tendulkar	India v Kenya	Paarl	2001-02
2nd	331	S.R.Tendulkar/R.Dravid	India v New Zealand	Hyderabad (Ind)	1999-00
3rd	237*	R.Dravid/S.R.Tendulkar	India v Kenya	Bristol	1999
4th	275*	M.Azharuddin/A.Jadeja	India v Zimbabwe	Cuttack	1997-98
5th	223	M.Azharuddin/A.Jadeja	India v Sri Lanka	Colombo (RPS)	1997-98
6th	161	M.O.Odumbe/A.V.Vadher	Kenya v Sri Lanka	Southampton	1999
7th	130	A.Flower/H.H.Streak	Zimbabwe v England	Harare	2001-02
8th	119	P.R.Reiffel/S.K.Warne	Australia v South Africa	Port Elizabeth	1993-94
9th	126*	Kapil Dev/S.M.H.Kirmani	India v Zimbabwe	Tunbridge Wells	1983
10th	106*	I.V.A.Richards/M.A.Holding	West Indies v England	Manchester	1984

BOWLING RECORDS
SIX WICKETS IN AN INNINGS

8-19	W.P.U.C.J Vaas	Sri Lanka v Zimbabwe	Colombo (SSC)	2001-02
7-15	G.D.McGrath	Australia v Namibia	Potchefstroom	2002-03
7-20	A.J.Bichel	Australia v England	Port Elizabeth	2002-03
7-30	M.Muralitharan	Sri Lanka v India	Sharjah	2000-01
7-36	Waqar Younis	Pakistan v England	Leeds	2001
7-37	Aqib Javed	Pakistan v India	Sharjah	1991-92
7-51	W.W.Davis	West Indies v Australia	Leeds	1983
6-12	A.Kumble	India v West Indies	Calcutta	1993-94
6-14	G.J.Gilmour	Australia v England	Leeds	1975
6-14	Imran Khan	Pakistan v India	Sharjah	1984-85
6-15	C.E.H.Croft	West Indies v England	Kingstown	1980-81
6-16	Shoaib Akhtar	Pakistan v New Zealand	Karachi	2001-02
6-18	Azhar Mahmood	Pakistan v West Indies	Sharjah	1999-00
6-19	H.K.Olonga	Zimbabwe v England	Cape Town	1999-00
6-20	B.C.Strang	Zimbabwe v Bangladesh	Nairobi	1997-98
6-22	F.H.Edwards	West Indies v Zimbabwe	Harare	2003-04
6-23	A.A.Donald	South Africa v Kenya	Nairobi	1996-97
6-23	A.Nehra	India v England	Durban	2002-03
6-23	S.E.Bond	New Zealand v Australia	Port Elizabeth	2002-03
6-25	S.B.Styris	New Zealand v West Indies	Port-of-Spain	2002
6-25	W.P.U.C.J Vaas	Sri Lanka v Bangladesh	Pietermaritzburg	2002-03
6-26	Waqar Younis	Pakistan v Sri Lanka	Sharjah	1989-90
6-28	H.K.Olonga	Zimbabwe v Kenya	Bulawayo	2002-03
6-29	B.P.Patterson	West Indies v India	Nagpur	1987-88
6-29	S.T.Jayasuriya	Sri Lanka v England	Moratuwa	1992-93
6-30	Waqar Younis	Pakistan v New Zealand	Auckland	1993-94
6-35	S.M.Pollock	South Africa v West Indies	East London	1998-99
6-35	Abdul Razzaq	Pakistan v Bangladesh	Dhaka	2001-02
6-39	K.H.MacLeay	Australia v India	Nottingham	1983
6-41	I.V.A.Richards	West Indies v India	Delhi	1989-90
6-42	A.B.Agarkar	India v Australia	Melbourne	2003-04
6-44	Waqar Younis	Pakistan v New Zealand	Sharjah	1996-97
6-49	L.Klusener	South Africa v Sri Lanka	Lahore	1997-98
6-50	A.H.Gray	West Indies v Australia	Port-of-Spain	1990-91
6-59	Waqar Younis	Pakistan v Australia	Nottingham	2001

The best for England is 5-15 by M.A.Ealham (v Z, Kimberley, 1999-00), for Bangladesh 4-36 by Saiful Islam (v SL, Sharjah, 1994-95), and for Kenya 5-24 by C.O.Obuya (v SL, Nairobi, 2002-03).

150 WICKETS IN A CAREER

		LOI	Balls	R	W	Avge	Best	4w	R/Over
Wasim Akram	P	356	18186	11812	**502**	23.52	5-15	23	3.89
Waqar Younis	P	262	12698	9919	**416**	23.84	7-36	27	4.68
M.Muralitharan	SL	224	12123	7646	**343**	22.29	7-30	16	3.78
J.Srinath	I	229	11935	8847	**315**	28.08	5-23	10	4.44
A.Kumble	I	251	13419	9530	**315**	30.25	6-12	10	4.26
S.M.Pollock	SA	208	10912	6783	**295**	22.99	6-35	15	3.72
S.K.Warne	A	193	10600	7514	**291**	25.82	5-33	13	4.25

		LOI	Balls	R	W	Avge	Best	4w	R/Over
Saqlain Mushtaq	P	169	8770	6275	288	21.78	5-20	17	4.29
W.P.U.C.J.Vaas	SL	228	11134	7714	285	27.06	8-19	7	4.15
G.D.McGrath	A	185	9784	6356	284	22.38	7-15	14	3.89
A.A.Donald	SA	164	8561	5926	272	21.78	6-23	13	4.15
Kapil Dev	I	225	11202	6945	253	27.45	5-43	4	3.72
S.T.Jayasuriya	SL	308	11290	9040	251	36.01	6-29	9	4.80
H.H.Streak	Z	180	9019	6813	227	30.01	5-32	7	4.53
C.A.Walsh	WI	205	10822	6915	227	30.46	5- 1	7	3.83
C.E.L.Ambrose	WI	176	9353	5430	225	24.13	5-17	10	3.48
C.J.McDermott	A	138	7460	5018	203	24.71	5-44	5	4.03
C.Z.Harris	NZ	238	10313	7374	199	37.05	5-42	3	4.29
B.K.V.Prasad	I	161	8129	6332	196	32.30	5-27	4	4.67
S.R.Waugh	A	325	8883	6764	195	34.68	4-33	3	4.56
A.B.Agarkar	I	127	6295	5363	193	27.78	6-42	9	5.11
C.L.Hooper	WI	227	9573	6957	193	36.04	4-34	3	4.36
D.Gough	E	121	6589	4694	188	24.96	5-44	10	4.27
J.H.Kallis	SA	190	7112	5590	184	30.38	5-30	4	4.71
L.Klusener	SA	159	6796	5323	182	29.24	6-49	7	4.69
Aqib Javed	P	163	8012	5721	182	31.43	7-37	6	4.28
Imran Khan	P	175	7462	4845	182	26.62	6-14	4	3.90
Abdul Razzaq	P	154	6713	4955	179	27.68	6-35	7	4.42
C.L.Cairns	NZ	180	6836	5446	163	33.41	5-42	3	4.78
Mushtaq Ahmed	P	144	7543	5361	161	33.29	5-36	4	4.26
Shoaib Akhtar	P	98	4572	3436	158	21.74	6-16	6	4.50
R.J.Hadlee	NZ	115	6182	3407	158	21.56	5-25	6	3.31
M.Prabhakar	I	130	6360	4534	157	28.87	5-33	6	4.27
M.D.Marshall	WI	136	7175	4233	157	26.96	4-18	6	3.54

The most for Bangladesh is 43 by Khaled Mahmud (53 LOI) and by Mohammad Rafique (54), and for Kenya 57 (61) by T.M.Odoyo.

HAT TRICKS

Jalaluddin	Pakistan v Australia	Hyderabad	1982-83
B.A.Reid	Australia v New Zealand	Sydney	1985-86
C.Sharma	India v New Zealand	Nagpur	1987-88
Wasim Akram	Pakistan v West Indies	Sharjah	1989-90
Wasim Akram	Pakistan v Australia	Sharjah	1989-90
Kapil Dev	India v Sri Lanka	Calcutta	1990-91
Aqib Javed	Pakistan v India	Sharjah	1991-92
D.K.Morrison	New Zealand v India	Napier	1993-94
Waqar Younis	Pakistan v New Zealand	East London	1994-95
Saqlain Mushtaq	Pakistan v Zimbabwe	Peshawar	1996-97
E.A.Brandes	Zimbabwe v England	Harare	1996-97
A.M.Stuart	Australia v Pakistan	Melbourne	1996-97
Saqlain Mushtaq	Pakistan v Zimbabwe	The Oval	1999
W.P.U.C.J Vaas	Sri Lanka v Zimbabwe	Colombo (SSC)	2001-02
Mohammad Sami	Pakistan v West Indies	Sharjah	2001-02
W.P.U.C.J Vaas[1]	Sri Lanka v Bangladesh	Pietermaritzburg	2002-03
B.Lee	Australia v Kenya	Durban	2002-03
J.M.Anderson	England v Pakistan	The Oval	2003

[1] The first three balls of the match. Took four wickets in opening over (W W W 4 wide W 0).

WICKET-KEEPING RECORDS
SIX DISMISSALS IN AN INNINGS

6	(6ct)	A.C.Gilchrist	Australia v South Africa	Cape Town	1999-00
6	(6ct)	A.J.Stewart	England v Zimbabwe	Manchester	2000
6	(5ct/1st)	R.D.Jacobs	West Indies v Sri Lanka	Colombo (RPS)	2001-02
6	(5ct/1st)	A.C.Gilchrist	Australia v England	Sydney	2002-03
6	(6ct)	A.C.Gilchrist	Australia v Namibia	Potchefstroom	2002-03

100 DISMISSALS IN A CAREER

Total			LOI	Ct	St
310‡	A.C.Gilchrist	Australia	180	272	38
264†‡	Moin Khan	Pakistan	192	195	69
248	M.V.Boucher	South Africa	165	237	11
233	I.A.Healy	Australia	168	194	39
220‡	Rashid Latif	Pakistan	164	182	38
206‡	R.S.Kaluwitharana	Sri Lanka	184	132	74
204‡	P.J.L.Dujon	West Indies	167	183	21
170	R.D.Jacobs	West Indies	133	144	26
165	D.J.Richardson	South Africa	122	148	17
165†‡	A.Flower	Zimbabwe	185	133	32
163†‡	A.J.Stewart	England	138	148	15
154‡	N.R.Mongia	India	139	110	44
136‡‡	A.C.Parore	New Zealand	148	111	25
124	R.W.Marsh	Australia	92	120	4
103	Salim Yousuf	Pakistan	86	81	22

The most for Bangladesh is 61 (68 LOI) by Khaled Masud, and for Kenya 37 (43) by K.O.Obuya.
† *Excluding catches taken in the field.* ‡ *Excluding matches when not wicket-keeper.*

FIELDING RECORDS

FIVE CATCHES IN AN INNINGS

5	J.N.Rhodes	South Africa v West Indies	Bombay	1993-94

100 CATCHES IN A CAREER
(Excluding catches taken while keeping wicket)

Total			LOI
156	M.Azharuddin	India	334
127	A.R.Border	Australia	273
120	C.L.Hooper	West Indies	227
111	S.R.Waugh	Australia	325
109	R.S.Mahanama	Sri Lanka	213
108	M.E.Waugh	Australia	244
105	J.N.Rhodes	South Africa	245
102	S.T.Jayasuriya	Sri Lanka	308
101	I.V.A.Richards	West Indies	187
101	S.P.Fleming	New Zealand	212

The most for England is 64 (120 LOI) by G.A.Hick, for Pakistan 93 (307) by Inzamam-ul-Haq, for Zimbabwe 86 (216) by GW Flower, for Bangladesh 13 (39) by Aminul Islam and by Mohammad Rafique (54), and for Kenya 20 (63) by S.O.Tikolo.

ALL-ROUND RECORDS

50 RUNS AND 5 WICKETS IN A MATCH

I.V.A.Richards	119	5-41	West Indies v New Zealand	Dunedin	1986-87
K.Srikkanth	70	5-27	India v New Zealand	Vishakhapatnam	1988-89
M.E.Waugh	57	5-24	Australia v West Indies	Melbourne	1992-93
L.Klusener	54	6-49	South Africa v Sri Lanka	Lahore	1997-98
Abdul Razzaq	70*	5-48	Pakistan v India	Hobart	1999-00
G.A.Hick	80	5-33	England v Zimbabwe	Harare	1999-00
Shahid Afridi	61	5-40	Pakistan v England	Lahore	2000-01
S.C.Ganguly	71*	5-34	India v Zimbabwe	Kanpur	2000-01
S.B.Styris	63*	6-25	New Zealand v West Indies	Port-of-Spain	2002
R.C.Irani	53	5-26	England v India	The Oval	2002
C.H.Gayle	60	5-46	West Indies v Australia	St George's	2002-03

1000 RUNS AND 100 WICKETS

England	I.T.Botham (2113/145)
Australia	S.P.O'Donnell (1242/108); S.K.Warne (1016/291); S.R.Waugh (7569/195)
South Africa	W.J.Cronje (5565/114); J.H.Kallis (6858/184); L.Klusener (3433/182); S.M.Pollock (2030/295)
West Indies	C.L.Hooper (5761/193); I.V.A.Richards (6721/118)
New Zealand	C.L.Cairns (4272/163); R.J.Hadlee (1751/158); C.Z.Harris (4250/199)
India	Kapil Dev (3782/253); M.Prabhakar (1858/157); R.J.Shastri (3108/129); S.R.Tendulkar (12921/114)
Pakistan	Abdul Razzaq (2959/179); Azhar Mahmood (1435/120); Imran Khan (3709/182); Mudassar Nazar (2654/111); Shahid Afridi (3887/131); Wasim Akram 3717/502)
Sri Lanka	U.D.U.Chandana (1179/101); P.A.de Silva (9284/106); H.D.P.K.Dharmasena (1196/137); S.T.Jayasuriya (9172/251); W.P.U.C.J.Vaas (1481/285)
Zimbabwe	G.W.Flower (6472/100); H.H.Streak (2646/227)

APPEARANCE RECORDS

250 MATCHES

356	Wasim Akram	Pakistan	283	Salim Malik	Pakistan
334	M.Azharuddin	India	273	A.R.Border	Australia
328	S.R.Tendulkar	India	269	A.Ranatunga	Sri Lanka
325	S.R.Waugh	Australia	262	Waqar Younis	Pakistan
308	P.A.de Silva	Sri Lanka	251	A.Kumble	India
308	S.T.Jayasuriya	Sri Lanka	250	Ijaz Ahmed	Pakistan
307	Inzamam-ul-Haq	Pakistan			

The most for England is 170 by A.J.Stewart, for South Africa 245 by J.N.Rhodes, for West Indies 238 by D.L.Haynes, for New Zealand 238 by C.Z.Harris, for Zimbabwe 216 by G.W.Flower, for Bangladesh 69 by Khaled Masud, and for Kenya 63 by S.O.Tikolo.

100 MATCHES AS CAPTAIN

LOI			W	L	T	NR	% Won (exc NR)
193	A.Ranatunga	Sri Lanka	89	95	1	8	48.10
178	A.R.Border	Australia	107	67	1	3	60.14
174	M.Azharuddin	India	90	76	2	6	53.57
152	S.P.Fleming	New Zealand	63	79	1	9	44.05
139	Imran Khan	Pakistan	75	59	1	4	55.55
138	W.J.Cronje	South Africa	99	35	1	3	73.33
118	S.T.Jayasuriya	Sri Lanka	66	47	2	3	57.39
115	S.C.Ganguly	India	61	50	–	4	54.95
109	Wasim Akram	Pakistan	66	41	2	–	60.55
108	I.V.A.Richards	West Indies	68	36	–	4	65.38
106	S.R.Waugh	Australia	67	35	3	1	63.80

The most for England is 56 by N.Hussain, for Zimbabwe 86 by A.D.R.Campbell, for Bangladesh 23 by Khaled Masud, and for Kenya 22 by S.O.Tikolo.

100 LOI UMPIRING APPEARANCES

145	D.R.Shepherd	England	June 1983	to	November 2003
118	S.A.Bucknor	West Indies	March 1989	to	February 2004
113	R.E.Koertzen	South Africa	December 1992	to	February 2004
107	D.L.Orchard	South Africa	December 1994	to	December 2003
100	R.S.Dunne	New Zealand	February 1989	to	February 2002

WOMEN'S TEST CRICKET RECORDS

1934-35 to 1 May 2004

RESULTS SUMMARY

	Opponents	Tests	E	A	NZ	SA	WI	I	P	SL	Ire	Drawn
England	Australia	40	6	10	–	–	–	–	–	–	–	24
	New Zealand	22	6	–	0	–	–	–	–	–	–	16
	South Africa	6	2	–	–	0	–	–	–	–	–	4
	West Indies	3	2	–	–	–	0	–	–	–	–	1
	India	9	1	–	–	–	–	0	–	–	–	8
Australia	New Zealand	13	–	4	1	–	–	–	–	–	–	8
	West Indies	2	–	0	–	–	0	–	–	–	–	2
	India	8	–	3	–	–	–	0	–	–	–	5
New Zealand	South Africa	3	–	–	1	0	–	–	–	–	–	2
	India	6	–	–	0	–	–	0	–	–	–	6
South Africa	India	1	–	–	–	0	–	1	–	–	–	–
West Indies	India	6	–	–	–	–	1	1	–	–	–	4
Pakistan	Sri Lanka	1	–	–	–	–	–	–	0	1	–	–
	Ireland	1	–	–	–	–	–	–	0	–	1	–
		121	17	17	2	0	1	2	0	1	1	80

	Tests	Won	Lost	Drawn	Toss Won
England	80	17	10	53	48
Australia	63	17	7	39	20
New Zealand	44	2	10	32	21
South Africa	10	–	4	6	6
West Indies	11	1	3	7	5†
India	30	2	5	23	14†
Pakistan	2	–	2	–	1
Sri Lanka	1	1	–	–	1
Ireland	1	1	–	–	1

† *Results of tosses in five of the six India v West Indies Tests in 1976-77 are not known*

TEAM RECORDS
HIGHEST INNINGS TOTALS

569-6d	Australia v England	Guildford	1998
525	Australia v India	Ahmedabad	1983-84
517-8	New Zealand v England	Scarborough	1996
503-5d	England v New Zealand	Christchurch	1934-35
497	England v South Africa	Shenley	2003
467	India v England	Taunton	2002
455	England v South Africa	Taunton	2003
427-4d	Australia v England	Worcester	1998
426-9d	India v England	Blackpool	1986
414	England v New Zealand	Scarborough	1996
414	England v Australia	Guildford	1998
404-9d	India v South Africa	Paarl	2001-02
403-8d	New Zealand v India	Nelson	1994-95

The highest totals for countries not included above are:

282	West Indies v Australia	Montego Bay	1975-76
316	South Africa v England	Shenley	2003
193-3d	Ireland v Pakistan	Dublin	2000
171	Pakistan v Sri Lanka	Colombo	1997-98

LOWEST INNINGS TOTALS

35	England v Australia	Melbourne	1957-58
38	Australia v England	Melbourne	1957-58
44	New Zealand v England	Christchurch	1934-35
47	Australia v England	Brisbane	1934-35
53	Pakistan v Ireland	Dublin	2000

The lowest innings totals for countries not included above are:

67	West Indies v England	Canterbury	1979
89	South Africa v New Zealand	Durban	1971-72
65	India v West Indies	Jammu	1976-77

BATTING RECORDS
1000 RUNS IN TESTS

			M	I	NO	HS	Avge	100	50
1935	J.A.Brittin	England	27	44	5	167	49.61	5	11
1594	R.Heyhoe-Flint	England	22	38	3	179	45.54	3	10
1301	D.A.Hockley	New Zealand	19	29	4	126*	52.04	4	7
1164	C.A.Hodges	England	18	31	2	158*	40.13	2	6
1110	S.Agarwal	India	13	23	1	190	50.45	4	4
1078	E.Bakewell	England	12	22	4	124	59.88	4	7
1007	M.E.Maclagan	England	14	25	1	119	41.95	2	6

HIGHEST INDIVIDUAL INNINGS

214	M.Raj	I v E	Taunton	2002
209*	K.L.Rolton	A v E	Leeds	2001
204	K.E.Flavell	NZ v E	Scarborough	1996
204‡	M.A.J.Goszko	A v E	Shenley	2001
200	J.Broadbent	A v E	Guildford	1998
193	D.A.Annetts	A v E	Collingham	1987
190	S.Agarwal	I v E	Worcester	1986
189	E.A.Snowball	E v NZ	Christchurch	1934-35
179	R.Heyhoe-Flint	E v A	The Oval	1976
177	S.C.Taylor	E v SA	Shenley	2003
176*	K.L.Rolton	A v E	Worcester	1998
167	J.A.Brittin	E v A	Harrogate	1998
161*	E.C.Drumm	E v A	Christchurch	1994-95
160	B.A.Daniels	E v NZ	Scarborough	1996
158*	C.A.Hodges	E v NZ	Canterbury	1984
155*	P.F.McKelvey	NZ v E	Wellington	1968-69

‡ *On debut*

5 HUNDREDS

				Opponents							
		M	I	E	A	NZ	SA	WI	IND	P	SL	IRE
5	J.A.Brittin (E)	27	44	–	3	1	–	–	1	–	–	–

HIGHEST PARTNERSHIP FOR EACH WICKET

1st	178	B.J.Haggett/B.J.Clark	A v I	Sydney	1990-91
2nd	235	E.A.Snowball/M.E.Hide	E v NZ	Christchurch	1934-35
3rd	309	L.A.Reeler/D.A.Annetts	A v E	Collingham	1987
4th	253	K.L.Rolton/L.C.Broadfoot	A v E	Leeds	2001
5th	138	J.Logtenberg/C.van der Westhuizen	SA v E	Shenley	2003
6th	132	B.A.Daniels/K.M.Leng	E v NZ	Scarborough	1996
7th	157	M.Raj/J.Goswami	I v E	Taunton	2002
8th	181	S.J.Griffiths/D.L.Wilson	A v NZ	Auckland	1989-90
9th	107	B.Botha/M.Payne	SA v NZ	Cape Town	1971-72
10th	78	E.Barker/H.Hegarty	E v A	Adelaide	1957-58
	78	S.Gupta/S.Chakraborty	I v A	Lucknow	1983-84

BOWLING RECORDS
50 WICKETS IN TESTS

Wkts			M	Balls	Runs	Avge	Best	5wI	10wM
77	M.B.Duggan	E	17	3734	1039	13.49	7- 6	5	–
68	E.R.Wilson	A	11	2885	803	11.80	7- 7	4	2
63	D.F.Edulji	I	20	5098†	1624	25.77	6- 64	1	–
60	M.E.Maclagan	E	14	3432	935	15.58	7- 10	3	–
57	R.H.Thompson	A	16	4304	1040	18.24	5- 33	1	–
56	S.Kulkarni	I	18	3320	1599	28.55	6- 99	5	–
55	J.Lord	NZ	15	3108	1049	19.07	6-119	4	1
50	E.Bakewell	E	12	2697	831	16.62	7- 61	3	1

† Excludes balls bowled in Sixth Test v West Indies 1976-77

TEN WICKETS IN A TEST

11- 16	E.R.Wilson	A v E	Melbourne	1957-58
11- 63	J.Greenwood	E v NZ	Canterbury	1979
11-107	L.C.Pearson	E v A	Sydney	2002-03
10- 65	E.R.Wilson	A v NZ	Wellington	1947-48
10- 75	E.Bakewell	E v WI	Birmingham	1979
10-107	K.Price	A v I	Lucknow	1983-84
10-118	D.A.Gordon	A v E	Melbourne	1968-69
10-137	J.Lord	NZ v A	Melbourne	1978-79

SEVEN WICKETS IN AN INNINGS

8-53	N.David	I v E	Jamshedpur	1995-96
7- 6	M.B.Duggan	E v A	Melbourne	1957-58
7- 7	E.R.Wilson	A v E	Melbourne	1957-58
7-10	M.E.Maclagan	E v A	Brisbane	1934-35
7-18	A.Palmer	E v A	Brisbane	1934-35
7-24	L.Johnston	A v NZ	Melbourne	1971-72
7-34	G.E.McConway	E v I	Worcester	1986
7-41	J.Burley	NZ v E	The Oval	1966
7-51	L.C.Pearson	E v A	Sydney	2002-03
7-61	E.Bakewell	E v WI	Birmingham	1979

HAT TRICK

E.R.Wilson	Australia v England	Melbourne	1957-58

WICKET-KEEPING AND FIELDING RECORDS
25 DISMISSALS IN TESTS

Total			Tests	Ct	St
58	C.Matthews	Australia	20	46	12
36	S.A.Hodges	England	11	19	17
28	B.Brentnall	New Zealand	10	16	12

EIGHT DISMISSALS IN A TEST

9 (8ct, 1 st)	C.Matthews	A v I	Adelaide	1990-91
8 (6ct, 2st)	L.Nye	E v NZ	New Plymouth	1991-92

SIX DISMISSALS IN AN INNINGS

8 (6ct, 2st)	L.Nye	E v NZ	New Plymouth	1991-92
6 (2ct, 4st)	B.Brentnall	NZ v SA	Johannesburg	1971-72

20 CATCHES IN THE FIELD IN TESTS

Total			Tests
25	C.A.Hodges	England	18
21	S.Shah	India	20
20	L.A.Fullston	Australia	12

APPEARANCE RECORDS
25 TEST MATCH APPEARANCES

27	J.A.Brittin	England	1979-98

TEST MATCHES RESULTS SUMMARY

Matches completed before 18 February 2004

	Opponents	Tests	E	A	SA	WI	NZ	I	P	SL	Z	B	Tied	Drawn
							Won by						Tied	Drawn
England	Australia	306	95	125	–	–	–	–	–	–	–	–	–	86
	South Africa	125	52	–	25	–	–	–	–	–	–	–	–	48
	West Indies	126	31	–	–	52	–	–	–	–	–	–	–	43
	New Zealand	85	38	–	–	–	7	–	–	–	–	–	–	40
	India	91	33	–	–	–	–	16	–	–	–	–	–	42
	Pakistan	60	16	–	–	–	–	–	10	–	–	–	–	34
	Sri Lanka	15	7	–	–	–	–	–	–	4	–	–	–	4
	Zimbabwe	6	3	–	–	–	–	–	–	–	0	–	–	3
	Bangladesh	2	2	–	–	–	–	–	–	–	–	0	–	–
Australia	South Africa	71	–	39	15	–	–	–	–	–	–	–	–	17
	West Indies	99	–	45	–	32	–	–	–	–	–	–	1	21
	New Zealand	41	–	18	–	–	7	–	–	–	–	–	–	16
	India	64	–	30	–	–	–	14	–	–	–	–	1	19
	Pakistan	49	–	21	–	–	–	–	11	–	–	–	–	17
	Sri Lanka	13	–	7	–	–	–	–	–	1	–	–	–	5
	Zimbabwe	3	–	3	–	–	–	–	–	–	0	–	–	–
	Bangladesh	2	–	2	–	–	–	–	–	–	–	0	–	–
South Africa	West Indies	15	–	–	10	2	–	–	–	–	–	–	–	3
	New Zealand	27	–	–	15	–	3	–	–	–	–	–	–	9
	India	14	–	–	7	–	–	2	–	–	–	–	–	5
	Pakistan	11	–	–	5	–	–	–	2	–	–	–	–	4
	Sri Lanka	13	–	–	8	–	–	–	–	1	–	–	–	4
	Zimbabwe	5	–	–	4	–	–	–	–	–	0	–	–	1
	Bangladesh	4	–	–	4	–	–	–	–	–	–	0	–	–
West Indies	New Zealand	32	–	–	–	10	7	–	–	–	–	–	–	15
	India	78	–	–	–	30	–	10	–	–	–	–	–	38
	Pakistan	39	–	–	–	13	–	–	12	–	–	–	–	14
	Sri Lanka	8	–	–	–	2	–	–	–	3	–	–	–	3
	Zimbabwe	6	–	–	–	4	–	–	–	–	0	–	–	2
	Bangladesh	2	–	–	–	2	–	–	–	–	–	0	–	–
New Zealand	India	44	–	–	–	–	9	14	–	–	–	–	–	21
	Pakistan	45	–	–	–	–	6	–	21	–	–	–	–	18
	Sri Lanka	20	–	–	–	–	7	–	–	4	–	–	–	9
	Zimbabwe	11	–	–	–	–	5	–	–	–	0	–	–	6
	Bangladesh	2	–	–	–	–	2	–	–	–	–	0	–	–
India	Pakistan	47	–	–	–	–	–	5	9	–	–	–	–	33
	Sri Lanka	23	–	–	–	–	–	8	–	3	–	–	–	12
	Zimbabwe	9	–	–	–	–	–	5	–	–	2	–	–	2
	Bangladesh	1	–	–	–	–	–	1	–	–	–	0	–	–
Pakistan	Sri Lanka	28	–	–	–	–	–	–	13	6	–	–	–	9
	Zimbabwe	14	–	–	–	–	–	–	8	–	2	–	–	4
	Bangladesh	6	–	–	–	–	–	–	6	–	–	0	–	–
Sri Lanka	Zimbabwe	13	–	–	–	–	–	–	–	8	0	–	–	5
	Bangladesh	3	–	–	–	–	–	–	–	3	–	0	–	–
Zimbabwe	Bangladesh	4	–	–	–	–	–	–	–	–	3	0	–	1
		1682	277	290	93	147	53	75	92	33	7	0	2	613

230

	Tests	Won	Lost	Drawn	Tied	Toss Won
England	816	277	239	300	–	392
Australia	648	290	175	181	2	328
South Africa	285	93	101	91	–	134
West Indies	405	147	118	139	1	214
New Zealand	307	53	120	134	–	157
India	371	75	123	172	1	188
Pakistan	299	92	74	133	–	140
Sri Lanka	136	33	52	51	–	73
Zimbabwe	71	7	40	24	–	42
Bangladesh	26	–	25	1	–	14

TEST CRICKET RECORDS

To 18 February 2004

TEAM RECORDS

HIGHEST INNINGS TOTALS

952-6d	Sri Lanka v India	Colombo (RPS)	1997-98
903-7d	England v Australia	The Oval	1938
849	England v West Indies	Kingston	1929-30
790-3d	West Indies v Pakistan	Kingston	1957-58
758-8d	Australia v West Indies	Kingston	1954-55
735-6d	Australia v Zimbabwe	Perth	2003-04
729-6d	Australia v England	Lord's	1930
708	Pakistan v England	The Oval	1987
705-7d	India v Australia	Sydney	2003-04
701	Australia v England	The Oval	1934
699-5	Pakistan v India	Lahore	1989-90
695	Australia v England	The Oval	1930
692-8d	West Indies v England	The Oval	1995
687-8d	West Indies v England	The Oval	1976
682-6d	South Africa v England	Lord's	2003
681-8d	West Indies v England	Port-of-Spain	1953-54
676-7	India v Sri Lanka	Kanpur	1986-87
674-6	Pakistan v India	Faisalabad	1984-85
674	Australia v India	Adelaide	1947-48
671-4	New Zealand v Sri Lanka	Wellington	1990-91
668	Australia v West Indies	Bridgetown	1954-55
660-5d	West Indies v New Zealand	Wellington	1994-95
659-8d	Australia v England	Sydney	1946-47
658-8d	England v Australia	Nottingham	1938
658-9d	South Africa v West Indies	Durban	2003-04
657-7d	India v Australia	Calcutta	2000-01
657-8d	Pakistan v West Indies	Bridgetown	1957-58
656-8d	Australia v England	Manchester	1964
654-5	England v South Africa	Durban	1938-39
653-4d	England v India	Lord's	1990
653-4d	Australia v England	Leeds	1993
652-7d	England v India	Madras	1984-85
652-7d	Australia v South Africa	Johannesburg	2001-02
652-8d	West Indies v England	Lord's	1973
652	Pakistan v India	Faisalabad	1982-83
650-6d	Australia v West Indies	Bridgetown	1964-65

The highest for Zimbabwe is 563-9d (v WI, Harare, 2001), and for Bangladesh 400 (v I, Dhaka, 2000-01).

LOWEST INNINGS TOTALS

26	New Zealand v England	Auckland	1954-55
30	South Africa v England	Port Elizabeth	1895-96
30	South Africa v England	Birmingham	1924
35	South Africa v England	Cape Town	1898-99
36	Australia v England	Birmingham	1902
36	South Africa v Australia	Melbourne	1931-32
42	Australia v England	Sydney	1887-88
42	New Zealand v Australia	Wellington	1945-46
42	India v England	Lord's	1974
43	South Africa v England	Cape Town	1888-89
44	Australia v England	The Oval	1896
45	England v Australia	Sydney	1886-87
45	South Africa v Australia	Melbourne	1931-32
46	England v West Indies	Port-of-Spain	1993-94
47	South Africa v England	Cape Town	1888-89
47	England v England	Lord's	1958

The lowest for West Indies is 51 (v A, Port-of-Spain, 1998-99), for Pakistan 53 (v A, Sharjah, 2002-03), for Sri Lanka 71 (v P, Kandy, 1994-95), and for Zimbabwe 63 (v WI, Port-of-Spain, 1999-00), and for Bangladesh 87 (v WI, Dhaka, 2002-03).

BATTING RECORDS
4000 RUNS IN A TEST CAREER

Runs			M	I	NO	HS	Avge	100	50
11174	A.R.Border	A	156	265	44	205	50.56	27	63
10927	S.R.Waugh	A	168	260	46	200	51.06	32	50
10122	S.M.Gavaskar	I	125	214	16	236*	51.12	34	45
9265	S.R.Tendulkar	I	111	180	18	241*	57.19	32	37
9157	B.C.Lara	WI	-102	180	5	375	52.32	24	43
8900	G.A.Gooch	E	118	215	6	333	42.58	20	46
8832	Javed Miandad	P	124	189	21	280*	52.57	23	43
8540	I.V.A.Richards	WI	121	182	12	291	50.23	24	45
8463	A.J.Stewart	E	133	235	21	190	39.54	15	45
8231	D.I.Gower	E	117	204	18	215	44.25	18	39
8114	G.Boycott	E	108	193	23	246*	47.72	22	42
8032	G.St A.Sobers	WI	93	160	21	365*	57.78	26	30
8029	M.E.Waugh	A	128	209	17	153*	41.81	20	47
7728	M.A.Atherton	E	115	212	7	185*	37.70	16	46
7624	M.C.Cowdrey	E	114	188	15	182	44.06	22	38
7558	C.G.Greenidge	WI	108	185	16	226	44.72	19	34
7525	M.A.Taylor	A	104	186	13	334*	43.49	19	40
7515	C.H.Lloyd	WI	110	175	14	242*	46.67	19	39
7487	D.L.Haynes	WI	116	202	25	184	42.29	18	39
7422	D.C.Boon	A	107	190	20	200	43.65	21	32
7249	W.R.Hammond	E	85	140	16	336*	58.45	22	24
7110	G.S.Chappell	A	87	151	19	247*	53.86	24	31
7039	G.Kirsten	SA	98	170	14	275	45.12	20	33
6996	D.G.Bradman	A	52	80	10	334	99.94	29	13
6971	L.Hutton	E	79	138	15	364	56.67	19	33
6868	D.B.Vengsarkar	I	116	185	22	166	42.13	17	35
6806	K.F.Barrington	E	82	131	15	256	58.67	20	35
6680	Inzamam-ul-Haq	P	91	150	16	329	49.85	18	35
6546	R.Dravid	I	75	130	16	233	57.42	16	32
6361	P.A.de Silva	SL	93	159	11	267	42.97	20	22
6227	R.B.Kanhai	WI	79	137	6	256	47.53	15	28

Runs			M	I	NO	HS	Avge	100	50
6215	M.Azharuddin	I	99	147	9	199	45.03	22	21
6149	R.N.Harvey	A	79	137	10	205	48.41	21	24
6080	G.R.Viswanath	I	91	155	10	222	41.93	14	35
5949	R.B.Richardson	WI	86	146	12	194	44.39	16	27
5821	R.T.Ponting	A	75	119	15	257	55.97	20	21
5807	D.C.S.Compton	E	78	131	15	278	50.06	17	28
5768	Salim Malik	P	103	154	22	237	43.69	15	29
5762	C.L.Hooper	WI	102	173	15	233	36.46	13	27
5552	G.P.Thorpe	E	83	151	19	200*	42.06	12	33
5486	J.H.Kallis	SA	75	123	20	189*	53.26	15	27
5444	M.D.Crowe	NZ	77	131	11	299	45.36	17	18
5430	N.Hussain	E	91	162	14	207	36.68	13	30
5410	J.B.Hobbs	E	61	102	7	211	56.94	15	28
5357	K.D.Walters	A	74	125	14	250	48.26	15	33
5345	I.M.Chappell	A	75	136	10	196	42.42	14	26
5334	J.G.Wright	NZ	82	148	7	185	37.82	12	23
5312	M.J.Slater	A	74	131	7	219	42.84	14	21
5258	S.T.Jayasuriya	SL	83	140	13	340	41.40	10	26
5248	Kapil Dev	I	131	184	15	163	31.05	8	27
5234	W.M.Lawry	A	67	123	12	210	47.15	13	27
5200	I.T.Botham	E	102	161	6	208	33.54	14	22
5138	J.H.Edrich	E	77	127	9	310*	43.54	12	24
5105	A.Ranatunga	SL	93	155	12	135*	35.69	4	38
5062	Zaheer Abbas	P	78	124	11	274	44.79	12	20
5037	J.L.Langer	A	71	118	6	250	44.97	17	20
4926	S.P.Fleming	NZ	79	137	9	274*	38.48	6	34
4882	T.W.Graveney	E	79	123	13	258	44.38	11	20
4869	R.B.Simpson	A	62	111	7	311	46.81	10	27
4794	A.Flower	Z	63	112	19	232*	51.54	12	27
4737	I.R.Redpath	A	66	120	11	171	43.45	8	31
4656	A.J.Lamb	E	79	139	10	142	36.09	14	18
4555	H.Sutcliffe	E	54	84	9	194	60.73	16	23
4554	D.J.Cullinan	SA	70	115	12	275*	44.21	14	20
4546	S.Chanderpaul	WI	71	119	15	140	43.71	9	29
4537	P.B.H.May	E	66	106	9	285*	46.77	13	22
4509	S.C.Ganguly	I	72	120	12	173	41.75	11	21
4502	E.R.Dexter	E	62	102	8	205	47.89	9	27
4488	M.L.Hayden	A	50	85	8	380	58.28	17	14
4455	E.de C.Weekes	WI	48	81	5	207	58.61	15	19
4415	K.J.Hughes	A	70	124	6	213	37.41	9	22
4409	M.W.Gatting	E	79	138	14	207	35.55	10	21
4399	A.I.Kallicharran	WI	66	109	10	187	44.43	12	21
4389	A.P.E.Knott	E	95	149	15	135	32.75	5	30
4378	M.Amarnath	I	69	113	10	138	42.50	11	24
4373	H.P.Tillekeratne	SL	80	125	24	204*	43.29	11	19
4372	H.H.Gibbs	SA	56	94	5	228	49.12	13	14
4356	I.A.Healy	A	119	182	23	161*	27.39	4	22
4334	R.C.Fredericks	WI	59	109	7	169	42.49	8	26
4236	R.A.Smith	E	62	112	15	175	43.67	9	28
4114	Mudassar Nazar	P	76	116	8	231	38.09	10	17
4052	Saeed Anwar	P	55	91	2	188*	45.52	11	25

The most for Bangladesh is 1840 by Habibul Bashar (52 innings).

750 RUNS IN A SERIES

Runs		Series		M	I	NO	HS	Avge	100	50
974	D.G.Bradman	A v E	1930	5	7	–	334	139.14	4	–
905	W.R.Hammond	E v A	1928-29	5	9	1	251	113.12	4	–
839	M.A.Taylor	A v E	1989	6	11	1	219	83.90	2	5
834	R.N.Harvey	A v SA	1952-53	5	9	–	205	92.66	4	3
829	I.V.A.Richards	WI v E	1976	4	7	–	291	118.42	3	2
827	C.L.Walcott	WI v A	1954-55	5	10	–	155	82.70	5	2
824	G.St A.Sobers	WI v P	1957-58	5	8	2	365*	137.33	3	3
810	D.G.Bradman	A v E	1936-37	5	9	–	270	90.00	3	1
806	D.G.Bradman	A v SA	1931-32	5	5	1	299*	201.50	4	–
798	B.C.Lara	WI v E	1993-94	5	8	–	375	99.75	2	2
779	E.de C.Weekes	WI v I	1948-49	5	7	–	194	111.28	4	2
774	S.M.Gavaskar	I v WI	1970-71	4	8	3	220	154.80	4	3
765	B.C.Lara	WI v E	1995	6	10	1	179	85.00	3	3
761	Mudassar Nazar	P v I	1982-83	6	8	2	231	126.83	4	1
758	D.G.Bradman	A v E	1934	5	8	–	304	94.75	2	1
753	D.C.S.Compton	E v SA	1947	5	8	–	208	94.12	4	2
752	G.A.Gooch	E v I	1990	3	6	–	333	125.33	3	2

HIGHEST INDIVIDUAL INNINGS

380	M.L.Hayden	A v Z	Perth	2003-04
375	B.C.Lara	WI v E	St John's	1993-94
365*	G.St A.Sobers	WI v P	Kingston	1957-58
364	L.Hutton	E v A	The Oval	1938
340	S.T.Jayasuriya	SL v I	Colombo (RPS)	1997-98
337	Hanif Mohammed	P v WI	Bridgetown	1957-58
336*	W.R.Hammond	E v NZ	Auckland	1932-33
334*	M.A.Taylor	A v P	Peshawar	1998-99
334	D.G.Bradman	A v E	Leeds	1930
333	G.A.Gooch	E v I	Lord's	1990
329	Inzamam-ul-Haq	P v NZ	Lahore	2001-02
325	A.Sandham	E v WI	Kingston	1929-30
311	R.B.Simpson	A v E	Manchester	1964
310*	J.H.Edrich	E v NZ	Leeds	1965
307	R.M.Cowper	A v E	Melbourne	1965-66
304	D.G.Bradman	A v E	Leeds	1934
302	L.G.Rowe	WI v E	Bridgetown	1973-74
299*	D.G.Bradman	A v SA	Adelaide	1931-32
299	M.D.Crowe	NZ v SL	Wellington	1990-91
291	I.V.A.Richards	WI v E	The Oval	1976
287	R.E.Foster	E v A	Sydney	1903-04
285*	P.B.H.May	E v WI	Birmingham	1957
281	V.V.S.Laxman	I v A	Calcutta	2000-01
280*	Javed Miandad	P v I	Hyderabad	1982-83
278	D.C.S.Compton	E v P	Nottingham	1954
277	B.C.Lara	WI v A	Sydney	1992-93
277	G.C.Smith	SA v E	Birmingham	2003
275*	D.J.Cullinan	SA v NZ	Auckland	1998-99
275	G.Kirsten	SA v E	Durban	1999-00
274*	S.P.Fleming	NZ v SL	Colombo (SSC)	2002-03
274	R.G.Pollock	SA v A	Durban	1969-70
274	Zaheer Abbas	P v E	Birmingham	1971
271	Javed Miandad	P v NZ	Auckland	1988-89
270*	G.A.Headley	WI v E	Kingston	1934-35
270	D.G.Bradman	A v E	Melbourne	1936-37

268	G.N.Yallop	A v P	Melbourne	1983-84
267*	B.A.Young	NZ v SL	Dunedin	1996-97
267	P.A.de Silva	SL v NZ	Wellington	1990-91
266	W.H.Ponsford	A v E	The Oval	1934
266	D.L.Houghton	Z v SL	Bulawayo	1994-95
262*	D.L.Amiss	E v WI	Kingston	1973-74
261	F.M.M.Worrell	WI v E	Nottingham	1950
260	C.C.Hunte	WI v P	Kingston	1957-58
260	Javed Miandad	P v E	The Oval	1987
259	G.M.Turner	NZ v WI	Georgetown	1971-72
259	G.C.Smith	SA v E	Lord's	2003
258	T.W.Graveney	E v WI	Nottingham	1957
258	S.M.Nurse	WI v NZ	Christchurch	1968-69
257*	Wasim Akram	P v Z	Sheikhupura	1996-97
257	R.T.Ponting	A v I	Melbourne	2003-04
256	R.B.Kanhai	WI v I	Calcutta	1958-59
256	K.F.Barrington	E v A	Manchester	1964.
255*	D.J.McGlew	SA v NZ	Wellington	1952-53
254	D.G.Bradman	A v E	Lord's	1930
251	W.R.Hammond	E v A	Sydney	1928-29
250	K.D.Walters	A v NZ	Christchurch	1976-77
250	S.F.A.F.Bacchus	WI v I	Kanpur	1978-79
250	J.L.Langer	A v E	Melbourne	2002-03

The highest for Bangladesh is 145 by Aminul Islam (v I, Dhaka, 2000-01).

18 HUNDREDS

							Opponents						
			200	Inn	E	A	SA	WI	NZ	I	P	SL	Z	B
34	S.M.Gavaskar	I	4	214	4	8	–	13	2	–	5	2	–	
32	S.R.Tendulkar	I	3	180	6	7	3	3	3	–	1	6	3	
32	S.R.Waugh	A	1	260	10	–	2	7	2	2	3	3	1	2
29	D.G.Bradman	A	12	80	19	–	4	2	–	4	–	–	–	
27	A.R.Border	A	2	265	8	–	–	3	5	4	6	1	–	
26	G.St A.Sobers	WI	2	160	10	4	–	–	1	8	3	–	–	
24	G.S.Chappell	A	4	151	9	–	–	5	3	1	6	–	–	
24	B.C.Lara	WI	6	180	6	8	2	–	1	1	–	5	1	–
24	I.V.A.Richards	WI	3	182	8	5	–	–	1	8	2	–	–	
23	Javed Miandad	P	6	189	2	6	–	2	7	5	–	1	–	
22	W.R.Hammond	E	7	140	–	9	6	1	4	2	–	–		
22	M.Azharuddin	I	–	147	6	2	–	–	2	–	3	5		
22	M.C.Cowdrey	E	–	188	–	5	3	6	2	3	3	–		
22	G.Boycott	E	1	193	–	7	1	5	2	4	3	–		
21	R.N.Harvey	A	2	137	6	–	8	3	–		–	–		
21	D.C.Boon	A	1	190	7	–	–	3	3	6	1	1	–	
20	R.T.Ponting	A	3	119	4	–	3	4	4	3	1	1		
20	K.F.Barrington	E	1	131	–	5	2	3	3	3	4	–		
20	P.A.de Silva	SL	2	159	2	1	–	2	5	8	–	1	1	
20	G.Kirsten	SA	3	170	5	2	–	3	1	3	2	1	1	2
20	M.E.Waugh	A	–	209	–	4	4	1	1	3	1			
20	G.A.Gooch	E	2	215	–	4	–	5	4	5	1	1	–	
19	L.Hutton	E	4	138	–	5	4	5	3	2	–	–		
19	C.H.Lloyd	WI	1	175	5	6	–	–	1	7	–	–		
19	C.G.Greenidge	WI	4	185	7	4	–	2	2	5	1	–		
19	M.A.Taylor	A	2	186	5	4	–	1	2	2	4	2	–	
18	Inzamam-ul-Haq	P	2	150	3	1	–	3	3	–	4	2	2	
18	D.L.Haynes	WI	2	202	5	5	–	2	3	4	–	–		
18	D.I.Gower	E	2	204	–	9	–	1	4	2	2	–	–	

The most for New Zealand is 17 by M.D.Crowe (131), for Zimbabwe 12 by A.Flower (112), and for Bangladesh 2 by Habibul Bashar (52). The most double hundreds by batsmen not included above is 4 by Zaheer Abbas (12 hundreds for Pakistan) and 3 by R.B.Simpson (10 for Australia).

HIGHEST PARTNERSHIP FOR EACH WICKET

1st	413	V.Mankad/Pankaj Roy	I v NZ	Madras	1955-56
2nd	576	S.T.Jayasuriya/R.S.Mahanama	SL v I	Colombo (RPS)	1997-98
3rd	467	A.H.Jones/M.D.Crowe	NZ v SL	Wellington	1990-91
4th	411	P.B.H.May/M.C.Cowdrey	E v WI	Birmingham	1957
5th	405	S.G.Barnes/D.G.Bradman	A v E	Sydney	1946-47
6th	346	J.H.W.Fingleton/D.G.Bradman	A v E	Melbourne	1936-37
7th	347	D.St E.Atkinson/C.C.Depeiza	WI v A	Bridgetown	1954-55
8th	313	Wasim Akram/Saqlain Mushtaq	P v Z	Sheikhupura	1996-97
9th	195	M.V.Boucher/P.L.Symcox	SA v P	Johannesburg	1997-98
10th	151	B.F.Hastings/R.O.Collinge	NZ v P	Auckland	1972-73
	151	Azhar Mahmood/Mushtaq Ahmed	P v SA	Rawalpindi	1997-98

BOWLING RECORDS
200 WICKETS IN TESTS

Wkts			M	Balls	Runs	Avge	5 wI	10 wM
519	C.A.Walsh	WI	132	30019	12688	24.45	22	3
491	S.K.Warne	A	107	29876	12624	25.71	23	6
485	M.Muralitharan	SL	85	28968	11130	22.94	39	12
434	Kapil Dev	I	131	27740	12867	29.64	23	2
431	R.J.Hadlee	NZ	86	21918	9612	22.29	36	9
430	G.D.McGrath	A	95	22374	9338	21.71	23	3
414	Wasim Akram	P	104	22627	9779	23.62	25	5
405	C.E.L.Ambrose	WI	98	22104	8500	20.98	22	3
383	I.T.Botham	E	102	21815	10878	28.40	27	4
382	A.Kumble	I	81	25868	10812	28.30	23	5
376	M.D.Marshall	WI	81	17584	7876	20.94	22	4
373	Waqar Younis	P	87	16224	8788	23.56	22	5
362	Imran Khan	P	88	19458	8258	22.81	23	6
355	D.K.Lillee	A	70	18467	8493	23.92	23	7
330	A.A.Donald	SA	72	15519	7344	22.25	20	3
326	S.M.Pollock	SA	80	17980	6893	21.14	16	1
325	R.G.D.Willis	E	90	17357	8190	25.20	16	—
309	L.R.Gibbs	WI	79	27115	8989	29.09	18	2
307	F.S.Trueman	E	67	15178	6625	21.57	17	3
297	D.L.Underwood	E	86	21862	7674	25.83	17	6
291	C.J.McDermott	A	71	16586	8332	28.63	14	2
266	B.S.Bedi	I	67	21364	7637	28.71	14	1
259	J.Garner	WI	58	13169	5433	20.97	7	—
252	J.B.Statham	E	70	16056	6261	24.84	9	1
249	M.A.Holding	WI	60	12680	5898	23.68	13	2
248	R.Benaud	A	63	19108	6704	27.03	16	1
246	G.D.McKenzie	A	60	17681	7328	29.78	16	3
242	B.S.Chandrasekhar	I	58	15963	7199	29.74	16	2
236	A.V.Bedser	E	51	15918	5876	24.89	15	5
236	Abdul Qadir	P	67	17126	7742	32.80	15	5
236	J.Srinath	I	67	15104	7196	30.49	10	1
235	G.St A.Sobers	WI	93	21599	7999	34.03	6	—
234	A.R.Caddick	E	62	13558	6999	29.91	13	1
229	D.Gough	E	58	11821	6503	28.39	9	—

Wkts			M	Balls	Runs	Avge	5 wI	10 wM
229	W.P.U.C.J.Vaas	SL	71	15637	6899	30.12	7	2
228	R.R.Lindwall	A	61	13650	5251	23.03	12	–
216	C.V.Grimmett	A	37	14513	5231	24.21	21	7
212	M.G.Hughes	A	53	12285	6017	28.38	7	1
207	Saqlain Mushtaq	P	48	13812	6002	28.99	13	3
202	A.M.E.Roberts	WI	47	11136	5174	25.61	11	2
202	J.A.Snow	E	49	12021	5387	26.66	8	1
200	J.R.Thomson	A	51	10535	5601	28.00	8	–

The most for Zimbabwe is 197 in 57 Tests by H.H.Streak and for Bangladesh 36 in 8 Tests by Mohammad Rafique.

35 WICKETS IN A SERIES

Wkts		Series	M	Balls	Runs	Avge	5 wI	10 wM
49	S.F.Barnes	E v SA	1913-14	4	1356	536	10.93	7	3
46	J.C.Laker	E v A	1956	5	1703	442	9.60	4	2
44	C.V.Grimmett	A v SA	1935-36	5	2077	642	14.59	5	3
42	T.M.Alderman	A v E	1981	6	1950	893	21.26	4	–
41	R.M.Hogg	A v E	1978-79	6	1740	527	12.85	5	2
41	T.M.Alderman	A v E	1989	6	1616	712	17.36	6	1
40	Imran Khan	P v I	1982-83	6	1339	558	13.95	4	2
39	A.V.Bedser	E v A	1953	5	1591	682	17.48	5	1
39	D.K.Lillee	A v E	1981	6	1870	870	22.30	2	1
38	M.W.Tate	E v A	1924-25	5	2528	881	23.18	5	1
37	W.J.Whitty	A v SA	1910-11	5	1395	632	17.08	2	–
37	H.J.Tayfield	SA v E	1956-57	5	2280	636	17.18	4	1
36	A.E.E.Vogler	SA v E	1909-10	5	1349	783	21.75	4	1
36	A.A.Mailey	A v E	1920-21	5	1465	946	26.27	4	2
36	G.D.McGrath	A v E	1997	6	1499	701	19.47	2	–
35	G.A.Lohmann	E v SA	1895-96	3	520	203	5.80	4	2
35	B.S.Chandrasekhar	I v E	1972-73	5	1747	662	18.91	4	–
35	M.D.Marshall	WI v E	1988	5	1219	443	12.65	3	1

The most for New Zealand is 33 by R.J.Hadlee (3 Tests v A, 1985-86), for Sri Lanka 30 by M.Muralitharan (3 Tests v Z, 2001-02), for Zimbabwe 22 by H.H.Streak (3 Tests v P, 1994-95), and for Bangladesh 17 by Mohammad Rafique (3 Tests v P, 2003).

15 WICKETS IN A TEST († On debut)

19- 90	J.C.Laker	E v A	Manchester	1956
17-159	S.F.Barnes	E v SA	Johannesburg	1913-14
16-136†	N.D.Hirwani	I v WI	Madras	1987-88
16-137†	R.A.L.Massie	A v E	Lord's	1972
16-220	M.Muralitharan	SL v E	The Oval	1998
15- 28	J.Briggs	E v SA	Cape Town	1888-89
15- 45	G.A.Lohmann	E v SA	Port Elizabeth	1895-96
15- 99	C.Blythe	E v SA	Leeds	1907
15-104	H.Verity	E v A	Lord's	1934
15-123	R.J.Hadlee	NZ v A	Brisbane	1985-86
15-124	W.Rhodes	E v A	Melbourne	1903-04
15-217	Harbhajan Singh	I v A	Madras	2000-01

The best analysis for South Africa is 13-165 by H.J.Tayfield (v A, Melbourne, 1952-53), for West Indies 14-149 by M.A.Holding (v E, The Oval, 1976), for Pakistan 14-116 by Imran Khan (v SL, Lahore, 1981-82), for Zimbabwe 11-257 by A.G.Huckle (v NZ, Bulawayo, 1997-98), and for Bangladesh 7-105 by Khaled Mahmud (v P, Multan, 2003).

NINE WICKETS IN AN INNINGS

10- 53	J.C.Laker	E v A	Manchester	1956
10- 74	A.Kumble	I v P	Delhi	1998-99
9- 28	G.A.Lohmann	E v SA	Johannesburg	1895-96
9- 37	J.C.Laker	E v A	Manchester	1956
9- 51	M.Muralitharan	SL v Z	Kandy	2001-02
9- 52	R.J.Hadlee	NZ v A	Brisbane	1985-86
9- 56	Abdul Qadir	P v E	Lahore	1987-88
9- 57	D.E.Malcolm	E v SA	The Oval	1994
9- 65	M.Muralitharan	SL v E	The Oval	1998
9- 69	J.M.Patel	I v A	Kanpur	1959-60
9- 83	Kapil Dev	I v WI	Ahmedabad	1983-84
9- 86	Sarfraz Nawaz	P v A	Melbourne	1978-79
9- 95	J.M.Noreiga	WI v I	Port-of-Spain	1970-71
9-102	S.P.Gupte	I v WI	Kanpur	1958-59
9-103	S.F.Barnes	E v SA	Johannesburg	1913-14
9-113	H.J.Tayfield	SA v E	Johannesburg	1956-57
9-121	A.A.Mailey	A v E	Melbourne	1920-21

The best analysis for Zimbabwe is 8-109 by P.A.Strang (v NZ, Bulawayo, 2000-01), and for Bangladesh 6-77 by Mohammad Rafique (v SA, Dhaka, 2002-03).

HAT TRICKS

F.R.Spofforth	Australia v England	Melbourne	1878-79
W.Bates	England v Australia	Melbourne	1882-83
J.Briggs	England v Australia	Sydney	1891-92
G.A.Lohmann	England v South Africa	Port Elizabeth	1895-96
J.T.Hearne	England v Australia	Leeds	1899
H.Trumble	Australia v England	Melbourne	1901-02
H.Trumble	Australia v England	Melbourne	1903-04
T.J.Matthews (2)[2]	Australia v South Africa	Manchester	1912
M.J.C.Allom[1]	England v New Zealand	Christchurch	1929-30
T.W.J.Goddard	England v South Africa	Johannesburg	1938-39
P.J.Loader	England v West Indies	Leeds	1957
L.F.Kline	Australia v South Africa	Cape Town	1957-58
W.W.Hall	West Indies v Pakistan	Lahore	1958-59
G.M.Griffin	South Africa v England	Lord's	1960
L.R.Gibbs	West Indies v Australia	Adelaide	1960-61
P.J.Petherick[1]	New Zealand v Pakistan	Lahore	1976-77
C.A.Walsh[3]	West Indies v Australia	Brisbane	1988-89
M.G.Hughes[3]	Australia v West Indies	Perth	1988-89
D.W.Fleming[1]	Australia v Pakistan	Rawalpindi	1994-95
S.K.Warne	Australia v England	Melbourne	1994-95
D.G.Cork	England v West Indies	Manchester	1995
D.Gough	England v Australia	Sydney	1998-99
Wasim Akram[4]	Pakistan v Sri Lanka	Lahore	1998-99
Wasim Akram[4]	Pakistan v Sri Lanka	Dhaka	1998-99
D.N.T.Zoysa[5]	Sri Lanka v Zimbabwe	Harare	1999-00
Abdul Razzaq	Pakistan v Sri Lanka	Galle	2000-01
G.D.McGrath	Australia v West Indies	Perth	2000-01
Harbhajan Singh	India v Australia	Calcutta	2000-01
Mohammad Sami	Pakistan v Sri Lanka	Lahore	2001-02
J.J.C.Lawson	West Indies v Australia	Bridgetown	2002-03
Alok Kapali	Bangladesh v Pakistan	Peshawar	2003

[1] On debut. [2] Hat trick in each innings. [3] Involving both innings. [4] In successive Tests. [5] His first 3 balls (second over of the match).

WICKET-KEEPING RECORDS
100 DISMISSALS IN TESTS†

Total				Tests	Ct	St
395	I.A.Healy	Australia		119	366	29
355	R.W.Marsh	Australia		96	343	12
274	M.V.Boucher	South Africa		71	264	10
270†	P.J.L.Dujon	West Indies		79	265	5
269	A.P.E.Knott	England		95	250	19
241†	A.J.Stewart	England		82	227	14
228	Wasim Bari	Pakistan		81	201	27
219	T.G.Evans	England		91	173	46
214	A.C.Gilchrist	Australia		51	195	19
201†	A.C.Parore	New Zealand		67	194	7
198	S.M.H.Kirmani	India		88	160	38
192	R.D.Jacobs	West Indies		57	183	9
189	D.L.Murray	West Indies		62	181	8
187	A.T.W.Grout	Australia		51	163	24
176	I.D.S.Smith	New Zealand		63	168	8
174	R.W.Taylor	England		57	167	7
165	R.C.Russell	England		54	153	12
152	D.J.Richardson	South Africa		42	150	2
151†	A.Flower	Zimbabwe		55	142	9
143†	Moin Khan	Pakistan		64	123	20
141	J.H.B.Waite	South Africa		50	124	17
130	Rashid Latif	Pakistan		37	119	11
130	K.S.More	India		49	110	20
130	W.A.S.Oldfield	Australia		54	78	52
112†	J.M.Parks	England		43	101	11
107	N.R.Mongia	India		44	99	8
104	Salim Yousuf	Pakistan		32	91	13
104	R.S.Kaluwitharana	Sri Lanka		44	82	22
101†	J.R.Murray	West Indies		31	98	3

The most for Bangladesh is 40 (37 ct, 3 st) by Khaled Masud in 23 Tests.
† Excluding catches taken in the field

25 DISMISSALS IN A SERIES

28	R.W.Marsh	Australia v England	1982-83
27 (inc 2st)	R.C.Russell	England v South Africa	1995-96
27 (inc 2st)	I.A.Healy	Australia v England (6 Tests)	1997
26 (inc 3st)	J.H.B.Waite	South Africa v New Zealand	1961-62
26	R.W.Marsh	Australia v West Indies (6 Tests)	1975-76
26 (inc 5st)	I.A.Healy	Australia v England (6 Tests)	1993
26 (inc 1st)	M.V.Boucher	South Africa v England	1998
26 (inc 2st)	A.C.Gilchrist	Australia v England	2001
25 (inc 2st)	I.A.Healy	Australia v England	1994-95
25 (inc 2st)	A.C.Gilchrist	Australia v England	2002-03

TEN DISMISSALS IN A TEST

11	R.C.Russell	England v South Africa	Johannesburg	1995-96
10	R.W.Taylor	England v India	Bombay	1979-80
10	A.C.Gilchrist	Australia v New Zealand	Hamilton	1999-00

SEVEN DISMISSALS IN AN INNINGS

7	Wasim Bari	Pakistan v New Zealand	Auckland	1978-79
7	R.W.Taylor	England v India	Bombay	1979-80

| 7 | I.D.S.Smith | New Zealand v Sri Lanka | Hamilton | 1990-91 |
| 7 | R.D.Jacobs | West Indies v Australia | Melbourne | 2000-01 |

FIVE STUMPINGS IN AN INNINGS

| 5 | K.S.More | India v West Indies | Madras | 1987-88 |

FIELDING RECORDS
100 CATCHES IN TESTS

Total			Tests	Total			Tests
181	M.E.Waugh	Australia	128	115	C.L.Hooper	West Indies	102
157	M.A.Taylor	Australia	104	112	S.R.Waugh	Australia	168
156	A.R.Border	Australia	156	110	R.B.Simpson	Australia	62
136	B.C.Lara	West Indies	102	110	W.R.Hammond	England	85
122	G.S.Chappell	Australia	87	109	G.St A.Sobers	West Indies	93
122	I.V.A.Richards	West Indies	121	108	S.M.Gavaskar	India	125
120	I.T.Botham	England	102	105	I.M.Chappell	Australia	75
120	M.C.Cowdrey	England	114	105	M.Azharuddin	India	99
117	S.P.Fleming	New Zealand	79	103	G.A.Gooch	England	118

The most for South Africa is 83 by G.Kirsten (98 Tests), for Pakistan 93 by Javed Miandad (124), for Sri Lanka 88 by H.P.Tillekeratne (69), for Zimbabwe 60 by A.D.R.Campbell (60) and for Bangladesh 12 by Habibul Bashar (26).

15 CATCHES IN A SERIES

| 15 | J.M.Gregory | | Australia v England | | 1920-21 |

SEVEN CATCHES IN A TEST

7	G.S.Chappell	Australia v England	Perth	1974-75
7	Yajurvindra Singh	India v England	Bangalore	1976-77
7	H.P.Tillekeratne	Sri Lanka v New Zealand	Colombo (SSC)	1992-93
7	S.P.Fleming	New Zealand v Zimbabwe	Harare	1997-98

FIVE CATCHES IN AN INNINGS

5	V.Y.Richardson	Australia v South Africa	Durban	1935-36
5	Yajurvindra Singh	India v England	Bangalore	1976-77
5	M.Azharuddin	India v Pakistan	Karachi	1989-90
5	K.Srikkanth	India v Australia	Perth	1991-92
5	S.P.Fleming	New Zealand v Zimbabwe	Harare	1997-98

APPEARANCE RECORDS
100 TEST MATCH APPEARANCES

168	S.R.Waugh	Australia	115	M.A.Atherton	England
156	A.R.Border	Australia	114	M.C.Cowdrey	England
133	A.J.Stewart	England	111	S.R.Tendulkar	India
132	C.A.Walsh	West Indies	110	C.H.Lloyd	West Indies
131	Kapil Dev	India	108	G.Boycott	England
128	M.E.Waugh	Australia	108	C.G.Greenidge	West Indies
125	S.M.Gavaskar	India	107	D.C.Boon	Australia
124	Javed Miandad	Pakistan	107	S.K.Warne	Australia
121	I.V.A.Richards	West Indies	104	M.A.Taylor	Australia
119	I.A.Healy	Australia	104	Wasim Akram	Pakistan
118	G.A.Gooch	England	103	Salim Malik	Pakistan
117	D.I.Gower	England	102	I.T.Botham	England
116	D.L.Haynes	West Indies	102	C.L.Hooper	West Indies
116	D.B.Vengsarkar	India	102	B.C.Lara	West Indies

The most for South Africa is 98 by G.Kirsten, for New Zealand 86 by R.J.Hadlee, for Sri Lanka 93 by P.A.de Silva and A.Ranatunga, for Zimbabwe 65 by G.W.Flower, and for Bangladesh 26 by Habibul Bashar.

100 CONSECUTIVE TEST APPEARANCES

153	A.R.Border	Australia	March 1979 to March 1994
107	M.E.Waugh	Australia	June 1993 to October 2002
106	S.M.Gavaskar	India	January 1975 to February 1987

50 TESTS AS CAPTAIN

93	A.R.Border	Australia	54	M.A.Atherton	England
74	C.H.Lloyd	West Indies	53	W.J.Cronje	South Africa
57	S.R.Waugh	Australia	50	I.V.A.Richards	West Indies
56	A.Ranatunga	Sri Lanka	50	M.A.Taylor	Australia
55	S.P.Fleming	New Zealand			

The most for India is 47 by M.Azharuddin and S.M.Gavaskar, for Pakistan 48 by Imran Khan, for Zimbabwe 21 by A.D.R.Campbell, and for Bangladesh 10 by Khaled Masud.

50 TEST UMPIRING APPEARANCES

86	S.A.Bucknor	(West Indies)	April 1989 to January 2004
78	D.R.Shepherd	(England)	August 1985 to January 2004
73	S.Venkataraghavan	(India)	January 1992 to January 2004
66	H.D.Bird	(England)	July 1973 to June 1996
51	D.B.Hair	(Australia)	January 1992 to December 2003

LEADING TEST AGGREGATES 2003

1000 RUNS

	M	I	NO	HS	Runs	Avge	100	50
R.T.Ponting (A)	11	18	3	257	1503	100.20	6	4
B C Lara (WI)	10	19	1	209	1344	74.66	5	5
M.L.Hayden (A)	12	21	4	380	1312	77.17	5	3
G.C.Smith (SA)	12	19	-	277	1198	63.05	4	2
H.H.Gibbs (SA)	12	19	1	228	1156	64.22	4	3
M.E.Trescothick (E)	13	24	3	219	1003	47.76	2	6

50 WICKETS

	M	O	R	W	Avge	Best	5wI	10wM
M.Ntini (SA)	12	469	1566	59	26.54	5-66	4	1
S.C.G.MacGill (A)	11	524.4	1688	57	29.61	5-56	4	1

TEST MATCH SCORES AND SERIES AVERAGES

WEST INDIES v AUSTRALIA (1st Test)

At Bourda, Georgetown, Guyana, on 10, 11, 12, 13 April 2003.
Toss: West Indies. Result: **AUSTRALIA** won by nine wickets.
Debuts: West Indies – D.S.Smith.

WEST INDIES

W.W.Hinds	c Langer b Hogg	10	lbw b MacGill		7
D.S.Smith	lbw b Lee	3	c Gilchrist b Gillespie		62
D.Ganga	b Gillespie	0	c Lee b Lehmann		113
*B.C.Lara	lbw b Bichel	26	hit wicket b Hogg		110
M.N.Samuels	c Hayden b Hogg	0	c Ponting b MacGill		7
S.Chanderpaul	lbw b Bichel	100	c Gilchrist b Gillespie		31
†R.D.Jacobs	not out	54	(9) c Lehmann b MacGill		11
V.C.Drakes	c Gilchrist b Bichel	0	(7) lbw b Gillespie		14
M.Dillon	lbw b MacGill	20	(8) lbw b Gillespie		0
P.T.Collins	st Gilchrist b MacGill	3	not out		1
J.J.C.Lawson	b Lee	0	lbw b Gillespie		0
Extras	(B 10, LB 2, W 3, NB 6)	21	(B 6, LB 13, W 1, NB 22)		42
Total		**237**			**398**

AUSTRALIA

J.L.Langer	c Hinds b Drakes	146	not out		78
M.L.Hayden	run out	10	c sub (N.Deonarine) b Lawson		19
R.T.Ponting	c Samuels b Drakes	117	not out		42
D.S.Lehmann	c sub (D.E.Bernard) b Drakes	6			
*S.R.Waugh	lbw b Dillon	25			
†A.C.Gilchrist	c and b Lawson	77			
G.B.Hogg	lbw b Collins	3			
A.J.Bichel	c Hinds b Drakes	39			
B.Lee	c Dillon b Drakes	20			
J.N.Gillespie	b Lawson	7			
S.C.G.MacGill	not out	4			
Extras	(B 18, LB 5, W 2, NB 10)	35	(B 1, LB 2, W 2, NB 3)		8
Total		**489**	(1 wicket)		**147**

AUSTRALIA	O	M	R	W		O	M	R	W	FALL OF WICKETS				
Lee	10.3	1	41	2	(3)	14	4	57	0		WI	A	WI	A
Gillespie	12	3	40	1		20.2	5	39	5	Wkt	1st	1st	2nd	2nd
Bichel	8	1	55	3	(5)	13	4	40	0	1st	9	37	52	77
Hogg	8	1	40	2	(2)	15	0	68	1	2nd	10	285	110	–
MacGill	12	4	49	2	(1)	31	5	140	3	3rd	47	300	295	–
Waugh						8	1	29	0	4th	47	319	303	–
Lehmann						4	0	6	1	5th	53	349	354	–
										6th	184	362	382	–
WEST INDIES										7th	184	447	384	–
Dillon	23	1	116	1		6	0	21	0	8th	222	473	391	–
Collins	23	1	96	1	(3)	6	2	14	0	9th	236	485	397	–
Lawson	21	0	111	2	(4)	9	2	31	1	10th	237	489	398	–
Drakes	26.1	5	93	5	(2)	8	0	28	0					
Samuels	21	6	49	0		9.1	1	41	0					
Ganga	1	0	1	0		4	0	9	0					

Umpires: E.A.R. de Silva (*Sri Lanka*) (23) and R.E.Koertzen (*South Africa*) (38).
Referee: M.J.Procter (*South Africa*) (8). **Test No. 1638/96 (WI394/A637)**

WEST INDIES v AUSTRALIA (2nd Test)

At Queen's Park Oval, Port-of-Spain, Trinidad, on 19, 20, 21, 22, 23 April 2003.
Toss: Australia. Result: **AUSTRALIA** won by 118 runs.
Debuts: West Indies – D.E.Barnard, C.S.Baugh.

AUSTRALIA

J.L.Langer	lbw b Dillon	25	lbw b Drakes		3
M.L.Hayden	lbw b Dillon	30	not out		100
R.T.Ponting	st Baugh b Samuels	206	c Baugh b Dillon		45
D.S.Lehmann	c Baugh b Drakes	160	b Dillon		66
†A.C.Gilchrist	not out	101			
G.B.Hogg	not out	17			
*S.R.Waugh					
A.J.Bichel					
B.Lee					
J.N.Gillespie					
S.C.G.MacGill					
Extras	(B 11, LB 7, W 7, NB 12)	37	(B 12, LB 6, W 1, NB 5)		24
Total	(4 wickets declared)	**576**	(3 wickets declared)		**238**

WEST INDIES

W.W.Hinds	c Hayden b Lee	20	b MacGill		35
D.S.Smith	c Gilchrist b Gillespie	0	lbw b Gillespie		0
D.Ganga	c Hayden b Lee	117	c Hayden b Gillespie		2
*B.C.Lara	b Hogg	91	c Hayden b MacGill		122
R.R.Sarwan	b Lee	26	c Lehmann b Bichel		34
M.N.Samuels	c Bichel b MacGill	68	lbw b Bichel		1
D.E.Bernard	b Gillespie	7	c Hayden b Bichel		4
†C.S.Baugh	hit wicket b MacGill	19	c Langer b Hogg		1
V.C.Drakes	lbw b Lee	24	not out		26
M.Dillon	lbw b Gillespie	0	c Bichel b Lee		13
P.T.Collins	not out	7	lbw b Gillespie		5
Extras	(B 4, LB 15, W 2, NB 8)	29	(B 25, LB 7, W 3, NB 10)		45
Total		**408**			**288**

WEST INDIES	O	M	R	W		O	M	R	W	FALL OF WICKETS				
											A	WI	A	WI
Dillon	28.5	1	124	2		18.2	0	64	2	Wkt	1st	1st	2nd	2nd
Collins	25	2	123	0	(4)	7	1	30	0	1st	49	4	12	2
Drakes	33	3	112	1	(2)	20	4	61	1	2nd	56	25	118	12
Samuels	26	2	111	1	(3)	21	1	65	0	3rd	371	183	238	107
Bernard	11	1	61	0						4th	542	258	–	213
Sarwan	2	0	7	0						5th	–	279	–	222
Hinds	7	0	20	0						6th	–	300	–	228
										7th	–	367	–	238
AUSTRALIA										8th	–	376	–	238
Lee	23	4	69	4		19	4	68	1	9th	–	384	–	270
Gillespie	28	9	50	3		17.2	3	36	3	10th	–	408	–	288
Bichel	12	1	58	0		13	3	21	3					
MacGill	27	4	98	2	(5)	20	6	53	2					
Hogg	22	3	98	1	(6)	13	1	58	1					
Waugh	7	2	16	0										
Lehmann					(4)	7	0	20	0					

Umpires: E.A.R. de Silva (*Sri Lanka*) (24) and R.E.Koertzen (*South Africa*) (39).
Referee: M.J.Procter (*South Africa*) (9).   **Test No. 1639/97 (WI395/A638)**

WEST INDIES v AUSTRALIA (3rd Test)

At Kensington Oval, Bridgetown, Barbados, on 1, 2, 3, 4, 5 May 2003.
Toss: West Indies. Result: **AUSTRALIA** won by nine wickets.
Debuts: West Indies – O.A.C.Banks, T.L.Best.

AUSTRALIA

J.L.Langer	c Chanderpaul b Banks	78	lbw b Lawson		0
M.L.Hayden	c Gayle b Drakes	27	not out		2
R.T.Ponting	run out	113			
D.S.Lehmann	lbw b Drakes	96	not out		4
*S.R.Waugh	b Lawson	115			
†A.C.Gilchrist	c Smith b Banks	65			
A.J.Bichel	c Lara b Banks	71			
B.Lee	b Lawson	11			
J.N.Gillespie	not out	18			
S.C.G.MacGill	b Lawson	0			
G.D.McGrath					
Extras	(B 3, LB 3, W 3, NB 2)	11	(B 2)		2
Total	(9 wickets declared)	**605**	(1 wicket)		**8**

WEST INDIES

C.H.Gayle	b Gillespie	71	st Gilchrist b MacGill		56
D.S.Smith	c Gilchrist b Gillespie	59	lbw b Lee		5
D.Ganga	c Bichel b Lehmann	26	lbw b Lee		6
R.R.Sarwan	c Gilchrist b Lee	40	lbw b MacGill		58
S.Chanderpaul	c Lee b MacGill	0	(6) c Gilchrist b Gillespie		21
O.A.C.Banks	c Ponting b Gillespie	24	(7) c Hayden b MacGill		32
†C.S.Baugh	c Ponting b MacGill	24	(8) run out		18
*B.C.Lara	lbw b Bichel	14	(5) lbw b Bichel		42
V.C.Drakes	c Lee b MacGill	11	b MacGill		0
T.L.Best	not out	20	c Bichel b MacGill		0
J.J.C.Lawson	st Gilchrist b MacGill	1	not out		5
Extras	(B 11, LB 16, NB 11)	38	(B 13, LB 25, W 1, NB 2)		41
Total		**328**			**284**

WEST INDIES	O	M	R	W		O	M	R	W		FALL OF WICKETS			
Lawson	32.3	4	131	3		1	0	2	1			A	WI	WI	A
Best	20	1	99	0							Wkt	1st	1st	2nd	2nd
Drakes	30	2	85	2							1st	43	139	14	0
Banks	40	2	204	3	(2)	1	0	2	0		2nd	151	142	31	–
Gayle	31	5	79	0	(3)	0.3	0	2	0		3rd	292	205	94	–
Sarwan	1	0	1	0							4th	331	206	187	–
											5th	444	245	195	–
AUSTRALIA											6th	568	245	256	–
McGrath	18	7	25	0		18	4	39	0		7th	580	281	256	–
Gillespie	21	9	31	3		28	11	37	1		8th	605	291	261	–
Lee	25	8	77	1	(4)	15	6	44	2		9th	605	324	265	–
MacGill	39.5	8	107	4	(3)	36	11	75	5		10th	–	328	284	–
Lehmann	9	2	26	1	(8)	1	0	4	0						
Bichel	16	3	35	1	(5)	12	2	35	1						
Ponting					(6)	2	0	6	0						
Waugh					(7)	4	1	6	0						

Umpires: D.R.Shepherd (*England*) (70) and S.Venkataraghavan (*India*) (65).
Referee: M.J.Procter (*South Africa*) (10).　　　　**Test No. 1640/98 (WI396/A639)**

WEST INDIES v AUSTRALIA (4th Test)

At Antigua Recreation Ground, St John's, Antigua, on 9, 10, 11, 12, 13 May 2003.
Toss: Australia. Result: **WEST INDIES** won by three wickets.
Debuts: None.

AUSTRALIA

J.L.Langer	c Banks b Lawson	42	c Lara b Gayle		111
M.L.Hayden	c Drakes b Lawson	14	run out		177
M.L.Love	b Banks	36	(4) c sub (M.N.Samuels) b Banks		2
D.S.Lehmann	c Jacobs b Lawson	7	(5) b Dillon		14
*S.R.Waugh	c Jacobs b Dillon	41	(6) not out		45
†A.C.Gilchrist	c Chanderpaul b Dillon	33	(3) c sub (M.N.Samuels) b Banks		6
A.J.Bichel	c sub (M.N.Samuels) b Lawson	34	c Smith b Dillon		0
B.Lee	c Jacobs b Lawson	3	c sub (S.C.Joseph) b Dillon		18
J.N.Gillespie	c Jacobs b Lawson	6	c Lara b Drakes		5
S.C.G.MacGill	c Sarwan b Lawson	2	c Lara b Dillon		0
G.D.McGrath	not out	5	c Ganga b Drakes		14
Extras	(B 2, LB 3, W 2, NB 4)	11	(B 4, LB 9, NB 12)		25
Total		**240**			**417**

WEST INDIES

C.H.Gayle	b McGrath	0	c Waugh b Lee		19
D.S.Smith	c Gilchrist b Lee	37	c Gilchrist b Gillespie		23
D.Ganga	c Gilchrist b Bichel	6	lbw b McGrath		8
V.C.Drakes	lbw b Lee	21	(9) not out		27
*B.C.Lara	c Langer b Bichel	68	(4) b MacGill		60
R.R.Sarwan	c and b Bichel	24	(5) c and b Lee		105
S.Chanderpaul	b McGrath	1	(6) c Gilchrist b Lee		104
†R.D.Jacobs	run out	26	(7) c Gilchrist b Lee		0
O.A.C.Banks	not out	16	(8) not out		47
M.Dillon	b Lee	9			
J.J.C.Lawson	c Love b MacGill	14			
Extras	(LB 8, W 3, NB 7)	18	(B 9, LB 9, W 1, NB 6)		25
Total		**240**	(7 wickets)		**418**

WEST INDIES	O	M	R	W	O	M	R	W		FALL OF WICKETS			
											A	WI	A	WI
Dillon	18	2	53	2	(2) 29	3	112	4		Wkt	1st	1st	2nd	2nd
Lawson	19.1	3	78	7	(1) 6	1	17	0		1st	27	1	242	48
Drakes	15	2	42	0	(4) 19	1	92	2		2nd	80	30	273	50
Banks	20	2	62	1	(3) 37	5	153	2		3rd	93	73	285	74
Gayle					13	1	30	1		4th	128	80	330	165
										5th	181	137	338	288
AUSTRALIA										6th	194	140	343	288
McGrath	17	6	44	2	25	10	50	1		7th	224	185	373	372
Gillespie	17	3	56	0	25	10	64	1		8th	231	197	385	–
Bichel	14	4	53	3	(5) 15	3	49	0		9th	233	224	388	–
Lee	15	2	71	3	(3) 23	4	63	4		10th	240	240	417	–
MacGill	2.3	0	8	1	(4) 35.5	8	149	1						
Waugh					5	0	25	0						

Umpires: D.R.Shepherd (*England*) (71) and S.Venkataraghavan (*India*) (66).
Referee: M.J.Procter (*South Africa*) (11).   **Test No. 1641/99 (WI397/A640)**

WEST INDIES v AUSTRALIA 2002-03

WEST INDIES – BATTING AND FIELDING

	M	I	NO	HS	Runs	Avge	100	50	Ct/St
B.C.Lara	4	8	–	122	533	66.62	2	3	4
O.A.C.Banks	2	4	2	47*	119	59.90	–	–	1
R.R.Sarwan	3	6	–	105	287	47.83	1	1	1
S.Chanderpaul	3	6	–	104	257	42.83	2	–	2
C.H.Gayle	2	4	–	71	146	36.50	–	2	1
D.Ganga	4	8	–	117	278	34.75	2	–	1
R.D.Jacobs	2	4	1	54*	91	30.33	–	1	4
D.S.Smith	4	8	–	62	189	23.62	–	2	2
V.C.Drakes	4	8	2	27*	123	20.50	–	–	1
M.N.Samuels	2	4	–	68	76	19.00	–	1	1
W.W.Hinds	2	4	–	35	72	18.00	–	–	2
C.S.Baugh	2	4	–	24	62	15.50	–	–	2/1
M.Dillon	3	5	–	20	42	8.40	–	–	1
P.T.Collins	2	4	–	7*	16	8.00	–	–	–
J.J.C.Lawson	3	5	1	14	20	5.00	–	–	–

Played in one Test: D.E.Bernard 7, 4; T.L.Best 20*, 0.

WEST INDIES – BOWLING

	O	M	R	W	Avge	Best	5wI	10wM
J.J.C.Lawson	88.4	8	370	14	26.42	7- 78	1	–
M.Dillon	123.1	7	490	11	44.54	4-112	–	–
V.C.Drakes	151.1	17	513	11	46.63	5- 93	1	–
O.A.C.Banks	98	9	421	6	70.16	3-204	–	–

Also bowled: D.E.Bernard 11-1-61-0; T.L.Best 20-1-99-0; P.T.Collins 61-6-263-1; D.Ganga 5-0-10-0; C.H.Gayle 44.3-6-111-1; W.W.Hinds 7-0-20-0; M.N.Samuels 77.1-10-266-1; R.R.Sarwan 3-0-8-0.

AUSTRALIA – BATTING AND FIELDING

	M	I	NO	HS	Runs	Avge	100	50	Ct/St
R.T.Ponting	3	5	1	206	523	130.75	3	–	3
S.R.Waugh	4	4	1	115	226	75.33	1	–	1
A.C.Gilchrist	4	5	–	101*	282	70.50	1	2	12/3
J.L.Langer	4	8	1	146	483	69.00	2	2	3
M.L.Hayden	4	8	2	177	379	63.16	2	–	7
D.S.Lehmann	4	7	1	160	353	58.83	1	2	2
A.J.Bichel	4	4	–	71	144	36.00	–	1	5
G.B.Hogg	2	2	1	17*	20	20.00	–	–	–
G.D.McGrath	2	2	1	14	19	19.00	–	–	–
B.Lee	4	4	–	20	58	14.50	–	–	4
J.N.Gillespie	4	4	1	18*	36	12.00	–	–	–
S.C.G.MacGill	4	4	1	4*	6	2.00	–	–	–

Played in one Test: M.L.Love 36, 2 (1 ct).

AUSTRALIA – BOWLING

	O	M	R	W	Avge	Best	5wI	10wM
J.N.Gillespie	168.4	53	353	17	20.76	5-39	1	–
B.Lee	144.3	33	490	17	28.82	4-63	–	–
A.J.Bichel	103	21	346	11	31.45	3-21	–	–
S.C.G.MacGill	204.1	46	679	20	33.95	5-75	1	–
G.B.Hogg	58	5	264	5	52.80	2-40	–	–

Also bowled: D.S.Lehmann 21-2-56-2; G.D.McGrath 78-27-158-3; R.T.Ponting 2-0-6-0; S.R.Waugh 24-4-76-0.

BANGLADESH v SOUTH AFRICA (1st Test)

At M.A.Aziz Stadium, Chittagong, on 24, 25, 26, 27 April 2003.
Toss: Bangladesh. Result: **SOUTH AFRICA** won by an innings and 60 runs.
Debuts: Bangladesh – Mohammad Salim; South Africa – A.C.Dawson, J.A.Rudolph and C.M.Willoughby.

BANGLADESH

Javed Omar	lbw b Dawson	28		c Boucher b Ntini	71
Mehrab Hossain	c Boucher b Pollock	6		lbw b Pollock	5
Habibul Bashar	c Gibbs b Dawson	60		c Boucher b Pollock	75
Mohammad Ashraful	c Dippenaar b Adams	12		c Smith b Willoughby	28
Akram Khan	c Rudolph b Adams	13	(7)	c Dippenaar b Adams	16
Alok Kapali	c Boucher b Adams	0	(5)	c Boucher b Adams	7
*Khaled Mahmud	b Ntini	6	(8)	st Boucher b Smith	1
†Mohammad Salim	not out	16	(6)	lbw b Adams	0
Tapash Baisya	c Dippenaar b Ntini	4	(10)	not out	0
Enamul Haque	b Adams	1	(11)	c and b Adams	11
Mashrafe Mortaza	st Boucher b Adams	20	(9)	c Pollock b Adams	0
Extras	(W 1, NB 6)	7		(B 5, LB 10, W 6, NB 2)	23
Total		**173**			**237**

SOUTH AFRICA

*G.C.Smith	c Salim b Baisya	16
H.H.Gibbs	c Salim b Mortaza	17
J.A.Rudolph	not out	222
H.H.Dippenaar	not out	177
N.D.McKenzie		
†M.V.Boucher		
S.M.Pollock		
P.R.Adams		
A.C.Dawson		
C.M.Willoughby		
M.Ntini		
Extras	(B 9, LB 6, W 2, NB 21)	38
Total	(2 wickets declared)	**470**

SOUTH AFRICA	O	M	R	W		O	M	R	W
Pollock	11	2	22	1		13	9	12	2
Ntini	17	4	45	2	(3)	16	4	37	1
Dawson	13	3	37	2	(4)	12	4	48	0
Willoughby	12	5	32	0	(2)	18	6	47	1
Adams	12.3	3	37	5		18.4	5	69	5
Smith						5	2	9	1

BANGLADESH	O	M	R	W
Mashrafe Mortaza	24	3	108	1
Khaled Mahmud	17	5	56	0
Tapash Baisya	23	8	70	1
Enamul Haque	33	10	81	0
Alok Kapali	18.5	2	71	0
Mohammad Ashraful	8	0	31	0
Habibul Bashar	7	0	38	0

FALL OF WICKETS			
	B	SA	B
Wkt	1st	1st	2nd
1st	14	38	7
2nd	97	41	138
3rd	100	–	173
4th	124	–	183
5th	124	–	185
6th	126	–	213
7th	136	–	224
8th	144	–	224
9th	147	–	224
10th	173	–	237

Umpires: B.F.Bowden (*New Zealand*) (4) and S.A.Bucknor (*West Indies*) (78).
Referee: C.H.Lloyd (*West Indies*) (22). **Test No. 1642/3 (B18/SA273)**

BANGLADESH v SOUTH AFRICA (2nd Test)

At Bangabandhu National Stadium, Dhaka, on 1, 2, 3, 4 May 2003.
Toss: South Africa. Result: **SOUTH AFRICA** won by an innings and 18 runs.
Debuts: South Africa – R.J.Peterson.

SOUTH AFRICA

*G.C.Smith	c Ashraful b Baisya	15
H.H.Gibbs	c Baisya b Rafique	21
J.A.Rudolph	st Salim b Ashraful	71
H.H.Dippenaar	c Mehrab b Rafique	1
N.D.McKenzie	lbw b Rafique	7
†M.V.Boucher	b Rafique	71
S.M.Pollock	lbw b Mortaza	41
R.J.Peterson	c Akram b Ashraful	61
A.C.Dawson	c Salim b Rafique	10
P.R.Adams	b Rafique	9
M.Ntini	not out	0
Extras	(B 6, LB 6, W 1, NB 5, PEN 5)	23
Total		**330**

BANGLADESH

Javed Omar	c sub (A.J.Hall) b Ntini	11	c Pollock b Adams	27
Mehrab Hossain	c Smith b Pollock	8	run out	14
Habibul Bashar	lbw b Pollock	14	c Boucher b Peterson	33
Mohammad Ashraful	c Pollock b Ntini	15	c Pollock b Peterson	23
Akram Khan	c Boucher b Ntini	13	c Rudolph b Ntini	23
Alok Kapali	run out	1	c Ntini b Dawson	23
*Khaled Mahmud	not out	20	c sub (A.J.Hall) b Peterson	0
†Mohammad Salim	c Boucher b Peterson	7	c Smith b Pollock	26
Mohammad Rafique	c Pollock b Dawson	0	c Boucher b Adams	18
Tapash Baisya	b Dawson	4	not out	8
Mashrafe Mortaza	c Dippenaar b Peterson	1	b Pollock	4
Extras	(LB 4, W 1, NB 3)	8	(B 5, W 1, NB 5)	11
Total		**102**		**210**

BANGLADESH	O	M	R	W		O	M	R	W
Tapash Baisya	19	5	67	1					
Mashrafe Mortaza	20	3	53	1					
Khaled Mahmud	14	6	36	0					
Mohammad Rafique	37.2	7	77	6					
Alok Kapali	11	2	33	0					
Mohammad Ashraful	10	0	42	2					
Mehrab Hossain	2	0	5	0					

SOUTH AFRICA	O	M	R	W		O	M	R	W
Pollock	8	3	21	2		8	1	21	2
Ntini	11	4	32	3		12	2	37	1
Dawson	7	2	20	2	(4)	10	5	12	1
Peterson	8.5	1	23	2	(3)	27	13	46	3
Adams	1	0	3	0		19	3	70	2
Smith						7	0	19	0

FALL OF WICKETS

Wkt	SA 1st	B 1st	B 2nd
1st	30	22	46
2nd	49	22	46
3rd	51	37	93
4th	63	53	119
5th	170	62	131
6th	219	66	139
7th	264	73	163
8th	294	77	190
9th	330	85	206
10th	330	102	210

Umpires: B.F.Bowden (*New Zealand*) (5) and S.A.Bucknor (*West Indies*) (79).
Referee: C.H.Lloyd (*West Indies*) (23).   **Test No. 1643/4 (B19/SA274)**

SRI LANKA v NEW ZEALAND (1st Test)

At P.Saravanamuttu Stadium, Colombo, on 25, 26, 27, 28, 29 April 2003.
Toss: New Zealand. Result: **MATCH DRAWN**.
Debuts: Sri Lanka – K.S.Lokuarachchi, R.A.P.Nissanka.

NEW ZEALAND

M.H.Richardson	b Vaas	85	(7) not out		6
M.J.Horne	c Dharmasena b Nissanka	4	(1) lbw b Lokuarachchi		42
*S.P.Fleming	not out	274	(2) not out		69
M.S.Sinclair	c Sangakkara b Dharmasena	17	(3) c sub (T.M.Dilshan) b Muralitharan		1
S.B.Styris	c Vaas b Dharmasena	63	(4) lbw b Lokuarachchi		8
J.D.P.Oram	c Lokuarachchi b Muralitharan	33	(5) c Kaluwitharana b Muralitharan		19
†R.G.Hart	c Jayawardena b Muralitharan	9	(6) c Sangakkara b Muralitharan		0
D.L.Vettori	lbw b Dharmasena	7			
P.J.Wiseman	not out	16			
D.R.Tuffey					
S.E.Bond					
Extras	(B 2, LB 3, W 1, NB 1)	7	(B 2, LB 5, NB 1)		8
Total	(7 wickets declared)	**515**	(5 wickets declared)		**161**

SRI LANKA

M.S.Atapattu	lbw b Tuffey	0
S.T.Jayasuriya	b Bond	50
W.P.U.C.J.Vaas	c Fleming b Bond	4
K.C.Sangakkara	c Oram b Wiseman	67
D.P.M.D.Jayawardena	b Hart b Oram	58
*H.P.Tillekeratne	b Bond	144
†R.S.Kaluwitharana	c Sinclair b Wiseman	76
H.D.P.K.Dharmasena	lbw b Vettori	31
K.S.Lokuarachchi	not out	28
R.A.P.Nissanka	lbw b Vettori	0
M.Muralitharan	lbw b Vettori	0
Extras	(LB 21, W 1, NB 3)	25
Total		**483**

SRI LANKA	O	M	R	W		O	M	R	W
Vaas	29	8	73	1		7	2	27	0
Nissanka	23	9	53	1		6	1	18	0
Dharmasena	40	7	132	3	(5)	16	7	21	0
Muralitharan	58.5	16	140	3	(3)	30	15	41	3
Lokuarachchi	18	2	83	0	(4)	19	2	47	2
Jayasuriya	6	0	29	0					

NEW ZEALAND	O	M	R	W
Tuffey	17	5	54	1
Bond	28	6	97	3
Oram	30	13	62	1
Vettori	33	8	94	3
Wiseman	41	13	127	2
Styris	3	0	28	0

FALL OF WICKETS

	NZ	SL	NZ
Wkt	1st	1st	2nd
1st	20	0	71
2nd	192	11	76
3rd	235	114	108
4th	392	134	133
5th	471	267	133
6th	486	374	–
7th	499	444	–
8th	–	483	–
9th	–	483	–
10th	–	483	–

Umpires: D.J.Harper (*Australia*) (29) and S.J.A.Taufel (*Australia*) (3).
Referee: G.R.Viswanath (*India*) (10).   **Test No. 1644/19 (SL130/NZ302)**

SRI LANKA v NEW ZEALAND (2nd Test)

At Asgiriya Stadium, Kandy, on 3 (*no play*), 4, 5, 6, 7 May 2003.
Toss: New Zealand. Result: **MATCH DRAWN**.
Debuts: None.

NEW ZEALAND

M.H.Richardson	c Sangakkara b Lokurachchi	55	c Kaluwitharana b Nissanka	55
M.J.Horne	c Kaluwitharana b Vaas	1	c Tillekeratne b Muralitharan	27
*S.P.Fleming	lbw b Nissanka	0	c Kaluwitharana b Dharmasena	33
M.S.Sinclair	lbw b Vaas	3	st Kaluwitharana b Muralitharan	0
S.B.Styris	c Tillekeratne b Muralitharan	32	c Muralitharan b Vaas	1
J.D.P.Oram	c Kaluwitharana b Lokurachchi	74	lbw b Muralitharan	16
†R.G.Hart	lbw b Muralitharan	31	c Kaluwitharana b Vaas	12
D.L.Vettori	run out	55	b Muralitharan	0
P.J.Wiseman	b Muralitharan	7	c Tillekeratne b Vaas	29
D.R.Tuffey	c Jayawardena b Nissanka	15	c Jayasuriya b Muralitharan	1
S.E.Bond	not out	10	not out	1
Extras	(B 3, LB 7, W 5, NB 7)	22	(B 1, LB 6, NB 1)	8
Total		**305**		**183**

SRI LANKA

K.C.Sangakkara	c Hart b Tuffey	10		not out	27
S.T.Jayasuriya	c Fleming b Wiseman	82		c Richardson b Bond	9
D.P.M.D.Jayawardena	c Hart b Oram	15		not out	32
*H.P.Tillekeratne	b Wiseman	93			
†R.S.Kaluwitharana	c Tuffey b Bond	20			
H.D.P.K.Dharmasena	c Fleming b Wiseman	5			
K.S.Lokurachchi	c Tuffey b Oram	20			
W.P.U.C.J.Vaas	b Oram	22			
M.S.Atapattu	retired hurt	2			
R.A.P.Nissanka	b Wiseman	6			
M.Muralitharan	not out	2			
Extras	(B 6, LB 11, NB 4)	21		(LB 4)	4
Total		**298**		(1 wicket)	**72**

SRI LANKA	O	M	R	W		O	M	R	W
Vaas	22	8	48	2		15.3	6	31	3
Nissanka	16.5	5	41	2		10	4	18	1
Muralitharan	34	10	90	3	(5)	39	18	49	5
Jayasuriya	8	0	24	0	(6)	7	0	20	0
Dharmasena	15	5	40	0	(3)	12	2	32	1
Lokurachchi	16	5	52	2	(4)	14	3	26	0

NEW ZEALAND	O	M	R	W		O	M	R	W
Tuffey	20	6	45	1		9	3	18	0
Bond	25	6	78	1		6	1	19	1
Oram	20	2	54	3					
Wiseman	32.3	4	104	4	(3)	9	4	20	0
Vettori					(4)	6	1	11	0

FALL OF WICKETS

	NZ	SL	NZ	SL
Wkt	1st	1st	2nd	2nd
1st	6	30	65	14
2nd	7	69	109	–
3rd	11	126	110	–
4th	71	169	115	–
5th	109	189	136	
6th	189	234	139	
7th	222	264	139	
8th	237	285	179	
9th	271	298	182	
10th	305	–	183	–

Umpires: D.J.Harper (*Australia*) (30) and S.J.A.Taufel (*Australia*) (4).
Referee: G.R.Viswanath (*India*) (11).   **Test No. 1645/20 (SL131/NZ303)**

ENGLAND v ZIMBABWE (1st Test)

At Lord's, London, on 22, 23, 24 May 2003.
Toss: Zimbabwe. Result: **ENGLAND** won by an innings and 92 runs.
Debuts: England – J.M.Anderson, A.McGrath; Zimbabwe – S.M.Ervine.

ENGLAND

M.E.Trescothick	c Ervine b Blignaut	59
M.P.Vaughan	b Streak	8
M.A.Butcher	c Vermeulen b Price	137
*N.Hussain	c Hondo b Friend	19
R.W.T.Key	c Taibu b Streak	18
†A.J.Stewart	c Taibu b Streak	26
A.McGrath	b Ervine	69
A.F.Giles	b Blignaut	52
S.J.Harmison	c Ebrahim b Ervine	0
M.J.Hoggard	c Ebrahim b Blignaut	19
J.M.Anderson	not out	4
Extras	(B 14, LB 27, W 3, NB 17)	61
Total		**472**

ZIMBABWE

D.D.Ebrahim	c McGrath b Butcher	68		c Key b Harmison	6
M.A.Vermeulen	b Anderson	1		c Trescothick b Butcher	61
S.V.Carlisle	c Trescothick b Hoggard	11		lbw b Butcher	24
G.W.Flower	c Key b Hoggard	3		c Trescothick b Harmison	26
†T.Taibu	c Hoggard b Harmison	25		c Butcher b McGrath	16
S.M.Ervine	lbw b Hoggard	4		c Trescothick b McGrath	4
*H.H.Streak	b Anderson	10		lbw b McGrath	11
A.M.Blignaut	c Butcher b Anderson	3		b Butcher	6
T.J.Friend	b Anderson	0		c Giles b Butcher	43
R.W.Price	not out	7		c Trescothick b Giles	26
D.T.Hondo	b Anderson	0		not out	0
Extras	(B 5, LB 1, W 1, NB 8)	15		(B 1, LB 6, W 3)	10
Total		**147**			**233**

ZIMBABWE	O	M	R	W		O	M	R	W
Streak	37	9	99	3					
Blignaut	26.1	4	96	3					
Hondo	14	4	45	0					
Ervine	22	5	95	2					
Friend	13	2	49	1					
Price	20	6	44	1					
Flower	1	0	3	0					
ENGLAND									
Hoggard	18	8	24	3	(2)	15	5	35	0
Anderson	16	4	73	5	(1)	15	4	65	0
Harmison	16	5	36	1		12	4	35	2
Butcher	5	2	8	1	(5)	12.5	0	60	4
Giles					(4)	8	2	15	1
McGrath						6	1	16	3

FALL OF WICKETS

	E	Z	Z
Wkt	1st	1st	2nd
1st	45	20	11
2nd	121	64	91
3rd	165	79	95
4th	204	104	128
5th	274	109	132
6th	342	129	150
7th	408	133	158
8th	408	133	168
9th	465	147	219
10th	472	147	233

Umpires: S.A.Bucknor (*West Indies*) (80) and D.L.Orchard (*South Africa*) (37).
Referee: C.H.Lloyd (*West Indies*) (24).   **Test No. 1646/5 (E805/Z66)**

ENGLAND v ZIMBABWE (2nd Test)

At Riverside, Chester-le-Street, on 5, 6, 7 June 2003.
Toss: England. Result: **ENGLAND** won by an innings and 69 runs.
Debuts: England – R.L.Johnson.

ENGLAND

M.E.Trescothick	c Taibu b Price	43
M.P.Vaughan	c Ervine b Streak	20
M.A.Butcher	b Hondo	47
*N.Hussain	c Taibu b Hondo	18
R.W.T.Key	c Flower b Hondo	4
†A.J.Stewart	lbw b Streak	68
A.McGrath	c Taibu b Blignaut	81
A.F.Giles	c Ervine b Streak	50
R.L.Johnson	c Streak b Blignaut	24
S.J.Harmison	c Vermeulen b Streak	11
J.M.Anderson	not out	12
Extras	(B 1, LB 5, W 7, NB 25)	38
Total		**416**

ZIMBABWE

D.D.Ebrahim	lbw b Anderson	6	lbw b Harmison	55
M.A.Vermeulen	lbw b Johnson	0	c McGrath b Anderson	0
S.V.Carlisle	lbw b Johnson	0	c Key b Anderson	28
G.W.Flower	c Trescothick b Anderson	8	b Anderson	16
†T.Taibu	lbw b Johnson	31	c Butcher b Giles	14
S.M.Ervine	c Stewart b Johnson	0	b Harmison	34
T.J.Friend	lbw b Johnson	0	not out	65
*H.H.Streak	lbw b Johnson	4	run out	3
A.M.Blignaut	c Anderson b Harmison	13	c Hussain b Anderson	12
R.W.Price	lbw b Harmison	17	c Stewart b Harmison	6
D.T.Hondo	not out	5	b Harmison	4
Extras	(B 5, LB 3, NB 2)	10	(B 6, LB 10)	16
Total		**94**		**253**

ZIMBABWE	O	M	R	W	O	M	R	W		FALL OF WICKETS		
											E	Z	Z
Streak	34.1	11	64	4						Wkt	1st	1st	2nd
Blignaut	23	4	95	2						1st	49	3	5
Hondo	22	1	98	3						2nd	109	3	65
Ervine	3	0	17	0						3rd	146	11	102
Price	40	9	105	1						4th	152	18	113
Friend	4	0	26	0						5th	156	23	131
Flower	1	0	5	0						6th	305	31	185
ENGLAND										7th	324	35	202
Anderson	10	2	30	2	23	8	55	4		8th	356	48	223
Johnson	12	4	33	6	22	7	67	0		9th	390	73	244
Harmison	9.1	3	22	2	21.4	4	55	4		10th	416	94	253
Giles	1	0	1	0	25	9	51	1					
Butcher					2	0	9	0					

Umpires: D.B.Hair (*Australia*) (45) and D.L.Orchard (*South Africa*) (38).
Referee: C.H.Lloyd (*West Indies*) (25).   **Test No. 1647/6 (E806/Z67)**

SRI LANKA v WEST INDIES (1st Test)

At Beausejour Stadium, Gros Islet, St Lucia, on 20, 21, 22, 23 (*no play*), 24 June 2003.
Toss: Sri Lanka. Result: **MATCH DRAWN**.
Debuts: West Indies – J.E.Taylor.

SRI LANKA

M.S.Atapattu	c Lara b Hinds	118	not out	50
S.T.Jayasuriya	c Banks b Collymore	8	not out	72
K.C.Sangakkara	lbw b Gayle	56		
D.P.M.DJayawardena	c Lara b Banks	45		
*H.P.Tillekeratne	b Collymore	13		
T.T.Samaraweera	c Jacobs b Collymore	11		
†R.S.Kaluwitharana	lbw b Collymore	2		
K.S.Lokuarachchi	c Lara b Collymore	15		
W.P.U.C.J.Vaas	c Jacobs b Gayle	38		
M.Muralitharan	lbw b Hinds	14		
R.A.P.Nissanka	not out	12		
Extras	(B 4, LB 5, W 5, NB 8)	22	(B 1, LB 2, NB 1)	4
Total		**354**	(0 wickets)	**126**

WEST INDIES

C.H.Gayle	lbw b Muralitharan	27
D.Ganga	lbw b Vaas	12
W.W.Hinds	run out	113
*B.C.Lara	c Kaluwitharana b Nissanka	209
R.R.Sarwan	c Atapattu b Muralitharan	7
M.N.Samuels	st Kaluwitharana b Muralitharan	8
†R.D.Jacobs	lbw b Muralitharan	13
O.A.C.Banks	not out	50
M.Dillon	c Atapattu b Lokuarachchi	2
C.D.Collymore	c and b Muralitharan	0
J.E.Taylor	not out	9
Extras	(B 4, LB 4, W 2, NB 17)	27
Total	(9 wickets declared)	**477**

WEST INDIES	O	M	R	W		O	M	R	W
Dillon	29	7	48	0		5	1	24	0
Collymore	29	5	66	5		3	0	8	0
Taylor	27	3	97	0	(4)	6	1	19	0
Hinds	11	4	28	2	(3)	4	0	25	0
Banks	33	8	74	1		10	0	28	0
Gayle	9.2	1	22	2					
Samuels	3	0	9	0	(6)	3	1	15	0
Sarwan	2	1	1	0	(7)	4	0	4	0

SRI LANKA	O	M	R	W
Vaas	39	5	116	1
Nissanka	21.3	1	108	1
Samaraweera	8	0	53	0
Muralitharan	50	10	138	5
Lokuarachchi	20	6	54	1

FALL OF WICKETS			
	SL	WI	SL
Wkt	1st	1st	2nd
1st	19	18	–
2nd	127	66	–
3rd	195	240	–
4th	228	262	–
5th	266	279	–
6th	269	305	–
7th	285	441	–
8th	288	447	–
9th	326	448	–
10th	354	–	–

Umpires: B.F.Bowden (*New Zealand*) (6) and D.J.Harper (*Australia*) (31).
Referee: Wasim Raja (*Pakistan*) (10).   **Test No. 1648/7 (WI398/SL132)**

SRI LANKA v WEST INDIES (2nd Test)

At Sabina Park, Kingston, Jamaica, on 27, 28, 29 June 2003.
Toss: West Indies. Result: **WEST INDIES** won by seven wickets.
Debuts: West Indies – F.H.Edwards; Sri Lanka – M.T.T.Mirando.

SRI LANKA

Batsman	Dismissal	R		Dismissal	R
M.S.Atapattu	c Gayle b Drakes	15		c Jacobs b Taylor	28
S.T.Jayasuriya	c Jacobs b Collymore	26		lbw b Collymore	13
K.C.Sangakkara	lbw b Edwards	75		c Jacobs b Collymore	12
D.P.M.D.Jayawardena	c Gayle b Edwards	10		c Jacobs b Edwards	32
*H.P.Tillekeratne	c Lara b Banks	13	(6)	b Collymore	7
†R.S.Kaluwitharana	c Samuels b Banks	10	(5)	b Taylor	23
H.D.P.K.Dharmasena	c Samuels b Collymore	6		c Lara b Collymore	20
W.P.U.C.J.Vaas	not out	12		c Lara b Collymore	21
M.T.T.Mirando	c Lara b Edwards	11		c Lara b Collymore	13
M.Muralitharan	b Edwards	0		c Sarwan b Collymore	6
R.A.P.Nissanka	c Gayle b Edwards	0		not out	0
Extras	(B 1, LB 17, W 2, NB 10)	30		(B 4, LB 6, W 2, NB 7)	19
Total		**208**			**194**

WEST INDIES

Batsman	Dismissal	R		Dismissal	R
C.H.Gayle	c Sangakkara b Nissanka	31		lbw b Vaas	0
W.W.Hinds	c Kaluwitharana b Nissanka	19		b Muralitharan	29
R.R.Sarwan	b Vaas	31		c Jayasuriya b Vaas	82
*B.C.Lara	lbw b Muralitharan	10		not out	80
M.N.Samuels	c Tillekeratne b Nissanka	14		not out	0
O.A.C.Banks	c Tillekeratne b Nissanka	2			
†R.D.Jacobs	lbw b Muralitharan	16			
V.C.Drakes	b Muralitharan	30			
J.E.Taylor	c Muralitharan b Dharmasena	1			
C.D.Collymore	c Sangakkara b Nissanka	13			
F.H.Edwards	not out	5			
Extras	(B 5, LB 3, W 6, NB 5)	19		(B 8, LB 3, W 4, NB 6)	21
Total		**191**		(3 wickets)	**212**

WEST INDIES	O	M	R	W		O	M	R	W
Collymore	15	6	28	2	(2)	16	2	57	7
Taylor	11	1	40	0	(4)	10	1	38	2
Drakes	18	3	54	1	(3)	11	3	29	0
Edwards	15.4	1	36	5	(1)	15	2	54	1
Banks	22	6	31	2		2	0	6	0
Gayle	4	3	1	0					

SRI LANKA	O	M	R	W		O	M	R	W
Vaas	15	4	33	1		12	2	54	2
Mirando	10	1	36	0		5	0	23	0
Nissanka	12.3	0	64	5		8	1	64	0
Muralitharan	11	3	23	3		15.4	1	48	1
Dharmasena	5	0	27	1		2	0	12	0

FALL OF WICKETS

	SL	WI	SL	WI
Wkt	1st	1st	2nd	2nd
1st	38	54	25	1
2nd	48	59	43	50
3rd	77	85	80	211
4th	109	107	118	
5th	129	110	118	
6th	140	123	138	
7th	192	162	173	
8th	204	163	176	
9th	208	175	184	
10th	208	191	194	

Umpires: D.B.Hair (*Australia*) (46) and R.B.Tiffin (*Zimbabwe*) (35).
Referee: Wasim Raja (*Pakistan*) (11).   **Test No. 1649/8 (WI399/SL133)**

AUSTRALIA v BANGLADESH (1st Test)

At Marrara Cricket Ground, Darwin, on 18, 19, 20 July 2003.
Toss: Australia. Result: **AUSTRALIA** won by an innings and 132 runs.
Debuts: None.

BANGLADESH

Hannan Sarkar	lbw b McGrath	0	c Gilchrist b Gillespie		35
Javed Omar	c Gilchrist b Gillespie	5	lbw b McGrath		5
Habibul Bashar	b Lee	16	b MacGill		54
Mohammad Ashraful	c Gillespie b McGrath	23	c Gilchrist b Lee		7
Al Sahariar	b Lee	0	c and b MacGill		36
Alok Kapali	lbw b MacGill	0	lbw b MacGill		0
†Khaled Masud	lbw b McGrath	11	c Gilchrist b MacGill		6
*Khaled Mahmud	c Gilchrist b MacGill	21	b Gillespie		5
Mashrafe Mortaza	c Gilchrist b Gillespie	3	(10) run out		15
Tapash Baisya	not out	2	(9) lbw b MacGill		4
Manjural Islam	c Langer b Lee	1	not out		0
Extras	(B 1, LB 5, W 6, NB 3)	15	(LB 6, W 2, NB 3)		11
Total		**97**			**178**

AUSTRALIA

J.L.Langer	lbw b Kapali	71
M.L.Hayden	b Mortaza	11
R.T.Ponting	c Omar b Baisya	10
D.S.Lehmann	c Omar b Mortaza	110
*S.R.Waugh	not out	100
M.L.Love	b Mortaza	0
†A.C.Gilchrist	b Manjural	43
B.Lee	run out	23
J.N.Gillespie	not out	16
S.C.G.MacGill		
G.D.McGrath		
Extras	(B 5, LB 8, W 7, NB 3)	23
Total	(7 wickets declared)	**407**

AUSTRALIA	O	M	R	W	O	M	R	W		FALL OF WICKETS		
											B	A
McGrath	13	6	20	3	10	0	25	1	Wkt	1st	1st	2nd
Gillespie	8	1	27	2	16	3	48	2	1st	4	13	8
Lee	8.2	2	23	3	12	5	34	1	2nd	26	43	89
MacGill	13	4	21	2	13.1	1	65	5	3rd	36	184	112
									4th	39	243	112
BANGLADESH									5th	40	244	112
Manjural Islam	24	4	78	1					6th	60	313	122
Mashrafe Mortaza	23	7	74	3					7th	87	377	143
Tapash Baisya	21.5	4	69	1					8th	91	–	152
Khaled Mahmud	28	2	98	0					9th	94	–	171
Alok Kapali	18	2	65	1					10th	97	–	178
Mohammad Ashraful	2	0	9	0								
Habibul Bashar	1	0	1	0								

Umpires: R.E.Koertzen (*South Africa*) (40) and D.R.Shepherd (*England*) (72).
Referee: M.J.Procter (*South Africa*) (12).   **Test No. 1650/1 (A641/B20)**

AUSTRALIA v BANGLADESH (2nd Test)

At Bundaberg Rum Stadium, Cairns, on 25, 26, 27, 28 July 2003.
Toss: Australia. Result: **AUSTRALIA** won by an innings and 98 runs.
Debuts: Bangladesh – Anwar Hossain Monir.

BANGLADESH

Hannan Sarkar	lbw b MacGill	76	c Hayden b MacGill		55
Javed Omar	c Gilchrist b Lee	26	lbw b Gillespie		8
Habibul Bashar	c and b MacGill	46	c Langer b Lee		25
Mohammad Ashraful	c Gilchrist b Gillespie	0	c Ponting b MacGill		0
Sanwar Hossain	b MacGill	46	c Ponting b MacGill		16
Alok Kapali	c Love b MacGill	5	c Langer b MacGill		17
†Khaled Masud	c Love b Gillespie	44	lbw b Gillespie		14
*Khaled Mahmud	lbw b MacGill	0	c Lee b MacGill		17
Tapash Baisya	c Gilchrist b McGrath	25	lbw b Gillespie		0
Mashrafe Mortaza	c Lee b Gillespie	8	not out		3
Anwar Hossain Monir	not out	0	b Gillespie		4
Extras	(LB 8, NB 11)	19	(LB 2, NB 2)		4
Total		**295**			**163**

AUSTRALIA

J.L.Langer	c Omar b Mortaza	1
M.L.Hayden	b Sanwar	50
R.T.Ponting	c Ashraful b Sanwar	59
D.S.Lehmann	c Ashraful b Baisya	177
*S.R.Waugh	not out	156
M.L.Love	not out	100
†A.C.Gilchrist		
B.Lee		
J.N.Gillespie		
S.C.G.MacGill		
G.D.McGrath		
Extras	(LB 11, W 1, NB 1)	13
Total	(4 wickets declared)	**556**

AUSTRALIA	O	M	R	W	O	M	R	W
McGrath	17	2	57	1	15	9	22	0
Gillespie	25	7	57	3	12.4	3	38	4
Lee	18	1	88	1	(4) 11	2	45	1
MacGill	24	9	77	5	(3) 20	3	56	5
Waugh	5	3	4	0				
Lehmann	3	1	4	0				

BANGLADESH	O	M	R	W
Mashrafe Mortaza	25	7	60	1
Tapash Baisya	26	5	96	1
Anwar Hossain Monir	21	4	95	0
Khaled Mahmud	19	3	75	0
Sanwar Hossain	30	2	128	2
Alok Kapali	14.2	0	69	0
Mohammad Ashraful	4	0	22	0

FALL OF WICKETS

Wkt	1st	1st	2nd
1st	47	14	12
2nd	155	105	87
3rd	156	132	90
4th	156	382	90
5th	170	–	123
6th	230	–	136
7th	230	–	156
8th	281	–	156
9th	295	–	156
10th	295	–	163

Umpires: R.E.Koertzen (*South Africa*) (41) and D.R.Shepherd (*England*) (73).
Referee: M.J.Procter (*South Africa*) (13).   **Test No. 1651/2 (A642/B21)**

ENGLAND v SOUTH AFRICA (1st Test)

At Edgbaston, Birmingham, on 24, 25 (*no play*), 26, 27, 28 July 2003.
Toss: South Africa. Result: **MATCH DRAWN**.
Debuts: None.

SOUTH AFRICA

*G.C.Smith	c Anderson b Giles	277	b Giles	85
H.H.Gibbs	c Butcher b Vaughan	179	b Anderson	9
G.Kirsten	c Stewart b Giles	44	c McGrath b Harmison	1
H.H.Dippenaar	c Butcher b Gough	22	not out	28
J.A.Rudolph	c Gough b Harmison	10	st Stewart b Giles	8
†M.V.Boucher	not out	15		
S.M.Pollock	not out	24		
R.J.Peterson				
D.Pretorius				
C.M.Willoughby				
M.Ntini				
Extras	(B 8, LB 11, NB 4)	23	(LB 2, NB 1)	3
Total	(5 wickets declared)	**594**	(4 wickets declared)	**134**

ENGLAND

M.E.Trescothick	b Ntini	31	not out	52
M.P.Vaughan	c Boucher b Pretorius	156	c Pollock b Peterson	22
M.A.Butcher	lbw b Ntini	13		
*N.Hussain	lbw b Pollock	1	(3) not out	23
A.McGrath	c Rudolph b Pretorius	34		
†A.J.Stewart	b Pretorius	38		
A.Flintoff	lbw b Pretorius	40		
A.F.Giles	b Pollock	41		
D.Gough	c Rudolph b Ntini	1		
S.J.Harmison	b Ntini	0		
J.M.Anderson	not out	0		
Extras	(B 19, LB 6, W 11, NB 17)	53	(B 8, LB 5)	13
Total		**408**	(1 wicket)	**110**

ENGLAND	O	M	R	W		O	M	R	W
Anderson	16	2	92	0	(2)	10	1	37	1
Gough	25	6	88	1					
Flintoff	25	6	97	0	(4)	2	0	16	0
Harmison	27	2	104	1	(1)	6	0	34	1
Giles	42	3	153	2	(3)	8	0	45	2
Butcher	2	0	15	0					
Vaughan	8	0	26	1					
SOUTH AFRICA									
Pollock	27.4	10	51	2		7	3	6	0
Ntini	28	8	114	4		4	0	38	0
Willoughby	20	7	46	0					
Pretorius	25	2	115	4		10	6	20	0
Peterson	22	9	57	0	(3)	13	3	33	1

FALL OF WICKETS

Wkt	SA 1st	E 1st	SA 2nd	E 2nd
1st	338	66	30	72
2nd	438	132	32	–
3rd	514	133	114	–
4th	552	222	134	–
5th	556	306	–	–
6th	–	311	–	–
7th	–	374	–	–
8th	–	398	–	–
9th	–	398	–	–
10th	–	408	–	–

Umpires: D.J.Harper (*Australia*) (32) and S.Venkataraghavan (*India*) (67).
Referee: R.S.Madugalle (*Sri Lanka*) (48). **Test No. 1652/121 (E807/SA275)**

ENGLAND v SOUTH AFRICA (2nd Test)

At Lord's, London, on 31 July, 1, 2, 3 August 2003.
Toss: South Africa. Result: **SOUTH AFRICA** won by an innings and 92 runs.
Debuts: None.

ENGLAND

M.E.Trescothick	b Ntini	6	c Adams b Ntini		23
*M.P.Vaughan	c sub (N.D.McKenzie) b Ntini	33	c Pollock b Hall		29
M.A.Butcher	c Hall b Pollock	19	c Kirsten b Hall		70
N.Hussain	b Hall	14	c Boucher b Ntini		61
A.McGrath	c Kirsten b Hall	4	c Boucher b Pollock		13
†A.J.Stewart	c Adams b Ntini	7	c Hall b Ntini		0
A.Flintoff	c Adams b Ntini	11	st Boucher b Adams		142
A.F.Giles	c Pollock b Hall	7	c Pollock b Ntini		23
D.Gough	c Adams b Pollock	34	c Adams b Pollock		14
S.J.Harmison	b Ntini	0	c Hall b Ntini		7
J.M.Anderson	not out	21	not out		4
Extras	(B 5, LB 3, W 1, NB 3, P 5)	17	(B 6, LB 5, W 3, NB 17)		31
Total		**173**			**417**

SOUTH AFRICA

*G.C.Smith	b Anderson	259
H.H.Gibbs	b Harmison	49
G.Kirsten	b McGrath	108
H.H.Dippenaar	c Butcher b Giles	92
J.A.Rudolph	c Stewart b Flintoff	26
†M.V.Boucher	b Anderson	68
S.M.Pollock	not out	10
A.J.Hall	not out	6
P.R.Adams		
D.Pretorius		
M Ntini		
Extras	(B 25, LB 21, W 5, NB 13)	64
Total	(6 wickets declared)	**682**

SOUTH AFRICA	O	M	R	W	O	M	R	W
Pollock	14.4	5	28	2	29	7	105	2
Ntini	17	3	75	5	31	5	145	5
Pretorius	4	0	20	0	(5) 3	0	16	0
Hall	10	4	18	2	(3) 24	6	66	2
Adams	3	0	19	0	(4) 20.1	1	74	1

ENGLAND	O	M	R	W
Gough	28	3	127	0
Anderson	27	6	90	2
Harmison	22	3	103	1
Flintoff	40	10	115	1
Giles	43	5	142	1
Butcher	6	1	19	0
McGrath	11	0	40	1

FALL OF WICKETS			
	E	SA	E
Wkt	1st	1st	2nd
1st	11	133	52
2nd	35	390	60
3rd	73	513	186
4th	77	580	208
5th	85	630	208
6th	96	672	208
7th	109	–	297
8th	112	–	344
9th	118	–	371
10th	173	–	417

Umpires: S.A.Bucknor (*West Indies*) (81) and D.B.Hair (*Australia*) (47).
Referee: R.S.Madugalle (*Sri Lanka*) (49).   **Test No. 1653/122 (E808/SA276)**

ENGLAND v SOUTH AFRICA (3rd Test)

At Trent Bridge, Nottingham, on 14, 15, 16, 17, 18 August 2003.
Toss: England. Result: **ENGLAND** won by 70 runs.
Debuts: England – R.J.Kirtley, E.T.Smith.

ENGLAND

M.E.Trescothick	c Boucher b Hall	24	c Adams b Pollock	0
*M.P.Vaughan	c Gibbs b Pollock	1	c Boucher b Pollock	5
M.A.Butcher	c Boucher b Ntini	106	b Hall	8
N.Hussain	lbw b Pollock	116	lbw b Pollock	30
E.T.Smith	c Boucher b Kallis	64	lbw b Hall	0
†A.J.Stewart	c Smith b Adams	72	c Boucher b Kallis	5
A.Flintoff	c Pollock b Hall	0	c Gibbs b Pollock	30
A.F.Giles	b Hall	22	c Boucher b Pollock	21
R.J.Kirtley	c Smith b Ntini	1	c Boucher b Ntini	3
S.J.Harmison	c Pollock b Adams	14	not out	2
J.M.Anderson	not out	0	lbw b Pollock	2
Extras	(B 9, LB 8, W 4, NB 4)	25	(B 4, LB 5, NB 3)	12
Total		**445**		**118**

SOUTH AFRICA

*G.C.Smith	hit wicket b Flintoff	35	lbw b Kirtley	5
H.H.Gibbs	b Harmison	19	c Giles b Harmison	28
J.A.Rudolph	c Stewart b Kirtley	15	lbw b Kirtley	0
J.H.Kallis	b Anderson	27	b Anderson	13
H.H.Dippenaar	lbw b Kirtley	0	c Smith b Anderson	1
N.D.McKenzie	c Trescothick b Anderson	90	b Kirtley	11
†M.V.Boucher	lbw b Flintoff	48	c Stewart b Kirtley	52
S.M.Pollock	c Kirtley b Anderson	62	b Flintoff	0
A.J.Hall	b Anderson	15	c Trescothick b Kirtley	0
P.R.Adams	b Anderson	13	c and b Kirtley	15
M.Ntini	not out	4	not out	3
Extras	(B 4, LB 19, W 3, NB 8)	34	(LB 2, NB 1)	3
Total		**362**		**131**

SOUTH AFRICA	O	M	R	W		O	M	R	W
Pollock	36	18	65	2		17.4	4	39	6
Ntini	33	3	137	2		13	5	28	1
Hall	24	6	88	3	(4)	6	2	6	2
Kallis	27	7	92	1	(3)	10	2	36	1
Adams	26.3	7	46	2					
ENGLAND									
Anderson	27.5	4	102	5	(4)	12	4	17	2
Kirtley	31	8	80	2	(1)	16.2	7	34	6
Flintoff	33	8	91	2	(2)	17	4	54	1
Harmison	17	3	42	1	(3)	11	2	24	1
Giles	10	3	24	0					
Vaughan	1	1	0	0					

FALL OF WICKETS				
	E	SA	E	SA
Wkt	1st	1st	2nd	2nd
1st	7	56	0	22
2nd	29	66	17	28
3rd	218	88	39	40
4th	322	88	39	41
5th	334	132	44	50
6th	347	261	76	71
7th	388	284	91	80
8th	408	309	114	81
9th	440	337	114	126
10th	445	362	118	131

Umpires: D.B.Hair (*Australia*) (48) and D.J.Harper (*Australia*) (33).
Referee: R.S.Madugalle (*Sri Lanka*) (50).   **Test No. 1654/123 (E809/SA277)**

ENGLAND v SOUTH AFRICA (4th Test)

At Headingley, Leeds, on 21, 22, 23, 24, 25 August 2003.
Toss: South Africa. Result: **SOUTH AFRICA** won by 191 runs.
Debuts: England – K.Ali; South Africa – M.Zondeki.

SOUTH AFRICA

*G.C.Smith	c Stewart b Kirtley	2	lbw b Bicknell	14
H.H.Gibbs	c Stewart b Bicknell	0	lbw b Kirtley	2
G.Kirsten	c Bicknell b Ali	130	lbw b Ali	60
J.H.Kallis	c Vaughan b Bicknell	6	c Stewart b Kirtley	41
N.D.McKenzie	c Stewart b Ali	4	c Bicknell b Flintoff	38
J.A.Rudolph	lbw b Ali	55	c Smith b Anderson	10
†M.V.Boucher	c Vaughan b Flintoff	16	c Stewart b Flintoff	39
A.J.Hall	c Smith b Flintoff	0	not out	99
M.Zondeki	c Butcher b Anderson	59	b Bicknell	7
M.Ntini	not out	32	lbw b Ali	8
D.Pretorius	c Stewart b Kirtley	9	b Kirtley	8
Extras	(LB 20, W 2, NB 7)	29	(B 7, LB 24, NB 8)	39
Total		**342**		**365**

ENGLAND

M.E.Trescothick	c and b Kallis	59	c Gibbs b Ntini	4
*M.P.Vaughan	b Ntini	15	c Gibbs b Kallis	21
M.A.Butcher	c Boucher b Kallis	77	c Hall b Kallis	61
N.Hussain	c and b Rudolph	42	lbw b Kallis	6
E.T.Smith	c Boucher b Kallis	0	c Smith b Hall	7
†A.J.Stewart	c Hall b Pretorius	15	c Boucher b Ntini	7
A.Flintoff	b Ntini	55	c Hall b Kallis	50
M.P.Bicknell	b Ntini	4	c Boucher b Kallis	15
K.Ali	c Boucher b Hall	1	c Kirsten b Kallis	9
R.J.Kirtley	c Boucher b Hall	1	c Kirsten b Hall	11
J.M.Anderson	not out	0	not out	0
Extras	(B 2, LB 17, W 6, NB 13)	38	(LB 9, W 2, NB 7)	18
Total		**307**		**209**

ENGLAND	O	M	R	W		O	M	R	W
Kirtley	29.4	10	74	2		21.5	7	71	3
Bicknell	27	11	50	2		22	3	75	2
Ali	22	3	80	3	(5)	14	2	56	2
Anderson	18	7	63	1		16	4	56	1
Flintoff	18	5	55	2	(3)	22	5	63	2
Vaughan						5	1	13	0

SOUTH AFRICA	O	M	R	W		O	M	R	W
Pretorius	19	1	100	1	(3)	9	3	27	0
Ntini	20.2	4	62	3	(1)	11	2	40	2
Hall	24	3	77	2	(2)	21.4	3	64	2
Zondeki	1.5	0	10	0	(5)	3	0	15	0
Kallis	20.1	7	38	3	(4)	17	4	54	6
Rudolph	2	1	1	1					

FALL OF WICKETS

	SA	E	SA	E
Wkt	1st	1st	2nd	2nd
1st	2	27	9	11
2nd	2	169	31	44
3rd	16	193	128	62
4th	21	197	139	81
5th	116	239	160	95
6th	142	261	219	169
7th	142	289	232	182
8th	292	293	281	189
9th	316	307	311	206
10th	342	307	365	209

Umpires: B.F.Bowden (*New Zealand*) (7) and S.J.A.Taufel (*Australia*) (5).
Referee: R.S.Madugalle (*Sri Lanka*) (51).   **Test No. 1655/124 (E810/SA278)**

ENGLAND v SOUTH AFRICA (5th Test)

At Kennington Oval, London, on 4, 5, 6, 7, 8 September 2003.
Toss: South Africa. Result: **ENGLAND** won by nine wickets.
Debuts: None.

SOUTH AFRICA

*G.C.Smith	run out	18	lbw b Bicknell		19
H.H.Gibbs	b Giles	183	c Stewart b Anderson		9
G.Kirsten	lbw b Giles	90	c Trescothick b Harmison		29
J.H.Kallis	run out	66	lbw b Harmison		35
N.D.McKenzie	c Stewart b Anderson	9	lbw b Flintoff		38
J.A.Rudolph	lbw b Bicknell	0	b Bicknell		8
†M.V.Boucher	c Stewart b Bicknell	8	c Stewart b Bicknell		25
S.M.Pollock	not out	66	c Thorpe b Harmison		43
A.J.Hall	lbw b Flintoff	1	c Smith b Bicknell		0
P.R.Adams	run out	1	not out		13
M.Ntini	b Anderson	11	c Smith b Harmison		1
Extras	(B 12, LB 10, W 4, NB 5)	31	(B 1, LB 7, NB 1)		9
Total		**484**			**229**

ENGLAND

M.E.Trescothick	c Rudolph b Ntini	219	not out		69
*M.P.Vaughan	c Gibbs b Pollock	23	c Boucher b Kallis		13
M.A.Butcher	lbw b Hall	32	not out		20
G.P.Thorpe	b Kallis	124			
E.T.Smith	lbw b Hall	16			
†A.J.Stewart	lbw b Pollock	38			
A.Flintoff	b Adams	95			
A.F.Giles	c Hall b Kallis	2			
M.P.Bicknell	lbw b Pollock	0			
S.J.Harmison	not out	6			
J.M.Anderson	not out	0			
Extras	(B 11, LB 18, W 9, NB 11)	49	(LB 4, NB 4)		8
Total	(9 wickets declared)	**604**	(1 wicket)		**110**

ENGLAND	O	M	R	W	O	M	R	W
Bicknell	20	3	71	2	24	5	84	4
Anderson	25	6	86	2	10	1	55	1
Harmison	27	8	73	0	19.2	8	33	4
Giles	29	3	102	2	10	2	36	0
Flintoff	19	4	88	1	6	2	13	1
Vaughan	5	0	24	0				
Butcher	3	0	18	0				

SOUTH AFRICA	O	M	R	W		O	M	R	W
Pollock	39	10	111	3		6	0	15	0
Ntini	31	4	129	1		8	0	46	0
Hall	35	5	111	2					
Kallis	34	5	117	2	(3)	5.2	0	25	1
Adams	17	2	79	1	(4)	3	0	20	0
Rudolph	6	1	28	0					

FALL OF WICKETS

	SA	E	SA	E
Wkt	1st	1st	2nd	2nd
1st	63	28	24	47
2nd	290	78	34	
3rd	345	346	92	
4th	362	379	93	
5th	365	480	118	
6th	385	489	150	
7th	419	502	193	
8th	421	502	193	
9th	432	601	215	
10th	484	–	229	

Umpires: S.J.A.Taufel (*Australia*) (6) and S.Venkataraghavan (*India*) (68).
Referee: R.S.Madugalle (*Sri Lanka*) (52).　　Test No. 1656/125 (E811/SA279)

ENGLAND v SOUTH AFRICA 2003

ENGLAND – BATTING AND FIELDING

	M	I	NO	HS	Runs	Avge	100	50	Ct/St
M.E.Trescothick	5	10	–	219	487	60.87	1	3	3
A.Flintoff	5	8	–	142	423	52.87	1	3	–
M.A.Butcher	5	9	1	106	406	50.75	1	3	4
N.Hussain	4	8	1	116	293	41.85	1	1	–
M.P.Vaughan	5	10	–	156	318	31.80	1	–	2
J.M.Anderson	5	8	7	21*	27	27.00	–	–	1
A.J.Stewart	5	8	–	72	182	22.75	–	1	14/1
A.F.Giles	4	6	–	41	116	19.33	–	–	1
E.T.Smith	3	5	–	64	87	17.40	–	1	5
A.McGrath	2	3	–	34	51	17.00	–	–	1
D.Gough	2	3	–	34	49	16.33	–	–	1
S.J.Harmison	4	6	2	14	29	7.25	–	–	–
M.P.Bicknell	2	3	–	15	19	6.33	–	–	2
R.J.Kirtley	2	4	–	11	16	4.00	–	–	2

Played in one Test: K.Ali 1, 9; G.P.Thorpe 124 (1 ct).

ENGLAND – BOWLING

	O	M	R	W	Avge	Best	5wI	10wM
R.J.Kirtley	98.5	32	259	13	19.92	6- 34	1	–
K.Ali	36	5	136	5	27.20	3- 80	–	–
M.P.Bicknell	93	22	280	10	28.00	4- 84	–	–
J.M.Anderson	161.5	35	598	15	39.86	5-102	1	–
S.J.Harmison	129.2	26	413	9	45.88	4- 33	–	–
A.Flintoff	182	44	592	10	59.20	2- 55	–	–
A.F.Giles	142	15	502	7	71.71	2- 45	–	–

Also bowled: M.A.Butcher 11-1-52-0; D.Gough 53-9-215-1; A.McGrath 11-0-40-1; M.P.Vaughan 19-2-63-1.

SOUTH AFRICA – BATTING AND FIELDING

	M	I	NO	HS	Runs	Avge	100	50	Ct/St
G.C.Smith	5	9	–	277	714	79.33	2	1	3
S.M.Pollock	4	6	3	66*	205	68.33	–	2	6
G.Kirsten	4	7	–	130	462	66.00	2	2	4
H.H.Gibbs	5	9	–	183	478	53.11	2	–	5
M.V.Boucher	5	8	1	68	271	38.71	–	2	17/1
H.H.Dippenaar	3	5	1	92	143	35.75	–	1	–
N.D.McKenzie	3	6	–	90	190	31.66	–	1	–
J.H.Kallis	3	6	–	66	188	31.33	–	1	1
A.J.Hall	4	7	2	99*	121	24.20	–	1	7
M.Ntini	5	6	3	32*	59	19.66	–	–	–
J.A.Rudolph	5	9	–	55	132	14.66	–	1	4
P.R.Adams	3	4	1	15	42	14.00	–	–	6
D.Pretorius	3	3	–	9	17	8.50	–	–	–

Played in one Test: M.Zondeki 59, 7. R.J.Peterson and C.M.Willoughby did not bat.

SOUTH AFRICA – BOWLING

	O	M	R	W	Avge	Best	5wI	10wM
S.M.Pollock	177	57	420	17	24.70	6- 39	1	–
J.H.Kallis	113.3	25	362	14	25.85	6- 54	1	–
A.J.Hall	144.4	29	430	16	26.87	3- 18	–	–
M.Ntini	196.2	33	814	23	35.39	5- 75	2	1
P.R.Adams	69.4	10	238	4	59.50	2- 46	–	–
D.Pretorius	70	12	298	5	59.60	4-115	–	–

Also bowled: R.J.Peterson 35-12-90-1; J.A.Rudolph 8-2-29-1; C.M.Willoughby 20-7-46-0; M.Zondeki 4.5-0-25-0.

PAKISTAN v BANGLADESH (1st Test)

At National Stadium, Karachi, on 20, 21, 22, 23, 24 August 2003.
Toss: Pakistan. Result: **PAKISTAN** won by seven wickets.
Debuts: Pakistan – Mohammad Hafeez, Shabbir Ahmed, Umar Gul, Yasir Hamid;
Bangladesh – Rajin Saleh.

BANGLADESH

Hannan Sarkar	c Rashid b Shabbir	41	lbw b Hafeez	30
Javed Omar	b Gul	1	lbw b Shoaib	13
Habibul Bashar	c Hafeez b Shoaib	71	c Shabbir b Kaneria	108
Sanwar Hossain	lbw b Shoaib	15	lbw b Shabbir	3
Rajin Saleh	c Gul b Kaneria	26	c Rashid b Shabbir	60
Alok Kapali	c Shabbir b Kaneria	46	b Kaneria	1
†Khaled Masud	lbw b Gul	19	st Rashid b Kaneria	22
*Khaled Mahmud	c Hamid b Kaneria	14	lbw b Shabbir	0
Tapash Baisya	c Taufiq b Shabbir	10	c Rashid b Shabbir	5
Mohammad Rafique	c Rashid b Shabbir	14	lbw b Shabbir	6
Mashrafe Mortaza	not out	9	not out	10
Extras	(B 3, LB 5, NB 14)	22	(LB 11, W 1, NB 4)	16
Total		**288**		**274**

PAKISTAN

Mohammad Hafeez	c Omar b Mortaza	2	b Rafique	50
Taufiq Umar	c Omar b Rafique	38	c Saleh b Baisya	4
Yasir Hamid	c Rafique b Mortaza	170	b Rafique	105
Inzamam-ul-Haq	c Saleh b Baisya	0	not out	35
Yousuf Youhana	c and b Saleh	46	not out	15
Misbah-ul-Haq	lbw b Mortaza	13		
*†Rashid Latif	not out	54		
Shoaib Akhtar	b Rafique	1		
Shabbir Ahmed	c Saleh b Rafique	6		
Danish Kaneria	c and b Mahmud	8		
Umar Gul	run out	0		
Extras	(LB 4, NB 4)	8	(LB 7, W 1)	8
Total		**346**	(3 wickets)	**217**

PAKISTAN	O	M	R	W		O	M	R	W		FALL OF WICKETS				
												B	P	B	P
Shoaib Akhtar	18	4	56	2		25	8	59	1	Wkt	1st	1st	2nd	2nd
Umar Gul	20	5	91	2		19	3	57	0	1st	9	5	19	10
Shabbir Ahmed	20.3	3	61	3	(4)	18.1	2	48	5	2nd	123	102	73	144
Danish Kaneria	21	6	58	3	(3)	38	12	85	3	3rd	123	103	83	170
Mohammad Hafeez	7	2	14	0		14	8	14	1	4th	146	234	194	–
										5th	176	270	195	–
BANGLADESH										6th	231	304	251	–
Mashrafe Mortaza	19	3	68	3		18	4	62	0	7th	251	307	251	–
Tapash Baisya	17	6	42	1		11	1	34	1	8th	252	323	254	–
Khaled Mahmud	17	2	74	1		6	3	8	0	9th	273	338	262	–
Mohammad Rafique	32	9	76	3		26	6	61	2	10th	288	346	274	–
Sanwar Hossain	9	0	23	0	(7)	5	1	23	0					
Alok Kapali	18	3	50	0	(5)	2	0	10	0					
Rajin Saleh	5	0	9	1	(6)	2	0	12	0					

Umpires: S.A.Bucknor (*West Indies*) (82) and T.H.Wijewardene (*Sri Lanka*) (3).
Referee: M.J.Procter (*South Africa*) (14).   Test No. 1657/4 (P293/B22)

PAKISTAN v BANGLADESH (2nd Test)

At Arbab Niaz Stadium, Peshawar, on 27, 28, 29, 30 August 2003.
Toss: Bangladesh. Result: **PAKISTAN** won by nine wickets.
Debuts: None.

BANGLADESH

Hannan Sarkar	c Rashid b Gul	6	c Taufiq b Shoaib Akhtar		7
Javed Omar	b Shoaib Akhtar	119	c Rashid b Shoaib Akhtar		0
Habibul Bashar	lbw b Shabbir	97	lbw b Gul		28
Mohammad Ashraful	c Rashid b Shoaib Akhtar	77	c Taufiq b Kaneria		7
Rajin Saleh	c Rashid b Kaneria	3	lbw b Shoaib Akhtar		6
Alok Kapali	c Rashid b Shoaib Akhtar	4	c Rashid b Shabbir		16
†Khaled Masud	lbw b Shoaib Akhtar	0	lbw b Shoaib Akhtar		0
*Khaled Mahmud	c Shabbir b Shoaib Akhtar	25	lbw b Kaneria		1
Mohammad Rafique	b Shoaib Akhtar	0	not out		9
Mashrafe Mortaza	b Gul	10	b Gul		14
Alamgir Kabir	not out	1	b Gul		4
Extras	(B 4, LB 5, W 1, NB 9)	19	(LB 2, NB 2)		4
Total		**361**			**96**

PAKISTAN

Mohammad Hafeez	c Masud b Mahmud	21	not out		102
Taufiq Umar	c Masud b Rafique	75	c Mortaza b Mahmud		43
Yasir Hamid	b Rafique	23	not out		18
Inzamam-ul-Haq	lbw b Rafique	43			
Yousuf Youhana	not out	64			
*†Rashid Latif	st Masud b Rafique	40			
Shoaib Malik	lbw b Rafique	0			
Shoaib Akhtar	b Mahmud	15			
Shabbir Ahmed	c Mortaza b Kapali	8			
Danish Kaneria	lbw b Kapali	0			
Umar Gul	lbw b Kapali	0			
Extras	(LB 1, NB 5)	6	(LB 1, W 1)		2
Total		**295**	**(1 wicket)**		**165**

PAKISTAN	O	M	R	W	O	M	R	W	FALL OF WICKETS				
Shoaib Akhtar	22.5	4	49	6	12	2	30	4		B	P	B	P
Umar Gul	27	3	67	2	(3) 4.5	1	16	3	Wkt	1st	1st	2nd	2nd
Shabbir Ahmed	25	7	73	1	(2) 7	2	21	1	1st	13	51	7	140
Danish Kaneria	41	11	110	1	10	3	27	2	2nd	180	84	20	–
Shoaib Malik	12	4	27	0					3rd	310	159	43	–
Mohammad Hafeez	10	4	26	0					4th	315	178	43	–
									5th	315	242	64	–
BANGLADESH									6th	315	250	64	–
Mashrafe Mortaza	18	6	48	0	7	1	26	0	7th	320	265	65	–
Alamgir Kabir	13	3	61	0	7.3	1	39	0	8th	320	289	75	–
Khaled Mahmud	21	6	42	2	14	5	28	1	9th	341	289	90	–
Mohammad Rafique	45	13	118	5	12	2	34	0	10th	361	295	96	–
Rajin Saleh	7	2	13	0									
Mohammad Ashraful	2	0	9	0	1	0	7	0					
Alok Kapali	2.1	1	3	3	(5) 6	0	30	0					

Umpires: S.A.Bucknor (*West Indies*) (83) and R.B Tiffin (*Australia*) (36).
Referee: M.J.Procter (*South Africa*) (15).   **Test No. 1658/5 (P294/B23)**

PAKISTAN v BANGLADESH (3rd Test)

At Multan Cricket Stadium on 3, 4, 5, 6 September 2003.
Toss: Bangladesh. Result: **PAKISTAN** won by one wicket.
Debuts: Pakistan – Farhan Adil, Salman Butt, Yasir Ali.

BANGLADESH

Hannan Sarkar	c Rashid b Gul	13		c Rashid b Gul	3
Javed Omar	c Younis b Gul	38		c Inzamam b Shabbir	16
Habibul Bashar	c Rashid b Ali	72		c Rashid b Gul	3
Mohammad Ashraful	lbw b Saqlain	12		c Salman b Shabbir	3
Rajin Saleh	run out	49		c Rashid b Gul	42
Alok Kapali	b Gul	11		c Rashid b Ali	22
†Khaled Masud	c Rashid b Gul	29	(8)	lbw b Shabbir	28
*Khaled Mahmud	lbw b Shabbir	19	(7)	lbw b Shabbir	2
Mohammad Rafique	b Shabbir	11		lbw b Gul	4
Tapash Baisya	lbw b Shabbir	0		not out	14
Manjural Islam	not out	0		c Younis b Saqlain	5
Extras	(B 4, LB 10, NB 13)	27		(B5, LB 2, W 2, NB 3)	12
Total		**281**			**154**

PAKISTAN

Mohammad Hafeez	lbw b Mahmud	21	(2)	c sub (Mashrafe Mortaza) b Manjural	18
Salman Butt	c Masud b Mahmud	12	(1)	c sub (Mashrafe Mortaza) b Manjural	37
Yasir Hamid	b Rafique	39		c sub (Mashrafe Mortaza) b Mahmud	18
Inzamam-ul-Haq	c Sarkar b Mahmud	10		not out	138
Younis Khan	c Masud b Mahmud	34		run out	0
Farhan Adil	lbw b Rafique	25		c Habibul b Rafique	8
*†Rashid Latif	c Kapali b Baisya	5		lbw b Mahmud	5
Saqlain Mushtaq	b Rafique	9		c Masud b Mahmud	11
Shabbir Ahmed	lbw b Rafique	4		lbw b Rafique	13
Umar Gul	b Rafique	0		run out	5
Yasir Ali	not out	0		not out	1
Extras	(B 1, LB 5, NB 5)	11		(LB 4, W 4)	8
Total		**175**		**(9 wickets)**	**262**

PAKISTAN	O	M	R	W		O	M	R	W		FALL OF WICKETS			
Shabbir Ahmed	25.2	3	70	3	(2)	23	6	68	4			B	P	B	P
Umar Gul	32	7	86	4	(1)	15	6	58	4		Wkt	1st	1st	2nd	2nd
Yasir Ali	14	4	43	1		6	1	12	1		1st	28	27	4	45
Saqlain Mushtaq	25	5	61	1		2.3	0	9	1		2nd	102	36	9	62
Mohammad Hafeez	3	1	7	0							3rd	136	50	23	78
											4th	166	121	41	81
BANGLADESH											5th	179	135	77	99
Manjural Islam	13	3	42	0		21	2	64	2		6th	241	152	91	132
Tapash Baisya	11	2	54	1		12	0	46	0		7th	248	154	111	164
Khaled Mahmud	13	1	37	4		28	9	68	3		8th	278	166	127	205
Mohammad Rafique	17.4	7	36	5		30	6	80	2		9th	278	170	137	257
											10th	281	175	154	–

Umpires: E.A.R.de Silva (*Sri Lanka*) (25) and R.B Tiffin (*Australia*) (37).
Referee: M.J.Procter (*South Africa*) (16). **Test No. 1659/6 (P295/B24)**

INDIA v NEW ZEALAND (1st Test)

At Sardar Patel Gujarat Stadium, Motera, Ahmedabad, on 8, 9, 10, 11, 12 October 2003.
Toss: India. Result: **MATCH DRAWN**.
Debuts: India – L.Balaji, A. Chopra.

INDIA

A.Chopra	c and b Vettori	42	c Styris b Vettori	31
V.Sehwag	lbw b Tuffey	29	c Hart b Oram	17
R.Dravid	c Hart b Oram	222	c Vincent b Wiseman	73
S.R.Tendulkar	c Astle b Styris	8	c Vettori b Wiseman	7
V.V.S.Laxman	c Wiseman b Vettori	64	c Vettori b Wiseman	44
*S.C.Ganguly	not out	100	b Wiseman	25
†P.A.Patel	not out	29	not out	5
Harbhajan Singh				
A.Kumble				
Zaheer Khan				
L.Balaji				
Extras	(B 2, LB 3, NB 1)	6	(B 4, LB 3)	7
Total	(5 wickets declared)	**500**	(6 wickets declared)	**209**

NEW ZEALAND

M.H.Richardson	b Zaheer	6	c Chopra b Kumble	21
L.Vincent	c Patel b Zaheer	7	b Kumble	67
*S.P.Fleming	b Zaheer	1	(4) c Laxman b Harbhajan	8
S.B.Styris	c Chopra b Harbhajan	34	(5) lbw b Kumble	0
N.J.Astle	st Patel b Harbhajan	103	(8) not out	51
C.D.McMillan	c Chopra b Sehwag	54	not out	83
J.D.P.Oram	c Dravid b Kumble	5	c Dravid b Harbhajan	7
†R.G.Hart	lbw b Balaji	15		
D.L.Vettori	c Dravid b Kumble	60		
P.J.Wiseman	c Laxman b Zaheer	27		
D.R.Tuffey	not out	2	(3) b Kumble	8
Extras	(B 4, LB 18, NB 4)	26	(B 4, LB 11, NB 12)	27
Total		**340**	(6 wickets)	**272**

NEW ZEALAND	O	M	R	W		O	M	R	W	FALL OF WICKETS				
											I	NZ	I	NZ
Tuffey	31	6	103	1		9	2	18	0	Wkt	1st	1st	2nd	2nd
Oram	33	8	95	1		8	0	39	1	1st	35	11	20	44
Styris	26	5	83	1						2nd	107	16	97	68
Vettori	44	9	128	2	(3)	16	0	81	0	3rd	134	17	118	83
McMillan	4	1	6	0						4th	264	108	166	86
Wiseman	21	0	80	0	(4)	11.5	0	64	4	5th	446	199	177	150
INDIA										6th	–	223	209	169
Zaheer Khan	23	3	68	4		10	1	36	0	7th	–	227	–	–
Balaji	26	7	84	1		11	4	21	0	8th	–	265	–	–
Kumble	35.1	11	58	2	(4)	39	12	95	4	9th	–	332	–	–
Harbhajan Singh	36	8	86	2	(3)	38	9	65	2	10th	–	340	–	–
Sehwag	8	2	17	1	(6)	2	2	0	0					
Tendulkar	3	2	5	0	(5)	7	0	19	0					

Umpires: R.E.Koertzen (*South Africa*) (42) and D.R.Shepherd (*England*) (74).
Referee: R.S.Madugalle (*Sri Lanka*) (53). **Test No. 1660/43 (1304/NZ366)**

INDIA v NEW ZEALAND (2nd Test)

At Punjab C.A.Stadium, Mohali, Chandigarh, on 16, 17, 18, 19, 20 October 2003.
Toss: New Zealand. Result: **MATCH DRAWN**.
Debuts: India – Yuvraj Singh.

NEW ZEALAND

M.H.Richardson	c Kumble b Harbhajan	145
L.Vincent	lbw b Kumble	106
S.B.Styris	lbw b Kumble	119
*S.P.Fleming	b Tendulkar	30
N.J.Astle	c Patel b Harbhajan	18
C.D.McMillan	not out	100
†R.G.Hart	b Kumble	11
D.L.Vettori	not out	48
P.J.Wiseman		
D.R.Tuffey		
I.G.Butler		
Extras	(B 21, LB 28, W 1, NB 3)	53
Total	(6 wickets declared)	**630**

INDIA

A.Chopra	c Astle b Tuffey	60	c Richardson b Wiseman	52
V.Sehwag	b Styris	130	c Fleming b Tuffey	1
R.Dravid	c Hart b Butler	13	c Fleming b Tuffey	5
S.R.Tendulkar	c Richardson b Vettori	55	b Tuffey	1
V.V.S.Laxman	not out	104	not out	67
Yuvraj Singh	c Hart b Tuffey	20	not out	5
†P.A.Patel	c Richardson b Vettori	18		
A.Kumble	run out	5		
Harbhajan Singh	run out	8		
L.Balaji	c Hart b Tuffey	4		
Zaheer Khan	c Hart b Tuffey	0		
Extras	(B 2, LB 1, W 2, NB 2)	7	(LB 4, W 1)	5
Total		**424**	(4 wickets)	**136**

INDIA	O	M	R	W		O	M	R	W		FALL OF WICKETS		
												NZ	I	I
Zaheer Khan	26	8	95	0							Wkt	1st	1st	2nd
Balaji	30	10	78	0							1st	231	164	6
Tendulkar	22	3	55	1							2nd	382	208	12
Kumble	66	18	181	3							3rd	433	218	18
Harbhajan Singh	48	7	149	2							4th	447	330	128
Sehwag	5.3	1	22	0							5th	507	364	–
Yuvraj Singh	1	0	1	0							6th	540	388	–
											7th	–	396	–
NEW ZEALAND											8th	–	408	–
Tuffey	29	5	80	4		14	4	30	3		9th	–	424	–
Butler	35	7	116	1		5	1	12	0		10th	–	424	–
Styris	19	7	40	1	(4)	4	2	4	0					
Vettori	56	24	84	2	(3)	23	8	40	0					
Wiseman	32	7	95	0		17	6	37	1					
McMillan	1	0	6	0		6	3	9	0					

Umpires: R.E.Koertzen (*South Africa*) (43) and D.R.Shepherd (*England*) (75).
Referee: R.S.Madugalle (*Sri Lanka*) (54). **Test No. 1661/44 (I305/NZ367)**

267

AUSTRALIA v ZIMBABWE (1st Test)

At W.A.C.A. Ground, Perth, on 9, 10, 11, 12, 13 October 2003.
Toss: Zimbabwe. Result: **AUSTRALIA** won by an innings and 175 runs.
Debuts: None.

AUSTRALIA

J.L.Langer	b Ervine	26
M.L.Hayden	c Carlisle b Gripper	380
R.T.Ponting	lbw b Ervine	37
D.R.Martyn	c Wishart b Gripper	53
*S.R.Waugh	c and b Ervine	78
D.S.Lehmann	c and b Ervine	30
†A.C.Gilchrist	not out	113
A.J Bichel		
B.Lee		
J.N.Gillespie		
S.C.G.MacGill		
Extras	(B 4, LB 10, W 1, NB 3)	18
Total	**(6 wickets declared)**	**735**

ZIMBABWE

D.D Ebrahim	b Gillespie	29		b Gillespie	4
T.R.Gripper	c Lehmann b Lee	53		c Gilchrist b Gillespie	0
M.A.Vermeulen	c Hayden b MacGill	38		c Gilchrist b Lee	63
S.V.Carlisle	c Hayden b MacGill	2		c Hayden b Lehmann	35
C.B.Wishart	c Gilchrist b Bichel	46		lbw b Bichel	8
C.N.Evans	b Bichel	22		b Lehmann	5
†T.Taibu	lbw b Gillespie	15		c Gilchrist b Bichel	3
*H.H.Streak	b Lee	9	(9)	not out	71
S.M.Ervine	c Waugh b Gillespie	6	(8)	b Bichel	53
A.M.Blignaut	lbw b Lee	0		st Gilchrist b Lehmann	22
R.W.Price	not out	2		c Waugh b Bichel	36
Extras	(LB 10, W 2, NB 5)	17		(B 4, LB 6, W 5, NB 6)	21
Total		**239**			**321**

ZIMBABWE	O	M	R	W	O	M	R	W
Streak	26	6	131	0				
Blignaut	28	4	115	0				
Ervine	31	4	146	4				
Price	36	5	187	0				
Gripper	25.3	0	142	0				
AUSTRALIA								
Lee	15	4	48	3	35	8	96	1
Gillespie	25.3	9	52	3	3	0	6	2
Bichel	21	2	62	2	(4) 28.2	15	63	4
MacGill	21	4	54	2	(3) 3.4	1	10	0
Lehmann	2	1	3	0	31.2	15	61	3
Waugh	5	1	10	0	(7) 8	2	26	0
Martyn					(6) 13	5	34	0
Ponting					5	1	15	0

	FALL OF WICKETS		
	A	Z	Z
Wkt	1st	1st	2nd
1st	43	61	2
2nd	102	105	11
3rd	199	120	110
4th	406	131	112
5th	502	199	118
6th	735	200	126
7th	–	231	126
8th	–	231	209
9th	–	231	247
10th	–	239	321

Umpires: S.Venkataraghavan (*India*) (69) and P.Willey (*England*) (25).
Referee: G.R.Viswanath (*India*) (12).

Test No. 1662/2 (A643/Z68)

AUSTRALIA v ZIMBABWE (2nd Test)

At Sydney Cricket Ground on 17, 18, 19, 20 October 2003.
Toss: Zimbabwe. Result: **AUSTRALIA** won by nine wickets.
Debuts: Australia – B.A.Williams; Zimbabwe – G.M.Ewing.

ZIMBABWE

D.D.Ebrahim	b Lee	9	c Katich b Williams	0
T.R.Gripper	c Gilchrist b Bichel	15	c Hayden b Katich	47
M.A.Vermeulen	lbw b Williams	17	c Waugh b Williams	48
S.V.Carlisle	c Ponting b Bichel	118	c Williams b Katich	5
C.B.Wishart	c Gilchrist b Williams	14	st Gilchrist b Katich	45
†T.Taibu	c Gilchrist b Hogg	27	c Ponting b Katich	35
*H.H.Streak	lbw b Hogg	14	run out	25
G.M.Ewing	c Martyn b Lee	2	c Gilchrist b Hogg	0
A.M.Blignaut	not out	38	c Williams b Katich	44
R.W.Price	c Williams b Bichel	20	lbw b Katich	0
N.B.Mahwire	c Gilchrist b Bichel	6	not out	1
Extras	(B 4, LB 12, W 3, NB 9)	28	(B 6, LB 5, W 1, NB 4)	16
Total		**308**		**266**

AUSTRALIA

J.L.Langer	c Streak b Blignaut	2	c Taibu b Streak	8
M.L.Hayden	c Carlisle b Blignaut	20	not out	101
R.T.Ponting	b Price	169	not out	53
D.R.Martyn	lbw b Price	32		
*S.R.Waugh	c Carlisle b Price	61		
S.M.Katich	b Price	52		
†A.C.Gilchrist	b Streak	20		
G.B.Hogg	c Ebrahim b Price	13		
A.J Bichel	c Wishart b Blignaut	5		
B.Lee	not out	6		
B.A.Williams	c and b Price	7		
Extras	(LB 2, W 1, NB 13)	16	(B 3, LB 3, NB 4)	10
Total		**403**	(1 wicket)	**172**

AUSTRALIA	O	M	R	W		O	M	R	W
Lee	23	5	78	2	(1)	16	8	56	2
Williams	23	6	58	2	(2)	19	5	64	0
Bichel	24.2	7	66	4	(3)	31	9	70	1
Hogg	23	8	49	2					
Waugh	4	0	7	0					
Katich	7	0	25	0	(4)	25.5	3	65	6
Martyn	3	1	9	0					
ZIMBABWE									
Streak	21	3	83	1		9	1	46	1
Blignaut	20	2	83	3		4	0	35	0
Mahwire	10	1	61	0					
Price	41.3	6	121	6	(3)	12.1	0	63	0
Ewing	11	1	53	0		3	0	20	0
Gripper					(4)	1	0	2	0

FALL OF WICKETS

	Z	A	Z	A
Wkt	1st	1st	2nd	2nd
1st	15	7	0	21
2nd	45	51	93	–
3rd	47	148	103	–
4th	95	283	114	–
5th	151	306	176	–
6th	218	347	212	–
7th	222	375	216	–
8th	243	384	230	–
9th	296	394	244	–
10th	308	403	266	–

Umpires: B.F.Bowden (*New Zealand*) (8) and S.Venkataraghavan (*India*) (70).
Referee: G.R.Viswanath (*India*) (13). **Test No. 1663/3 (A644/Z69)**

PAKISTAN v SOUTH AFRICA (1st Test)

At Gaddafi Stadium, Lahore, on 17, 18, 19, 20, 21 October 2003.
Toss: South Africa. Result: **PAKISTAN** won by eight wickets.
Debuts: Pakistan – Asim Kamal.

SOUTH AFRICA

*G.C.Smith	c Kamal b Sami	33		c Taufiq b Shoaib Akhtar	12
H.H.Gibbs	c Taufiq b Kaneria	27		c Taufiq b Shoaib Akhtar	59
G.Kirsten	retired hurt	53	(6)	c Youhana b Kaneria	46
J.H.Kallis	c Moin b Kaneria	29		c Moin b Shoaib Akhtar	18
H.H.Dippenaar	c Farhat b Shoaib Malik	24	(3)	c Youhana b Shoaib Akhtar	27
N.D.McKenzie	lbw b Shoaib Akhtar	0	(5)	b Kaneria	14
†M.V.Boucher	c Farhat b Shoaib Malik	72		c Farhat b Kaneria	15
S.M.Pollock	b Shoaib Malik	28		b Kaneria	18
P.R.Adams	not out	18		lbw b Kaneria	0
A.Nel	lbw b Shoaib Akhtar	0		b Mushtaq	0
M.Ntini	c Kamal b Shoaib Malik	8		not out	0
Extras	(LB 5, NB 23)	28		(B 1, LB 11, NB 20)	32
Total		**320**			**241**

PAKISTAN

Taufiq Umar	c and b Adams	111		b Adams	63
Imran Farhat	b Adams	41		c Gibbs b Smith	58
Yasir Hamid	c Boucher b Pollock	16		not out	20
*Yousuf Youhana	c Boucher b Nel	8			
Asim Kamal	b Nel	99			
Shoaib Malik	b Adams	47	(4)	not out	8
†Moin Khan	lbw b Adams	37			
Shoaib Akhtar	st Boucher b Adams	1			
Mohammad Sami	b Adams	0			
Mushtaq Ahmed	not out	14			
Danish Kaneria	c Smith b Adams	0			
Extras	(B 2, LB 17, W 2, NB 6)	27		(LB 6, W 5, NB 4)	15
Total		**401**		**(2 wickets)**	**164**

PAKISTAN	O	M	R	W		O	M	R	W	FALL OF WICKETS				
Shoaib Akhtar	14	1	62	2		14.3	2	36	4		SA	P	SA	P
Mohammad Sami	13	2	66	1		19.3	0	77	0	*Wkt*	*1st*	*1st*	*2nd*	*2nd*
Mushtaq Ahmed	18	1	80	0		8	1	18	1	1st	52	109	43	134
Danish Kaneria	21	2	65	2	(5)	28.3	8	46	5	2nd	84	151	104	141
Shoaib Malik	17	4	42	4	(4)	14	0	52	0	3rd	154	160	108	–
										4th	159	223	149	–
SOUTH AFRICA										5th	229	322	149	–
Pollock	22	7	48	1		7	2	21	0	6th	282	363	192	–
Ntini	28	4	88	0		6	0	24	0	7th	302	366	237	–
Adams	45	11	128	7	(5)	11	1	57	1	8th	307	366	238	–
Nel	27	5	67	2	(3)	5	1	13	0	9th	320	401	241	–
Kallis	18	3	37	0	(4)	6	1	30	0	10th	–	401	241	–
Smith	8	1	14	0		5.1	2	13	1					

Umpires: D.B.Hair (*Australia*) (49) and N.A.Mallender (*England*) (1).
Referee: C.H.Lloyd (*West Indies*) (26). **Test No. 1664/10 (P280/SA296)**

PAKISTAN v SOUTH AFRICA (2nd Test)

At Iqbal Stadium, Faisalabad, on 24, 25, 26, 27, 28 October 2003.
Toss: South Africa. Result: **MATCH DRAWN**.
Debuts: None.

SOUTH AFRICA

*G.C.Smith	c Inzamam b Shabbir	2	lbw b Shabbir		65
H.H.Gibbs	lbw b Mushtaq	98	lbw b Kaneria		20
H.H.Dippenaar	c Taufiq b Shabbir	4	lbw b Shoaib		21
J.H.Kallis	c Taufiq b Kaneria	10	(6) lbw b Razzaq		43
G.Kirsten	c Taufiq b Razzaq	54	(4) c Taufiq b Razzaq		118
N.D.McKenzie	c Mushtaq b Shabbir	27	(5) c Taufiq b Kaneria		35
†M.V.Boucher	b Razzaq	27	b Razzaq		0
S.M.Pollock	run out	16	not out		30
R.J.Peterson	c sub (Misbah-ul-Haq) b Shabbir	4	c Inzamam b Shabbir		17
P.R.Adams	c Taufiq b Kaneria	14	not out		9
M.Ntini	not out	16			
Extras	(LB 1, W 1, NB 4)	6	(B 1, LB 7, W 2, NB 3)		13
Total		**278**	(8 wickets declared)		**371**

PAKISTAN

Taufiq Umar	c Gibbs b Adams	68	c Smith b Peterson		71
Imran Farhat	c Peterson b Pollock	128	lbw b Kallis		8
Yasir Hamid	c Gibbs b Pollock	21	c Dippenaar b Ntini		17
*Inzamam-ul-Haq	lbw b Pollock	23	lbw b Ntini		60
Asim Kamal	c Pollock b Ntini	1	c Boucher b Adams		38
Shoaib Malik	c Smith b Pollock	9	(7) not out		23
Abdul Razzak	c sub (J.A.Rudolph) b Ntini	37	(6) b Pollock		10
†Moin Khan	c Gibbs b Kallis	18	not out		9
Mushtaq Ahmed	lbw b Pollock	6			
Shabbir Ahmed	not out	24			
Danish Kaneria	c Smith b Pollock	0			
Extras	(B 3, LB 8, W 1, NB 1)	13	(B 1, LB 1, NB 4)		6
Total		**348**	(6 wickets)		**242**

PAKISTAN	O	M	R	W	O	M	R	W	FALL OF WICKETS				
										SA	P	SA	P
Shabbir Ahmed	26	8	74	4	34.3	10	70	2	Wkt	1st	1st	2nd	2nd
Abdul Razzaq	22	4	68	2	18	3	70	3	1st	6	137	42	18
Danish Kaneria	33.1	10	68	2	37	6	100	2	2nd	20	178	93	46
Shoaib Malik	5	0	19	0	26	5	70	1	3rd	40	248	128	125
Mushtaq Ahmed	13	1	48	1	12	3	53	0	4th	148	251	213	187
									5th	195	257	303	209
SOUTH AFRICA									6th	212	261	303	209
Pollock	29.2	9	78	6	22	12	27	1	7th	236	293	325	–
Ntini	29	9	64	2	20	7	45	2	8th	247	309	358	–
Kallis	22	4	57	1	19	6	51	1	9th	250	339	–	–
Peterson	8	1	40	0	(5) 15	6	21	1	10th	278	348	–	–
Adams	25	5	82	1	(4) 20	2	75	1					
Smith	3	0	16	0	2	0	21	0					

Umpires: D.J.Harper (*Australia*) (34) and S.J.A.Taufel (*Australia*) (7).
Referee: C.H.Lloyd (*West Indies*) (27).   **Test No. 1665/11 (P281/SA297)**

BANGLADESH v ENGLAND (1st Test)

At Bangabandhu National Stadium, Dhaka, on 21, 22, 23, 24, 25 October 2003.
Toss: Bangladesh. Result: **ENGLAND** won by seven wickets.
Debuts: Bangladesh – Enamul Haque II (*unrelated to Enamul Haque – 10 Tests 2000-01 to 2002-03*); England – G.J.Batty, R.Clarke.

BANGLADESH

Hannan Sarkar	b Hoggard	20		c Trescothick b Hoggard	59
Javed Omar	c Clarke b Harmison	3	(7)	lbw b Hoggard	27
Habibul Bashar	c Trescothick b Harmison	2		c Trescothick b Batty	58
Rajin Saleh	c Read b Harmison	11	(2)	c Read b Harmison	8
Alok Kapali	b Batty	28	(4)	c Butcher b Harmison	12
Mushfiqur Rahman	lbw b Hoggard	34	(5)	not out	46
†Khaled Masud	lbw b Clarke	51	(6)	c Hussain b Giles	7
*Khaled Mahmud	b Hoggard	4		lbw b Harmison	18
Mohammad Rafique	b Harmison	32		c Read b Harmison	1
Mashrafe Mortaza	b Harmison	11		c Trescothick b Hoggard	1
Enamul Haque II	not out	0		lbw b Hoggard	0
Extras	(B 2, LB 3, NB 2)	7		(LB 10, NB 3, Pen 5)	18
Total		**203**			**255**

ENGLAND

M.E.Trescothick	c Mahmud b Haque	113		st Masud b Rafique	32
*M.P.Vaughan	b Rafique	48		not out	81
M.A.Butcher	lbw b Mushfiqur	0		lbw b Rafique	8
N.Hussain	c Masud b Mushfiqur	0		lbw b Mortaza	17
G.P.Thorpe	c Saleh b Mortaza	64		not out	18
R.Clarke	b Rafique	14			
†C.M.W.Read	c Masud b Haque	1			
G.J.Batty	c Masud b Mortaza	19			
A.F.Giles	c sub (Aftab Ahmed) b Rafique	19			
S.J.Harmison	lbw b Mortaza	0			
M.J.Hoggard	not out	6			
Extras	(LB 4, W 2, NB 5)	11		(B 1, LB 1, W 1, NB 5)	8
Total		**295**		**(3 wickets)**	**164**

ENGLAND	O	M	R	W	O	M	R	W	FALL OF WICKETS			
Hoggard	23	6	55	3	27	11	48	4		**B**	**E**	**B**	**E**
Harmison	21.5	9	35	5	25	8	44	4	*Wkt*	*1st*	*1st*	*2nd*	*2nd*
Clarke	6	1	18	1	(5) 15	6	31	0	1st	12	137	12	64
Batty	21	6	43	1	(3) 20	2	65	1	2nd	24	140	120	86
Giles	12	1	47	0	(4) 52	4	52	1	3rd	38	140	140	128
									4th	40	175	148	—
BANGLADESH									5th	72	224	176	—
Mashrafe Mortaza	23	6	41	3	11	2	46	1	6th	132	225	219	—
Mushfiqur Rahman	17	6	55	2	3	1	16	0	7th	148	266	248	—
Khaled Mahmud	17	7	45	0	3	1	14	0	8th	182	267	254	—
Mohammad Rafique	35.3	9	84	3	13.2	0	57	2	9th	198	267	255	—
Enamul Haque II	23	8	53	2	7	0	27	0	10th	203	295	255	—
Rajin Saleh	2	0	9	0	2	0							
Alok Kapali	3	1	4	0									

Umpires: Alim Dar (*Pakistan*) (1) and E.A.R.de Silva (*Sri Lanka*) (26).
Referee: Wasim Raja (*Pakistan*) (12).　　　　　　　　　　　**Test No. 1666/1 (E812/B25)**

BANGLADESH v ENGLAND (2nd Test)

At M.A.Aziz Stadium, Chittagong, on 29, 30, 31 October, 1 November 2003.
Toss: Bangladesh. Result: **ENGLAND** won by 329 runs.
Debuts: England – M.J.Saggers.

ENGLAND

M.E.Trescothick	c Mushfiqur b Mahmud	60	(7) not out		1
*M.P.Vaughan	c Masud b Mortaza	54	run out		25
M.A.Butcher	b Rafique	6	(1) c Masud b Rafique		42
N.Hussain	c Masud b Mortaza	76	(3) c and b Rafique		95
G.P.Thorpe	b Mortaza	0	(4) lbw b Rafique		54
R.Clarke	c Sarkar b Mortaza	55	lbw b Haque		27
†C.M.W.Read	c Saleh b Haque	37	(5) not out		38
A.F.Giles	lbw b Mushfiqur	6			
R.L.Johnson	c Masud b Mushfiqur	6			
M.J.Saggers	lbw b Rafique	1			
M.J.Hoggard	not out	0			
Extras	(B 8, LB 5, W 7, NB 5)	25	(B 4, W 1, NB 6)		11
Total		**326**	(5 wickets declared)		**293**

BANGLADESH

Hannan Sarkar	lbw b Clarke	28	c Read b Johnson		4
Javed Omar	c Vaughan b Johnson	2	c Read b Saggers		18
Habibul Bashar	c Butcher b Hoggard	18	run out		21
Rajin Saleh	c Read b Johnson	32	c Read b Clarke		9
Alok Kapali	c Butcher b Clarke	0	(6) c Saggers b Johnson		19
Mushfiqur Rahman	c Read b Saggers	28	(5) run out		6
†Khaled Masud	c sub (P.D.Collingwood) b Johnson	0	c Read b Johnson		15
*Khaled Mahmud	c sub (P.D.Collingwood) b Johnson	15	c Vaughan b Johnson		33
Mohammad Rafique	not out	12	c Read b Hoggard		0
Mashrafe Mortaza	b Johnson	1	absent hurt		
Enamul Haque II	c Hoggard b Saggers	9	(10) not out		1
Extras	(LB 1, NB 6)	7	(B 4, LB 5, W 1, NB 2)		12
Total		**152**			**138**

BANGLADESH	O	M	R	W		O	M	R	W	FALL OF WICKETS				
											E	B	E	B
Mashrafe Mortaza	28	11	60	4		4	0	23	0	Wkt	1st	1st	2nd	2nd
Mushfiqur Rahman	18.3	6	50	2		5	0	41	0	1st	126	6	66	5
Khaled Mahmud	23	8	46	1	(4)	14	3	64	0	2nd	133	44	70	33
Mohammad Rafique	37	15	63	2	(3)	29	3	106	3	3rd	134	61	208	51
Enamul Haque II	23	4	81	1		14	5	40	1	4th	134	63	231	58
Alok Kapali	4	0	12	0						5th	250	107	290	70
Rajin Saleh	2	1	1	0	(6)	1	0	15	0	6th	313	110	–	91
										7th	313	126	–	108
ENGLAND										8th	321	138	–	126
Hoggard	20	3	64	1		12	3	37	1	9th	326	139	–	138
Johnson	21	6	49	5		12.1	1	44	4	10th	326	152	–	–
Clarke	13	5	24	2	(5)	1	0	4	1					
Saggers	12.1	3	29	2		7	1	33	1					
Giles					(3)	5	1	11	0					

Umpires: Alim Dar (*Pakistan*) (2) and E.A.R.de Silva (*Sri Lanka*) (27).
Referee: Wasim Raja (*Pakistan*) (13).   Test No. 1667/2 (E813/B26)

ZIMBABWE v WEST INDIES (1st Test)

At Harare Sports Club on 4, 5, 6, 7, 8 November 2003.
Toss: Zimbabwe. Result: **MATCH DRAWN**.
Debuts: Zimbabwe – S.Matsikenyeri, V.Sibanda.

ZIMBABWE

V.Sibanda	c Jacobs b Edwards	18	c Ganga b Collymore		16
T.R.Gripper	c Lara b Taylor	41	lbw b Drakes		26
M.A.Vermeulen	c Hinds b Edwards	8	c Chanderpaul b Edwards		2
S.V.Carlisle	c Lara b Collymore	8	lbw b Drakes		10
C.B Wishart	c Jacobs b Hinds	47	b Drakes		34
S.Matsikenyeri	c Jacobs b Edwards	57	not out		46
†T.Taibu	b Edwards	83	b Drakes		21
*H.H.Streak	not out	127	(9) not out		7
A.M.Blignaut	c Gayle b Drakes	91	(8) c Jacobs b Collymore		13
R.W.Price	lbw b Edwards	2			
N.B.Mahwire	not out	1			
Extras	(B 1, LB 5, W 3, NB 15)	24	(B 8, LB 2, W 2, NB 13)		25
Total	**(9 wickets declared)**	**507**	**(7 wickets declared)**		**200**

WEST INDIES

C.H.Gayle	lbw b Streak	14	c Taibu b Price		13
W.W.Hinds	c Blignaut b Mahwire	79	c Carlisle b Streak		24
D.Ganga	b Mahwire	73	b Price		16
*B.C.Lara	c Mahwire b Price	29	lbw b Streak		1
R.R.Sarwan	lbw b Price	9	st Taibu b Gripper		39
S.Chanderpaul	lbw b Streak	36	c Sibanda b Price		39
†R.D.Jacobs	c Vermeulen b Price	5	not out		60
V.C.Drakes	c Streak b Price	31	c Taibu b Blignaut		4
J.E.Taylor	c Wishart b Price	9	c Matsikenyeri b Blignaut		3
C.D.Collymore	not out	11	c Vermeulen b Price		1
F.H.Edwards	c Matsikenyeri b Price	18	not out		1
Extras	(B 7, LB 7, W 3, NB 4)	21	(B 1, LB 1, W 1, NB 3)		6
Total		**335**	**(9 wickets)**		**207**

WEST INDIES	O	M	R	W		O	M	R	W		FALL OF WICKETS			
Collymore	29	6	131	1		15	2	59	2			Z	WI	Z	WI
Edwards	34.3	3	133	5		16	5	52	1		*Wkt*	*1st*	*1st*	*2nd*	*2nd*
Hinds	15	6	40	1							1st	26	50	21	37
Drakes	34	4	85	1	(3)	20	2	67	4		2nd	35	127	27	37
Taylor	9.4	4	32	1							3rd	58	179	60	38
Gayle	19.2	6	38	0							4th	112	211	90	73
Sarwan	9	0	35	0	(4)	1	0	12	0		5th	154	215	107	103
Chanderpaul	1	0	7	0							6th	233	240	152	171
Ganga	1	1	0	0							7th	314	290	175	184
											8th	482	294	–	194
ZIMBABWE											9th	495	309	–	204
Blignaut	14	3	68	0	(2)	14	2	50	2		10th	–	335	–	–
Streak	28	9	74	2	(1)	15	7	28	2						
Mahwire	25	7	75	2	(4)	2	0	10	0						
Price	37.2	13	73	6	(3)	38	11	88	4						
Matsikenyeri	2	0	10	0	(6)	2	0	6	0						
Gripper	8	1	21	0	(5)	12	5	23	1						

Umpires: B.F.Bowden (*New Zealand*) (9) and S.J.A.Taufel (*Australia*) (8).
Referee: G.R.Viswanath (*India*) (14). **Test No. 1668/5 (Z70/WI400)**

ZIMBABWE v WEST INDIES (2nd Test)

At Queens Sports Club, Bulawayo, on 12, 13, 14, 15, 16 November 2003.
Toss: West Indies. Result: **WEST INDIES** won by 128 runs.
Debuts: None.

WEST INDIES

C.H.Gayle	c Taibu b Blignaut	47	lbw b Streak		0
W.W.Hinds	st Taibu b Price	81	c Carlisle b Price		28
D.Ganga	c Matsikenyeri b Price	23	c Carlisle b Blignaut		8
*B.C.Lara	c Wishart b Blignaut	191	b Streak		1
R.R.Sarwan	c Vermeulen b Price	65	c Wishart b Blignaut		9
S.Chanderpaul	c Wishart b Price	15	lbw b Streak		15
†R.D.Jacobs	c Gripper b Streak	1	c Blignaut b Price		10
O.A.C.Banks	lbw b Blignaut	3	c Vermeulen b Price		16
M.Dillon	c Matsikenyeri b Price	19	not out		27
C.D.Collymore	not out	16	b Price		0
F.H.Edwards	c Taibu b Blignaut	0	b Blignaut		0
Extras	(B 1, LB 12, W 2, NB 5)	20	(B 5, LB 3, W 4, NB 2)		14
Total		**481**			**128**

ZIMBABWE

V.Sibanda	c and b Edwards	2	c Lara b Dillon		0
T.R.Gripper	b Dillon	1	c Ganga b Banks		8
M.A.Vermeulen	b Banks	118	b Hinds		24
S.V.Carlisle	b Edwards	11	c Jacobs b Banks		9
C.B Wishart	lbw b Collymore	96	c Jacobs b Hinds		13
S.Matsikenyeri	b Collymore	8	(7) run out		5
†T.Taibu	c Gayle b Collymore	27	(8) lbw b Collymore		1
*H.H.Streak	lbw b Dillon	3	(9) not out		33
A.M.Blignaut	lbw b Collymore	31	(6) lbw b Banks		3
R.W.Price	c Ganga b Banks	35	b Collymore		4
N.B.Mahwire	not out	8	b Dillon		4
Extras	(B 17, LB 4, W 1, NB 15)	37			–
Total		**377**			**104**

ZIMBABWE	O	M	R	W	O	M	R	W	FALL OF WICKETS
Streak	24	4	87	1	15	2	39	3	
Blignaut	20	4	86	4	14.4	6	29	3	
Mahwire	15	3	79	0	(4) 2	0	16	0	
Price	43	1	199	5	(3) 21	7	36	4	
Gripper	5	1	17	0					

WEST INDIES									
Hinds	6	2	18	0	(3) 9	2	20	2	
Edwards	15	3	48	2					
Dillon	34	13	57	0	(1) 8	2	17	2	
Collymore	24	5	70	4	(2) 15	7	29	2	
Banks	41.1	13	106	2	(4) 15	2	35	3	
Gayle	6	1	23	0					
Sarwan	7	0	34	0	(5) 2	1	3	0	

Wkt	WI 1st	Z 1st	WI 2nd	Z 2nd
1st	73	5	0	0
2nd	146	10	17	32
3rd	161	31	21	33
4th	351	185	51	54
5th	389	201	51	56
6th	394	279	82	62
7th	422	289	82	63
8th	449	302	127	67
9th	475	336	127	75
10th	481	377	128	104

Umpires: R.E.Koertzen (*South Africa*) (44) and S.J.A.Taufel (*Australia*) (9).
Referee: G.R.Viswanath (*India*) (15).   Test No. 1669/6 (Z71/WI401)

SRI LANKA v ENGLAND (1st Test)

At Galle International Stadium on 2, 3, 4, 5, 6 December 2003.
Toss: Sri Lanka. Result: **MATCH DRAWN**.
Debuts: Sri Lanka – K.A.D.M.Fernando; England – P.D.Collingwood.

SRI LANKA

M.S.Atapattu	c Read b Flintoff	29	st Read b Batty		35
S.T.Jayasuriya	c Collingwood b Giles	48	c Trescothick b Giles		17
†K.C.Sangakkara	lbw b Johnson	71	run out		19
D.P.M.D.Jayawardena	c Collingwood b Giles	17	not out		86
*H.P.Tillekeratne	c Read b Giles	0	lbw b Batty		1
T.T.Samaraweera	c Read b Flintoff	45	c Trescothick b Giles		1
U.D.U.Chandana	lbw b Flintoff	21	(8) lbw b Giles		19
H.D.P.K.Dharmasena	lbw b Batty	27	(9) lbw b Hoggard		2
W.P.U.C.J.Vaas	not out	22	(7) c Collingwood b Giles		19
K.A.D.M.Fernando	c Collingwood b Batty	4	c Trescothick b Flintoff		1
M.Muralitharan	c Read b Giles	38	c Collingwood b Batty		13
Extras	(B 5, LB 2, W 1, NB 1)	9	(B 4, LB 9)		13
Total		**331**			**226**

ENGLAND

M.E.Trescothick	c Sangakkara b Muralitharan	23	b Jayasuriya		24
*M.P.Vaughan	b Muralitharan	24	c Tillekeratne b Fernando		8
M.A.Butcher	c Sangakkara b Jayasuriya	51	c Sangakkara b Vaas		54
G.P.Thorpe	lbw b Vaas	43	c Vaas b Muralitharan		10
P.D.Collingwood	c Jayasuriya b Muralitharan	1	c Tillekeratne b Dharmasena		36
A.Flintoff	lbw b Muralitharan	1	c Tillekeratne b Vaas		0
†C.M.W.Read	c Tillekeratne b Muralitharan	0	c Jayawardena b Muralitharan		14
G.J.Batty	c Jayasuriya b Dharmasena	4	b Muralitharan		26
A.F.Giles	c Atapattu b Muralitharan	18	not out		17
R.L.Johnson	c Atapattu b Muralitharan	26	b Muralitharan		3
M.J.Hoggard	not out	6	not out		0
Extras	(B 12, LB 8, NB 8)	28	(B 10, LB 1, NB 7)		18
Total		**235**	(9 wickets)		**210**

ENGLAND	O	M	R	W	O	M	R	W	FALL OF WICKETS				
Hoggard	20	4	49	0	9	2	33	1		SL	E	SL	E
Johnson	17	5	54	1	7	2	28	0	Wkt	1st	1st	2nd	2nd
Flintoff	23	7	42	3	17	5	32	1	1st	76	56	26	16
Collingwood	4	0	12	0					2nd	88	67	72	62
Batty	31	5	98	2	23.2	7	55	3	3rd	132	142	72	73
Giles	32.5	9	69	4	(4) 40	14	63	4	4th	132	143	78	125
Vaughan					(6) 1	0	2	0	5th	202	151	85	125
									6th	238	155	123	148
SRI LANKA									7th	239	177	163	170
Vaas	12	2	25	1	14	4	23	2	8th	279	183	179	204
Fernando	3	1	21	0	4	0	29	1	9th	291	208	180	208
Dharmasena	24	6	55	1	(7) 18	8	36	1	10th	331	235	226	–
Muralitharan	31.4	15	46	7	(5) 37	18	47	4					
Chandana	13	2	24	0	(6) 11	2	24	0					
Jayasuriya	17	2	44	1	(4) 21	5	31	1					
Samaraweera					(8) 2	0	3	0					

Umpires: D.J.Harper (*Australia*) (35) and S.Venkataraghavan (*India*) (71).
Referee: C.H.Lloyd (*West Indies*) (28).　　　　　**Test No. 1670/13 (E814/SL134)**

SRI LANKA v ENGLAND (2nd Test)

At Asgiriya Stadium, Kandy, on 10, 11, 12, 13, 14 December 2003.
Toss: Sri Lanka. Result: **MATCH DRAWN**.
Debuts: None.

SRI LANKA

M.S.Atapattu	lbw b Kirtley	11	lbw b Giles		8
S.T.Jayasuriya	c Read b Giles	32	b Kirtley		27
†K.C.Sangakkara	run out	34	c Collingwood b Giles		10
D.P.M.D.Jayawardena	c Kirtley b Giles	45	b Flintoff		52
T.M.Dilshan	c Trescothick b Flintoff	63	st Read b Batty		100
*H.P.Tillekeratne	c Butcher b Flintoff	45	c Thorpe b Giles		20
T.T.Samaraweera	lbw b Giles	3	not out		23
W.P.U.C.J.Vaas	lbw b Kirtley	32	c Vaughan b Kirtley		20
H.D.P.K.Dharmasena	lbw b Giles	29	not out		7
K.A.D.M.Fernando	not out	51			
M.Muralitharan	b Giles	19			
Extras	(B 1, LB 15, NB 2)	18	(LB 6, W 1, NB 5)		12
Total		**382**	(7 wickets declared)		**279**

ENGLAND

M.E.Trescothick	c Dilshan b Muralitharan	36	c Jayawardena b Vaas		14
*M.P.Vaughan	c Jayawardena b Muralitharan	52	c Dilshan b Muralitharan		105
M.A.Butcher	st Sangakkara b Dharmasena	4	st Sangakkara b Muralitharan		6
N.Hussain	lbw b Vaas	10	c Sangakkara b Vaas		17
G.P.Thorpe	lbw b Muralitharan	57	c Sangakkara b Muralitharan		41
P.D.Collingwood	c Sangakkara b Vaas	28	c Jayawardena b Dharmasena		24
A.Flintoff	b Muralitharan	16	lbw b Muralitharan		19
†C.M.W.Read	lbw b Jayasuriya	9	not out		18
G.J.Batty	c Dilshan b Vaas	38	not out		25
A.F.Giles	c Jayawardena b Vaas	16			
R.J.Kirtley	not out	3			
Extras	(B 16, LB 10, NB 8)	34	(B 5, LB 6, NB 5)		16
Total		**294**	(7 wickets)		**285**

ENGLAND	O	M	R	W	O	M	R	W	FALL OF WICKETS			
										SL	E	SL	E
Kirtley	33	10	109	2	17	4	62	2		*1st*	*1st*	*2nd*	*2nd*
Flintoff	24	5	60	2	15	3	40	1	Wkt	1st	1st	2nd	2nd
Giles	37.4	7	116	5	22	3	101	3	1st	20	89	33	24
Collingwood	9	3	13	0	(6)	3	0	12	0	2nd	76	100	41	50
Batty	18	3	59	0	(4)	11	1	47	1	3rd	84	119	53	90
Vaughan	5	0	9	0	(5)	3	0	11	0	4th	187	119	206	167
									5th	201	177	212	208
SRI LANKA									6th	206	202	243	233
Vaas	24.2	4	77	4	29	7	59	2	7th	270	205	272	239
Fernando	7	0	36	0	7	1	21	0	8th	278	256	–	–
Dharmasena	19	3	63	1	7	2	74	1	9th	354	279	–	–
Muralitharan	40	18	60	4	56	28	64	4	10th	382	294	–	–
Jayasuriya	24	6	32	1	17	2	45	0					
Tillekeratne					1	0	1	0					
Samaraweera					1	1	0	0					
Dilshan					1	1	0	0					

Umpires: Alim Dar (*Pakistan*) (3) and D.J.Harper (*Australia*) (36).
Referee: C.H.Lloyd (*West Indies*) (29).　　　　　　　**Test No. 1671/14 (E815/SL135)**

SRI LANKA v ENGLAND (3rd Test)

At Sinhalese Sports Club, Colombo, on 18, 19, 20, 21 December 2003.
Toss: England.Result: **SRI LANKA** won by an innings and 215 runs.
Debuts: None.

ENGLAND

M.E.Trescothick	c Jayawardena b Muralitharan	70	c sub (M.G.Vandort) b Vaas	0
*M.P.Vaughan	c Jayawardena b Chandana	18	c Jayasuriya b Fernando	14
M.A.Butcher	c Sangakkara b Fernando	23	b Jayasuriya	37
N.Hussain	lbw b Vaas	8	c Sangakkara b Muralitharan	11
G.P.Thorpe	lbw b Muralitharan	13	st Sangakkara b Muralitharan	19
A.Flintoff	c and b Muralitharan	77	(7) c Sangakkara b Fernando	30
G.J.Batty	c Atapattu b Chandana	14	(6) st Sangakkara b Muralitharan	0
†C.M.W.Read	not out	17	lbw b Jayasuriya	0
A.F.Giles	run out	10	b Fernando	13
R.J.Kirtley	lbw b Vaas	1	b Muralitharan	12
J.M.Anderson	lbw b Vaas	1	not out	1
Extras	(B 4, LB 8, NB 1)	13	(B 2, LB 8, NB 1)	11
Total		**265**		**148**

SRI LANKA

†K.C.Sangakkara	c Trescothick b Kirtley	31
S.T.Jayasuriya	c Trescothick b Flintoff	85
T.T.Samaraweera	run out	142
D.P.M.D.Jayawardena	c sub (P.D.Collingwood) b Flintoff	134
T.M.Dilshan	b Giles	83
*H.P.Tillekeratne	b Giles	12
U.D.U.Chandana	c Vaughan b Kirtley	76
W.P.U.C.J.Vaas	run out	9
M.Muralitharan	not out	21
C.R.D.Fernando	not out	1
M.S.Atapattu		
Extras	(B 7, LB 16, W 5, NB 6)	34
Total	(8 wickets declared)	**628**

SRI LANKA	O	M	R	W		O	M	R	W
Vaas	17	5	64	3		7	2	25	1
Fernando	12	3	55	1		12	4	27	3
Samaraweera	4	1	11	0					
Chandana	26	7	82	2	(3)	13	7	18	0
Muralitharan	40	21	40	3	(4)	27	9	63	4
Jayasuriya	2	1	1	0	(5)	9	6	5	2

ENGLAND	O	M	R	W
Kirtley	31	4	131	2
Anderson	24	5	85	0
Flintoff	18	0	47	2
Giles	65	16	190	2
Batty	41	4	137	0
Vaughan	1	0	5	0
Trescothick	2	0	10	0

FALL OF WICKETS

	E	SL	E
Wkt	1st	1st	2nd
1st	78	71	0
2nd	108	138	22
3rd	114	400	44
4th	135	428	82
5th	139	456	82
6th	226	582	84
7th	236	605	84
8th	258	606	124
9th	259	–	137
10th	265	–	148

Umpires: Alim Dar (*Pakistan*) (4) and S.A.Bucknor (*West Indies*) (85).
Referee: C.H.Lloyd (*West Indies*) (30).   Test No. 1672/15 (E816/SL136)

SRI LANKA v ENGLAND 2003-04

SRI LANKA – BATTING AND FIELDING

	M	I	NO	HS	Runs	Avge	100	50	Ct/St
D.P.M.D.Jayawardena	3	5	1	134	334	83.50	1	2	7
T.M.Dilshan	2	3	–	100	246	82.00	1	2	3
T.T.Samaraweera	3	5	1	142	214	53.50	1	–	
S.T.Jayasuriya	3	5	–	85	209	41.80	–	1	3
U.D.U.Chandana	2	3	–	76	116	38.66	–	1	–
K.C.Sangakkara	3	5	–	71	165	33.00	–	1	9/4
M.Muralitharan	3	4	1	38	91	30.33	–	–	1
K.A.D.M.Fernando	2	3	1	51*	56	28.00	–	1	–
W.P.U.C.J.Vaas	3	5	1	32	102	25.50	–	–	1
H.D.P.K.Dharmasena	2	4	1	29	65	21.66	–	–	
M.S.Atapattu	3	4	–	35	83	20.75	–	–	3
H.P.Tillekeratne	3	5	–	45	78	15.60	–	–	4

Played in one Test: C.R.D.Fernando 1*.

SRI LANKA – BOWLING

	O	M	R	W	Avge	Best	5wI	10wM
M.Muralitharan	231.4	109	320	26	12.30	7-46	1	1
C.R.D.Fernando	24	7	82	4	20.50	3-27	–	–
W.P.U.C.J.Vaas	103.2	24	273	13	21.00	4-77	–	–
S.T.Jayasuriya	90	22	158	5	31.60	2- 5	–	–
H.D.P.K.Dharmasena	87	19	228	4	57.00	1-36	–	–
U.D.U.Chandana	63	18	148	2	74.00	2-82	–	–

Also bowled: T.M.Dilshan 3-1-10-0; K.A.D.M.Fernando 21-2-107-1; T.T.Samaraweera 8-3-20-0; H.P.Tillekeratne 1-0-1-0.

ENGLAND – BATTING AND FIELDING

	M	I	NO	HS	Runs	Avge	100	50	Ct/St
M.P.Vaughan	3	6	–	105	221	36.83	1	1	2
G.P.Thorpe	3	6	–	57	183	30.50	–	1	1
M.A.Butcher	3	6	–	54	175	29.16	–	2	1
M.E.Trescothick	3	6	–	70	167	27.83	–	1	6
A.Flintoff	3	6	–	77	143	23.83	–	1	–
G.J.Batty	3	6	1	38	117	23.40	–	–	–
P.D.Collingwood	2	4	–	36	89	22.25	–	–	6
A.F.Giles	3	5	1	18	74	18.50	–	–	–
C.M.W.Read	3	6	2	18*	49	12.25	–	–	5/2
N.Hussain	2	4	–	17	46	11.50	–	–	–
R.J.Kirtley	3	3	1	12	16	8.00	–	–	1

Played in one Test: J.M.Anderson 1, 1*; M.J.Hoggard 6*, 0*; R.L.Johnson 26, 3.

ENGLAND – BOWLING

	O	M	R	W	Avge	Best	5wI	10wM
A.Flintoff	97	20	221	9	24.55	3- 42	–	–
A.F.Giles	197.3	49	539	18	29.94	5-116	1	–
R.J.Kirtley	81	18	302	6	50.33	2- 62	–	–
G.J.Batty	124.2	20	396	6	66.00	3- 55	–	–

Also bowled: J.M.Anderson 24-5-85-0; P.D.Collingwood 16-3-37-0; M.J.Hoggard 29-6-82-1; R.L.Johnson 24-7-82-1; M.E.Trescothick 2-0-10-0; M.P.Vaughan 10-0-27-0.

AUSTRALIA v INDIA (1st Test)

At Woolloongabba, Brisbane, on 4, 5, 6, 7, 8 December 2003.
Toss: India. Result: **MATCH DRAWN**.
Debuts: Australia – N.W.Bracken.

AUSTRALIA

J.L.Langer	lbw b Agarkar	121	(2) c Patel b Agarkar		0
M.L.Hayden	c Laxman b Zaheer	37	(1) c Sehwag b Harbhajan		99
R.T.Ponting	c Patel b Zaheer	54	c Sehwag b Nehra		50
D.R.Martyn	run out	42	not out		66
*S.R.Waugh	hit wicket b Zaheer	0	not out		56
S.M.Katich	c Patel b Zaheer	16			
†A.C.Gilchrist	c Laxman b Zaheer	0			
A.J.Bichel	c Laxman b Agarkar	11			
J.N.Gillespie	run out	8			
N.W.Bracken	not out	6			
S.C.G.MacGill	c Chopra b Agarkar	1			
Extras	(B 4, LB 7, W 2, NB 14)	27	(B 4, NB 9)		13
Total		**323**	(3 wickets declared)		**284**

INDIA

A.Chopra	c Hayden b Gillespie	36	c Langer b Bracken		4
V.Sehwag	c Hayden b Bracken	45	c Martyn b Bracken		0
R.Dravid	c Hayden b Gillespie	1	not out		43
S.R.Tendulkar	lbw b Gillespie	0			
*S.C.Ganguly	c Gillespie b MacGill	144			
V.V.S.Laxman	c Katich b MacGill	75	(4) not out		24
†P.A.Patel	c Bichel b Gillespie	37			
A.B.Agarkar	c Hayden b Bichel	12			
Harbhajan Singh	not out	19			
Zaheer Khan	b MacGill	27			
A.Nehra	lbw b MacGill	0			
Extras	(LB 6, W 1, NB 6)	13	(NB 2)		2
Total		**409**	(2 wickets)		**73**

INDIA	O	M	R	W		O	M	R	W		FALL OF WICKETS				
Zaheer Khan	23	2	95	5		3	0	15	0			A	I	A	I
Nehra	15	4	51	0	(3)	19	1	89	1		Wkt	1st	1st	2nd	2nd
Agarkar	25.1	5	90	3	(2)	12	3	45	1		1st	73	61	6	4
Harbhajan Singh	14	1	68	0		21	1	101	1		2nd	162	62	146	4
Ganguly	1	0	8	0							3rd	268	62	156	–
Tendulkar					(5)	2	0	9	0		4th	275	127	–	–
Sehwag					(6)	5	1	21	0		5th	275	273	–	–
											6th	276	329	–	–
AUSTRALIA											7th	302	362	–	–
Gillespie	31	12	65	4		5	1	17	0		8th	310	362	–	–
Bracken	26	5	90	1		4	1	12	2		9th	317	403	–	–
Bichel	28	6	130	1	(4)	3	0	12	0		10th	323	409	–	–
MacGill	26.1	4	86	4	(3)	4	0	32	0						
Waugh	7	3	16	0											
Katich	2	0	16	0											

Umpires: S.A.Bucknor (*West Indies*) (84) and R.E.Koertzen (*South Africa*) (45).
Referee: M.J.Procter (*South Africa*) (17).　　　　**Test No. 1673/61 (A645/I368)**

AUSTRALIA v INDIA (2nd Test)

At Adelaide Oval on 12, 13, 14, 15, 16 December 2003.
Toss: Australia. Result: **INDIA** won by four wickets.
Debuts: India – I.K.Pathan.

AUSTRALIA

J.L.Langer	c Sehwag b Kumble	58	lbw b Agarkar		10
M.L.Hayden	c Patel b Pathan	12	c Sehwag b Nehra		17
R.T.Ponting	c Dravid b Kumble	242	c Chopra b Agarkar		0
D.R.Martyn	c Laxman b Nehra	30	c Dravid b Tendulkar		38
*S.R.Waugh	b Nehra	30	c Dravid b Tendulkar		42
S.M.Katich	c Sehwag b Agarkar	75	c Nehra b Agarkar		31
†A.C.Gilchrist	c Sehwag b Agarkar	29	b Kumble		43
A.J.Bichel	c Chopra b Kumble	19	b Agarkar		1
J.N.Gillespie	not out	48	c Patel b Agarkar		3
B.A.Williams	b Kumble	0	not out		4
S.C.G.MacGill	lbw b Kumble	0	b Agarkar		1
Extras	(B 1, LB 7, W 1, NB 4)	13	(B 2, LB 2, W 1, NB 1)		6
Total		**556**			**196**

INDIA

A.Chopra	c and b Bichel	27	lbw b Gillespie		20
V.Sehwag	c Hayden b Bichel	47	st Gilchrist b MacGill		47
R.Dravid	c Bichel b Gillespie	233	not out		72
S.R.Tendulkar	c Gilchrist b Bichel	1	lbw b MacGill		37
*S.C.Ganguly	run out	2	c Katich b Bichel		12
V.V.S.Laxman	c Gilchrist b Bichel	148	c Bichel b Katich		32
†P.A.Patel	c Ponting b Katich	31	b Katich		3
A.B.Agarkar	c MacGill b Katich	11	not out		0
A.Kumble	lbw b MacGill	12			
I.K.Pathan	c and b MacGill	1			
A.Nehra	not out	0			
Extras	(B 4, LB 2, W 2, NB 2)	10	(B 3, LB 6, W 1)		10
Total		**523**	(6 wickets)		**233**

INDIA	O	M	R	W		O	M	R	W
Agarkar	26	1	119	2		16.2	2	41	6
Pathan	27	3	136	1		7	0	24	0
Nehra	25	3	115	2		7	2	21	1
Kumble	43	3	154	5		17	2	58	1
Sehwag	5	0	21	0	(6)	3	0	12	0
Tendulkar	1	0	3	0	(5)	6	0	36	2

AUSTRALIA	O	M	R	W		O	M	R	W
Gillespie	40.5	13	106	1		10.2	2	22	1
Williams	23	7	72	0		14	6	34	0
Bichel	28	3	118	4	(4)	11.4	1	35	1
MacGill	44	8	143	2	(3)	24.4	3	101	2
Katich	16	3	59	2		8	1	22	2
Waugh	9	2	15	0		4	0	10	0
Ponting	1	0	4	0					

FALL OF WICKETS

	A	I	A	I
Wkt	1st	1st	2nd	2nd
1st	22	66	10	48
2nd	135	81	18	79
3rd	200	83	44	149
4th	252	85	109	170
5th	390	388	112	221
6th	426	447	183	229
7th	473	469	184	–
8th	556	510	188	–
9th	556	518	192	–
10th	556	523	196	–

Umpires: R.E.Koertzen (*South Africa*) (46) and D.R.Shepherd (*England*) (76).
Referee: M.J.Procter (*South Africa*) (18).   Test No. 1674/62 (I646/A369)

AUSTRALIA v INDIA (3rd Test)

At Melbourne Cricket Ground on 26, 27, 28, 29, 30 December 2003.
Toss: India. Result: **AUSTRALIA** won by nine wickets.
Debuts: None.

INDIA

A.Chopra	c Katich b MacGill	48		c Gilchrist b Bracken	4
V.Sehwag	c Bracken b Katich	195		c Williams b Lee	11
R.Dravid	c Martyn b Waugh	49		c Gilchrist b Lee	92
S.R.Tendulkar	c Gilchrist b Lee	0	(5)	c Gilchrist b Williams	44
*S.C.Ganguly	c Langer b Lee	37	(4)	b Bracken	73
V.V.S.Laxman	c Hayden b MacGill	19		c Hayden b MacGill	18
†P.A.Patel	c Gilchrist b Bracken	0		not out	27
A.B.Agarkar	run out	0		b Williams	1
A.Kumble	c Langer b Williams	3		lbw b Williams	0
Zaheer Khan	not out	0		c Hayden b Williams	1
A.Nehra	c Gilchrist b MacGill	0		c Hayden b MacGill	0
Extras	(LB 3, W 1, NB 11)	15		(B 4, LB 3, W 1, NB 7)	15
Total		**366**			**286**

AUSTRALIA

J.L.Langer	c Tendulkar b Agarkar	14		lbw b Agarkar	2
M.L.Hayden	lbw b Kumble	136		not out	53
R.T.Ponting	st Patel b Kumble	257		not out	31
†A.C.Gilchrist	c Nehra b Kumble	14			
D.R.Martyn	c Patel b Agarkar	31			
*S.R.Waugh	lbw b Kumble	19			
S.M.Katich	c Chopra b Kumble	29			
B.Lee	c Laxman b Kumble	8			
N.W.Bracken	c and b Tendulkar	1			
B.A.Williams	not out	10			
S.C.G.MacGill	lbw b Agarkar	0			
Extras	(B 4, LB 8, W 5, NB 17, PEN 5)	39		(B 4, LB 2, W 1, NB 4)	11
Total		**558**		(1 wicket)	**97**

AUSTRALIA	O	M	R	W		O	M	R	W		FALL OF WICKETS				
												I	A	I	A
Lee	27	7	103	2		22	3	97	2			A	I	A	A
Bracken	28	6	71	1		25	13	45	2		Wkt	1st	1st	2nd	2nd
Williams	20	6	66	1		22	5	53	4		1st	141	30	5	9
MacGill	15	3	70	3		26.5	5	68	2		2nd	278	264	19	–
Katich	4	0	18	1		4	0	16	0		3rd	286	295	126	–
Waugh	9	0	35	1							4th	311	373	160	–
											5th	350	437	253	–
INDIA											6th	353	502	258	–
Agarkar	33.2	5	115	3		7	2	25	1		7th	353	535	271	–
Zaheer Khan	25	4	103	0							8th	366	542	271	–
Nehra	29	3	90	0	(2)	6	3	16	0		9th	366	555	277	–
Kumble	51	8	176	6	(3)	6.2	0	43	0		10th	366	558	286	–
Tendulkar	13	0	57	1											
Sehwag					(4)	3	0	7	0						

Umpires: B.F.Bowden (*New Zealand*) (10) and D.R.Shepherd (*England*) (77).
Referee: M.J.Procter (*South Africa*) (19).   **Test No. 1675/63 (A647/I370)**

AUSTRALIA v INDIA (4th Test)

At Sydney Cricket Ground on 2, 3, 4, 5, 6 January 2004.
Toss: India. Result: **MATCH DRAWN**.
Debuts: None.

INDIA

A.Chopra	b Lee	45	c Martyn b Gillespie		2
V.Sehwag	c Gilchrist b Gillespie	72	c Gillespie b MacGill		47
R.Dravid	lbw b Gillespie	38	not out		91
S.R.Tendulkar	not out	241	not out		60
V.V.S.Laxman	b Gillespie	178			
*S.C.Ganguly	b Lee	16			
†P.A.Patel	c Gilchrist b Lee	62			
A.B.Agarkar	b Lee	2			
I.K.Pathan	not out	13			
A.Kumble					
M.Kartik					
Extras	(B 4, LB 5, W 4, NB 25)	38	(LB 3, W 1, NB 7)		11
Total	(7 wickets declared)	**705**	(2 wickets declared)		**211**

AUSTRALIA

J.L.Langer	c Patel b Kumble	117	c Sehwag b Kartik		47
M.L.Hayden	c Ganguly b Kumble	67	c Dravid b Kumble		30
R.T.Ponting	lbw b Kumble	25	c and b Pathan		47
D.R.Martyn	c and b Kumble	7	c sub (Yuvraj Singh) b Kumble		40
*S.R.Waugh	c Patel b Pathan	40	c Tendulkar b Kumble		80
S.M.Katich	c Sehwag b Kumble	125	not out		77
†A.C.Gilchrist	b Pathan	6	st Patel b Kumble		4
B.Lee	c Chopra b Kumble	0			
J.N.Gillespie	st Patel b Kumble	47	(8) not out		4
N.W.Bracken	c Agarkar b Kumble	2			
S.C.G.MacGill	not out	0			
Extras	(B 6, LB 9, W 3, NB 20)	38	(B 6, LB 7, W 2, NB 13)		28
Total		**474**	(6 wickets)		**357**

AUSTRALIA	O	M	R	W		O	M	R	W	FALL OF WICKETS				
											I	A	I	A
Lee	39.3	5	201	4		12.2	2	75	0	*Wkt*	*1st*	*1st*	*2nd*	*2nd*
Gillespie	45	11	135	3		7	2	32	1	1st	123	147	11	75
Bracken	37	13	97	0	(4)	8	0	36	0	2nd	128	214	73	92
MacGill	38	5	146	0	(3)	16	1	65	1	3rd	194	229	–	170
Waugh	2	0	6	0						4th	547	261	–	196
Katich	17	1	84	0						5th	570	311	–	338
Martyn	9	1	27	0						6th	671	341	–	342
INDIA										7th	678	350	–	–
Agarkar	25	3	116	0		10	2	45	0	8th	–	467	–	–
Pathan	26	3	80	2	(3)	8	1	26	1	9th	–	473	–	–
Kumble	46.5	7	141	8	(2)	42	8	138	4	10th	–	474	–	–
Kartik	19	1	122	0		26	5	89	1					
Ganguly	1	1	0	0										
Tendulkar					(5)	6	0	36	0					
Sehwag						2	0	10	0					

Umpires: B.F.Bowden (*New Zealand*) (11) and S.A.Bucknor (*West Indies*) (86).
Referee: M.J.Procter (*South Africa*) (20).   **Test No. 1676/64 (A648/I371)**

AUSTRALIA v INDIA 2003-04

AUSTRALIA – BATTING AND FIELDING

	M	I	NO	HS	Runs	Avge	100	50	Ct/St
R.T.Ponting	4	8	1	257	706	100.85	2	2	1
S.M.Katich	4	6	1	125	353	70.60	1	2	3
M.L.Hayden	4	8	1	136	451	64.42	1	3	9
J.L.Langer	4	8	–	121	369	46.12	2	1	3
S.R.Waugh	4	7	–	80	267	44.50	–	2	–
D.R.Martyn	4	7	1	66*	254	42.33	–	1	3
J.N.Gillespie	3	5	2	48*	110	36.66	–	–	2
A.C.Gilchrist	4	6	–	43	96	16.00	–	–	10/1
B.A.Williams	2	3	2	10*	14	14.00	–	–	1
A.J.Bichel	2	3	–	19	31	10.33	–	–	4
N.W.Bracken	3	3	1	6*	9	4.50	–	–	1
B.Lee	2	2	–	8	8	4.00	–	–	–
S.C.G.MacGill	4	5	1	2	2	0.50	–	–	2

AUSTRALIA – BOWLING

	O	M	R	W	Avge	Best	5wI	10wM
J.N.Gillespie	139.1	41	377	10	37.70	4- 65	–	–
S.M.Katich	51	5	215	5	43.00	2- 22	–	–
B.A.Williams	79	24	225	5	45.00	4- 53	–	–
A.J.Bichel	70.4	10	295	6	49.16	4-118	–	–
S.C.G.MacGill	194.4	29	711	14	50.78	4- 86	–	–
N.W.Bracken	128	38	351	6	58.50	2- 12	–	–
B.Lee	100.5	17	476	8	59.50	4-201	–	–

Also bowled: D.R.Martyn 9-1-27-0; R.T.Ponting 1-0-4-0; S.R.Waugh 31-5-82-1.

INDIA – BATTING AND FIELDING

	M	I	NO	HS	Runs	Avge	100	50	Ct/St
R.Dravid	4	8	3	233	619	123.80	1	3	4
V.V.S.Laxman	4	7	1	178	494	82.33	2	1	5
S.R.Tendulkar	4	7	2	241*	383	76.60	1	1	3
V.Sehwag	4	8	–	195	464	58.00	1	3	8
S.C.Ganguly	4	6	–	144	284	47.33	1	1	1
P.A.Patel	4	6	1	62	160	32.00	–	1	8/3
A.Chopra	4	8	–	48	186	23.25	–	–	5
Zaheer Khan	2	3	1	27	28	14.00	–	–	1
I.K.Pathan	2	2	1	13*	14	14.00	–	–	1
A.B.Agarkar	4	6	1	12	26	5.20	–	–	1
A.Kumble	3	3	–	12	15	5.00	–	–	1
A.Nehra	3	4	1	0*	0	0.00	–	–	2

Played in one Test: Harbhajan Singh 19*; M.Kartik did not bat.

INDIA – BOWLING

	O	M	R	W	Avge	Best	5wI	10wM
A.Kumble	206.1	27	710	24	29.58	8-141	3	1
A.B.Agarkar	154.5	23	596	16	37.25	6- 41	1	–
Zaheer Khan	51	6	213	5	42.60	5- 95	1	–
S.R.Tendulkar	28	–	141	3	47.00	2- 36	–	–
I.K.Pathan	68	7	266	4	66.50	2- 80	–	–
A.Nehra	101	16	382	4	95.50	2-115	–	–

Also bowled: S.C.Ganguly 2-1-8-0; Harbhajan Singh 35-2-169-1; M.Kartik 45-6-211-1; V.Sehwag 18-1-71-0.

SOUTH AFRICA v WEST INDIES (1st Test)

At The Wanderers, Johannesburg, on 12, 13, 14, 15, 16 December 2003.
Toss: South Africa. Result: **SOUTH AFRICA** won by 189 runs.
Debuts: None.

SOUTH AFRICA

*G.C.Smith	c Lara b Edwards	132		c sub (D.R.Smith) b Drakes	44
H.H.Gibbs	b Collymore	60		retired hurt	6
J.A.Rudolph	c Lara b Drakes	2		c Sarwan b Hinds	44
J.H.Kallis	b Dillon	158		lbw b Hinds	44
M.van Jaarsveld	lbw b Dillon	73	(6)	run out	15
N.D.McKenzie	c Jacobs b Edwards	8	(8)	not out	9
†M.V.Boucher	c Ganga b Collymore	27	(5)	st Jacobs b Sarwan	18
S.M.Pollock	c Jacobs b Hinds	30	(7)	b Collymore	10
R.J.Peterson	c Jacobs b Hinds	25		not out	18
A.Nel	b Hinds	0			
M.Ntini	not out	22			
Extras	(B 4, LB 7, W 4, NB 9)	24		(B 2, LB 3, W 6, NB 7)	18
Total		**561**		(6 wickets declared)	**226**

WEST INDIES

W.W.Hinds	c Peterson b Nel	10		b Ntini	0
D.Ganga	c Peterson b Ntini	60		lbw b Ntini	10
R.R.Sarwan	c Boucher b Pollock	21	(4)	lbw b Pollock	8
*B.C.Lara	c Van Jaarsveld b Nel	202	(5)	b Pollock	5
S.Chanderpaul	b Ntini	34	(6)	c Nel b Pollock	74
†R.D.Jacobs	c Boucher b Ntini	4	(7)	b Nel	25
V.C.Drakes	lbw b Kallis	21	(3)	b Ntini	6
M.Dillon	b Ntini	13	(9)	b Ntini	7
C.H.Gayle	c Kallis b Ntini	8	(8)	c Boucher b Nel	26
F.H.Edwards	c McKenzie b Nel	0	(11)	not out	0
C.D.Collymore	not out	0	(10)	lbw b Pollock	0
Extras	(B 12, LB 15, W 4, NB 5)	36		(B 10, LB 6, NB 11)	27
Total		**410**			**188**

WEST INDIES	O	M	R	W		O	M	R	W		FALL OF WICKETS				
												SA	WI	SA	WI
Edwards	27	3	102	2		13	0	60	0		Wkt	1st	1st	2nd	2nd
Dillon	36	7	96	2		10	0	26	0		1st	149	43	72	5
Collymore	26	2	118	2	(4)	9	3	19	1		2nd	160	94	145	18
Drakes	29	5	92	1	(3)	10	2	21	1		3rd	240	141	158	25
Ganga	4	0	26	0							4th	372	266	180	41
Sarwan	9	0	37	0	(5)	10	0	40	1		5th	398	278	188	43
Hinds	17.4	3	79	3	(6)	11	0	55	2		6th	456	314	206	141
SOUTH AFRICA											7th	510	380	–	168
Pollock	30	7	65	1		17	6	31	4		8th	520	405	–	176
Ntini	32	9	94	5		14	4	53	4		9th	520	409	–	188
Nel	32.5	11	78	3		13	3	49	2		10th	561	410	–	188
Kallis	22	6	53	1		4	0	21	0						
Peterson	13	2	76	0		3	0	18	0						
Smith	4	0	17	0											

Umpires: D.B.Hair (*Australia*) (50) and S.J.A.Taufel (*Australia*) (10).
Referee: R.S.Madugalle (*Sri Lanka*) (55).   **Test No. 1677/12 (SA282/WI402)**

SOUTH AFRICA v WEST INDIES (2nd Test)

At Kingsmead, Durban, on 26, 27, 28, 29 December 2003.
Toss: South Africa. Result: **SOUTH AFRICA** won by an innings and 65 runs.
Debuts: None.

WEST INDIES

W.W.Hinds	c Boucher b Pollock	0		b Nel	11
D.Ganga	c Pollock b Ntini	6		lbw b Pollock	12
R.R.Sarwan	c Kallis b Pollock	4		b Ntini	114
*B.C.Lara	c Pollock b Ntini	72		c McKenzie b Hall	11
S.Chanderpaul	c Hall b Ntini	0	(7)	c McKenzie b Ntini	109
C.S.Baugh	c Kallis b Nel	21	(5)	c Ntini b Kallis	2
†R.D.Jacobs	lbw b Nel	58	(6)	c Kirsten b Rudolph	15
V.C.Drakes	c Boucher b Nel	67		c Rudolph b Nel	4
M.Dillon	b Ntini	6		c Gibbs b Nel	0
A.Sanford	c Hall b Ntini	15		not out	18
F.H.Edwards	not out	1		c Boucher b Ntini	5
Extras	(LB 6, NB 8)	14		(LB 16, W 1, NB 11)	28
Total		**264**			**329**

SOUTH AFRICA

*G.C.Smith	c Sarwan b Edwards	14
H.H.Gibbs	b Sanford	142
J.A.Rudolph	c Ganga b Sanford	36
J.H.Kallis	c Sarwan b Dillon	177
G.Kirsten	c Drakes b Sarwan	137
N.D.McKenzie	c Jacobs b Drakes	32
†M.V.Boucher	lbw b Drakes	12
S.M.Pollock	not out	38
A.J.Hall	c sub (D.R.Smith) b Sarwan	32
M.Ntini	c Lara b Sanford	0
A.Nel		
Extras	(LB 9, W 6, NB 23)	38
Total	(9 wickets declared)	**658**

SOUTH AFRICA	O	M	R	W		O	M	R	W
Pollock	23	3	59	2		22	9	42	1
Ntini	25.5	8	66	5		26	8	72	3
Hall	10	2	51	0	(4)	13	3	20	1
Nel	13	4	43	3	(3)	18	3	68	3
Kallis	4	0	30	0		11	3	20	1
Rudolph	2	0	9	0		23	3	91	1

WEST INDIES	O	M	R	W
Dillon	33	5	111	1
Edwards	25	1	115	1
Sanford	38.2	4	170	3
Sarwan	21	2	65	2
Drakes	30	3	113	2
Hinds	13	2	50	0
Ganga	6	1	25	0

FALL OF WICKETS

	WI	SA	WI
Wkt	1st	1st	2nd
1st	0	38	31
2nd	4	99	32
3rd	15	267	78
4th	17	516	95
5th	50	562	130
6th	148	572	243
7th	172	599	271
8th	191	649	271
9th	261	658	317
10th	264	–	329

Umpires: D.B.Hair (*Australia*) (51) and S.J.A.Taufel (*Australia*) (11).
Referee: R.S.Madugalle (*Sri Lanka*) (56).   **Test No. 1678/13 (SA283/WI403)**

SOUTH AFRICA v WEST INDIES (3rd Test)

At Newlands, Cape Town, on 2, 3, 4, 5, 6 January 2004.
Toss: South Africa. Result: **MATCH DRAWN**.
Debuts: West Indies – D.Mohammed, D.R.Smith.

SOUTH AFRICA

*G.C.Smith	c Lara b Sanford	42	b Edwards		24
H.H.Gibbs	c Jacobs b Sanford	33	c Gayle b Sarwan		142
J.A.Rudolph	lbw b Mohammed	101	c Jacobs b Drakes		0
J.H.Kallis	lbw b Sanford	73	not out		130
G.Kirsten	c Sanford b Edwards	16	not out		10
N.D.McKenzie	b Mohammed	76			
P.R.Adams	b Edwards	0			
†M.V.Boucher	not out	122			
S.M.Pollock	c Jacobs b Edwards	9			
M.Ntini	c Jacobs b Mohammed	18			
A.Nel	c Jacobs b Sanford	4			
Extras	(B 6, LB 12, W 2, NB 18)	38	(B 3, LB 7, W 8, NB 11)		29
Total		**532**	(3 wickets declared)		**335**

WEST INDIES

C.H.Gayle	lbw b Pollock	116	c Gibbs b Ntini		32
D.Ganga	b Nel	17	c Boucher b Ntini		10
R.R.Sarwan	c McKenzie b Nel	44	c Gibbs b Ntini		69
*B.C.Lara	b Nel	115	c Boucher b Nel		86
W.W.Hinds	c Boucher b Kallis	13	b Pollock		25
D.R.Smith	c Kallis b Nel	20	not out		105
†R.D.Jacobs	c Pollock b Ntini	23	not out		9
V.C.Drakes	c Boucher b Nel	20			
D.Mohammed	c Kallis b Pollock	36			
A.Sanford	run out	0			
F.H.Edwards	not out	0			
Extras	(B 6, LB 7, NB 10)	23	(B 2, LB 7, W 2, NB 7)		18
Total		**427**	(5 wickets)		**354**

WEST INDIES	O	M	R	W		O	M	R	W
Drakes	26	7	64	0	(4)	20	0	68	1
Edwards	30	3	132	3	(1)	14	0	86	1
Sanford	37	4	132	4	(2)	8	1	38	0
Smith	2	0	4	0					
Mohammed	33	5	112	3		6	0	30	0
Gayle	10	0	39	0	(3)	9	3	34	0
Hinds	7	2	31	0					
Sarwan					(6)	19	1	69	1

SOUTH AFRICA	O	M	R	W		O	M	R	W
Pollock	24	6	88	2		17	3	64	1
Ntini	20	1	105	1		21	4	82	3
Nel	28.1	8	87	5		21	5	57	1
Kallis	21	8	64	1		16	3	38	0
Adams	19	1	70	0		22	3	103	0
Rudolph						1	1	0	0
Kirsten						2	1	0	0

FALL OF WICKETS

	SA	WI	SA	WI
Wkt	1st	1st	2nd	2nd
1st	70	126	48	28
2nd	90	183	50	47
3rd	162	187	301	203
4th	304	224	—	224
5th	305	252	—	296
6th	305	306	—	—
7th	315	361	—	—
8th	461	409	—	—
9th	513	426	—	—
10th	532	427	—	—

Umpires: D.J.Harper (*Australia*) (37) and S.Venkataraghavan (*India*) (72).
Referee: R.S.Madugalle (*Sri Lanka*) (57).   **Test No. 1679/14 (SA284/WI404)**

SOUTH AFRICA v WEST INDIES (4th Test)

At Centurion Park, (Verwoerdburg), Pretoria, on 16, 17, 18, 19, 20 January 2004.
Toss: West Indies. Result: **SOUTH AFRICA** won by ten wickets.
Debuts: None.

SOUTH AFRICA

*G.C.Smith	c Jacobs b Collymore	139	not out	23
H.H.Gibbs	c Ganga b Sarwan	192	not out	8
J.A.Rudolph	b Edwards	37		
J.H.Kallis	not out	130		
G.Kirsten	c and b Sarwan	10		
N.D.McKenzie	c Lara b Dillon	40		
†M.V.Boucher	c Edwards b Smith	13		
S.M.Pollock	not out	1		
A.J.Hall				
M.Ntini				
A.Nel				
Extras	(B 1, LB 17, W 12, NB 12)	42	(B 4, W 10, NB 1)	15
Total	(6 wickets declared)	**604**	(0 wickets)	**46**

WEST INDIES

C.H.Gayle	c McKenzie b Ntini	77	c McKenzie b Ntini	107
D.Ganga	c Kallis b Ntini	7	b Ntini	0
R.R.Sarwan	b Ntini	13	lbw b Pollock	119
*B.C.Lara	c Boucher b Nel	34	lbw b Nel	6
S.Chanderpaul	c Pollock b Nel	42	c Gibbs b Kallis	27
D.R.Smith	c Boucher b Kallis	39	b Ntini	0
†R.D.Jacobs	c Boucher b Nel	8	lbw b Pollock	3
V.C.Drakes	b Ntini	35	c Gibbs b Pollock	4
M.Dillon	b Ntini	30	c Smith b Pollock	29
C.D.Collymore	b Pollock	4	not out	13
F.H.Edwards	not out	0	b Nel	10
Extras	(LB 7, NB 5)	12	(B 4, LB 11, W 7, NB 8)	30
Total		**301**		**348**

WEST INDIES	O	M	R	W	O	M	R	W
Dillon	31	5	109	1	2	0	17	0
Edwards	24	2	128	1	1.4	0	25	0
Drakes	33	5	101	0				
Collymore	26	5	91	1				
Gayle	7	0	39	0				
Sarwan	14	0	55	2				
Smith	13	1	42	1				
Ganga	10	0	21	0				

SOUTH AFRICA	O	M	R	W		O	M	R	W
Pollock	16.2	6	46	1		32	10	69	4
Ntini	20	7	49	5		28	4	99	3
Nel	18	6	64	3		15.4	2	64	2
Hall	11	0	65	0	(5)	0.2	0	4	0
Kallis	12	4	46	1	(4)	16	4	49	1
Smith	3	1	7	0		8.4	1	24	0
Rudolph	2	0	17	0		6	0	24	0

FALL OF WICKETS

	SA	WI	WI	SA
Wkt	1st	1st	2nd	2nd
1st	301	22	18	—
2nd	373	37	32	—
3rd	422	139	99	—
4th	446	142	273	—
5th	532	195	277	—
6th	567	224	278	—
7th	—	241	284	—
8th	—	280	309	—
9th	—	301	322	—
10th	—	301	348	—

Umpires: D.R.Shepherd (*England*) (78) and S.Venkataraghavan (*India*) (73).
Referee: R.S.Madugalle (*Sri Lanka*) (58).   **Test No. 1680/15 (SA285/WI405)**

SOUTH AFRICA v WEST INDIES 2003-04

SOUTH AFRICA – BATTING AND FIELDING

	M	I	NO	HS	Runs	Avge	100	50	Ct/St
J.H.Kallis	4	6	2	177	712	178.00	4	1	6
H.H.Gibbs	4	7	2	192	583	116.60	3	1	5
G.C.Smith	4	7	1	139	418	69.66	2	–	1
G.Kirsten	3	4	1	137	173	57.66	1	–	1
M.V.Boucher	4	5	1	122*	192	48.00	1	–	13
N.D.McKenzie	4	5	1	76	165	41.25	–	1	6
J.A.Rudolph	4	5	–	101	220	36.66	1	–	1
A.J.Hall	2	1	–	32	32	32.00	–	–	2
S.M.Pollock	4	5	2	38*	88	29.33	–	–	4
M.Ntini	4	3	1	22*	40	20.00	–	–	1
A.Nel	4	2	–	4	4	2.00	–	–	1

Played in one Test: P.R.Adams 0; R.J.Peterson 25, 18* (2 ct); M.van Jaarsveld 73, 15 (1 ct).

SOUTH AFRICA – BOWLING

	O	M	R	W	Avge	Best	5wI	10wM
M.Ntini	186.5	45	620	29	21.37	5-49	3	–
A.Nel	159.4	42	510	22	23.18	5-87	1	–
S.M.Pollock	181.2	50	464	16	29.00	4-31	–	–
J.H.Kallis	106	28	321	5	64.20	1-20	–	–

Also bowled: P.R.Adams 41-4-173.0; A.J.Hall 34.2-5-140-1; G.Kirsten 2-1-1-0; R.J.Peterson 16.0-2-94-0; J.A.Rudolph 34-4-141-1; G.C.Smith 15.4-2-48-0.

WEST INDIES – BATTING AND FIELDING

	M	I	NO	HS	Runs	Avge	100	50	Ct/St
B.C.Lara	4	8	–	202	531	66.37	2	2	5
C.H.Gayle	3	6	–	116	366	61.00	2	1	1
D.R.Smith	2	4	1	105*	164	54.66	1	–	–
R.R.Sarwan	4	8	–	119	392	49.00	2	1	4
S.Chanderpaul	3	6	–	109	286	47.66	1	1	–
V.C.Drakes	4	7	–	67	157	22.42	–	1	1
R.D.Jacobs	4	8	1	58	145	20.71	–	1	10/1
A.Sanford	2	3	1	18*	33	16.50	–	–	1
D.Ganga	4	8	–	60	122	15.25	–	1	3
M.Dillon	3	6	–	30	85	14.16	–	–	–
W.W.Hinds	3	6	–	25	59	9.83	–	–	–
C.D.Collymore	2	4	2	13*	18	9.00	–	–	–
F.H.Edwards	4	7	4	10	16	5.33	–	–	1

Played in one Test: C.S.Baugh 21, 2; D.Mohammed 36.

WEST INDIES – BOWLING

	O	M	R	W	Avge	Best	5wI	10wM
W.W.Hinds	48.4	7	215	5	43.00	3- 79	–	–
R.R.Sarwan	73	3	266	6	44.33	2- 55	–	–
D.Mohammed	39	5	142	3	47.33	3-112	–	–
A.Sanford	83.2	9	340	7	48.57	4-132	–	–
C.D.Collymore	61	10	228	4	57.00	2-118	–	–
F.H.Edwards	134.4	9	648	8	81.00	3-132	–	–
M.Dillon	112	17	359	4	89.75	2- 96	–	–
V.C.Drakes	148	22	459	5	91.80	2-113	–	–

Also bowled: D.Ganga 20-1-72-0; C.H.Gayle 26-3-112-0; D.R.Smith 15-1-46-1.

NEW ZEALAND v PAKISTAN (1st Test)

At Seddon Park, Hamilton, on 19, 20, 21, 22, 23 December.
Toss: Pakistan. Result: **MATCH DRAWN**.
Debuts: None.

NEW ZEALAND

M.H.Richardson	run out	44	c Moin b Gul		15
L.Vincent	c Inzamam b Shabbir	8	c Farhat b Sami		4
*S.P.Fleming	lbw b Gul	192	c Moin b Sami		0
S.B.Styris	c Taufiq b Kaneria	33	c Taufiq b Sami		20
C.D.McMillan	c Taufiq b Kaneria	22	run out		2
C.L.Cairns	c Moin b Shabbir	11	b Gul		0
J.D.P.Oram	b Shabbir	6	not out		23
†R.G.Hart	c Youhana b Shabbir	10	b Sami		0
D.L.Vettori	not out	137	c Taufiq b Sami		20
D.R.Tuffey	b Gul	35	not out		1
I.G.Butler	c Farhat b Shabbir	7			
Extras	(B 4, LB 12, W 9, NB 33)	58	(LB 4, W 1, NB 6)		11
Total		**563**	(8 wickets)		**96**

PAKISTAN

Imran Farhat	c Hart b Oram	20
Taufiq Umar	c Butler b Tuffey	27
Yasir Hamid	lbw b Tuffey	80
Yousuf Youhana	c Vincent b Tuffey	28
*Inzamam-ul-Haq	lbw b Tuffey	51
Abdul Razzaq	c Hart b Tuffey	48
†Moin Khan	lbw b Oram	137
Mohammad Sami	c Hart b Vettori	25
Shabbir Ahmed	c Hart b Butler	8
Umar Gul	c Vettori b Butler	3
Danish Kaneria	not out	0
Extras	(LB 4, W 11, NB 21)	36
Total		**463**

PAKISTAN	O	M	R	W		O	M	R	W
Mohammad Sami	27	2	126	0		16	4	44	5
Shabbir Ahmed	43.2	9	117	5		10	7	10	0
Umar Gul	31	5	118	2		8.1	2	25	2
Abdul Razzaq	18	2	74	0	(5)	3	1	7	0
Danish Kaneria	32	6	112	2	(4)	4	2	6	0

NEW ZEALAND	O	M	R	W
Tuffey	33	8	87	5
Butler	23.4	6	113	2
Oram	23	7	55	2
Cairns	17	0	60	0
Vettori	36	3	117	1
Styris	12	4	27	0

FALL OF WICKETS

	NZ	P	NZ
Wkt	1st	1st	2nd
1st	16	47	13
2nd	117	55	13
3rd	217	134	42
4th	249	209	42
5th	266	256	42
6th	274	285	47
7th	314	437	52
8th	439	453	95
9th	538	462	–
10th	563	463	–

Umpires: S.J.Davis (*Australia*) (6) and D.L.Orchard (*South Africa*) (34).
Referee: B.C.Broad (*England*) (1).   **Test No. 1681/44 (NZ306/P298)**

NEW ZEALAND v PAKISTAN (2nd Test)

At Basin Reserve, Wellington, on 26, 27, 28, 29, 30 December.
Toss: New Zealand. Result: **PAKISTAN** won by seven wickets.
Debuts: New Zealand – R.A.Jones.

NEW ZEALAND

M.H.Richardson	c Youhana b Shabbir	82		c Moin b Shoaib	41
L.Vincent	b Shoaib	0		lbw b Shoaib	4
*S.P.Fleming	lbw b Shoaib	0		lbw b Kaneria	24
R.A.Jones	b Razzak	16		c Moin b Shoaib	7
S.B.Styris	c Moin b Shoaib	36	(6)	b Shoaib	0
C.D.McMillan	lbw b Shabbir	26	(7)	not out	3
†R.G.Hart	c Farhat b Shoaib	19	(10)	b Shoaib	0
J.D.P.Oram	c Moin b Shabbir	97		lbw b Shabbir	3
D.L.Vettori	c Yasir b Sami	44		lbw b Shabbir	0
D.R.Tuffey	not out	9	(5)	run out	13
I.G.Butler	c Moin b Shoaib	4		b Shoaib	0
Extras	(B 5, LB 14, W 3, NB 11)	33		(LB 4, W 1, NB 3)	8
Total		**366**			**103**

PAKISTAN

Imran Farhat	c Hart b Oram	20		c Hart b Oram	14
Taufiq Umar	c Oram b Tuffey	16		lbw b Vettori	34
Yasir Hamid	b Butler	3		c Hart b Butler	59
Yousuf Youhana	c Fleming b Vettori	60		not out	88
*Inzamam-ul-Haq	lbw b Oram	34		not out	72
Abdul Razzaq	b Butler	26			
†Moin Khan	c Vettori b Butler	19			
Mohammad Sami	c Hart b Butler	4			
Shoaib Akhtar	b Butler	0			
Shabbir Ahmed	not out	0			
Danish Kaneria	lbw b Butler	0			
Extras	(B 4, LB 3, W 1, NB 6)	14		(B 4, LB 2, NB 4)	10
Total		**196**		(3 wickets)	**277**

PAKISTAN	O	M	R	W	O	M	R	W		FALL OF WICKETS			
											NZ	P	NZ	P
Shoaib Akhtar	20.3	5	48	5	18	3	30	6		*Wkt*	*1st*	*1st*	*2nd*	*2nd*
Mohammad Sami	30	12	64	1	(3)	4	12	0		1st	1	27	8	37
Shabbir Ahmed	37	8	87	3	(2) 17	5	20	2		2nd	1	30	43	75
Danish Kaneria	32	5	86	0	9	2	18	1		3rd	41	60	73	156
Abdul Razzaq	23	6	62	1	5	1	19	0		4th	94	112	95	–
										5th	145	168	95	–
NEW ZEALAND										6th	171	171	96	–
Tuffey	24	9	46	1	14	5	41	0		7th	247	194	101	–
Butler	20	6	46	6	18.5	1	100	1		8th	327	195	102	–
Oram	22	5	49	2	9	1	34	1		9th	361	196	103	–
Vettori	22	6	47	1	(5) 23	5	59	1		10th	366	196	103	–
Styris	2	1	1	0	(4) 6	1	26	0						
McMillan					4	0	11	0						

Umpires: E.A.R.de Silva (*Sri Lanka*) (28) and D.L.Orchard (*South Africa*) (40).
Referee: B.C.Broad (*England*) (2).   Test No. 1682/45 (NZ307/P299)

TEST MATCH CHAMPIONSHIP SCHEDULE

2004	Mar	West Indies host England
		Pakistan host India
	Apr	Zimbabwe host Sri Lanka
	May	England host New Zealand
		West Indies host Bangladesh
		Zimbabwe host Australia
	Jun	Australia host Sri Lanka
	Jul	England host West Indies
	Aug	Sri Lanka host South Africa
	Oct	Pakistan host Zimbabwe
		Bangladesh host New Zealand
		India host Australia
	Nov	India host South Africa
		Zimbabwe host England (tbc)
		Bangladesh host Sri Lanka
	Dec	Australia host West Indies
		Australia host Pakistan
		New Zealand host Sri Lanka
		South Africa host England
2005	Feb	New Zealand host Australia
		South Africa host Zimbabwe
	Mar	Pakistan host Sri Lanka
		West Indies host South Africa
	Apr	India host Bangladesh
	May	England host Bangladesh
		West Indies host Pakistan
	Jun	England host Australia
	Jul	Sri Lanka host West Indies
	Sep	Super Test Series in South Africa
		Zimbabwe host New Zealand
	Oct	Australia host West Indies
		South Africa host New Zealand
		Zimbabwe host India
	Nov	India host Sri Lanka
		Pakistan host England
	Dec	Australia host South Africa
		New Zealand host Zimbabwe
2006	Jan	Australia host Sri Lanka
		India host Pakistan
	Feb	New Zealand host West Indies
		India host England
		South Africa host Australia
		Sri Lanka host Bangladesh
	Mar	Sri Lanka host Pakistan
	Apr	West Indies host Zimbabwe
		Bangladesh host Australia
	May	England host Sri Lanka
		West Indies host India
	Jun	England host Pakistan
	Jul	England host Sri Lanka
	Aug	Zimbabwe host South Africa
	Sep	Zimbabwe host Australia
	Oct	Australia host New Zealand
		Pakistan host Zimbabwe
		Bangladesh host India
		Sri Lanka host South Africa
	Nov	Australia host England
	Dec	Pakistan host West Indies
		South Africa host India
		New Zealand v Bangladesh
2007	Jan	Australia host New Zealand
	Feb	Bangladesh host England
		New Zealand host India
		South Africa host Pakistan
		Sri Lanka host Zimbabwe
		West Indies host Australia
	Apr	*World Cup in West Indies*
	Jun	England host India
	Aug	Sri Lanka host New Zealand
	Sep	Zimbabwe host Pakistan
	Oct	India host Zimbabwe
		Bangladesh host New Zealand
		Pakistan host South Africa
		Sri Lanka host England
	Nov	Australia host Sri Lanka
	Dec	Australia host India
		New Zealand host Sri Lanka
		South Africa host West Indies
		Zimbabwe host Bangladesh
2008	Feb	India host West Indies
		New Zealand host England
		Bangladesh host Sri Lanka
		Pakistan host Australia
		South Africa host Zimbabwe
	Mar	Bangladesh host South Africa
	Apr	West Indies host New Zealand
	May	England host Zimbabwe
		West Indies host Sri Lanka
	Jun	England host South Africa
	Jul	Sri Lanka host India
	Sep	Sri Lanka host Australia
		Zimbabwe host West Indies
	Oct	India host South Africa
		Pakistan host New Zealand
	Nov	Australia host Pakistan
		West Indies host Bangladesh
	Dec	Australia host West Indies
		New Zealand host Pakistan
		South Africa host England
		Zimbabwe host Sri Lanka
2009	Jan	South Africa host India
		Bangladesh host Zimbabwe
		Australia host Pakistan
	Feb	New Zealand host Australia
		West Indies host England
	Mar	Pakistan host India
	Apr	West Indies host Zimbabwe
		South Africa host Bangladesh
	May	England host New Zealand
	Jun	England host Australia
	Jul	Sri Lanka host West Indies
	Sep	Pakistan host Bangladesh
	Oct	India host New Zealand
		South Africa host Sri Lanka
		Zimbabwe host England
		Bangladesh host West Indies
	Nov	Australia host Zimbabwe
		Pakistan host England
	Dec	Australia host South Africa
		India host Sri Lanka
		New Zealand host West Indies

SECOND XI FIXTURES 2004

No symbol	Second XI Championship	3 days
*	Second XI Championship	4 days
†	Second XI Trophy	1 day

APRIL

28-30	Northampton	Northants v Lancs

MAY

4-6	Chesterfield	Derbys v Yorks
	Manchester (OT)	Lancs v Warwicks
5-7	Cardiff	Glam v Glos
11-13	Southampton	Hants v Surrey
12-14	Chester-le-St	Durham v Yorks
	Panteg	Glam v Notts
	Kenilworth Wardens	Warwicks v Northants
	Belper Meadows	Derbys v Leics
18-20	Cheam	Surrey v Durham
	Leicester	Leics v Warwicks
19-21	Nottingham (Boots)	Notts v Northants
	Taunton	Somerset v Glam
24	Southampton	†Hants v Glam
25-27	Bristol	Glos v Lancs
	Knowle & Dorridge	Warwicks v Notts
26-28	Northampton	Northants v Surrey
	Southampton	Hants v Sussex

JUNE

1-3	Hove	Sussex v Surrey
1-4	Liverpool	*Lancs v Durham
2-4	Hinckley	Leics v Notts
	Cheltenham C	Glos v Warwicks
4	Taunton	†Somerset v Hants
7	Bristol (WI)	†Glos v Hants
8	Kidderminster	†Worcs v Glam
9-11	Southgate	Middx v Essex
	Milton Keynes	Northants v Leics
	Hastings	Sussex v Warwicks
9	Lydney	†Glos v Glam
11	Cheltenham CC	†Glos v Worcs
15-17	Crosby	Lancs v Surrey
	Hatherley & Reddings	Glos v Hants
16-18	Notts Unity	Notts v Derbys
17	Neath	†Glam v Worcs
21	Northampton	†Northants v Leics
22	Sunderland	†Durham v Notts
	Cheadle Hulme	†Lancs v Yorks
	Horsham	†Sussex v Surrey
23-25	Hove	Sussex v Hants
23	Sunderland	†Durham v Yorks
	Luton	†Minor C v Leics
	Gowerton	†Glam v Somerset

	Canterbury	†Kent v MCC YC
24	Pudsey Congs CC	†Yorks v Lancs
	Denby	†Derbys v Notts
	Hinckley	†Leics v Minor C
	Northampton	†Northants v Middx
25	Wellbeck	†Notts v Derbys
	Seaton Carew	†Durham v Lancs
	The Oval	†Surrey v MCC YC
28	Farnsfield CC (tbc)	†Notts v Lancs
	Derby	†Derbys v Yorks
	Hinckley	†Leics v Middx
	Coventry/N Wwk	†Warwicks v Northants
	Southampton	†Hants v Glos
	Shenley	†MCC YC v Surrey
	Wickford	†Essex v Kent
29	Notts Unity (tbc)	†Notts v Yorks
	The Oval	†Surrey v Kent
30	Nelson CC	†Lancs v Derbys
	Milton Keynes	†Minor C v Middx
	Southampton	†Hants v Somerset

JULY

1	Glossop	†Derbys v Lancs
	Nottingham (Boots)	†Notts v Durham
	Dorridge	†Warwicks v Leics
	Milton Keynes	†Minor C v Northants
	Banstead	†Surrey v Essex
	Shenley	†MCC YC v Sussex
2	Winchmore Hill	†Middx v Northants
	Southampton	†Hants v Worcs
	Taunton	†Somerset v Glos
5	Bradford & Bingley	†Yorks v Notts
	Barnt Green	†Worcs v Hants
	Banstead	†Surrey v Sussex
6	tba	†Lancs v Notts
	York	†Yorks v Durham
	Ealing	†Middx v Minor C
	Hinckley	†Leics v Warwicks
	Usk	†Glam v Hants
	Old Hill	†Worcs v Glos
	Canterbury	†Kent v Surrey
	Bishop's Stortford	†Essex v Sussex
7	Sandiacre CC	†Derbys v Durham
	Harborne	†Warwicks v Minor C
8	Bristol (WI)	†Glos v Somerset
	Chelmsford	†Essex v MCC YC
	Canterbury	†Kent v Sussex

9	Middleton CC	†Lancs v Durham	4-6	Worcester	Worcs v Derbys
	Oakham School	†Leics v Northants		Worksop CC	Notts v Kent
	Canterbury	†Kent v Essex		Bristol	Glos v Essex
12-14	Nottingham (Boots)	Notts v Surrey		Leeds	Yorks v Leics
12	Norton	†Durham v Derbys		Taunton	Somerset v Sussex
	Northampton	†Northants v Warwicks		Sutton	Surrey v Middx
	Hastings	†Sussex v MCC YC	9 (10)	tba	†Trophy Semi-Finals
13	Castleford	†Yorks v Derbys	11-13	Dunstall CC	Derbys v Durham
14-16	S Northumberland	Durham v Lancs		North Perrott	Somerset v Glos
14	Northampton	†Northants v Minor C		Blackpool	Lancs v Yorks
	W Brom Dartmouth	†Warwicks v Middx		Guildford	Surrey v Hants
	Ombersley	†Worcs v Somerset		Canterbury	Kent v Warwicks
	High Wycombe	†MCC YC v Essex	16-18	Denby	Derbys v Notts
	Eastbourne	†Sussex v Kent		Stamford Bridge	Yorks v Durham
15	Luton	Minor C v Warwicks	17-19	Chelmsford	Essex v Lancs
	Ammanford	†Glam v Glos		Barnt Green	Worcs v Glam
	Uxbridge (Vine L)	†MCC YC v Kent		Hinckley	Leics v Yorks
16	Richmond	†Middx v Leics		Basingstoke	Hants v Kent
	Millfield S	†Somerset v Worcs	18-20	Stirlands CC	Sussex v Glos
	Eastbourne	†Sussex v Essex		Stratford-u-Avon	Warwicks v Somerset
20-22	Coggleshall	Essex v Hants		Uxbridge (Vine L)	Middx v Northants
	Oakham S	Leics v Derbys	23-25	Nottingham (Boots)	Notts v Durham
	Maidstone	Kent v Sussex		Bristol	Glos v Worcs
	Lytham (tbc)	Lancs v Notts	24-26	Leeds	Yorks v Derbys
20	Uxbridge	†Middx v Warwicks	25-27	Hastings	Sussex v Middx
21-23	Northampton	Northants v Yorks		Billericay	Essex v Surrey
	Uxbridge	Middx v Warwicks		Hinckley	Leics v Northants
21	Taunton	†Somerset v Glam	31-Sep 2	Purley	Surrey v Yorks
23	Coggleshall	†Essex v Surrey		Bournemouth (SC)	Hants v Middx
26-28	Hartlepool	Durham v Leics	31-Sep 3	Moseley	*Warwicks v Worcs
27-30	Worksop C	*Notts v Lancs	**SEPTEMBER**		
	Bristol	*Glos v Warwicks	1-3	Halstead	Essex v Kent
28-30	Beckenham	Kent v Surrey		Northampton	Northants v Glam
	Kidderminster	Worcs v Somerset		Derby	Derbys v Lancs
	Billericay	Essex v Middx	6 (7)	tba	†Trophy Final
AUGUST			8-10	Hove	Sussex v Essex
2-4	Darlington	Durham v Northants		Manchester (OT)	Lancs v Worcs
3-5	Cardiff	Glam v Hants		Nottingham (Boots)	Notts v Leics
3-6	Walmley	*Warwicks v Lancs		Northampton	Northants v Somerset

MINOR COUNTIES CHAMPIONSHIP
FIXTURES 2004

3-day matches. † Noon start (1st day)

	Venue	Div	Match
MAY			
23-25	†Dunstable	E	Beds v Staffs
	Falkland CC	W	Berks v Cheshire
	†Colwall	W	Herefords v Wilts
	Jesmond	E	Northumb v Cambs
24-26	Netherfield	E	Cumb v Suffolk
	Bridgnorth	W	Salop v Cornwall
30-Jun 1	Bovey Tracey	W	Devon v Oxon
	†Bournemouth (DP)	W	Dorset v Wales MC
	†Hertford	E	Herts v Bucks
JUNE			
13-15	Finchampstead	W	Berks v Dorset
	†Gerrards Cross	E	Bucks v Cumb
	Oxton	W	Cheshire v Devon
	†Sleaford	E	Lincs v Beds
	Challow & Childrey	W	Oxon v Salop
	Longton	E	Staffs v Norfolk
	Bury St Edmunds	E	Suffolk v Northumb
	†Swansea	W	Wales MC v Herefords
	Trowbridge	W	Wilts v Cornwall
27-29	Truro	W	Cornwall v Oxon
	†Barrow	E	Cumb v Cambs
	Bournemouth (DP)	W	Dorset v Cheshire
	Kington	W	Herefords v Devon
	Long Marston	E	Herts v Lincs
	†Jesmond	E	Northumb v Beds
	Ipswich (Ransomes)	E	Suffolk v Staffs
	†South Wilts	W	Wilts v Wales MC
JULY			
11-13	Bedford S	E	Beds v Herts
	†Beaconsfield.	E	Bucks v Northumb
	March	E	Cambs v Norfolk
	Alderley Edge	W	Cheshire v Wilts
	Camborne	W	Cornwall v Berks

	Venue	Div	Match
	Grantham	E	Lincs v Suffolk
	Bicester	W	Oxon v Herefords
	Whitchurch	W	Salop v Dorset
	Stone	E	Staffs v Cumb
	†Pontypridd	W	Wales MC v Devon
28-30	†March	E	Cambs v Herts
	Norwich (MP)	E	Norfolk v Bucks
AUGUST			
1-3	†Bishop's Stortford	E	Herts v Staffs
	Norwich (MP)	E	Norfolk v Lincs
	Shifnal	W	Salop v Berks
8-10	†Luton T & Ind CC	E	Beds v Bucks
	†Reading	W	Berks v Wales MC
	Exmouth	W	Devon v Cornwall
	Bournemouth (DP)	W	Dorset v Herefords
	Cleethorpes	E	Lincs v Cumb
	Norwich (MP)	E	Norfolk v Northumb
	Banbury	W	Oxon v Cheshire
	Mildenhall	E	Suffolk v Cambs
	Corsham	W	Wilts v Salop
22-24	Marlow	W	Bucks v Suffolk
	†March	E	Cambs v Beds
	†Chester (BH)	W	Cheshire v Salop
	St Austell	W	Cornwall v Dorset
	†Carlisle	E	Cumb v Norfolk
	†Exmouth	W	Devon v Wilts
	Kingsland	W	Herefords v Berks
	Jesmond	E	Northumb v Herts
	Leek	E	Staffs v Lincs
	†Abergavenny	W	Wales MC v Oxon
SEPTEMBER			
12-14	(tba – W Div)		**CHAMPIONSHIP FINAL**

MCCA KNOCK-OUT TROPHY FIXTURES 2004

† Noon start

FIRST ROUND – JUNE 6

1	†Colwall	Herefords v Salop
2	Copdock	Suffolk v Bucks
3	†Banbury	Oxon v Wales MC
4	Jesmond	Northumb v Lincs

SECOND ROUND – JUNE 20

5	Brockhampton/Oswestry	Winner # 1 v Wilts
6	March	Cambs v Cumb
7	Bournemouth (DP)	Dorset v Norfolk
8	Cheadle Hulme	Cheshire v Berks
9	Harpenden	Herts v Winner # 3
10	Porthill Park	Staffs v Winner # 4
11	Luton Town & Indians CC	Beds v Cornwall
12	Torquay	Devon v Winner # 2

QUARTER-FINALS – JULY 4

13	Welwyn Garden City/(tba)	Winner # 9 v Winner # 8
14	Torquay/(tba)	Winner # 12 v Winner # 11
15	Leek/(tba)	Winner # 10 v Winner # 6
16	Bournemouth (DP)/ Norwich (MP)	Winner # 7 v Winner # 5

SEMI-FINALS – AUGUST 15 (Reserve AUGUST 16)

17	(tba)	Winner # 13 v Winner # 14
18	(tba)	Winner # 16 v Winner # 15

FINAL – SEPTEMBER 6 (No reserve day)

19	Lord's	

PRINCIPAL FIXTURES 2004

CC1   Frizzell County Championship (1st Div)
CC2   Frizzell County Championship (2nd Div)
CGT   Cheltenham & Gloucester Trophy
FCF   First-Class Friendly
LOI   NatWest Limited-Overs International
F   Floodlit

NL1   National League (1st Division)
NL2   National League (2nd Division)
TM   npower Test Match
T20   Twenty20 Cup
UCCE   Univ Centre of Cricketing Excellence

Fri 9 – Mon 12 April
FCF   Lord's   MCC v Sussex

Sat 10 – Mon 12 April
FCF   Durham   Durham UCCE v Durham
FCF   Taunton   Somerset v Loughboro' UCCE
     Worcester   Worcs v Cardiff UCCE
     Leeds   Yorks v Brad/Leeds UCCE
FCF   Cambridge   Cambridge UCCE v Essex
FCF   Oxford   Oxford UCCE v Surrey

Fri 16 – Mon 19 April
CC2   Cardiff   Glamorgan v Derbyshire
CC1   Bristol   Glos v Kent
CC2   Southampton   Hampshire v Durham
CC1   Northampton   Northants v Lancashire
CC1   The Oval   Surrey v Sussex
CC1   Birmingham   Warwicks v Middlesex

Fri 16 – Sun 18 April
FCF   Oxford   Oxford UCCE v Notts

Wed 21 – Sat 24 April
CC2   Chester-le-St   Durham v Notts
CC1   Canterbury   Kent v Worcs
CC1   Lord's   Middlesex v Surrey
CC1   Hove   Sussex v Lancashire
CC2   Leicester   Leics v Glamorgan
CC2   Taunton   Somerset v Derbyshire
CC2   Leeds   Yorkshire v Essex

Wed 21 – Fri 23 April
FCF   Bristol   Glos v Loughboro' UCCE
FCF   Northampton   Northants v Durham UCCE
FCF   Cambridge   Cambridge UCCE v Warwicks

Sun 25 April
NL2   Chester-le-St   Durham v Notts
NL1   Canterbury   Kent v Glos
NL2   Lord's   Middlesex v Sussex
NL1   Northampton   Northants v Lancashire
NL2   Taunton   Somerset v Derbyshire
NL1   The Oval   Surrey v Glamorgan
NL1   Birmingham   Warwicks v Hampshire
NL2   Leeds   Yorkshire v Leics

Wed 28 April – Sat 1 May
CC2   Derby   Derbyshire v Durham

CC2   Chelmsford   Essex v Somerset
CC2   Southampton   Hampshire v Leics
CC2   Nottingham   Notts v Yorkshire
CC1   The Oval   Surrey v Northants
CC1   Birmingham   Warwicks v Glos
CC1   Worcester   Worcs v Sussex

Wed 28 – Fri 30 April
     Cardiff   Glamorgan v Cardiff UCCE
FCF   Oxford   Oxford UCCE v Kent

Sun 2 May
NL2   Derby   Derbyshire v Durham
NL1   Bristol   Glos v Glamorgan
NL1   Southampton   Hampshire v Essex
NL1   Manchester   Lancashire v Kent
NL2   Leicester   Leics v Scotland
NL2   Nottingham   Notts v Yorkshire
NL2   Worcester   Worcs v Sussex

Mon 3 – Wed 5 May
FCF   Cambridge   Brit U v New Zealanders

Mon 3 May
NL1   Chelmsford   Essex v Warwicks
NL1   Cardiff   Glamorgan v Northants
NL2   Leicester   Leics v Derbyshire
NL2   Lord's   Middlesex v Durham
NL1   The Oval   Surrey v Hampshire
NL2   Leeds   Yorkshire v Scotland

Tue 4 May
NL2   Worcester   Worcs v Notts

Wed 5 May (*Reserve 6 May*)
CGT   Round 2 (*see p 302*)

Fri 7 – Mon 10 May
CC2   Chester-le-St   Durham v Essex
CC2   Southampton   Hampshire v Derbyshire
CC1   Canterbury   Kent v Glos
CC1   Northampton   Northants v Sussex
CC1   Lord's   Middlesex v Lancashire
CC2   Nottingham   Notts v Glamorgan
FCF   Worcester   Worcs v New Zealanders

Fri 7 – Sun 9 May
     Bradford   Brad/Leeds UCCE v Leics

Fri 7 May

| NL2 | Edinburgh | Scotland v Somerset |

Sun 9 May

| NL2 | Taunton | Somerset v Yorkshire |
| NL1 | Birmingham | Warwicks v Surrey |

Wed 12 – Sat 15 May

CC2	Cardiff	Glamorgan v Essex
CC1	Bristol	Glos v Northants
CC1	Manchester	Lancashire v Worcs
CC2	Leicester	Leics v Notts
CC2	Taunton	Somerset v Durham
CC1	Birmingham	Warwicks v Surrey
CC2	Leeds	Yorkshire v Hampshire

Wed 12 – Fri 14 May

| FCF | Hove | Sussex v Loughboro' UCCE |
| FCF | Cambridge | Cambridge UCCE v Middx |

Thu 13 – Sun 16 May

| FCF | Canterbury | Kent v New Zealanders |

Sun 16 May

NL1	Cardiff	Glamorgan v Essex
NL1	Bristol	Glos v Surrey
NL1	Manchester	Lancashire v Hampshire
NL2	Leicester	Leics v Notts
NL2	Worcester	Worcs v Durham
NL2	Leeds	Yorkshire v Sussex
NL2	Edinburgh	Scotland v Middlesex

Tue 18 – Fri 21 May

| CC1 | Worcester | Worcs v Glos |

Wed 19 – Sat 22 May

CC2	Derby	Derbyshire v Somerset
CC2	Chester-le-St	Durham v Glamorgan
CC2	Chelmsford	Essex v Leics
CC1	Northampton	Northants v Kent
CC1	The Oval	Surrey v Middlesex
CC1	Horsham	Sussex v Warwicks
CC2	Leeds	Yorkshire v Notts

Wed 19 – Fri 21 May

| | Southampton | Hants v Cardiff UCCE |
| | Bradford | Brad/Leeds UCCE v Lancs |

Thu 20 – Mon 24 May

| TM1 | Lord's | England v New Zealand |

Sun 23 May

NL2	Derby	Derbyshire v Somerset
NL1	Bristol	Glos v Hampshire
NL1	Manchester	Lancashire v Glamorgan
NL1	Northampton	Northants v Kent
NL2	Nottingham	Notts v Middlesex
NL1	The Oval	Surrey v Essex
NL2	Horsham	Sussex v Leics
NL2	Leeds	Yorkshire v Worcs

Tue 25 – Fri 28 May

CC2	Derby	Derbyshire v Glamorgan
CC1	Manchester	Lancashire v Middlesex
CC2	Nottingham	Notts v Durham
CC2	Taunton	Somerset v Essex
CC1	The Oval	Surrey v Kent
CC1	Hove	Sussex v Northants
CC1	Birmingham	Warwks v Worcs

Wed 26 and Sat 29 May *(Reserve 27, 30 May)*

| CGT | | Round 3 *(see p 302)* |

Fri 28 – Mon 31 May

| FCF | Leicester | Leics v New Zealanders |

Mon 31 May

NL2	Chester-le-St	Durham v Derbyshire
NL1	Southampton	Hampshire v Kent
NL2	Lord's	Middlesex v Somerset
NL2	Nottingham	Notts v Sussex
NL1	Birmingham	Warwks v Glamorgan
NL2	Edinburgh	Scotland v Yorkshire

Wed 2 – Sat 5 June

CC2	Chelmsford	Essex v Yorkshire
CC2	Swansea	Glamorgan v Somerset
CC1	Bristol	Glos v Surrey
CC2	Southampton	Hampshire v Notts
CC1	Tunbridge W	Kent v Lancashire
CC2	Oakham S	Leics v Derbyshire
CC1	Lord's	Middlesex v Warwicks
CC1	Northampton	Northants v Worcs

Thu 3 – Mon 7 June

| TM2 | Leeds | England v New Zealand |

Sun 6 June

NL2	Derby	Derbyshire v Middlesex
NL2	Chester-le-St	Durham v Scotland
NL1	Swansea	Glamorgan v Glos
NL1	Southampton	Hampshire v Warwickshire
NL1	Tunbridge W	Kent v Lancashire
NL2	Oakham S	Leics v Worcs
NL1	Northampton	Northants v Essex
NL2	Hove	Sussex v Somerset

Tue 8 – Fri 11 June

| CC2 | Chester-le-St | Durham v Yorkshire |

Tue 8 June

| NL2 | Derby | Derbyshire v Scotland |
| NL1 | FChelmsford | Essex v Hampshire |

Wed 9 – Sat 12 June

CC2	Chelmsford	Essex v Hampshire
CC2	Cardiff	Glamorgan v Leics
CC1	Gloucester	Glos v Middlesex
CC1	Manchester	Lancashire v Sussex
CC2	Bath	Somerset v Notts

| CC1 | Birmingham | Warwks v Northants |
| CC1 | Worcester | Worcs v Kent |

Wed 9 – Fri 11 June

| FCF | Derby | Derbyshire v Durham UCCE |

Thu 10 – Mon 14 June

| TM3 | Nottingham | England v New Zealand |

Sun 13 June

NL1	Gloucester	Glos v Northants
NL2	Lord's	Middlesex v Notts
NL2	Bath	Somerset v Leics
NL1	The Oval	Surrey v Kent
NL1	Birmingham	Warwks v Lancashire
NL2	Worcester	Worcs v Yorkshire

Tue 15 and Wed 16 June (*Reserve 16/17 June*)

| CGT | | Quarter-Finals |

Wed 16 June

| | Belfast | Ireland v West Indies |
| | Derby/Worcester | Derbys/Worcs v New Zealanders |

Thu 17 June

| | Belfast | Ireland v West Indies |

Fri 18 – Mon 21 June

CC2	Southampton	Hampshire v Somerset
CC1	Lord's	Middlesex v Worcs
CC2	Nottingham	Notts v Derbyshire
CC1	The Oval	Surrey v Glos
CC1	Stratford (*tbc*)	Warwks v Lancashire
CC2	Leeds	Yorkshire v Leics

Fri 18 June

| | FChelmsford | Essex v New Zealanders |

Sat 19 June

| | Cardiff | Wales v England |
| | FHove | Sussex v West Indians |

Sun 20 June

| NL2 | Edinburgh | Scotland v Durham |
| | Northampton | Northants v New Zealanders |

Mon 21 June

| | Beckenham (*tbc*) | Kent v West Indians |

Wed 23 – Sat 26 June

CC2	Derby	Derbyshire v Essex
CC2	Cardiff	Glamorgan v Durham
CC2	Southampton	Hampshire v Yorkshire
CC1	Beckenham (*tbc*)	Kent v Warwicks
CC2	Taunton	Somerset v Leics
CC1	Arundel	Sussex v Glos
CC1	Worcester	Worcs v Surrey

Wed 23 June

| | Shenley | Middlesex v West Indians |

Thu 24 June

| LOI | FManchester | England v New Zealand |
| | Lord's | Cambridge U v Oxford U |

Fri 25 June

| NL1 | FManchester | Lancashire v Northants |

Sat 26 – Tue 29 June

| CC1 | Liverpool | Lancashire v Northants |

Sat 26 June

| LOI | Birmingham | New Zealand v West Indies |

Sun 27 June

LOI	Nottingham	England v West Indies
NL2	Derby	Derbyshire v Worcs
NL1	Cardiff	Glamorgan v Surrey
NL1	Beckenham (*tbc*)	Kent v Warwicks
NL2	Leicester	Leics v Middlesex
NL2	Taunton	Somerset v Durham
NL2	Arundel	Sussex v Yorkshire
NL2	Edinburgh	Scotland v Notts

Mon 28 June – Thu 1 July

| FCF | Oxford | Oxford U v Cambridge U |

Mon 28 June

| NL1 | FChelmsford | Essex v Glos |

Tue 29 June

| LOI | FChester-le-St | England v New Zealand |

Wed 30 Jun

NL2	FHove	Sussex v Durham
NL2	Edinburgh	Scotland v Sri Lanka A
	Leicester	Brit U v Sri Lanka A

Thu 1 July

| LOI | FLeeds | England v West Indies |

Fri 2 July

T20	Derby	Derbyshire v Yorkshire
T20	FChelmsford	Essex v Hampshire
T20	Maidstone (*tbc*)	Kent v Middlesex
T20	Manchester	Lancashire v Leics
T20	Northampton	Northants v Glamorgan
T20	Nottingham	Notts v Durham
T20	FHove	Sussex v Surrey
T20	Birmingham	Warwks v Somerset
T20	Worcester	Worcs v Glos

Sat 3 July

LOI	Cardiff	New Zealand v West Indies
T20	The Oval	Surrey v Hampshire
	Leeds	Yorkshire v Sri Lanka A

Sun 4 July

LOI	Bristol	England v New Zealand
NL2	Chester-le-St	Durham v Leics
NL1	Maidstone	Kent v Essex

NL1	Manchester	Lancashire v Glos
NL2	Nottingham	Notts v Derbyshire
NL2	Hove	Sussex v Scotland
NL1	Birmingham	Warwks v Northants
NL2	Worcester	Worcs v Somerset
NL2	Leeds	Yorkshire v Middlesex

Mon 5 July

NL2	Richmond	Middlesex v Scotland
	Chester-le-St	Durham v Sri Lanka A
T20	Maidstone (tbc)	Kent v Essex
T20	Luton	Northants v Worcs
T20	Taunton	Somerset v Glamorgan

Tue 6 July

LOI	Lord's	England v West Indies

Wed 7 July

	Worcester	Worcs v Sri Lanka A
T20	FChelmsford	Essex v Surrey
T20	Leicester	Leics v Durham
T20	Richmond	Middlesex v Sussex
T20	Nottingham	Notts v Yorkshire

Thu 8 July

LOI	Southampton	New Zealand v West Indies
T20	Derby	Derbyshire v Lancashire
T20	Cardiff	Glamorgan v Warwicks
T20	Northampton	Northants v Glos
T20	Leeds	Yorkshire v Leics

Fri 9 July

	Cardiff	Glamorgan v Sri Lanka A
T20	Chester-le-St	Durham v Lancashire
T20	Bristol	Glos v Somerset
T20	Nottingham	Notts v Derbyshire
T20	The Oval	Surrey v Kent
T20	FHove	Sussex v Hampshire
T20	Birmingham	Warwks v Worcs

Sat 10 July (*Reserve 11 July*)

LOI	Lord's	NatWest Series Final

Sun 11 July

NL2	Chester-le-St	Durham v Yorkshire
NL1	Southampton	Hampshire v Lancashire
NL2	Leicester	Leics v Sussex
NL2	Southgate	Middlesex v Derbyshire
NL1	Northampton	Northants v Glamorgan
NL2	Nottingham	Notts v Somerset
NL1	The Oval	Surrey v Glos
NL1	Birmingham	Warwks v Essex

Mon 12 July

	Hove	Sussex v Sri Lanka A
T20	Southgate	Middlesex v Essex
T20	Birmingham	Warwks v Northants

Tue 13 – Thu 15 July

FCF	Arundel	MCC v West Indians

Tue 13 July

T20	Chester-le-St	Durham v Derbyshire
T20	Southampton	Hampshire v Middlesex
T20	Canterbury	Kent v Sussex
T20	Leicester	Leics v Notts
T20	Taunton	Somerset v Worcs

Wed 14 July

	Canterbury	Kent v Sri Lanka A
T20	Cardiff	Glamorgan v Glos
T20	Leeds	Yorkshire v Lancashire

Thu 15 July

T20	Derby	Derbyshire v Leics
T20	Chester-le-St	Durham v Yorkshire
T20	FChelmsford	Essex v Sussex
T20	Bristol	Glos v Warwicks
T20	Southampton	Hampshire v Kent
T20	Manchester	Lancashire v Notts
T20	Lord's	Middlesex v Surrey
T20	Taunton	Somerset v Northants
T20	Worcester	Worcs v Glamorgan

Sat 17 – Mon 19 July

FCF	Shenley	West Indies v Sri Lanka A

Sat 17 July (*Reserve 18 July*)

CGT		Semi-Finals

Sun 18 July

NL2	Derby	Derbyshire v Sussex
NL2	Chester-le-St	Durham v Middlesex
NL1	Cardiff	Glamorgan v Warwicks
NL1	Southampton	Hampshire v Northants
NL1	Canterbury	Kent v Surrey
NL1	Manchester	Lancashire v Essex
NL2	Taunton	Somerset v Worcs
NL2	Leeds	Yorkshire v Notts

Mon 19 July

T20		Quarter-Finals

Tue 20 July

NL1	FCanterbury	Kent v Hampshire

Wed 21 – Sat 24 July

CC2	Chester-le-St	Durham v Derbyshire
FCF	Swansea	Glamorgan v Sri Lanka A
CC1	Cheltenham	Glos v Lancashire
CC2	Leicester	Leics v Essex
CC1	Guildford	Surrey v Warwicks
CC2	Scarborough	Yorkshire v Somerset

Wed 21 July

NL2	FHove	Sussex v Notts
NL2	FWorcester	Worcs v Middlesex

Thu 22 – Mon 26 July
TM1   Lord's   England v West Indies

Thu 22 – Sun 25 July
CC1   Worcester   Worcs v Middlesex

Fri 23 – Mon 26 July
CC2   Nottingham   Notts v Hampshire
CC1   Hove   Sussex v Kent

Sun 25 July
NL1   Southend   Essex v Northants
NL1   Cheltenham   Glos v Lancashire
NL2   Leicester   Leics v Durham
NL1   Guildford   Surrey v Warwicks
NL2   Scarborough   Yorkshire v Somerset

Tue 27 – Fri 30 July
CC1   Manchester   Lancashire v Warwicks
CC2   Leicester   Leics v Durham
FCF   Taunton   Somerset v Sri Lanka A

Tue 27 July
NL1   ^FThe Oval   Surrey v Northants

Wed 28 – Sat 31 July
CC2   Derby   Derbyshire v Yorkshire
CC2   Southend   Essex v Notts
CC1   Cheltenham   Glos v Worcs
CC1   Southgate   Middlesex v Kent

Wed 28 July
NL1   ^FCardiff   Glamorgan v Hampshire

Thu 29 July – Mon 2 August
TM2   Birmingham   England v West Indies

Thu 29 July – Sun 1 August
CC2   Cardiff   Glamorgan v Hampshire
CC1   Northampton   Northants v Surrey

Sat 31 July
NL1   ^FManchester   Lancashire v Warwicks

Sun 1 August
NL1   Cheltenham   Glos v Kent
NL2   Southgate (tbc) Middlesex v Yorkshire
NL2   Cleethorpes   Notts v Durham
NL2   Taunton   Somerset v Sussex
NL2   Worcester   Worcs v Derbyshire
NL2   Edinburgh   Scotland v Leics

Tue 3 – Fri 6 August
CC2   Southampton   Hampshire v Essex
CC1   Canterbury   Kent v Sussex
CC1   Lord's   Middlesex v Glos
CC2   Taunton   Somerset v Glamorgan
CC1   The Oval   Surrey v Worcs

Tue 3 August
NL2   ^FDerby   Derbyshire v Leics

Wed 4 August
NL1   ^FNorthampton   Northants v Warwicks

Thu 5 – Sat 7 August
FCF   tba   Derbys/Leics/Durham/
                    Yorks v West Indians

Sat 7 August
T20   Birmingham   Semi-Finals/Final

Sun 8 August
NL2   Chester-le-St Durham v Worcs
NL1   Canterbury   Kent v Glamorgan
NL2   Lord's   Middlesex v Leics
NL1   Northampton   Northants v Notts
NL2   Hove   Sussex v Derbyshire

Mon 9 August
NL1   ^FChelmsford   Essex v Lancashire
NL1   ^FSouthampton Hampshire v Surrey

Tue 10 – Fri 13 August
CC1   Lord's   Middlesex v Sussex

Tue 10 August
NL2   ^FLeeds   Yorkshire v Derbyshire

Wed 11 – Sat 14 August
CC2   Southampton   Hampshire v Glamorgan
CC2   Nottingham   Notts v Leics
CC1   Whitgift S   Surrey v Lancashire
CC1   Birmingham   Warwks v Kent
CC1   Worcester   Worcs v Northants

Wed 11 August
NL2   ^FChester-le-St   Durham v Somerset

Thu 12 – Mon 16 August
TM3   Manchester   England v West Indies

Thu 12 – Sun 15 August
CC2   Leeds   Yorkshire v Derbyshire

Fri 13 – Mon 16 August
CC2   Chester-le-St Durham v Somerset

Fri 13 August
NL1   ^FBristol   Glos v Essex

Sun 15 August
NL1   Southampton   Hampshire v Glamorgan
NL2   Lord's   Middlesex v Worcs
NL2   Nottingham   Notts v Leics
NL1   Whitgift S   Surrey v Lancashire
NL1   Birmingham   Warwks v Kent
NL2   Edinburgh   Scotland v Sussex

Tue 17 August
NL2   ^FHove   Sussex v Worcs
NL1   ^FBirmingham   Warwks v Glos

300

Wed 18 – Sat 21 August

CC2	Colchester	Essex v Durham
CC1	Canterbury	Kent v Surrey
CC1	Northampton	Northants v Middlesex
CC2	Taunton	Somerset v Hampshire

Wed 18 August

NL2	FDerby (tbc)	Derbyshire v Notts
NL2	FLeicester	Leics v Yorkshire

Thu 19 – Mon 23 August

TM4	The Oval	England v West Indies

Thu 19 – Sun 22 August

CC2	Derby	Derbyshire v Notts
CC1	Bristol	Glos v Warwicks
CC2	Leicester	Leics v Yorkshire
CC1	Hove	Sussex v Worcs

Sun 22 August

NL1	Colchester	Essex v Kent
NL1	Colwyn Bay	Glamorgan v Lancashire
NL1	Northampton	Northants v Hampshire
NL2	Taunton	Somerset v Scotland

Tue 24 – Fri 27 August

CC2	Derby	Derbyshire v Leics
CC2	Chester-le-St	Durham v Hampshire
CC2	Colwyn Bay	Glamorgan v Yorkshire
CC1	Manchester	Lancashire v Kent
CC1	Northampton	Northants v Glos
CC1	Birmingham	Warwks v Sussex

Tue 24 August

NL2	FTaunton	Somerset v Middlesex
NL2	Worcester	Worcs v Scotland

Wed 25 August

NL1	FChelmsford	Essex v Surrey
NL2	FNottingham	Notts v Worcs

Thu 26 August

NL2	Nottingham	Notts v Scotland
	Taunton	Somerset v Indians

Sat 28 August (Reserve Sun 29 August)

CGT	Lord's	Final

Sat 28 August

	tba	Essex/Glamorgan or Leics v Indians

Sun 29 August

NL2	Derby	Derbyshire v Yorkshire
NL2	Chester-le-St	Durham v Sussex
NL1	Cardiff	Glamorgan v Kent
NL2	Leicester	Leics v Somerset
NL1	Northampton	Northants v Surrey

Mon 30 August

NL1	Southampton	Hampshire v Glos

Tue 31 August – Fri 3 September

CC1	Worcester	Worcs v Warwicks

Tue 31 August

NL1	FManchester	Lancashire v Surrey

Wed 1 – Sat 4 September

CC2	Leicester	Leics v Hampshire
CC2	Scarborough	Yorkshire v Durham

Wed 1 September

LOI	Nottingham	England v India

Thu 2 – Sun 5 September

CC2	Chelmsford	Essex v Glamorgan
CC1	Manchester	Lancashire v Surrey

Thu 2 September

NL2	FHove	Sussex v Middlesex

Fri 3 – Mon 6 September

CC1	Canterbury	Kent v Northants
CC2	Nottingham	Notts v Somerset

Fri 3 September

LOI	The Oval	England v India

Sat 4 – Tue 7 September

CC1	Hove	Sussex v Middlesex

Sat 4 September

NL1	Bristol	Glos v Warwicks

Sun 5 September

LOI	Lord's	England v India
NL2	Worcester	Worcs v Leics
NL2	Scarborough	Yorkshire v Durham
NL2	Edinburgh	Scotland v Derbyshire

Mon 6 September

NL1	FChelmsford	Essex v Glamorgan

Tue 7 September

NL1	FCanterbury	Kent v Northants

Wed 8 September

NL2	FTaunton	Somerset v Notts

Thu 9 – Sun 12 September

CC2	Chester-le-St	Durham v Leics
CC2	Chelmsford	Essex v Derbyshire
CC1	Bristol	Glos v Sussex
CC1	Lord's	Middlesex v Northants
CC1	Worcester	Worcs v Lancashire

Fri 10 – Mon 13 September

CC2	Cardiff	Glamorgan v Notts
CC2	Taunton	Somerset v Yorkshire

Thu 16 – Sun 19 September

CC2	Derby	Derbyshire v Hampshire
CC1	Canterbury	Kent v Middlesex
CC1	Manchester	Lancashire v Glos

CC2	Leicester	Leics v Somerset		CC1	Hove	Sussex v Surrey
CC1	Northampton	Northants v Warwicks		CC2	Leeds	Yorkshire v Glamorgan
CC2	Nottingham	Notts v Essex				

ICC CHAMPIONS TROPHY

LIMITED-OVERS INTERNATIONALS

(One reserve day for each match)

SEPTEMBER

Fri 10	The Oval	New Zealand v USA	Wed 15	Southampton	West Indies v Bangladesh
	Birmingham	England v Zimbabwe	Thu 16	The Oval	Australia v New Zealand
Sat 11	Southampton	India v Kenya	Fri 17	Southampton	England v Sri Lanka
Sun 12	Birmingham	South Africa v Bangladesh	Sat 18	The Oval	South Africa v West Indies
Mon 13	Southampton	Australia v USA	Sun 19	Birmingham	India v Pakistan
Tue 14	Birmingham	Pakistan v Kenya	Tue 21	Birmingham	Winner Pool A v Winner Pool D
	The Oval	Sri Lanka v Zimbabwe	Wed 22	Southampton	Winner Pool B v Winner Pool C
			Sat 25	The Oval	Final

CHELTENHAM & GLOUCESTER TROPHY FIXTURES 2003

Round 2 – Wed 5 May (*reserve 6 May*)

19	Reading	Berkshire v Kent
18	March	Cambs v Northants
17	Alderley Edge	Cheshire v Hampshire
25	Derby	Derbyshire v Somerset
21	Exmouth	Devon v Leics
13	Bournemouth (DP)	Dorset v Yorkshire
26	Chester-le-St	Durham v Sussex
23	Kingsland (Luct'ns)	Herefords v Worcs
4	Amsterdam (VRA)	Holland v Glos
11	Clontarf	Ireland v Surrey
15	tba	Lincs v Glamorgan
20	Edinburgh	Scotland v Essex
22	Wellington CC	Shropshire v Warwicks
12	Stone	Staffs v Lancashire
14	Lamphey	Wales MC v Middlesex

24 Westbury CC Wiltshire v Notts

Round 3 – Wed 26 May (*reserve 27 May*)

30 Winner # 21   v   Winner # 13

Sat 29 May (reserve 30 May)

27	*Winner # 23*	v	Winner # 25
28	*Winner # 26*	v	Winner # 12
29	*Winner # 14*	v	Winner # 15
31	*Winner # 24*	v	Winner # 20
32	*Winner # 22*	v	Winner # 19
33	*Winner # 16*	v	Winner # 17
34	*Winner # 11*	v	Winner # 18

Quarter-Finals 15/16 (16/17) June
Semi-Finals 17 (18) July
Final Lord's 28 (29) August

UNDER-19 CRICKET

TEST MATCH SERIES
England v Bangladesh

TM1	Leeds (*tbc*)	Wed 28 – Sat 31 July
TM2	Taunton	Tue 10 – Fri 13 August
TM3	Cardiff	Tue 17 – Fri 20 August

LIMITED-OVERS INTERNATIONALS
England v Bangladesh

LOI	Arundel	Tue 24 August
LOI	Hove	Thu 26 August
LOI	Hove	Fri 27 August

WOMEN'S CRICKET

WOMEN'S TEST MATCH
England v New Zealand

| TM1 | Scarborough | Sat 21 – Tue 24 August |

WOMEN'S LIMITED-OVERS
England v New Zealand

T20	Hove	Thu 5 August
LOI	Hove	Fri 6 August
LOI	ᶠChelmsford	Tue 10 August
LOI	Northampton	Fri 13 August

| LOI | Derby | Sun 15 August |
| LOI | Manchester | Tue 17 August |

WOMEN'S SUPER 4s

Sat 15 May	Taunton – King's College
Sun 23 May	Taunton – King's College
Sun 30 May	Reading CC
Mon 31 May	Reading CC
Sun 13 Jun	Caythorpe
Sat 19 Jun	Loughborough U

FIELDING CHART

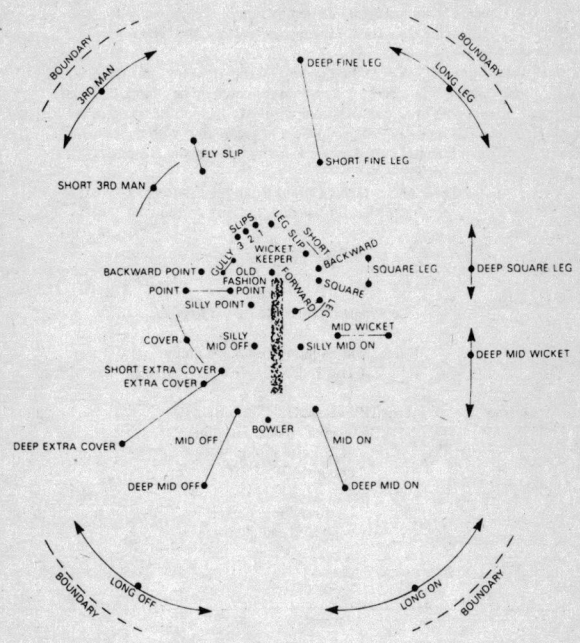

Cover photographs: (*Front*) Brian Lara © Reuters;
(*Back*) Michael Vaughan © Getty Allsport

ISBN 0 7553 1297 X

Typeset by
Letterpart Limited, Reigate, Surrey

Printed and bound in Great Britain by
Clays Ltd, St Ives plc

HEADLINE BOOK PUBLISHING
A division of Hodder Headline
338 Euston Road
London NW1 3BH

www.headline.co.uk
www.hodderheadline.com